Native Diasporas

BORDERLANDS AND TRANSCULTURAL STUDIES

Series Editors

Pekka Hämäläinen
Paul Spickard

| EDITED BY GREGORY D. SMITHERS & BROOKE N. NEWMAN

Native Diasporas

Indigenous Identities
and Settler Colonialism
in the Americas

University of Nebraska Press | Lincoln & London

Library of Congress Cataloging-in-Publication Data

Smithers, Gregory D., 1974–
Native diasporas: indigenous identities and settler colonialism in the Americas /
Gregory D. Smithers, Brooke N. Newman.
pages   cm. — (Borderlands and transcultural studies)
Includes bibliographical references and index.
ISBN 978-0-8032-3363-8 (pbk.: alk. paper) — ISBN 978-0-8032-5530-2 (epub)
ISBN 978-0-8032-5531-9 (mobi) — ISBN: 978-0-8032-5529-6 (pdf)
1. Indians of North America—Ethnic identity. 2. Indians of North America—Migrations. 3.
Indians of North America—Relocation. 4. Forced migrations—United States—History. 5. United
States—Race relations. 6. United States—Colonization. 7. United States—Social policy. I. Title.
E98.E85S55 2014
970.004'97—dc23
2013044686

Set in Sabon by Renni Johnson.

| Contents

List of Illustrations | vii

Preface | ix

Gregory D. Smithers and Brooke N. Newman

Introduction: "What Is an Indian?"—The Enduring Question of American Indian Identity | 1

Gregory D. Smithers

Part 1. Adapting Indigenous Identities for the Colonial Diaspora

1. Indigenous Identities in Mesoamerica after the Spanish Conquest | 31

   Rebecca Horn

2. Rethinking the Middle Ground: French Colonialism and Indigenous Identities in the *Pays d'en Haut* | 79

   Michael A. McDonnell

3. Identity Articulated: British Settlers, Black Caribs, and the Politics of Indigeneity on St. Vincent, 1763–1797 | 109

   Brooke N. Newman

4. Religion, Race, and the Formation of Pan-Indian Identities in the Brothertown Movement, 1700–1800 | 151

   Linford D. Fisher

5. "Decoying Them Within": Creek Gender Identities and the Subversion of Civilization | 187

   Felicity Donohoe

Part 2. Asserting Native Identities through Politics, Work, and Migration

6. Mastering Language: Liberty, Slavery, and Native Resistance in the
   Early Nineteenth-Century South | 209
   James Taylor Carson

7. Resistance and Removal: Yaqui and Navajo Identities in the
   Southwest Borderlands | 235
   Claudia B. Haake

8. Progressivism and Native American Self-Expression in the Late
   Nineteenth and Early Twentieth Century | 273
   Joy Porter

9. Mixed-Descent Indian Identity and Assimilation Policy | 297
   Katherine Ellinghaus

10. "All Go to the Hop Fields": The Role of Migratory and Wage Labor
    in the Preservation of Indigenous Pacific Northwest Culture | 317
    Vera Parham

**Part 3. Twentieth-Century Reflections on Indigenous and Pan-Indian
Identities**

11. Tribal Institution Building in the Twentieth Century | 349
    Duane Champagne

12. Disease and the "Other": The Role of Medical Imperialism in
    Oceania | 385
    Kerri A. Inglis

13. "Why Injun Artist Me": Acee Blue Eagle's Diasporic Performative | 411
    Bill Anthes

14. Asserting a Global Indigenous Identity: Native Activism Before and
    After the Cold War | 443
    Daniel M. Cobb

15. From Tribal to Indian: American Indian Identity in the Twentieth
    Century | 473
    Donald L. Fixico

Contributors | 497

Index | 503

Illustrations

3.1 "Map of the Island of St Vincent" | 120

3.2 "Chatoyér, the Chief of the Black Charaibes" | 127

3.3 "A Leeward Islands Carib Family" | 130

3.4 "Pacification with the Maroon Negroes" | 136

13.1 "Acee Blue Eagle Wearing Feathered Headdress" | 412

13.2 "Smoke Signals" | 414

13.3 "Man on Horseback and Two Pheasants" | 415

13.4 "Close Up and Comedy of Acee Blue Eagle" | 416

13.5 "Blue Deer" | 417

13.6 "Asah Dancing" | 423

13.7 "Blue Eagle Trademark" | 432

13.8 Pin with blue eagle logo | 433

13.9 "The Emergence of a Legend," 1 | 435

13.10 "The Emergence of a Legend," 2 | 436

Preface

This volume had its genesis in Hawai'i in 2008. While strolling through one of the Big Island's many lush, tropical gardens, we spotted an elderly gentleman taking pleasure in the solitude of his pickup truck and a quiet cigarette. Given that Hawaiians spend an unusually large amount of time sitting in their automobiles, this was not a particularly atypical early-evening scene. What was unexpected was the bumper sticker on the back of this elderly gentleman's vehicle: "Proud to be Cherokee." Here, in the middle of the Pacific Ocean, was a very public declaration of indigeneity. However, it was not an expression of indigenous identity that tied the owner of the vehicle to the native inhabitants of the Hawaiian Islands. Instead, this gentleman identified with a distant land, culture, and people. This chance encounter crystallized in our minds the importance that so many people attach to an indigenous identity—or, as this volume contends, to indigenous *identities*. These identities are as much geographically mobile and culturally fluid as they are fixed to a specific piece of land.

Since this fortuitous encounter, a number of the contributors to this volume have responded to our calls and joined us at professional conferences to discuss the interconnections between indigenous identity and human mobility; others have graciously agreed to our request to prepare essays specifically for this volume. It is our hope that this collection will contribute to the extension of a vibrant debate about the meaning(s) of indigenous identities in the Caribbean, the mainland Americas, and in those Pacific Islands touched by European and Euro-American colonialism. Having said that, we recognize that the comparative and transnational aspects of this volume constitute a departure from recent ethnohistorical studies, with the majority focusing on localized indigenous identities. While a number of the contributors here present localized case studies of indigenous identities, the overarching thrust of this volume is to place these localized analyses into a larger comparative and transnational context.

We hope, therefore, that this collection highlights the value of collaborative scholarship and centers our historical gaze on indigenous understandings of self-identification, community, and culture. Additionally, the volume is designed to address the enduring conception in Western popular culture of indigenous peoples as unchanging historical relics. By focusing on indigenous identities since Columbus's initial voyage to the Americas in 1492, we aim to show how indigenous people were not "doomed" or completely "eliminated" from world history but crafted a multitude of identities to sustain and enrich indigenous life. In this respect, *Native Diasporas* represents the fulfillment of historian Alexandra Harmon's call for more historical analysis of indigenous identities.

This volume was completed while the editors enjoyed postdoctoral research support. Brooke Newman would like to thank the John Carter Brown Library at Brown University and the National Endowment for the Humanities for generously providing a long-term fellowship in 2010–11. The excellent staff members at the John Carter Brown Library were a pleasure to work with, and she would especially like to acknowledge Lynne Harrell, Kimberly Nusco, and Ken Ward for their frequent assistance with rare books and manuscripts and Leslie Tobias-Olsen and John Minichiello for help with images. Gregory Smithers would like to acknowledge the postdoctoral support he received from the Center for Historical Research at the Ohio State University during the 2010–11 academic year. He thanks Alan Gallay in particular for being a warm and gracious host. Finally, we would both like to acknowledge the support this volume has received from the University of Nebraska Press. In particular, our thanks go to Matthew Bokovoy for championing the project from the beginning and for providing his own expert insights. Finally, our gratitude toward Paul Spickard and Pekka Hämäläinen, editors of the Borderlands and

Transcultural Studies book series, is boundless. Thank you both for the insights and guidance you brought to this collection.

Gregory D. Smithers
Brooke N. Newman
Virginia Commonwealth University

Native Diasporas

Introduction

"What Is an Indian?"—The Enduring Question
of American Indian Identity

Gregory D. Smithers

On May 26, 1826, the Cherokee leader and editor of the *Cherokee Phoenix*, Elias Boudinot, delivered "An Address to the Whites" at the First Presbyterian Church in Philadelphia.[1] Fresh faced, mission educated, and politically ambitious, the twenty-two-year-old Boudinot outlined his answer to arguably the most vexing question in American history: "What is an Indian?"[2] Boudinot delivered his answer at a time when debate over the removal of Native Americans from the Southeast raged. This seething political backdrop made his address as much a political argument about indigenous land rights as it was a statement on Indian identity. Boudinot understood that for most Native Americans in the American Southeast, land rights and indigeneity were intimately intertwined. He therefore defended Cherokee claims to ancestral lands by declaring: "You here behold an *Indian*. My kindred are *Indians*, and my fathers sleeping in the wilderness grave—they too were *Indians*. But I am not as my fathers were—broader means and nobler influences have fallen upon me."[3]

In the years following this speech, Elias Boudinot became an infamous figure in Cherokee history. His role in signing the Treaty of New Echota (1835), an agreement between the Cherokee Treaty Party and the United States government, which federal authorities used to justify Indian removal, earned Boudinot many enemies. Among the

Cherokees, Boudinot's political opponents believed that his about-face in championing emigration and signing the Treaty of New Echota had breached Cherokee blood law. Boudinot, like John Ridge and other prominent Treaty Party men, had thus given away land without communal consultation. For his sins, Boudinot ultimately met with a brutal death, his skull split open with a tomahawk in at least six places, his body brutally beaten, and his right hand "cut off."[4]

Embedded within this violent and very personal story is a complex tale of identity articulation, formation, and change. In May 1826 Boudinot set himself up as a model example of the modern Indian. He was educated, articulate, well dressed, and politically knowledgeable. These characteristics exemplified what he and other southeastern Indian leaders believed were the requisite qualities needed to legitimately claim their sovereign right to their homelands. Here was an appeal to land rights based on an identity, as Boudinot saw it, rooted in his biological connection to "my fathers sleeping in the wilderness grave" and to the social and cultural abilities of the nineteenth-century Indian to adapt and maintain a sense of Indianness amid the onslaught of the American republic's territorial expansion. However, the power of that onslaught, Boudinot came to believe, would eventually prove too great a threat to the continued existence of the Cherokee people. By the 1830s, therefore, Boudinot felt that the survival of a recognizable Cherokee identity rested on accepting terms with the Americans and emigrating west of the Mississippi River.

Boudinot's articulation of Indian identity was but one of many ways in which Native Americans adapted and rearticulated their indigeneity in the early nineteenth century. And given the violent manner in which his life ended, it is possible to glimpse just how contentious—indeed, life threatening—the embrace of one type of indigenous identity over another has been. If we reverse our historical gaze and survey indigenous history throughout the Americas in the sixteenth, seventeenth, and eighteenth centuries, a litany of historical case studies emerges that underscores the importance of identity to life and death among American Indians. Similarly, shifting to the modern era, the nineteenth, twentieth, and the twenty-first centuries, one is struck by how scholars, political activists, and American Indian leaders remained (and remain) divided over this deceptively simple question: "What is an Indian?"

The historical study of American Indian identity is no small matter. It is the very stuff of politics, economy, culture, and social being. Without identity, these elements of history are meaningless; their structures collapse. Beginning in the Americas of the sixteenth and seventeenth centuries, all attempts to answer the question of indigeneity have met with varying degrees of disagreement, dismay, and, more often than not, confusion.[5] Why? An answer must begin with the recognition that after Columbus unexpectedly arrived in the Americas in 1492, instigating multiple forms of European colonialism in the centuries that followed, the Americas became a confusing historical stage on which the most intense sorts of human dramas played out. Life/death, violence/peace, love/hate, hospitality/suspicion, and generosity/greed all existed in unequal and at times unpredictable measures in the colonial societies that Indians ultimately shared with Europeans and Africans. As Melissa Meyer observes, addressing the complexities of American Indian identity in such contexts demands that we keep in mind that "marrying across group boundaries, forming alliances, amalgamating, and splintering have characterized the social relations of human beings, American Indian groups among them, as much as cohesion and persistence, and perhaps more so."[6]

Native Diasporas: Indigenous Identities and Settler Colonialism in the Americas examines how indigenous peoples articulated a sense of self, or more accurately from a Native American perspective, a "soul," and community amid the changes wrought by European colonialism in the Caribbean, mainland Americas, and the Pacific Islands. The chapters in this volume explore the articulation and rearticulation of indigeneity through the speeches, cultural products and productions, intimate relations, and political and legal practices of colonizing and colonized peoples. The volume focuses therefore on the plurality of indigenous identities from the Caribbean, throughout the Americas, and across the vast Pacific world.[7] Grouped thematically, and in roughly chronological order, the chapters in this volume highlight how indigenous identities after 1492 cannot be reduced to a single racial "essence" or in terms of cultural "otherness," but were complex amalgams of Native and European worlds colliding, overlapping, and intersecting at different moments and places. Stated differently, the following chapters recognize the very different chronological, spatial, and ideological contexts in which indigenous identities have been constructed and contested since the early modern era of exploration, expansion, and colonialism.[8]

Acknowledging that American Indian identities were (and are) fluid tells us very little about those identities across space and over time. A more productive approach to indigenous identities demands that we analyze the social, political, economic, and cultural structures that produced both disjunctures and patterns in the way indigenous Americans spoke about themselves in relation to one another and in relation to colonizers. Understood in this way, we see how American Indian identities are, as Alexandra Harmon argues, "layered."[9] For indigenous peoples, this layering of identity has been a product of their own adaptive social, cultural, and political skills. As Harmon explains, "Indianness has been defined and redefined in continual give-and-take between outsiders' ascriptions and insiders' self-representations, between government policy and actual practice, between national or international forces and local conditions, between the adverse and the beneficial consequences of being Indian, and between Indians with differing self-conceptions."[10]

The use of the term "diaspora" in the title of this volume is designed to underscore how the contributors endeavor to center indigenous identities in the context of colonialism's many regimes of power and knowledge throughout the Caribbean, the Americas, and the Pacific.[11] The term diaspora is derived from the ancient Greek term *diasperien*, meaning "to sow or scatter seed."[12] For some of the indigenous groups and individuals described in this volume, this definition certainly applies. Individuals such as Acee Blue Eagle (see Bill Anthes's essay) and groups such as the Cherokees, Shawnees, Comanches, and Seminoles were, to borrow a phrase from James Clifford, "traveling cultures."[13] Forced by the pressures of intertribal conflict and the exclusionary impulses of settler colonial regimes of power, indigenous individuals and groups strove to maintain a coherent sense of group identity by transporting, innovating, and adapting their concepts of land, kinship, spirituality, cultural self-representation, and so forth to new homelands and different mediums of communication. Eliminated from the land of their ancestors, as many were during the early nineteenth century, they endured as indigenous peoples through creative and adaptive processes.

Increasingly, scholars of diaspora theorize that different forms of transnational encounters can be highlighted to better understand the formation of diasporic communities. These scholars contend that a nuanced approach to transnationalism opens analytical spaces for us to examine the flow of ideas and cultures across natural and politically constructed borders. Such analysis helps us understand how the larger structures of colonialism impacted the ways in which indigenous people envisioned, heard, and experienced the world around them. This type of analytical focus also illuminates the small, localized, and/or individualized ways in which specific aspects of larger colonial structures were reinterpreted and incorporated into indigenous cultural practices and self-representations.[14] For some of the indigenous groups and individuals presented in this volume, transnational processes of diplomacy or economy had profound consequences for identity formation at the local level. These groups did not have to migrate away from the lands that their ancestors once knew to feel the pangs of uncertainty that migration underscored for those American Indians who found themselves migrating to a new land and an uncertain future. For "the people who stayed," to borrow the title from a recent anthology, the overlapping European and African diasporas made familiar coastlines, landscapes, and river systems seem utterly foreign.[15]

It is also worth remembering, as several of the chapters in part 1 of this volume indicate, that the social, cultural, or political boundaries designed to place points of demarcation between the colonizer and colonized were still very much up for grabs in the sixteenth and seventeenth centuries. This should remind us that the history of Native America, as with all history, is more than the linear retelling of contact, "middle ground," violence, population decline, and forced adaptation. For many Native Americans, the story of identity is much more complex and challenging than this standard formulation of Western historiography can imagine.[16]

In contrast to the methodological agility that the contributors to this volume are proposing, a different, more rigid paradigm has emerged among colonial and postcolonial scholars. This paradigm anchors analysis of colonialism around concepts of land and the "elimination" of indigenous peoples. The leading proponent of this paradigm is Patrick Wolfe. Wolfe argues that settler colonialism was a "zero-sum game" that aimed solely to eliminate indigenous populations. According to Wolfe and the scholars who follow his lead, European settler colonialism in North America and elsewhere imposed structures that effectively worked to eliminate Native populations. Settlers, Wolfe argues, wanted the land inhabited by indigenous communities so they could expand their own colonial economies and sociopolitical systems.[17] While there were moments in the history of the Americas when European colonists committed social, political, and economic abuses against Native peoples in the Americas, when an "eliminationist" or "exterminationist" motive no doubt animated the actions of colonists and colonizers, we must be careful not to overlook the important roles that indigenous people played as actors in, for example, trade, diplomacy, and labor. If the history of settler colonialism in the Americas is presented as one long example of indigenous peoples succumbing to the onslaught of colonialism, we run the risk of presenting a tidy narrative in which "natives" are essentially eliminated, to borrow from Wolfe, from the histories of the Americas by the end of the nineteenth century.[18]

Tidiness of historical narrative, however, should not be confused with completeness of story.[19] There is no question that settler colonialism— and other forms of colonialism, for that matter—had profound impacts on the lives of indigenous peoples throughout the Americas. But understanding what it meant to claim an indigenous identity in the Caribbean, the mainland Americas, and the Pacific Islands after 1492 demands that we carefully and respectfully endeavor to recover those aspects of life that gave meaning to the cultural, socioeconomic, political, and biological identities of Native peoples. The historical study of indigenous identity is not an exercise in cultural boosterism or historical exoticism; instead, it should constitute an attempt to cut to the very heart of what has made life meaningful for indigenous peoples in the Caribbean, Americas, and Pacific Islands since the arrival of European colonizers and colonists in the early sixteenth century. The "contest of cultures," as one scholar puts it, had very real social, economic, and political implications for American Indian identities.[20]

American Indian history and indigenous studies have both enjoyed something of a renascence over the past two decades. Historians of colonial America, for example, have busied themselves emphasizing how America's original peoples negotiated new challenges to community, family, and personal identity in the wake of European expansion and the formation of nation-states throughout the Americas. Scholarship by Richard White, James Lockhart, Anthony Pagden, Daniel Usner, Jean O'Brien, Karen Ordahl Kupperman, Amy Turner Bushnell, Daniel Richter, Inga Clendinnen, Kathleen Duval, Alan Taylor, and Pekka Hämäläinen has produced important new insights that broaden our historical understanding of how indigenous peoples responded and adapted to different forms of European colonialism.[21] Much of this recent literature emphasizes the importance of crosscultural encounters and negotiations between European settlers and indigenous peoples in sixteenth-, seventeenth-, and early eighteenth-century America. Using treaty minutes, correspondence, and travelers' accounts, historians have highlighted the changing fortunes of Native American peoples in colonial America by presenting a more indigenous-centered perspective on trade relations, political meetings, treaties, and the dispossession of tribal lands.

This flurry of scholarship represents an important intervention in the historiographical debate about Indian-European relations in the colonies of early modern America. While the above-named scholars do not uniformly agree with each other's arguments, collectively they have offered an important counterbalance to a previous generation of scholarship that focused on the racial (and racist) attitudes of European colonizers toward American Indians, and the death and destruction visited upon indigenous communities through disease transfer and outbreaks of colonial violence. One of the most famous examples of this type of scholarship was Francis Jennings's seminal (and recently re-released) *The Invasion of America* (1976). Jennings's work, a major contribution to the "new social history" of the 1960s and 1970s, detailed how English colonizers constructed an image of themselves as the carriers of "civilization," a grandiose self-perception that contrasted sharply with the English characterization of indigenous peoples as "savages."[22] Jennings, like many of his contemporaries during the 1960s and 1970s, constructed the racial binary of civilized-savage to describe colonial relations between Europeans and Indians, and to explain what one scholar termed the "American Holocaust" of Native Americans.[23] If there existed any sense of Indian identity in the historiography from this era, it was an identity characterized by death, disease, violence, dispossession of land, and a collective sense of victimization.

The writing of history has always been, and remains, a political act. This was especially the case for Francis Jennings and many of the fellow historians of his generation who were unhappy with the teleological, unproblematic, and smugly progressive narratives that dominated American history writing during the first half of the twentieth century. The "new social history" that Jennings and his contemporaries made such profound contributions to challenged American readers with a darker version of their colonial and national histories. The rise of the American Indian Movement (AIM) played a significant role in fueling this challenge. AIM was a pan-Indian political effort to challenge past interpretations of Native American history and culture. AIM activists also asserted a sense of cultural autonomy and political independence. In 1972 representatives from AIM brought a list of their demands to lawmakers in Washington DC. This twenty-point manifesto, entitled the "Trail of Broken Treaties," demanded:

1. Restoration of treaty making (ended by Congress in 1871).
2. Establishment of a treaty commission to make new treaties (with sovereign Native Nations).

3. Indian leaders to address Congress.

4. Review of treaty commitments and violations.

5. Unratified treaties to go before the Senate.

6. All Indians to be governed by treaty relations.

7. Relief for Native Nations for treaty rights violations.

8. Recognition of the right of Indians to interpret treaties.

9. Joint Congressional Committee to be formed on reconstruction of Indian relations.

10. Restoration of 110 million acres of land taken away from Native Nations by the United States.

11. Restoration of terminated rights.

12. Repeal of state jurisdiction on Native Nations.

13. Federal protection for offenses against Indians.

14. Abolishment of the Bureau of Indian Affairs.

15. Creation of a new office of Federal Indian Relations.

16. New office to remedy breakdown in the constitutionally prescribed relationships between the United States and Native Nations.

17. Native Nations to be immune to commerce regulation, taxes, trade restrictions of states.

18. Indian religious freedom and cultural integrity protected.

19. Establishment of national Indian voting with local options; free national Indian organizations from governmental controls.

20. Reclaim and affirm health, housing, employment, economic development, and education for all Indian people.[24]

Coming on the heels of the civil rights movement, the activism of AIM's participants emphasized concepts such as "renewal," "resurgence," "self-determination," and "sovereignty."[25] This activism inspired a generation of historians to reconsider the importance of these concepts against a backdrop of disease, violence, and dramatic declines in indigenous populations. For example, historians and demographers highlighted how the American Indian population in the United States fell sharply, from approximately 600,000 to 228,000, between 1800 and

1890. Scholars used such data to support historical representations of
American Indians as the victims of settler colonialism's train of evils,
which began with disease transfer, continued with racism, violence,
and the loss of ancestral homelands, and culminated in the late nineteenth and early twentieth centuries with the "cultural genocide" per-
petrated by the Bureau of Indian Affairs' system of boarding schools.[26]

Until very recently, then, historians have portrayed American Indian history in particularly grim terms. Thus, historians of early America such as White, Richter, Usner, and others have over the past two
decades breathed new life into American Indian history by building
a more nuanced scholarship. The vigorous application of ethnohistorical methodologies and the influence of late twentieth- and early twenty-first-century racial politics have driven these changes. For
scholars of colonial America, American Indian identity was the product not simply of disease transfer and frontier violence but also of the
delicate diplomatic relations between Europeans and Indians, and the
agency of Native Americans to tie their identities consciously to individualized and group-centered connections to the land, spirituality,
migration, language, cultural practices, work, and so forth.[27]

But perhaps the fastest growing (and largest) body of recent research on American Indian societies comes from an interdisciplinary
group of scholars devoted to understanding Native American identity
in fresh, meaningful, and methodologically innovative ways. For example, Eva Marie Garroutte has proposed that "radical indigenism,"
a methodology that requires scholars to "enter," not merely observe,
indigenous philosophies, represents a framework to move us beyond
simplistic descriptions of Native American identities and illuminate
the content that gives indigenous identities their meaning.[28] Other
scholars, such as C. Matthew Snipp and Daniel Heath Justice, have
discussed the resilience and adaptability of Native American identities by exploring issues such as rates of reproduction, accessibility to
healthcare facilities, the importance of English and Indian literacies in
the articulation of Native American identities, and the incorporation
and/or exclusion of mixed-race people (white-Indian, black-Indian, or
Latina/o-Indian) from tribal membership.[29]

Given the rapid growth in scholarship about Indian-European and Indian-African intermixture, the broader historical significance of mixed-race indigenous identities warrants our considered attention. Since the early modern era, mixing between Native Americans and European outsiders has occurred on many levels. These interactions took place at the level of the political, the social, the economic and mercantile, and the intimate. Such categories of analysis often overlapped in the lived experiences of Indians, Africans, and Europeans. These relations were shaped by the charged and regularly changing power dynamics of colonial and settler colonial societies. From the mixed-race "go-between" who acted as interpreter and mediator in trade and political transactions between indigenous and colonial Europeans, to the syncretism of many Native American spiritual belief systems and changes in the gendered social structures of indigenous communities since the sixteenth and seventeenth centuries, American Indian identity has demonstrated its resilience, dynamism, and adaptability. As John and Jean Comaroff note, the forces unleashed by colonial ventures in the early modern and modern worlds "played into local forms and conditions in unexpected ways, changing known structures into strange hybrids."[30] This was the case for the indigenous as well as for European- and African-descended peoples of the Americas.

The concept of hybridity has become central to most recent studies of racial and ethnic groups, communities, and the development of nation-states in the Americas. Implicit in this analysis has been an increasingly sophisticated appreciation for the importance of race and gender in restructuring Native American identities.[31] Scholarship by Ann Marie Plane, James Brookes, Theda Perdue, Lucy Murphy, Jennifer Spear, Tiya Miles, Fay Yarbrough, Katherine Ellinghaus, Gregory Smithers, and Eva Marie Garroutte has explored the intricacies of interracial sex and marriage from the early modern period of colonization to the present, and from the Atlantic to the Pacific Ocean worlds.[32] This research has shed important light on the historical, sociological, and cultural dimensions of a "hybrid," "half-blood," and/ or "mixed-race" identity. Thus, the historical significance of racial and cultural mixing in Native American history has, to borrow from the Russian linguist M. M. Bakhtin, provided us with even clearer evidence that "the idea of metamorphosis (transformation)" is critical to understanding the formation of Native American identities.[33]

At the dawn of the twenty-first century, the idea of human hybridity and the metamorphosis of identities are generally celebrated as markers of an inclusive and accepting society. This was not always the case. Among early modern Spanish, French, and English colonizers, human metamorphosis was both a source of curiosity and a concern. Building on medieval cultural traditions in which Europeans identified people on the basis of "*gens, natio*, 'blood,' 'stock,' etc.," early modern Europeans strove vigorously to fit the landscape and peoples of the Americas into their proto-racial and proto-ethnic worldviews.[34] There existed a degree of comfort, as Stephen Greenblatt has explained, in colonizers setting themselves apart and above indigenous peoples by envisioning "the radical otherness of the American lands and peoples."[35] However, as the categorical hardening of human identities quickened after the eighteenth-century Enlightenment, the realities of colonial encounters among Indians-Africans-Europeans belied Enlightenment classifications by producing a dizzying array of creole cultures and biologically mixed peoples. Far from such hybridity being a source of celebration, it became, particularly in the Anglo-colonial world, a point of deep social and governmental anxiety. How does one govern a colony, for example, when it is virtually impossible to clearly identify discrete groups of human beings?[36]

Indigenous Americans were not immune from these concerns. For many, the value of centuries-old traditions of diplomacy, adoption, kinship, and seasonal migrations suddenly changed as Native Americans scrambled to make sense of their place in a much broader, more interconnected world.[37] For tribes occupying land on the Spanish colonial borderlands, or along the eastern seaboard of British and French North America, and what ultimately became the American South, once-nurturing community environments became "shatter zones" where disease and warfare altered human relations. The result was a restructuring of indigenous societies and governance, and the initiation of the process of ethnogenesis, or the social and cultural creation of new identities.[38]

"History," Don José Ortega y Gasset once observed, "is the ever flow-ing river of ethnogenesis."[39] This has been the case for Native Amer-ican groups such as the Catawbas, Shawnees, Comanches, Creeks, and Navajos, among many others. The identities these groups nur-tured after 1492 revolved around the interconnections between colo-nial politics and economy, migration, cultural adaption, and sexual intermixture with Europeans and Euro-Americans.[40] For instance, Su-san Sleeper-Smith contends that in seventeenth-century New France, Native American women enjoyed relatively greater opportunities to assert their own conceptions of identity and influence over the colo-nial context. Some of these women married French traders, and the European men they married in turn became dependent on indige-nous women for supplies of fresh food.[41] In other cases, indigenous women suffered a considerable loss of social influence and political power within Native communities. This was the case for Cherokee women during the late eighteenth and early nineteenth centuries. For the Cherokees, long caricatured by European observers for prac-ticing what they saw as a "petticoat government," the transition to a patriarchal society put an end to matriarchal concepts of property in-heritance and clan membership. The Cherokees, as Boudinot insisted in 1826, had changed and adapted to the "modern" world. They were now a "civilized" patriarchal society.[42]

Recent studies of racial and cultural mixture have highlighted his-torical changes in the "living web of interrelationships."[43] From the early modern era to our present day, the manner and context in which individuals preserve and act on these "interrelationships" has shaped, and been shaped by, the way bodily features were/are read by others and in language and cultural practices, and also by where—and with whom—Indians, Europeans, Africans (and African Americans) lived. In other words, this recent scholarship has opened new vistas to our understanding of how racial and ethnic identities were mapped onto Native America, and how indigenous Americans engaged in their own social remapping.[44]

One of the most famous historical examples of the contested na-ture of this mapping and remapping of indigenous identities is the

Seminole Indians. For much of the nineteenth century, the Seminoles strove to maintain a sense of themselves as distinctive from the neighboring Creek Indians. They did this, much as the Cherokees and other southern tribes did, by jealously guarding their land and slaves.[45] This determination, and their close, daily interaction with people of African descent, in turn fueled tension between the Seminoles and their slaves. Some of these slaves absconded from their Seminole masters and formed maroon communities in Florida. In these contraband communities, the Seminole maroons gave birth to a new identity: the black Seminoles.

Historian Kevin Mulroy has devoted his academic career to studying the Seminoles. His research reveals how the black Seminoles self-consciously differentiated themselves from other enslaved people of African descent by emphasizing "the term *Seminoles*" in articulations of their identity.[46] Such assertions of indigenous identity remain to this day a point of contention between Seminoles and black Seminoles, much as it remains controversial in Cherokee, Creek, and Choctaw communities.[47]

It is worth noting, however, that while Seminole leaders attempt to invalidate the indigenous identities of the black Seminoles by emphasizing their biological connection to a distant African ancestry, the black Seminoles have, since at least the nineteenth century, insisted on a group name, language, and cultural practices that underscore their self-identification as indigenous.[48] There exist other historical examples of such self-identifications, for instance, the Garifuna in Central America, the modern-day descendants of the Black Caribs, whom British settlers delegitimized as a Native people before forcibly removing them from the Caribbean in the late eighteenth century (see Newman's essay in this collection).

So what is an Indian? What makes one "indigenous"? Is it blood or culture? Language or spirituality? The possession of a fixed homeland, or geographical movement and mobility? The answer is not simple. All these things can constitute the component parts of an indigenous identity in the twenty-first century, just as they did in previous centuries. If we begin to look beyond Western constructions of indigeneity—those concepts that became embedded in New World colonial cultures and continue to resonate today—and re-center Native American actors in our histories of colonialism, we start to see these complex "layered" and adaptable cultures for what they are: meaningful expressions of indigenous identities that structure the lived experiences of individuals and communities. There are many examples of such expressions in our twenty-first-century world. One testimonial strikes me as particularly poignant. It is the autobiographical reflections of Steve Russell. Writing of his mixed Cherokee-Scottish lineage in 1999, Russell explained that while he has nothing against the Scots, he has no notion of what it is to be Scottish. "I was born and raised in Oklahoma," Russell reflected, "and it is Cherokee language and Cherokee lore and Cherokee people that tell me who I am."[49] Russell's self-consciously chosen identity is rich with the themes that run through this volume. His personal family history, the location of his birth, the acquisition of Cherokee language skills, and the internalization of Cherokee folkways tell Russell who he is and where he has come from.

Russell's personal account of indigenous identity echoes Greg Dening's insistence that "our pasts suffuse our presents." These "pasts" are "transformed, translated, interpreted, and encapsulated" in ways that help us to make sense of our identities in the present.[50] Of course, this process does not happen in a vacuum; it occurs in relation to other people and their articulated understanding of the past. For indigenous peoples across the Caribbean, the Americas, and into the Pacific, this relational articulation of self occurs amid an enduring cacophony of stereotypes—some of which are flattering, others offensive. In the United States, some of these stereotypes are embedded in the nation's racial culture. Indians are supposed to look, act, and speak one way, Euro-Americans another. In many cases, the tourism industry perpetuates these racial stereotypes. Take a trip to Cherokee, North Carolina, for instance, and one will see "authentic" Eastern Cherokees selling souvenirs from roadside tepees. The Cherokees did not live in tepees, but never mind the details, an "authentic" holiday experience awaits. Indeed, the word Cherokee is splashed on everything from children's underwear to automobiles and aircrafts. If such crude consumerism is not to one's taste, then perhaps solace can be found at collegiate and professional sports venues throughout the United States. Here one will find teams with nicknames like the "Chiefs," "Braves," "Sioux," and "Seminoles." Presumably, nicknames of this nature are meant to evoke masculine qualities of leadership, courage, and a warrior spirit. That Native Americans are branded and introduced to the vast majority of Americans in this way suggests that white Americans remain disengaged from the settler colonial history that made the appropriation of these symbols of indigeneity both possible and palatable.[51] And for indigenous Americans, this milieu of historical amnesia and simplistic stereotyping makes the presentation of Native American identities—like that articulated by Steve Russell—that much more challenging.[52]

The contributors to this volume confront the historical and contemporary complexities of indigenous identities. The following chapters are grouped in a thematic and roughly chronological order. In part 1, "Adapting Indigenous Identities for the Colonial Diaspora," the authors analyze the construction and reconstruction of indigenous identities during the sixteenth, seventeenth, and eighteenth centuries. Rebecca Horn and Michael McDonnell analyze the complex and diverse Native cultures, political structures, and notions of identity encountered by early Spanish and French explorers, traders, missionaries, and colonialists, respectively. Brooke Newman, Linford Fisher, and Felicity Donohoe extend the narrative of Native identities into the eighteenth century and the era of revolutions that transformed settler colonial and plantation societies in North America and the Caribbean. Newman, Fisher, and Donohoe present original arguments based on groundbreaking research that force us to rethink the nature of indigenous identity in relation to concepts of race and human difference, Christianity, gender, and sexuality.

As a whole, part 1 demonstrates that the formation of colonial societies and nation-states in the Americas from the seventeenth to the early nineteenth century bore witness to various forms of European expansion and settlement in the Caribbean islands and mainland Americas. These included efforts to establish trading and military posts, plantation agriculture, and missionary schools, the creation of permanent sites of European colonial settlement, and the negotiation of racial and gendered identities in the nascent American republic. Through their engagements with Spanish, Dutch, French, and British colonizers, and ultimately, the founding generation of the American republic, indigenous Americans negotiated different forms of European expansion, economic and political systems, and varying degrees of violence. With an emphasis on the ways in which indigenous peoples adapted their identities to the colonial worlds encircling them, part 1 thus attempts to integrate historical discussion of what Michael McDonnell has referred to as "stories from the bottom up, [and] facing east."[53]

Part 2, "Asserting Native Identities through Politics, Work, and Migration," takes us into the long nineteenth century, a period of dramatic and at times traumatic changes for American Indians. The authors focus on the challenges that confronted Native American people and their collective understanding of identity following the political rise of the United States. Much has been written on Native American policy in the American republic, from the policy of "expansion with honor" to the Removal Act (1830), Dawes Severalty Act (1887), and beyond.[54] The chapters in part 2 provide fresh insights into American relations with Native Americans during the nineteenth and early twentieth centuries.

Chapters by James Taylor Carson, Claudia Haake, Joy Porter, Katherine Ellinghaus, and Vera Parham focus on Native American articulations of identity in letters, speeches, political documents, oral traditions, work practices, and cultural self-representations, through movement over space and time and with reference to the lens of racial "purity" and concepts of "mixed-race" identity. These chapters provide original insights into indigenous identities in the context of changing political structures, the law, "Indian" policies, and the migration of English- and Spanish-speaking peoples into Native American lands.

Part 3, "Twentieth-Century Reflections on Indigenous and Pan-Indian Identities," addresses some of the major twentieth-century challenges to indigenous identities. Chapters by Duane Champagne,

Kerri Inglis, Bill Anthes, Daniel Cobb, and a brilliant retrospective by Donald Fixico, explore Native American notions of individual and group identities by focusing on changing indigenous conceptions of sovereignty and self-government, education, medicine, cultural self-representation, political activism, and self-reflection. These chapters demonstrate the richness of Native American identities and highlight how different historical forces throughout the Atlantic and Pacific worlds contributed to the reshaping of American Indian identities during the twentieth century.

Many stories of indigenous life remain untold, some of which may never be told for lack of archival sources or absence of collective memory to breathe renewed life and meaning into them. But if the chapters in this volume demonstrate anything, much like the life and death of the Cherokee leader Elias Boudinot, it is that economic, political, and sociocultural structures at a "macro" level of analysis can reveal new historical insights when interpreted at the "micro," or local, level of human interaction. As the forthcoming chapters highlight, the intersection and overlapping of these different levels of analysis are shaped and reshaped by changes in colonial power, by the impact of disease and violence, and by the myriad ways in which indigenous peoples adapted, interpreted, and/or discarded the material and intellectual elements of colonialism. Indigenous peoples from the Caribbean to the Pacific Islands might have suffered dramatic declines in population and the dispossession of land after 1492, but as this volume insists, indigenous identities have not been "eliminated." Standing Bear, the Ponca chief who doggedly resisted late nineteenth-century American imperialism, expressed this sentiment when he declared, "I am a man."[55]

Notes

1. Elias Boudinot, *An Address to the Whites: Delivered in the First Presbyterian Church, on the 26th of May, 1826* (Philadelphia: William F. Geddes, 1826).

2. For a different perspective on the purpose of this speech, see William G. McLoughlin and Walter H. Conser Jr., "'The First Man Was Red': Cherokee Responses to the Debate Over Indian Origins, 1760–1860," *American Indian Quarterly* 41, no. 2 (June 1989): 244.

3. Boudinot, *An Address to the Whites*, 3–4.

4. Brian Hicks, *Toward the Setting Sun: John Ross, the Cherokees, and the Trail of Tears* (New York: Atlantic Monthly Press, 2011), 236–27. On Cherokee removal, see John Ehle, *Trail of Tears: The Rise and Fall of the Cherokee Nation* (New York: Doubleday, 1988); William Anderson, ed., *Cherokee Removal: Before and After* (Athens: University of Georgia Press, 1991); Robert Conley, *The Cherokee Nation: A History* (Albuquerque: University of New Mexico Press, 2005); Theda Perdue and Michael Green, *The Cherokee Removal: A Brief History with Documents* (Boston: Bedford/St. Martin's, 2005).

5. On the theoretical aspects of this point, see Arturo J. Aldama, *Disrupting Savagism: Intersecting Chicana/o, Mexican Immigrant, and Native American Struggles for Self-Representation* (Durham NC: Duke University Press, 2001); Eva Marie Garroutte, *Real Indians: Identity and the Survival of Native America* (Berkeley: University of California Press, 2003). For a poignant example of personal reflections on the issue of identity, see Patricia Hilden, *When Nickels Were Indians* (Washington DC: Smithsonian Institute, 1997).

6. Melissa L. Meyer, "Race and Identity in Indian Country," *Ethnohistory* 51, no. 4 (2004): 800. See also William E. Unrau, *Mixed-Bloods and Tribal Dissolution: Charles Curtis and the Quest for Indian Identity* (Lawrence: University Press of Kansas, 1989); James F. Brooks, ed., *Confounding the Color Line: The Indian-Black Experience in North America* (Lincoln: University of Nebraska Press, 2002); Circe Sturm, *Blood Politics: Race, Culture, and Identity in the Cherokee Nation of Oklahoma* (Berkeley: University of California Press, 2002); Tiya Miles, *Ties that Bind: The Story of an Afro-Cherokee Family in Slavery and Freedom* (Berkeley: University of California Press, 2005), 111; Celia E. Naylor, *African Cherokees in Indian Territory: From Chattel to Citizens* (Chapel Hill: University of North Carolina Press, 2008), 10–13; Claudio Saunt, "The Native South: An Account of Recent Historiography," *Native South* 1, no. 1 (2008): 50; Fay A. Yarbrough, *Race and the Cherokee Nation: Sovereignty in the Nineteenth Century* (Philadelphia: University of Pennsylvania Press, 2008). See also the following important essay and response in *Ethnohistory*: Theda Perdue, "Race and Culture: Writing the Ethnohistory of the South," *Ethnohistory* 51, no. 4 (2004): 701–23; Claudio Saunt, Barbara Krauthamer, Tiya Miles, Celia Naylor, and Circe Sturm, "Rethinking Race and Culture in the Early South," *Ethnohistory* 53, no. 2 (2006): 399–405.

7. Katrina Gulliver, "Finding the Pacific World," *Journal of World History* 22, no. 1 (2011): 83–100.

8. N. Jayaram, "Introduction: The Study of Indian Diaspora," in *The Indian Diaspora: Dynamics of Migration*, ed. N. Jayaram (New Delhi and Thousand Oaks CA: Sage, 2004), 20; Robbie F. Ethridge, *From Chicaza to Chickasaw: The European*

Invasion and the Transformation of the Mississippian World, 1540–1715 (Chapel Hill: University of North Carolina Press, 2010), 1–3.

9. Alexandra Harmon, "Wanted: More Histories of Indian Identity," *A Companion to American Indian History*, ed. Philip J. Deloria and Neal Salisbury (Malden MA: Blackwell Publishing, 2004), 254. See also Alexandra Harmon, *Indians in the Making: Ethnic Relations and Indian Identities around Puget Sound* (Berkeley: University of California Press, 1998), 3–4; Shari M. Huhndorf, *Mapping the Americas: The Transnational Politics of Contemporary Native Culture* (Ithaca NY: Cornell University Press, 2009), 7.

10. Harmon, "Wanted: More Histories of Indian Identity," 255.

11. Ann Laura Stoler, *Race and the Education of Desire: Foucault's History of Sexuality and the Colonial Order of Things* (Durham NC: Duke University Press, 1995), 1.

12. Jana Evans Braziel and Anita Mannur, "Nation, Migration, Globalization: Points of Contention in Diaspora Studies," in *Theorizing Diaspora: A Reader*, ed. Jana Evans Braziel and Anita Mannur (Malden MA: Blackwell Publishing, 2003), 1.

13. James Clifford, "Travelling Cultures," in *Cultural Studies*, ed. Lawrence Grassberg, Cary Nelson, Paula Treichler (New York: Routledge, 1992), 96; Andre Levy, "Diasporas through Anthropological Lenses: Contexts of Postmodernity," *Diaspora* 9, no. 1 (2000): 137–57. See also Stanley J. Stein and Barbara H. Stein, *Silver, Trade, and War: Spain and America in the Making of Early Modern Europe* (Baltimore: Johns Hopkins University Press, 2000), ch. 2.

14. M. Kearney, "The Local and the Global: The Anthropology of Globalization and Transnationalism," *Annual Review of Anthropology* 24 (1995): 548; Hae-Kyung Um, "Listening Patterns and Identity of the Korean Diaspora in the Former USSR," *British Journal of Ethnomusicology* 9, no. 2 (2000): 121–42; Alisse Waterston, "Bringing the Past into the Present: Family Narratives of Holocaust, Exile, and Diaspora: The Story of My Story," *Anthropological Quarterly* 78, no. 1 (2005): 57; Gabriel Sheffer, "Transnationalism and Ethnonational Diasporism," *Diaspora* 15, no. 1 (2006): 121–45; Robin Cohen, Global Diasporas: An Introduction, 2nd ed. (New York: Routledge, 2008); Ted C. Lewellan, *The Anthropology of Globalization: Cultural Anthropology Enters the 21st Century* (Westport CT: Greenwood Publishing, 2002); Stuart Hall, "Cultural Identity and Diaspora," in *Theorizing Diaspora: A Reader*, ed. Jana Evans Braziel and Anita Mannur (Malden MA: Blackwell Publishing, 2003), 233–46.

15. Geary Hobson, Janet McAdams, and Kathryn Walkiewicz, eds., *The People Who Stayed: Southeastern Indian Writing after Removal* (Norman: University of Oklahoma Press, 2010).

16. Rubin Patterson, "Transnationalism: Diaspora-Homeland Development," *Social Forces* 84, no. 4 (2006): 1891–1907; Kevin Kenny, "Diaspora and Comparison: The Global Irish as a Case Study," *Journal of American History* 90, no. 1 (2003): 134–62.

17. Patrick Wolfe, *Settler Colonialism and the Transformation of Anthropology: The Politics and Poetics of an Ethnographic Event* (London: Cassell, 1999), 2; Wolfe, "Land, Labor, and Difference: Elementary Structures of Race," *American Historical Review* 106, no. 3 (2001): 866–905; Wolfe, "Settler Colonialism and the Elimination of the Native," *Journal of Genocide Research* 8, no. 4 (2006): 387–410. Similarly, see Richard Harris Cole, *Making Native Space: Colonialism, Resistance, and Reserves in British Columbia* (Vancouver: University of British Columbia Press, 2002); Scott L. Morgensen, "The Biopolitics of Settler Colonialism: Right Here, Right Now," *Settler Colonial Studies* 1, no. 1 (2011): 52–76.

18. Leo Spitzer, *Lives in Between: The Experience of Marginality in a Century of Emancipation* (New York: Hill and Wang, 1989), 8–9; Daniel H. Usner, *American Indians in the Lower Mississippi Valley: Social and Economic Histories* (Lincoln: University of Nebraska Press, 1998).

19. Although to be fair to adherents to the Wolfeian paradigm, Marxist and neo-Marxist historians have for almost half a century emphasized themes of "declension and dependency." A classic example of the Native American "declension" argument is Henry F. Dobyns, *Their Number Become Thinned: Native American Population Dynamics in Eastern North America* (Knoxville: University of Tennessee Press, 1983). For analysis, see Gary C. Anderson, *The Indian Southwest, 1580–1830: Ethnogenesis and Reinvention* (Norman: University of Oklahoma Press, 1999), 4.

20. James Axtell, *The Invasion Within: The Contest of Cultures in Colonial North America* (New York: Oxford University Press, 1985); Shari Michelle Huhndorf, *Going Native: Indians in the American Cultural Imagination* (Ithaca NY: Cornell University Press, 2001).

21. Richard White, *The Middle Ground: Indians, Empires, and Republics in the Great Lakes Region, 1650–1815* (New York: Cambridge University Press, 1991); James Lockhart, *The Nahuas after the Conquest: A Social and Cultural History of the Indians of Central Mexico, Sixteenth through Eighteenth Centuries* (Stanford CA: Stanford University Press, 1992); Anthony Pagden, *The Fall of Natural Man: The American Indian and the Origins of Comparative Ethnology* (New York: Cambridge University Press, 1992); Daniel H. Usner, *Indians, Settlers, and Slaves in a Frontier Exchange Economy: The Lower Mississippi Valley Before 1783* (Chapel Hill: University of North Carolina Press, 1992); Jean O'Brien, *Dispossession by Degrees: Indian Land and Identity in Natick, Massachusetts, 1650–1790* (New York: Cambridge University Press, 1997); Karen Ordahl Kupperman, *Indians and English:*

Facing Off in Early America (Ithaca NY: Cornell University Press, 2000); Amy Turner Bushnell, "Spain's Conquest by Contract: Pacification and the Mission System in Eastern North America," in *The World Turned Upside-Down: The State of Eighteenth-Century American Studies at the Beginning of the Twenty-First Century*, ed. Michael V. Kennedy and William G. Shade (London: Rosemont Publishing, 2001), 289–320; Daniel Richter, *Facing East from Indian Country: A Native History of Early America* (Cambridge MA: Harvard University Press, 2001); Inga Clendinnen, *Ambivalent Conquests: Maya and Spaniard in Yucatan, 1517–1570* (New York: Cambridge University Press, 2003); Kathleen Duval, *The Native Ground: Indians and Colonists in the Heart of the Continent* (Philadelphia: University of Pennsylvania Press, 2006); Alan Taylor, *The Divided Ground: Indians, Settlers and the Northern Borderland of the American Revolution* (New York: Alfred A. Knopf, 2006); Pekka Hämäläinen, *The Comanche Empire* (New Haven CT: Yale University, 2008).

22. Francis Jennings, *The Invasion of America: Indians, Colonialism, and the Cant of Conquest* (1976; repr., Chapel Hill: University of North Carolina Press, 2010), 8. See also Roy Harvey Pearce, *Savagism and Civilization: A Study of the Indian and the American Mind* (Berkeley: University of California Press, 1953); Robert F. Berkhofer, *The White Man's Indian: Images of the American Indian, from Columbus to the Present* (New York: Vintage Books, 1979).

23. David E. Stannard, *American Holocaust: The Conquest of the New World* (New York: Oxford University Press, 1992).

24. Troy R. Johnson, *Red Power: The Native American Civil Rights Movement* (New York: Chelsea House, 2007), 54–55; Kenneth Saul Stern, *Loud Hawk: The United States versus the American Indian Movement* (Norman: University of Oklahoma Press, 1994), 327.

25. For analysis, see Stephen Cornell, *The Return of the Native: American Indian Political Resurgence* (New York: Oxford University Press, 1990); Troy R. Johnson, *The Occupation of Alcatraz: Indian Self-Determination and the Rise of Indian Activism* (Urbana: University of Illinois Press, 1996); Joane Nagel, *American Indian Ethnic Renewal: Red Power and the Resurgence of Identity and Culture* (New York: Oxford University Press, 1997).

26. For a synthesis of population analyses, see Russell Thornton, "Aboriginal Population Size of North America," in *A Population History of North America*, ed. Michael R. Haines and Richard H. Steckel (New York: Cambridge University Press, 2000), 9–50.

27. Claudio Saunt has rejected calls to see Native American identity as a product of settler colonial relations. He insists that indigenous identity remains tied to the land. See Claudio Saunt, "The Indians' Old World," *William and Mary Quarterly* 68, no. 2 (2011): 215–18. On the significance of disease in postcontact Native

American history, see Alfred W. Crosby, "Virgin Soil Epidemics as a Factor in the Aboriginal Depopulation of America," *William and Mary Quarterly* 33, no. 2 (1976): 189–99; Dean R. Snow and Kim M. Lanphear, "European Contact and Indian Depopulation in the Northeast: The Timing of the First Epidemics," *Ethnohistory* 35, no. 1 (1988): 15–33; David S. Jones, "Virgin Soils Revisited," *William and Mary Quarterly* 60, no. 4 (2003): 703–42. On the significance of colonial violence in Native American history, see Ned Blackhawk, *Violence over the Land: Indians and Empires in the Early American West* (Cambridge MA: Harvard University Press, 2006); Alfred Cave, "Genocide in the Americas," in *The Historiography of Genocide*, ed. Dan Stone (Basingstoke: Palgrave Macmillan, 2008), 273–95; Karl Jacoby, "'The Broad Platform of Extermination': Nature and Violence in the Nineteenth-Century North American Borderlands," *Journal of Genocide Research* 10, no. 2 (2008): 249–67; Gregory D. Smithers, "Rethinking Genocide in North America," in *The Oxford Handbook of Genocide Studies*, ed. Donald Bloxham and A. Dirk Moses (New York: Oxford University Press, 2010), 322–41; Pekka Hämäläinen, "Lost in Transitions: Suffering, Survival, and Belonging in the Early Modern Atlantic World," *William and Mary Quarterly* 68, no. 2 (2011): 219–23. The study of European-Indian diplomacy has a rich historiography. For some key examples, see Wilbur R. Jacobs, *Diplomacy and Indian Gifts: Anglo-French Rivalry along the Ohio and Northwest Frontiers, 1748–1763* (Stanford CA: Stanford University Press, 1950); John P. Reid, *A Better Kind of Hatchet: Law, Trade, and Diplomacy in the Cherokee Nation during the Early Years of European Contact* (University Park: Pennsylvania State University Press, 1976); Roger A. Williams Jr., *Linking Arms Together: American Indian Treaty Visions of Law and Peace, 1600–1800* (New York: Routledge, 1999); Timothy J. Shannon, *Iroquois Diplomacy on the Early American Frontier* (New York: Viking, 2009).

28. Eva Marie Garroutte, *Real Indians: Identity and the Survival of Native America* (Berkeley: University of California Press, 2003), 10, 101, 107. See also the essays in Clifford E. Trafzer, ed., *American Indian Identity: Today's Changing Perspectives* (Sacramento: Sierra Oaks Publishing Co., 1985)

29. Daniel Heath Justice, *Our Fire Survives the Storm: A Cherokee Literary History* (Minneapolis: University of Minnesota Press, 2006); C. Matthew Snipp, "Who Are American Indians? Some Observations about the Perils and Pitfalls of Data for Race and Ethnicity," *Population Research and Policy Review* 5 (1986): 237–52. See also William Lorenz Katz, *Black Indians: A Hidden History* (New York: Simon and Schuster, 1986); Russell Thornton, "Tribal Membership Requirements and the Demography of 'Old' and 'New' Native Americans," *Population Research and Policy Review* 16 (1997): 33–42; Linda M. Alcoff, *Visible Identities: Race, Gender, and the Self* (New York: Oxford University Press, 2006), 208, 235, 283; Lauren L. Basson,

White Enough to Be American? Race Mixing, Indigenous People, and the Boundaries of State and Nation (Chapel Hill: University of North Carolina Press, 2008).

30. John Comaroff and Jean Comaroff, *Ethnography and the Historical Imagination* (Boulder CO: Westview Press, 1992), 5. See also Greg Dening, *History's Anthropology: The Death of William Gooch* (Lanham MD: University Press of America, 1988), 3.

31. *Journal of American History* 88, no. 3 (December 2001); *William and Mary Quarterly*, 3rd ser., 70, no. 1 (January 2003); a special forum on "Amalgamation and the Historical Distinctiveness of the United States" in *American Historical Review* 108, no. 5 (December 2003); and two special editions, *Frontiers* 23, no. 2 (2002), and 29, issue 2–3 (2008) dealing with race, gender, and indigenous women.

32. Ann Marie Plane, *Colonial Intimacies: Indian Marriage in Early New England* (Ithaca NY: Cornell University Press, 2000); James F. Brooks, *Captives and Cousins: Slavery, Kinship, and Community in the Southwest Borderlands* (Chapel Hill: University of North Carolina Press, 2001); Theda Perdue, *"Mixed Blood" Indians: Racial Construction in the Early South* (Athens: University of Georgia Press, 2005); Lucy E. Murphy, *A Gathering of Rivers: Indians, Métis, and Mining in the Great Lakes, 1737–1832* (Lincoln: University of Nebraska Press, 2000); Jennifer Spear, *Race, Sex, and Social Order in Early New Orleans* (Baltimore: Johns Hopkins University Press, 2009); Tiya Miles, *Ties that Bind: The Story of an Afro-Cherokee Family in Slavery and Freedom* (Berkeley: University of California Press, 2005); Fay Yarbrough, *Race and the Cherokee Nation: Sovereignty in the Nineteenth Century* (Philadelphia: University of Pennsylvania Press, 2008); Katherine Ellinghaus, *Taking Assimilation to Heart: Marriages of White Women and Indigenous Men in the United States and Australia, 1887–1937* (Lincoln: University of Nebraska Press, 2006); Gregory Smithers, *Science, Sexuality, and Race in the United States and Australia, 1780s–1890s* (New York: Routledge, 2009); Eva Marie Garroutte, *Real Indians*.

33. M. M. Bakhtin, *The Dialogic Imagination: Four Essays*, ed. Michael Holquist, trans. Caryl Emerson and Michael Holquist (Austin: University of Texas Press, 1981), 112, 352. See also Spitzer, *Lives in Between*, 28.

34. J. H. Elliot, *The Old World and the New, 1492–1650* (1970; Cambridge: Cambridge University Press, 2000), 16, 21, passim; Taylor, *American Colonies*, xii; Benjamin Isaac, *The Invention of Racism in Classical Antiquity* (Princeton NJ: Princeton University Press, 2004), 37; Robert Bartlett, *The Making of Europe: Conquest, Colonization, and Cultural Change 950–1350* (New York: Penguin Books, 1993), 197. See also Roxann Wheeler, *The Complexion of Race: Categories of Difference in Eighteenth-Century British Culture* (Philadelphia: University of Pennsylvania Press, 2000).

35. Stephen Greenblatt, *Marvelous Possessions: The Wonder of the New World* (Chicago: University of Chicago Press, 1991), 54. See also John Speed, *The Theatre*

of the Empire of Great-Britain (London: Thomas Basset, 1676), 43; William Cronon, *Changes in the Land: Indians, Colonists, and the Ecology of New England* (New York: Hill and Wang, 1983), 54–61, 76–77.

36. Paul R. Spickard, *Mixed Blood: Intermarriage and Ethnic Identity in Twentieth-Century America* (Madison: University of Wisconsin Press, 1989); Philippa Levine, *Prostitution, Race, and Politics: Policing Venereal Disease in the British Empire* (New York: Routledge, 2003), ch. 7; Gregory D. Smithers, "The 'Pursuits of the Civilized Man': Race and the Meaning of Civilization in the United States and Australia, 1790s–1850s," *Journal of World History* 20, no. 2 (2009): 245–72; Peggy Pascoe, *What Comes Naturally: Miscegenation Law and the Making of Race in America* (New York: Oxford University Press, 2009).

37. Russell Thornton, *Studying Native America: Problems and Prospects* (Madison: University of Wisconsin Press, 1998), 232–24.

38. Wilbur Zelinsky, "Seeing Beyond the Dominant Culture," in *Understanding Ordinary Landscapes*, ed. Paul Groth and Todd W. Bressi (New Haven CT: Yale University Press, 1997), 158; Peter Turchin, *Historical Dynamics: Why States Rise and Fall* (Princeton NJ: Princeton University Press, 2003), 63; Robbie Ethridge, *From Chicaza to Chickasaw: The European Invasion and the Transformation of the Mississippian World, 1540–1714* (Chapel Hill: University of North Carolina Press, 2010).

39. Don José Ortega y Gasset quoted in Eduardo Seda Bonilla, *Ethnogenesis: Foundations of Thought and Action* (Victoria BC: Trafford Publishing, 2005), 14.

40. James H. Merrell, *The Indians' New World: Catawbas and Their Neighbors from Contact through the Era of Removal* (Chapel Hill: University of North Carolina Press, 1989); David G. Moore, *Catawba Valley Mississippians: Ceramics, Chronology, and Catawba Indians* (Jackson: University Press of Mississippi, 2002); William C. Sturtevant, "Creek into Seminole," in *North American Indians in Historical Perspective*, ed. Eleanor B. Leacock and Nancy O. Lurie (Long Grove IL: Waveland Press, 1988), 2:92–128; Joseph M. Hall, *Making an Indian People: Creek Formation in the Colonial Southeast, 1590–1735* (Madison: University of Wisconsin Press, 2001); Cameron B. Wesson, "Mississippian Sacred Landscapes: The View from Alabama," in *Mississippian Towns and Sacred Spaces: Searching for an Architectural Grammar*, ed. R. Barry Lewis and Charles Stout (Tuscaloosa: University of Alabama Press, 1998), 108; G. C. Anderson, *The Indian Southwest, 1580–1830*.

41. Susan Sleeper-Smith, *Indian Women and French Men: Rethinking Cultural Encounter in the Western Great Lakes* (Amherst: University of Massachusetts Press, 2001), 75.

42. On the Cherokees, see Yarbrough, *Race and the Cherokee Nation*.

43. Nathan Irvin Huggins, *Black Odyssey: The African American Ordeal in Slavery* (1977; repr., New York: Vintage Books, 1990), 7. See also Gary B. Nash, *Red,*

White, and Black: The Peoples of Early North America (New York: Prentice Hall, 1992); Colin G. Calloway, *New Worlds for All: Indians, Europeans, and the Remaking of Early America* (Baltimore: Johns Hopkins University Press, 1997).

44. Timothy J. Reiss, "Mapping Identities: Literature, Nationalism, Colonialism," in *Debating World Literature*, ed. Christopher Prendergast (London: Verso, 2004), 146.

45. Kevin Mulroy, *Freedom on the Border: The Seminole Maroons in Florida, the Indian Territory, Coahuila, and Texas* (Lubbock: Texas Tech University Press, 1993), 33. For further analysis of the black Seminoles, see Daniel F. Littlefield, *Africans and Seminoles: From Removal to Emancipation* (Jackson: University Press of Mississippi, 1977); Kevin Mulroy, *The Seminole Freedmen: A History* (Norman: University of Oklahoma Press, 2007). On race mixing among the Creeks, see Gary Zellar, *African Creeks: Estelvste and the Creek Nation* (Norman: University of Oklahoma Press, 2007).

46. Mulroy, *Freedom on the Border*, 22, 178.

47. Sigmund Sameth, "Creek Negroes: A Study in Race Relations" (MA thesis, University of Oklahoma, 1940); Katja May, *African Americans and Native Americans in the Creek and Cherokee Nations, 1830s to 1920s: Collision and Collusion* (New York: Garland, 1996); Gary W. Zellar, "'If I Ain't One, You Won't Find Another One Here': Race, Identity, Citizenship, and Land; The African Creek Experience in the Indian Territory and Oklahoma, 1830–1910" (PhD diss., University of Arkansas, 2003); Barbara Krauthamer, "In Their 'Native Country': Freedpeople's Understandings of Culture and Citizenship in the Choctaw and Chickasaw Nations," in *Crossing Waters, Crossing Worlds*, ed. Tiya Miles and Sharon P. Holland (Durham NC: Duke University Press), 100–20; Circe Sturm, "Blood Politics, Racial Classification, and Cherokee Nation Identity: The Trials and Tribulations of the Cherokee Freedmen," in Brooks, *Confounding the Color Line*, 223–58; Zellar, *African Creeks*; Yarbrough, *Race and the Cherokee Nation*, ch. 7.

48. Mulroy, *Freedom on the Border*, 176.

49. Steve Russell, "Identity as Survival," *Peace Review* 11, no. 2 (1999): 299.

50. Dening, *History's Anthropology*, 2.

51. Debra Merskin, "Winnebagos, Cherokees, Apaches, and Dakotas: The Persistence of Stereotyping of American Indians in American Advertising Brands," *Howard Journal of Communications* 12 (2001): 159–69; *Do All Indians Live in Tipis? Questions and Answers from the National Museum of the American Indian* (Washington DC: Smithsonian Institute, 2007).

52. For a recent collection of Native American voices and self-representation, see Gerald McMaster and Clifford E. Trafzer, eds., *Native Universe: Voices of Indian America* (Washington DC: Smithsonian Institute, 2004); David Cuillier and

Susan D. Ross, "Gambling with Identity: Self-Representation of American Indians on Official Tribal Websites," *Howard Journal of Communications* 18, no. 3 (2008): 197–219.

53. Michael A. McDonnell, "Paths Not Yet Taken, Voices Not Yet Heard: Rethinking Atlantic History," in *Connected Worlds: History in Transnational Perspective*, ed. Ann Curthoys and Marilyn Lake (Canberra: ANU E Press, 2006), 45–61, quote on 45.

54. Francis P. Prucha, *Americanizing the American Indians* (Cambridge MA: Harvard University Press, 1973), 100, passim; Berkhofer, *The White Man's Indian*, 149–52; Eric Cheyfitz, "Savage Law: The Plot against American Indians in *Johnson and Graham's Lessee v. M'Intosh* and *The Pioneers*," in *Cultures of United States Imperialism*, ed. Amy Kaplan and Donald E. Pease (Durham NC: Duke University Press, 1993), 113.

55. Joe Starita, *"I Am a Man": Chief Standing Bear's Journey for Justice* (New York: St. Martin's Press, 2008).

Part 1

Adapting Indigenous Identities for the Colonial Diaspora

| Chapter 1

Indigenous Identities in Mesoamerica after the Spanish Conquest

Rebecca Horn

Of all the European powers, Spain encountered the greatest diversity of indigenous societies in the Americas, ranging from the fully sedentary empires of Mesoamerica and the Andes to the small bands of hunters and gatherers scattered through the arid northern reaches of Mexico or the deep grasslands of southern Argentina. Each of these indigenous groups surely had its own notions of identity, though available Spanish-language sources tell us relatively little about them.[1] In this regard, Mesoamerica stands apart; it was the only part of Spanish America—indeed, the Americas as a whole—that after the conquest developed a widespread tradition of writing in indigenous languages using the Latin alphabet introduced by Europeans. This tradition, carried out by indigenous scribes in their home communities over roughly three centuries of Spanish rule, produced thousands and thousands of documents that recorded local legal matters in genres modeled on (but not identical to) Spanish ones—a corpus unique in the Americas in terms of its size, complexity, and duration. Written in such indigenous languages as Nahuatl, Mixtec, and Maya, these "notarial" documents include testaments, land records, petitions, and minutes of city council meetings, among others. Mesoamericans also produced alphabetic and pictorial manuscripts, including historical annals, community histories, and genealogies that were neither produced by official community scribes nor based primarily on European documentary genres. Together, these two broad types of indigenous-language sources convey a complex and variegated sense of indigenous identities in Mesoamerica, hardly evident in Spanish-language sources or available for other parts of the Americas.

Drawing heavily on recent scholarship based on indigenous-language sources, this chapter explores indigenous identities in Mesoamerica in the three centuries after the Spanish conquest.[2] It argues that across Mesoamerica, indigenous identities were highly localized, with individuals defined by membership in an indigenous polity. Social status was highly differentiated, including (at least initially) the fundamental distinction between noble and commoner. Leaders of indigenous communities employed diverse strategies to retain or acquire certain benefits, ranging from campaigns for recognition and privilege from Spanish authorities to legal suits lodged in Spanish courts to protect community lands, strengthening collective identities in the process. Indigenous-language manuscripts often played a critical role in these efforts, helping to create common understandings of ethnic identity, community origins and history, and for leaders, legitimacy to govern. Hardly static, indigenous identities shifted over time in ways that reflect preconquest traditions and regional diversity as well as the nature, timing, and intensity of Spanish intrusion. Indigenous communities throughout Mesoamerica adopted European-introduced animals, crops, and material goods, along with Hispanic-style government, religion, and markers of social status. In addition, Mesoamericans came to terms with the common experience of Spanish rule and the presence of new groups—Spaniards, blacks, and persons of mixed ancestry— that also played a role in the construction of individual and community identities over time. Yet in the end, indigenous-language sources counter any traditional notion of a homogeneous "Indian" identity; Mesoamericans continued to identify themselves primarily by membership in a Native community (in contrast to a racialized pan-Indian identity) throughout the colonial period and beyond.[3]

The modern term Mesoamerica (literally, "Middle America") refers to a cultural region that at the time of the Spanish conquest extended in the north to the upper reaches of central Mexico and in the south to the northern reaches of present-day Central America, including Guatemala and parts of Honduras and El Salvador.[4] Through centuries of interaction, the region came to share certain cultural features, including complex polities, pronounced social stratification, intensive, permanent agriculture, elaborate trade and tribute systems, and such impressive cultural achievements as monumental stone architecture, fine craft production, sophisticated writing/painting traditions, a calendar, and a vigesimal counting system. For all these reasons, Mesoamerica proved enormously appealing to Spaniards, who in the sixteenth century concentrated their activities there, along with the Andean highlands, the only other region of the Americas that boasted such complex indigenous societies; together, Mesoamerica and Peru became the center of the early Spanish American empire. Estimates of the Mesoamerican population at the time of the Spanish invasion remain a topic of heated debate, with the most extensive demographic research presenting figures just for central Mexico ranging from 11 million to 25 million.[5] The region had many distinct language and cultural groups, some quite small in size and geographic range, others larger and more dominant.

Indigenous-language research has the longest tradition for three core Mesoamerican groups. The Nahuatl-speaking peoples, or Nahuas, constituted the major linguistic-cultural group in central Mexico, which bore the brunt of the Spanish presence. The Ñudzahuis (Mixtecs) and Yucatec Mayas inhabited the southern regions of Mesoamerica, at some distance from the center of Spanish colonial life and the commercial trunk line from silver mines to transatlantic port. Relatively few Spaniards ended up either in the Mixteca, a culturally and linguistically diverse region, or in the more homogeneous Yucatan.[6] Those who did largely clustered along the main highways that connected Mexico City with Oaxaca City, Yucatan, and Guatemala or in Spanish regional administrative and commercial centers. Indigenous-language scholarship, now well advanced, allows comparative approaches within Mesoamerica, highlighting regional variation in indigenous responses to the changes introduced by Spaniards. With time, many individuals permanently left indigenous communities to reside either in urban areas or on Spanish estates. Throughout the colonial period, however, the majority of Mesoamericans remained in their home communities scattered across the countryside, speaking Native languages, cultivating traditional crops, recognizing the authority of local rulers, and negotiating changing notions of individual and collective identities.[7]

In Mesoamerica, indigenous peoples hardly experienced the widespread dislocation and dispersal (diaspora) characteristic of the Native groups in many other parts of the Americas examined in this volume. Rather, most Mesoamericans confronted the profound changes initiated by Spanish conquest and settlement, including the large-scale migration of Spaniards and Africans to the region and the growth of populations of mixed ancestry, in the context of home communities. Individual and group identities thus remained framed by the institutional and social structures that defined everyday community life: the indigenous state and its constituent parts, gender and status hierarchies, and religious institutions and practices. Linked so firmly to local communities and practices, identity in Mesoamerica never became a matter of simply being an "Indian"; rather, Mesoamerican identities reflected the complexities of local indigenous life across time and place.

The Indigenous State

Indigenous-language scholarship has at long last put to rest any lingering notion of a homogeneous "Indian" identity in Mesoamerica after the Spanish conquest, instead highlighting individual identity as rooted in membership in the indigenous state.[8] Indigenous-language sources rarely adopted the Spanish term *indio*; rather, they typically identify individuals as members of an indigenous regional state—known as *altepetl* in Nahuatl, *ñuu* in Ñudzahui (Mixtec), and *cah* in Maya.[9] Central to Mesoamerican sociopolitical organization before and after the Spanish conquest, these states formed the basis of empire. The so-called Aztec empire had been made up of separate, autonomous states that, when given the opportunity, allied with Spaniards to overthrow the Mexican imperial rulers at Tenochtitlan. Although the Aztec empire

was destroyed during the Spanish conquest, the individual states survived.[10] Indeed, after the Spanish conquest, indigenous states throughout Mesoamerica were initially strengthened, forming as they did the
basis for Spanish civil and ecclesiastical jurisdictions that the Spaniards
had no interest or capability to cut from whole cloth.[11]

The precise nature and internal organization of the indigenous
state in Mesoamerica varied by region and culture group, with important implications for postconquest adjustments. In central Mexico,
the heartland of the Nahuatl-speaking peoples, the indigenous state
was called *altepetl*. The term altepetl "is a slightly altered form of the
metaphorical doublet *in atl, in tepetl*, 'the water(s), the mountain(s),'
and thus it refers in the first instance to territory, but what is meant is
primarily an organization of people holding sway over a given territory."[12] Each altepetl considered itself a separate people with a shared
origin tradition (often rooted in migration in the distant past) and
ethnic identity, as well as allegiance to a dynastic ruler or *tlatoani* (pl.
tlatoque) and an ethnic god; along with the central marketplace, the
ruler's palace and the main temple served as the physical embodiment
of altepetl identity and sovereignty. Each altepetl was composed of
constituent parts, known as *calpolli* or *tlaxilacalli*, each a microcosm
of the whole, typically with its own god, distinctive name, leader with
distinctive title, and portion of altepetl territory. Overall, organization of the altepetl was cellular or modular, with a number of "relatively equal, relatively separate and self-contained constituent parts
of the whole," among which rotated certain responsibilities according to a ranked order of preference.[13] In sum, a designated territory,
set of constituent parts, and established dynastic ruler constituted the
main criteria to be an altepetl.

The Ñudzahui ñuu and the Maya cah shared many of the core features of the Nahua altepetl. Ñudzahui-language documents typically
identify individuals as affiliated with a specific ñuu, as, for example,
"*tay ñuu Yucunduchi*, 'person from the ñuu of Etlantongo,' or simply
tay ñuu, 'person from a ñuu.'"[14] Some ñuu were also known as *yuhuitayu*—a term that referred to a marriage alliance between the hereditary rulers of two ñuu.

The term *yuhuitayu* is a metaphorical doublet: *yuhui* is "reed mat," and tayu is "seat" or "pair" (depending on tonal pronunciation). Tayu is a tone pun or metaphor for both the seat of rulership and the married, ruling couple. . . . As a metaphorical doublet representing an actual place, the yuhuitayu is comparable to the Nahuatl term for the local ethnic state, *altepetl*, a combining form of *atl*, "water," and *tepetl*, "hill." The symbol of the yuhuitayu represented an institution that joined the resources and rulerships of two ñuu without compromising their autonomy and separateness.[15]

Images of the royal couple, typically seated together on a reed mat facing each other, found in Ñudzahui codices, *lienzos* (pictorial records painted on cloth), and maps, symbolized the yuhuitayu and represented its autonomy and high status. Similar to the altepetl, the yuhuitayu also had constituent parts (called *siqui, siña*, and *dzini*, depending on the locale) that carried distinctive names, represented segments of the whole, and were bound together by ethnicity, common origin, and economic and political ties; for Ñudzahuis, as with Nahuas, these subunits represented the primary site of identity beyond the level of the household, with Ñudzahui-language documents typically identifying an individual by membership in a particular one.

In contrast, no parallel term to (Nahuatl) calpolli/tlaxilacalli and (Ñudzahui) siqui/siña/dzini emerges from the Yucatec Maya—language documents, leaving it unclear whether such subunits formed part of cah organization; Maya-language documents typically refer to an individual cah member as *cahnal* (pl. *cahalob*), "cah member," and *ah cahnal*, "he who resides (or was born in) the cah of."[16] In Yucatan, the primary collective term of identity between the level of the cah and the household was *chibal* (pl. *chibalob*)—the patronymic group. Members of a chibal, or those who shared a patronymic, "formed a kind of extended family, most of whose members seem to have pursued their common interests wherever possible through political factionalism, the acquisition and safeguarding of land, and the creation of marriage-based alliances with other chibalob of similar or higher socioeconomic status."[17]

The "chibal was in many ways a substitute for a calpolli-type sub-unit in that it formed a partial basis for identity, economic organization, and sociopolitical faction within each cah."[18] Differences in the internal structure of the indigenous state affected how Mesoamericans responded to the changes imposed by Spaniards after the conquest, evident in such diverse realms as municipal organization, office holding, and even personal naming patterns.

Far from being destroyed by the Spanish conquest, the indigenous state was initially strengthened, as "[e]verything the Spaniards organized outside their own settlements in the sixteenth century—the encomienda, the rural parishes, Indian municipalities, the initial administrative jurisdictions—was built solidly on individual, already existing altepetl."[19] Spaniards first gained access to the resources of indigenous communities through the *encomienda*, a grant of Indian tribute and labor awarded (almost always) to a Spaniard for service to the crown, initially through participation in the conquest. In central Mexico, where the indigenous state was relatively large, one altepetl typically became first an encomienda and then a parish and a municipality, with its own Hispanic-style town council, or *cabildo*, introduced by Spanish officials beginning around the mid-sixteenth century. In the Mixteca, with many small indigenous states (coupled with a weak Spanish presence and thus relatively weaker demand for encomienda grants), multiple units of yuhuitayu, ñuu, and siqui usually became an encomienda grant, parish, and municipality.[20] With time, and especially with indigenous population decline, the encomienda waned in importance and many individual grants reverted to the crown. Increasingly, direct royal government extended into the countryside, with several encomiendas—and thus indigenous states—typically designated one royal jurisdiction (*corregimiento*). Internally, tribute largely continued to be collected and labor drafts organized through the traditional authority of the dynastic ruler, with subunits (at least in the case of the Nahua altepetl and Ñudzahui yuhuitayu/ñuu) taking turns in the customary manner.

Early on, Spaniards designated what they perceived to be the central settlement of an encomienda as a *cabecera* (head town) and the

remaining settlements as *sujetos* (subject towns). By elevating one settlement above others, the Spanish cabecera-sujeto arrangement violated the indigenous principle of equal constituent parts, at least in
the case of the Nahua altepetl and Ñudzahui yuhuitayu/ñuu, where
it clearly underlay indigenous organization. Moreover, since the original criterion for cabecera status was an indigenous rulership, the designation of a cabecera-sujeto arrangement effectively disenfranchised
the rulers from those entities that had not received official Spanish
recognition. As Kevin Terraciano states concerning the Ñudzahuis:
"Disputed successions and claims of yuhuitayu status undoubtedly existed before the conquest, but the new order gave undue advantage to
a few prominent places to the exclusion of others. As a center of local
government, administration, writing, economic enterprise, tribute
collection, and religious authority, the cabecera became more powerful than any of its parts."[21]

Resenting their subordinate status and hoping to rid themselves
of tribute and labor obligations to the cabecera, the leaders of sujetos sought autonomy. The timing varied regionally. In central Mexico, the move by sujetos to gain independence was in full swing by the
early seventeenth century, whereas in the Mixteca it occurred much
later. Everywhere, it picked up momentum with time as internal and
external pressures for independence mounted decade by decade up
to 1800.[22] Throughout Mesoamerica, bids for independence by sujetos
fragmented the indigenous state, leading eventually to smaller entities often recognized by Spaniards simply as undifferentiated pueblos.
Fragmentation, however, should not be considered simply a process
of decline, as traditionally portrayed by scholars; the tendency toward
autonomy was an inherent characteristic of the Nahua altepetl and
Ñudzahui ñuu, with postconquest circumstances providing new incentives for old tendencies. Nonetheless, the simplification of indigenous sociopolitical organization represented an undeniable secular
trend. However altered, indigenous entities survived throughout the
colonial period as corporate bodies and sites of individual and collective identities. Such indigenous terms as altepetl/tlaxilacalli, yuhuita-
yu/ñuu, and cah are found in indigenous-language documents as long

as they continued to be produced—in contrast to the virtual absence of such Spanish terms as cabecera, sujeto, and pueblo.[23] Among the Nahuas, the smaller entities kept the whole rationale in terms of just themselves and almost stopped speaking of the older altepetl. Over time, the result was an even stronger micro-patriotism concentrated on even smaller units instead of an expanding ethnicity. Moreover, as the function of interregional communication of all kinds was increasingly taken over by Spanish mechanisms, the smaller entities became ever more isolated from each other.

As part of the broader attempt to refashion indigenous states into Hispanic-style municipalities, Spanish authorities introduced the *cabildo*, or municipal council, beginning around the mid-sixteenth century.[24] Although based on the Spanish model, indigenous cabildos never replicated it exactly; rather, they differed in ways that reflected preconquest traditions of political authority and governance. Most strikingly, indigenous cabildos included a position not found on Spanish ones—the governor (using the Spanish loanword *gobernador*). It was presumably a concession to the role of the indigenous ruler whom the Spaniards called *cacique*, a term of Caribbean origin that Spaniards carried throughout Spanish America. Initially, the (male) ruler filled the position, a pattern reflected in such titles as *cacique y gobernador* and *señor* (natural ruler) *y gobernador* and (incorporating Native titles for rulers) *yya toniñe gobernador* (in the Mixteca) and *batab-gobernador* (in Yucatan). Even though Spanish law required annual election of cabildo officers, caciques tended to serve repeatedly, conforming to the preconquest custom of lifetime hereditary rule. Overall, "in these formative years, the governorship permanently took on a great deal of the aura, powers, and characteristics of the preconquest rulership."[25]

Similar to the governorship, indigenous municipalities adapted other cabildo offices to fit local traditions. These offices included *alcaldes* (judges) and *regidores* (councilmen), whose titles were drawn from Spanish tradition but who were selected from the same group of prominent nobles that would have governed alongside the ruler before the conquest. In contrast to Spanish practices, indigenous communities ranked alcaldes higher than regidores in social terms, associated even minor municipal offices with noble status, and did not maintain a strict boundary between cabildo officers and a larger body of nobles involved in municipal affairs. Regional traditions also emerge. Nahua and Ñudzahui cabildo officers represented specific districts of the indigenous state (yet another departure from Spanish traditions) whereas in the Yucatan they represented patronymic groups. In diverse ways, indigenous communities adopted a Spanish institution and transformed it to suit their own needs and traditions. Most importantly, they identified with it—the cabildo (or *oficiales de república*, as town officials were known in the late colonial period) became the corporate manifestation of altepetl, ñuu, and cah identity.

The creation of the governorship nonetheless profoundly altered preconquest practices, with long-term implications for political authority and power in indigenous communities. Right away, the designation of a single governor in complex polities with multiple rulers created one recognized head and consolidated rule that had not existed before the conquest. Moreover, even though in many places rulers and those high-ranking nobles eligible for the rulership continued to dominate indigenous cabildos, the rulership and governorship separated with time—except in Yucatan, where Maya cahob never developed a tradition of a rulership (*batabil*) separate from the governorship, and the system of annual election never took root. In the end, the broader pattern led to the creation of an entirely new political position and hierarchy, with the loss of authority for many hereditary rulers. And notably in the Mixteca, where the marriage of a male ruler and a female ruler created the yuhuitayu, it also resulted in the widespread exclusion of women from official political positions, with the subsequent loss of political power and material resources that that process entailed. Formal political authority increasingly became defined as masculine.

Once established, indigenous government lasted in its basic form until independence.[26] It was involved in all aspects of community life, including the dispensation of local justice, sponsorship of religious festivities, confirmation of inheritance rights and land transfers, collection of tribute and organization of public labor service, expenditure of municipal funds, and maintenance of community buildings, among others. As the official governing body that oversaw internal legal matters, it also produced (through the municipal notaries associated with it) a vast body of indigenous-language documentation that tells us so much about community life and culture in the postconquest era. Based on a Spanish model and initially imposed by Spanish authorities, the cabildo along with the local patron saint quickly became the emblem of corporate pride and identity for indigenous communities across Mesoamerica. It symbolized the tradition of local autonomy and constituted the primary instrument of corporate representation—to Spanish authorities and in Spanish courts and also in relation to other indigenous corporations. In this guise, the cabildo worked to protect the integrity of community lands, challenge tribute and labor abuses, defend local residents in myriad ways, seek privileges for the corporate body, and overall promote the status and well-being of the community. As a political body staffed by the most prominent male members of the local community, it also served the social, political, and economic interests of those who governed, a reflection of the profound cleavages of rank and status present in indigenous communities before and after the conquest.

Rank and Status

Pronounced social stratification characterized Mesoamerican communities in the pre- and postconquest periods, framing notions of individual and group identity. At the time of the conquest, the distinction between the hereditary categories of noble and commoner was basic to indigenous social and political life, with fine gradations within each group, constituting overall a broad social continuum of wealth and status.[27] Elaborate vocabularies to indicate key social categories had developed among diverse Mesoamerican groups in the preconquest period. For the Nahuas, these categories included *tlatoani* (pl. *tlatoque*), "ruler"; *teuctli* (pl. *teteuctin*), "lord"; *pilli* (pl. *pipiltin*), "noble"; and *macehualli* (pl. *macehualtin*), "commoner." In the possessed form, macehualli meant "subject, vassal," whereas the unpossessed form meant "commoner" (originally, macehualli meant "human being"). Among the Ñudzahuis, key social categories were *yya toniñe* (lord ruler) and *yya dzehe toniñe* (lady ruler) for the hereditary rulers of a yuhuitayu; *yya* (male lord) and *yya dzehe* (female lord) for the highest-ranking lords of a ñuu, who descended directly from a ruling couple; *toho* and *toho dzehe* for noblemen and noblewomen, who could not claim descent on both sides from rulers; *ñandahi* for commoner, or person from a ñuu liable to community labor, apparently in addition to the dependents who lived on the lands of nobles. Similarly, two broad hereditary categories characterized Maya society: *almehen*, "noble" (pl. *almehenob*), which included the ruler or *batab*, and *macehual* (from the Nahuatl macehualli, apparently a preconquest loanword; pl. *macehualob*), "commoner." In Yucatan, the term macehual meant "commoner" and "subject, vassal," similar to the term macehualli in central Mexico.

Throughout preconquest Mesoamerica, commoners constituted the vast majority of people resident in indigenous communities. Most commoners held land through membership in an individual district (Nahua calpolli/tlaxilacalli or Ñudzahui *siqui, siña*, and *dzini*) of the indigenous state. In turn, they delivered tribute in goods and performed community labor, working in a system of ordered rotation (Nahua *coatequitl*; Ñudzahui *tniño*) alongside their neighbors and under the supervision of district leaders, whether at the lord's palace, local temple, marketplace, or lands held by prominent nobles. Another group of commoners resided permanently on lands held by nobles—not community land distributed directly by district authorities. These dependent laborers did not participate in community labor drafts but maintained themselves and their families through service to the noble establishment, contributing to its productive capacity. Dependents typically originated from outside the local indigenous state—through conquest, migration, or simply destitution—yet apparently were not sharply distinguished as a separate group from ordinary commoners.[28] Mesoamerican communities also included slaves who likewise tended to originate outside the local district and whose relationship to ordinary commoners was ambiguous.

Far fewer in numbers, nobles constituted a privileged minority with its own hierarchy of ranked status.[29] The most illustrious were the lords

of noble lineages that possessed buildings, lands, and dependents—
called *teccalli* in Nahuatl and *aniñe* in Ñudzahui.[30] The relationship
between these noble establishments and the districts through which
ordinary commoners received land and fulfilled tribute obligations
was controversial among both Nahuas and Ñudzahuis. In the eastern Nahua region, noble houses (teccalli) were so prominent that they
might have subverted and replaced the calpolli/tlaxilacalli structure,
a situation not dissimilar to Ñudzahui aniñe and the subunits of the
ñuu.[31] Noble status conferred various privileges, most strikingly ex-
emption from the community labor service performed by commoners. Yet nobles also carried out a wide range of administrative duties,
including the organization of the community labor draft itself, in
addition to various reciprocal obligations that constituted serious responsibilities. Commoners sought protection and aid from local authorities in times of need.

In contrast to Nahua and Ñudzahui practices, Yucatec Mayas, nobles and commoners alike, were organized into *chibal*—the patronymic
group. Consequently, an individual's identity rested on cah membership, hereditary status (noble or commoner), and chibal affiliation.
The Mayas maintained a taboo on marriage within the chibal, thereby creating marriage alliances between chibalob—and consequently multi-chibal households. Together, these households constituted a
network of chibal interest groups that reached across the cah—and beyond. Patronymic groups thus created connections between autonomous Yucatec Maya states. At times one prominent patronymic group
came to dominate a larger region of multiple cahob, the larger region
on occasion becoming known by the name of the dominant chibal.
Matthew Restall argues that patronymic groups also reinforced the
distinction between noble and commoner since chibalob tended to
consist of families at similar socioeconomic levels.

Throughout Mesoamerica, the distinction between noble and commoner was marked in multiple ways, including material wealth, physical adornment, codes of behavior, and access to specialized knowledge.
High-ranking nobles lived in large, finely decorated (stone or adobe)
palaces, dressed in intricately woven textiles, and adorned themselves

with elaborate jewelry and headdresses.[32] They commanded numerous servants and sponsored sumptuous feasts. They controlled large landholdings, typically divided into numerous separate plots in scattered locations that at times were worked by dependent laborers resident on the land. Nobles learned elaborate speech forms, were familiar with the conventions of pictographic writing, and had access to specialized spiritual knowledge and substances.[33]

After the conquest, Spaniards recognized Mesoamerican rulers as high-ranking lords entitled to certain rights and privileges, including patrimonial lands and tribute in goods and labor. Eschewing indigenous terms, Spaniards referred to indigenous rulers as *caciques* (male) and *cacicas* (female). As crucial intermediaries between Spanish authorities and indigenous commoners, caciques interacted closely with Spaniards, employing various strategies, legal and otherwise, to shore up their position within the new social and political order.[34] Don Juan de Guzmán—the great mid-sixteenth-century ruler of Coyoacan, a prominent altepetl located southwest of Mexico City—vividly illustrates this pattern.

While maintaining ties with the ruling families of other altepetl, don Juan de Guzmán also enjoyed close relations with Spanish authorities. He spoke some Spanish, aided the Spaniards in suppressing the Mixtón rebellion in western Mexico in the 1540s, and on occasion hunted with the viceroy. As the viceroy stated, he "was always treated like a Spaniard." Don Juan de Guzmán actively sought the confirmation and protection of rights associated with the rulership from Spanish authorities; he petitioned the king for favors and called attention to the services rendered to the crown by his father and brother. Royal *cédulas* (orders) issued in 1534 and 1545 confirmed his landholdings as private property, creating a *cacicazgo*, or the entailed estate of a cacique based on the Spanish model of *mayorazgo*. A royal cédula of 1551 granted him a coat of arms, and Viceroy Mendoza authorized him to carry a sword "after the Spanish manner." And in 1553 don Juan de Guzmán requested that the king grant him and his heirs the office of governor (the grant was not forthcoming, however). Don Juan also complained to the king that Spaniards treated Coyoacan commoners as if they were slaves, and in the 1550s he brought suit against [don Hernando de] Cortés for usurping land and demanding excessive labor and tribute. Finally, shortly before his death in 1569, don Juan and [his wife] doña Mencía founded a *capellanía*, or ecclesiastical endowment, at the Dominican monastery in Coyoacan.[35]

The quintessential sixteenth-century indigenous ruler, don Juan de Guzmán—along with others like him across Mesoamerica—used visual culture to reinforce the hierarchy of indigenous political authority in New Spain. The coat of arms awarded to a royal lineage or the privilege to ride on horseback or carry a sword visually reminded public audiences of the power and status of indigenous rulers and the high-ranking noblemen and noblewomen closely associated with them. Indigenous authorities willingly incorporated Spanish "insignia of power" into their existing repertory in the sixteenth century and later. Pictorial manuscripts illustrate this pattern, depicting Native lords wearing Spanish-style shirts and trousers and holding the *vara* (Spanish staff of office) while covered with a Native cape and seated on a reed mat—the pre-Hispanic symbol of political authority. At times, pictorial manuscripts portray rulers with a turquoise diadem, a pre-Hispanic convention that symbolizes political authority.[36]

Although Nahua women might influence royal succession, they ruled in their own right only in exceptional cases, primarily in the absence of a male heir to the throne. In contrast, Ñudzahui women were recognized as hereditary rulers, reflecting the practice in which a marriage alliance between a hereditary male and female ruler, each from a separate, autonomous ñuu, created the yuhuitayu. Spanish authorities acknowledged this tradition of political alliance through royal marriage with the legal notion of *conjunta persona*, or "joint person" rule, which legally recognized female rulers and their right to patrimony, or *cacicazgo* (rights, properties, and dependents associated with the royal lineage).[37] Spanish authorities and Ñudzahui commoners alike continued to recognize male and female caciques in many places throughout the colonial period. Nonetheless, Spanish rule accorded specific advantages to male over female rulers, which, together with the creation of the exclusively male cabildo, led to their ultimate exclusion from official political decision making in Ñudzahui communities. A series of images of the ruler doña Catalina de Peralta in the *Codex Sierra*, a pictorial manuscript that records community accounts in the mid-sixteenth century, visually depict this transition. Heir to the throne of Santa Catalina Texupa, doña Catalina de Peralta claimed possession of the lordly establishment (aniñe) and its properties and received confirmation as cacique from Spanish authorities in 1569. Reflecting her royal status, the earliest entries in the codex portray her seated prominently in front of the royal palace and the unnamed (male) governor, likely her spouse, who "derived his position from her authority in the community." Later, doña Catalina disappears from the manuscript, after which "a full cabildo appears for the first time" with the governor now "seated in front of a body of nobles who represent various offices of the cabildo." "The evolution of the full cabildo seems to have eclipsed the cacica's prominent position."[38]

With time, indigenous rulers increasingly found themselves competing with Spaniards for the tribute and labor of commoners, and they struggled to preserve privileges increasingly restricted by Spanish law. In general, the privileges of Mesoamerican lords diminished with time; the loss of land, servants, and income was common throughout the region, though greatest in central Mexico, where the Spanish presence hit hardest earliest. Catastrophic demographic decline severely cut into tribute deliveries and weakened labor drafts. At the same time, the lords' traditional obligations—to feed the nobles who served at the palace and the workers who performed labor service, to sponsor community feasts, to redistribute goods and services to local nobles—persisted, placing many lords in an increasingly compromised situation and leading to their frequent complaints that "they could no longer fulfill the social responsibilities that represented and sustained their authority."[39]

Social distinctions based on the hereditary categories of noble and commoner eroded with time, most clearly in central Mexico where the Spanish presence was felt most immediately and strongly. Judging by the documentary record, the Nahuatl terms for noble (pilli) and lord (teuctli) had fallen into disuse by the mid-seventeenth century. By the late colonial period, the concept of the tlatoani as a dynastic ruler of an altepetl had all but disappeared; the meaning of the term itself broadened and weakened, coming to mean "no more than a prominent person."[40] A similar trend occurred in the Mixteca. Ñudzahui terminology of nobility, including yya and toho, persisted in indigenous-language documents as long as they continued to be produced, although by the beginning of the eighteenth century references to specific individual yya and toho became less frequent. Even the reverential speech characteristic of the nobility began to fade by the end of the sixteenth century.[41] And as with the Nahuas, the cultural meaning of such terms may have also changed, referring simply to "important persons."[42] Apparently, the least change occurred in Yucatan, where almehen, the Native term for noble, persisted throughout the colonial period. Whether this continuity in terminology represents continuity in meaning is unclear.

In central Mexico, the demise of the preconquest terminological system of nobility and lordship parallels the decline of ruling dynastic lineages, but it by no means indicates the unequivocal leveling of Nahua society. In many communities an upper social, economic, and political group persisted up to independence, distinguished by its monopoly of local government and church offices, claim to large estates, including landholdings, and general political dominance in the local scene over generations. Most such late colonial political dynasties had no claim to be heirs of a preconquest ruling lineage, even though some bore similarities to the tlatoani lineages of the sixteenth century. In larger towns, two or three political dynasties might vie for the governorship and political dominance; the origins of each, whether a tlatoani lineage or not, mattered relatively little.[43] Ñudzahui noble privileges also diminished with time. Lords also complained of diminished access to labor and tribute, and demographic decline meant their base of support weakened. Yet not all dependents disappeared. Whereas in central Mexico, Nahua nobles could no longer boast of large numbers of dependents that worked patrimonial lands (except in the eastern region with its robust tradition of noble houses), among the Ñudzahuis "many yya and toho managed to retain many lands and a steady supply of labor throughout this period. In some parts of the Mixteca, the lord-dependent structure persisted well into the eighteenth century."[44] And in Yucatan, many chibal dynasties retained political and economic prominence throughout the colonial period.

For commoners, membership in a Native community, allegiance to a Native lord, and liability to provide tribute and labor constituted central elements of social identity. Like nobles, commoners fell along a broad continuum of wealth and status, with some employed in such specialized high-prestige occupations as long-distance trade or silver- and goldsmithing that also included nobles among their practitioners. Indeed, the boundaries between the two hereditary groups overlapped and were more porous than strictly rigid; commoners even had (limited) opportunities to ascend into the ranks of the nobility, assuming along the way outward markings strongly associated with noble status. In general, however, commoners were associated with the essential tasks of agricultural work (for men) and weaving (for women). "These roles were so basic that Spanish officials described the oficio [work] of some people in generic terms, as *trabajo de indio*, or 'Indian work.'"[45]

This gendered division of labor was fundamental to Mesoamerican ideology, practice, and identity, yet it "was not so strict as to prohibit men and women from performing a variety of duties that did not conform to an idealized division or specialization."[46] Both men and women performed multiple kinds of tasks. In addition to working in the fields, men filled the community labor drafts that cleared fields, constructed buildings, and transported goods. In addition to spinning and weaving, women performed various tasks around the household complex, activities that often led them to the fields and local marketplaces. They reproduced and reared children, prepared food (especially labor-intensive maize grinding) and drink, raised small animals, cultivated garden plots, provisioned the marketplace with goods and comestibles, and at times assisted with the harvest of crops. Women also worked outside the household complex as midwives and healers. And in the Nahua cultural region, evidence suggests that before the

conquest women also traditionally staffed separate hierarchies in religious, political, and economic spheres that paralleled those of men.

Social identity thus rested on gender as well as community affiliation and rank. Scholars consider Mesoamerican gender relations to be
complementary—male and female roles were considered equally critical to the survival and well-being of households and communities—
at the same time that they acknowledge regional variation.[47] Stronger
patriarchal tendencies characterized Maya groups, reflected in an emphasis on male leadership and descent reckoned primarily through
the male line. In contrast, Ñudzahuis harbored an ideology of complementarity among noblemen and noblewomen that allowed equally for male and female rule. The Nahuas fell somewhere in between,
as gender hierarchy flourished alongside gender complementarity and
parallelism.[48] Scholars continue to debate the extent to which the imposition of Spanish ideologies of patriarchy and gender hierarchy led
to the widespread diminution of the status of indigenous women after the conquest. Some scholars emphasize the narrowing of women's
roles; intensification of tribute and labor demands; resort to Spanish
legal precepts prejudicial to women; and introduction of religious beliefs "that stressed women's passivity, enclosure, purity, and honor."[49]
Others point to the persistence of gender complementarity at different times and in different places.

Indigenous-language research indicates the tremendous complexity of postconquest gender norms in indigenous communities, highlighting both change and continuity, along with significant regional
variation.[50] The gendered division of labor continued throughout the
colonial period, with women's work remaining critical to the well-
being of household and community. Indigenous women continued to
own, inherit, and bequeath landed property. In the Mixteca, Ñudzahui noblewomen continued to exercise informal political power and
control considerable resources, including land, labor, and prestige
goods, throughout the eighteenth century. Some Nahua noblewomen
displayed considerable local authority, at times dominating lineages
(often, it is true, when adult men had died out), playing an important
role in the marriage alliances of the next generation.[51] Women also

actively participated in the religious life of their communities and as
defenders of community interests.[52]

Nevertheless, Spanish gender norms had an unmistakable impact,
especially with time. The introduction of the Hispanic-style cabildo
excluded indigenous women from formal political office in their communities, as we have seen. In later years, women served less often as
witnesses to official documents, a reflection of the Spanish notion that
only adult males constituted legitimate witnesses to legal procedure.[53]
And in eighteenth-century central Mexico, gendered terms at times replaced traditional gender-neutral ones to refer to small children and
spouses, pointing "to Spanish gender distinctions reaching into areas of
Nahuatl kinship terminology that had previously not been affected."[54]
These diverse examples of change and continuity in indigenous gender
norms and practices suggest the complexity and subtlety of the topic,
one that will benefit from future research in various realms of postconquest indigenous life. Whatever the case, throughout Mesoamerica,
women and men continued to equate their identity with membership
in the corporate group and the social rank and status of their families.[55]

In the postconquest period, personal names came to distinguish
Mesoamericans from Spaniards and to create social distinctions (based
on status, gender, and other criteria) within indigenous communities,
with time going far "toward replacing traditional social categories"
of hereditary (noble and commoner) status.[56] Personal names thus
marked social identity and status throughout colonial Mesoamerica,
and certain features were shared regionwide, most notably the widespread adoption of Spanish given names and the honorific noble titles
don and *doña*. Yet indigenous naming patterns were neither identical
to Spanish ones nor uniform throughout colonial Mesoamerica, a reflection of regional differences in preconquest practices and the timing and intensity of Spanish intrusion. Broadly speaking, the Maya
emphasis on lineage (and retention of indigenous patronymics) contrasted sharply with the virtual absence of family or lineage names
among Nahuatl and Ñudzahui speakers. Even so, Nahua and Ñudzahui patterns differed in significant ways, especially in terms of gender
and the timing of the transition to Spanish names.[57]

Personal names created a finely tuned system of social differentiation, at least among Nahuatl and Ñudzahui speakers. The most illustrious Spanish surnames, reserved for indigenous rulers or high-ranking nobles, indicated the highest social status. They originated with famous conquerors, encomenderos, or royal officials and included such renowned examples as Cortés, Guzmán, and Mendoza. At times, the Spaniard had actually served as a baptismal sponsor. But these surnames also spread independent of direct baptismal sponsorship, though clearly still with some oversight, as only the most prominent indigenous nobles were eligible recipients. Less prestigious surnames included Spanish patronymics—Gómez, Hernández, Jiménez, Juárez, López, Pérez, and Sánchez, among others—that carried a decidedly plebeian tone among Spaniards. Other indigenous nobles might bear the name of an actual saint (e.g., doña Catalina de Sena), a name based on Christian lore or doctrine (e.g., Juan de la Cruz or Gaspar de los Reyes), or a name characteristic of ecclesiastics, commonly a saint's name adopted at the time a friar took vows (e.g., Cristóbal de San Pedro). These ecclesiastical names apparently served as a model for indigenous commoners who had had no Spanish baptismal sponsor. With time, the repetitive "de San" (or de Santo) element was dropped, leaving two Spanish first names: Cristóbal Pedro (drawing on the example above) or the archetype Juan Diego or Juana María. These double first names ranked lowest on the social scale and constituted the norm for ordinary commoners from the time they were adopted up until independence. With full Spanish names, the primary distinction was between those individuals (largely ordinary commoners) who carried two Spanish first names and those with all other types of Spanish surnames, which generally indicated higher social status.

Consistent with kinship principles, neither Nahua nor Ñudzahui names in the preconquest period bore any relation to family or lineage, although among Nahuas "in certain royal dynasties the same names were used in succeeding generations, at intervals, thus associating a set of names with a specific dynasty and rulership."[58] A similar pattern prevailed after the adoption of Spanish surnames. The only names that tended to be carried in the same family and passed on to children and grandchildren were the highest-ranking Spanish surnames that tended to be associated with those prominent families involved in office holding, at times having originated in a great ruler in the sixteenth century. Consider, for example, the ruling family of Coyoacan that carried the surname Guzmán across generations, its origins harking back to the great mid-sixteenth-century tlatoani don Juan de Guzmán mentioned above.[59] Indeed, some governing families maintained the same surname from the sixteenth into the eighteenth century. Most Spanish surnames, however, bore no relation to lineage, and members of Nahua and Ñudzahui families typically had entirely different second names.

The variable naming typical of Nahua and Ñudzahui families differs dramatically from Maya patterns, in which the patronymic so unambiguously emphasized lineage. After the conquest, Mayas adopted a Christian first name, and evidence from Maya-language sources suggests that Christian first names for females were no more conservative than for males. The Mayas also retained the culturally significant patronymic—with no widespread adoption of Spanish surnames throughout the sweep of the colonial period. Maya patronymics reflected the general status of a particular chibal (patronymic group) in a given cah. But they never conveyed the fine-tuned distinctions of social differentiation and identity characteristic of the diverse Spanish surnames adopted in Nahua and Ñudzahui communities.

Mesoamericans also adopted the Spanish honorific titles of don and (its feminine form) doña though their use varied by cultural group.[60] Among Spaniards, the don or doña was acquired at birth and carried for the duration of an individual's life. "The don was primarily a matter of family and birthright; all the sons of a don were also don from the hour of their birth to the hour of their death."[61] At the time of the conquest, only the highest Spanish nobility carried the title don, though the feminine form, doña, was more widespread among the women of noble families. After the conquest, Spaniards awarded the don to most recognized (male) indigenous rulers at the time of baptism. With time, however, Mesoamericans used the title in ways that diverged from customary Spanish practice. The Nahuas apparently equated the title with office holding—a prominent male would be without it until accession to high office, when he would acquire it. The use of doña was initially more restricted than with Spaniards, "presumably because the noblewomen did not ordinarily hold an office or head a [noble house]."[62] Ñudzahui and Maya peoples also adopted the terms don and doña. In contrast to Nahuas, however, their use of the terms remained far more conservative, being restricted to the highest-ranking lords throughout the entire colonial period.

Personal names thus created distinctions both within indigenous communities and between Indians and Spaniards. A Maya patronymic clearly identified an individual as an Indian at the same time that, along with the presence or absence of the honorific title don or doña, it provided a minimal measure of status within a community (or region), depending on the reputation of a given chibal. In Nahua and Ñudzahui communities, Spanish names functioned in similar yet arguably more subtle ways. Double first names became the norm for ordinary people and identified the bearer as an Indian who lacked the rank and status of those individuals who carried Spanish surnames—a system that itself provided clues as to the ethnic identity and social rank of an individual. The prominent surname Cortés, for example, became one of the most common names among indigenous nobles in central Mexico. Someone with that name was most likely to be an Indian; if he also carried the title don, it was almost a certainty. Certain Spanish saints' names and patronymics—Santiago and Juárez, among others—also became characteristically "Indian." The use of the title don with a plebeian-sounding patronymic, as in don Pedro Jiménez, would not occur among Spaniards until a late time, before which it would have been utterly ridiculous.[63] An individual with such a name could only be an Indian nobleman. And because the transition from indigenous to Spanish names occurred at different times in cabeceras and outlying areas, names also provided clues to one's residence or one's status as either a minor or prominent official. In the end, naming patterns identified individuals as Indians while at the same time constituting a fine-tuned register of rank and status within indigenous communities that approximated the older terminology.

Indigenous Christians

As naming patterns suggest, Mesoamericans received Christian baptism in the wake of conquest, initiating the process by which they
became Christians. Traditionally, scholars have focused on the early stages of the so-called spiritual conquest, especially the efforts and
methods of friars and the success or failure of "conversion."[64] Recent
research based on indigenous-language sources has shifted scholarly
attention to the experiences and perspectives of Mesoamericans and
the centuries-long emergence of indigenous Christianities—and identities as indigenous Christians.[65] Ecclesiastical texts, including ser-
mons, catechisms, confessional guides, and religious plays, together
with the diverse indigenous-language documents produced in local
communities, constitute critical sources on Native religious expressions and identities in diverse regions of Mesoamerica throughout
the colonial period.[66]

Perhaps not surprisingly, the indigenous state held as central a place
in religious life as it did in the political sphere.[67] Each encomienda
(itself based on an indigenous state) typically became a parish (doc-
trina), with the cabecera also serving as the seat of the ecclesiastical
jurisdiction. In central Mexico, the process of creating parishes began
as early as the 1520s and was largely complete by the 1540s; in Oaxaca and Yucatan it occurred later, as did conquest itself. A parish initially received much of its revenue through the encomienda, so that
indigenous labor and tribute maintained the clergy stationed there,
with everything functioning through the internal organization and
working mechanisms of the indigenous municipality. Native authorities functioned as crucial intermediaries. Religious orders initially
administered rural indigenous parishes, the most prominent being
Franciscans, Dominicans, and Augustinians. With time, these parishes were secularized, that is, turned over to secular clergy, the process
not complete even in central Mexico until the eighteenth century.[68]

In the sixteenth century, the friars assigned to administer indigenous parishes oversaw major construction campaigns, with monastery churches rising near if not literally on the same site (and often

built from the same stones) as the preconquest temple. Like the preconquest temple, the Christian church (along with the cabildo) became the primary symbol of local sovereignty and identity. Local
residents enthusiastically participated in its construction and adornment, as they had with the temple in an earlier time. With time and
the fragmentation of indigenous jurisdictions, a secondary wave of
church construction occurred, as each newly independent community sought its own symbol of local autonomy. Indeed, at times a sujeto
constructed a church before it had actually acquired independence,
precisely to bolster its claim to autonomy.

The religious order associated with a parish became inextricably intertwined with local identity. Indigenous communities at times em-
barked on legal suits and even threatened violent resistance when royal
officials attempted to assign either another religious order or secular
clergy to the local parish. Indigenous entities often thought of the order in charge of the parish as part of their own identity, especially in
the early period. But local residents were also concerned with the potential loss of sacred property—the church and its devotional objects—
which, having been constructed by and maintained through the labor
and financial contributions of their forebears, they considered right-
fully theirs.[69] As one scholar states: "Attempts to assert control over the
local church buildings and property did not just symbolize their attachment to their parishes; these items *represented* their community, in the
broadest meaning of the term, and parishioners' claims on sacred property were also claims about community identity."[70] The church building likewise represented "the locus of community memory," because
it "made visible and tangible a sixteenth-century history [of indigenous
labor] perhaps otherwise only dimly remembered."[71]

As Spaniards, clerics assigned to a parish were outsiders to the local
community, rotated at fairly short intervals, and in any case were often
absent, seeing to their own interests or other matters in nearby urban
areas. The indigenous staff of the church, emerging out of the local
scene, thus took on special importance, representing the community
and mediating between the priest and parishioners. As James Lockhart states in regard to the Nahuas: "No wonder that the local people

considered themselves sole owners of their churches."[72] The highest-ranking church official—called *fiscal* (*de la iglesia*) among Nahuas and Ñudzahuis, and *maestro* (*de la iglesia*) among Mayas—served as the primary aide to the priest and general manager of the parish church, seeing to its smooth operation both in terms of religious observances and financial matters. The fiscal (or maestro) was a person of high social standing, drawn from the same group of prominent nobles who served on the cabildo, maybe at some point even taking a turn as alcalde or governor himself. Second-ranking to the cacique, the fiscal supervised a staff of "church people," including singers, musicians, sacristans, constables, custodians, and a notary clerk (*escribano de la iglesia*). Although initially each parish would have had a single fiscal, with the creation of new parishes the number of fiscales proliferated, at least among the Nahuas and Ñudzahuis, where the fragmentation of the indigenous polity occurred. "Perhaps the greatest single responsibility of both sets of [ecclesiastical and cabildo] officials, from the indigenous point of view, was to maintain the splendor of the church, the saint's cult, and the festivities as a unified expression of [corporate] well-being and religious devotion."[73]

More than anything, religion in postconquest Mesoamerica concerned saints.[74] Promoted by clerics, each parish church was dedicated to the patron saint of the community (an analog to the preconquest ethnic god), who became the sacred symbol of the community, unifying its constituent parts. The patron saint's feast day represented the height of a community's calendrical cycle of religious festivities, with participation of all the prominent town officials as well as the general populace, displaying the strength and internal organization of the municipality with great pomp and ceremony. Christian saints also constituted a central focus of household and personal devotions; each household sought to possess an image of a saint, with a separate "saint's house," or building, that the saint occupied. The cult seems to have emerged gradually, with the mature form not evident until the late seventeenth century, at least among the Nahuas. In the mature complex, each individual is ideally identified with a particular saint (image), and that saint with the household the individual will create;

the saint and the individual hold land jointly. Thus, the saint symbolizes the household's identity, much as the patron saint did for the
community. Indigenous-language testaments indicate that both men
and women possessed the images of saints, which they inherited, be-
queathed, and maintained. Heirs were charged with "serving" the
saint, acts of devotion that included providing flowers, incense, and
candles; keeping the images clean and in good repair; and sweeping
as a sacred act. In general, the household saints were not the same as
the community patron saint. Whenever possible, individuals brought
their personal or household saints to the community church to be
blessed and displayed publicly, at times risking their appropriation
by the community as a whole.

Cofradías (lay brotherhoods or confraternities) became a standard
feature of Mesoamerican communities during the seventeenth and
eighteenth centuries, representing another manifestation of the central
role of saints in indigenous religion. Spanish clerics initially encouraged the foundation of cofradías in Native communities—in central
Mexico campaigns began in earnest in the late sixteenth century—and
local people soon took the initiative. They proliferated until every indigenous municipality had one (or more). Each cofradía was dedicated to a saint, although at least in the Nahua region rarely (if ever) to
the patron saint of the community. However, cofradía officers were
drawn from the same group of prominent nobles who served in other secular and ecclesiastical posts. Interestingly, evidence also suggests
that women were active participants in lay brotherhoods, apparently
even serving as officers, a phenomenon not seen (at least from available documentation) in formal institutions in indigenous Mesoamerican communities in the postconquest period.[75]

The mature saint complex, as expressed in both community patron
saints and household saints, continued in Mesoamerica throughout
the colonial and into the national period. A significant change occurred with the emergence of regional devotions, which transcended
the boundaries of indigenous municipalities, especially the renowned
Virgin of Guadalupe, today the patron saint of Mexico.[76] Devotion
to the Virgin of Guadalupe initially reached beyond its base near

Mexico City through the efforts of Spanish clerics, building momentum in indigenous communities after the mid-seventeenth century. In the later period, indigenous-language documents refer to images of Guadalupe, to chapels devoted to her, and to interest in her apparition story—more so than anything seen with any other saint. This regionwide, multiethnic phenomenon in the later period paradoxically reflects the fragmentation of the indigenous state, along with the rise of bilingualism and the increased day- to-day interactions between individual Mesoamericans and Spaniards, a process most pronounced in central Mexico.

Overall, Mesoamericans came to identify as Christians. "Native people who underwent baptism and participated in Christian ceremonies were choosing to represent themselves as Christians, whatever they understood Christianity to be."[77] Certainly, Mesoamerican religious beliefs and practices differed in significant ways from those of Spaniards, though available documentation tells us more about outward behaviors than personal faith. Mesoamericans selectively responded "to the devotional options presented them by the friars [and thus] exerted considerable control over the creation of their church."[78] This indigenous church was characterized by its "intense ceremonialism" and "exuberant pageantry"—the incorporation of music, song, and dance; public processions; elaborate decorations, including the massive consumption of flowers; and dramatic performances with Native actors in costume, all a carryover from preconquest devotional practices.[79] Regional traditions also played a role, as different Mesoamerican groups interpreted Christian concepts and texts in somewhat distinct ways, a reflection largely of preconquest regional traditions.[80] At the same time, in family homes and outlying spaces outside the public arena, relatively unchanged indigenous practices persisted, as suggested by the periodic idolatry campaigns by Spanish clerics. An immediate and concrete illustration is the unique collection of Nahuatl incantations compiled by a priest in the early seventeenth century as a guide for other priests to recognize and root out idolatrous practices.[81] Yet identity as Christians remained at the core of both individual and corporate bodies. Indeed, in the later period, the coming of Christianity represented foundational acts in the histories of indigenous communities, reinforcing corporate identities, sovereignty, and boundaries.[82]

Collective Identities

The leaders of indigenous communities employed diverse strategies to advance the economic and political interests of their communities, in addition to their own lineages and factions, which in the end also helped maintain and create collective identities. As with other aspects of indigenous life in the colonial period, these efforts drew on both indigenous and Spanish traditions and succeeded most fully when they paralleled one another in significant ways. Indigenous communities valued local church and civic buildings as an expression of municipal pride and autonomy; championed corporate and dynastic privilege; utilized writing to claim and protect corporate and dynastic pretensions; and considered history central to the construction of identity. Indigenous communities maintained and created collective identities that separated themselves from outsiders, whether indigenous or Spanish. These strategies and identities were not static but rather changed with time.

Collective identities rested first and foremost with the corporate body and were manifested in both material and symbolic forms. The central spaces and structures of the municipality—the plaza, church, civic buildings, marketplace, and residence of the cacique—each represented municipal autonomy and pride, much as similar ones had done before the conquest. Sacred and ritual objects, including altarpieces, religious images, vestments, and chapels, served as the focus of local devotions and as symbols of a common identity, the patron saint considered symbolic protector and possessor of the community. Once established, the cabildo constituted a critical component of municipal identity and irrefutable evidence of its independent status. Its officers actively sought confirmation of territorial boundaries from Spanish authorities and privileges to enhance its reputation and prestige, whether a municipal coat of arms or a prestigious title like *ciudad* or *villa*, drawn from the civic hierarchy of Spanish municipalities.[83]

Tlaxcala, a large and important central Mexican altepetl, which early on allied with the Spaniards, so successfully campaigned for rewards in recognition of its role in the defeat of Tenochtitlan that it generated deep-seated resentment from neighboring groups not similarly recognized.[84] Once granted, these rewards and privileges reinforced and encouraged a sense of collective identity.

Writing constituted a central element in Native efforts to advance the economic and political interests of local leaders and communities, strengthening collective identities in the process. At the time of the conquest, Mesoamerica claimed a longstanding tradition of painting/writing, with the position of scribe commensurate with noble status.[85] This tradition facilitated the adoption of alphabetic writing in indigenous communities when Spaniards introduced it after the conquest; it soon became an autonomous, self-perpetuating tradition. The introduction of alphabetic writing did not immediately displace pictorial writing, although with time the latter largely fell away.[86] Each cabildo typically had one or more official notary clerk closely associated with it who produced documents concerned with day-to-day legal matters, including testaments, land sale records, petitions, election records, and minutes of cabildo meetings. Largely based on Spanish models, though never replicating them exactly, these notarial or mundane documents (as they are known in the field today) reflect the integrity and vitality of the indigenous corporate body, actively involved in the management of local affairs as well as external relations with Spaniards.[87]

The centrality of the corporate body to indigenous identity is also reflected in the branch of colonial-era manuscript production that includes diverse genres based primarily on preconquest ones and produced by individuals (or collaborative teams) working more autonomously than the official notaries associated with the cabildo. Arranged chronologically, with year-by-year entries, annals record events of interest to the local scene, creating a history that both reflected and promoted the autonomy and identity of a particular community, at least from the perspective of the author(s).[88] Genealogies trace royal lineage and succession to support a dynastic family's claim to power, property, and status as well as to undercut the pretensions of its rivals.[89] At times, dynastic genealogies were incorporated into cartographic histories—manuscripts that interweave history and geography, visually depicting the significant places and events in a community's past, including migrations, conquests, foundations, sacred landscapes, and boundaries, among others.[90] Manuscripts known as primordial titles (*títulos*), produced in the later period (none before the late seventeenth century), also present community histories, in this case typically with detailed boundary descriptions together with the recounting of mythic and historical events, similar to cartographic histories.[91] Maps produced in official settings likewise presented a local vision of territoriality and history.[92]

These complex, fascinating, and diverse manuscripts typically drew on both written (pictorial and alphabetic) texts and oral traditions as sources and might be directed to either Spanish or indigenous audiences. Regardless of the intended audience, they served to promote local interests and secure rights for caciques and their communities. The detailed boundary descriptions that form such a prominent feature of primordial titles point to their use as legal evidence of corporate landownership, in response to encroachment either by Spaniards or other indigenous communities. Genealogical documents embedded in primordial titles or cartographic histories reflect efforts by caciques to prove their legitimate social and political status or to secure rights to land.[93] Early on, a cacique might use pictorial manuscripts to make the case, switching to a written (alphabetic) testament when it appeared to be a more effective instrument to achieve similar ends.[94]

History occupies a prominent place in these pictorial and alphabetic texts. They present a vision of the past that is used to verify historical claims—to municipal autonomy, legitimacy to rule, and rights to land—and to create a shared history to reinforce collective memory and thus collective identity. Communities preserved these manuscripts locally, perhaps storing them in a locked chest housed in the home of the cacique or other prominent resident, to be drawn upon in ritualized public settings. History is nonetheless both partial and partisan. These manuscripts privilege certain events, places, and identities—and

exclude others. They are also "at once corporate in focus and factional in perspective," with the narrative presented as if it represents the
whole corporate group but instead actually emphasizes the lineage
or faction of the writer(s).[95] They betray deep-rooted factionalism between the interests of communities and caciques, ethnic majorities
and minorities, and rival political dynasties, all of which have played
such a central role in Mesoamerican culture and society across time.[96]
However factionalized, the Native community nonetheless remained
at the center of indigenous history making and identity formation.

Throughout the colonial period, indigenous identity remained firmly rooted in the microethnicity of the Native community. Notably,
the Spanish term *indio* ("Indian") virtually never appears in Nahuatl-,
Ñudzahui-, or Yucatec Maya—language documents written by indigenous notaries.[97] Nonetheless, some broader notions of ethnic identity are evident, whether used in distinction to other indigenous groups
or to the Spaniards, blacks, and the ever-growing population of persons of mixed ancestry.[98] Judging from indigenous-language sources,
the broad ethnic labels commonly used today—Nahua, Ñudzahui,
and Maya—were not unknown in the colonial period as descriptors
of self-identity, a reflection in each case of a shared culture and common language. Yet, with the exception of Ñudzahuis, these broader
ethnic terms do not frequently appear in indigenous-language documents written by indigenous notaries. The Nahuas "emphasized the
narrow ethnicity of the local altepetl and calpolli-tlaxilacalli rather
than broader ethnic categories . . . even when the contrast between indigenous and Spanish was specifically at issue."[99] In the sixteenth century, Nahua notaries used the phrase *nican titlaca*, "we people here," to
refer to the broader group of indigenous people.[100] In the seventeenth
and eighteenth centuries, macehualli became the primary term used
(in the plural) "as a designation for indigenous people, regardless of
rank, as opposed to Spaniards, blacks, or those of mixed descent."[101]
Similarly, the term Maya appears rarely in Maya-language documents,
being limited to references to language.[102] And, as with the Nahuas,
the term macehualli (sing. *macehual*; pl. *macehualob*) "came close to acquiring its colonial central Mexican meaning of 'indigenous people.'"[103]

Still, some sense of the broader ethnic group is apparent in the use in Maya-language documents of the blanket term *dzul* (pl. *dzulob*), "foreigner," to refer to outsiders, whether indigenous or Spanish.[104]

In striking contrast, the term *Ñudzahui* commonly appears in Ñudzahui-language documents, used "in reference to the region, language, individuals and groups of people, communities, material objects, flora and fauna, and the ritual calendar."[105] "People from the Mixteca Alta called themselves *tay ñudzahui*, 'people from the rain place.'"[106] These references to Ñudzahui ethnicity largely occurred in the context of changes in the late seventeenth century, especially the growth in the number of Spanish speakers in cabeceras and the (related) intensification of competition for resources, that "tested the boundaries of Ñudzahui ethnicity."[107] And they occur primarily when "contact with other ethnic or racial groups provided the context of expression."[108] Terraciano argues that this pattern reflects the complex multiethnic nature of the Mixteca and the substantial changes that took shape over the course of the colonial period. In this context, the Ñudzahuis constituted a much smaller group than the dominant and widely scattered Nahuas, who apparently gave little thought to being Nahuas, whereas the Ñudzahuis were challenged on every side.[109] With the Yucatec Mayas, the relative lack of emphasis on the language group might reflect their isolation from other groups due to their location on the peninsula.

The diverse changes that affected indigenous communities as reflected in shifting terms of self-identification also created the context for many individuals to leave their Native communities altogether. Some left for perceived opportunities in urban areas or on nearby Spanish estates. Others sought to escape the legal category of "Indian" imposed by the Spanish state, as well as the obligations it implied, including the payment of tribute and the performance of labor. To do so successfully, Indians might not only change residence, and thus no longer identify as a member of an indigenous community, but also take advantage of alterations in other markers of ethnic identity, including language, clothing, hairstyle, and so on, that occurred spontaneously among groups in close contact with Spaniards, to claim an identity as a mestizo, a group that was not liable to tribute payment or labor. Such a move entailed the loss of rights derived from membership in an indigenous community at the same time that it deprived the community of its own people.

Conclusion

The widespread tradition of writing in indigenous languages and the rich and diverse source materials it produced over the course of the colonial period provide scholars with the opportunity to explore Mesoamerican identities in ways not otherwise possible. Indigenous-language sources tell us first of all that identity among the indigenous peoples of colonial Mesoamerica was never homogeneous: no simple "Indian" identity emerged over the course of the colonial period. Rather, indigenous identities were complex and constituted at different levels—the corporate community and its constituent parts; hierarchical rank and status; gender norms and expectations; and religious expressions and practices. The precise nature of these identities varied by time and place, influenced both by preconquest regional diversity and the nature, intensity, and timing of the Spanish intrusion as well as interaction with neighboring indigenous groups.[110]

Strong regional diversity characterized Mesoamerica both before and after the conquest. A growing body of scholarship based on documents written in Nahuatl, Ñudzahui, and Yucatec Maya allows comparison among Mesoamerican cultural regions, shedding light on different preconquest traditions and their impact on Native adaptations to changes initiated by Spaniards. A striking example concerns the Ñudzahui tradition of joint male-female rulership and its implications for changes in Native political authority with the introduction of the exclusively male Hispanic-style cabildo after the conquest. But overall it is the Maya region that stands apart. The Maya indigenous state had no apparent constituent parts and no apparent fragmentation along internal lines as occurred in both the Nahua and Ñudzahui regions. Maya gender relations were characterized by heightened patriarchy, with the patronymic group constituting a distinct form of social organization that accounted for, among other things, naming patterns that diverged significantly from Nahua and Ñudzahui ones. The office of governor never separated from the ruler.

In the end, the comparative approach within Mesoamerican studies that I have explored in such detail here illustrates the general idea that identities reflect basic structures, and change in identities grows out of structural change—especially (but not only) the corporate entities (however defined across region and time) that served as the fundamental framework for indigenous life before and after the Spanish conquest. Arguably, we see this point illustrated most clearly in the Nahua sphere, due both to its longer tradition of indigenous-language research and the stronger (and earlier) Spanish presence. Here, Spanish intrusion penetrated deepest, creating larger commonalities across region and ethnicity, and the consequent weakening of the great old complex altepetl. Indigenous communities responded in superficially paradoxical ways: on the one hand, by cultivating a supra-altepetl devotion to the Virgin of Guadalupe; and on the other, by placing greater emphasis on the tiniest entities, both tlaxilacalli seen as altepetl and the household saint cult to symbolize the household. Future indigenous-language research promises to deepen our understanding of this complex relationship between structure and identity, especially as scholars increasingly turn to Mesoamerican languages that to date have had no longstanding scholarly tradition, a trend thankfully already well under way.

Notes

1. For a succinct discussion of indigenous groups in Spanish America, especially Mesoamerica and the Andes, see Kevin Terraciano, "Indigenous Peoples in Colonial Spanish American Society," in *A Companion to Latin American History*, ed. Thomas H. Holloway (Malden MA: Blackwell Publishing, 2008), 124–45.

2. For overviews of indigenous-language research on Mesoamerica, known in the field as the New Philology, see Matthew Restall, "A History of the New Philology and the New Philology in History," *Latin American Research Review* 38, no. 1 (2003): 113–34; and James Lockhart, "Introduction: Background and Course of the New Philology," in *Sources and Methods for the Study of Postconquest Mesoamerican Ethnohistory*, ed. James Lockhart, Lisa Sousa, and Stephanie Wood

(Eugene OR: Wired Humanities Projects, University of Oregon), e-book, http://
whp.uoregon.edu/Lockhart/index.html. For collections of indigenous-language
documents published in (English) translation, see Arthur J. O. Anderson, Frances Berdan, and James Lockhart, eds., *Beyond the Codices* (Berkeley: University
of California Press, 1976); and Matthew Restall, Lisa Sousa, and Kevin Terraciano, eds., *Mesoamerican Voices: Native-Language Writings from Colonial Mexico,
Oaxaca, Yucatan, and Guatemala* (Cambridge: Cambridge University Press, 2005).

3. In view of space considerations and the broad audience of this volume, I
limit references to English-language literature largely published in the last two
decades.

4. For introductions to Mesoamerica on a wide range of topics both before
and after the Spanish conquest, see Richard E. W. Adams and Murdo J. McLeod,
eds., *The Cambridge History of the Native Peoples of the Americas*, vol. 2: *Mesoamerica* (Cambridge: Cambridge University Press, 2000); and Davíd Carrasco, ed., *The
Oxford Encyclopedia of Mesoamerican Cultures: The Civilizations of Mexico and Central America*, 3 vols. (Oxford: Oxford University Press, 2001).

5. William M. Denevan, ed., *The Native Population of the Americas in 1492*,
2nd ed. (Madison: University of Wisconsin Press, 1992), xxi.

6. In the Mixteca, Zapotecs outnumbered Ñudzahuis, and current research sug-
gests that the documentary corpus written in Zapotec is as large if not larger than
Ñudzahui-language materials. For a recent study that utilizes Zapotec-language
sources, see María de los Angeles Romero Frizzi, "The Power of the Law: The
Construction of Colonial Power in an Indigenous Region," in *Negotiation within
Domination: New Spain's Indian Pueblos Confront the Spanish State*, ed. Ethelia Ruiz
Medrano and Susan Kellogg (Boulder: University Press of Colorado, 2010), 107–35.

7. In the following, I rely heavily on James Lockhart, *The Nahuas after the
Conquest: A Social and Cultural History of the Indians of Central Mexico, Sixteenth
through Eighteenth Centuries* (Stanford CA: Stanford University Press, 1992); Kevin Terraciano, *The Mixtecs of Colonial Oaxaca: Ñudzahui History, Sixteenth through
Eighteenth Centuries* (Stanford CA: Stanford University Press, 2001); and Matthew Restall, *The Maya World: Yucatec Culture and Society, 1550–1850* (Stanford
CA: Stanford University Press, 1997). These works follow an earlier generation
of studies based largely on Spanish-language materials, including most notably
Charles Gibson, *The Aztecs under Spanish Rule: A History of the Indians of the Valley of Mexico, 1519–1810* (Stanford CA: Stanford University Press, 1964); Nancy Farriss, *Maya Society under Colonial Rule* (Princeton NJ: Princeton University Press,
1984); and Ronald Spores, *The Mixtec Kings and Their People* (Norman: University of Oklahoma Press, 1967) and *The Mixtecs in Ancient and Colonial Times* (Norman: University of Oklahoma Press, 1984).

8. In the following I emphasize the indigenous state as the critical context for understanding identity in the pre- and postconquest periods. Recent archaeological research has shed light on the complex history of identity formation and the ways in which identities were drastically shifting in preconquest Mesoamerica. See Frances F. Berdan, John K. Chance, Alan R. Sandstrom, Barbara L. Stark, James Taggart and Emily Umberger, *Ethnic Identity in Nahua Mesoamerica: The View from Archaeology, Art History, Ethnohistory, and Contemporary Ethnography* (Salt Lake City: University of Utah Press, 2008); and Michael E. Smith and Frances F. Berdan, eds., *The Postclassic Mesoamerican World* (Salt Lake City: University of Utah Press, 2003). For a synthetic overview of this archaeological research, see Susan Kellogg, "The Gods Depart: Riddles of the Rise, Fall, and Regeneration of Mesoamerica's Indigenous Societies," in *A Companion to Mexican History and Culture*, ed. William H. Beezley (Marlton MA: Wiley-Blackwell, 2011).

9. For discussions of the altepetl, ñuu, and cah before and after the Spanish conquest, see Lockhart, *The Nahuas After the Conquest*, 14–58; Terraciano, *The Mixtecs of Colonial Oaxaca*, 102–32; and Restall, *The Maya World*, 13–40, respectively.

10. On what is becoming known in the field as the New Conquest History, which emphasizes indigenous roles in and perspectives of the conquest based largely on indigenous-language documents, see Susan Schroeder, ed., *The Conquest All Over Again: Nahuas and Zapotecs Thinking, Writing, and Painting Spanish Colonialism* (Eastbourne UK: Sussex Academic Press, 2010); Susan Schroeder, David E. Taváez, Anne J. Cruz, and Cristián Roa-de-la-Carrera, eds. and trans., *Chimalpahin's Conquest: A Nahua Historian's Rewriting of Francisco López de Gómera's "La conquista de México"* (Stanford CA: Stanford University Press, 2010); Florine Asselbergs, *Conquered Conquistadors: The Lienzo de Quauhquechollan; A Nahua Vision of the Conquest of Guatemala*, new ed. (Boulder: University Press of Colorado, 2008); Laura E. Matthew and Michel R. Oudijk, eds., *Indian Conquistadors: Indigenous Allies in the Conquest of Mesoamerica* (Norman: University of Oklahoma Press, 2007); Matthew Restall and Florine Asselbergs, eds., *Invading Guatemala: Spanish, Nahua, and Maya Accounts of the Conquest Wars* (University Park: Pennsylvania State University Press, 2007); Matthew Restall, *Seven Myths of the Spanish Conquest* (Oxford: Oxford University Press, 2003); Lisa Sousa and Kevin Terraciano, "The 'Original Conquest' of Oaxaca: Nahua and Mixtec Accounts of the Spanish Conquest," *Ethnohistory* 50, no. 2 (2003): 349–400; Stephanie Wood, *Transcending Conquest: Nahua Views of Spanish Colonial Mexico* (Norman: University of Oklahoma Press, 2003); Matthew Restall, *Maya Conquistador* (Boston: Beacon Press, 1998); and James Lockhart, ed. and trans., *We People Here: Nahuatl Accounts of the Conquest of Mexico* (Berkeley: University of California Press, 1993).

11. For an excellent, succinct introduction to Spanish policy toward Indians in Mesoamerica, see María Elena Martínez, *Genealogical Fictions: Limpieza de Sangre, Religion, and Gender in Colonial Mexico* (Stanford CA: Stanford University Press, 2008), 91–105.

12. Lockhart, *The Nahuas after the Conquest*, 14.

13. Lockhart, *The Nahuas after the Conquest*, 14.

14. Terraciano, *The Mixtecs of Colonial Oaxaca*, 103.

15. Terraciano, *The Mixtecs of Colonial Oaxaca*, 103–4.

16. Restall, *The Maya World*, 13 and 15.

17. Restall, *The Maya World*, 17. Maya-language documents rarely actually use the term *chibal*, instead typically referring to the chibal by name.

18. Restall, *The Maya World*, 28.

19. Lockhart, *The Nahuas after the Conquest*, 14.

20. For the Nahua pattern of a one-to-one relationship and variations from it, see Lockhart, *The Nahuas after the Conquest*, 28–30, and Gibson, *The Aztecs under Spanish Rule*, 9–97. For Ñudzahuis, see Terraciano, *The Mixtecs of Colonial Oaxaca*, 119. In Yucatan, Spanish-designated jurisdictions also rested on the indigenous state (in this case, the cah), although the general relationship is not entirely clear. See Restall, *The Maya World*, 24–40, and Farriss, *Maya Society*, 147–52.

21. Terraciano, *The Mixtecs of Colonial Oaxaca*, 129.

22. Spanish and indigenous interests converged in sujetos' bids for autonomy. With the decline of the *repartimiento*, Spaniards no longer relied on the indigenous state for labor recruitment. Indigenous demographic recovery also coincided with increased Spanish recognition of pueblo status, official campaigns to verify titles to municipal land, and the wave of construction of smaller, secondary churches in settlements outside the cabecera.

23. Note that in the eighteenth century the term *barrio* (district) appears consistently as a Spanish loanword in Nahuatl- and Ñudzahui-language documents.

24. On indigenous cabildos, see Lockhart, *The Nahuas after the Conquest*, 30–52; Terraciano, *The Mixtecs of Colonial Oaxaca*, 182–95; Restall, *The Maya World*, 51–83. For an excellent study of Nahua town government and factional politics in central Mexico, see Robert Haskett, *Indigenous Rulers: An Ethnohistory of Town Government in Colonial Cuernavaca* (Albuquerque: University of New Mexico Press, 1991).

25. Lockhart, *The Nahuas after the Conquest*, 31.

26. Local government was hardly static, however. Notable changes in the terminology and practices of office holding in both Nahua and Ñudzahui regions occurred in the late colonial period.

27. On social differentiation, see Lockhart, *The Nahuas after the Conquest*, 94–140; Terraciano, *The Mixtecs of Colonial Oaxaca*, 133–57; and Restall, *The Maya World*, 87–97.

28. Scholars once considered the dependents that worked the lands held by noble lineages as a distinct group separate from the ordinary commoners who received land directly from district authorities. Native-language terms, however, suggest that Nahua and Ñudzahui societies did not distinguish between them so sharply. Although Nahuas referred to the dependents of nobles by various terms, they used *macehualli* most frequently. Ñudzahuis had no separate term for dependents, referring to them with the same term as ordinary commoners: *ñandahi*.

29. Both Nahua and Ñudzahui peoples considered anyone who was not a commoner a noble (Nahuatl: pilli; Ñudzahui: toho and yya).

30. The teccalli was associated in particular with the eastern Nahua region. The situation of the noble house in the western region is less clear; the *tecpan* (palace) does not seem to be a full equivalent.

31. On the teccalli, also see John K. Chance, "The Noble House in Colonial Puebla, Mexico: Descent, Inheritance, and the Nahua Tradition," *American Anthropologist* 102 (2000): 485–502.

32. For an excellent study of the repertoire of elite attire and other attributes of rank as expressions of identity in central Mexico in the Late Postclassic period (ca. 1350–1520) and the sixteenth century, see Justyna Olko, *Turquoise Diadems and Staffs of Office: Elite Costume and Insignia of Power in Aztec and Early Colonial Mexico* (Warsaw: Polish Society for Latin American Studies and Centre for Studies on the Classical Tradition, University of Warsaw, 2005). For a general study of Mesoamerican clothing in the preconquest period, see Patricia Rieff Anawalt, *Indian Clothing before Cortés: Mesoamerican Costumes from the Codices* (Norman: University of Oklahoma Press, 1981).

33. Speech patterns distinguished nobles from commoners (as well as individuals by age, gender, and region). Nobles spoke in a high register (called *huehuetlatolli* in Nahuatl). Indeed, "polite and flowery speech of the lords was so elaborate that the meaning of its complex metaphors and conventions often eluded commoners." (Terraciano, *The Mixtecs of Colonial Oaxaca*, 134). See Lockhart, *The Nahuas after the Conquest*, 140; and Terraciano, *The Mixtecs of Colonial Oaxaca*, 77–81. For an important study of huehuetlatolli, see Frances Karttunen and James Lockhart, eds., *The Art of Nahuatl Speech: The Bancroft Dialogues*, Nahuatl Studies Series, 2 (Los Angeles: UCLA Latin American Center, 1987).

34. For the argument that Spanish policies reconstituted pre-Hispanic dynasties, see Martínez, *Genealogical Fictions*, 105–12.

35. Rebecca Horn, *Postconquest Coyoacan: Nahua-Spanish Relations in Central Mexico, 1519–1650* (Stanford CA: Stanford University Press), 49.

36. Olko, *Turquoise Diadems and Staffs of Office*, 469–91. On visual images of colonial-era rulers, also see William L. Barnes, "Secularizing for Survival: Changing Depictions of Central Mexican Rule in the Early Colonial Period," in *Painted Books and Indigenous Knowledge: Manuscript Studies in Honor of Mary Elizabeth Smith*, ed. Elizabeth Hill Boone (New Orleans: Tulane University Middle American Research Institute, 2005), 319–44.

37. Terraciano, *The Mixtecs of Colonial Oaxaca*, 169. Also see Ronald Spores, "Mixteca Cacicas: Status, Wealth, and the Political Accommodation of Native Elite Women in Early Colonial Oaxaca," in *Indian Women of Early Mexico*, ed. Susan Schroeder, Stephanie Wood, and Robert Haskett (Norman: University of Oklahoma Press, 1997), 184–97.

38. Terraciano, *The Mixtecs of Colonial Oaxaca*, 187–88.

39. Terraciano, *The Mixtecs of Colonial Oaxaca*, 147.

40. Lockhart, *The Nahuas after the Conquest*, 133.

41. Terraciano, *The Mixtecs of Colonial Oaxaca*, 78.

42. Terraciano, *The Mixtecs of Colonial Oaxaca*, 137.

43. Lockhart, *The Nahuas after the Conquest* 136–38. For an excellent discussion of political factionalism in Nahua communities in central Mexico, see Haskett, *Indigenous Rulers*. For late colonial caciques in central Mexico, see John K. Chance, "The Caciques of Tecali: Class and Ethnic Identity in Late Colonial Mexico," *Hispanic American Historical Review* 76, no. 2 (1996): 475–502, and "Indigenous Ethnicity in Colonial Central Mexico," in Berdan et al., *Ethnic Identity in Nahua Mesoamerica*, 133–49; and Joyce Marcus and Judith Francis Zeitlin, eds., *Caciques and Their People: A Volume in Honor of Ronald Spores* (Ann Arbor: University of Michigan Museum of Anthropology, 1994). For late colonial caciques in the Mixteca, see John K. Chance, "From Lord to Landowner: The Predicament of the Late Colonial Mixtec Cacique," *Ethnohistory* 57, no. 3 (2010): 445–66, and "The Mixtec Nobility under Colonial Rule," in *Códices, Caciques, y Comunidades*, ed. Maarten Jansen and Luis Reyes García, Cuadernos de Historia Latinoamerica, no. 5 (Ridderkerk, Netherlands: Asociación de Historiadores Latinoamericanistas Europeos, 1997), 161–78.

44. Terraciano, *The Mixtecs of Colonial Oaxaca*, 144. Also see the classic work by William B. Taylor that first demonstrated the retention of substantial landholdings by indigenous communities in late colonial Oaxaca: *Landlord and Peasant in Colonial Oaxaca* (Stanford CA: Stanford University Press, 1972). It is true that the lord-dependent structure also persisted to a certain extent into the eighteenth century in the eastern Nahua region, where the noble house (teccalli) was so pronounced.

45. Terraciano, *The Mixtecs of Colonial Oaxaca*, 139.

46. Terraciano, *The Mixtecs of Colonial Oaxaca*, 139.

47. For excellent discussions of women and gender in Spanish America before and after the conquest, see Susan Kellogg, *Weaving the Past: A History of Latin America's Indigenous Women from the Prehispanic Period to the Present* (Oxford: Oxford University Press, 2005), 18–89; Karen Powers, *Women in the Crucible of Conquest: The Gendered Genesis of Spanish American Society, 1500–1600* (Albuquerque: University of New Mexico Press, 2005); Arnold Bauer, *Goods, Power, History: Latin America's Material Culture* (Cambridge: Cambridge University Press, 2001), 27–33; Susan Migden Socolow, *The Women of Colonial Latin America* (Cambridge: Cambridge University Press, 2000); Susan Schroeder, Stephanie Wood, and Robert Haskett, eds., *Indian Women of Early Mexico* (Norman: University of Oklahoma Press, 1997); Steve J. Stern, *The Secret History of Gender: Women, Men, and Power in Late Colonial Mexico* (Chapel Hill: University of North Carolina Press, 1997); Susan Kellogg, *Law and the Transformation of Aztec Culture, 1500–1700* (Norman: University of Oklahoma Press, 1995).

48. For a thoughtful discussion of regional differences in Mesoamerican gender systems, see Kellogg, *Weaving the Past*, 18–41.

49. Kellogg, *Weaving the Past*, 53.

50. See Lockhart, *The Nahuas after the Conquest*, 74–79, 83–87, 90–92, 226–27, and 238–39; Terraciano, *The Mixtecs of Colonial Oaxaca*, 353–54; Restall, *The Maya World*, 121–40. Testaments are a particularly rich source for the roles of indigenous women and men. See Jonathan Truitt, "Courting Catholicism: Nahua Women and the Catholic Church in Colonial Mexico City," *Ethnohistory* 57, no. 3 (2010): 415–44; Caterina Pizzigoni, *Testaments of Toluca* (Stanford CA and Los Angeles: Stanford University Press and UCLA Latin American Center Publications, 2007); Susan Kellogg and Matthew Restall, eds., *Dead Giveaways: Indigenous Testaments of Colonial Mesoamerica and the Andes* (Salt Lake City: University of Utah Press, 1998); Matthew Restall, *Life and Death in a Maya Community: The Ixil Testaments of the 1760s* (Lancaster CA: Labyrinthos, 1995); and S. L. Cline and Miguel León-Portilla, eds., *The Testaments of Culhuacan* (Los Angeles: UCLA Latin American Center Publications, 1984).

51. Robert Haskett, "Activist or Adulteress? The Life and Struggle of Doña Josefa María of Tepoztlan," in Schroeder, Wood, and Haskett, *Indian Women of Early Mexico*, 145–63; Pizzigoni, *Testaments of Toluca*.

52. Truitt, "Courting Catholicism"; Stephanie Wood, "Gender and Town Guardianship in Mesoamerica: Directions for Future Research," *Journal de la Société des Américanistes* 84 (1998): 243–76; William B. Taylor, *Drinking, Homicide, and Rebellion in Colonial Mexican Villages* (Stanford CA: Stanford University Press, 1979).

53. Pizzigoni, *Testaments of Toluca*, 31.

54. Pizzigoni, *Testaments of Toluca*, 19.

55. Sexuality arguably was another important aspect of identity in Mesoamerica. For the literature on Mesoamerican sexuality based on indigenous-language sources, see Sonya Lipsett-Rivera, "Language as Body and Body as Language: Religious Thought and Cultural Syncretism," in *Religion in New Spain*, ed. Susan Schroeder and Stafford Poole (Albuquerque: University of New Mexico Press, 2007), 66–82; John Chuchiak, "Secrets behind the Screen: *Solicitantes* in the Colonial Diocese of Yucatan and the Yucatec Maya, 1570–1785," in Schroeder and Poole, *Religion in New Spain*, 83–109; Pete Sigal, *From Moon Goddesses to Virgins: The Colonization of Yucatecan Maya Sexual Desire* (Austin: University of Texas Press, 2000); Pete Sigal, ed., *Infamous Desire: Male Homosexuality in Colonial Latin America* (Chicago: University of Chicago Press, 2003); Pete Sigal and John F. Chuchiak IV, eds., "Sexual Encounters/Sexual Collisions: Alternative Sexualities in Colonial Mesoamerica," special issue, *Ethnohistory* 54, no. 1 (2007).

56. Lockhart, *The Nahuas after the Conquest*, 118.

57. On naming patterns, see Lockhart, *The Nahuas after the Conquest*, 117–30; Terraciano, *The Mixtecs of Colonial Oaxaca*, 150–57; and Restall, *The Maya World*, 41–50. For Nahuas, also see Rebecca Horn, "Gender and Social Identity: Nahua Naming Patterns in Postconquest Central Mexico," in Schroeder, Wood, and Haskett, *Indian Women of Early Mexico*, 105–22. The early sixteenth-century censuses from the Cuernavaca region represent a rich source for preconquest Nahua names. See *The Book of Tributes: Early Sixteenth-Century Nahuatl Censuses from Morelos*, Nahuatl Studies Series, 4 (Los Angeles: UCLA Latin American Center Publications, 1993). For a preliminary discussion of naming patterns among Chocho-speakers based on Chocho-language documents, see Terraciano, *The Mixtecs of Colonial Oaxaca*, 156–57.

58. Lockhart, *The Nahuas after the Conquest*, 118.

59. Horn, *Postconquest Coyoacan*, 45–55.

60. For discussions of don and doña, see Lockhart, *The Nahuas after the Conquest*, 125–27; Terraciano, *The Mixtecs of Colonial Oaxaca*, 156; and Restall, *The Maya World*, 46.

61. Lockhart, *The Nahuas after the Conquest*, 126.

62. Lockhart, *The Nahuas after the Conquest*, 126.

63. Lockhardt, *The Nahuas after the Conquest*, 130.

64. For the classic work on the "spiritual conquest," see Robert Ricard, *The Spiritual Conquest of Mexico: An Essay on the Apostolate and the Evangelizing Methods of the Mendicant Orders in New Spain, 1523–1572* (1933; repr., Berkeley: University of California Press, 1966). Important recent studies include Patricia Lopes

Don, *Bonfires of Culture: Franciscans, Indigenous Leaders, and the Inquisition in Early Mexico, 1524–1540* (Norman: University of Oklahoma Press, 2010); Viviana Díaz Balsera, *The Pyramid under the Cross: Franciscan Discourses of Evangelization and the Nahua Christian Subject in Sixteenth-Century Mexico* (Tucson: University of Arizona Press, 2005); James Krippner-Martínez, *Rereading the Conquest: Power, Politics, and the History of Early Colonial Michoacán, Mexico, 1521–1565* (University Park: Pennsylvania State University Press, 2001); Fernando Cervantes, *The Devil in the New World: The Impact of Diabolism in New Spain* (New Haven CT: Yale University Press, 1994); and Inga Clendinnen, *Ambivalent Conquests: Maya and Spaniard in Yucatan, 1517–1570* (Cambridge: Cambridge University Press, 1987).

65. A critical text in this historiographical shift is Louise M. Burkhart, *The Slippery Earth: Nahua-Christian Moral Dialogue in Sixteenth-Century Mexico* (Tucson: University of Arizona Press, 1989).

66. For Nahuatl theater, see Louise M. Burkhart, "The Destruction of Jerusalem as Colonial Nahuatl Historical Drama," in Schroeder, *The Conquest All Over Again*, 74–100; Barry D. Sell and Louise M. Burkhart, eds., *Nahuatl Theatre*, 4 vols. (Norman: University of Oklahoma Press, 2004–2009); and Louise M. Burkhart, *Holy Wednesday: A Nahua Drama from Early Colonial Mexico* (Philadelphia: University of Pennsylvania Press, 1996). For confessional guides, see Barry D. Sell, "'Perhaps Our Lord, God, Has Forgotten Me': Intruding into the Colonial Nahua (Aztec) Confessional," in Schroeder, *The Conquest All Over Again*, 181–205; and Barry D. Sell and John Frederick Schwaller, eds., *A Guide to Confession Large and Small in the Mexican Language, 1634, by Bartolomé de Alva* (Norman: University of Oklahoma Press, 1999). For primordial titles, see citations below.

67. The following discussion draws on Lockhart, *The Nahuas after the Conquest*, 203–6; Terraciano, *The Mixtecs of Colonial Oaxaca*, 252–317; and Restall, *The Maya World*, 148–65.

68. For a magisterial study of the relationship between priests and parishioners in late colonial Mexico, see William B. Taylor, *Magistrates of the Sacred: Priests and Parishioners in Eighteenth-Century Mexico* (Stanford CA: Stanford University Press, 1996).

69. For a fascinating discussion of the rhetoric used by residents of Indian parishes faced with reform in late colonial Mexico City, see Matthew D. O'Hara, "Stone, Mortar, and Memory: Church Construction and Communities in Late Colonial Mexico City," *Hispanic American Historical Review* 86, no. 4 (2006): 647–80, and *A Flock Divided: Race, Religion, and Politics in Mexico, 1749–1857* (Durham NC: Duke University Press, 2010), 91–122.

70. O'Hara, "Stone, Mortar, and Memory," 657. Emphasis in original.

71. O'Hara, "Stone, Mortar, and Memory," 658.

72. Lockhart, *The Nahuas after the Conquest*, 210.

73. Lockhart, *The Nahuas after the Conquest*, 215.

74. For a detailed study of the cult of the saints in eighteenth-century central Mexico based on Nahuatl testaments, see Stephanie Wood, "Adopted Saints: Christian Images in Nahua Testaments of Late Colonial Toluca," *The Americas* 47, no. 3 (1991): 259–94. Also see Pizzigoni, *Testaments of Toluca*, 22–25.

75. Also see Truitt, "Courting Catholicism."

76. On the Virgin of Guadalupe, see Lisa Sousa, Stafford Poole, and James Lockhart, eds., *The Story of Guadalupe: Luis de la Vega's "Huei tlamahuiçoltica" of 1649*, Nahuatl Studies Series, 5 (Los Angeles and Stanford CA: UCLA Latin American Studies Center and Stanford University Press, 1998); and Stafford Poole, *Our Lady of Guadalupe: The Origins and Sources of a Mexican National Symbol, 1531–1797* (Tucson: University of Arizona Press, 1995). Also see Jeanette Favrot Peterson, "Canonizing a Cult: A Wonder-Working Guadalupe in the Seventeenth Century," in Schroeder and Poole, *Religion in New Spain*, 125–56; and William B. Taylor, "The Virgin of Guadalupe in New Spain: An Inquiry into the Social History of Marian Devotion," *American Ethnologist* 14 (1987): 9–33.

77. Louise M. Burkhart, "Pious Performances: Christian Pageantry and Native Identity in Early Colonial Mexico," in *Native Traditions in the Postconquest World*, ed. Elizabeth Hill Boone and Tom Cummins (Washington DC: Dumbarton Oaks, 1998), 362.

78. Burkhart, "Pious Performances," 362.

79. Louise Burkhart uses the term "ethnic church." She states: "Through the combined agency of the Nahuas and friars, the Nahua church did develop as a separate church with its own customs and traditions, and these customs provided for a rich and complex ritual life. Borrowed elements, such as the musical instruments, were employed in distinctive ways: their Old World origins did not preclude their functioning as both ethnic markers and tools of native devotion in the new context." See Burkhart, "Pious Performances," 367.

80. See Mark Z. Christensen, "The Tales of Two Cultures: Ecclesiastical Texts and Nahua and Maya Catholicisms," *The Americas* 66, no. 3 (January 2010): 353–77.

81. See J. Richard Andrews and Ross Hassig, trans. and eds., *Treatise on the Heathen Superstitions That Today Live among the Indians Native to This New Spain, 1629* (Norman: University of Oklahoma Press, 1984). Also see David Tavárez, "The Passion according to the Wooden Drum: The Christian Appropriation of a Zapotec Ritual Genre in New Spain," *The Americas* 62, no. 3 (2006): 413–44.

82. Robert Haskett, "Conquering the Spiritual Conquest in Cuernavaca," in Schroeder, *The Conquest All Over Again*, 226–60, and *Visions of Paradise: Primordial Titles and Mesoamerican History in Cuernavaca* (Norman: University of Oklahoma

Press, 2005); Serge Gruzinski, *The Conquest of Mexico: The Incorporation of Indian Societies into the Western World, 16th to 18th Centuries* (Cambridge: Polity Press, 1993); James Lockhart, "Views of Corporate Self and History in Some Valley of Mexico Towns, Seventeenth and Eighteenth Centuries," in *Nahuas and Spaniards: Postconquest Central Mexican History and Philology* (Los Angeles and Stanford CA: UCLA Latin American Center Publications and Stanford University Press, 1991), 39–64; and Stephanie Wood, "The Cosmic Conquest: Late-Colonial Views of the Sword and Cross in Central Mexican *Títulos*," *Ethnohistory* 38, no. 2 (1991): 176–95.

83. For municipal coats of arm, see María Castañada de la Paz, "Central Mexican Indigenous Coats of Arms and the Conquest of Mesoamerica," *Ethnohistory* 56, no. 1 (2009): 125–61; and Robert Haskett, "Paper Shields: The Ideology of Coats of Arms in Colonial Mexican Primordial Titles," *Ethnohistory* 42, no. 1 (1996): 99–126.

84. On Tlaxcala, see the classic work by Charles Gibson, *Tlaxcala in the Sixteenth Century* (New Haven CT: Yale University Press, 1952). For a recent discussion, see R. Jovita Baber, "Empire, Indians, and the Negotiation for the Status of City in Tlaxcala, 1521–1550," in Medrano and Kellogg, *Negotiation within Domination*, 19–44; and Travis Barton Kranz, "Visual Persuasion: Sixteenth-Century Tlaxcalan Pictorials in Response to the Conquest of Mexico," in Schroeder, *The Conquest All Over Again*, 41–73. For recent work that concerns the campaigns of various indigenous allies, see the citations to the New Conquest History above. Yanna Yannakakis notes that some indigenous allies may have claimed Tlaxcalan identity to advance their own campaigns for privileges. See Yanna Yannakakis, *The Art of Being In-Between: Native Intermediaries, Indian Identity, and Local Rule in Colonial Oaxaca* (Durham NC: Duke University Press, 2008), 204.

85. For Mesoamerican pictorial traditions, see Elizabeth Hill Boone, ed., *Painted Books and Indigenous Knowledge: Manuscript Studies in Honor of Mary Elizabeth Smith* (New Orleans: Tulane University Middle American Research Institute, 2005); Elizabeth Hill Boone, *Stories in Red and Black: Pictorial Histories of the Aztecs and Mixtecs* (Austin: University of Texas Press, 2002); Walter Mignolo, ed., *Writing Without Words: Alternative Literacies in Mesoamerica and the Andes* (Durham NC: Duke University Press, 1994); and Joyce Marcus, *Mesoamerican Writing Systems: Propaganda, Myth, and History in Four Ancient Civilizations* (Princeton NJ: Princeton University Press, 1992).

86. For the relationship between pictorial and alphabetic representation, see Terraciano, *The Mixtecs of Colonial Oaxaca*, 15–65; Boone and Mignolo, *Writing Without Words*; Lockhart, *The Nahuas after the Conquest*, 326–73; Gruzinski, *The Conquest of Mexico*, 6–69; Frances Karttunen, "Nahuatl Literacy," in *The Inca and*

Aztec States, ed. George Collier, Renato Rosaldo, and John Wirth (New York: Academic Press, 1982), 395–417.

87. For scholarship based on Nahuatl-language notarial records, for which we have the longest tradition, see Pizzigoni, *Testaments of Toluca*; Horn, *Postconquest Coyoacan*; Kellogg, *Law and the Transformation of Aztec Culture*; Haskett, *Indigenous Rulers*; and S. L. Cline, *Colonial Culhuacan, 1580–1600: A Social History of an Aztec Town* (Albuquerque: University of New Mexico Press, 1986). For a comparative approach to indigenous testaments in Mesoamerica and the Andes, see Kellogg and Restall, *Dead Giveaways*.

88. Annals originate primarily in central Mexico. See Camilla Townsend, *Here in This Year: Seventeenth-Century Nahuatl Annals of the Tlaxcala-Puebla Valley* (Stanford CA: Stanford University Press, 2010); Camilla Townsend, "Don Juan Buenaventura Zapata y Mendoza and the Notion of Nahua Identity," in Schroeder, *The Conquest All Over Again*, 144–80; Dana Leibsohn, *Script and Glyph: Pre-Hispanic History, Colonial Bookmaking, and the "Historia Tolteca-Chichimeca"* (Washington DC: Dumbarton Oaks Research Library and Collection, 2009); Lori Boornazian Diel, *The Tira de Tepechpan: Negotiating Place Under Aztec and Spanish Rule* (Austin: University of Texas Press, 2008); James Lockhart, Susan Schroeder, and Doris Namala, eds., *Annals of His Time: Don Domingo de San Antón Muñón Chimalpahin Quauhtlehuanitzin* (Stanford CA: Stanford University Press, 2006); J. O. Anderson and Susan Schroeder, eds., *Codex Chimalpahin: Society and Politics in Mexico Tenochtitlan, Tlatelolco, Texcoco, Culhuacan, and Other Nahua Altepetl in Central Mexico*, 2 vols. (Norman: University of Oklahoma Press, 1997).

89. Barbara E. Mundy, "At Home in the World: Elites and the Teozacoalco Map-Genealogy," in Boone, *Painted Books and Indigenous Knowledge*, 363–81; Joseph W. Whitecotton, *Zapotec Elite Ethnohistory: Pictorial Genealogies from Eastern Oaxaca* (Nashville: Vanderbilt University Publications in Anthropology, 1990).

90. Florine Asselbergs, *Conquered Conquistadors*; and Dana Leibsohn, "Primers for Memory: Cartographic Histories and Nahua Identity," in Boone and Mignolo, *Writing Without Words*, 161–87.

91. On primordial titles, see David Tavárez, "Representations of Spanish Authority in Zapotec Calendrical and Historical Genres," in Schroeder, *The Conquest All Over Again*, 206–25; Robert Haskett, "Conquering the Spiritual Conquest in Cuernavaca," in Schroeder, *The Conquest All Over Again*, 226–60; Haskett, *Visions of Paradise*; Stephanie Wood, *Transcending Conquest*; Sousa and Terraciano, "The 'Original Conquest' of Oaxaca"; Restall, *Maya Conquistador*; Stephanie Wood, "The Social vs. Legal Context of Nahuatl *Títulos*," in Boone and Cummins, *Native Traditions in the Postconquest World*, 201–31; Gruzinski, *The Conquest of Mexico*, 98–145; Lockhart, "Views of Corporate Self and History in Some Valley of Mexico Towns."

92. Dana Leibsohn, "Mapping after the Letter: Indigenous Cartography in New Spain," in *The Language Encounter in the Americas, 1492–1800*, ed. Edward G. Gray and Norman Fiering (New York: Berghahn Books, 2000), 119–51; Barbara Mundy, *The Mapping of New Spain: Indigenous Cartography and the Maps of the Relaciones Geográficas* (Chicago: University of Chicago Press, 1996); Dana Leibsohn, "Colony and Cartography: Shifting Signs on Indigenous Maps of New Spain," in *Reframing the Renaissance: Visual Culture in Europe and Latin America, 1450–1650*, ed. Claire J. Farago (New Haven CT: Yale University Press, 1995), 264–81; and Serge Gruzinski, "Colonial Indian Maps in Sixteenth-Century Mexico: An Essay in Mixed Cartography," *RES* 13 (1987): 46–61.

93. For the ways in which Spanish legal procedures influenced indigenous histories and genealogies, see Martínez, *Genealogical Fictions*, 112–22.

94. See Terraciano, *The Mixtecs of Colonial Oaxaca*, 50.

95. Leibsohn, "Primers for Memory," 161.

96. Stephanie Wood, "Testaments and Títulos: Conflict and Coincidence of Cacique and Community Interests in Central Mexico," in Kellogg and Restall, *Dead Giveaways*, 85–111; Leibsohn, "Primers for Memory."

97. For Nahuatl, see Lockhart, *The Nahuas after the Conquest*, 8, 115–16, and *Nahuas and Spaniards*, 8; for Yucatec Maya, see Restall, *The Maya World*, 13; and for Ñudzahui, see Terraciano, *The Mixtecs of Colonial Oaxaca*, 319, 320, and 328. For the exceptional use of *indio* in a Nahuatl annal, see Townsend, "Don Juan Buenaventura Zapata y Mendoza," in Schroeder, *The Conquest All Over Again*, 162–65.

98. A growing literature on ethnicity in pre- and postconquest Mesoamerica has emerged in recent years. See Berdan et al., *Ethnic Identity in Nahua Mesoamerica*; John K. Chance and Barbara L. Stark, "Ethnicity," in *Archaeology of Ancient Mexico and Central America: An Encyclopedia*, ed. Susan Toby Evans and David L. Webster (New York: Garland Publishing, 2001), 236–39; Frederic Hicks, "Ethnicity," in *The Oxford Encyclopedia of Mesoamerican Cultures*, 1:388–92; Elizabeth M. Brumfiel, Tamara Salcedo, and David K. Schaer, "The Lip Plugs of Xaltocan: Function and Meaning in Aztec Archaeology," in *Economies and Polities in the Aztec Realm*, ed. Mary G. Hodge and Michael E. Smith, Studies on Culture and Society, 6 (Albany: Institute of Mesoamerican Studies, University at Albany, State University of New York, 1994), 113–31.

99. Lockhart, *The Nahuas after the Conquest*, 115. Also see the excellent discussion of ethnicity in a comparative Mesoamerican framework, from which I benefit here, in Terraciano, *The Mixtecs of Colonial Oaxaca*, 329–31.

100. Lockhart, *The Nahuas after the Spanish Conquest*, 115, and *We People Here*, 13.

101. Lockhart, *The Nahuas after the Spanish Conquest*, 114. Also see Townsend, *Here in This Year*, 42–43.

102. Restall, *The Maya World*, 14, 15, and 18.

103. Restall, *The Maya World*, 16.

104. Restall, *The Maya World*, 16.

105. Terraciano, *The Mixtecs of Colonial Oaxaca*, 320. ("Mixtec" is in origin a Nahuatl word coined by imperial overlords, later to be adopted by modern scholars, who now increasingly prefer "Ñudzahui" as the preferred ethnic term of self-description.)

106. Terraciano, *The Mixtecs of Colonial Oaxaca*, 319.

107. Terraciano, *The Mixtecs of Colonial Oaxaca*, 328.

108. Terraciano, *The Mixtecs of Colonial Oaxaca*, 328.

109. Current research suggests that the Zapotecs, the other major ethnic group in the Mixteca, had a term (*zaa*) that referred to their general ethnicity and, similar to the Ñudzahui, was used in reference to plants, objects, and so on.

110. For a discussion of "stages" of cultural change as reflected in language contact phenomena in a comparative framework, see James Lockhart, "Three Experiences of Culture Contact: Nahua, Maya, and Quechua," in Boone and Cummins, *Native Traditions in the Postconquest World*, 31–51.

Chapter 2

Rethinking the Middle Ground
French Colonialism and Indigenous Identities
in the *Pays d'en Haut*

Michael A. McDonnell

At least since the publication of Richard White's *The Middle Ground* in 1991, scholars have been aware of the critical importance of the *pays d'en haut* (or upper Great Lakes region) in one of the greatest transformations of modern history—the birth of the Atlantic world. In his masterful work, White showed that the French empire in North America was predicated on the creation of a "middle ground"—a process, as well as a place—between Europeans and Indians. A place "in between cultures, peoples, and in between empires and the nonstate world of villages"; a process whereby diverse groups of people came together and negotiated something new out of a series of mutual, creative and often expedient misunderstandings. The creation of this middle ground, in turn, was dependent on a rough balance of power, a mutual need or desire for what the other side offered, and an inability by either side to compel change. In the *pays d'en haut*, this middle ground held sway for a remarkably long time—at least until the creation of the new American republic.[1]

White forced scholars to focus their attention on this previously neglected region, and obliged us to pay close heed to the process at work. But though Native Americans were at the heart of his study, White's work was not necessarily focused on Native Americans. White set out to write a history of European-Indian relations—an imperial history, even while complicating our notions of imperialism. As a result of this, however, Native Americans remain strangely distant in his book—at times almost as incomprehensible to the reader as they were to seventeenth-century Europeans. In part, this was a deliberate and necessary strategy—as White notes, Native Americans *were* often incomprehensible to the Europeans they encountered. Though we may pretend to know more about them than contemporaries did, White asserts, we probably don't, especially given that we can only glimpse this world through the confused eyes of European sources.[2]

White's methodology is at its best, then, when exploring the complex nuances of the daily (re-)creation of a middle ground when Native and newcomer came together. But the larger narrative arc of White's story, when told from these same confused European sources, tells an all too familiar story. It alienates Native Americans from both the region and their own history. Indigenous identities are mere creations of a European imaginary.[3] Algonquians are from the start described as "shattered peoples"—"refugee" and "remnant" groups who had been hammered against the anvil of punishing Iroquois attacks in the first half of the seventeenth century. These shattered groups then used an "imported imperial glue" to reconstruct a village world in the *pays d'en haut*. This new world—the middle ground—"sustained, and was in turn sustained by, the French empire." Indigenous identities, it seems, were almost an artifact of European imperial rule. Seen only through the eyes of European scribes, White's cast of characters then appear on stage only when called, or noticed, by imperial officials. They remain a volatile, fleeting, and ephemeral—even if important—presence throughout the colonial period. Finally, White's story comes to an end with the establishment of the American republic and the apparent imbalance of power that resulted. Europeans eventually dispossessed, made dependent, and removed the nations created by the middle ground of the *pays d'en haut*—returning us to a more familiar tale. The middle ground ceased to exist; along with it, so too did the people of the *pays d'en haut*. Ultimately, the glimpse White gave us of the Native Americans of the *pays d'en haut* foreclosed rather than engendered further discussion, despite the rich complexity of the tale he told.[4]

This chapter, in contrast, is an attempt to rethink the early history of the *pays d'en haut* and in particular to follow the dictates of Daniel Richter and others to face east rather than west. It is a preliminary effort to view the history of this region from the perspective of Michilimackinac rather than Montreal.[5] Yet in trying to comprehend these events from an indigenous perspective, it quickly becomes clear that we need a much more nuanced understanding of indigenous identities in the region than historians of colonial North America have generally been able to reconstruct. Fortunately, there has been a recent spate of indigenous-centered histories throughout the Americas that have helped balance our older accounts of European imperialism. More specifically, too, recent studies of migration, family and kinship networks, and especially the importance of doodemic (or clan) associations among the Anishinaabeg in particular have begun to point the way toward an understanding of this period and place that is based more on the centrality of family and kinship than nation and tribe.[6] It is becoming clear that in an important sense, early seventeenth-century Jesuits—many of whom lived with and among at least some of the nations of the Lakes—appreciated these distinctions and different associations much more finely than did eighteenth-century imperial officials, nineteenth-century governments, and modern historians.

Starting with an exploration of what we now know about indigenous identities in the region, this chapter will draw on this new work to sketch out an alternative history of French-Indian relations in the *pays d'en haut*, focused particularly on Michilimackinac. A more nuanced understanding of indigenous identities during this period helps makes better sense of the world that French explorers, traders, and missionaries encountered and tried to describe in the Great Lakes. It also helps us understand Native patterns of warfare, trade, migration, and marriage—patterns that structured relations with the French in important ways. In turn, tracing the history of French-Indian relations through this period reveals important clues about the continuities in indigenous identities in this era. While Europeans coined different names for the peoples they encountered, consistencies in the patterns of warfare, trade, and marriage during the French colonial period give us some indication that indigenous identities remained coherent, and relatively stable, even in this period of supposedly great change. From Anishinaabe perspectives, the French had made limited inroads in the Michilimackinac region, even after 150 years of colonization.

From the perspective of the arriving French, the *pays d'en haut* seemed, as Richard White notes, a world of "dim shadows"—a "fragmentary, distorted world." Jesuit missionaries and early explorers, desperate to get some purchase on an alien world, glimpsed what they thought was a world shattered by persistent and horrific Iroquois attacks. They listened to tales of long-running wars between Algonquian- and Iroquois-speaking groups, often told by Huron intermediaries who struggled most in the territory between the two. Unable to comprehend what they encountered, they heard what they could. Thus, when the Hurons themselves were finally uprooted and scattered in 1649, accompanying French missionaries believed that they were only the last to suffer. And when Jesuits and Hurons alike found refuge among small communities of Algonquians to their north and west, the French concluded that these peoples were only the remnants of much larger groups of Indians similarly hammered by the Iroquois. Not finding densely settled villages and towns as they had done in Iroquoia and Huronia, early French visitors believed that they were seeing a world that had collapsed.[7]

The world of the *pays d'en haut* may have been in flux at the moment of contact with the French, but it was unlikely in a state of collapse. Indeed, put into a long-term context, most indigenous accounts of the Native peoples of the Great Lakes stress the expansion and consolidation of the peoples who called themselves Anishinaabe across the region in the centuries leading to the arrival of Europeans. Meaning "human beings" or "original peoples," Anishinaabe was a self-referent used by multiple groups of Algonquian-speaking peoples who jostled for space in the *pays d'en haut* with other Algonquian speakers along with Siouian and Iroquoian speakers in the region. The Anishinaabeg had come to the Lake Huron region from the east at least a few hundred years prior to the arrival of the Europeans, mixing with others in the Great Lakes. Oral traditions and archaeological evidence suggest that they had most recently come from the Ottawa River valley and moved steadily northwest, possibly under earlier pressure from Iroquois groups to their south.[8]

Over time, and as they merged with the indigenous peoples they encountered in the region, we have come to recognize three main groups of Anishinaabeg, at least in the upper Great Lakes. Those who continued to move farther northwest, into the pine forests north of Lakes Huron and Superior, have become known as the Ojibwes. Those who moved into the more fertile ecological zone of the Carolinian forest of southern Lake Michigan became known as the Potawatomis. The people who would come to be known as the Odawas, or Ottawas, stayed in the dynamic transitional Canadian-Carolinian forest zone between these two—mainly around the shores of northern Lake Huron. This transitional zone created multiple ecosystems, and ranged from the more northern zone—like boreal forests around Michilimackinac to the southern-influenced broadleaf forests around the southern part of Georgian Bay.[9]

By the time the French arrived in the *pays d'en haut*, the Anishinaabeg had come to occupy most of the region and dominated the upper reaches of the Great Lakes and surrounding rivers. But they did not occupy the region in a way that made sense to the French. There were many clusters of peoples who lived in towns and villages of varying sizes, most often at strategic or resource-rich lakeshore locations such as La Pointe, Sault Sainte Marie, or Michilimackinac. These were more or less permanent villages, most often occupied during the summer months. In the winter, the population of these villages would disperse, and smaller family groups would hunt away from the main villages. Sometimes in parallel with this seasonal mobility was a longer-term mobility, as small groups sometimes joined larger communities in another village for a year or more, to trade, or for safety.[10]

Adding to the Europeans' confusion, the particular groupings at summer villages and around winter camps did not make for easy identification by the visitors. Villages were often multiethnic, and even multilingual, with Siouan and Iroquoian speakers mixed with Anishinaabemowin speakers. Though the French often tried to designate

villages as "Saulteur" or "Ottawa," observers on the ground almost invariably noted the presence of numerous other "nations" at any particular village site.[11]

The French were quick to believe that these mobile multiethnic
villages must have been communities of refugees, brought together
under pressure of Iroquois attacks, shattered at their real source. But
as historians have recently uncovered, they were stable, cohesive, and
coherent communities to the peoples who lived in them. As Michael
Witgen has written, they were held together by "strands of real and
fictive kinship" that had been established through trade, language,
and intermarriage. These strands intersected and crisscrossed over a
vast space, knitting together disparate peoples and places across the
Great Lakes. They connected winter bands and village communities
across the *pays d'en haut*. And they shifted across time, as trading and
kinship relations changed.[12]

Indeed, though the split into the nations we now know as Ojibwe,
Potawatomi, and Odawa has come to define the way we think about
the Anishinaabeg of the northern Great Lakes, more recent work on
the social and political organization of the Anishinaabeg suggests that
another layer of identity was in play in the seventeenth century and
shaped relations in the area in profound ways. Perhaps the most important glue holding these communities together was the doodem. Heidi Bohaker's pathbreaking work on kinship networks among eastern
Algonquian-speaking Anishinaabe peoples would suggest that doodemag, or kinship networks, "operated as an important component
of Anishinaabe collective identities" during the early contact period
and likely prior to it. Doodem identities, usually ascertained from pic-
tographs and based on some kind of other-than-human progenitor,
were inherited from fathers and implied an obligation toward those
in the same lineage. As a result, "Nindoodemag shaped marriage and
alliance patterns and facilitated long-distance travel; access to community resources was also negotiated through these networks."[13]

Origin stories, linguistic evidence, and later historical sources suggest that these relationships shaped, and continue to shape, Anishinaabe worlds in powerful and complex ways. Yet they did so in very

different ways than Europeans might have imagined. For example, Anishinaabe collective identities were not grounded in a particular geographic space—they were not based on continuous possession, occupation, and defense of particular places but rather were based in shared descent, in spiritual practices, and in origin stories. Thus, drawing on well-established interdisciplinary methodologies, Bohaker has shown that the Anishinaabeg of the *pays d'en haut* had an entirely different method for organizing their sociopolitical world than the Europeans they encountered. Uncomprehending, the French could only grope for the words to describe it.[14]

Doodem relations, for example, often underpinned the mobility that so confounded European commentators. In particular, people participated in widespread, expected, and politically negotiated seasonal movements often based on doodem relationships. It was a deeply embedded cultural practice that served a range of social and political functions. Dispersals, for example, helped avoid overhunting of game during the winter. Aggregations, on the other hand, allowed young people opportunities to meet marriage partners and visit relatives. But patterns of dispersion and aggregation defied easy description. When under attack, for example, Anishinaabeg could and did negotiate with distant doodem communities for protection and alliance. When they did so, they drew on a tradition of long-distance travel throughout the region. Keen to map out the political geography of the Great Lakes, the French were mystified by these movements. These annual movements in patterns of aggregation and dispersal "thoroughly unsettled even the earliest European notions of civilized society." But it is unlikely the Anishinaabeg were refugees—as Richard White asserts—when they were among their own kin.[15]

This mobility did not mean that place was unimportant to the Anishinaabeg. Indeed, as Bohaker notes, the *aadizookaanag* teach that Anishinaabe political geography is inextricably tied to the spiritual landscape of the Great Lakes region. This landscape was home to a more inclusive category of personhood that could include people in the form of animals, or animals in the form of humans. And these other-than-human forms gave life to different doodemag. They were also often associated with particular sites. Thus doodem identity is and was intimately tied to place, and Anishinaabeg moved through a "spiritually charged geography."[16]

In this respect, Michilimackinac was one of several important sites to the Anishinaabeg of the *pays d'en haut*. Its rich natural resources, its strategic location, and its accessibility made it an attractive place for permanent residents and visitors alike. It was one of the most important cultural, social, and political crossroads in North America before and after the arrival of Europeans. But for the Anishinaabeg of the upper country, the land and vital surrounding waters of Michilimackinac were also the key to their cosmology as seen in numerous origin stories, or *aadizookaanag*. In many of these stories, Michilimackinac is literally the birthplace and center of the world. Mackinac Island was also the native country of Michabous, the Great Hare—an important doodem identity.[17]

By the 1670s, if not earlier, there were at least four distinct doodemag living in and around Michilimackinac who came to be known as the four nations of Odawas (the Sables, Sinagos, Kiskakons, and Nassauekuetons). There were likely more. Diverse doodemag that became known as the Saulteurs, or Ojibwes, for example, were also associated with the region.[18] Certainly, it had been and was again becoming a central gathering place for Anishinaabeg from all around the lakes. One Jesuit noted that the area "forms the key and the door, so to speak, for all the peoples of the South, as does the Sault for those of the North; for in these regions there are only those two passages by water for very many Nations, who must seek one or the other of the two if they wish to visit the French settlements." The abundant fisheries and fertile soil of the area attracted many "tribes" to the area, and with the end of the war with the Iroquois in sight, many more "nations" were planning their return to the region, "each to its own country."[19] The return of these different "nations" only makes sense if we see them as doodem identities, and the movements in this region as part of a greater pattern of annual—or longer—negotiated migrations.

Equally significantly, these doodem identities were also key to Anishinaabe expansion before *and* during the French colonial period.

The Anishinaabeg had a long history of creating alliances with their culturally and politically distinct neighbors, as evidenced by early reports of mixed communities of Ochateguins (Wendats) and Algonquins (Ottawa River Anishinaabeg), and also the Kiskakon Odawas and the Tionontates (Petuns).[20] Marriages were particularly important in creating new, geographically diverse and widespread kinship networks that were often the basis of lateral alliances. Daughters and sisters were key to these new relations, as women made important connections by marrying men from different doodemag who lived in different communities. Travelers could then rely on the hospitality of kin as they voyaged throughout the region. War chiefs could also count on the support of in-laws as allies across long distances. In the absence of formal alliances, such relationships were crucial for maintaining and expanding commercial and military ties in a world in flux. Such kinship alliances ensured an ever-thickening and expanding network of relations throughout the Great Lakes. This network of relations helped the Anishinaabeg consolidate their hold on the Great Lakes and even to expand during this period.[21]

This understanding of Anishinaabe identity also throws important new light on the practice of intermarriage. While much has been made of the importance of mixed marriages in maintaining the French alliance with Algonquian nations, it is clear that they were an extension of existing Anishinaabe practices, and they were a necessity in the Anishinaabe-dominated world of posts such as Michilimackinac. From Anishinaabe perspectives, for most of the colonial period the French maintained a relatively tiny post—and presence—at the strategic crossroads of Michilimackinac. They were clearly there at the invitation of thousands of Anishinaabeg who lived along the shores of the nearby Great Lakes. With a French post in their midst, the Anishinaabeg took advantage. They grew corn, fished, hunted, and supplied sugar for the garrison, the local *habitants*, the constant stream of traders and explorers who passed through, and the French commanders at the post. The Anishinaabeg also positioned themselves as key players in an expanding trade empire. After the wars with the Iroquois in the seventeenth century, the Anishinaabeg became an important link between the French to the east and the thousands of western Indians of all nations who made the journey to Michilimackinac each spring to trade furs and renew their friendships and alliances. Never in a position to coerce the Anishinaabeg, the French were dependent on the hospitality and goodwill of their more numerous neighbors and hosts. To facilitate the fur trade, the French were forced to make alliances of the diplomatic and intimate kind.[22]

This was particularly true when the French stopped the official fur trade at the western posts in the 1690s. Most fur traders left stranded in the region were thus more vulnerable to random plundering and predation. Many quickly married into Algonquian families. While references to interracial marriages in the region were rare before the 1690s, the sudden (and temporary) withdrawal of the French posts in the *pays d'en haut* corresponded with a sudden rise in the number of reported relationships between French men and Algonquian women at the turn of the century. Through marriage, French fur traders—*coureurs de bois*—may have been attempting to establish the necessary kin connections with Indians that would allow them to keep trading safely in the area.[23] But if French traders saw advantages to more intimate relationships with Native women—and flattered themselves that Native women liked "the French better than their own Countrymen"—they could do so only because their Algonquian trading partners also sought new opportunities.[24] Well-connected Indian women actively sought fur-trade husbands who would be of benefit to their kin relations.[25]

Though much is made of these relationships in creating a "middle ground" between the French and Indians, their importance to the Anishinaabeg may be overstated. It is clear that the practice of intermarrying likely stemmed from doodemic practices that predated the arrival of Europeans and continued through the era of imperialism. Though intermarriages with Algonquians may have been important to Europeans, for Algonquians they were not unusual, nor uncommon. Nor is it clear exactly how new French men were incorporated into the doodem. They certainly had some influence that reflected a different kind of status than unincorporated French men. But there is much work yet to be done to understand the nature of these new kinds of relationships and their meanings to both French and Anishinaabe communities and individuals. In the meantime, though we know these relationships and their offspring often served as important cultural conduits between the Anishinaabeg and the French, we can infer that their importance and impact have likely been overestimated by both contemporary French observers whose only insights into Anishinaabe worlds came via these people, and by subsequent historians who have reconstructed Anishinaabe-European relations on the very thin evidentiary base left by these relatively rare relationships. What they do reveal, however, is the protean nature of doodemic relationships and the incorporative nature of Anishinaabe identities in the Great Lakes.

As the example of mixed marriages demonstrates, greater understanding of these different layers of identity—a pan-Anishinaabe identity, composed of interconnected and expanding doodemag—allows us to make more sense of French-Indian relations at the macro and micro level.[26] At the macro level, for example, understanding Anishinaabe identity in this way bolsters later nineteenth-century Anishinaabe historians' claims that the French colonial period was but a small part of their history before the nineteenth century—a history that was dominated instead by accounts of Anishinaabe expansion. Indeed, the French may have been right about landing in the middle of an epic war in the early seventeenth century, but later Anishinaabe historians, recounting the tales of elders, assured their readers that these were wars of expansion and consolidation. Anishinaabe accounts of the sixteenth and seventeenth centuries are full of stories of battles, wars, and migrations as they first fought the Mascoutens and Winnebagos to expand into the Michigan peninsula, and then the Iroquois over control of southern Ontario. Later, they did battle with the Fox and Dakotas over territory to the south and west of Lake Superior. Thus in Anishinaabe histories recorded in the nineteenth century, Algonquians stood in the middle of a dynamic and expanding world. Theirs was a history of consolidation, not collapse.[27]

Significantly, in these histories the French only figured as supporting actors on the periphery of an Anishinaabe world. They were commercial associates who often supplied the arms necessary for Anishinaabe success. They reacted to Anishinaabe trading initiatives, and they joined them as allies in their long wars with rivals. But the French were never dominant partners. Traders and explorers such as Radisson and Des Grosseilliers may have boasted that they were conquering "Caesars" on their trips through the *pays d'en haut* in the late 1650s and early 1660s, but the "poore miserable" Indians they encountered later claimed the vulnerable French only survived with their help. One account notes some young Ojibwes found the two isolated venturers on the verge of starvation, brought them to their village, "where, being nourished with great kindness, their lives were preserved."[28]

In these Anishinaabe accounts, the coming of the French was noted as part of a larger story, but only a part. More important were the numerous and long-standing rivalries and relationships with nations and tribes east, west, north, and south of them, and especially the Iroquois. In all of these Native-authored histories, the Anishinaabeg—not the French—stand in the middle of a complex web of social relations, all of which had to be constantly negotiated and renegotiated. In all these narratives, the seasonal rhythms of the annual fur trade, hunt, fishing, and agricultural pursuits remained relatively undisturbed. In all these stories, continuities are emphasized over decline, and Europeans often stood at the periphery of these stories. From the perspective of the majority of Anishinaabeg, the European presence was limited in the *pays d'en haut* over the course of the seventeenth and even eighteenth centuries.[29]

At the level of French-Indian relations, recognizing that a greater Anishinaabe alliance—composed of interconnected doodemag across the Great Lakes—was in play compels us to acknowledge the many claims made that the French inadvertently stepped into the middle of an already raging Algonquian-Iroquois war. From the start of their association with the French, the Anishinaabeg were keen to manipulate their relations with the newcomers to their advantage. Indeed, in hindsight, Champlain's first forays to the Great Lakes were used by the Anishinaabeg to initiate a relationship with the French that would help keep the Iroquois off balance and at bay on their southeastern flanks. Within a few months of meeting Anishinaabe warriors on the banks of the French River, Champlain formalized the alliance proffered several years previously by the allied Wendats, accompanying a large expedition of about five hundred mixed warriors south of Lake Ontario to an Oneida town. In doing so, Champlain had, wittingly or not, enmeshed the French in a world of Indian warfare.[30]

The alliance came at a tremendous cost. These early Huron-French attacks on the Iroquois renewed an almost century-long war, marked by ferocious attacks, temporary truces, and diplomatic intrigues between all parties concerned. Significantly, however, though these conflicts have often been seen as pitting European-allied Indians against other European-allied Indians, closer scrutiny shows that Europeans were often merely bit players in a drama unfolding on a nearly continental scale. Seen in this light, the French did not drag Indians into European conflicts; Indians dragged Europeans into Native conflicts.

The French only saw the tip of the iceberg of these wars. And they most often glimpsed it through the eyes of Jesuit missionaries who reported on the Iroquois victories over the Hurons in 1649–50. The French also witnessed the flight of at least some Anishinaabeg from the southern Georgian Bay region. But if war with the Iroquois forced some Anishinaabeg to relocate among kin living elsewhere around the lakes, the movement was merely temporary. At worst, if Iroquois attacks on the Wendat peoples in 1649–50 compelled some Anishinaabeg to move north and west of Sault Sainte Marie, by 1655 they were back on the offensive. Though the French were often unaware of the major conflicts, sometime between 1653 and 1655 a multination force soundly defeated an Iroquois war party near Sault Sainte Marie. By 1662, Anishinaabe war parties consisting of hundreds if not thousands of warriors launched punitive counterattacks deep into Iroquois territory.[31] Though it would not be clear to the French for some time, the Anishinaabeg had by then put the Iroquois on the back foot.[32] As Bohaker asserts, then, far from being destabilized by the attacks of the Haudenosaunees, by the 1660s at the latest, most Anishinaabe peoples had "survived, regrouped, and reestablished themselves on land in which their ancestors had been buried."[33]

While Richard White's depiction of the Algonquians as refugees in the seventeenth century has given rise to an overemphasis on their need for French help and protection against the Iroquois, the French struggled to try and mediate between the two. Indeed, Anishinaabe relations with all their allies, including the French, were shaped by the need to keep the Iroquois threat to a minimum. But they were also increasingly designed to keep the balance of power between themselves and the French. The Anishinaabeg of Michilimackinac, in particular, did not hesitate to raise the threat of an Algonquian-Iroquois-English alliance in order to strengthen their hand against the French.[34]

Recent scholarship has also made clear that as the Anishinaabeg secured their southeastern flanks, they also pursued an independent strategy southwest of Michilimackinac against the Fox. As Brett Rushforth has shown, the French were initially keen to bring the Fox into a trading and military alliance against the Iroquois. But most other Algonquian-speaking nations around the *pays d'en haut*—including the Anishinaabeg—detested them. The source of this animosity is not clear, but the absence of doodem relations with the Fox speaks of a long-standing rivalry and enmity. With the arrival of the French, the Anishinaabeg tolerated French overtures to the Fox only while the Iroquois threat was at its height. Even as that conflict began winding down, Anishinaabe attacks on the Fox increased.[35]

When the French concluded a more formal peace with the Iroquois, they also established a post at Detroit, threatening the hold the Anishinaabeg had over the developing trade between the French and western nations. War was virtually inevitable when Fox warriors attacked Anishinaabe Ojibwes near the southeastern corner of Lake Superior in 1703 and 1708, triggering resentment among allied doodemag from Michilimackinac to Bjekwanong (near present-day Detroit). Thus, when the French invited the Fox to live at the new post at Detroit, they met a disastrous fate at the hands of the Anishinaabeg and related groups.[36]

This was only the beginning of an increasingly destructive, decades-long wasting war with the Fox encouraged by the Anishinaabeg and allied groups of Algonquians to curb the Fox, their relations with the French, and their role in the new trade. The Algonquians' most successful strategy, as Rushforth has argued, was to raid Fox villages for captives, then sell or give these to the French, driving a deep wedge between the French and their potential allies, the Fox. Even while officially pushing for peace, French colonists' demands for slaves helped ensure that the Fox would be alienated from the French. Thus, "in addition to illuminating the role of Indian slavery in structuring the western alliance system, the wars also powerfully illustrate the ways in which Indians shaped the contours of the alliance to their advantage against French wishes." The French could not control these independent strategies. They never fully understood the separate and long history of rivalries between the Anishinaabeg and other Algonquian-speaking groups such as the Fox.[37]

At the same time, though, recognizing the importance of doodemic identities to the Anishinaabeg also helps us comprehend the history of the region at the micro-level. Early French explorers and Jesuits in the region, for example, struggled to understand the nature of Anishinaabe movements and the plural identities found at any one place. Yet the earliest names ascribed to Algonquian-speaking "nations" were most often doodemag such as Amikwa (beaver), Kiskakon (cut-tail, or catfish), and Sinago (gray squirrel). Early accounts express a wide variety of names. The French used the terms *nation* or *nations* to describe these doodemag identities, but they also seemed to have a sense that this did not correspond with what they knew of nations.[38]

For politically charged reasons, the French quickly reverted to shorthand descriptors. In 1666–67, for example, Father Allouez noted his mission to the "Outaouacs, Kiskakoumac, and Outaousinagouc" (the Odawas, Kiskakons, and Sinagos). He grouped the three "nations" together, he said, because "they have the same tongue, the Algonquin, and form collectively one village." Allouez also noted, though, that the Odawas claimed the Ottawa River as their own, and that no nation might use it without their permission. All the nations who thus used the river to trade with the French, then, "bear the general name of Outaouacs, under whose auspices they make the journey," even though they were "of widely different nations."[39]

Within a few years, this shorthand seemed commonplace. As the Jesuits explained in 1670–71, "the name Outaouacs has been given to all the Savages" of the *pays d'en haut*, "although of different Nations, because the first to appear among the French were the Outaouacs."[40] At the same time, the French began making distinctions between Algonquian-speaking communities in the region based on their geographic location. The Odawas became most commonly associated with the Michilimackinac area and Manitoulin Island, the Saulteurs, or Ojibwes, with the falls at Sault Sainte Marie,[41] and the Potawatomis with Green Bay and subsequently the region south and west of Michilimackinac. They also recognized a relationship between these nations and others they identified as Nipissing, Algonquin, and Mississauga.[42] Europeans, then, quickly divided up the indigenous peoples they encountered on geopolitical terms that made most sense to them—language and geography. But officials and representatives on the ground, as it were, were aware that there was more to these divisions than met the eye. In almost all their descriptions of these different groups, early Jesuit commentators were compelled to acknowledge the presence of different "nations" living among each village or location.[43]

The French continued to acknowledge this dual identity for most of the seventeenth century, even if they did not quite fully grasp its full contours. For example, when two French traders were killed near Sault Sainte Marie by a mixed group of Menominees and Saulteurs, Daniel Greysolon Dulhut—who was in the midst of trying to establish a French post at Michilimackinac—knew he had to tread carefully. One of the accused had a brother, sister, and uncle in the village of the Kiskakons. To be sure, before meting out any punishment, he consulted all the chiefs of the Sables, Sinagos, Kiskakons, Saulteurs, Mississaugas, Hurons, and Amikwas who were living in and around Michilimackinac.[44] A few years later, at the Great Peace of Montreal in 1701, the French were compelled to acknowledge formally doodemag as political entities. They named twenty-five distinct Native American political entities in the preamble to the treaty, noting some of the more important doodemag—or at least

those with which they were more familiar. For example, they listed the
Outaouacs du Sable, Kiskakons, Sinagos, and Nation de la Fourche (or
Nassauekuetons). But as Heidi Bohaker notes, they also clearly missed
some doodemag. There were in fact as many as thirty-eight distinct pic-
tographs on the treaty representing different doodemag.[45]

Over time, this early—and fuzzy—acknowledgment of doodemag
identities seemed to give way to a greater emphasis on more geographically based notions of nation. Despite continuing evidence to con-
tradict such notions, the French began dividing up the Algonquian
"nations" with more certainty and regularity, referring increasingly
to the Saulteurs and Odawas of Michilimackinac, for example, and
the Potawatomis of St Joseph's River. And though references to the
"Michilimackinac Indians" (and after 1741, the "L'Arbre Croche Ottawas") sometimes implicitly recognized the mixed communities that
were better represented by doodem labels, such terms increasingly became a catchall for Indians in the region to distinguish them from the
"Detroit Indians" or the Indians of the Sault. Ironically, then, even as
some French men married into these doodemag, and as French knowledge of the politics of the *pays d'en haut* seemed to grow, shorthand
descriptors tended to obscure French understanding of the continuing impact of doodem identities (and thus ours, too).

At times, the Anishinaabeg seemed happy to allow the French to
gloss these differences. Indeed, at least some doodem chiefs relied on
French officials' ignorance of the extent of their authority and were
only too happy to allow the French to believe they represented "the
Ottawa" of Michilimackinac. Often, doodem chiefs parlayed this ignorance into more numerous gifts at formal councils in Montreal.
Some were also able to use this ignorance to gain influence not just
in French councils but among their Anishinaabe brethren too. The
early eighteenth-century history of Anishinaabe relations reveals a
constant jockeying for position among different chiefs vis-à-vis their
relations with the French. As relations with the French became more
important over the course of the first half of the eighteenth century,
there is some evidence to suggest that doodem chiefs who could claim
French favor held more authority in Anishinaabe councils.

At the same time, Anishinaabe doodem chiefs could continue to construct an independent foreign policy from the French—often under cover of their vaunted lack of authority over their warriors. Indeed, as the French complained, complex and extended negotiations in Montreal for peace and for war with "representatives" of each nation often broke down when those representatives returned to Michilimackinac. The chiefs' lack of compelling authority over younger warriors has become a commonplace among historians of early North America. Yet we have only begun to glimpse that the lines of authority may have been quite different from what we have come to expect, and in fact doodem chiefs were happy to manipulate this confusion.

Savvier French officials, especially post commanders with extensive experience of Anishinaabe-French relations, had a more realistic sense of the limits of different chiefs' authority. Invariably, this contributed to growing conflict between post commanders in the *pays d'en haut* and officials in Montreal, or the metropole, as the former demanded ever-greater quantities of "presents" to influence the numerous chiefs who held authority over their doodemag. Officials at arm's length increasingly wanted single representatives of "nations" to deal with and treat.

Constant French efforts to systematize and order their relations with indigenous peoples in the Great Lakes may have obscured our view of Anishinaabe identities in the eighteenth century, but it is clear that kinship relations continued to play an important, and sometimes crucial, role in the politics of the *pays d'en haut*—particularly in frustrating that very imperial order about which the French dreamed. One important example might suffice. In the 1740s the French struggled with continuous defections from their alliance and constant rumors of a more general uprising and conspiracies among the northern Indians. A significant source of the problems that plagued Indian-French relations during this period was the thickening trade relations with the English that many southern nations enjoyed and the northern nations coveted. As both English traders and new Indians villages sprawled out along the Ohio River and its tributaries, southern Anishinaabeg began to join them in ever-greater numbers, most likely as an extension of doodem marriages and kinship practices. One of the centers of this "rebel" activity was Pickawillany—a new village established by an upstart and previously minor Miami chief, Memeskia (also known as La Demoiselle, or Old Briton), of mixed Piankashaw-Miami descent.

By 1750 the French were desperate to strike a blow against Memeskia, believing that by doing so they could stop the British trade offensive into the heart of territory they claimed. They called upon all their indigenous allies in the Great Lakes to join them in an expedition against Pickawillany. But despite repeated promises of support, most of the Indians of the Great Lakes refused to budge. The problem lay in the thick web of intermarriages among the nations of the *pays d'en haut*. The commandant of St. Joseph's River post, for example, said that he could not control the nations there because the rebellious Miamis were near relatives.[46] There was also a report that the Odawas had blocked a French expeditionary party at Detroit because, they claimed, the Miamis had intermarried with them and they could not let them attack their relations. There was even one report that Memeskia's son was married to an Odawa woman.[47] French officials despaired. In April 1752, after surveying the sentiments of many of the nations of the *pays d'en haut*, the French governor concluded that very few had acted against Memeskia, and even those who "promised wonders" were only deceiving the French, for "at heart, they preserve the same feelings of attachment for those rebels to whom they are connected by blood."[48]

The standoff was finally resolved by a surprise blow of approximately 250 warriors from the Michilimackinac region led by Charles Langlade, himself of mixed French-Anishinaabe (Nation de la Fourche) descent. With reports of numbers of Saginaw, St. Joseph's, and Detroit Indians at Pickawillany, Anishinaabeg from Michilimackinac had to tread carefully to avoid initiating a complex civil war among the nations of the *pays d'en haut*. Yet those relations may have also held the key to the success of the expedition. Indeed, descriptions of the attack suggest that the event was carefully stage-managed. Langlade and his allies allegedly surprised the village when most of the male warriors were out hunting. At about 9:00 a.m., Langlade and the

Indian warriors charged the stockade, catching women in the corn-
fields and forcing the few warriors who remained in the village to attempt a defense from within the stockade. After a short siege, during
which Langlade ritually and symbolically killed, boiled, and ate the
heart of Memeskia, who they had managed to capture, the defenders
gave up the English in their midst in return for the women and children captured. With four captured traders and £3,000 worth of goods,
most of the attackers returned the captured women to the defenders,
as promised, and headed northward. Reports of the number of casualties vary, but English accounts note only seven dead—Memeskia,
an Englishman, one Mingo, one Shawnee, and three Miamis. This
was no "massacre"; it was a clinical extraction.[49] It was also successful.
Because of the limited Indian casualties, the strength of the alliances
of the attackers, and the weakness of the Memeskia's new alliances,
there were no repercussions among the Indians of the *pays d'en haut*.
Instead, the raid worked to persuade many wavering nations that the
English were ultimately weak. With few exceptions, the nations of
the *pays d'en haut* allied with the French during the war that followed.

In hindsight, of course, the attack on Pickawillany seemed a pyrrhic
victory, especially for the Anishinaabeg of Michilimackinac. The attack has been considered the first battle of the impending Seven Years'
War. Though other French initiatives show that it was more generally indicative of a renewed interest in the area that would have led to
conflict eventually, the raid was certainly instrumental in stopping
the British trade offensive in the Ohio Valley, and most importantly,
in securing the allegiances of most of the peoples of the *pays d'en haut*
for the French throughout the coming conflict.[50] In turn, the Seven
Years' War is often seen as the beginning of the end of Native American independence in the *pays d'en haut*, as it was quickly followed by
the American Revolution and the creation of a new republic in North
America. Unable to play off competing European powers in the new
world after 1783, nations such as the Odawa, Ojibwe, and Potawatomi were defeated, dispossessed, and removed by a restless, expansionist, and ultimately racist new United States.[51]

But the attack on Pickawillany also suggests that we need to look much more closely at the politics of the *pays d'en haut* in the post-French period, too. The enduring strength of kinship alliances throughout the Great Lakes at the end of the French colonial period points to the need to trace these relationships through the Revolutionary era and beyond. Though British and American officials had an increasingly clouded view of doodem politics, these relationships continued to shape Anishinaabe life, and consequently relations with Europeans and Americans. One need only consider the fact that in 1763 Pontiac, the Odawa, led a surprise attack at Detroit, while Odawas at Michilimackinac saved the British garrison there. To fully comprehend these influences, we need to rethink our view of Native American identity and historicize the rise of nations such as the Odawa, Potawatomi, and Ojibwe. Though these labels became a convenient way for the new republic to organize and deal with the peoples of the *pays d'en haut* in the nineteenth century, it is still not clear when, how, and to what extent diverse Native peoples themselves adopted and embraced these labels. While the Odawas, Potawatomis, and Ojibwes of northern Michigan may have been relabeled and removed (with mixed results), the enduring relationships at the heart of kinship relations were more difficult to eradicate.[52]

In the long run, viewing events from indigenous perspectives helps us think very differently about the narrative arc of European-Indian relations, but particularly about the enduring continuities in indigenous identities across time. Seen from this vantage point, Richard White's middle ground becomes less a tale of accommodation between disparate, ephemeral Native groups and burgeoning centralized empires, and more a story of multigenerational continuity in which French, and later English, officials played a less significant role than we might have imagined. Finally, such an approach will raise questions about how we understand Native histories and indigenous identities in the post-French era. From an indigenous perspective, while the middle ground described by White may have closed, Native Americans in the region did not simply disappear with it. While the middle ground may have been crucial to the creation of new empires and Euro-American nations, the conflicted boundaries of those political entities mattered less to the peoples who inhabited this region than the persistent and enduring ties of kinship and family. Moreover, recognizing that the "tribe" or "nation" may have been only one layer of a more complex identity, we may yet be able to write nuanced histories of Native peoples that account for long-term continuities and the persistence of the people of the *pays d'en haut* in the very face of dispossession, removal, and the phenomenon of the so-called vanishing Indian.[53]

Notes

1. Richard White, *The Middle Ground: Indians, Empires, and Republics in the Great Lakes Region, 1650–1815* (New York: Cambridge University Press, 1991), ix–xv; Richard White, "Creative Misunderstandings and New Understandings," *William and Mary Quarterly* 3rd ser., 63, no. 1 (2006): 9–11. Compellingly written, richly detailed, and conceptually innovative, White's book has had an impact far beyond the historiography of the Great Lakes.

2. For the incomprehensibleness of this world, see White's comments in "Creative Misunderstandings," 12–14; White, *Middle Ground*, xi–xiv.

3. White was not really interested in "real" identities. Instead, he was keen to explore the perceived, imagined, and fictive identities generated by the European-Indian encounter. But in doing so, he implicitly brushes aside the reality that there were Native identities independent of the fictive imagined identities perceived by the French.

4. White, *Middle Ground*, 1–3, and *passim*. Again, White's Eurocentrism in rewriting the history of the *pays d'en haut* is implicit in his focus on the middle ground. This was only one dimension of the history of the Great Lakes. For another more explicit argument that overplays the role of French imperialism in the *pays d'en haut*, see Gilles Havard, *Empire et Métissages: Indiens et Français dans le Pays d'en Haut, 1660–1715* (Paris: Presses de l'université de Paris-Sorbonne, 2003). For a sense of the effect of White's narrative on subsequent historians, see Jeremy Adelman and Stephen Aaron, "From Borderlands to Borders: Empires, Nation-States, and the Peoples in Between in North American History," *American Historical Review* 104, no. 3 (1999): 817–23. For an extended discussion of some of these themes, see Michael A. McDonnell, "Dancing with Shadows: Biography and the Making and Remaking of the Atlantic World," in *Transnational Lives*, ed. Desley Deacon, Penny Russell, and Angela Woollacott (Basingstoke: Palgrave Macmillan, 2010). Heidi Bohaker also critiques White along these lines in her article

"*Nindoodemag:* The Significance of Algonquian Kinship Networks in the Eastern Great Lakes Region, 1600–1701," *William and Mary Quarterly* 63, no. 1 (2006): esp. 50–51, discussed in more detail below.

5. Daniel Richter, *Facing East from Indian Country: A Native History of Early America* (Cambridge MA: Harvard University Press, 2001). For an extended discussion of the need to view these events—even the formation of the Atlantic world—from indigenous perspectives, see Michael A. McDonnell, "Paths Not Yet Taken, Voices Not Yet Heard: Rethinking Atlantic History," in *Connected Worlds: History in Transnational Perspective*, ed. Anne Curthoys and Marilyn Lake (Canberra: Australian National University Press, 2005), 46–62.

6. This chapter will focus mainly on the Anishinaabeg of the Michilimackinac area, and especially the Odawas there. For a sample of this rich and exciting indigenous-centered literature, see James Lockhart, *The Nahuas after the Conquest: A Social and Cultural History of the Indians of Central Mexico, Sixteenth through Eighteenth Centuries* (Stanford CA: Stanford University Press, 1992); Ned Blackhawk, *Violence over the Land: Indians and Empires in the Early American West* (Cambridge MA: Harvard University Press, 2006); Pekka Hämäläinen, *The Comanche Empire* (New Haven CT: Yale University Press, 2008); Joshua Aaron Piker, *Okfuskee: A Creek Indian Town in Colonial America* (Cambridge MA: Harvard University Press, 2004); and Alexandra Harmon, *Indians in the Making: Ethnic Relations and Indian Identities around Puget Sound* (Berkeley: University of California Press, 1998). For recent works on the Anishinaabeg and their neighbors more specifically, see D. Peter Macleod, "The Anishinabeg Point of View: The History of the Great Lakes Region to 1800 in Nineteenth-Century Mississauga, Odawa, and Ojibwa Historiography," *Canadian Historical Review* 73, no. 2 (1992): 206–7; Michael J. Witgen, "An Infinity of Nations: How Indians, Empires, and Western Migration Shaped National Identity in North America" (PhD diss., University of Washington, 2004); Witgen, *An Infinity of Nations: How the Native New World Shaped Early North America* (Philadelphia: University of Pennsylvania Press, 2012); Witgen, "The Rituals of Possession: Native Identity and the Invention of Empire in Seventeenth-Century Western North America," *Ethnohistory* 54, no. 4 (2007): 639–68; Andrew Sturtevant, "'Inseparable Companions' and Irreconcilable Enemies: The Hurons and Odawas of French Detroit, 1701–1738," *Ethnohistory* 60, no. 3 (Summer 2013): 219–43; Brett Rushforth, "Slavery, the Fox Wars, and the Limits of Alliance," *William and Mary Quarterly*, 3rd ser., 63, no. 1 (2006): 53–59; Rushforth, *Bonds of Alliance: Indigenous and Atlantic Slaveries in New France* (Chapel Hill: University of North Carolina Press, 2012); Bohaker, "*Nindoodemag*: The Significance of Algonquian Kinship Networks"; Bohaker, "*Nindoodemag*: Anishinaabe Identities in the Eastern Great Lakes Region, 1600

to 1900" (PhD diss., University of Toronto, 2006); and William James Newbigging, "The History of the French-Ottawa Alliance: 1613–1763" (PhD diss., University of Toronto, 1995).

7. White, *Middle Ground*, 1–9. White notes that it was a world dimly perceived
by the French, but then proceeds to tell the tale from French perspectives alone.
He also fails to note the Algonquians' different sociopolitical organization from
that of the better-known Hurons and Iroquois—or at least what the difference
might have made to French perceptions.

8. Newbigging, "French-Ottawa Alliance," 28–36, 87; Witgen, "Rituals of Possession," 645; Blackbird, *History of the Ottawa*, 79–85; Francis Assikinack, "Legends and Traditions of the Odahwah," *Canadian Journal of Industry, Science, and
Art* 3, no. 14 (1858): 115–25. Assikinack says the Odawas did not arrive at Manitoulin Island until about 1500, but archaeological evidence suggests new influences
that may have been brought about by the arrival of Algonquian-speaking peoples
from the east as early as 1200, and possibly as early as 1000 (Newbigging, "French-
Ottawa Alliance," 34n20, 40; Cleland, *Rites of Passage*, 23–27; Tanner, *Atlas*, 24–28).

9. Newbigging, "French-Ottawa Alliance," 28–38, 41–44, 47–48, 89–94. Newbigging points out that Ojibwe and Odawa migration stories are virtually the
same. Cf. William W. Warren, *History of the Ojibway People* (St. Paul: Minnesota
Historical Society Press, 1984), 81–82, whose 1852 relation of his mother's Ojibwe
people notes that the separation of the Anishinaabeg took place at Michilimackinac "from natural causes, and the partition has been more distinctly defined,
and perpetuated through locality."

10. Witgen, "Rituals of Possession," 647–48.

11. Witgen, "Rituals of Possession," 647–48.

12. Witgen, "Rituals of Possession," 648. Witgen notes that the Algonquian-
speaking peoples were named as nations by the French for the purposes of possession. In reality, they shifted shape depending on location and relations with
their hosts and neighbors.

13. Bohaker, "*Nindoodemag*: The Significance of Algonquian Kinship Networks," 25–26. The importance of kinship in understanding Native identities
has long been asserted, but it has only recently been taken seriously by historians. See Raymond J. DeMallie, "Kinship: The Foundation for Native American
Society," in *Studying Native America: Problems and Prospects*, ed. Russell Thornton (Madison: University of Wisconsin Press, 1998), 306–56. James McClurken,
in his study of the Odawas, also noted the relationship between nindoodemag
and trading relations. Noting that the word *ota'wa'* means to trade, McClurken
asserts that the families who emerged as the Odawa nation were middlemen for
the Huron-Chippewa trade and each Odawa family "owned" different routes.

These routes were geographical paths as well as a set of trading relations along the way. Marriages were often arranged to turn trading partners into family members and so extend kinship ties. Trade routes could only be used by the families who pioneered them and who maintained the gift exchange and kinship ties that assured safe passage (See James A. Clifton, George L. Cornell, and James M. McClurken, *Peoples of the Three Fires: The Ottawa, Potawatomi, and Ojibway of Michigan* (Grand Rapids: Michigan Indian Press, 1986), 11.

14. Bohaker, "*Nindoodemag*: The Significance of Algonquian Kinship Networks," 43. Nineteenth-century indigenous commentators such as Francis Assikinack were well aware of these divisions, though they spoke of them in the past. Assikinack noted that the tribes were again subdivided into section or families according to their "Ododams"—"that is their devices, signs"—and members of each family kept themselves distinct from the other members of the tribe. In large villages, all members of an ododam would live in separate and distinct areas. Some of the families were more influential than others and had to consent to convening councils, others were distinguished by their bravery or eloquence, and some for their "filibustering propensities." Though there was a head chief of the whole tribe, his authority was "merely nominal," as authority was divided up between the heads of the ododam families. Assikinack also talked about parallel war chiefs and civil chiefs, but it is not clear whether these existed within the ododam structure, on top of it, or indeed were the ododam chiefs themselves (Assikinack, "Legends and Traditions of the Odahwah," 119–20).

15. Bohaker, "*Nindoodemag*," 38.

16. Bohaker, "*Nindoodemag*," 37–38.

17. See Tracy Neal Leavelle, *The Catholic Calumet: Colonial Conversions in French and Indian North America* (Philadelphia: University of Pennsylvania Press, 2012), 26–28, 40; Rueben Gold Thwaites, *The Jesuit Relations and Allied Documents: Travels and Explorations of the Jesuit Missionaries in New France, 1610–1791* (New York: Pageant Books, 1959), 54:199–203 (hereafter *JR*); La Potherie in Emma H. Blair, ed., *The Indian Tribes of the Upper Mississippi Valley and Region of the Great Lakes* (Cleveland: Arthur H. Clark, 1912), 1:283–88; Raudot, *Memoir*, quoted in W. Vernon Kinietz, *The Indians of the Western Great Lakes, 1615–1760* (Ann Arbor: University of Michigan Press, 1965), 379; and *JR* 67:153–61. See also Bohaker, "*Nindoodemag*: Anishinaabe Identities," 240.

18. In 1679 the Jesuits claimed that there were 1,300 mostly Kiskakon Odawas alone who belonged to their mission at St. Ignace (*JR* 61:103). A 1683 report also notes the presence of most of the main Odawa nindoodems at Michilimackinac. See E. M. Sheldon, *The Early History of Michigan: From the First Settlement to 1815* (New York: A. S. Barnes, 1874), 43–59.

19. *JR* 55:157.

20. Bohaker, *"Nindoodemag*: The Significance of Algonquian Kinship Networks," 38; Newbigging, "French-Ottawa Alliance," 95n28; Bruce Trigger, *Natives and Newcomers: Canada's "Heroic Age" Reconsidered* (Vancouver: UBC Press), 149–63.

21. Bohaker, *"Nindoodemag*: The Significance of Algonquian Kinship Networks," 47–48.

22. For Michilimackinac, see White, *Middle Ground*, 42–45; "Relation of Sieur de Lamothe Cadillac . . ." 1718, *Wisconsin Historical Society, Collections* 16 (1902): 350 (hereafter *WHC*); Helen Hornbeck Tanner, *Atlas of Great Lakes Indian History* (Norman: University of Oklahoma Press, 1987), 31; *JR* 55: 135–167. There may have been as many as six thousand to seven thousand Odawa, Huron, and Ojibwa peoples living within a pistol shot of the straits in the early eighteenth century (see Jacqueline Louise Peterson, "The People in Between: Indian-White Marriage and the Genesis of Métis Society and Culture in the Great Lakes Region, 1680–1830" [PhD diss., University of Illinois at Chicago Circle, 1981], 38).

23. Richard White speculates the sudden rise of marriages may have been a reaction to formal French attempts to force coureurs de bois out of the *pays d'en haut*, culminating in the abandonment of western posts in the late 1690s.

24. Peterson, "People in Between," 59–60.

25. On the "tender ties" that helped sustain the fur trade, see especially Susan Sleeper-Smith, *Indian Women and French Men: Rethinking Cultural Encounter in the Western Great Lakes* (Amherst: University of Massachusetts Press, 2001); Sylvia Van Kirk, *Many Tender Ties: Women in Fur Trade Society, 1679–1870* (Norman: University of Oklahoma Press, 1983); Van Kirk, "The Custom of the Country: An Examination of Fur Trade Practices," in *Essays on Western History*, ed. Lewis H. Thomas (Edmonton: University of Alberta Press, 1976), 49–68; Van Kirk, "The Role of Native Women in the Fur Trade Society of Western Canada, 1670–1830," *Frontiers* 7, no. 3 (1984): 76–80; Van Kirk, "'Women in Between': Indian Women in Fur Trade Society in Western Canada," in *Out of the Background: Readings on Canadian Native History*, ed. Robin Fisher and Kenneth Coates (Toronto: Copp Clark Pitman Ltd., 1988), 150–66; Jennifer S. H. Brown, *Strangers in Blood: Fur Trade Company Families in Indian Country* (1980; repr., Norman: University of Oklahoma Press, 1996).

26. The following paragraphs are drawn from Michael McDonnell, *Negotiating Empires: French, Anishinaabe, and Métis Communities in the Making and Unmaking of the Atlantic World* (New York: Hill and Wang, 2014).

27. The extent to which the Anishinaabeg were pushed back across the Great Lakes, and indeed, fought back against the Iroquois, is contested terrain. For a sample of two opposing views on these questions, see especially Leroy V. Eid,

"The Ojibwa-Iroquois War: The War the Five Nations Did not Win," *Ethnohistory* 26, no. 4 (1979): 297–324, who draws on oral stories and testimony to assert that the Odawas and Ojibwes especially hit back at the Iroquois in the latter half of the seventeenth century, and on the work of J. A. Brandão, who has mounted a vigorous argument against Eid based on an exhaustive reading of the surviving written evidence (see especially Brandão and William A. Starna, "The Treaties of 1701: A Triumph of Iroquois Diplomacy," *Ethnohistory* 43, no. 2 (1996): 209–44, and Brandão, "'Your Fyre Shall Burn No More': Iroquois Policy towards New France and Her Native Allies to 1701" (PhD diss., York University, 1994). Though the details might never be clearly understood, Brandão's work in particular makes it clear that conflict was endemic throughout this period, and it was devastating. The escalation of warfare in the southern Great Lakes region in the seventeenth century has been the subject of many works and numerous interpretations. One of the best works on the subject, especially from the Iroquois perspective, is Richter, *Ordeal of the Longhouse*, esp. chapters 1–7.

28. Macleod, "The Anishinabeg Point of View," 206–7. Michael Witgen's recent book, *An Infinity of Nations*, takes up this theme in more detail.

29. Macleod, "Anishinabeg Point of View," 194–210.

30. Trigger, *Natives and Newcomers*, 180–81. See Brandão, "'Your Fyre Shall Burn No More,'" ch. 5, for the long-standing nature of conflicts between the Hurons, Algonquians, and Iroquois.

31. Newbigging, "French-Ottawa Alliance," 126, 132–35. The first Odawa fur fleet arrived in Montreal in 1653, which points to the fact that not only were the Odawa not all on the run westward, but that they were not particularly worried about the Iroquois threat to such trips. It is likely that they were there in order to cement their alliance with the French at this crucial moment in the conflict with the Iroquois (Newbigging, "French-Ottawa Alliance," 160–65; *JR* 41:77–79.

32. Gilles Havard, *The Great Peace of Montreal of 1701: French-Native Diplomacy in the Seventeenth Century* (Montreal: McGill-Queen's University Press, 2001), 89, believes the tide began to turn against the Iroquois around 1662, when the Iroquois suffered a major defeat by the Ojibwes, Odawas, and Nipissings near Lake Superior, which was no doubt linked to an epidemic among the Iroquois that same year.

33. Bohaker, "*Nindoodemag*: The Significance of Algonquian Kinship Networks," 45; For continued hostilities with the Odawas and Hurons while the French enjoyed relative peace with the Iroquois, see Ralph Flenley, ed. and trans., *A History of Montreal, 1640–1672: From the French of Dollier de Casson* (London: J. M. Dent and Sons, 1928), 207; Newbigging, "French-Ottawa Alliance," 136–137; *JR* 44: 205; Tanner, *Atlas*, 31.

34. Havard, *Great Peace*, 81. Cf. Monseignat, Relation de ce qui s'est passé de plus remarquable au Canada, novembre, 1690 AN CIIA, 11:6, Library and Archives of Canada, Ottawa; also in NYCD IX, 463, cited in John R. Brodhead, Berthold Fernow, and E. B. O'Callaghan, eds., *Documents Relative to the Colonial History of New York*, vol. 9 of 15 (Albany: Weed, Parsons, 1858–73); Louise Phelps Kellogg, *The French Régime in Wisconsin and the Northwest* (Madison: State Historical Society of Wisconsin, 1925), 244–45; *JR* 64:29.

35. Rushforth, "Slavery, the Fox Wars, and the Limits of Alliance," 53–59.

36. Rushforth, "Slavery, the Fox Wars, and the Limits of Alliance," 61.

37. Rushforth, "Slavery, the Fox Wars, and the Limits of Alliance," 54–57; Newbigging, "French-Ottawa Alliance," 323. As Rushforth and Newbigging note, the Fox Wars did not result from a failure of the French to mediate, as Richard White claimed, but rather because the Anishinaabeg were determined to eliminate a serious threat to their authority in their territory.

38. Bohaker, "*Nindoodemag*: The Significance of Algonquian Kinship Networks," 34–35, 36–37. One early Jesuit noted of Lake Huron that "the Eastern and Northern shores of this Lake are inhabited by various Algonquin Tribes,—Outaouakamigouek, Sakahiganiriouik, Aouasanik, Atchougue, Amikouek, Achirigouans, Nikikouek, Michisaguek, Paouitagoung,—with all of which we have a considerable acquaintance." *Relation de ce qvi s'est Passe . . .* in *JR* 33:149.

39. *JR* 51:79–81.

40. They did the same for the Algonquian-speaking Illinois, "who are very numerous and dwell toward the South, since the first who visited point saint Esprit to trade were called Ilinois." *JR* 55:205–7.

41. *JR* 51:119–20; 54:131–33; 62:191–93.

42. *JR* 62:191–93; Bohaker, "*Nindoodemag*: The Significance of Algonquian Kinship Networks," 24–25.

43. See, for example, *JR* 62:191–93; 54:131–33; 57:13–15; 54:203–5.

44. See Sheldon, *Early History of Michigan*, 43–59; White, *Middle Ground*, 77–82.

45. Bohaker, "*Nindoodemag*: The Significance of Algonquian Kinship Networks," 24–25.

46. Longueuil to the French minister, April 21, 1752, *WHC* 18:104–5 (reprint from NY Col. Docs, x, 245–51).

47. Kellogg, *French Régime*, 419; *WHC* 18:104–8; Thomas Cresap to Governor Dinwiddie, November 20, 1751–January 23, 1752, in Charles A. Hanna, *The Wilderness Trail, or the Ventures and Adventures of the Pennsylvania Traders on the Allegheny Path* (New York: G. P. Putnam's Sons, 1911), 2:282–85.

48. Longueuil to the French minister, April 21, 1752, *WHC* 18:108–9; NYCD 10:247. Longueuil also noted that that web of relations was only getting worse.

He noted that every party of Indians who went to the Miami village left people there "to increase the rebel forces."

49. See White, *Middle Ground*, 230–31, 233–34; R. David Edmunds, "Picka-willany: French Military Power versus British Economics," *Western Pennsylvania Historical Magazine* 58 (1975): 182–83; Paul Trap, "Charles Langlade" (undated, un-published manuscript), 4:8–10. Initial details of the attack come mainly from Eng-lish sources, and primarily from the eyewitness accounts of the two surviving Englishmen, Thomas Burney and Andrew McBryer. See especially the journal of William Trent and related papers: Alfred T. Goodman, ed. *Journal of Captain William Trent from Logstown to Pickawillany, A D 1752* (Cincinnati: Robert Clarke and Co., for William Dodge, 1871; repr., [New York]: Arno Press, 1971), 87–89, and also the collected letters in Hanna, *The Wilderness Trail*, 2:289. Despite their claims of being reassured by wampum belts before the attack, there is a good chance that Memeskia's village had been warned of the impending attack, and thus some may have fled. Trent notes that on June 27, they met a Mingo man named Powell, who had been in Detroit twenty days before and had seen three hundred French and Indians set off, either to persuade the Twightwees to come back to the French, or "else to cut them off" (85). On the number of dead, Ed-munds notes that the escaped traders said there were six dead—La Demoiselle, the British trader, and four pro-British Indians. Burney later said there were fif-teen people killed (see Samuel Hazzard, ed., *Pennsylvania Colonial Records*, vol. 5 of 16 [Philadelphia: State of Pennsylvania, printed by J. Severns, 1851–53], 599). Volwiler, the biographer of Irish-born fur trader George Croghan, appears to have taken his figure of thirty dead from contemporary newspaper accounts (see Albert T. Volwiler, *George Croghan and the Westward Movement, 1741–1782* [Cleve-land: Arthur Clark Company, 1926], 79).

50. See, for example, Lawrence Henry Gipson, *The British Empire before the American Revolution* (New York: Knopf, 1958), 4:224; George Chalmers, *An In-troduction to History of the Revolt of the American Colonies* (Boston: James Mun-roe, 1845), 2:263–64. See, for general accounts of Langlade's raid and its context, Francis Jennings, *The Founders of America: How Indians Discovered the Land, Pio-neered in It, and Created Great Classical Civilizations, How They Were Plunged into a Dark Age by Invasion and Conquest, and How They are Reviving* (New York: Nor-ton, 1993), 287–90; Jennings, *Empire of Fortune: Crowns, Colonies, and Tribes in the Seven Years' War in America* (New York: Norton, 1988), 49–57; Ian K. Steele, *Warpaths: Invasions of North America* (New York: Oxford University Press, 1994), 179–83; White, *Middle Ground*, 220–234; Edmunds, "Pickawillany," 169–84; Greg-ory H. Dowd, *A Spirited Resistance: The North American Indian Struggle for Unity, 1745–1815* (Baltimore: Johns Hopkins University Press, 1992), 23–24; W. J. Eccles,

The Canadian Frontier, 1534–1760 (1969; repr., Albuquerque: University of New Mexico Press, 1979), 160–64. Cf. R. Douglas Hurt, *The Ohio Frontier: Crucible of the Old Northwest, 1720–1830* (Bloomington: Indiana University Press, 1996), who says it was on the morning of June 21, 1752, that the first shots of a new French and Indian War were fired (35).

51. For a recent interpretation along these lines, see Adelman and Aaron, "From Borderlands to Borders," esp. 839–41. The apparent end of this story also seems to confirm a historiographical trajectory cultivated among colonial American historians about racial attitudes, too—one that begins hopeful, and ends with the hardening of increasingly racialized attitudes in the late eighteenth century. See, for example, Jane Merritt, *At the Crossroads: Indians and Empires on a Mid-Atlantic Frontier, 1700–1763* (Chapel Hill: University of North Carolina Press, 2003).

52. Francis Assikinack, for example, an Odawa from Manitoulin Island, noted the nindoodem divisions, but in 1858 spoke of them in the past. (Assikinack, "Legends and Traditions of the Odahwah," 119–20). Yet at least as late as 1835, dozens of Odawa and Ojibwe "chiefs" from all across the Great Lakes signed a document naming Augustin Hamelin Jr. as "head chief" to act on their behalf, and drew their nindoodem images in place of their signatures. In this, we see all three layers of identity in play ("To all whom it may concern the chiefs of the Ottawa Tribe . . . ," May 3, 1835, MS 669, Edward E. Ayer Manuscript Collection, Newberry Library, Chicago). This perhaps should not be so surprising. We have little trouble in acknowledging that someone from Wales might variously and simultaneously identify themselves as Welsh, British, and European, depending on the context, and yet still make most important decisions on the basis of relationships with kin and community.

53. We now know that the Anishinaabeg and other Indian populations in the northern Great Lakes especially had achieved a stable pattern distribution and growth as early as 1810—patterns that would persist throughout the nineteenth century. Any history of the people of the *pays d'en haut* has to account for the continuities that have sustained these figures, as well as the discontinuities of the imperial middle ground. Tanner, *Atlas of Great Lakes Indian History*, 12, 96, 100, 175–79. For more discussion of this issue, see McDonnell, "'Il a Epousé une Sauvagesse': Indian and Métis Persistence across Imperial and National Borders," in *Moving Subjects: Gender, Mobility, and Intimacy in an Age of Global Empire*, ed. Tony Ballantyne and Antoinette Burton (Urbana: University of Illinois Press, 2008), 149–71. Again, Michael Witgen's richly complex new book, *An Infinity of Nations*, deals with many of these same themes.

Chapter 3

Identity Articulated
British Settlers, Black Caribs, and the Politics of Indigeneity
on St. Vincent, 1763–1797

Brooke N. Newman

"The savage, with the name and title, thinks he inherits the qualities, the rights, and the property, of those whom he may pretend to supersede: hence he assimilates himself by name and manners, as it were to make out his identity, and confirm the succession."[1] So wrote Sir William Young, Second Baronet, in *An Account of the Black Charaibs in the Island of St. Vincent's* (1795), an edited compilation of the original papers of his late father, also Sir William Young, former chief commissioner for the sale of lands in the Ceded Islands and a major proponent of dispossessing Native peoples in the service of British colonial expansion. Long recognized in Europe as "neutral" territory, until formally allotted to Britain by article 9 of the Treaty of Paris concluding the Seven Years' War (1756–63) on February 10, 1763, the Ceded Islands, as they became known, of St. Vincent, Grenada, Dominica, and Tobago, offered the Crown and British investors the opportunity to cultivate areas of the Lesser Antilles hitherto only semideveloped by independent French, British, and Dutch colonists. Yet a glitch remained. Although France agreed to deliver the Ceded Islands to Britain in exchange for St. Lucia, and the restoration of Guadeloupe and Martinique, European negotiators had flagrantly disregarded the extant Native inhabitants of the Lesser Antilles, and St. Vincent particularly; "the Charaibes not being mentioned in the whole transaction," one contemporary reported, "as if no such people existed."[2]

The significant Carib presence on St. Vincent would not be ignored for long, however. Soon after the ink dried on the Treaty of Paris, British land commissioners, executive officials, and administrators began to create an ethnographic portrait of the island's Native community. In official correspondence and published accounts they divided and juxtaposed the Vincentian Carib population into, as William Young II later put it, "two nations of people of very different origin and pretensions": the Yellow or Red Caribs, whom they deemed "the original natives," and the Black Caribs, "principally the descendants of Runaway negroes from Barbadoes and the other Neighboring Islands."[3] From the beginning, the elder Young and others maintained that the dominant Carib group on the island—the so-called Black Caribs—consisted primarily of fugitive Africans who, desperate to prevent their return to slavery, had gone to great lengths to masquerade as Natives. "Thus these Negroes not only assumed the national appellation of Charaibs," wrote Young II, "but individually their Indian names; and they adopted many of their customs." Worse still, the Black Caribs had not simply appropriated the identity of the aboriginal Natives on a superficial level; they ultimately aimed "to destroy the Red Charaibs, and carry off their women, and seemed in full career to the extirpation of the original inhabitants."[4]

What does it mean for William Young, senior and junior, and other interested parties to have focused so intensely on the assumed identity of the Black Caribs of St. Vincent, both in their communications with imperial authorities and in retrospective accounts intended for public view? Historians Bernard Marshall, Michael Craton, Paul Thomas, and Robin Fabel argue that British commentators, cognizant that the Black Caribs occupied territory ripe for large-scale agricultural development, accentuated their Africans origins in an attempt to neutralize their ancestral claims to property.[5] The British, as Peter Hulme shows, were determined to see the Native peoples occupying the most fertile section of the island as overwhelmingly African, in descent, complexion, facial features, hair texture, and temperament, rather than

Carib.[6] The available evidence confirms this interpretation yet also raises fundamental questions about eighteenth-century understandings of indigeneity, race, and the territorial rights (or lack thereof) of independent mixed communities on newly colonized lands: Could part-black populations claim Native property rights? At what point did biological amalgamation with outsiders compromise a Native group's indigenous status, generating dilemmas of both sovereignty and identity? "All colonial encounters involved dispossessing people of their land but justifications differed," Cole Harris observes.[7] Casting themselves as harbingers of progress and profit, British land commissioners characterized the appropriation of Vincentian resources, including Native lands, as an inevitable result of imperial conquest. That the hybrid Caribs opposed their dispossession by British colonizers and used legal language to put forward counterclaims, not just to land rights but to sovereignty in their own country, both baffled and angered St. Vincent's nascent white establishment.[8] From the British viewpoint, the bulk of the Vincentian Carib population, composed of savage men and women whose ancestry marked them as a foreign and enslaveable people, could make neither a valid claim to landownership nor a valid claim to Native sovereignty.

It is clear that the negative association of the Black Caribs with blackness, slavery, and Africa played an important rhetorical role in British justifications for, and retellings of, their eventual expulsion from St. Vincent. But this narrow perspective is not the only one that matters. Attending to the struggle for colonial dominion on St. Vincent also offers an opportunity to push beyond the narratives the British told themselves, to the various means through which the Black Caribs—phenotypically black but culturally and linguistically Carib—articulated a corporate identity distinct from that of other African diaspora communities. "Members of all groups," James Sidbury and Jorge Cañizares-Esguerra recently point out, responded to pan-Atlantic shifts and localized contingencies by "seeking to reembed themselves into communities, creating new identities rooted in the transformations that forged the early modern Atlantic world."[9] If the Black Caribs positioned themselves as a people native to the Caribbean, how should we think through such a self-identification now, knowing that their modern-day descendants, the Garifuna of Central America, share modern West African genetic traits and a genotype thought to resemble closely that of the original West Africans in the West Indies?[10] Is indigeneity (and hence indigenous rights) more about a "pure," localized lineage and evidence of lengthy residence in a fixed territorial space, as British officials came to insist, or a culturally constructed sense of belonging that draws upon historically rooted practices, beliefs, and landscapes, as the behavioral patterns of the Black Caribs suggest?

To begin to answer these questions, this chapter attempts to read against the grain of the imperial archive, foregrounding indigenous experiences and placing them in dialogue with the views and objectives of the Europeans who created the historical narrative. Returning to materials from the traditional source base, I provide alternate analyses of official state correspondence, published accounts, and visual imagery produced by, or on behalf of, Britons seeking to deprive the Black Caribs of their lands, liberty, and identity as a hybrid Native community. By highlighting some of the central themes in the commonly recited story of the Black Caribs' origin, I hope to show how the localized processes of colonialism and ethnogenesis that forged the Black Caribs as a new people linked across time and space to changing understandings of racial and ethnic identities in metropolitan Britain. In considering the vehement disavowal of the Black Caribs' indigeneity, I argue that British imperial aims in the Caribbean emerged together with an increasingly racialized pan-Atlantic discourse of difference, undercutting the rights of ethnic groups who impeded expansionist colonial projects and challenged the racial order. For the Black Caribs, such a merger of political interests and discursive constructions of human difference resulted in violence, dispossession, and attempted erasure.

Colonial Ethnography and Discourses of Dispossession

While questions about any historical group's collective identity are difficult to answer, they are doubly so for the mixed Afro-Carib community that lived on St. Vincent during the seventeenth and eighteenth centuries, whom the British termed the Black Caribs. European identity regimes and political imperatives pervade the surviving historical records pertaining to the Black Caribs, a culturally and ethnically blended people whose refusal to acquiesce to British colonial aims in the 1760s sparked a Franco-Anglo-Carib conflict that lasted well into the 1790s. For centuries, the story of their existence on and forcible removal from St. Vincent has remained a one-sided tale, told on behalf of victors who saw no reason to acknowledge the remarkable, tenuous nature of their survival in an era of ongoing political upheaval, warfare, and Native decimation. Willingly joining forces with the French on numerous occasions, even after signing a treaty with the British in 1773 whereby they agreed to acknowledge King George III as "their rightful sovereign" and "submit themselves to the Laws and Obedience of His Majesty's Government," the Black Caribs' political savvy only intensified contemporary claims that they were duplicitous Africans masquerading as Caribs.[11] Securing the Black Caribs' deportation en masse to Honduras in 1797, British colonial officials sought to ensure that their land rights, traditions, and historical memories on St. Vincent would not last. And they have not lasted—at least not in the traditional sense.[12] Consequently, historians seeking to recreate the lives, perspectives, or initiatives of the Black Caribs during the final phase of Native resistance to European hegemony in the Caribbean must reach into the charged ether of the early modern past, turning to depictions produced in the course of their contact and violent conflict with British colonists.

Generated in the context of a long series of hostilities, late-eighteenth-century British representations of Black Caribs are largely negative and also point toward broader cultural trends related to emerging notions of racially marked and gendered selves. The long eighteenth century saw the transformation of British understandings of personal and collective identity, from identity conceived of as fluid, multiple, and changeable to identity connoting a fixed inner essence, with gender and racial categories in particular being ascribed a relatively stable set of core characteristics beginning in approximately the 1780s. Imperial expansion overseas, encounters and conflicts with non-European peoples, and the American War of Independence helped contribute to this new configuration in British conceptions of identity and the social and cultural changes it engendered.[13] Moreover, in an age of feverish Enlightenment classification, in which a number of people backed by metropolitan and colonial patrons—natural philosophers, scientific travelers, physicians, botanists, and sailors—sought to gather, order, and control knowledge, pinning down the allegedly "essential" characteristics of the various ethnic groups peopling the Atlantic became a project of considerable consequence.[14] The nearly thirty-five-year Franco-Anglo-Carib struggle on St. Vincent occurred in the midst of this drive for colonial knowledge and mastery, and a more robust division between black and white, European and Other, in Britain and the wider British world.[15]

Immediately after France ceded St. Vincent to Britain in 1763, British observers began offering estimates of the total Native population with which settlers would have to contend as they transformed the island into a site of flourishing, profit-rich sugar plantations. These figures ranged anywhere from one thousand to five thousand Caribs.[16] "St. Vincent is fruitful & healthy," wrote one observer who produced a survey for the Crown in the early 1760s, with "about 2000 Caribbes . . . on the Western Side of the Island."[17] Another highly specific report counted 1,138 Caribs and their twenty-eight slaves on St. Vincent, with "the chief settlements of the Indians [being] to the windward and about the middle of the island at a place called the grand sable, the lands very good."[18] The elder Sir William Young initially speculated that "about 2000 natives" inhabited the eastern portion of the island, but in the same breath he dismissed their indigeneity, claiming that the majority "owe their origin to a ship freighted with negroes from Africa to Barbadoes, and wrecked on these coasts." Of the "original natives," whom Young characterized as "of an innocent and timid nature," only a few of their descendants "of a yellow complexion" remained, living fearfully apart from the more numerous body of African intruders.[19]

British surveyors, agents, settlers, and legislators produced a confusion of terminology in relation to St. Vincent's indigenous population, sometimes using various spellings of the identifying terms "Caribs" and "Black Caribs" interchangeably and on other occasions differentiating explicitly between these two groups for ethnographic or ideological purposes ("Native Caribs, "Yellow Caribs," "aborigines," "original Indians," and "Red Caribs" as opposed to "Black Caribs," "negroes," "African Negroes," "the free Negroes," or "the Blacks"). As a result, accounts of the ethnic composition of the Vincentian Native community differed wildly, with the majority stating that only a few hundred Yellow Caribs (hereafter referred to as the Island Caribs) remained, pushed nearly to extinction by a large, fierce group of African maroons. In 1719 agent Thomas Weir informed the Lords for Trade and Plantations that it would take a significant force to defeat "the Negroes of St. Vincent, in which Island by best Report are 4,000 Negroes."[20] Seventy-six years later, when William Young II looked back on the Vincentian Carib community his father faced in the mid-1760s, he estimated that approximately three thousand Black Caribs and only one hundred "Red Charaibs, or Indians," resided on the island, "so reduced were that aboriginal people!"[21] The West Indian historian Bryan Edwards concurred, characterizing St. Vincent's mid-eighteenth-century Island Carib population as a "miserable remnant" of an authentic aboriginal community destroyed over the course of several generations by a formidable "race of people" non-native to the region, though "long distinguished, however improperly, by the name of the *Black* Charaibes."[22]

Whatever the numbers or ethnic composition of the Vincentian indigenous population, neither of which observers found possible to fix precisely, it was clear enough to British land commissioners and other white settlers, such as the Methodist missionary George Davidson, that the Black Caribs possessed "the most extensive and finest part" of the island.[23] Davidson, who later published a detailed ethnographic and historical account of the Vincentian Caribs, explained that a group of marooned blacks had come to dominate "the most valuable part of the island" beginning in 1700, when the French divided St. Vincent longitudinally to separate French settlers and their native allies from the more hostile, independent Black Carib majority.[24] Such a compromise proved pragmatic for the French, who contented themselves with cultivating less labor- and capital-intensive commercial crops, including coffee, cocoa, and tobacco, on the hillier Caribbean side of St. Vincent.[25] In the wake of the Seven Years' War, as European control of St. Vincent changed hands, the victors deemed this earlier Franco-Carib agreement invalid: the British set their sights on the entire island, not a portion of it. Indeed, to Sir William Young the elder and other land commissioners appointed to survey the Ceded Islands and assess their potential for large-scale sugar production, St. Vincent stood out as "an admirable good island," and the windward section in particular. "The richness of the soil, and the face of the country, are perfectly adapted for the growth of sugar," wrote Young in 1764; "there seems great reason to expect, that it will very soon be classed among the best, most valuable of our sugar colonies."[26]

Young and his fellow commissioners envisioned St. Vincent as becoming the second-best British sugar colony in export production, after Jamaica, but with a larger, more diverse population of white settlers. Jamaica's failure as a stable settler society, they anticipated, would be rectified by St. Vincent, where a flourishing white community could keep the island profitable as well as secure.[27] To fulfill this plan, the commissioners sought to open up the underdeveloped windward side of St. Vincent to would-be sugar planters and set aside smallholdings in less fertile areas for poor white settlers. Only the Black Caribs stood in the way. Relocating them to tracts in the interior was thus perceived as a precondition to settlement and an economic necessity. It also guaranteed the island's safety, by preventing French forces from nearby St. Lucia from landing undetected on the windward side.[28] Regarding the Native population, as Vincentian planters and merchants later explained to the Duke of Portland, the objective was to create a "settlement in some Quarter of the Island, adequate to their Comfort and Wants, but deemed least suitable for forming sugar Plantations."[29] But would the Black Caribs acquiesce to such plans? Young thought they would. In an early assessment, he argued that the Black Caribs, though "a free people" born in "a state of nature" and "usually represented as turbulent and dangerous," were in fact "quiet and well disposed," educated by French missionaries to speak French

and practice Roman Catholicism. According to Young's initial prediction, the Vincentian Caribs would respond to the British takeover
by selecting one of two equally reasonable courses: they would either
migrate to the French-controlled colonies of St. Lucia or Martinique
or, once acclimated to British rule and "assured of the enjoyment of
their lands, freedom, favor and protection," remain on their allotted
settlement and "be gained over to our cause, and even rendered useful."[30] In making this prediction, Young projected his own expectations and desires onto the Carib community, assuming they would
abandon the island and turn to the French for protection or fall into
line and ally themselves with the British. Either result would clear the
way for the island's development.

To Sir William Young's surprise, the Black Caribs chose neither
course and proved a much greater obstacle than British officials had
anticipated. In June 1768 Vincentian authorities, on behalf of King
George III, sent the French priest Abbé Valladares on a tour through
Carib country to relay news of their intended resettlement, "to be carried into effect with the gentlest hand, and in the mildest manner." The
Black Caribs responded by questioning the legitimacy of the British
Crown. "What king was this, of Great Britain?" they demanded.[31] The
commissioners' decision soon after to drive a road through the windward side of St. Vincent to facilitate a full survey of cultivatable lands,
irrespective of Black Carib opposition, prompted armed bands of warriors to harass the road builders and surveyors and the troops attending them, obstructing access to Carib territory and grinding progress
to a halt. Tensions soon escalated. At a legislative meeting held the following spring, on May 10, 1769, Harry Alexander, Esq., president of the
Council of St. Vincent, declared that the Black Caribs had "assembled
themselves in Arms, denied any Subjection to the Crown of Great Britain and Stopped the Progress of his Majesty's Service with Survey of
and Carrying a road of Communication thro' that part of this Island
claimed by them." Although Alexander "wished much to punish" the
Black Caribs for this act of defiance, he admitted that his hands were
tied by King George III, who had "forbid[den] any Coercive force to be
made use of till his further pleasure shall be known."[32]

The British Crown preferred a policy of "gentle assimilation," in the words of P. J. Marshall, whereby the Caribs would come to understand that the king had allocated lands for the use and enjoyment of his "loving subjects" and meant to protect them.[33] However, the Black Caribs made it clear that they had no intention of submitting to the British, relocating to a reservation, or compromising at their own expense. As anger mounted between the two groups, the imperial government received reports from colonists, agents, legislators, and land commissioners in St. Vincent stating that the Black Caribs, though having failed to cultivate the valuable and extensive tract of land in their possession, stood obstinately in the way of the island's productive settlement. Such vigorous opposition to "Progress," they protested, constituted an act of "Ingratitude" and an "Audacious Insult to Government"; surely it demonstrated that the Black Caribs were nothing but a "worthless set of Savages," the king's lenient treatment of whom would "hurt his faithful, loyal and obedient Subjects."[34]

From the British perspective, the Black Caribs underlined their recalcitrance at a meeting held between the commissioners and forty Carib chiefs at Morne Garou in 1771. Joseph Chatoyér, their principal leader and spokesman during times of war, declared the Black Caribs a free and sovereign people, outside the bounds of either British or French royal authority, ready to defend their territory from foreign encroachments. In the wake of this failed parlay, Vincentian legislators, settlers, and agents began to agree that no other alternative remained but "the reduction of the Charibbs," who were then to "be totally and absolutely removed from this Island," perhaps to another area in the Caribbean or some place in Africa, the part of the world where these foreigners had presumably originated.[35] It is clear, however, that their removal was contemplated prior to the Morne Garou meeting. In 1770 an anonymously published tract, written from the point of view of a "Canibal of St. Vincent," highlighted the Black Caribs' reliance upon secluded fortifications to outmaneuver their well-armed enemies. Through this work (usually attributed to Sir William Young the elder), the author intended to rectify "the present *unprotected* state of our new-ceded islands, at this critical juncture," by familiarizing

British military commanders with the guerilla techniques practiced by truculent "Cannibals" in heavily wooded islands. Putting words into the mouth of a fictional Black Carib, the tract underlined the group's non-Native status and the pressing strategic need to expel them from St. Vincent: "The English Baccaras are not cruel; they will not extirpate us, though we will deserve it, for extirpating the natives, who gave us shelter in our distress; they must therefore find us land somewhere, as they must have possession of ours, to secure the quiet of the island, in case of a war with the French Baccaras."[36] Rather than mere victims of British imperialism, the Black Caribs were themselves accused of criminal acts of conquest and dispossession.

In September 1772, failed negotiations between the two parties accelerated into full-fledged conflict, and under the command of General Dalrymple, the British deployed troops against the Black Caribs in an effort to secure control of St. Vincent. The subsequent First Carib War of 1772–73, which led to a significant loss of British troops from disease, generated negative publicity in Britain, and sparked an unprecedented parliamentary debate about Native territorial rights in areas recently incorporated into the empire. The British press questioned whether colonization—and the voracious land-grabbing and forceful dispossession of Native peoples that inevitably ensued—was really compatible with the basic principles of humanity.[37] For colonists in St. Vincent, the conflict was a necessary step toward subduing and removing "the Free Negroes (improperly termed Charaibs)," a non-native people fiercely possessive of "the Country they chose to occupy," despite their dubious claim to the land and "disposition little worthy of Royal Favour, or of Sovereign Protection."[38] Still, in April 1773, when it became apparent that the plan for removal had failed, the two parties agreed to a treaty. A northern section of the island, "from the river Byera to Point Espagniol on the one side, and from the river Analibou to Point Espagniol on the other side," was set aside for the residence of the Black Caribs (fig. 3.1). In exchange, the Black Caribs, represented by twenty-eight chiefs, swore oaths of loyalty to the British Crown and agreed to permit the construction of

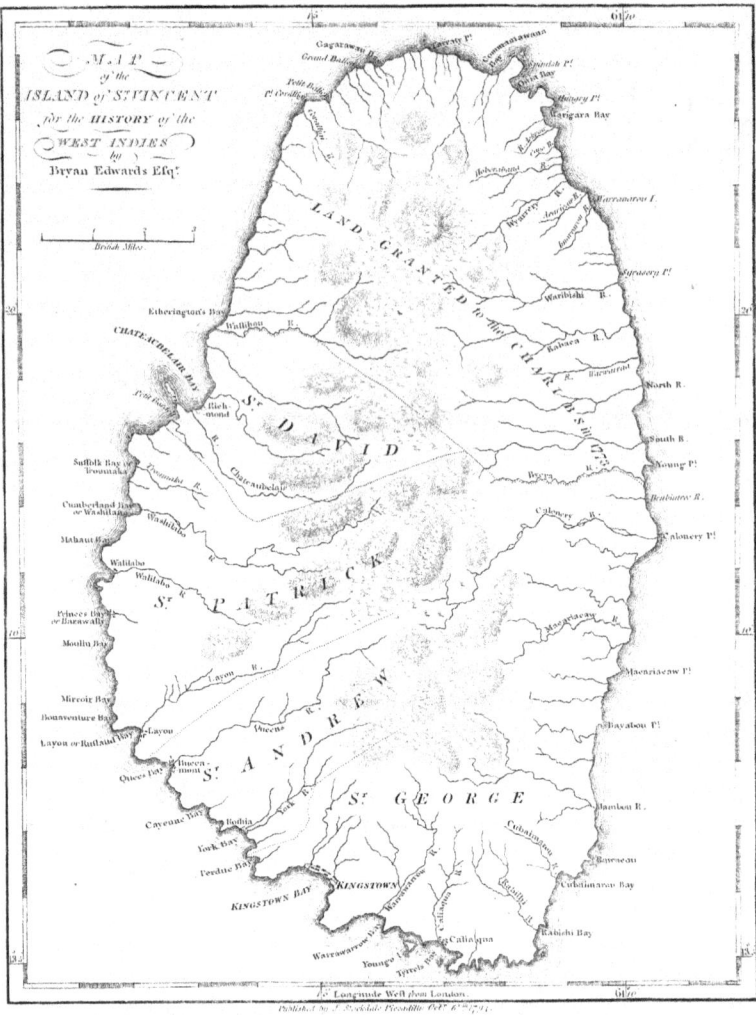

Fig. 3.1. "Map of the Island of St Vincent for the History of the West Indies by Bryan Edwards, Esq." London, 1794. Courtesy of the John Carter Brown Library at Brown University.

roads and batteries, return runaway slaves to their owners, and cease communications with the French, among other things.[39] While the treaty brought some relief to the frustrated administrators in St. Vincent, in the years that followed the Black Caribs largely disregarded the agreement and continued to operate independently and maintain friendly relations with their French allies. The Black Caribs may have sworn allegiance to the king of a distant land for the sake of political expediency, but their primary concern remained the preservation of their territory, autonomy, and way of life.

Constructing a "Black Carib" Identity

But who were these supposed African usurpers whom British officials so eagerly sought to dispossess? By the mid-eighteenth century, Europeans had long circulated modified versions of essentially the same origin narrative for the group known as the Black Caribs. According to the most common account, which cannot be tied to a definitive authorial source, the Black Caribs originated with an unintended catastrophe of European colonialism: the wreck on Bequia, a small island south of St. Vincent, of a single Dutch, Spanish, or Portuguese slave ship headed from the Bight of Benin to Barbados and caught up in a hurricane sometime between 1635 and 1675. Invited to the mainland of St. Vincent by a party of Island Caribs, the surviving Africans found themselves at the mercy of the Vincentian aboriginal community, the members of which either kindly offered them asylum and "restored them to liberty," according to one version of the story, or "made slaves of them, and set them to work," according to another.[40]

In the latter version of the origin narrative, best captured by William Young II, the shipwrecked Africans are explicitly identified as belonging to "a warlike Moco tribe."[41] The only eighteenth-century reference to the African ethnicity of the Black Caribs, Young's contention that they were Mocos is illuminating. By this time, British slaveowners preferred to avoid purchasing Africans deemed Moco due to their reputation for committing suicide rather than submitting to enslavement. As James Grainger stated in his poem *The Sugar-Cane* (1764): "But fly, with care, the Moco-nation; they themselves destroy."[42] But that was not all. In his popular history of the West Indies, Bryan Edwards claimed that the Moco tribe belonged to the "Ebo nation" of the Gold Coast and had long been, "without doubt, accustomed to the shocking practice of feeding on human flesh."[43] While accusations of cannibalism commonly appeared in European descriptions of Caribs in the three centuries after Columbus's arrival, what should we make of William Young II's connection between the Black Caribs and the Mocos of Africa?[44] Contemporaries often linked the Ibo and Moco (Bight of Biafra) due to their belief that these groups shared closely related languages.[45] The Moco tribe, Philip Curtin argues, most likely consisted of "a diverse range of peoples and cultures shipped from slave ports on the lower Cross River" in modern day Nigeria and Cameroon rather than one particular, identifiable group.[46] Moreover, the Black Carib origin tale specifies that the shipwrecked African slaves originated from the Bight of Benin, not the Bight of Biafra. Thus it makes sense to assume that Young's presentation of the Mocos as the African ancestors of the Black Caribs was most effective at the symbolic level, evoking images of fierceness and unredeemable savagery in the minds of educated British readers.

Within the parameters of this tale, it is unsurprising, then, to learn that dominating a large body of aggressive Africans proved challenging for the Island Caribs. Allegedly, upon discovering that their Moco slaves "proved restive and indocile servants," St. Vincent's aboriginal population determined to put to death all male children born to the Africans and to reserve the females. "This cruel policy occasioned a sudden insurrection of the Blacks, who massacred such of the Caribs they could take by surprise," detailed Young. The rebellious Moco Africans then fled to the wooded, mountainous northeast area of St. Vincent, where "they found many other Negroes from the neighbouring Islands." Driven by hunger and the desire to rule St. Vincent, or so the narrative continues, the Africans descended into the fertile valleys occupied by the Island Caribs, killing the males they took in war and seizing the women. In a short time, they "formed a nation, now known by the name of Black Charaibs; a title themselves arrogated, when entering into a contest with their ancient masters."[47]

Scholars generally agree that in their accounts of the fragmentation and disappearance of St. Vincent's aboriginal community, the British made a conscious decision to highlight the shipwreck narrative, in which the descendants of a specific tribe of Africans arose, phoenix-like and grasping, from a wreckage of the Middle Passage to drive out the Island Caribs and usurp their Native identity.[48] Insisting that the unexpected arrival of the shipwrecked Africans constituted a major turning point in the seamless history of the Vincentian Caribs, eighteenth-century commentators strove to demonstrate the profound disturbance posed by this rupture. Sir William Young senior's account, published in London in 1764, emphasized that although an aboriginal people had once inhabited St. Vincent, a band of fierce Africans had "gradually extirpated, or reduced [them] to their obedience."[49] "The Negroes commonly called black Charibbs," agreed the Council of St. Vincent in a letter to the Crown in May 1769, ravaged the island, "forcing from their Habitations, the original Yellow or Red Charibbs a harmless and well affected People who first offered them Asylum."[50] This tale of ruthless Africans dominating meek, peaceful Natives became the formative origin narrative circulating in Britain. Colonial histories written in the late eighteenth and nineteenth centuries stressed that the Black Caribs, realizing their superiority in both strength and numbers, had forcibly driven the Island Caribs to the leeward part of the island or off St. Vincent completely, to the islands of Trinidad and Tobago.[51]

The purported intention of the Black Caribs' project, to merge with and then supplant the Native population on St. Vincent, is central to this well-recited narrative. It lays the groundwork for the assertion that the emergence of the hybrid ethnic group known as the Black Caribs came at the direct expense of the original Natives, who were described by the British in terms reminiscent of the prototypical noble savage as "harmless," "innocent," and "well affected." The Black Caribs, rather than integrating with the Island Carib population, and subsequently ensuring the survival of their indigenous beliefs, customs, and bloodlines, sought to erase and replace them—to steal their Native identity. Too helpless and outnumbered to prevent their own destruction, the Island Caribs reportedly fled the island or turned to Europeans for assistance, inviting French settlers to occupy sections of their lands as a buffer against Black Carib encroachments. Whether or not this narrative is valid, in 1700, Claude Thomas d'Amblimont, the governor of Martinique, intervened in Vincentian Carib affairs, imposing a boundary line, known as the Barre de l'Isle, between the two groups. The Black Caribs were granted the western half of the island, and the Island Caribs and any European settlers the eastern portion.[52] This part of the story, at least, is well documented and suggests that the French acknowledged the Black Caribs as a separate, sovereign people.

Yet according to contemporaries, the Barre de l'Isle failed to improve relations between the two groups on St. Vincent. If anything, it exacerbated existing conflicts. Island Caribs complained that large numbers of unwelcome "negroes" continually raided their territory, stealing their women and girls. "It is not possible for the Caribs to rescue them," remarked the traveler Pére Labat in the early eighteenth century, "as the negroes, who are a much braver race and in far superior numbers, only laugh at them, ill-treat them, and possibly will one day make them work as their slaves."[53] Meanwhile, the presence of the black slaves who had accompanied their French masters to St. Vincent terrified the Black Caribs, a people who, though descended from Africans, had not yet understood the full implications of their ancestry. As the Abbé Reynal recounted, the "black Caribs, shocked at the thought of resembling men who were degraded by slavery, and fearing that some time or other their colour, which betrayed their origin, might be made a pretence for enslaving them . . . flattened the foreheads of all their children as soon as they were born."[54] The critical point here is that although vulnerability to enslavement threatened indigenous populations throughout the Lesser Antilles, the Black Caribs alone bore a striking resemblance to enslaved Africans. This superficial similarity prompted the Black Caribs to take slaves themselves, as proof of their independent status, and to alter their physical appearance and align it with traditional Carib practices.

Europeans had for years associated flattened foreheads with the Native peoples of the Caribbean. Raymond Breton, the first French missionary to spend time among the Caribs of Guadeloupe in the 1630s and 1640s, noted that women pressed the foreheads of their infants by hand or with a board immediately after giving birth.[55] Decades later, Labat commented that the Caribs were not unpleasant to look at "except that their foreheads were flat and sloped." "This is not natural," he clarified, "but as soon as a child is born they tie a piece of board over its forehead to press it flat."[56] In mimicking this venerable Carib practice, commentators insisted, the Black Caribs' goal was simple: to distinguish themselves physically from runaway slaves, liable for recapture and enslavement. And apparently it worked. As Sir William Young the elder put it, "the black Charibbs are easily distinguished from any other negroes, by a custom they have of flattening the foreheads of their infants, in order that their race may be kept distinct."[57]

George Davidson, the Methodist missionary who lived near the boundary of the Black Caribs' territory on St. Vincent during the 1780s, claimed to have pieced together the true origins of the Black Caribs by talking to the Natives themselves. He reported that, upon first encountering large numbers of enslaved Africans, the Black Caribs had feared that their similarity to blacks marked them as an inferior and enslaveable people. According to Davidson's account, the Black Caribs, "differing so little from the negroes whom they saw employed in the occupations of the field, soon perceived the necessity of a discrimination founded on more obvious marks than that of complexion; and therefore adopted a plan of flattening their childrens' foreheads."[58] Betrayed by their bodies as the descendants of Africans, agreed the Abbé Reynal, the Black Caribs fought back, "imprinting an indelible mark of distinction upon their tribe, that might be a perpetual token of their independence." Rather than accepting the arbitrary classification system devised by Europeans to justify African subjugation, the Black Caribs used their bodies as a canvas upon which to inscribe and proclaim their uniqueness as a blended, autonomous community. Thus with dark skin and heads altered by design, "the next generation appeared as a new race," as Reynal put it, conveying their distinctive Afro-Carib identity through the language Europeans understood best: visible signifiers.[59] Alexander Anderson, the manager of St. Vincent's botanical garden in the late 1790s, powerfully captured this evident fusion when he described the Black Caribs as a "peculiar race and from accidental causes different from all other tribes of men. Altho' originally Africans, from the mixture and connection with American Indians they were what we may call a hybrid race from the two."[60]

Anderson's use of the term "accidental" to describe how marooned Africans redefined themselves as an indigenous people was by no means common at the time. Most British observers preferred to assign blame, presenting the Black Caribs as a people born of displacement, bloodshed, and willful dissimulation: just as the Black Caribs did not inadvertently reduce the Island Caribs, neither did they acquire their appearance and customs by chance. But this crude understanding of the Black Caribs' self-identification presupposes that identity is something either invented or imposed, rather than an act of positioning brought about when groups realign and articulate their sense of self at particular conjunctures.[61] To complete their transformation into a new race of people no longer connected to Africa, and hence protected from the indignities of slavery, the descendants of the original shipwrecked Africans self-consciously adopted Carib names, raiding practices, methods of travel, and cultural and religious traditions. In addition to flattening the skulls of their infants with a board, they ate cassava roots and drank fermented cassava beer (*ouicou*); went mostly naked, wearing only a strip of cloth over their groins in the Carib manner; painted their bodies with an orange dye derived from the flowers of the roucou tree; and buried their dead in a seated position in a round hole beneath the floor of their huts.[62] They also cohabitated with Carib females captured in raids in an attempt to provide males with multiple wives and, perhaps, to infuse their community with aboriginal blood, a practice that resulted in offspring of "tawney and mixed complexion."[63] Within a few short decades of repositioning themselves as indigenous, the Black Caribs, "or rather Negroes, Invaders and destroyers of the original Charaib or Indian of the Country," as the British settlers of St. Vincent later described them, had transformed themselves into "a new race," readily distinguishable from other Africans.[64]

While British and French observers expressed a slight sense of awe for the capacity of a group of shipwrecked Africans to adapt culturally and biologically to their new environs, they tended to fixate overwhelmingly on the Black Caribs' failed attempt to erase the embodied evidence of their ancestral connection to Africa. In one of the earliest recorded European encounters with the Black Caribs, Pére Labat, for example, described their unsuccessful effort to mimic the aboriginal peoples of the Caribbean by transforming their skin color: "The

Fig. 3.2. Agostino Brunias, "Chatoyér, the Chief of the Black Charaibes in St. Vincent with His Wives" (ca. 1773). Oil on canvas. Courtesy of the National Library of Jamaica. Thanks to Yvonne Fraser-Clarke, head of Special Collections at the National Library of Jamaica, for helping the author acquire a digital copy of this rarely reproduced painting.

negroes in St. Vincent paint themselves red like the Indians, but it is easy to distinguish them, for in feature and build they are entirely unlike the Caribs."[65] The ancestors of "this doubly savage race," agreed the Abbé Raynal many decades later, may have mixed with Carib females, but their descendants "have preserved more of the primitive colour of their fathers, than of the lighter hue of their mothers."[66] Sexual relations between African males and Island Carib females, concurred Davidson, had resulted in "a motley mixture, such as we now see; but in which the negro-colour and features chiefly prevail."[67]

The ethnographic portrait of the Black Caribs favored by British observers, in which they are a fierce, "motley" people, predominantly African in nature and appearance, is well captured in Agostino Brunias's painting *Chatoyér, the Chief of the Black Charaibes in St. Vincent with His Wives* (fig. 3.2). Brunias, a London-based Italian painter, left England in 1770 to accompany William Young I as he began his appointment as the first British governor of Dominica. Based on Dominica as Young's personal painter, Brunias also frequented Barbados, St. Vincent, and St. Christopher, chronicling everyday life in Britain's oldest and youngest Caribbean colonies. After leaving for England to exhibit several of his paintings at the Society of Arts in London in the mid-1770s, just as Young's appointment came to an end, Brunias returned to the British West Indies and lived out the remainder of his life on Dominica, where he died on April 2, 1796.[68] His genre paintings, and the embellished engravings produced from them for inclusion in popular printed works by authors such as Bryan Edwards, are the richest visual sources available documenting European perceptions of the Black and Island Caribs during the late eighteenth century.[69]

Created in approximately 1773, the subject of Brunias's painting is Joseph Chatoyér, the principal chief of the Black Caribs during the latter decades of the eighteenth century, and two of his wives, who are at work gathering food in a rugged, uncultivated landscape. Presumably the gray, mountainous, sparsely vegetated background represents an area within the Black Caribs' territory. The absence of signs of human civilization, such as buildings, gardens, or roads, suggests that the Black Caribs inhabit an empty wilderness, uncultivated and hence ripe for the picking. The skin tone of the three figures is presented as dark brown, the women's hair is displayed in tight black curls, and the whites of the figures' eyes are prominent. Because of the positioning of the three figures, the eye is led immediately to the female crouched in the middle of the composition and then to Chatoyér, standing poised and alert on the right. Garbed in a hybrid costume, Chatoyér wears a loose loincloth in the Carib tradition accompanied by an African-style head wrap or turban. He stands guard and smokes thoughtfully while his bare-breasted wives serve as beasts of burden, carrying baskets laden with plantains. Well armed with a knife and cutlass, Chatoyér is a serious, threatening figure, ready for battle at a moment's notice. Taken together, the symbols in the painting do far more than represent a scene of everyday life in Carib country as witnessed by an outsider. They signal that the Black Caribs are savage and potentially dangerous, like the landscape they inhabit, as well as strikingly African in appearance and physically robust. Just as the painting as a whole accentuates the connections between the Black Caribs and African slaves, so too does it reinforce their failure to improve their territory.

This rare visual representation of the Black Caribs stands in marked contrast to Agostino Brunias's contemporaneous portrait of an Island Carib family (fig. 3.3). Although the subjects of both paintings are scantily clad, the Island Caribs wear distinctive Native dress—cotton girdles with red feathers attached. They have olive-colored skin and long, straight hair tied with a white ribbon in the man's case or swept up with shells and bunches of feathers in the women's. The women are adorned additionally with shell necklaces and ribbons stained dark red. Congregating outside a hut with a thatched roof and interior hammock, the family members appear engaged in pleasantries while a small child rests near the breast of the seated Island Carib female. Standing to the right smoking a pipe, the male Island Carib is positioned in this composition in a similar manner as Chatoyér, but he lacks weapons and consequently appears harmless. Here, the women are involved in what appears to be childcare and conversation rather than manual labor. In portraying this particular group of Island Caribs in a peaceful, domestic setting, Brunias has created a recognizable image of a noble savage family whose indigeneity is indisputable.

In contrast, the repeated insistence on the visible manifestations of African ancestry among the Vincentian Carib population helps clarify how proponents of British colonization strove to expose the Black Caribs as imposters and invalidate their claims to indigenous rights to land

Fig. 3.3. Agostino Brunias, "A Leeward Islands Carib Family Outside a Hut" (ca. 1780). Oil on canvas. Courtesy of the Yale Center for British Art, Paul Mellon Collection.

and to self-governance. This occurred at a time when, as Lisa Ford describes, legal complexity and ambiguity characterized settler-indigenous relations in the British Atlantic Empire; despite British claims to sovereignty in treaties and charters, "perfect settler sovereignty" did not yet exist.[70] Consequently, although British settlers declared dominion in St. Vincent through the power of a treaty excluding Native peoples, they nonetheless expected and needed the island's hybrid indigenous community to play along. When the Native population refused, British land commissioners and officials denied that they had any rights at all. The Black Caribs were runaway slaves who had lost their spurious title to any illegitimately acquired lands on St. Vincent with the signing of the 1763 Treaty of Paris. Moreover, as "African Negroes" the Black Caribs were not only counterfeit Caribs, they were a barbarous and inferior people, incapable of improving the island or sharing it with civilized settlers subject to the laws of the British nation. Sir William Young the elder claimed that these were "an idle, ignorant, and savage people, subject to no law or discipline, and scarcely acknowledging subordination to any chief."[71] Indeed, so long as these "Charaibs" remained on St. Vincent, where they neither belonged nor held jurisdiction, it would be necessary to introduce "some code of Laws adapted to their comprehension and calculated to make them useful Subjects," argued colonists.[72] Disregarding the Black Caribs' identity as a sovereign indigenous people with land rights, British settlers condescended to consider them subjects—but undeserving subjects.

Assuming an Indigenous Identity

Casting the Black Caribs as false Natives or lawless black foreigners belies the ethnic diversity, cultural complexity and adaptability, and rapid growth of their mixed community on the island of St. Vincent over the course of the seventeenth and eighteenth centuries. But roughly disentangling the threads that bound the Black Caribs to the Island Caribs did have its advantages. "Such a simple genesis was a convenient myth for Englishmen," observes Michael Craton, for they could "portray the Black Caribs as bloody usurpers with less right to the island than the British."[73] Hence Britain's subjugation or removal of the Black Caribs from St. Vincent constituted neither a breach of treaty nor an act of inhumanity but rather the unavoidable and just outcome of their ancestors' unnatural usurpation of the lands and identity of the Island Caribs. That the British continued to tussle with the descendants of Africans over land that did not belong to them was another matter: simply "usurping the Indian Name of Charaib" could not transform marooned blacks into an indigenous people with legal rights.[74]

While the myth of the Black Caribs' origins may have suited British imperial goals, it is far more plausible that the group whom the British referred to as the Black Caribs emerged slowly and organically over the course of a century, as a result of intermarriage, interethnic alliances, and concubinage between Island Caribs and marooned, shipwrecked, or runaway persons of African descent, rather than from one transformative incident.[75] As early as 1668, Lord William Willoughby, governor of Barbados and nominal governor over St. Vincent, St. Lucia, and Dominica, commented that St. Vincent was "inhabited only by Indians and Blacks," presumably living in egalitarian communities, with "none proper to impower as Governor."[76] Already the island had become a place where Africans and Island Caribs coexisted and mingled independently. For Europeans to have documented anywhere from one thousand to five thousand Black Caribs living on St. Vincent in the early eighteenth century indicates a lengthier and more complex process of Afro-Carib amalgamation and cultural syncretism than the traditional narrative allows.[77] A statement made in 1719 by a Mr. Weir, writing to the Lords of Trade and Plantations, cited that, "by best Report," four thousand "Negroes" inhabited St. Vincent. He did not mention the Island Caribs.[78] In an earlier report produced in 1700 for the French government, Claude Thomas d'Amblimont observed that while many of the Native Caribs hoped that the Black Caribs would leave St. Vincent, "there are a great many of these Blacks allied with some of the Caraibes and who live together on good terms." "It is a very steadfast sentiment that they prefer to see two thousand Negroes settled in their island, than to see disembarking here only 50 armed Frenchmen," he concluded.[79] In this age of colonial encounters and conflicts, Carib relations on St. Vincent were far more complicated than initial appearances might have indicated.

By all accounts, the blended community of Afro-Caribbean peoples that came to inhabit St. Vincent had forged an entirely new identity, self-selecting advantageous elements from a variety of cultures—Island Carib, African, European—and incorporating them into their group. While they may have looked more African than Carib in facial features, hair texture, and complexion, particularly to European observers seeking to gauge their ancestry, the Black Caribs' dress, diet, manner of travel, and social and religious customs suggested a strong attachment to Carib cultural traditions. Like the Island Caribs, both men and women went seminaked, with a cord wrapped around their middles from which hung a long piece of cloth dyed orange with the flowers of the roucou tree and open on the left side. Women wore garters below each knee; single women and widows omitted the right garter. Both men and women protected themselves from sunburn and insect bites by decorating their bodies daily with a thick, red mixture of roucou dye and castor oil.[80] Pére Labat said this same mixture made the Island Caribs "look like boiled lobsters."[81] Before going on a war expedition or attending an important meeting, men painted black lines on their face and bodies. The diet of the Black Caribs consisted of fish and game, including wild rabbit and pigeon, and cassava root cakes and beer, supplemented by plantains, yams, and other root vegetables.[82]

Black Carib males maintained several wives, who lived separate from one another in small wooden houses with thatched roofs made of bundles of reeds. Due to their position of importance in times of war, headmen, or chiefs, maintained as many as six wives. The need for additional women to assume these roles often prompted raids, just as it did among the Island Caribs.[83] Women performed the agricultural labor and prepared food for their families; men were responsible for hunting, fishing, and defense. Excellent navigators by sea, the Black Caribs felled trees and fashioned small canoes and pirogues according to Carib custom, some of which were large enough to hold dozens of men. On St. Vincent they lived in small autonomous villages or districts, no more than two or three miles in length, with a chief, or headman, who headed councils and exerted his authority solely during wartime.[84] Like the Island Caribs, the Black Carib community was decentralized and egalitarian, and this continually perplexed the British colonists with whom they interacted.[85] Some men grew commercial crops such as cotton and tobacco for sale in the marketplaces of Martinique and St. Vincent. The Carib chief Chatoyér and his brother, Du Vallée, owned small cotton plantations, purchased with loans from "English gentlemen" and worked by African slaves.[86]

Owing to a long history of frequent contact with Europeans, particularly French settlers and missionaries, the Black Caribs accumulated a sophisticated knowledge of European languages, mores, firearms, and agricultural techniques. They would travel frequently to the markets of Martinique to exchange their cotton and tobacco for "muskets, gunpowder, flints, ball, and cutlasses, some wine, and an inferior kind of rum," in the words of one British colonist.[87] Decades before the Seven Years' War, another observer reported that leading a successful expedition against "the Negroes of St. Vincent" would be a difficult undertaking, owing to their "being acquainted with the use of a Musket."[88] Maintaining their freedom and independence in an age of nearly constant political hostility required knowledge and possession of arms and ammunition, and it was to the French that the Black Caribs turned to arm themselves. Of the European powers with whom they repeatedly came into contact, the Black Caribs greatly preferred the more amenable French to the British, who clamored to survey and possess their lands and relocate the Black Carib community to the interior of St. Vincent.

The Black Caribs' attachment to the French, and absorption of a number of their customs, ranging from their use of the French language and French names to their propensity for wine, provoked deep resentment and suspicion among British settlers.[89] Correspondence between colonists and imperial authorities is replete with condemnations of the Black Caribs' communication with the nearby French islands, particularly after the treaty assigning them the northern third of St. Vincent in 1773 specified the following: "No undo intercourse with the French islands to be allowed."[90] Yet communications between the French-ruled islands and the Vincentian Caribs would continue. The enduring Franco–Black Carib alliance enraged Governor Valentine Morris, who in 1779, during the American War of Independence, surrendered St. Vincent to a French force led by Charles Marie de Trolong, Chevalier du Rumain, and aided by the Black Caribs. After the British regained St. Vincent under the terms of the Treaty of Versailles in 1783, Morris placed the blame for the loss of St. Vincent squarely on the shoulders of the "treacherous" Black Caribs, who, as he complained to Lord Lambden, used their alliance with the French

to gain firearms, though "offensive Weapons are by no means necessary to them, who live by fishing or Grain, Fruits, and Vegetables; nor
do they use them but for annoyance."[91]

On February 10, 1783, Morris wrote to William Petty, the Second Earl
of Shelburne and prime minister from July 1782 to March 1783, seeking the restoration of his position as governor of St. Vincent and proposing stipulations with the French respecting the Black Caribs. The
Black Caribs, Morris specified, were "a numerous body of turbulent
people" hostile to the British and "completely armed by the French at
their Islands" prior to the French invasion in 1779. Morris advised the
British government to disarm the Black Caribs, for "if left in the possession of those arms, they will be highly dangerous to the colony, as
they use arms, My Lord, only for annoyance or parade, living on the
fruits and other produce of the earth." He also recommended that
"the court of France should also expressly stipulate never more to furnish them with arms or ever to suffer them to land on their islands,
unless they produce the governor of St Vincent's permission in writing for their voyage; without this, the inhabitants of the French islands
will (for gain) furnish them, to the most imminent danger of the colony."[92] Morris sought to outmaneuver the shrewd Black Caribs by undercutting their ability to negotiate with a longstanding European ally.

British attempts therefore to pigeonhole the Black Caribs as the
crude descendants of Africans intent on mimicking Carib practices
too easily obscure the sophistication of this blended indigenous community and the complicated process of ethnogenesis from which it
emerged. However, as Neil Whitehead points out, "ethnogenesis was
not just a matter of self-identification, but also overt manipulation
by colonial regimes." The contemporary emphasis on the "Black" element of Black Carib identity, with all the negative connotations accompanying blackness, "really originates in a political opposition to
colonial designs."[93] Although Island and Black Caribs overlapped culturally and linguistically, British commentators insisted well into the
nineteenth century, as Charles Shephard did in 1831, that they were
"two distinct races of men," whose differing appearance and manners
"plainly corresponded with those of different portions of the globe."

PACIFICATION *with the* MAROON NEGROES.

Drawn from the life by Agostino Brunias.   From an original painting in the possession of Sir Wm Young Bart F.R.S

Published 1 Jan.y 1801 by J. Stockdale Piccadilly.

Fig. 3.4. Scott, "Pacification with the Maroon Negroes." Based on a painting by Agostino Brunias. London, 1801. Courtesy of the John Carter Brown Library at Brown University.

Island Caribs were descended from "Aborigines of the island"; Black Caribs were the descendants of Africans.[94] This tendency to collapse Black Caribs and Africans is encapsulated in the engraving, "Pacification with the Maroon Negroes," included in Bryan Edward's *The History, Civil and Commercial, of the British Colonies in the West Indies* (fig. 3.4). Though the engraving purports to be based on an original painting by Agostino Brunias depicting peace negotiations between Jamaican Maroons and British authorities in 1738 (several decades before Brunias visited the Caribbean), the original Brunias painting is widely recognized as a visual representation of the peace concluded between the Black Carib chiefs and General Dalrymple at the end of the First Carib War in St. Vincent in 1773.[95] To Edwards, the visible differences between "Maroon Negroes" and Black Caribs were apparently too inconsequential to acknowledge.

Africanizing the Black Caribs and denying their self-articulated indigeneity, both at the time and in retrospect, had distinct advantages for British planters, land commissioners, and historians. By the eighteenth century, African-descended individuals made up the overwhelming majority of slaves in the Caribbean, and Europeans throughout the Americas had consciously placed Africans into a new racialized category of enslaveable peoples. Europeans not only characterized Africans as "heathens," outside the fold of the Christian faith and hence unable to attain salvation, they also deemed them barbarous and bestial and therefore condemned to a subservient existence. Intersecting race and gender ideologies informed European travelers' perceptions that African women's possession of animalistic bodies and degraded familial and community roles served to justify their enslavement by Europeans.[96] Cast as excessively passionate, lacking in government, religion, or proper gender norms, and questionably human, Africans were judged incapable of assuming a civilized European, or Christian, identity. Africans' dark skin color only served to heighten their status as inferior outsiders legally subject to the possibility of enslavement.[97] Although the British in particular had remained open to the enslavement of Amerindians and Caribs in their plantation colonies, they generally viewed Native peoples sympathetically as tawnier, simplistic

versions of white-skinned Europeans.[98] More importantly, vast numbers of the New World's aboriginal population had long since been
depleted by disease and war, and Britons deemed their surviving ancestors unfit for hard labor in hot climates.

At the same time that British settlers exploited concepts of racial difference to justify their colonial strategy on St. Vincent, the Black Caribs used the intense Anglo-French rivalry in the Caribbean, and the
presence of disaffected slaves, to their advantage. Defending their territory on St. Vincent—and thereby preserving their autonomy, identity, and traditional way of life—trumped all other considerations.
Faced with growing numbers of British settlers eager to purloin their
lands and populate them with sugar plantations, the Black Caribs thus
sought out allies among French smallholders and marooned and runaway slaves, organizing a formidable, multifaceted anti-British military
campaign. In 1769 the Council of St. Vincent reported that the Black
Caribs regularly enticed slaves to join them and forsake their British
masters, "detaining others by Force, who accidentally fall into their Islands promising them their Liberty, Arms, and Lands, provided they
would Join and Assist them in totally extirpating the white Inhabitants."[99] A goal of total extirpation may have been a fanciful claim, but
fears of an alliance between Black Caribs and enslaved Africans, not to
mention the French, remained constant among British planters. When
the First Carib War ended in a stalemate, article 8 of the treaty signed
by both parties required the Black Caribs to round up and deliver all
runaway slaves in their possession and to report discovery of any future fugitives.[100] Planters complained bitterly thereafter that the terms
of the treaty were too "indulgent" and ineffective, owing to "the un-
steady Disposition of these Savages" and their refusal to either honor or
fully comprehend civilized agreements. In March 1774 St. Vincent assembly members reported "a very recent instance of the perfidy of the
Caraibs in carrying off a considerable number of our Negroes to the
French Islands." A year later they expressed fear for the colony's safety,
admitting that the Black Caribs' "ill designs" could be executed at any
time "by the Slaves they had embodied during the War and who have
been kept by them in Arms ever since prepared for any Violence."[101]

In 1783, when the Treaty of Versailles reinstated the British on St. Vincent after a four-year period in which the French, aided by the Black Caribs, took possession of the island, British settlers drew up a list of grievances against the Black Caribs. In 1779, dissatisfied with British rule, the Black Caribs had sent their chief, Chatoyér, to the Comte d'Estaing, governor general of the French windward islands, at Martinique, inviting him to attack St. Vincent. Once d'Estaing appeared off the coast, "they openly revolted from us, took Arms, and assisted the French to subdue the Colony." During the French occupation, the Black Caribs "usurped Lands belonging to British subjects, some of whom they have murthered, and others they have driven off their plantations, and burned their Houses." In short, though they cast the Black Caribs as nothing more than savages incapable of civility or the comprehension of British law, settlers on St. Vincent still recognized the Black Caribs as "a dangerous Enemy in the Heart of our Island."[102] The key to subjugating these blacks, planters insisted, was to sever their ties to the French, without whom they would be powerless, for the Black Caribs would "never venture an attack unsupported by their friends the French."[103]

What the Black Caribs thought of such accusations is unknown, but their repeated attempts to protect their territory throughout the relatively tranquil 1780s suggest that they knew what was at stake in the prevention of British settlement in Carib country. Fortunately, preserved in the historical record are the words and actions of specific Black Caribs who challenged settlers determined to build houses in a portion of the two thousand acres ceded to the British in February 1773. For example, on June 28, 1785, a Mr. Rose complained to the St. Vincent council that two Black Carib chiefs, Louison and Will, had prevented him from building a house for his slaves near the center of his estate at Colonarie. Informing Mr. Rose that he could not build there, Louison and Will threw down the posts and ordered Carib children to fill up the holes with dirt. Mr. Rose threatened to report them to the governor, but "Will replied I might do it when I choose." Ten days later, coming upon Mr. Rose's slaves at work on the house, Louison and Will threw the timber collected for the project down a steep hill. Louison then confronted Mr. Rose, who insisted that he would build his house and apply to the general for assistance if necessary. Louison "replied with great vehemence, at the same time flourishing his Cutlass, that he would sooner die than permit me to build any Houses whatever," detailed Mr. Rose.[104] The Black Caribs continued to regard the acres ceded to the settlers as their ancestral lands, and few settlers successfully built in the area while Black Caribs remained on the island.

By the mid-1790s tensions between British settlers and the Black Caribs had reached a breaking point, as the unrest developing out of the French and Haitian Revolutions sparked the Second Carib War (1795–97). Fed up with the British, the Black Caribs found allies in the minority population of French smallholders and free coloreds who had remained unhappily on St. Vincent under British rule and in a group of recently imported African slaves. They sought out additional assistance from the French islands, and as Michael Craton notes, there was a great deal of traffic in ideas, people, and arms between St. Vincent and St. Lucia, Martinique, and Guadeloupe after 1793.[105] Following the initiation of armed conflict on March 8, 1795, forces led by the Carib chiefs Chatoyér and Du Vallée made significant gains, attacking Chateau Belair, a village on the eastern side of the island; seizing Dorsetshire Hill above Kingstown, where they hoisted a national flag; killing British settlers and torching sugar estates north of the Yambou River; and closing in on Kingstown, the capital. Only the arrival of reinforcements from outside the island enabled the British to launch a successful assault on Dorsetshire Hill in mid-March, during which Chatoyér and a number of other Black Caribs and their French allies were killed and nearly fifty taken prisoner.[106]

On March 28, within weeks of Chatoyér's death, Governor James Seton issued a proclamation declaring the Black Caribs' recent attack a treasonable plot designed not for the "fair and avowed object of Conquest, but for the Purpose of exterminating the English inhabitants in the Colony." Prompted by "Motives of Rapine and Murder," the Black Caribs were nothing but "Traitors to their own King and Country" and lawless savages, an enemy to whom the laws of war simply could not apply.[107] There is, of course, nothing in the historical record to indicate that the British allowed the Black Caribs to issue a response to this allegation. Two days later Governor Seton made his own intentions crystal clear to the Duke of Portland, admitting his desire to "totally exterminate this savage & merciless Race of Charaibs, with whom no Treaties are binding, no Favours conciliating, nor any laws Divine or human restraining."[108] But the war lingered for another year, owing to the Black Caribs' secret knowledge of such a mountainous and woody island, unsportsmanlike use of guerilla tactics, and possession of savage bodies "inured to the climate," as Governor Seton explained it.[109] Despite these advantages, the Black Caribs were no match for General Ralph Abercromby's force of seventeen thousand men, a third of which arrived in St. Vincent in June 1796 to bring the war to an end. In October 1796, five thousand Black Caribs surrendered to British forces, bringing the "horrid, butchering war with the Caribs" to its conclusion.[110] Their deportation to Central America soon followed, as did the official forfeit of all Black Carib lands to the Crown. By the end of the eighteenth century, the colonial government's objective of dispossessing the Black Caribs and erasing their presence on St. Vincent was complete.

But this is not the end of the story. As a blended, resilient people with a lineage-based and culturally constructed sense of indigeneity, the Black Caribs did not cease to exit because the British forced them to relocate from their island home in the Caribbean to Honduras. Collectively forged—and continually forced to reposition themselves— as a result of European settler colonialism, the African slave trade, interethnic alliances, warfare, and historical contingency, the surviving Black Carib community engaged, once again, in the difficult and painful process of identity realignment. In a new land, among new and unfamiliar people, they reconceived the way they connected to their ancestors, to one another, and to an alien environment, while retaining a common identity as a people. Although British colonizers forced them to abandon long-held tribal lands in St. Vincent in 1797, the Black Caribs reembedded themselves in Central America and elsewhere in the world, giving rise to modern-day descendants who, like their ancestors before them, chose to articulate their own identity by renaming themselves the Garifuna.

Notes

1. William Young, *An Account of the Black Charaibs in the Island of St. Vincent's; with the Charaib Treaty of 1773, and other Original Documents. Compiled from the Papers of the Late Sir William Young* (London: J. Sewell, Knight, and Triphook, 1795), 8.

2. Bryan Edwards, *The History, Civil and Commercial, of the British Colonies in the West Indies*, 2 vols. (London: Printed for John Stockdale, 1793), 1:377.

3. Young, *An Account of the Black Charaibs*, 5; "Letter to His Majesty, At a Meeting of the Council at Kingstown, St. Vincent, on Wednesday 24 May 1769," Colonial Office and Predecessors: St. Vincent Sessional Papers, 1769–1775 (hereafter CO), National Archives, Kew, England, CO 263/1/nf.

4. Young, *An Account of the Black Charaibs*, 8, 11.

5. Bernard Marshall, "The Black Caribs: Native Resistance to British Penetration into the Windward Side of St. Vincent, 1763–1773," *Caribbean Quarterly* 19, no. 4 (1973): 4–19; Michael Craton, *Testing the Chains: Resistance to Slavery in the British West Indies* (Ithaca NY: Cornell University Press, 1982), 21–23; Michael Craton, "The Black Caribs of St. Vincent: A Reevaluation," in *The Lesser Antilles in the Age of European Expansion*, ed. Robert L. Paquette (Gainesville: University Press of Florida, 1996), 71–85; Paul Thomas, "The Caribs of St. Vincent: A Study in Imperial Maladministration," *Journal of Caribbean History* 18, no. 2 (1984): 60–74; Robin E. Fabel, *Colonial Challenges: Britons, Native Americans, and Caribs, 1759–1775* (Gainesville: University Press of Florida, 2000), 152–86.

6. Peter Hulme, "Black, Yellow, and White on St. Vincent: Moreau de Jonnès Carib Ethnography," in *The Global Eighteenth Century*, ed. Felicity A. Nussbaum (Baltimore: Johns Hopkins University Press, 2003), 182–94; Peter Hulme, *Colonial Encounters: Europe and the Native Caribbean, 1492–1797* (1986; repr., New York: Routledge, 1992), 242–63.

7. Cole Harris, *Making Native Space: Colonialism, Resistance, and Reserves in British Columbia* (Vancouver: University of British Columbia Press, 2002), 48.

8. As Saliha Belmessous argues, in their dealings with Native peoples, the British and other European colonizers understood that it was one thing for indigenous communities to claim ownership and quite another for them to make a case for sovereignty: "that is, when they made claims to a particular territory with delimited borders and upon which they had established the law of the land, determining, for example, who could come and live on that territory." The Black Caribs resisted British colonization by claiming both ownership and sovereignty. Belmessous, "Introduction: The Problem of Indigenous Claim Making in Colonial History," in *Native Claims: Indigenous Law Against Empire, 1500–1920*, ed. Saliha Belmessous (New York: Oxford University Press, 2012), 5.

9. James Sidbury and Jorge Cañizares-Esguerra, "Mapping Ethnogenesis in the Early Modern Atlantic," *William and Mary Quarterly* 68, no. 2 (2011): 185.

10. Michael H. Crawford, "Foundations of Anthropological Genetics," in *Anthropological Genetics: Theory, Methods, and Applications*, ed. Michael H. Crawford (New York: Cambridge University Press, 2007), 10–11; D. F. Roberts, "Migration in the Recent Past: Societies with Records," in *Biological Aspects of Human Migration*, ed. C. G. Nicholas Mascie-Taylor and Gabriel W. Lasker (New York: Cambridge University Press, 2009), 52–53; Lorena Madrigal, *Human Biology of Afro-Caribbean Populations* (New York: Cambridge University Press, 2006), xii–xiii.

11. "A Treaty of Peace and Friendship concluded by His Excellency Major General Dalrymple on the part of His Brittanick Majesty and the Chiefs of the peace or Security of the Colony in St. Vincent, 17 February 1773," CO 263/1/nf.

12. The Black Caribs have survived in British Honduras and elsewhere in the world through their modern-day ancestors, the Garifuna. The Garifuna are discussed in Christopher Taylor, *The Black Carib Wars: Freedom, Survival, and the Making of the Garifuna* (Oxford: University Press of Mississippi, 2012); Paul Christopher Johnson, *Diaspora Conversions: Black Carib Religion and the Recovery of Africa* (Berkeley: University of California Press, 2007); Mark Anderson, *Black and Indigenous: Garifuna Activism and Consumer Culture in Honduras* (Minneapolis: University of Minnesota Press, 2009); Sarah Chon England, "Creating a Global Garifuna Nation? The Transnationalization of Race, Class, and Gender Politics in the Garifuna Diaspora" (PhD diss., University of California, Davis, 2000).

13. On British notions of identity in the long eighteenth century, see Dror Wahrman, *The Making of the Modern Self: Identity and Culture in Eighteenth-Century England* (New Haven CT: Yale University Press, 2006); Dror Wahrman, "The English Problem of Identity in the American Revolution" *American Historical Review* 106, no. 4 (2001): 1236–62; Kathleen Wilson, *The Island Race: Englishness, Empire, and Gender in the Eighteenth Century* (New York: Routledge, 2003); Felicity Nussbaum, *The Limits of the Human: Fictions of Anomaly, Race, and Gender in the Long Eighteenth Century* (New York: Cambridge University Press, 2003); Roxann Wheeler, *The Complexion of Race: Categories of Difference in Eighteenth-Century British Culture* (Philadelphia: University of Pennsylvania Press, 2000).

14. Gathering scientific knowledge in the early modern Atlantic is analyzed in James Delbourgo and Nicholas Dew, eds., *Science and Empire in the Atlantic World* (New York: Routledge, 2008); Susan Scott Parish, *American Curiosity: Cultures of Natural History in the Colonial British Atlantic World* (Chapel Hill: University of North Carolina Press, 2006).

15. On the importance of this period to changing concepts of "whiteness," particularly in reference to the British Caribbean, see Christer Petley, "'Home'

and 'This Country': Britishness and Creole Identity in the Letters of a Transatlantic Slaveholder," *Atlantic Studies* 6, no. 1 (2009): 43–61; Brooke N. Newman, "Gender, Sexuality, and the Formation of Racial Identities in the Eighteenth-Century Anglo-Caribbean World," *Gender and History* 22, no. 3 (2010): 585–602; Trevor Burnard, "West Indian Identity in the Eighteenth Century," in *Assumed Identities: The Meanings of Race in the Atlantic World*, ed. John D. Garrigus and Christopher Morris (Arlington: University of Texas Press, 2010), 71–87.

16. Kenneth F. Kiple and Kriemhild C. Ornelas, "After the Encounter: Disease and Demographics in the Lesser Antilles," in Paquette, *The Lesser Antilles in the Age of European Expansion*, 53; Fable, *Colonial Challenges*, 150; Marshall, *The Black Caribs*, 4.

17. "Abstract of several Informations & plans relative to the settling of Grenada, Tobago St. Vincent & Dominico, April 1763, George Grenville, Americana: Miscellany re: American & West Indian Colonies, [c. 1670]–1770," Stowe Collection, Grenville Correspondence, 32 folders, Henry E. Huntington Library, San Marino CA, STG Box 12.

18. "State of the Island of St. Vincent in 1763," Shelburne Papers, vol. 74, West India Miscellaneous Papers, f. 122, William Clements Library, Ann Arbor MI.

19. Sir William Young, *Considerations which may Tend to Promote the Settlement of our New West-India Colonies, by Encouraging Individuals to Embark in the Undertaking* (London: Printed for James Robson in New Bondstreet, 1764), 9; Sir William Young, *Authentic Papers Relative to the Expedition Against the Charibbs, and the Sale of Lands in the Island of St. Vincent* (London: Printed for J. Almon, opposite Burlington House, in Piccadilly, 1773), 6.

20. "Copy of a Letter from Mr Weir to the Lords Comm[is]s[ione]rs for Trade & Plantations dated at St. Lucia the 20th of June 1719," CO 260/3/nf.

21. Young, *An Account of the Black Charaibs*, 18.

22. Edwards, *The History, Civil and Commercial, of the British Colonies in the West Indies*, 1:378.

23. Young, *Authentic Papers Relative to the Expedition Against the Charibbs*, 5.

24. George Davidson, "The Copy of a Letter . . . containing a Short History of the Caribbs" [July 24, 1787] in *The Case of the Caribbs in St. Vincent's*, ed. Thomas Coke (Dublin[?], n.p., 1788), 8.

25. Craton, "The Black Caribs of St. Vincent," 72.

26. Young, *Considerations which may Tend to Promote the Settlement of our New West-India Colonies*, 9, 11.

27. Jamaica's failure as an Anglicized settler society has been well documented by Trevor Burnard. See esp. Burnard, "Not a Place for Whites? Demographic Failure and Settlement in Comparative Context: Jamaica, 1655–1780," in *Jamaica*

in Slavery and Freedom: History, Heritage and Culture, ed. Kathleen E. A. Monteith and Glen Richards (Mona: University of the West Indies Press, 2002), 73–88.

28. Richard H. Grove, *Green Imperialism: Colonial Expansion, Tropical Island Edens and the Origins of Environmentalism, 1600–1860* (New York: Cambridge University Press, 1995), 282; Craton, "The Black Caribs of St. Vincent," 74.

29. "Memorial to His Grace the Duke of Portland of the Planters & Merchants concerned in the Island of St. Vincent," May 9, 1795, St. Vincent Original Correspondence, November 5, 1794–September 8, 1796, CO 260/13/178.

30. Young, *Considerations which may tend to Promote the Settlement of our New West-India Colonies*, 10.

31. Young, *An Account of the Black Charaibs*, 38.

32. "Saint Vincent, At a Meeting of the Council at Kingstown on Wednesday the 10th of May 1769," CO 263/1/nf.

33. P. J. Marshall, *The Making and Unmaking of Empires: Britain, India, and America, c. 1750–1783* (New York: Oxford University Press, 2005), 194.

34. "Saint Vincent, At a Meeting of the Council at Kingstown on Wednesday the 10th of May 1769," CO 263/1/nf.

35. "Extract of a letter from Governor Leyborne to the Earl of Hillsborough, Dated St. Vincent, 18 June 1772," Hardwicke Papers, vol. 168, Papers relating to the West Indian Islands, 1734–1803, Add MS 35916, f. 124, British Library, London; "Saint Vincent, At a Meeting of the Council at Kingstown the 25th day of November 1772," CO 263/1/nf.

36. Anonymous [Sir William Young?], *A New System of Fortification, Constructed with Standing Timber, &c. Or the Sentiments of a West-India Savage on the Art of War* (London: Printed for J. Millan, near Whitehall, 1770), preface, 4, 13.

37. The parliamentary debate is discussed at length in Fabel, *Colonial Challenges*, 183–93, and in Jack P. Greene, *Encountering Empire and Confronting Colonialism in Eighteenth-Century Britain* (New York: Cambridge University Press, 2013), prologue. For a broader perspective on the debates sparked by British attempts to seize indigenous property after the Seven Years' War, see Christopher Leslie Brown, *Moral Capital: Foundations of British Abolitionism* (Chapel Hill: University of North Carolina Press, 2006), 155–61, 222–26.

38. "Memorial to His Grace the Duke of Portland," May 9, 1795, CO 260/13/178.

39. The terms of the treaty are detailed in Young, *An Account of the Black Charaibs*, 90–97.

40. Members of the St. Vincent Council, Bryan Edwards, and the Abbé Raynal maintained that the Island Caribs were a harmless people who offered asylum to the shipwrecked Africans. For these accounts, see, respectively, "Saint Vincent, At a Meeting of the Council at Kingstown on Wednesday the 24th of May

1769," CO 263/1/nf; Edwards, *The History, Civil and Commercial, of the British Colonies in the West Indies*, 1:395; Abbé Raynal, *Philosophical and Political History of the Settlements and Trade of the Europeans in the East and West Indies*, 10 vols., trans. J. O. Justamond (London: printed for W. Strahan and T. Cadell in the Strand, 1783) 6:378–79. Quote in Raynal, *Philosophical and Political History*, 6:378. In contrast, Sir William Young II claimed that the Island Caribs enslaved the Africans, a decision that ultimately led to their downfall. Quote in Young, *An Account of the Black Charaibs*, 6.

41. Young, *An Account of the Black Charaibs*, 7.

42. James Grainger, *The Sugar-Cane: A Poem in Four Books* (London: Printed for R. and J. Dodsley, in Pall-mall, 1764), lines 101–2.

43. Edwards, *The History, Civil and Commercial, of the British Colonies in the West Indies*, 2:70.

44. European discourses of Carib cannibalism are analyzed in Neil L. Whitehead, "'Carib Cannibalism': The Historical Evidence," *Société des Americanistes* 70 (1984): 69–87; Philip P. Boucher, *Cannibal Encounters: Europeans and Island Caribs, 1492–1763* (Baltimore: Johns Hopkins University Press, 1992); Peter Hulme, "Introduction: The Cannibal Scene," in *Cannibalism and the Colonial World*, ed. Francis Barker, Peter Hulme, and Margaret Iversen (New York: Cambridge University Press, 1998), 1–38.

45. Michael Mullin, *Africa in America: Slave Acculturation and Resistance in the American South and the British Caribbean, 1736–1831* (Urbana: University of Illinois Press, 1992), 282, 287.

46. Philip Curtin, *The Atlantic Slave Trade: A Consensus* (Madison: University of Wisconsin Press, 1969), 188.

47. Young, *An Account of the Black Charaibs*, 7.

48. Johnson, *Diaspora Conversions*, 69–70; Craton, "The Black Caribs of St. Vincent," 72; Craton, *Testing the Chains*, 147; Hulme, *Colonial Encounters*, 226; Hulme, "Black, Yellow, and White on St. Vincent," 185.

49. Young, *Considerations which may tend to Promote the Settlement of our New West-India Colonies*, 9–10.

50. "Saint Vincent, At a Meeting of the Council at Kingstown on Wednesday the 24th of May 1769," CO 263/1/nf.

51. Representative examples are Davidson, *The Case of the Caribbs in St. Vincent*, 8; Charles Shephard, *An Historical Account of the Island of Saint Vincent* (London: Printed by W. Nicol, Cleveland Row, St. James's, 1831), 25.

52. Fabel, *Colonial Challenges*, 145–46; Boucher, *Cannibal Encounters*, 101.

53. Pére Labat, *The Memoirs of Pére Labat 1693–1705*, trans. John Eaden (London: Frank Cass and Company, 1970), 137.

54. Raynal, *Philosophical and Political History*, 6:380.

55. Raymond Breton, "Of the Origin, Mores, Religion, and Other Customs of the *Caraibes* Commonly Called Savages, Ancient Inhabitants of Guadeloupe (1647)," in *Wild Majesty: Encounters with Caribs from Columbus to the Present Day*, ed. Peter Hulme and Neil L. Whitehead (Oxford: Clarendon Press, 1992), 113.

56. Labat, *The Memoirs of Père Labat*, 70.

57. Young, *Authentic Papers Relative to the Expedition Against the Charibbs*, 6.

58. Davidson, *The Case of the Caribbs in St. Vincent*, 10.

59. Raynal, *Philosophical and Political History*, 6:381.

60. Alexander Anderson, "Alexander Anderson and the Carib War in St. Vincent (1798)" in Hulme and Whitehead, *Wild Majesty*, 229.

61. Tania Murray Li, "Environment, Indigeneity, and Transnationalism," in *Liberation Ecologies: Environment, Development, Social Movements*, ed. Richard Peet and Michael Watts (1996; repr., New York: Routledge, 2004), 309.

62. Edwards, *The History, Civil and Commercial, of the British Colonies in the West Indies*, 1:401; Young, *An Account of the Black Charaibs*, 7; Davidson, *The Case of the Caribbs in St. Vincent*, 13–14, 17.

63. Young, *An Account of the Black Charaibs*, 8.

64. "Memorial to His Grace the Duke of Portland," May 9, 1795, CO 260/13/179.

65. Labat, *The Memoirs of Père Labat*, 139.

66. Raynal, *Philosophical and Political History*, 6:379.

67. Davidson, *The Case of the Caribbs in St. Vincent*, 7.

68. Patricia Mohammed, "The Emergence of a Caribbean Iconography in the Evolution of Identity," in *New Caribbean Thought: A Reader*, ed. Brian Meeks and Folke Lindahl (Mona: University of the West Indies Press, 2001), 250–52.

69. On Agostino Brunias's life and paintings, see Kay Dian Kriz, "Marketing Mulattresses in the Paintings and Prints of Agostino Brunias" in Nussbaum, *The Global Eighteenth Century*, 195–96; Beth Fowkes Tobin, *Picturing Imperial Power: Colonial Subjects in Eighteenth-Century British Painting* (Durham NC: Duke University Press, 1999), 13–73; Simon Gikandi, *Slavery and the Culture of Taste* (Princeton NJ: Princeton University Press, 2011), 188–90.

70. Lisa Ford, *Settler Sovereignty: Jurisdiction and Indigenous Peoples in America and Australia* (Cambridge MA: Harvard University Press, 2010), 20.

71. Young, *Authentic Papers Relative to the Expedition Against the Charibbs*, 6.

72. "At a Meeting of His Majesty's Privy Council, held at their house in Kingstown on Tuesday the 28th of June 1785," Minutes of Assembly, St. Vincent, 1784–1788, CO 263/3/nf.

72. Craton, *Testing the Chains*, 147.

74. "Memorial to His Grace the Duke of Portland," May 9, 1795, CO 260/13/179.

75. Boucher, *Cannibal Encounters*, 102–3; Johnson, *Diaspora Conversions*, 63–64; Craton, *Testing the Chains*, 147.

76. "Extract of a Letter from the Lord William Willoughby, dated 9 July 1668, to the Lords of the Council," CO 260/3/nf.

77. Boucher, *Cannibal Encounters*, 97.

78. "Copy of a Letter from Mr Weir to the lords Comm[issioners] for trade and Plantations dated at St. Lucia the 20th of June 1719," CO 260/3/nf.

79. D'Amblimont quoted in Neil L. Whitehead, "Black Read as Red: Ethnic Transgression and Hybridity in Northeastern South America and the Caribbean," in *Beyond Black and Red: African-Native Relations in Colonial Latin America*, ed. Matthew Restall (Albuquerque: University of New Mexico Press, 2005), 237.

80. Davidson, *The Case of the Caribbs in St. Vincent*, 17.

81. Labat, *The Memoirs of Père Labat*, 71.

82. Davidson, *The Case of the Caribbs in St. Vincent*, 13–14.

83. Philip Boucher, *France and the American Tropics to 1700* (Baltimore: Johns Hopkins University Press, 2008), 31–32.

84. Davidson, *The Case of the Caribbs in St. Vincent*, 11, 14, 18.

85. Virginia Kerns, *Women and the Ancestors: Black Carib Kinship and Ritual* (1983; repr., Urbana: University of Illinois Press, 1997), 30.

86. Young, *An Account of the Black Charaibs*, 106–7.

87. Davidson, *The Case of the Caribbs in St. Vincent*, 19.

88. "Copy of a letter from Mr. Weir, 20 June 1719," CO 260/3/nf.

89. Young, *Considerations which may tend to Promote the Settlement of our New West-India Colonies*, 10.

90. "A Treaty of Peace and Friendship concluded by His Excellency Major general Dalrymple on the part of His Brittanick Majesty and the Chiefs of the peace or Security of the Colony in St. Vincent, 17 February 1773," CO 263/1/nf.

91. "Valentine Morris to Lord Lambden, St. Vincent's, 2nd February 1783," CO 260/3/nf.

92. "Valentine Morris to the Earl of Shelburne, February 10 1783," Shelburne Papers, vol. 78, West India Information, f. 63, William Clements Library.

93. Whitehead, "Black Read as Red," 238.

94. Shephard, *An Historical Account*, 21.

95. Craton, "The Black Caribs of St. Vincent," 82.

96. Jennifer Morgan, "'Some Could Suckle over Their Shoulder': Male Travelers, Female Bodies, and the Gendering of Racial Ideology, 1500–1770," *William and Mary Quarterly* 54, no. 1 (1997): 167–92.

97. Franklin W. Knight, "Introduction: Race and Identity in the New World," in *Assumed Identities: The Meanings of Race in the Atlantic World*, ed.

John D. Garrigus and Christopher Morris (Arlington: University of Texas Press, 2010), 8.

98. Karen Ordahl Kupperman, *Indians and English: Facing Off in Early America* (Ithaca NY: Cornell University Press, 2000), 58–59.

99. "Saint Vincent, At a Meeting of the Council at Kingstown on Wednesday the 24th May 1769," CO 263/1/nf.

100. "At a Meeting of his Excellency the General and the members of the Council at Kingstown 17th May 1773," CO 263/1/nf.

101. "At a Meeting of the Council at Kingstown 16th March 1774" and "At a Meeting of the Council at Kingstown on Wednesday the 22nd of March 1775," CO 263/1/nf.

102. "Governor Lincoln to Lord North, St. James's street, St. Vincent, 6 April 1783," CO 260/3/nf.

103. "At a Meeting of the Assembly on Monday the 19th of December 1785," CO 263/3/nf.

104. CO 263/3/nf.

105. Craton, *Testing the Chains*, 191.

106. "Governor Seton to the Duke of Portland, Fort Charlotte, St. Vincent, 16 March 1795," CO 260/13/13–14.

107. CO 260/13/13–14.

108. "Governor Seton to the Duke of Portland, Fort Charlotte, St. Vincent, 30 March 1795," CO 260/13/29.

109. "Governor Seton to the Duke of Portland, Fort Charlotte, St. Vincent, 23 June 1795," CO 260/13/71.

110. "From Robert Bisset, Jr., to Robert Bisset Esq., Forbe's Ridge, St. Vincent, 27 July 1796," CO 260/13/252.

| Chapter 4

Religion, Race, and the Formation of Pan-Indian Identities in the Brothertown Movement, 1700–1800

Linford D. Fisher

On November 7, 1785, representatives from seven American Indian nations in New England gathered on Oneida land in New York—250 miles away from their homelands—and created a new town called Eeyawquittoowauconnuck, or "Brotherton."[1] In addition to electing a few town officers—a clerk, trustees, and two fence viewers—and laying out two central streets in the town, the representatives also agreed "to live in Peace, and in Friendship . . . both in their Religious and Temporal Concerns."[2] This collective move to Brothertown, New York, by disparate Native communities from southern New England represents wider fascinating trends among Native American communities in eighteenth-century North America, namely, tribal melding and migration. A century and a half of English colonization completely reshaped the physical landscape, drastically reduced Native landholdings, and triggered depopulation of Indian communities through disease and warfare. In response to many of these challenges, Native communities increasingly remade themselves, fashioning new identities around new and old forms of association.

As a point of entrée into these larger issues of changing Native identity and coping with colonization in British North America, this chapter analyzes the Brothertown movement of the 1770s and 1780s in the broader Native history of the region. This large-scale intertribal migration to Brothertown, New York, in 1785 exemplifies many of the external and internal pressures felt by Native communities in the mid-eighteenth century, including land loss, increasing intermarriage with non-Indians, internal tribal divisions, and ever-present indebtedness. The Brothertown Natives implicitly, and at times explicitly, redefined identity in several ways that on the surface seemed somewhat contradictory. Instead of relying on older tribal associations in identity formation, the Brothertowns chose association based upon the shared experiences of an indigenized version of Euro-American Christianity. While such intertribality was far from new in the eighteenth century, the Brothertown movement is especially interesting because it was designed specifically as a Christian Indian settlement. The settlement's founders appointed the famed and aged Mohegan minister Samson Occom as its town preacher, who agreed to make Brothertown his "Home and Center."[3] At the same time these tribal distinctions were being minimized in favor of a shared Christianity, however, the Brothertowns (and New England Natives as a whole) increasingly sought to preserve a "true" or pure Indian identity vis-à-vis blacks or mulattos by restricting landownership in Brothertown to racially pure Indians. The Brothertown movement, in short, was prompted by growing discontentment with treatment by whites, ongoing land loss, racial concerns about intermarriage with blacks, and a desire to create a specifically Christian Indian community.

Early Native Identity and Ethnogenesis

North American indigenous populations discovered strangers on their shores starting shortly after Columbus's accidental landing in the present-day Caribbean in 1492. English exploration of the northeastern coast of the North American landmass started as early as 1497 with the crown-backed explorations of John Cabot. After a fateful second voyage in 1498 in which John Cabot and three of his ships were lost at sea, English exploration halted for three-quarters of a century. Although Spanish, French, and Dutch traders and explorers frequented the eastern seaboard of North America throughout the sixteenth century, and the English attempted settlements at Roanoke in 1585 and 1587, it was not until 1607 that the English were able to establish a humble but permanent outpost they called Jamestown, in present-day Virginia (although by this time or shortly thereafter the French, Dutch, and Spanish each had North American claims as well).[4]

Identifying cohesive social groups was undoubtedly confusing at first for both Natives and Europeans along the eastern coast of North America. Indian narrations of first contacts come decades after the events, when identities were more learned. Even so, Indians recalled the first time meeting "the Dutch" or "the English" or "the Spanish"— the less precise and broader identity designation "European" was a rarely used descriptor in the early years of encounter (and indeed it seems more a convenient construction by later historians than anything else). In similar ways, English, French, and Dutch explorers reported meeting "Indians," but they often recorded with surprising frequency the tribal and community names of the populations they encountered.

Although Native societies at the time of contact had some sense of national or tribal distinctions, "identity" formation was not firm. Tribal boundaries were often overlapping, sometimes contained within larger confederacies, and could be amended, altered, or even obliterated by cultural processes such as adoption, intermarriage, alliance-building, and the ritual submission of defeated enemies. Jamestown, for example, was settled in the middle of a large collection of Indian communities that were confederated in a tributary relationship under the powerful chief Wahunsenacawh (also called Powhatan) and were referred to as the Powhatans, even as they retained their own local tribal identities. And as recent scholars have argued, Powhatan initially attempted to incorporate the English in Jamestown within his tributary confederation, as the capture and ritual "saving" of Captain John Smith by Pocahontas suggests.[5] Indian communities were also intricately interconnected through marriage and kinship in ways that usually defied "tribal" boundaries. Euro-American observers and, later, historians and anthropologists have often reified tribal distinctions when in fact tribal affiliation was fluid and changing. The seventeenth-century Mohegan sachem Uncas, for instance, was arguably part Mohegan, Pequot, and Narragansett since his paternal great-grandfather, Woipequand, was a Pequot sachem; Woipequand's wife, Mukunnup, was the daughter of a principal sachem of the Narragansetts, and Uncas's mother was descended from Tamaquawshad, the chief sachem of the Mohegan. Intertribal marriages were probably in part strategic but were not enough to prevent martially related communities from waging war against each other. Uncas himself married first the sister and then the daughter of Sassacus, the Pequot sachem against whom Uncas rebelled and joined with the English in the Pequot War (1636–38).[6] Similarly, in the eighteenth century, the Mohegan Samson Occom's family illustrated this common tribal intermingling. Samson's mother, Sarah, married Joshua Occom, a Mohegan, but her younger brother married a Narragansett. Growing up, Samson Occom had cousins among the Narragansetts and the Pequots, and possibly among the Western Niantics.[7] Samson's aunt Hannah Justice Samson married into the Poquiantup family of Niantics, further connecting Samson to that Native community.[8] Samson himself married a Montaukett, with the result that he as Mohegan was related through kinship networks to the Pequots, Narragansetts, Niantics, and Montauketts.

Perhaps the greatest factor affecting Native identities on the eastern seaboard of North America was European diseases, or the so-called virgin soil epidemics.[9] The loss of 85 to 95 percent of the indigenous populations in the Americas during the first one hundred years of contact through disease and conquest was devastating socially, economically, spiritually, and psychologically. In response to rapid population loss, land dispossession, and increasing loss of political and cultural sovereignty, some Native communities often decided that joining other area Indian communities was the most effective strategy for survival. By pooling agricultural, trade, and spiritual resources, communities were redefined, strengthened, and better able to respond to the most devastating consequences of colonialism. Historians of colonialism often refer to this process as *ethnogenesis*.[10] Perhaps the most well-documented example of this is the Catawbas, a name that after 1701 referred to a large collection of disparate Indian communities within the English colony of Carolina.[11]

In some ways, however, these new beginnings were not so new. Archaeological evidence from the precontact period indicates that for millennia bands of Natives formed and reformed across North America in response to warfare, environmental factors, and cycles of trade.[12] Nonetheless, the invasion of Europeans accelerated this process. At times, this involved nothing less than full-scale attempted extermination, as with the Pequots in the northeast. After waging a bloody and largely unjustified war against the large and powerful Pequot nation in 1636–38, the English gathered up and distributed the remaining Pequots between the English, Narragansetts, and Mohegans, in hopes of eliminating the Pequots as a distinct nation. A 1638 treaty between the remaining Connecticut Indians and the English stipulated that all Pequots who remained in New England (either enslaved by the colonists or newly adopted into Indian towns) "shall no more be called Pequots, but Narragansets and Moheagans, and as their men."[13] Within a decade Pequot communities had reassembled on small portions of their land, and eventually the word "Pequett" reappeared on the pages of official colonial records.[14] Similar wars and uprisings punctuated the seventeenth century in the English colonies, most notably the two Powhatan "uprisings" in Virginia in 1622 and 1644, as well as the pan-Indian uprising in New England, King Philip's War (1675–76).

By the eighteenth century, war, disease, land loss, and economic hardship had further reduced the populations of many Indian communities in British North America. New patterns of subsistence emerged; instead of seasonal migration based on agricultural and hunting considerations, Native communities stayed put year round, planted more crops, hunted less, and raised domesticated animals like hogs. With altered modes of subsistence came new kinds of labor opportunities, as Indians of all ages hired themselves out to work on local farms, crafted baskets and spoons for sale and trade, and—for young men—joined the growing fleet of whaling and merchant ships in coastal towns. Native villages, facing shrinking community and natural resources, often moved to new locations, many times joining other Indian groups in the process. In some cases, these mergers created entirely new communities in which the older affiliations were muted or replaced by a new identifying name. Such was the case with the Western Niantics in eastern Connecticut, who by the early eighteenth century had joined the Narragansetts in Rhode Island. Sometimes ethnogenesis led to a local relocation, as in the case of the Weatinock, Potatuck, and Paugusset Indians from the New Milford area in southwestern Connecticut, who in approximately 1728 founded a new Indian settlement twelve miles up the Housatonic River, which they called "Pishgochti-goch" (Pachgatgoch), under the leadership of the Pequot Mawehu.[15] Another example of this tribal melding occurred in 1725, when the Tunxis near Farmington in central Connecticut were joined by the Wangunks of Middletown and the Quinnipiacs of East Haven, two smaller communities that were trying to cope with population reductions and land losses. In subsequent decades these communities were frequently referred to as the "Farmington Indians," even by other Natives like Joseph Johnson.[16]

Occasionally, however, larger-scale migrations and ethnic blending took place within a more fixed framework of tribal identity. The most famous eighteenth-century migrations in the Northeast involved the Six Nations of the Iroquois Confederacy. The Tuscarora nation of North Carolina, for example, after their crushing defeat at the hands of the English colonists who were aided by many Catawbas, Creeks, and Cherokees in the Tuscarora War of 1711–13, requested and received permission from the Five Nations of the Iroquois Confederacy (Mohawk, Oneida, Cayuga, Onondaga, and Seneca) to move onto Iroquois lands in the Susquehanna River watershed in New York. In late 1713 and the spring of 1714, between fifteen hundred and two thousand Tuscarora men, women, and children made the six-hundred-mile trek along well-worn north—south Indian trails in the backcountry of English settlements. Within a few years the Tuscarora had been adopted as the sixth member of the Iroquois Confederacy.[17] Given that such arrangements were mutually beneficial, the Six Nations over time received into the longhouse (meetinghouse of the tribal chiefs) other Indian communities struggling to maintain their own cultural vitality. In many cases, this resulted in the creation or expansion of intertribal villages that still remained underneath the umbrella of the Six Nations. The town of Onoquaga in New York was one such example,

for although it reported itself to non-Natives as an Oneida town, by
the 1770s it contained Tuscaroras, Delawares, Mahicans, Shawnees,
Mohawks, Cayugas, Nanticokes, and Oneidas.[18]

Intertribality

In many areas, however, local Native communities sustained their
own identity even as they increasingly leaned upon other regional Indian towns for support and cultural solidarity. Throughout the seventeenth and early eighteenth centuries, New England Indian nations
in Connecticut, Rhode Island, and on Long Island, New York, were
far more connected to each other through trade and marriage than
they were with Native communities in Massachusetts, New York, and
on Cape Cod and Martha's Vineyard. Although such cultural interrelatedness clearly had roots in the decades and centuries prior to the
arrival of Europeans, the experience of colonialism helped forge an
interdependence and cohesion that was, if nothing else, more intense
and accelerated than would have been otherwise.

The eighteenth century was a period of increasing intertribal activity and cultural consolidation. The connections between eighteenth-
century Native communities are evidenced by the periodic intertribal
meetings and dances that were called to elect leaders, prepare for war,
deal with communal issues, create alliances with neighboring tribes,
and commemorate important festivals in the lunar year. In 1723, when
the Mohegan sachem Caesar passed away, the Mohegans invited the
Niantics and Pequots to Mohegan for a lengthy meeting to elect a new
sachem.[19] Similarly, on September 10, 1736, a large group of Mohegans,
Niantics, and Pequots held a "black dance" to elect a new leader to replace Ben Uncas II, with whom they were unhappy.[20]

By the mid-eighteenth century, however, Natives in southern New
England began forming intertribal connections in a new and important
way, namely, around the shared experience of European Christianity.
Although the encounter with Protestant Christianity had its roots in
the seventeenth century, it was not until the opening decades of the
eighteenth century that these particular Native communities in Connecticut, Rhode Island, and on Long Island, New York, demonstrated

any long-term openness to education and missionaries. Throughout the 1720s and 1730s, many of these Native communities in Connecticut and Rhode Island had experienced decades of fairly regular instruction in basic literacy and reformed Protestantism. During the period of intense religious revivalism of the 1730s and 1740s in New England (usually referred to as the First Great Awakening), many Indian individuals participated by attending indoor and outdoor evangelistic services marked by theatrical preaching and boisterous singing. Over time, dozens of Natives joined local pro-revival churches. The awakening, for many of these Indians, was a logical culmination of a longer evangelization process, although such affiliations did not always last as long as historians have assumed. For those Natives who did affiliate with local English churches—often up to half the adult population in each Indian community—Christianity seemingly became a meaningful way of ordering their worlds.[21]

In the decades following the First Great Awakening, then, Christianized Indians across southern New England began to forge networks in ways that followed old intertribal ties but were reinforced by new rituals and ideas. The basis for this emerging network was an indigenized form of Reformed Protestantism that became for many an important way of redefining their religious lives and practices in a way that, at times, complemented ongoing Native cultural traditions. An awareness of these shared religious practices, ideas, and experiences was facilitated by a cadre of itinerant Native preachers and teachers who increasingly held Native Christian services on Native lands. It is important to note the similarities and differences between this movement and other pan-tribal movements in the eighteenth century, particularly those that involved elements of nativism—a call to a recovery of Native traditional practices and a rejection of European cultural and religious influences. These nativist movements, as Gregory Dowd has argued, began in the early 1740s in the mid-Atlantic and Midwest and resurfaced in a variety of communities through the early 1800s.[22] Native prophets and visionaries like the Neolin (Delaware) and Pontiac (Ottawa) gave inspiration for and leadership to movements that resulted in violent conflicts between Europeans and

Natives from a wide range of Native nations. Nonetheless, although there are a few common elements between the Brothertown movement and the nativist impulse—shared disillusionment, promoting separation from Europeans—in practice the two were very different. At no time during the Brothertown movement was military resistance ever discussed as an option nor were there any visions of or conversations with the Master of Life (the Indian deity from whom Neolin and others received visions). Furthermore, Brothertown was an explicit embrace of an indigenized version of Reformed Protestantism, not a rejection of Christianity altogether.

The Idea of Brothertown

Disillusionment was nevertheless widespread among Natives in southeastern New England. In the years following the Great Awakening in southern New England, American Indians did not find that the connections of Christian fellowship with local whites had significantly increased their social or economic status, or even produced an inkling of change in how they were perceived or treated. In the face of ongoing defeat in local land controversies, the continual erosion of Native traditional life and subsistence on reserved lands, the dramatic changes in labor patterns, and the heavy losses of Indian males in colonial wars, Natives began talking about a radical move away from their ancestral lands to new territory to the west, far from the influences and pressures of Anglo-European settlers and governments.

The very idea of a large-scale, voluntary Indian migration must have seemed ludicrous to many eighteenth-century observers at a variety of levels. Most significantly, these same Native communities had fought for their land rights in local courts for the preceding century and a half and now proposed leaving these lands entirely. As we have seen, however, such migrations were not unusual in the colonial period, especially in response to external pressures and extraordinary circumstances. What made the New England Indians' adoption and migration distinctive, then, was not the proposed destination or the distance of the migration (250 miles—less than half the distance of the Tuscarora migration) nor even the diverse composition of the adoptive migrants, but rather the fact that they wanted their new community to be for racially pure Christian Indians (more on this below). The New England Indians seeking refuge represented portions of seven Indian towns, according to the Mohegan Joseph Johnson: Farmington, Mohegan, Niantic, Mashantucket Pequot, Eastern Pequot, Narragansett, and Montauk. But within these seven towns were represented perhaps as many as ten to twelve distinct Indian communities (the Farmingtons and Montauketts, in particular, were certainly a combination of tribal groups from each respective region).[23] Along with the shared experiences of colonialism and intermarriage, a vibrant network of indigenized Christianity was a major element that unified these communities.

The first concrete Native reference to such a possible move was in a letter from the Narragansett Tobias Shattock to Eleazar Wheelock on October 2, 1767. Shattock's letter detailed the ongoing problems the Narragansetts faced with regard to the loss and sale of tribal lands. Shattock was interested in the possibility that Wheelock could help the Narragansetts secure land outside Rhode Island for them to settle upon, perhaps even in New York. "If we shou'd move to or near Onida," Shattock suggested, "we shall be of great service to You in promoting your worthy Design."[24] Couching a possible relocation within the goals of Wheelock's Design (of creating Christianized, Anglicized allies out of the powerful Six Nations) was more than just savvy diplomacy; all proposed migrations by the Christianized New England Indians in the 1760s, 1770s, and 1780s included a strong component of potential religious outreach to western nations, even after Wheelock and other non-Natives ceased to be so involved.[25] Nonetheless, in a letter dated November 30, 1767, Shattock revealed that the Narragansetts were vigorously pursuing their own resolutions to the land controversy in New England. First, if they could raise sufficient funds, they planned to send Shattock to England to present the Narragansett case against the colony of Rhode Island and various settlers. If that failed, Shattock indicated they would take up Wheelock's prior offer to send the case to the Earl of Dartmouth, to see if he could influence people in London to help protect their land. If all these appeals failed, however, the Sam Niles (antisachem) group of the Narragansetts agreed they would "try to Secure what we are in possession of, & dispose of the Same, & Imbrace Sr. Williams offer."[26] In other words, if they lost their present land case, they were going to get free and clear titles to the land they did own, sell them, and move elsewhere. Sir William Johnson, the British superintendent for Indian affairs (northern colonies), at Wheelock's request had become involved in the Narragansett land case and apparently offered to secure lands for the Narragansett in New York, barring all other possible solutions.

This specific idea of relocation to New York surfaced among only a few of these New England Indian communities in the late 1760s and had mostly died out by 1770. This was perhaps because Wheelock himself—who would have naturally provided much of the direction, resources, and vision for it—was busy moving his own Indian Charity School to Hanover, New Hampshire, where he renamed it Dartmouth College (after a prominent British sponsor). When the idea of a joint, multitribal migration to New York resurfaced in the early 1770s, it did so in earnest and became quickly associated with the Mohegan Joseph Johnson. Not only did he spearhead the initiative, but he also provided the critical personal link to the Oneidas themselves, conducting his negotiations in 1774 on the foundation of an almost decade-long friendship built on prior evangelistic missionary trips to New York he had taken under the sponsorship of Eleazar Wheelock.

Joseph Johnson Jr. was born in 1751 in Mohegan, Connecticut, the son of Joseph and Betty (Garrett) Johnson. Johnson was born into a Mohegan family and community that was fairly Christianized, given their individual and collective experiences of education, lectures, and church services from the 1730s onward through the First Great Awakening.[27] Joseph Johnson Sr. died in September 1758 while leading a scouting expedition near Lake George in New York for British forces in the French and Indian War. In December 1758, just a few months after his father's death, the seven-year-old Joseph Johnson was sent to Eleazar Wheelock's Indian Charity School in Lebanon, Connecticut. Johnson's eight years under Wheelock's tutelage were formative—especially given his young age. In November 1766, at the age of fifteen, Johnson was sent on his first mission to serve as an assistant teacher

at the Oneida village of Kanonwalohale. Part of his training under
Wheelock included instruction in the Iroquoian languages such as
Oneida and Mohawk, but undoubtedly his grasp of languages so unfamiliar to his own would have been feeble at best (as other Wheelock
missionaries reported linguistic difficulties of their own).

Somewhere along the way, Johnson became disillusioned with his
missionary assignment. Over the course of the year 1768, Johnson increasingly drank heavily and kept concubines, thereby defying the
Christian principles Wheelock sent him to inculcate. Although Johnson seemed to have smoothed things over with the Oneidas through a
public confession of his sins—which the Oneidas promised to "Bury
in Oblivion and let things be as if it never happened so"—his actions
proved to those around him that Johnson had all along worked "under *pretence* of regard" to Wheelock and his Design. By December
1768 Johnson had fled his post in Oneida to Providence, Rhode Island, where he felt too "ashamed"—and too unhappy—to return to
Wheelock's service.[28]

Johnson spent the next several years in relative silence. No letters
or journals from Johnson survive from this time, although he later
reported that he worked first as a schoolteacher in Providence and
later on a whaling ship, during which time he sailed as far east as the
Azores and to many islands in the West Indies, including Antigua,
Grenada, the Virgin Islands, and "Portireco" (Puerto Rico).[29] In October 1771, at the age of twenty-one, Johnson returned from his whaling
expeditions—having seen much of the world indeed, but perhaps not
having made as much money as he had hoped—and took up residence
at Mohegan working on his uncle's farm.[30] In November 1771 Johnson
experienced a prolonged season of religious turmoil that culminated
in a reconversion of sorts. His journal entries from November 5, 1771,
onward, indicate an articulation of his own sinfulness and a corresponding attention to Christian devotional practices such as reading
the Bible, praying, and reading classic Puritan and Reformed devotional works like Richard Baxter's *The Saints' Everlasting Rest* (1650) in
addition to regularly attending local Indian worship services at Mohegan and Groton (as well as Anglo-American services on occasion).

Johnson went public with the particulars of his spiritual transformation in May 1772, when he penned a "publick dedication" to "the living God," and sometime in November of that same year in an open letter "to All Enquiring Friends."[31]

With this renewed sense of purpose, Johnson poured his energies into local Indian communities. In November 1772, at Occom's suggestion, Johnson moved fifty-five miles northwest of Mohegan to Farmington, Connecticut (west of Hartford), to serve as a schoolteacher among the Natives there.[32] By the early 1770s the Farmington community was an intertribal amalgam of Christianized Natives that had direct ties to Pequot and Mohegan communities in the southeastern part of the state and the Narragansetts in Rhode Island. A key element in fostering even greater connections between subsets of these Indian communities in southern New England was the shared experience of Indian Christian practices, usually centered around joint Christian worship services. On Saturday, February 1, 1772, for example, Johnson traveled to Groton to spend time with friends and family, in particular his uncle Benjamin Garrett and close friend Sampson Paukanop.[33] In the early evening, the "Indians of Narragansett arrived and held a conference" there. After the service, James Niles Jr. (nephew of the Narragansett Separate minister Sam Niles) spent the night with Johnson, and they stayed up almost the whole night talking. The next day, Sunday, this intertribal group of Mohegans, Pequots, and Narragansetts held another lengthy meeting, in which there was "Exhorting, Singing, Praying," until the evening, when they finally took part in the "Lords supper."[34] Even while at the much more distantly located Farmington community, Johnson recorded that his Indian friends from Groton and Mohegan visited him and joined in their collective meetings.[35]

As an outgrowth of this already-existing, Christianity-enhanced intertribalness, many of the Indian communities again began to talk more seriously about the possibility of a westward migration. On March 13, 1773, a "Vast number of People Men, Women, and Children," all Christian Indians from Pequot (Groton and Stonington), Farmington, Niantic (Lyme), Montaukett (Long Island), Narragansett (Charlestown, Rhode Island), and Mohegan, met at Mohegan to consider the advantages of a joint settlement.[36] Part of the purpose of this meeting, it seems, was to explore the possibility of relocation as well as discuss possible destinations. "Some were of a Mind to go southward as far as to Ohio, and some not so far that way," Joseph Johnson recalled. Others suggested that "it would not do to live so far from the English."[37] Indians wanted distance, but apparently not too much of it. During the course of the meeting each Indian community agreed to send one or two representatives to scope out which destination might make the most sense, but not until after the community cycles of planting and harvesting were over.[38]

Johnson spent the summer of 1773 at Farmington, teaching his students and writing letters to friends, supporters, and colonial officials, including Samson Occom, Jonathan Trumbull (the governor of Connecticut), Eleazar Wheelock, and Andrew Oliver (treasurer of the Boston Commissioners for the New England Company, a London-based missionary society for Native Americans). Although conversations regarding the potential migration were undoubtedly taking place among the various Indian communities of southern New England after the March 1773 meeting, Johnson's letters do not capture this ongoing dialogue. He was instead focused on securing the support of Sir William Johnson, who was in turn in communication with the Oneida Indians about the possibility of a settlement on Oneida lands. With these preliminary negotiations taken care of and most of the harvest season past, Johnson returned to the task of organizing a party of representatives to make the first of several trips to New York. On October 13, 1773, Johnson penned a letter on behalf of the Farmington Indians to "all our Indian Brethren, at Mohegan, Nihantuck [Niantic], Pequtt [Mashantucket Pequot], Stonington [Eastern Pequot], Narragansett, and Montauk," urging them to "remember the Affair, of which we So earnestly talked last Spring at the Town of Mohegan." "We beg that ye would this once more take this Affair under your deliberate Considerations," Johnson pleaded, "Let it not drop through, Since we have Encouragements on every Side." Joseph Johnson's hard work to secure the support of Sir William Johnson paid off, and Sir William agreed to give his support, just as he had done to the Narragansetts in 1767 and the Montauketts on earlier occasions. As a result, Sir William invited representatives from the New England Indians to New York to possibly broker a land deal.[39]

Accordingly, Joseph Johnson's proposal in his letter to the Indian communities suggested that each group should "Send a Man, out of Each Tribe, that they may go with us, and Seek a Country for our Brethren." All such representatives were to meet at Farmington by October 23, 1773, in order to set out by October 25 for their planned meeting with Sir William Johnson. The document was signed by eight Farmington Indians plus Joseph Johnson.[40] In the end, not a single town sent a representative to Farmington, and Joseph Johnson and Elijah Wimpey (from Farmington) were the only ones willing to make the arduous journey.[41] At Johnson Hall in Johnstown, New York, they met with Sir William Johnson, who told them that the Oneidas agreed earlier in October to grant the New England Indians ten square miles, or approximately sixty-four hundred acres (an amount Johnson later persuaded the Oneida to increase).

Upon Joseph Johnson's return to New England in November 1773, he took time off from his busy schedule of negotiations, traveling, and writing to indulge in a meaningful relationship he had been pursuing. On December 2, 1773, Joseph Johnson and Tabitha Occom (Samson's daughter) were married in Norwich, with the Reverend Ephraim Judson performing the ceremony. Very few details of the event are provided by either Johnson or his new father-in-law, Samson Occom, who laconically reported to Wheelock that Johnson "lately tooke one of my Daughters to Wife."[42] Although a service seems to have been conducted in Norwich at an Anglo-American church, it is probable that a parallel celebration of sorts was held in Mohegan shortly thereafter, since such interwoven and dual participation had long been a feature of Christian Indian life.

Within a few weeks, however, Johnson and the same group of Farmington Indians issued another letter to the seven communities of New England Natives, this time taking them to task for an apparent cooling toward the idea of migration. "We are Sorry to See So much Coldness, Luke warmness, and indifference amongst you,

as ye have discovered since last March 1773," Johnson and his Farmington friends chided. They had promised to return to New York in
January 1774, this time with more representatives, to meet with the
Oneida chiefs to formally request and receive a sufficient land grant.
"What shall we think of you, if ye do not send one out of Each Town,
or Tribe[?]," Johnson queried. Even more importantly, what would Sir
William Johnson and the Oneidas think? They were, after all, expect-
ing a representative from each community, and having only two Indians show up again would hardly do. Johnson renewed his plea for at
least one representative from each of the seven communities to meet
at Farmington on January 1, 1774.[43]

In the end, however, only three individuals met in Farmington to accompany Johnson: Jacob Fowler (Montaukett), Samuel Tobias (Narragansett), and Elijah Wympy (Farmington).[44] Only one of these Indians
actually lasted the whole trip (perhaps Jacob Fowler, Johnson's brother-
in-law); the other two turned back for health reasons. The Indian communities had their reasons for not sending more representatives—most
of them practical rather than ideological. It was, after all, wintertime,
and with a "great body of snow" on the ground it was hardly an appropriate season for traveling great distances or adequately assessing
the proposed land once they were there. Furthermore, there was a lot
of "bad News" circulating in New England about New York, mostly related to the rising standoff between pro- and anti-British populations in the colonies. Although the first shots of what would become
the American Revolution were half a year away, tensions were palpa-
ble in many areas of the colonies and backcountry. "We heard that it
was dangerous times," Johnson later explained to the Oneidas. "We
h[e]ard that there was a considerable talk of war among the Indians
in these Parts, which News discouraged many of our Brethren," even
though Sir William Johnson assured them otherwise.[45]

Ultimately, Johnson's negotiations at Oneida were successful. All that
was left for Johnson to do was to convince his fellow Indians in New
England that the enormous undertaking the migration represented was
worth the risk and effort. As it turns out, this was easier said than done.
In May 1774, after several months of trying to rally support, Johnson

confided to Occom: "The Mohawk affair has brought me very low, as I have had no help worth mentioning, since I undertook for the Indians. I am almost ready to say that I will undertake no more for such unthankful, ungrateful, and unmanly Indians."[46] By mid-1774, however, the idea of a collective migration was again beginning to take firm root among at least a few individuals in the various Indian towns. On May 19, 1774, the Farmington Indians Elijah Wimpey, Solomon Mossuck, and Samuel Adams (not the Boston politician and patriot) petitioned the Connecticut General Assembly for permission to sell their lands near Hartford in anticipation of their planned migration westward. "Being Straitned where we now dwell," they explained, "[we] think it will be best for ourselves & our Children . . . to Sell our Interest in this Colony to accept the kind invitation of our bretheren & to remove with our females to the Oneida."[47] The General Assembly accordingly appointed a committee to oversee and authorize the sale of Farmington lands.[48] By the summer of 1774, the migration began to look more and more possible. Joseph Johnson reported to Sir William Johnson on July 8, 1774, that "As for our Intentions of removing from these Parts we are as Engaged as Ever and perhaps more so."[49] Even the Narragansetts showed renewed interest in such a relocation. On August 22, 1774, North Stonington minister Joseph Fish recorded in his journal that he preached at the Indian schoolhouse in Charlestown to only five "Indian Hearers." Although Indian attendance at his monthly lectures had been on the decline for years, the absences this Sunday were particularly poignant since "Many of the Heads of the Tribe (and *Sam Niles* for one,) are gone off, with a view to Settle beyond Albany." Fish's conclusion, that the "Indians in General Are determined not to hear Me Any More," was accurate, but he missed the larger importance of the plans that were taking place.[50]

Nonetheless, things progressed rather slowly. On October 4, 1774, the Oneidas finally sent a deed for land in Oneida country—drawn up by Guy Johnson, Sir William Johnson's nephew and successor— to Joseph Johnson and the New England Indians.[51] By early 1775, concrete plans for the move were in place, with a multistage strategy for settlement. The first step was to send "men that are able to endure hardships to go and work or break the way through, or prepare a Sort of Shelter for themselves and (—?) to live in, and raise little Somewhat to eat for them and (—?)." After this initial stage, when rudimentary shelters were in place and crops planted, the "families" and "aged Men and Women" could then move to the new town.[52] In February 1775 Johnson reported that a group of fifty-eight "young men" planned to depart for their new lands on March 13, 1775. These fifty-eight individuals came from Indian towns throughout New England: ten from Mohegan, twenty from Narragansett, ten from Farmington, five from Niantic, and thirteen from Montauk. The Mashantuckets and Eastern Pequots were, according to Johnson, "so deeply involved in debt" that they could not send anyone for the initial settlement, although Occom was working with the creditors of a few individuals to make their involvement possible.[53]

Motivations for Migration

Why would these Indian individuals and communities even consider such a risky, costly, and disruptive migration in the first place? Motivations for moving to New York undoubtedly varied widely from individual to individual; the migration hardly meant the same thing to everybody. It was an event full of potential and contradictory meanings. Nonetheless, there do seem to be some core shared experiences and assumptions regarding treatment by whites in New England and the possibilities of a better life in New York. And perhaps most importantly, the clearest ideological point of connection was their Native Christianity, which provided a stronger point of connection between the potential émigrés than did their respective tribal affiliations. Whether such connections constituted a formal sense of "identity" at this early phase is doubtful, but it is clear that this sense of consciousness was forming slowly.

At the most basic level, one major motivation for migration seems to have been long-term resentment and frustration at their circumstances in New England. "They have a very great and rooted Prejudice against White People," Occom explained of the New England Indians, "and they have too much good reason for it, they have been imposed upon."[54] By the late 1760s there was widespread disillusionment among Native communities on a variety of fronts, including labor relations, educational opportunities, prejudice in the legal system, alcohol sales, burdensome debt, and general racial disparagement.

As part of this wider backdrop of general disillusionment, however, the clearest immediate context for migration was land loss, particularly at the hands of white Christians.[55] Gideon Hawley, a longtime missionary at Onaquaga, observed such resentment in 1761: "That the more acquainted Indians are with white people, even professing Christians, the more prejudiced they are against our nation & the more averse to getting footing in their country. Have we not already ousted them of the greatest part and even of almost every tract of the best land on the vastly extended sea-shore?"[56] Every New England Indian community that participated in the relocation had in the years prior to the migration been handed several major defeats in ongoing land struggles against either specific colonies, their own sachems, or both. The Mohegan land controversy, for example, received its final hearing and eventual ruling against the Mohegan on June 11, 1771, in London.[57] It was an unsurprising and yet extremely disheartening end to a series of defeats since 1704 (officially, at least, this date being when British monarchs got involved, but local controversies existed decades before 1704). Occom's stolid reporting of the decision in a letter to Long Island minister Samuel Buell masked the emotional intensity the issue held with many Indian families and communities: "the grand Controversy, Which has Subsisted between the Colony of Connecticut and the Mohegan Indians above 70 years we hear is finally Decided, and it is in Favour of the Colony."[58] The Narragansetts, as described earlier, similarly had run out of choices and in the 1760s even sent Tobias Shattock to London as a last-ditch effort to win rights to their land, a move that also was unsuccessful. Given these apparent dead ends, the best option, it seemed, was to find more land elsewhere. And in New York, according to the reports of Joseph Johnson and others who went, there was lots of it.

The appeal of starting over with new lands in New York, then, was threefold: there would be more land; it was less threatened by white encroachment; and it was allotted to individuals, not sachems or the community as a whole (which was seen as a good thing, given the way sachems often controlled and squandered land in the eighteenth century). And indeed, in the settlement that later became Brothertown in the 1780s, individuals and families were given grants of 50 to 170 acres, with clearly defined boundaries of individual ownership.[59] More than just the land itself, the move to Brothertown represented the escape from constant pressures and land encroachments by colonists.

In addition to—but not separate from—the ever-present issue of land, another motivation for migration had a distinctly Christian, evangelistic bent to it. The clearest articulation of this impulse came from a seeming latecomer to the idea, Samson Occom. Despite Occom's familiarity with the plans and later leadership in the second attempted (and successful) relocation in the 1780s, during this first effort in the 1770s he seems rather aloof—committing himself only if the movement succeeded. On November 10, 1773, while Joseph Johnson and Elijah Wimpey were busy meeting with Sir William Johnson at Johnson Hall, Occom wrote to the English gentlemen in Britain who had been placed in charge of overseeing the funds raised by Occom during his tour of the British Isles in the late 1760s. In this letter, he requested £50 per year toward his many and various services among the Indians of New England (since Wheelock had proved unwilling to support Occom). Occom gives a clear vision of the planned migration, although his perspective is certainly filtered through his own education, experiences, hopes, and desires:

> There is a motion among the tribes of Indians around here, to unite together and Seek for a New Settlement among the Western Indians, Their view is if they can find room, to embody together both in Civil and Religious State, their Main View is, to Introduce the Religion of Jesus Christ by their example—among the benighted Indians in the Wilderness, and also Introduce Agriculture amongst them. . . . If this Can be effected it Will be the likeliest way to bring the Indians heart to Consider the Christian Religion, and to bring to Husbandry—they have very Prejudice against the English ministers and all English, but

if a number of [Regular] Indian Christians went amongst them and
Set good Example before them they may think and be Convinced, that
there was in the Christian Religion, I am promoting the thing and encouraging the Indians all I can, and if they Shall Succeed, I shall go
with them all my Heart.[60]

For Occom, Johnson, and others, the relocation represented a fresh
start and a distinct sense of purpose. "I really feel engaged on my Part,
and greatly encouraged," Johnson confided to a sponsor. "The prospects
of great future good to my poor brethren in these parts, and also those
that inhabit the western Wilderness animates my Soul to press forward.
I greatly desire the Prosperity of my sinking Nation.—O that I might,
by the Grace of God, be beneficial not only to the bodies, but to the precious, exceeding precious Souls of my poor Indian Brethren."[61] It is possible, as David Silverman has argued, that the migration to New York
and the evangelization of the "western nations" represented a possible
regaining of God's favor for the Indians. At times, Occom does seem to
promote this idea when he speaks of God's curse on Indians as a whole,
and he sometimes states outright that evangelizing other Indian nations
will remove that curse.[62] At other times, however, Occom seems to believe the opposite—that the Indians have been cursed no more severely than other nations, whether white or black.[63]

Racial and Christian separatism also motivated some migrants. Occom's observation that the Indians of New England had "very great and
rooted Prejudice against White People" was only half the story; many
Natives increasingly exhibited a prejudice against blacks and any Indians who intermarried with them. Similarly, some Christian Indians
increasingly desired to remove themselves from their nonprofessing Indian community members. The movement to emigrate to New York
reflected many of the very real racial and religious tensions contained
within many of the participating Native communities. The push for
migration cannot be correctly understood apart from the practical desire by some of the leaders to pursue Indian racial and Christian purity.

Although it is easy to quickly read reified racial categories into
eighteenth-century discourse about ethnic difference, ideas about

race emerged slowly over time in New England, as they did elsewhere. "Racial purity" (for lack of a better term) became an increasingly important issue over the course of the eighteenth century.
Until approximately the 1730s and 1740s, "mulattoes" or individuals
of mixed ethnicities (white-black, white-Indian, or black-Indian) were
not looked down upon so strongly by Natives. This was in part because of the relative isolation of many Indian communities, the lower numbers of blacks in New England in the early decades of the
eighteenth century, and the early infrequency of intermarriage between Africans and Indians. As Indian labor and patterns of settlement changed over time, and as more blacks arrived against their will
in New England's ports and to serve in English households and work
on farms, intermixing, cultural exchange, and intermarriage became
more common. Even so, there is evidence that intermarriage between
blacks and Indians was not entirely forbidden or discouraged, even
in English churches. In the three Stonington, Connecticut, churches, for example, three mixed marriages took place: in 1739, 1742, and
1752.[64] Indian-black marriages became more frequent as Indian males
joined colonial militias and never returned from battle, particularly
during the French and Indian War (1754–63). Widows and younger females searching for spouses or replacement partners often looked to
the growing enslaved and free African populations in the neighboring urban centers like New London, Stonington, Lyme, and Norwich
in Connecticut, and Charlestown in Rhode Island. Although Indian communities were not initially inclined to look unfavorably upon
such marriages, over time they created real internal problems in individual communities, as local Indian lands became a place of refuge
for a variety of persons of color, often those who were unemployed.

Within each Native community, then, tension arose over how to
handle these perceived intrusions. Indian leaders differed greatly on
how to respond to the challenges of racial and ethnic mixing. In 1765,
for example, the Mohegan sachem Ben Uncas III and Samson Occom
disagreed over whether or not to allow mulattoes onto Mohegan lands
(Occom favored it in this case, although by the 1780s he had changed
his mind).[65] A similar problem existed among the Narragansetts. When

Edward Deake first arrived in Charlestown, Rhode Island, in 1765 as
their schoolteacher, he counted seventy-three families, 151 school-aged
children, and "a considerable Number of mixtures as melatoes and
mustees which the tribe Disowns, and Sundry families of Indians
which properly Belongs to other tribes."[66] This presence of outsider
Indians and Indians of mixed ethnicities continued to cause considerable consternation among the Mohegans as well. In 1774 Zachary
Johnson complained to the General Assembly that "many Interlopers
from other tribes & Straggling Indians and Mulattoes have crowded
in upon said Lands, whereby many Difficulties and Disputes have aris-
en."[67] In response, the General Assembly formed a committee and set
up specific laws governing the occupancy and sale of lands.[68]

The problem escalated considerably when local Anglo governments
threatened to (and in some cases did) stop recognizing individuals of
mixed ethnicities as "authentic" Indians. Individuals who were not
"pure" Indians, for instance, were not counted in Anglo tallies of the
Indian populations, which had direct consequences in terms of colony
assistance and the public perception of land required by each Native
nation. Joseph Johnson, very aware of the contestation of authentic
Indian identity in the late eighteenth century, refers to himself in several letters to Anglo-American friends as a "True Mohegan."[69] Similarly, in his suggestion to Governor Trumbull regarding land allotments,
Johnson suggests that any income from land rental should be distributed equally among the Mohegans, but with one major caveat: that
only those who are "True Mohegan Indian[s]" should receive the disbursements.[70] Authentic Native identity was increasingly tied to survival, and many Natives feared that as their tribal rolls became filled
with individuals and families of mixed ethnicities, the possibilities for
ongoing, autonomous existence were slowly slipping away. In other
words, identity and sovereignty were inextricably linked.

The proposed Christian Indian community in Oneida country was
designed to circumvent this problem entirely by creating a place for racially "pure" Indians. The deed for Oneida lands granted to the New
England Indians stated in no uncertain terms the concerns of Indians
at this time. The deed described a large tract of land (in terms of local

landmarks but unspecified in total acreage) granted "to the New England Indians, & their Posterity, without Power of Alienation," without any restrictions at all except one: "that the same shall not be possessed by any Persons deemed of the said Tribes who are descended from, or have intermixed with Negroes, or Mulatoes."[71] Put simply, this was land for "true" or racially pure Indians only. All the dozens of mixed ethnicity or intermarried Indians or Africans on Indian lands around New England—Christian or not—need not apply. Foregrounding racial purity in determining the membership of the proposed new settlement naturally cut across other possible ways of deciding who was in and who was out. Although Indians left New England in some small part to escape the influence of non-Christian Indians, by enforcing a "racial purity" principle those who migrated automatically excluded or designated as second-class residents of the settlement their Christian relatives and friends who might have intermarried with non-Indians.

In practice, at least after the mid-1780s, when the settlement actually got underway, people of mixed ethnicities (and even white people) certainly lived on the land, either as renters, leasers, squatters, or relatives of "pure" Indians. But the leadership of Brothertown, as the settlement eventually was named, was rather uncompromising about who could *own* the land. In 1796, for example, the case of Sarah Pendleton (formerly Potteogue), a Narragansett Indian, came before the Brothertown leadership council. Sarah had some years prior married James Pendleton, who was "a decendant from a negro man, and a woman who was part white and part negro." The two had several children together. In the mid-1790s it appears they moved to Brothertown and requested a plot of land—as they would have been allowed to do given their affiliation with the Narragansetts. When James' mixed ethnicity was revealed, however, Sarah's request for land was flatly denied. "It has been an immemorial custom among all the nations as well Narragansetts as others from whom the Brothertown Indians descended," the Brothertown leaders asserted, "that if any indian woman or girl married a negro man, or any one who had a mixture of negro blood, she forfeited all her rights and privileges as an individual of the Nation from she and they decended and particularly all right and title to lands belonging to the Tribe or Tribes to whom they belonged."[72] Indians who had married partners of mixed ethnic heritages automatically disqualified themselves from future landownership; if a "pure" Indian woman already owned land, through such a marriage she forfeited the rights to her land, as the Brothertown leadership council affirmed repeatedly in future years.

Also embedded in the rhetoric of migration to Brothertown was a pointed critique of the colonial practice—or pretense—of Christianity. In his speech to the Oneidas in January 1774, Johnson highlighted the discernible gap between actions of the English Christians and the moral standards understood by Indian Christians in their reading of the Bible: "So now Brethren, we leave the English those who have acted unjustly towards us in New England, I say we leave them all in the hands of that God who knoweth all things, and will reward every one according to their deeds whether good or Evil."[73] Racial and Christian purity, then, along with land considerations formed the backbone of motivations for migration to New York.

Despite these years of preparation, wider political, military, and cultural developments brought the plans for migration to a standstill between 1775 and 1784. Most immediately, the start of the American Revolution redirected the energy of most of the leaders of the migration and made the migration too hazardous to undertake. Although by April 14, 1775, Johnson and the first group had reached Oneida to clear some land, plant corn and potatoes, and build temporary housing, Johnson at least did not remain there for long. And eventually all fifty-eight Natives who had moved in the spring of 1775 were forced back to either Stockbridge, Massachusetts, or—more embarrassingly—their home communities in New England before the year was out. Neither the eventual American victory in the war nor the future possibility (and success) of relocating was apparent to the hundreds of Indian families who hunkered down during the long and lean war years and watched as their husbands, fathers, sons, and brothers went off to fight, often never to return. Nor could the leaders of the migration have foreseen the suffering they were spared by not being on the fertile Oneida lands in 1779 when the Clinton-Sullivan Campaign stormed through the homelands of the Oneidas and the Six Nations, burning crops, destroying food supplies, pillaging homes, and killing men, women, and children, even as they admired the technological, architectural, and agricultural sophistication of the Iroquois.[74] The war also claimed the lives of dozens, if not hundreds, of New England Natives and stole away the twenty-five-year-old leader of the migration movement, Joseph Johnson, who died sometime between mid-1776 and May 1777.[75]

Ultimately, it was Samson Occom who saw the planned migration to New York come to fruition after the war ended. In the spring of 1784, just half a year after the Treaty of Paris brought an official end to the hostilities, Occom renewed the call to move to New York. On May 8, twenty Indian families sailed from New London down the Long Island Sound and up the Hudson River to Albany, where they most likely transferred their belongings to horses and wagons and made their way westward to the tract of land given to them by the Oneidas.[76] By the fall of 1784, Occom reported that once again the idea of migration had found a lot of traction among the same seven Indian communities in New England. When he had returned to Mohegan in late summer of that year, after having helped the first group of migrants reach New York, he said that Indians from Montauk and Narragansett had come to see him, "and they say out of each of these Places many are getting ready to move into that Country as fast as they can."[77] In New York in November 1785, for the first time, the New England Indians organized themselves into a "Body Politick" and officially gave a name to their settlement: Eeyawquittoowauconnuck, or simply "Brotherton" in English.[78] By 1795 approximately 135 individuals from the original seven Indian villages had migrated, including Occom, who moved his family to Brothertown in 1789.[79]

The Brothertown Indians were joined in Oneida country in this postwar period by some of the Mahicans from along the Housatonic River in western Massachusetts who had been residing in and near the mission town of Stockbridge since the 1730s and 1740s. When the New England Indians who had taken refuge at Stockbridge during the Revolutionary War once again made their way to Oneida country in 1784, many of the Stockbridge Indians decided to relocate as well.[80]

The Oneidas granted the Stockbridge Indians a tract of land six miles square just southwest of Brothertown, which they promptly named "New Stockbridge."[81]

Conclusion

In the end, the creation of Brothertown and the subsequent trickle of migration over time reshaped New England Indian demographics, although not as dramatically as historians have supposed. In some cases, the removal of key families and leaders did make it more difficult for Indian communities to maintain a viable political, social, and cultural presence. As a result of the migration in 1784–85, as archaeologist Kevin McBride has observed, "the Tunxis, Wangunk, Quinnipiac, and Western Niantic tribes disappeared from the region," while the "communities at Narragansett, Mohegan, Montauk, Pawcatuck and Mashantucket struggled to maintain their culture and identity on reservations that were significantly reduced in area and with populations just a fraction of their former size."[82]

For those who did leave New England, history merely repeated itself in their new location, with more land loss, intermarriage, and settler encroachment. In 1818, in another attempt to escape more land intrusions, the Brothertown Indians tried to move even farther west, first to southern Indiana, along the White River, but when that did not work out, they ultimately moved to Wisconsin, along the Fox River. The continual struggle to maintain racial purity did not disappear either, even after the move to Wisconsin. In 1855 Thomas Commuck, a Brothertown Indian of Narragansett ancestry, reported to the Wisconsin Historical Society that "already has inter-marriage with the whites so changed the Brothertowns, in complexion, that three-quarters of them would be readily considered as white, where they were not known, and in another generation our Indian blood will probably become so intermixed with the general mass of mankind."[83]

The leaders of the migration attempts to New York in the 1770s and 1780s, however, could not have known all of this. Given their increasingly constricted situation in New England with regard to land, economic opportunity, and proximity to racial and religious "others," a migration to New York seemed to provide a solution to many of the most pressing problems facing Indian communities. The coordinated migration to Brothertown (and beyond) reveals Native identities in the British colonies that were fragmentary and dissolving, even amid the emergence of newer religiously and racially based identities that overlapped, merged with, and at times even obliterated older tribal/ band and kinship groupings and loyalties. And yet, the fact that the Brothertown Nation of Indians still maintains a vibrant—but not yet federally recognized—presence in Wisconsin testifies to the power of ethnogenesis and the importance of religion and collective agency in maintaining tribal sovereignty.

Notes

1. Journal entry for Monday, November 7, 1785. Samson Occom, *The Collected Writings of Samson Occom, Mohegan*, ed. Joanna Brooks (New York: Oxford University Press, 2006), 308. Occom rendered the town name as "Brotherton," but later historians and present-day Natives have used the slightly different spelling of "Brothertown." The literature on Brothertown is growing. See especially David J. Silverman, *Red Brethren: The Brothertown and Stockbridge Indians and the Problem of Race in Early America* (Ithaca NY: Cornell University Press,2010); Brad D. E. Jarvis, *The Brothertown Nation of Indians: Land Ownership and Nationalism in Early America, 1740–1840* (Lincoln: University of Nebraska Press, 2010).

2. Journal entry for Monday, November 7, 1785. Occom, *Collected Writings*, 309.

3. Journal entry for Monday, November 7, 1785. Occom, *Collected Writings*, 309.

4. On European exploration and English settlements, see Karen Ordahl Kupperman, *The Jamestown Project* (Cambridge MA: Belknap Press of Harvard University Press, 2007); J. H. Parry, *The Age of Reconnaissance: Discovery, Exploration, and Settlement, 1450 to 1650* (New York: Praeger, 1969); John Huxtable Elliott, *The Old World and the New 1492–1650* (Cambridge: Cambridge University Press, 1970); Patricia Seed, *Ceremonies of Possession in Europe's Conquest of the New World, 1492–1640* (New York: Cambridge University Press, 1995).

5. See, for example, Daniel K. Richter, *Facing East from Indian Country: A Native History of Early America* (Cambridge MA: Harvard University Press, 2001), ch. 3.

6. Henry A. Baker, *History of Montville, Connecticut, Formerly the North Parish of New London from 1640 to 1896* (Hartford CT: Press of the Case Lockwood and Brainard Company, 1896), 5–6.

7. Will Ottery and Rudi Ottery, *A Man Called Sampson* (Camden ME: Penobscot Press, 1989), 77–78.

8. Occom, *Collected Writings*, 54n34.

9. For more on the "virgin soil" epidemics, see Alfred W. Crosby, *The Columbian Exchange: Biological and Cultural Consequences of 1492*, 30th anniv. ed. (Westport CT: Praeger, 2003).

10. See, for example, Jonathan D. Hill, *History, Power, and Identity: Ethnogenesis in the Americas, 1492–1992* (Iowa City: University of Iowa Press, 1996). Also Gary Clayton Anderson, *The Indian Southwest, 1580–1830: Ethnogenesis and Reinvention* (Norman: University of Oklahoma Press, 1999).

11. James Hart Merrell, *The Indians' New World: Catawbas and Their Neighbors from European Contact through the Era of Removal* (New York: W. W. Norton, 1991), 93–95.

12. Neal Salisbury, "The Indians' Old World: Native Americans and the Coming of Europeans," *William and Mary Quarterly* 53, no. 3 (1996): 435–58.

13. Connecticut, Uncas, and John Mason, *Governor and Company of Connecticut, and Moheagan Indians* (London: W. and J. Richardson, 1769), 34.

14. J. Hammond Trumbull and Charles J. Hoadly, eds., *The Public Records of the Colony of Connecticut, 1636–1776* (Hartford CT: Lockwood and Brainard Company, 1850), 1:185. The Massachusetts Bay Company General Court apparently granted land to the Pequots in 1646, a grant that the colony of Connecticut affirmed in 1649. See "New England Company Collection, 1649–1775, American Antiquarian Society," Folder 2, Worcester MA; Trumbull and Hoadly, *Public Records of the Colony of Connecticut* (1872), 1:185.

15. Some scholars prefer the alternate form of this term, Schaghticoke (also Scaticook), but this is often easily confused with the Scatacook (also Scaticook) community near Albany, New York. Both Pachgatgoch and Schaghticoke mean roughly the same thing—the place where two rivers join together. "Pishgochti-goch" is an Algonkian word meaning "where the waters meet." And indeed, Mawehu's community settled where the Ten Mile River joins the Housatonic. See Trudie Lamb Richmond, "Spirituality and Survival in Schaghticoke Basket-Making," in *A Key into the Language of Woodsplint Baskets*, ed. Ann McMullen and Russell G. Handsman (Washington CT: American Indian Archaeological Institute, 1987), 111. For more background on Mawehu and the Pachgatgoch Indians during the Great Awakening, see Linford D. Fisher, "'I Believe They Are Papists!': Natives, Moravians, and the Politics of Conversion in Eighteenth-Century Connecticut," *New England Quarterly* 81, no. 3 (2008): 410–37. Several good anthropological studies of the Pachgatgoch are also available: Corinna Dally-Starna and William A. Starna, "Picturing Pachgatgoch: An Eighteenth

Century American Indian Community in Western Connecticut," *Northeast Anthropology*, no. 67 (2004): 1–22; Dally-Starna and Starna, "American Indians and Moravians in Southern New England," in *Germans and Indians: Fantasies, Encounters, Projections*, ed. Colin G. Calloway, Gerd Gmünden, and Susanne Zantop (Lincoln: University of Nebraska Press, 2002).

16. Ottery and Ottery, *A Man Called Sampson*, 42. Another attempted small-scale relocation occurred in 1703 when the Scatacook Indians north of Albany, New York, made plans to move to Mohawk territory. When New York officials learned of the plan, they spent a considerable amount of time attempting to dissuade the Scatacooks, in part, perhaps, because the Scatacooks represented a buffer of sorts between the English settlements in New York and the Canadian Indians. See "Propositions Made to the Schakook Indians Meet at Shinnechtady," July 6, 1703, Gilder Lehrman Manuscript Collection, Gilder Lehrman Institute of American History, New York City, doc. GLC03107.02072. A subset of the Mohawks themselves eventually moved northward into French Canada in the early eighteenth century, and colonial leaders in New York at one point floated the highly improbable idea of moving the Mohawks, Onondagas, and Oneidas to lands just outside Albany. "Observations made by Robert Livingston Secretary of Indian Affairs," April 1700, Gilder Lehrman Manuscript Collection, doc. GLC03107.02051.

17. Daniel K. Richter, *The Ordeal of the Longhouse: The Peoples of the Iroquois League in the Era of European Colonization* (Chapel Hill: University of North Carolina Press, 1992), 238–39. For more on the Tuscarora War from the Catawba perspective, see Merrell, *Indians' New World*. On the practice of raids and warfare as slave supply in the south, see Alan Gallay, *The Indian Slave Trade: The Rise of the English Empire in the American South, 1670–1717* (New Haven CT: Yale University Press, 2002).

18. Colin G. Calloway, *The American Revolution in Indian Country: Crisis and Diversity in Native American Communities* (New York: Cambridge University Press, 1995), 110–11.

19. "Thomas Rose's deposition, dated May 30th, 1738 in Norwich," in Connecticut, Uncas, and Mason, *Governor and Company of Connecticut*, 235.

20. "Deposition of Joseph Tracy, Jr., and Jabez Crocker, May 29, 1738," in Connecticut, Uncas, and Mason, *Governor and Company of Connecticut*, 235. Although Tracy and Crocker hint strongly but do not say explicitly that there were Niantics and Pequots present, the signatures and marks on subsequent documents indicate that other tribes were indeed in attendance and involved in the proceedings.

21. For more on the Indian Great Awakening, see Linford D. Fisher, "'Traditionary Religion': The Great Awakening and the Shaping of Native Cultures in

Southern New England, 1736–1776" (PhD diss., Harvard University, 2008). Also Linford D. Fisher, "'It provd But Temporary, & Short lived': Pequot Affiliation in the First Great Awakening," *Ethnohistory* 59, no. 3 (2012): 465–88.

22. Gregory Evans Dowd, *A Spirited Resistance: The North American Indian Struggle for Unity, 1745–1815* (Baltimore: Johns Hopkins University Press, 1992). See also Alfred A. Cave, *Prophets of the Great Spirit: Native American Revitalization Movements in Eastern North America* (Lincoln: University of Nebraska Press, 2006).

23. It is also helpful to remember that other prior examples of Christian Indian settlements existed in the seventeenth and eighteenth centuries. John Eliot most famously pioneered this model in the mid-seventeenth century with his organization of Indian "Praying Towns" across Massachusetts. As Lisa Brooks has noted, Occom would have been familiar with at least one of these Praying Towns that survived into the eighteenth century: Natick, Massachusetts. Similarly, the creation of Stockbridge, Massachusetts, in the 1730s was another Christian Indian town experiment. But an additional (and often unrecognized) influence would have come from New Jersey. David Brainerd, shortly before his death, relocated the Christian Delawares in central New Jersey (around 160 in mid-1747) to a new town he called Bethel. His brother, John Brainerd, continued his mission at Bethel (later renamed Brotherton) after David's death in 1747. Thomas S. Kidd, *The Great Awakening: The Roots of Evangelical Christianity in Colonial America* (New Haven CT: Yale University Press, 2007), 201. New England Indians who attended Wheelock's school undoubtedly heard of the New Jersey town of Bethel/Brotherton from the Delaware students who also came to study with Wheelock.

24. Tobias Shattock to Eleazar Wheelock, October 2, 1767, *Microfilm Edition of the Papers of Eleazar Wheelock* (Hanover NH: Dartmouth College Library, 1971), 767552. Also printed in James Dow McCallum, *The Letters of Eleazar Wheelock's Indians* (Hanover NH: Dartmouth College Publications, 1932), 207.

25. For a more complete explication of racial dynamics in the founding of Brothertown, see Silverman, *Red Brethren*.

26. Tobias Shattock to Eleazar Wheelock, November 30, 1767, *Wheelock Papers*, 767630.2

27. Laura Murray, "Reading Joseph Johnson," in *To Do Good to My Indian Brethren: The Writings of Joseph Johnson, 1751–1776*, ed. Joseph Johnson and Laura J. Murray (Amherst: University of Massachusetts Press, 1998), 11. Much of the biographical sketch that follows is taken in part from Murray's helpful summary of Johnson's life.

28. Joseph Johnson to Eleazar Wheelock, December 28, 1768, and Samuel Kirkland to Eleazar Wheelock, December 29, 1768, in Johnson and Murray, *To Do Good*, 76, 77. Italics in original.

29. Joseph Johnson to Enquiring friends, or to Strangers, undated but perhaps c. 1773, in Johnson and Murray, *To Do Good*, 192.

30. See Johnson's journals, which begin in October 1771. Johnson and Murray, *To Do Good*, 92ff.

31. Joseph Johnson's Dedication, May 24, 1772, in Johnson and Murray, *To Do Good*, 147. For the open letter, see Joseph Johnson to all Enquiring Friends, in Johnson and Murray, *To Do Good*, 178. Although this document is not dated, in it Johnson notes that he is "at present" employed as a teacher in Farmington, and Johnson's journals record that he starting serving in that capacity on November 23, 1772.

32. November 18, 1772, in Johnson and Murray, *To Do Good*, 151.

33. Johnson's mother, Elizabeth, was a Garrett before she married Joseph Johnson Sr. Although it is not clear, Benjamin Garrett was possibly Elizabeth's brother and therefore a Pequot.

34. February 2, 1772, in Johnson and Murray, *To Do Good*, 133.

35. On Sunday, December 20, 1772, for example, Joseph Sunsaman (Pequot) and Robert Ashpo (Mohegan) arrived and participated in services in the forenoon and afternoon. Johnson and Murray, *To Do Good*, 162.

36. Johnson and Murray, *To Do Good*, 182. Occom was also in attendance. Occom, *Collected Writings*, 165.

37. Joseph Johnson's Speech to the Oneidas, in Johnson and Murray, *To Do Good*, 207.

38. This can be inferred from Johnson's October 1773 letter to all these same communities, in which he says: "Brethren, if the men chosen last Spring [March 1773] be backward to go to the Mohawk Country be so good as to Send others in their room." Farmington Indians to "All our Indian Brethren," October 13, 1773, in Johnson and Murray, *To Do Good*, 200.

39. Farmington Indians to "All our Indian Brethren," October 13, 1773, in Johnson and Murray, *To Do Good*, 198–99.

40. Farmington Indians to "All our Indian Brethren," 200.

41. Samson Occom to Eleazar Wheelock, January 6, 1774, in Occom, *Collected Writings*, 205. Although, oddly enough, Joseph Johnson told the Oneidas in his first speech to them, on January 20, 1774, that nine Indians went to see Sir William Johnson in the fall of 1773. Joseph's letter to the other Indian communities after his return in November 1773, however, indicates that fewer people than he expected went to New York in October. Joseph Johnson's Speech to the Oneidas, January 20, 1774, in Johnson and Murray, *To Do Good*, 208. Also see: To the Indians Concerning Oneida Lands, December 24, 1773, in Johnson and Murray, *To Do Good*, 203–4.

42. Samson Occom to Eleazar Wheelock, January 6, 1774, in Johnson and Murray, *To Do Good*, 205, 205n.

43. To the Indians Concerning Oneida Lands, December 24, 1773, in Johnson and Murray, *To Do Good*, 203–4.

44. See Samson Occom to Eleazar Wheelock, January 6, 1774, and Joseph Johnson's Speech to the Oneidas, January 20, 1774, in Johnson and Murray, *To Do Good*, 209.

45. Johnson and Murray, *To Do Good*, 208.

46. Joseph Johnson to Samson Occom, May 25, 1774, in Johnson and Murray, *To Do Good*, 230–31. The "unmanly" charge is striking but was not entirely uncommon in Native ridicule of the English or other Indian communities. For some seventeenth-century examples of this, see R. Todd Romero, "'Ranging Foresters' and 'Women-Like Men': Physical Accomplishment, Spiritual Power, and Indian Masculinity in Early-Seventeenth-Century New England," *Ethnohistory* 52, no. 2 (2006): 281–329.

47. Quote comes from Johnson and Murray, *To Do Good*, 230–31. The actual document is dated May 2, 1774. Indian Papers, Connecticut State Library, Hartford CT, ser. 1 (A), vol. 2, doc. 193.

48. May 1774; Charles J. Hoadly, ed., *Public Records of Connecticut* (1987), 14:292.

49. Joseph Johnson to Sir William Johnson, July 8, 1774, in Johnson and Murray, *To Do Good*, 239.

50. Entry for August 22, 1774, in Cheryl L. Simmons and William S. Simmons, eds., *Old Light on Separate Ways: The Narragansett Diary of Joseph Fish, 1765–1776* (Hanover NH: University Press of New England, 1982), 107. Ironically enough, however, Sam Niles must not have liked what he saw, for he ended up staying in Rhode Island.

51. Deed to Oneida Lands, October 4, 1774, in Johnson and Murray, *To Do Good*, 242–43.

52. Joseph Johnson to John Rodgers, February 15, 1775, in McCallum, *Letters of Eleazar Wheelock's Indians*, 189.

53. Joseph Johnson to John Rodgers, February 15, 1775, in McCallum, *Letters of Eleazar Wheelock's Indians*, 189. It is interesting to note, however, that the Pequots were making modest gains in their land claims during the same time that planning for the migration was underway. It is tempting to read their reserve as a result of this land renegotiation. The Mashantucket Pequots successfully petitioned the Connecticut General Assembly in May 1773 to have 989 acres (and sixty-eight rods) of land laid out for them, land that had been promised to them by the assembly in 1761. This redrawing of Mashantucket boundaries seems to have satisfied them for a short while. In May 1785, however, the

Mashantucket Pequots once again petitioned the General Assembly, declaring that despite the measures that were taken in 1772 and 1773, "our Tribe find ourselves Interrupted in the Possession of our Lands by your People round about Cutting & Destroying our Timber & Crouding their Improvements in upon our Lands." The ongoing (and in some cases, increased) pressure upon their lands undoubtedly convinced some families and subgroups after the Revolutionary War that such a drastic move westward was necessary. For the 1773 General Assembly decision, see *Records of Connecticut*, 14:130. The original petition can be found in Indian Papers, Connecticut State Library, ser. 1, vol. 2, doc. 243a. For the 1785 petition, see Indian Papers, Connecticut State Library, ser. 1, vol. 2, doc. 248.

54. As quoted in Bernd Peyer, *The Tutor'd Mind: Indian Missionary-Writers in Antebellum America* (Amherst: University of Massachusetts Press, 1997), 81.

55. Kevin McBride has persuasively argued that the general loss of land in the eighteenth century was a "catalyst" for the movement, a contention the various records seem to confirm. McBride, "Shallow Christians" (unpublished manuscript, 2006), 14.

56. Gideon Hawley, September 17, 1761, as quoted in Harold William Blodgett, *Samson Occom* (Hanover NH: Dartmouth College Publications, 1935), 77.

57. Jonathan Trumbull, Trumbull Papers, Collections of the Massachusetts Historical Society, ser. 5, vol. 9, 482.

58. Samson Occom to Samuel Buell, [January] 1773, in Occom, *Collected Writings*, 104.

59. These figures come from an allotment chart in the Hamilton College Archives that date to a 1795 allotment. It is possible the original allotments in the mid-1780s were larger. Brothertown, New York, Allotment of Lands, Hamilton College Archives, Clinton NY.

60. To the Officers of the English Trust for Moor's Indian Charity School, November 10, 1773, in Occom, *Collected Writings*, 108.

61. Joseph Johnson to John Rodgers, February 15, 1775, in McCallum, *Letters of Eleazar Wheelock's Indians*, 189.

62. See Silverman, *Red Brethren*. Also David J. Silverman, "To Become a Chosen People: The Missionary Work and Missionary Spirit of the Brothertown and Stockbridge Indians, 1775–1835" (paper presented at the Annual Meeting of the American Historical Association, Washington DC, 2008).

63. "Some Times I am ready to Conclude," says Occom, speaking of Indians generally, "that they are under Great Curse from God,—But When I look and view the nations of the World I Cant See that they are under Greater Curse than other nations." "I believe all Adamites are under a Curse," Occom concluded.

"The Most Remarkable and Strange Situation and Appearance of Indian Tribes in this Great Continent" (1783). Occom, *Collected Writings*, 58–59.

64. As tallied by the author from the manuscript records at the Connecticut State Library of the First, Second, and East Stonington churches. See Fisher, "'Traditionary Religion'," appendix.

65. Benjamin Uncas to Thomas Fitch, May 18, 1765, in William Samuel Johnson Papers, Connecticut Historical Society. As cited in Johnson and Murray, *To Do Good*, 173, 306n112.

66. Edward Deake to Joseph Fish, December 5, 1765, in Simmons and Simmons, *Old Light on Separate Ways*, 22. Mustees, like mulattoes, were mixed-race individuals.

67. "Memorial of Zachary Johnson, Simon Joyjoy, and the Rest of the Tribe of the Mohegan Indians," May 1774, in Indian Papers, Connecticut State Library, ser. 1, vol. 2, 310.

68. Indian Papers, Connecticut State Library, ser. 1, vol. 2, 312a; *Records of Connecticut*, 14:314.

69. Joseph Johnson to Jonathan Trumbull, October 11, 1773, in Johnson and Murray, *To Do Good*, 196–97.

70. Joseph Johnson to Jonathan Trumbull, October 11, 1773, Johnson and Murray, *To Do Good*, 197. In many ways, this prefigured by two hundred years the same policy that Indian nations implemented in the twentieth century upon receiving U.S. federal recognition and determining who should be considered official members and—more importantly—who gets to share in earnings disbursements from casino profits.

71. Deed to Oneida Lands, October 4, 1774, in Johnson and Murray, *To Do Good*, 242–43.

72. "The claim of Sarah Pendleton," September 26, 1796, Hamilton College Archives.

73. Joseph Johnson's Speech to the Oneidas, January 20, 1774, in Johnson and Murray, *To Do Good*, 206–7.

74. Johnson and Murray, *To Do Good*, 176. See also Alan Taylor, *The Divided Ground: Indians, Settlers, and the Northern Borderland of the American Revolution* (New York: Alfred A. Knopf, 2006). For a rich description of the Oneida towns, see Calloway, *The American Revolution in Indian Country*, 12, 124–25.

75. The date of Johnson's death is unknown; various scholars give it within this time range. For the 1777 date, see Christopher Bickford, *Farmington in Connecticut* (Canaan NH: Phoenix Pub., 1981), 165. Also Johnson and Murray, *To Do Good*, xvii.

76. Occom's journal entries for May 8–17, 1784, in Occom, *Collected Writings*, 285–86. See also Muriel D'Agostino, "Leader of the Broken Tribes—Samson Occom" (BA Honors thesis, Hamilton College, n.d.), 58.

77. Samson Occom to Solomon Welles, September 26, 1784, in Occom, *Collected Writings*, 125.

78. Journal entry for Monday, November 7, 1785, in Occom, *Collected Writings*, 308. Although it is unclear whether there was a definite connection, it is interesting that a Christian Delaware settlement in New Jersey founded in 1759 was also named "Brotherton." George D. Flemming, *Brotherton: New Jersey's First and Only Indian Reservation and the Communities of Shamong and Tabernacle That Followed* (Medford NJ: Plexus Publishing, 2005), ch. 4.

79. Ottery and Ottery, *A Man Called Sampson*, 46. Occom's daughter, Christiana, her children, and her mother-in-law accompanied the first group of Indians to New York in May 1784, but Occom apparently did not move his own household until 1789. See Occom's journal entry for May 25, 1774, in Occom, *Collected Writings*, 286. Brad Jarvis has a helpful graph of this breakdown. See Jarvis, *The Brothertown Nation of Indians*, 114.

80. In September 1784, Occom noted that the Stockbridge Indians (as he calls them) had been to Oneida during the summer "and Planted much Corne," and were planning a larger move in the fall of 1784. Samson Occom to Solomon Welles, September 26, 1784, in Occom, *Collected Writings*, 125. By 1785, when he passed through Stockbridge en route to Oneida, he noted that approximately two-thirds of the Stockbridge Indians had removed to New York. Thursday, September 29, 1785, in Occom, *Collected Writings*, 300.

81. William DeLoss Love, *Samson Occom and the Christian Indians of New England*, 1st Syracuse University Press ed. (Syracuse NY: Syracuse University Press, 2000), 243–46. See also Rachel M. Wheeler, "Women and Christian Practice in a Mahican Village," *Religion and American Culture* 13, no. 1 (2003): 27–67; Rachel M. Wheeler, "Living Upon Hope: Mahicans and Missionaries, 1730–1760" (PhD diss., Yale University, 1999); Corinna Dally-Starna and William A. Starna, "A Comment on 'Mahican Life and Moravian Missions,'" *Northeast Anthropology*, no. 65 (2003): 53–65.

82. McBride, "Shallow Christians," 2.

83. Thomas Commuck, "Sketch of the Brothertown Indians," in *Wisconsin Historical Collections* (Manchester: Wisconsin Historical Society, 1859), 291–98.

| Chapter 5

"Decoying Them Within": Creek Gender Identities and the Subversion of Civilization

Felicity Donohoe

As the eighteenth century drew to a close, a group of American settlers in Tensaw, Alabama, breathed a sigh of relief after narrowly avert-
ing a bloody encounter—and certain death—at the hands of Creek
Indian men. The Creek warriors, determined to resist encroaching
American settlement, were halted by the Creek chief's deputy, Sophia Durant, the elder sister of Alexander McGillivray. Durant, aged
forty-four and only two weeks away from giving birth, rode to Hickory Ground where the recalcitrant chiefs were duly summoned, chas-
tised, and subdued. The Alabama planter and amateur historian Albert
James Pickett described the event:

> In the summer of 1790, while McGillivray was at New-York, the Creeks
> threatened to descend upon the Tensaw settlers, and put the whole
> of them to death. Mrs. Durant mounted a horse, with a negro wom-
> an upon another, and set out from Little river, camped out at night,
> and, on the fourth day, arrived at Hickory Ground, where she assem-
> bled the Chiefs, threatened them with the vengeance of her brother
> upon his return, which caused the arrest of the ringleaders, and put a
> complete stop to their murderous intentions. Two weeks afterwards,
> this energetic and gifted woman was delivered of twins, at the Hick-
> ory Ground.[1]

This account focused on a number of features that reveal something of the character of Sophia Durant. The heroic, Boudicca-like charge while heavily pregnant at an advanced age presents an image of a politically powerful woman, so confident in her authority that she felt comfortable arresting the violent intentions of her kinsmen. Pickett's narrative also reveals how traditionally masculine virtues of physical power, economic success, and respect among warriors had significant implications for Native American women.[2] With few archival sources available to allow the historian to reconstruct the lives of Creek women, such accounts afford a rare look at the influential Native American women who operated in the Southeast during the early years of the American republic. Even if Durant only attracted historical attention because she displayed exceptional leadership qualities, her story allows us to reexamine changes in socioeconomic and cultural life for indigenous women in the American South during the early republic.

Sophia Durant was a member of the powerful Wind clan, a matrilineal society famous for its strong female leaders.[3] One of these women, Sehoy Marchand, was Sophia Durant's grandmother. Marchand married her first husband, Captain Francois Marchand from Fort Toulouse, in 1721. She gave birth to another influential Wind clan woman, Sehoy II, Durant's mother, who married Scottish trader Lachlan McGillivray and had a number of children: three with Lachlan and others with Malcolm McPherson.[4] With traditional matrilineal powers on her side, Sehoy McGillivray used her status as clan matron to engineer a marriage for her daughter Jeannet to a European man, and produced Chief Alexander McGillivray, the youngest of the three.[5]

Wind clan women were thus well acquainted with the benefits of interracial unions. Like other southeastern Native Americans, these unions became such a common occurrence that European observers complained that Indian women exercised too much power in selecting one, and sometimes multiple, husbands. For Native American women, however, marriage to European outsiders reflected their influence over issues such as marriage and clan adoption. Indigenous women would have gone into such marriages aware that the children produced by the union would inherit their clan status, with maternal uncles providing the educational and material support that Europeans associated with a father's responsibilities.[6]

When in 1770 Sophia, at the age of twenty-four, married a white man, the sixteen-year-old trader Benjamin Durant, she did so safe in the knowledge that her children would inherit her clan identity.[7] The indomitable Durant, therefore, was representative of a number of crucial aspects of Creek female identity during the late eighteenth and early nineteenth centuries. Although her possession of slaves, wealth, and military command was perhaps exceptional, her marital choice and political clout were not particularly unusual among Creek women. After all, Durant grew up witnessing Indian-European marriage alliances and acquiring insights into colonial society from the white men who married in to Creek society. Her actions and decisions, moreover, were endorsed by tradition and matrilineal privilege.

However, by the end of the century those traditions were under assault both from outside Creek society and from within. Creek women thus found themselves innovating traditions that had long given meaning to Creek life, innovations that were designed to meet the overwhelming pressures from within as well as outside Creek society. Change was afoot, and it was not necessarily to the advantage of Creek women.

For Creek women like Sophia Durant, the pressures that impacted their lives were twofold. One set came in the form of the desire by the new American republic to incorporate Indians into their vision of an industrious, "civilized," and masculine nation peopled by independent, "heroic artisans" and their supportive wives and offspring.[8] The American male archetype of the early republic was "vigorous, manly and direct, not effete and corrupt like the supposed Europeans. He was plain rather than ornamented, rugged rather than luxury seeking, a liberty loving common man or natural gentleman rather than an aristocratic oppressor or servile minion."[9] Such a vision of masculinity required indigenous women to relinquish their traditional rights to authority and submit to both their husbands and President Washington's Indian policy of "expansion with honor."[10]

The second challenge to Creek women came from within Native American society. At the same time that the American republic came into existence, the Nativist Indian movement sought to undermine the Euro-American "civilization" imperative, demanding a return to traditional practices and lifestyles, and insisting that Indian women also return to indigenous men as first-choice husbands and fathers.[11] Both these developments spanned the former mainland colonies and affected the lives of the Shawnees, Cherokees, Choctaws, Delawares or Lenapes, Senecas, and Wyandots, in addition to the Creeks.[12]

In this context, Sophia Durant represented an unusual—yet in many ways typical—Indian woman. She was unusual in that she was recorded by name in historical documents and has a position within that record that underscores the significance of prevailing gendered ideals in late eighteenth- and early nineteenth-century America. Although a multitude of Creek male identities are acknowledged in the sources, such as warrior, shaman, chief, and elder, most Creek women are collectively represented simply as "women."[13] As a result, indigenous women share a one-dimensional and homogenous set of historical experiences as "women" that disregards the significance of age, social role, material conditions, marital status, and/or maternal circumstance in shaping women's lives.[14]

Recovering the complexity of Creek female life and identity is hampered by the scarcity of archival sources, many of which were authored by male travelers, traders, and Indian agents. The narratives these authors constructed were overwhelmingly shaped by their patriarchal worldview, a perspective that assumed the subordination and impoverishment of women within Indian nations.[15] Although historians have observed the gendered nature of these narratives, how Native American women understood and constructed their own identities remains underdeveloped.[16] This chapter emphasizes the complex, fluid, and adaptable nature of Creek female identities during the late eighteenth and early nineteenth centuries. Creek women, like Sophia Durant, struggled to both retain and construct their own sense of self (or soul) that would help them cope with internal and external social pressures at a turning point in the settler colonial history of North America.

Sophia Durant, long accustomed to wielding social and political power among her own people, represents an indigenous woman forced to grapple with Euro-American gender ideals at the end of the eighteenth century. Bridging old and new worlds, Durant accepted some of the advantages of "civilized" life while rejecting less palatable ones. Additionally, she modified her Creek matrilineal values to incorporate American patriarchal practices that benefited her life. Following the American Revolution, these gender ideals emphasized male ambition, independence, and controlled aggression. Such qualities were well suited to life as an independent farmer and to participation in public and political life. In contrast, the ideal American woman was a dutiful "wife"; she gave birth to and raised children who would grow to become virtuous republican citizens.

The United States government's Indian agents, in addition to missionaries, were informed in their work among the Creeks by these American gender ideals, which clashed with Creek gender norms in stark ways. Speaking to the Creeks in 1782, John Martin, governor of Georgia, further emphasized the apparent dependency and powerlessness of indigenous women and the dire situation encountered by those who had lost their husbands, saying, "We always desired you to remain at home quietly and Peaceably, and to mind your hunting & Support your women and children in peace & happiness."[17] Still preferring to hunt rather than farm, Creek men adhered to principles that mandated extended periods away from home for hunting. This traditional way of life determined material and economic independence for women and allowed, as Durant's life demonstrates, a significant degree of female authority over males.[18]

Often credited with bringing civilization to the Creeks, Indian agent Benjamin Hawkins, a former U.S. senator and confidant of Presidents Washington and Jefferson, spent almost thirty years among them.[19] Although his ultimate goal was to seek more effective means of civilizing Indian males through information acquired from, and

cooperation with, Indian women, his time spent with them also provided striking insights into the changes Native women underwent
in this period. For the most part the women are presented as dynamic, strong individuals directing their own fates as much as possible.
Nonetheless, the literature generated from Hawkins's accounts preferred to characterize women as more gentle and malleable.[20] Samuel L. Mitchill MD, writing in the *American Monthly Magazine and
Critical Review* in 1818, recognized Hawkins's particular success with
women, attributing it to his ability to woo them with gentle words,
"soothing arts," "kind treatment," and a promise to help them pro-
cure provisions and clothes.[21] Hawkins did appear to be instrumental
in introducing weaving and spinning to many willing Indian wom-
en, among other skills such as counting and weighing.

However, British and American officials, aided by ambitious settlers, had worked hard throughout the eighteenth century to promote
the virtues of a civilized life to the Creek people and had laid considerable groundwork for the homogenization of Native women.[22] By the
time of Hawkins's arrival, then, women were well versed in a number of Euro-American roles in addition to other less "delicate" jobs
as alcohol traders, food and fur traders, shamans, council speakers,
warriors, and healers.[23] Hawkins's softly-softly approach was therefore either unnecessary or nonexistent, and any "success" with wom-
en could be attributed more to their versatility and flexible response
to change, and less to Hawkins's "soothing arts."

Sophia Durant's life story straddled "traditional" and "civilized"
lifeways. From a Euro-American perspective of Indian society, indigenous women were alternately characterized as prostitutes and wives,
killers and nurturers, mothers and mercenaries, drudges and queens.
Few Creek women were said to possess elements of all these traits.[24]
Durant, though, came close.

In her role as mother, Durant had her first child at the age of twenty-
nine. By 1796, the year Benjamin Hawkins arrived in Creek country,
she had given birth to eleven children.[25] The age of twenty-nine was
quite advanced to have a first child in this period, and it is possible
she had married another man prior to meeting Benjamin Durant.

Benjamin was a French Huguenot trader from South Carolina who met "pretty, dark-eyed Sophia" after "coming to her mother's house." He won a brawl to prove his exceptional fighting skills and then went to live on the estate of Sophia Durant's father, Lachlan McGillivray, before marrying Sophia in 1770.[26]

Their married life reflected the malleability of gender ideals in the Native South during the early republic. Benjamin was successful in business, becoming a wealthy man; but in other areas, Benjamin and Sophia's marriage ran counter to early republican gender ideals.[27] For instance, during the Siege of Savannah in 1779, with her son Lachlan and husband, Benjamin, away fighting, Sophia asserted her authority by single-handedly managing the family business concerns. During the Redstick War with the Americans and their Choctaw allies in 1813, Sophia Durant took a similarly prominent role.[28] Such public engagement in business matters suggests that Durant was determined to shape specific aspects of her own identity, irrespective of emerging American gender norms. Indeed, she appears to have exploited the flexibility of these evolving ideals.[29]

Despite appearing to opt out of a traditional matrilineal Creek identity by marrying Benjamin, Durant's informal status as a trader suggests that she cultivated a sense of independence not entirely out of step with traditional Creek gender roles and in preference to an identity as a "helpmate" to her husband.[30] In other words, Durant subverted "civilized" values to help her rearticulate matrilineal privilege to suit the changing world around her. Superficially, Durant was Benjamin's wife; in her own construction of self—and borrowing from Euro-American and Creek ideals—Durant likely saw herself as a Creek matriarch who enjoyed significant tribal and economic authority.[31] By appropriating Euro-American ideals, Durant transformed them in practice and, in the process, undermined patriarchy's effectiveness as a tool of Anglo-American "civilization."[32]

Not all Creek women traded or worked in ways that enabled them to enjoy the type of authority that Sophia Durant exercised. Most Creek women (and men for that matter), scratched out a living by engaging in subsistence agriculture, trading small quantities of fowl and hogs, or weaving baskets and making clothing, and hunting for additional meat. An example of this hardscrabble existence was provided by Edmond Atkin, who in 1757 reported the situation of one friendly Indian, Aleck, mico of Cussitah: "In truth he was poor & unable to maintain his family in his own country, in the manner they had lived. His Wives therefore were often complaining, that they did not live so well there as they had done."[33] Aleck had requested twenty cows and calves or a stock of forty head of cattle to start off his civilized life: not an inconsiderable demand. Although he may have sought advancement for his own ends, it appeared that he was unable to hunt to provide enough for his wives and children, and they had pressured him to change and adapt in order to respond to their needs and overcome the perils of poverty.

Aleck's possession of multiple wives presents one of the most obvious points of departure for Creek and white masculine ideals. As a man with multiple wives he practiced polygamy and had undoubtedly been successful in hunting or business: one simply could not afford to provide for several wives and children otherwise. The women, too, appeared to be traditionally Creek in that they had accepted life within a polygamous marriage. However, his capitulation to their demands for cattle revealed how Creek women were a significant force in shaping their own fortunes by adopting practices such as cattle raising. Their insistence on Aleck's economic advancement could certainly be viewed as traditional, but on marrying a man of wealth, his wives would have expected him to maintain his wealth in order to honor marital commitments—and he was evidently disappointing in this department, hence the demand for change. His inability to recover, or seek divorce, would have been perceived as a failure of his masculine Creek duties, and although his failings would not have lowered his wives' social status (their status derived from their clan, not their husband), it did present an inconvenience for women who had grown accustomed to, or had been promised, certain material standards.

The account does present a rather clichéd view of a group of nagging women and their hapless, henpecked husband, but their concern was that he provide for his *children*, rather than themselves. This was a fundamental responsibility of fathers and is a crucial distinction in comprehending the priorities and events that helped determine social and economic change at the hands of women. Whether farming as the method of his advancement was his or his wives' choice is unknown, but given the aversion to farming and cattle practices by Creek men, it is probable the wives had advanced this option and would have undertaken the cattle raising as an extension of their agricultural practices.

Finally, Aleck's situation also provides some insight into the rather weakened position of a male within a polygamous marriage. He was subject to collective pressure from his wives and to the ever-present but less obvious pressure from the community. Knowing that their husband was an ally of the British and a man of influence among the Lower Creeks, Aleck's wives were aware of the leverage they held and used it to full advantage, initially requesting land within the white towns but eventually remaining among the Creeks. It was also notable that his wives were united in their demands, and that Aleck and Edmond Atkin were the tools to realize their ambitions rather than obstacles. In this interesting case, the women provided the focus and impetus for change, using social customs and gendered pressures to force Euro-American practices on their husband. The blend of traditional femininities with a modernizing vision shows a fluid and flexible outlook on the changing colonial landscape, and contrasts with Aleck's restricted and weakened masculine position. Fortunately for Aleck, he could have saved his Creek masculinity by refraining from farming and handing the reins of production over to his wives.

As forerunners to Sophia Durant and her trading enterprise, Aleck's wives indicate the roots of female ambition and the determination of women to take advantage of opportunities as they arose. Forty years later, however, Creek women remained critical of male shortcomings, asserting that "they performed almost all the labor, the men assisted but little and that in the corn."[34] For women who had children to feed, poverty may have prompted them to seek other ways to survive, and some hunted with their husbands, leaving their offspring at home for up to three months with an elder child as supervisor.[35] Creek historian Claudio Saunt has argued that the increasing masculinization of the fur trade throughout the eighteenth century eclipsed women's contribution in this arena.[36] Although some women and men did hunt together, women's exclusion from the trade led them to seek alternative means of acquiring the goods now denied to them, such as producing baskets and other saleable goods. Other women may have used different avenues. On August 16, 1798, R. Thomas, a clerk to the Indian agency, reported that some Indian warriors and young men had crossed the boundary lines and plundered houses, taking "household utensils" and "children's cloathing."[37] These men sought goods for their own trade purposes, of course, and they were likely "trading" with women, too. But women may also have raised "thieving" parties as well as war parties (despite the possibility of punishment from tribal leaders) and demanded necessities such as children's clothes.[38] The danger of such a raid would have made it an attractive enterprise to adventure-seeking younger men also. For women seeking to avoid material poverty, the call-to-arms was an effective use of matrilineal privilege.

Lacking winter clothes and blankets, and living in impoverished abodes, Creek women seemed poorer than the neighboring Cherokees in Euro-American eyes.[39] However, Creek women like Durant did not see themselves in this light—certainly not enough to justify swapping her particular brand of matrilineal privilege for patriarchal protection and a finer house. Durant's priorities lay less with household or domestic concerns and focused more on her own financial enterprises. She differed from the generations of women before her in that she no longer physically worked in her own fields, which were now worked by her slaves.[40] The cultivation of the earth held a deep spiritual and cosmological significance for Creek women and other Indian nations, a place where female power was both derived and recognized, and in this sense Durant had adopted a modern means of cultivating both the earth and her powers.[41]

Durant may have rejected the immediate power that working the land offered her, but she retained the authority of her clan matron position, keeping one foot in the past and another in the future as she navigated social changes and selected suitable marriage partners for her children to advance familial interests. To accomplish these ends, Creek women of Durant's social standing actively engineered marriages. Traveler Louis Milfort, for example, claimed he had little interest in Creek women but agreed to marry one of Sophia's sisters—as encouraged by female members of her family—recognizing that it afforded him full acceptance in the nation and that it pleased Alexander McGillivray, brother to his bride, Jeannet.

Despite Milfort's somewhat reluctant acceptance of the women's proposal, the account suggests that they left him very little option but to consent to the marriage, fully aware of their bargaining position and quite determined that the relationship should be at least physically consummated, despite his blushes.[42] The arrangement of marriages to specially selected white men highlights the conflation of past and present social systems where matrilineal privilege allowed patriarchal trade and economic practices to gain traction. Women who arranged marriages on behalf of their daughters still expected obedience and respect for their authority, and such decisions were made with an eye to their own futures as much as their daughters'. Hawkins himself was faced with a determined matchmaking mother, and when he declined the invitation to marry her daughter, he explained his reasons by extolling the benefits of a Euro-American marriage. His claims fell on deaf ears. Convinced of matrilineal superiority, "She would not consent that the woman and children should be under the direction of the father, and the negotiation ended there."[43]

Despite historical records that often refer to older women in denigrating terms, matrons continued to hold considerable power, especially postmenopausal women who now claimed an enhanced spiritual and social authority with their advanced age.[44] The maneuverings of these women had the potential to cause unrest, particularly when dealing with younger generations. Hawkins noted that the children seemed "exceedingly" afraid of white people, and when he asked the mothers for the reason, they claimed the older townspeople had remembered the white people from previous violent encounters and "had been much horrified by the whites, that the old people remembered their former situation and sufferings and frequently spoke of them. That these tales were listened to by the children and made an impression which showed itself in the manner I had observed."[45]

Stories of this nature emphasized how a traditional pastime and generational division among women about what civilization could offer for their individual needs and circumstances produced new divisions in Creek society. This should not be confused with enmity or hostility among women, which characterized many male differences, such as those that became evident in the Nativist movement.[46] Within the Nativist movement, different views on how best to deal with rapid social changes resulted in opposition and bloodshed between opposing groups of men: those who supported conciliation and accommodation with whites, and those who rejected it. Conversely, a variety of feminine identities seemed to coexist relatively harmoniously, as several generations shared different views on the benefits of Euro-American civilization. Older women appeared to retain more traditional values, and although they had no mouths to feed, they expected care from relatives and obedience.

Women of Durant's generation had different needs—many of her children were grown, but she had a commercial enterprise to steer and a political voice.[47] As a woman of standing, Durant's authority also came with advanced age and was reflected in the weighty words of other matrons who could be scathing and contemptuous, sometimes of Indian men and occasionally of white men, too.[48] Creek women thus expressed their displeasure for white men in terms such as these:

> When white men have come into our nation, they have never studied the good of the women, nor endeavoured to better their oppressed condition. All they have hitherto done is to make our situation more wretched. They have employed every art to raise and shorten our petticoats, and have thereby left us more exposed and naked than they found us.... You, father, commiserate our condition.... You come to lengthen our petticoats, and extend them over us from the hips to the ankles. Father, we will follow your advice: speak and we will obey.[49]

Such commentaries demonstrate how Creek women identified themselves as "oppressed"; they also highlight how Creek women were critical of the duplicitous behavior of white men. Thus, accepting the
"gift" of "civilization" was conditional and based on an appreciation
and respect for Creek social roles.

Many younger Creek women saw white men and American civilization as vehicles to help them continue their self-sufficient lives.
The "lengthening" of their petticoats suggested a welcome return to
their previous dignified state vis-à-vis greater authority by separating
their experiences and needs from Indian males' concerns. Durant's
identity, for example, was rooted in her matrilineal status, but Euro-
Americans like Hawkins preferred to focus on her "poor and dirty"
state and the "small hut" she lived in, giving only a token nod to her
clan matron role.[50] Other Creek women sought out wage labor, and in
the eyes of Euro-Americans, those who did so had forfeited an identity
of poverty-stricken "savage" for that of industrious wage earner. However, these working women continued to assert their economic role as
yet another face of the fluid matrilineal role. The matriline reinforced
their Native identity, not their position as a civilized wage earner.

Although sources detailing the changing patterns of Creek women's
work, politics, and social life are sparse, some conclusions can be drawn
about the reworking of indigenous gender identities. An overview of
the century reveals that women who had traditionally worked the land
alongside their various other roles as shamans, council leaders, traders, mothers, and matrons now viewed the land and its female power
in different terms. Though women still sought sustenance from their
fields and gardens, those who were able to do so extended those lands
and began to include cattle and other animals within enclosures, despite potential problems with theft.[51] Women's cosmological identification with the land altered the concept of "production," taking on
much wider implications. No longer merely for subsistence farming,
land was also for cattle, cotton, and other livestock. Other women were
more restricted in available land, however, and by the time of Hawkins's
arrival, many towns and their associated lands had become smaller.

Some plots rarely produced enough food for a woman and her family, and women subsequently extended their skills to include more manufactures to boost finances, allowing them to purchase food and others goods and offering opportunities for active engagement in the colonial and early American economy.[52] When husbands were away on extended hunts, these women became the sole providers for their children, adding to the burden of childcare provision and undermining the importance of adult males in children's lives. As hunts extended farther and lasted longer, even the visible presence of males in towns was diminished, except for elders or those who adopted cattle raising.[53]

At the other end of the Creek matrilineal scale, women with particular status utilized servants and slaves for financial advancement. Mary Musgrove, for example, was educated and literate, and did not appear to pick up a hoe in her lifetime, yet her manipulation of matrilineal authority was evident in the way she achieved financial security and social status, acting as a valuable aid to General James Oglethorpe in negotiations with the Creeks.[54] Furthermore, her marriages to white men such as her servant Jacob Matthews allowed her to overcome a number of patriarchal practices that excluded full access to her wealth based on her gender under colonial law.[55] Durant, some sixty years later, still reflected matrilineal entitlement as a wealthier, higher-status "colonial" woman with eighty slaves, a plantation under her control, and a powerful younger brother within her clan. Although women such as Musgrove and Durant were far less prominent by the end of the century, evidence of female authority and ability to manipulate clan fortunes was still present into the nineteenth century.[56]

Perhaps the biggest change for women was the sheer volume of white men who moved into the Southeast over the century. These men presented greater marital options for Creek women. Some women married to white men abandoned their place in the matriarchy, but they often chose to flex their rights within a patriarchal marriage while also keeping close connections with kinswomen, old and young. However, when Creek towns reduced in size and women moved into more remote areas with their families, chances for daily contact with other women outside collective paid farming, weaving, or spinning work

were more limited. These women, therefore, remained conduits of kinship connections and extended their economic and familial authority into Euro-American households. While contact with white men
had its drawbacks, these women took advantage of opportunities often with an eye to their children's (and therefore their clan's) status,
and they subsequently adopted potentially useful skills. Whether this
was education (as in Musgrove's case), spinning, language, or food-
production talents, there was no evidence of conflict among wom-
en regarding their personal choices. This differed from men, whose
choices were limited to traditional masculinities versus concession
to civilization, a choice underscored by the rise of Nativism. Notable
for their flexibility and willingness to accommodate new customs,
matrilines were a means to expand the repertoire of female identities, withstanding a great deal of change while retaining essential Indian feminine values.[57]

Notes

The chapter title, "Decoying Them Within," is from James Adair, *The History of
the American Indians; Particularly Those Nations Adjoining to the Mississippi East
and West Florida, Georgia, South and North Carolina and Virginia* (London: E. &
C. Dilly, 1775), 145. When Adair asked a Chickasaw man the reason for harsh pun-
ishments for women, he claimed that with "the lurking enemy for ever pelting
them without, and the women decoying them within . . . all their beloved brisk
warriors would soon be spoiled, and their habitations turned to a wild waste."
Unwittingly, he revealed the extent to which women's decisions affected the fortunes of the nation.

1. Albert James Pickett, *History of Alabama, and Incidentally of Georgia and
Mississippi, from the Earliest Period* (Charleston: Walker and James, 1851), 2:127.

2. E. Anthony Rotundo, *American Manhood: Transformations in Masculinity from the Revolution to the Modern Era* (New York: Basic Books, 1993), 10–28.

3. Pickett, *History of Alabama*, 73; William Bartram, *William Bartram on the
Southeastern Indians*, ed. Gregory A. Waselkov and Kathryn E. Holland Braund
(Lincoln: University of Nebraska Press, 1995), 189; Michael D. Green, "Mary Musgrove: Creating a New World," in *Sifters: Native American Women's Lives*, ed. Theda Perdue (Oxford: Oxford University Press, 2001), 30.

4. Gregory A. Waselkov, *A Conquering Spirit: Fort Mims and the Redstick War
of 1813–1814* (Tuscaloosa: University of Alabama Press, 2006), 37.

5. Louis LeClerc Milfort, *Memoirs; or a Quick Glance at my Various Travels and my Sojourn in the Creek Nation* (Paris, 1802), ch. 54, http://homepages.rootsweb.ancestry.com/~cmamcrk4/mlfrttoc.html.

6. Theda Perdue, *Cherokee Women: Gender and Culture Change, 1700–1835* (Lincoln: University of Nebraska Press, 1998), 178; Claudio Saunt, *A New Order of Things: Property, Power, and the Transformation of the Creek Indians, 1733–1816* (New York: Cambridge University Press, 1999), 89; Gregory D. Smithers, "The 'Pursuits of the Civilized Man': Race and the Meaning of Civilization in the United States and Australia, 1790s–1850s," *Journal of World History* 20, no. 2 (2009): 245–72.

7. Waselkov, *A Conquering Spirit*, 37. Primary sources often describe the early marriages of Indian women, usually in their teens. See John Lawson, *A New Voyage to Carolina* (London, 1709), 29, http://docsouth.unc.edu/nc/lawson/lawson.html.

8. Michael S. Kimmel, "Masculinity as Homophobia" in *Race, Class, and Gender in the United States: An Integrated Study*, ed. Paula S. Rothenberg, 7th ed. (New York: Worth, 2007), 89.

9. Douglass C. Baynton, "Disability and the Justification of Inequality in American History," in Rothenberg, *Race, Class, and Gender*, 96.

10. Thomas Jefferson, *Notes on the State of Virginia* (London, 1787), 101–2. For discussion of "expansion with honor," see Gregory D. Smithers, *Science, Sexuality, and Race in the United States and Australia, 1780s–1890s* (New York: Routledge, 2009), 25–27.

11. David Eugene Wilkins, "The Criminal Code of Tenskwatawa (Shawnee Prophet c.1805)," in *Documents of Native American Political Development: 1500s to 1933* (Oxford: Oxford University Press, 2009), 48–50; John Sugden, "Early Pan-Indianism; Tecumseh's Tour of the Indian Country, 1811–1812," *American Indian Quarterly* 10, no. 4 (1986): 275; Gregory Evans Dowd, "Thinking and Believing: Nativism and Unity in the Ages of Pontiac and Tecumseh" in *American Encounters: Natives and Newcomers from European Contacts to Indian Removal, 1500–1850*, ed. Peter C. Mancall and James H. Merrell (New York: Routledge, 2000), 380–403. For details on traditional clan structures, see John R. Swanton, *The Indian Tribes of North America* (Washington DC: Smithsonian Institution, 1952).

12. Dowd, "Thinking and Believing," 380–403.

13. Often "women" are found in older secondary sources listed under indexes. More modern scholarship devotes chapters to women's experiences rather than as participants throughout the narratives. For example, see Saunt, *A New Order of Things*, 139–63.

14. Linda Stone and Nancy P. McKee, eds., *Gender and Culture in America* (New Jersey: Prentice Hall, 1999), 23.

15. Jefferson, *Notes*, 101–2; Benjamin Hawkins, "Letters of Benjamin Hawkins" in *The Collected Works of Benjamin Hawkins, 1796–1810*, ed. H. Thomas Foster (Tuscaloosa: University of Alabama Press, 2003), 43.

16. For some examples on the higher profile afforded to Indian women's history, see Gunlög Fur, *A Nation of Women: Gender and Colonial Encounters among the Delaware* (Philadelphia: University of Pennsylvania Press, 2009); James Axtell, ed., *The Indian Peoples of Eastern America: A Documentary History of the Sexes* (New York: Oxford University Press, 1981); Perdue, *Cherokee Women*; Helen C. Rountree, "Powhatan Indian Women: The People Captain John Smith Barely Saw," *Ethnohistory* 45, no. 1 (1998): 1–29.

17. Governor John Martin Letter Books, "19th July, 1782, To the Tallassee King & the Head Men and Warriors of the Upper and Lower Creek Nation," in "Official Letters of Governor John Martin, 1782–1783," *Georgia Historical Quarterly* 1, no. 4 (1917): 313.

18. Hawkins, *Letters*, 20, 21, 28, 29, 52, 56; Waselkov, *A Conquering Spirit*, 22.

19. Hawkins, *Collected Works*, vii.

20. For a more detailed discussion on this topic and conceptions of appropriate or desired female behavior, see Mary Beth Norton, *Liberty's Daughters: The Revolutionary Experience of American Women, 1750–1800* (Ithaca NY: Cornell University Press, 1996), 110–14.

21. Samuel L. Mitchill MD, "Progress of the Human Mind from Rudeness to Refinement: Exemplified in the Methods Pursued by Col. Benjamin Hawkins to Civilise Certain Tribes of Savages," *American Monthly Magazine and Critical Review* 3, no. 5 (September 1818): 359.

22. Robbie Franklyn Ethridge, *Creek Country: The Creek Indians and Their World* (Chapel Hill: University of North Carolina Press, 2003), 149.

23. Alcohol and trading: Peter C. Mancall, *Deadly Medicine: Indians and Alcohol in Early America* (Ithaca NY: Cornell University Press, 1995), 57; Bartram, *The Southeastern Indians*, 65; Kathryn E. Holland Braund, *Deerskins and Duffels: The Creek Indian Trade with Anglo-America, 1685–1815* (Lincoln: University of Nebraska Press, 1993), 75, 77. Official speaking: Pickett, *History of Alabama*, 127; Gretchen M. Bataille, ed., *Native American Women, A Biographical Dictionary* (New York: Garland Publishing, 1993), 180–81, 272–73. Warriors: Henry Timberlake, *The Memoirs of Lt. Henry Timberlake: The Story of a Soldier, Adventurer, and Emissary to the Cherokees, 1756–1765*, ed. Duane H. King (Cherokee NC: Museum of the Cherokee Indian Press, 2007), 36; Horatio Bardwell Cushman, *History of the Choctaw, Chickasaw, and Natchez Indians* (Greenville TX: Headlight, 1899), 335; Bernard Romans, *A Concise Natural History of East and West Florida* (New York, 1776), 75. Healers: Cushman, *History of the Choctaw*, 416.

24. Romans, *A Concise Natural History*, 41, 43; Diron D'Artaguiette, "Journal

of Diron D'Artaguiette," in *Travels in the American Colonies*, ed. Newton D. Mereness (New York: Macmillan, 1916), 73; Lawson, *A New Voyage*, 174; Cushman, *History of the Choctaw*, 232; John Pope, *A Tour through the Southern and Western Territories of the United States of North America* (Richmond, 1792), 60; Bartram, *The Southeastern Indians*, 47.

25. Hawkins, *Letters*, 43.

26. Waselkov, *A Conquering Spirit*, 40.

27. Pickett, *History of Alabama*, 127; Waselkov, *A Conquering Spirit*, 36. Alexander became chief in 1783. Durant's status and role as interpreter would have increased her political profile thereafter.

28. Pickett, *History of Alabama*, 126, 322–23; George Cary Eggleston, *Red Eagle and the Wars with the Creek Indians of Alabama* (New York: Dodd, Mead, 1878), 221; Waselkov, *A Conquering Spirit*, 166–67.

29. Pickett, *History of Alabama*, 126–27. For other examples of changing roles, see Holland Braund, *Deerskins and Duffels*, 181; Waselkov, *A Conquering Spirit*, 39; Ethridge, *Creek Country*, 143–45.

30. Bartram, *The Southeastern Indians*, 77.

31. Referring to Durant's authority and business skills, Hawkins said, "She and her sister Mrs. Weatherford keep the command absolute of everything from their husbands." Hawkins, *Letters*, 43.

32. Hawkins, *Letters*, 20.

33. Edmond Atkin to Governor Henry Ellis, January 25, 1760, Henry Ellis Papers, 1757–1760, MS 942, Georgia Historical Society, Savannah. Aleck's wives were Yuchi but matrilineal. Swanton, *The Indian Tribes*, 118.

34. Hawkins, *Letters*, 21.

35. Hawkins was entertained by the young daughters of a hunting couple who acted as hosts in the absence of their parents. Hawkins, *Letters*, 23.

36. Saunt, *A New Order*, 144.

37. Hawkins, *Letters*, 497.

38. Hawkins, *Letters*, 464. One Indian woman and a man were held responsible for the death of a man named Harrison in retaliation for an earlier killing. Although the woman had not struck the blow, she had most likely raised the war party and thus her role was deemed central to the affair.

39. Hawkins, *Letters*, 21, 28, 29.

40. Hawkins, *Letters*, 43.

41. Dowd, "Thinking and Believing," 388.

42. Milfort, *Memoirs*, ch. 54.

43. Hawkins, *Letters*, 85.

44. Perdue, *Cherokee Women*, 36, 39.

45. Hawkins, *Letters*, 23.

46. For more discussion on this, see Karl Davis, "'Remember Fort Mims': Reinterpreting the Origins of the Creek War," *Journal of the Early Republic* 22, no. 4 (2002): 611–36; Theron A. Nunez Jr., "Creek Nativism and the Creek War of 1813–1814," *Ethnohistory* 5, no. 1 (1958): 1–47; Dowd, "Thinking and Believing," 388; Gregory Evans Dowd, *A Spirited Resistance: The North American Indian Struggle for Unity, 1745–1815* (Baltimore: Johns Hopkins University Press, 1993), 154–60, 169.

47. Hawkins, *Letters*, 43.

48. Perdue, *Cherokee Women*, 36, 39; Hawkins, *Letters*, 85; Pickett, *History of Alabama*, 127; Allen D. Candler, *Colonial Records of the State of Georgia*, August 10, 1749 (Atlanta: Franklin Printing and Publishing Company, 1906), 260. Mrs. Bosomworth was Mary Musgrove of the Creeks. Her sense of authority is very evident in this entry.

49. Mitchill, "Progress of the Human Mind," 360.

50. Hawkins, *Letters*, 43.

51. Hawkins, *Letters*, 31, 32; Holland Braund, *Deerskins and Duffels*, 76–80.

52. Hawkins, *Letters*, 20–23.

53. Hawkins, *Letters*, 22, 30.

54. Bataille, *Native American Women*, 180.

55. For examples of women who maneuvered around colonial law and gender tradition, see Ben Marsh, "The Very Sinews of a New Colony: Demographic Determinism and the History of Early Georgia Women, 1732–1752," in *Gender, Race, and Religion in the Colonization of the Americas*, ed. Nora E. Jaffary (Hampshire: Ashgate Publishing, 2007), 39–53.

56. Waselkov believes Sophia Durant's daughter Elizabeth persuaded her siblings to adopt the Redsticks' cause: Waselkov, *A Conquering Spirit*, 39, 166–67.

57. Anthropologist Linda Stone demonstrates that matrilineal societies are notable by their flexibility and power-sharing, thus improving their abilities to withstand a great deal of change. Linda Stone, *Kinship and Gender: An Introduction* (Boulder CO: Westview Press, 1997).

Part 2

Asserting Native Identities through Politics, Work, and Migration

Chapter 6

Mastering Language
Liberty, Slavery, and Native Resistance in the
Early Nineteenth-Century South

James Taylor Carson

Centuries ago, the people who inhabited the region we know today as the American South encountered for the first time a different people who had come from Europe to take gold, slaves, and other commodities from their land and deliver to them the one faith that would, to the newcomers' minds, save their souls. The men who represented the clans, towns, and confederacies that encountered them, however, saw those outsiders who hoveled by the sea as useful if uncouth people. Nonetheless, they often, but not always, spoke to them graciously in a language rich with hospitality, welcome, and belonging. Such words were invariably accompanied by bowls of food to share and by displays of sacred items to open the straight white paths that had always carried good intentions between one people and another. On one occasion, for example, a Yamacraw leader's wife presented the founders of Georgia two bottles, one containing milk and one containing honey, to welcome them to their promised land. Two delegates from the Creek town of Coweta likewise told Georgia's founders a vivid story that began in the hole in the ground from which they had crawled and the red rivers they had crossed on their long walk before they found the smooth and clear white paths that had brought them to their homeland and that now promised to open before James Oglethorpe and his fellow trustees as well. In talks with the governor of South Carolina,

Cherokee diplomats passed around a white wing as a token of their
new peace with their Creek neighbors, while Chickasaw diplomats
beseeched the English in Charles Town to assuage their needs and to
protect their women and children as would be expected of any close
friend. Choctaws meanwhile invoked the powers of white earth, white
wings, and sacred fire to bind them to their new neighbors.[1]

If, however, the invaders denied the offers of food and welcome
or turned their backs on the good feelings that white objects promised, then sharp words, or worse, hatchets would follow and open
crooked red paths that bespoke enmity and perhaps even war. In either the white or the red case, however, the expectations and rules
of engagement in the colonial South were rooted in indigenous symbols and forms of knowledge where memory, agreement, and whole-
ness challenged European assumptions about literacy, hierarchy, and
separation. Those people who had come with such high aspirations
and imperial convictions had little choice but to comply with their
hosts until such time as their press of numbers and control of trade
enabled them to attempt to turn the tables.[2]

In 1793, when Eli Whitney invented the cotton gin that made up-
land cotton a viable cash crop for the thousands of small farmers who
populated the hills, Georgia and the territory that became the states
of Mississippi and Alabama were home to 32,800 "Indians," 53,400
"whites," and 30,000 "blacks." By 1840 the same region was home to
922,000 "whites" and 737,000 "blacks." The census takers failed to
note the presence of any remaining Cherokees, Creeks, Choctaws,
and Chickasaws, though some remained, hiding and waiting until
they could safely reassert their public identities once more. Something more, however, than the providential unfolding of America had
happened in the South in the first half of the nineteenth century. Between 1830 and 1840 the federal and state governments expelled from
their homes an indigenous population of nearly 50,000 people and
appropriated for commercial sale their land and improvements. It is
tempting to simply say those people were "Indians" and that is what
happened when "civilization" met "Indians." That story, after all, has
been told and retold for generations, but let's see if we can agree for

a few moments that they were not "Indians." That they had names. That they were mothers, fathers, children, Baptists, Methodists, Catholics, slaveowners, cotton farmers, basket weavers, market vendors, cowboys, and dreamers. And that they were southerners whose ancestors had inhabited the land for millennia.[3]

Against an invasion that had begun almost three centuries before, they had first struggled mightily to defend their families and fields from brutal Spanish conquistadors and the diseases that had followed in their wake. By the early nineteenth century, however, they faced state and federal governments who sought to pressure them to abandon their land. In response, the South's first peoples undertook to change their leadership structures and notions of law in order to more effectively protect their lives and their land, but before we go any further, make no mistake about it—their struggle will result in the deaths of thousands of people. So while much of the discussion that follows focuses on the process of learning and using the power of words to defend oneself and one's people, lives were on the line.

This story, however, begins before the deaths, in the creation of a new kind of language and a new way of being that saw the people and their leaders adopt to varying degrees the language of liberty and slavery that structured life in the Anglo- and African-American slave society of the early nineteenth-century South. Notions of liberty and enslavement had fired the colonists' early struggles against their imperial oppressors and then informed political rhetoric in the new republic even though such ideas embodied an irreconcilable tension between freedom and its absence. As Native slaveholders began to speak about liberty and slavery, they pushed their way into larger political and cultural debates in the United States, discussions that without their participation contemplated their destruction or removal. Oddly enough, their practice of slavery and their adoption of the language of liberty and slavery gave them the voice they needed to fight, albeit at great cost to their descendants, who struggle to this day to cope with the many shadows slavery has cast over their lives.

On July 4, 1827, a group of twelve men, eleven of whom owned slaves, met to discuss the formation of a union designed to protect personal liberty and defend national sovereignty. But the men who met, discussed, debated, and in the end signed the document were Cherokees. Not Americans. Or were they? For the historian who wrote the most extensive study of the 1827 Cherokee Constitution, the document was "a Cherokee version of the American Constitution to suit Cherokee needs."[4] Indeed, it is reasonable to argue that the 1827 Cherokee Constitution was modeled after the American one because it clearly was. The resulting constitution recognized three branches of government, created a bicameral legislature, instituted a bill of rights, and established a judicial system of district courts overseen by a supreme court. Also like its counterpart, the document addressed only obliquely the ownership of enslaved people. Unlike the slave codes of the states that surrounded them, however, Cherokee law sought to curtail the behavior of the owners more than the enslaved. But if the Cherokee founders took some of their inspiration from their neighbors' founding document, they intended to use it to defend themselves against the self-same model. In their document's first article the authors declared that "the Sovereignty and Jurisdiction of this Government shall extend over the Country within the boundaries above described, and the lands therein are, and shall remain, the common property of the Nation."[5] Never mind the fact that Cherokees swore also to defend their land as a common treasury for all who belonged to the nation. No such clause appeared in the United States' constitution, and no such words were to be found in the American Revolution's republican legacy except for perhaps on its most radical fringes.

Around the same time, ideas of race and color as markers of social status and innate capacity were on the rise. Scientific breakthroughs in Europe and Anglo-America crystallized ideas that had been floating around for centuries and supported arguments that some men were inherently inferior to others and that skin color was a reliable index for such difference. First peoples in the South had told stories for centuries about the prototypical "red," "black," and "white" men, but it was not until the early nineteenth century that racism was apparently making inroads in their societies. And as with their neighbors, it was the people Creeks called *luste*, Chickasaws called *lusau*,

Choctaws *lausau*, and Cherokees termed *enecka*—"black people"—who
bore the most powerful stigma of all. Ownership of enslaved people
varied widely. A federal census of the Choctaws in 1830 counted 17,963
Choctaws but only 512 enslaved people. Their Chickasaw neighbors
to the north, however, who numbered between five thousand and six
thousand individuals, held 1,156 people in bondage, a huge proportion
of the nation's overall population, a statistic that probably owes something to the eighteenth-century Chickasaws' notoriety as the region's
most prolific slavers, only then they were trading in Native, not African, people. Cherokee slave ownership resembled that of the Choctaws more than the Chickasaws, with sixteen hundred slaves living
among sixteen thousand Cherokees. Creek slave ownership figures
were probably comparable.[6]

Still, traditions of adoption, kinship, and marriage remained powerful, and such conventions could at times cut across the hardening lines
of race that citizens across the country were drawing and redrawing
every day. For such reasons, first peoples either practiced or accepted
a kind of slavery that looked very much like that of their neighbors.
But historians have found here and there in slavery's daily operation
examples of Cherokees or Creeks or Choctaws who acted not in reference to prevailing notions of race but instead drew from deeper
cultural reserves to fashion unique approaches to the complications
and opportunities that came with human bondage. Nevertheless, enslaved people in the nations were owned as property and fundamentally construed as "black" as opposed to "red" or "white." Whether
"black" men, women, and children were held in South Carolina or
in the Cherokee Nation, rights in property and beliefs in blackness
stood as a fundamental consensus that bound Native and non-Native
slaveholders no matter what other particularities might divide them.[7]

The mastery of, in effect, a new kind of language and knowledge
by Creek, Cherokee, Chickasaw, and Choctaw leaders to buttress their
values, concerns, and claims enabled a new kind of resistance to American encroachment at a time when, nearly to a man, they agreed that
gunfire would get them nowhere. Instead they used language to back
federal and state governments into practical and rhetorical corners

from which there were few escapes. If their use of language, however, ultimately failed to thwart the land cessions and the comprehensive expulsion of their people, it nonetheless signaled a new form of engagement between first peoples and American imperialism that had long-lasting consequences for each side.

Such questions and concerns have been studied before. The new forms of information, knowledge, and rhetoric that arose out of colonial contact situations constitute a central problem in what are often called postcolonial studies. Scholars disagree, however, about the nature and depth of indigenous resistance to the power of the invader or the diasporic societies that confronted them and the adoption of new forms of knowledge, such as writing, and the forms of communication that follow from it. Any change in communication causes other changes, some intentional, some unwitting. Writing, in particular, gnaws at the power and propriety of memory as embodied by either individuals or community mores and puts in its place a kind of disembodied knowledge that exists independently of the people who value it. It uproots what was implicit in a culture, what informed people's most basic assumptions, and sets such implications outside culture so that they become subject to the kind of disembodied dissection and deconstruction that was unknown before literacy stalked the land. Once knowledge leaves the body for the page, the relational nature of oral narration and memory falls away to be usurped by the static and discrete powers of alphabetical organization and permanent records. Written words detach everything they touch, but at the same time, they lay the groundwork for the kind of abstract and universal thought that, according to the children of the Enlightenment in the early nineteenth-century American South, transcended cultural boundaries and justified the dispossession of cultural beings.[8]

Speaking broadly, it is fair to say that some scholars have concluded that indigenous appropriations of European literacy signified acceptance of Europeans on European terms, and therefore, an implicit accommodation of the larger colonial enterprise.[9] Other scholars, however, have emphasized the originality of indigenous appropriations of the colonizers' discourses, literacies, and languages and are reluctant to cast such counterdiscourses as pale imitations of the conquerors' agendas.[10] Each perspective has its merits, but literacy reflected not so much a scale that slides between resistance and surrender but a tool for empowering particular leaders' novel ideas. Cherokees, for example, saw literacy as an effective tool they could use to resist their forced expulsion while at the same time accommodating the vision of "civilization" put before them by early federal policy makers. In a different way, the Creek leader Alexander McGillivray used letters to conjure for the benefit of his Spanish and American correspondents a Creek Nation that he presumed to lead, when on the ground no such thing existed. But the nation first promised in letters took shape over time, and the rise of literacy allowed for the centralization of power and recalibration of Creek values that made McGillivray's dream possible.[11]

Can we still say, not quite two centuries after the ratification of the Cherokee Constitution, that the document was modeled after the U.S. Constitution? At what point could such a document be inherently Cherokee, Choctaw, or Creek as well, or even American in the hemispheric rather than in the United States sense? When can they own who they were and are, and not be considered as part this or part that? We do not have a word in English to articulate the full extent of the blended world Cherokees, Creeks, Choctaws, and Chickasaws, and even Anglo-Americans and African Americans, inhabited in those days. Our inability today to imagine social forms that can, as anthropologist Bernard Cohn put it, unite "the European colonialist and the indigene . . . in one analytic field" leaves us nothing but short.[12]

When cotton prices began to rise in the early 1800s, men on the make knew that slaves and land were safe bets, and some of the best land to be had lay in the belts of black soil that undulated across present-day Georgia, Alabama, and Mississippi and were under the government and occupation of the South's first peoples. If that land was going to be opened to U.S. citizens and the enslaved people they owned, it had to be taken. In one case, Mississippi governor Thomas Holmes put to the state assembly that because the state depended on land tax revenues to fund the roads and bridges necessary to carry the invaders on their way, the vast stretch of untaxed land under Choctaw and Chickasaw occupation and jurisdiction had to be acquired, emptied, opened for sale, repopulated, assessed, and taxed. Without a new parcel of taxable land, he concluded, the state would be forced to levy oppressive taxes on citizens residing within its current bounds, which would both stifle the state's growth and turn away subsequent waves of invaders. Holmes's successor, George Poindexter, added that further land cessions would open interstate commerce with Tennessee and Alabama. With the free and easy movement of cotton, Poindexter predicted that the state's population not only would increase but also would become more prosperous, more industrious, and in the end, more virtuous. By establishing a close relationship between land cessions, expulsion, taxation, and the invaders' moral and economic prosperity, the two governors articulated a cogent and powerful set of conditions that required federal action.[13]

Such action came in 1825. The Treaty of Indian Springs ceded to the United States all Creek land in Georgia and some in Alabama. But it was a fraud negotiated by interested federal officers and a bought rump of Creek men. After the rightful Creek leaders raced as much as one could in those days of stagecoaches to Washington to denounce the Senate's ratification of the treaty, President John Quincy Adams abrogated it and called for another, more honest, agreement. The new 1826 Treaty of Washington, negotiated with official representatives of the Creek national council, replaced the old treaty and outraged the governor of Georgia.[14] George M. Troup warned secretary of war John C. Calhoun that if those people remained in Georgia "public opinion would . . . fix them in a middle status between the negro and the white man, and that as long as they survive this degradation, without the possibility of attaining the elevation of the latter, they would gradually sink to the conditions of the former." Troup thereafter dedicated himself to driving Creeks and Cherokees out of the state, but the inability of the Adams administration to keep pace with his social engineering project frustrated him. "There is such a radical difference of opinion between the authorities of Georgia and of the United States," Troup lamented, "that the harmony and tranquility of the two Governments . . . can never be maintained . . . until those Indians have been removed."[15] Joining the governor, the editor of the Augusta *Constitutionalist* asked, "Are we the *slaves* of the United States Government, and therefore bound to close our lips against *her* taunts?"[16] No one who lives in a slave society wants to be a slave, and in a way, the Treaty of Washington controversy made Georgians frame their world as an enslaved one and then place the Creeks on the dark side of that balance. Political society in Georgia argued more or less to a man that the state government should not "brook the insolence" of those who had dared to challenge the Treaty of Indian Springs.[17]

Like his Georgia and Mississippi counterparts, Alabama governor John Murphy deplored the abrogation of the Indian Springs treaty because he had counted on it to leverage the complete expulsion of the Creeks from his state and to attract slaveholders who, he believed, would increase the state's productivity, revenue, and what he called "respectability." He regretted the "crisis" that had arisen and argued that the Creeks ought to be sent across the Mississippi River in order to save them from the inevitable extinction that awaited them at the bottom of the South's racial pile. Indeed, to leave them where they were, he admitted, "would neither comport with the justice, generosity, or humanity, of a liberal and Christian people." But charity only went so far. "We have a claim," he threatened, "which will not be denied."[18]

One year after the debacle of the Treaty of Indian Springs and in anticipation of similar pressures being brought to bear on them, the Cherokees wrote their constitution. Almost to the day, the Georgia senate condemned it.[19] A state senate resolution offered an elaborate reading of colonial and federal law to argue that "Indians" had only a "possessory" right to land that could not take precedence over Georgia's constitutional rights.[20] Cherokees of course resented the implications of the Georgia senate report and asked how the relatively new constitutional rights that Georgians enjoyed could trump their own human rights when they had been there first and had in fact welcomed those first invaders who had stumbled into the mountains almost three centuries before. The nation's principal chiefs, John Ross and George Hicks, described as "preposterous" the senate resolution denouncing their constitution. "Our ancestors," they wrote, "from time immemorial possessed this country."[21]

Notwithstanding their protests that their constitution was a threat to neither Georgia nor the United States, Cherokees asked why no one had ever before informed them that they could not set up their own government when they had ably adopted other facets of Anglo-American culture presented to them by "the illustrious Washington, Jefferson, Madison and Monroe."[22] They viewed the first treaties they had signed with the United States as a "gigantic silver pipe which Gen. Washington placed in the hands of the Cherokees" and as a "golden chain which Mr. Jefferson attached to the charter of our rights." By juxtaposing silver pipes, golden chains, and the language of liberty, Cherokee chiefs fashioned a discourse to underpin the defense of their property and persons. At the same time, they refused to adopt wholesale Anglo notions of natural or contractual rights and instead maintained what historian Cynthia Cumfer has described as "a specifically Cherokee kind of mutuality" that acknowledged the antiquity of their possession of the land, the precariousness of their claims to liberty, and the strength of relationships built around a silver pipe that each side could smoke and a golden chain that each side could grasp and polish from time to time.[23]

Cherokee republicanism, if we may call it that, meant that men like John Ross and Elijah Hicks could engage American politicians and policy makers in English on terms with which their counterparts were intimately familiar but which at the same time could be deployed on behalf of Cherokees. Unless Andrew Jackson upheld the promises of Washington and Jefferson, one Cherokee newspaper reader wrote, the "sun of liberty" would sink forever behind "the appalling cloud of despotism."[24] Another contributor to the *Cherokee Phoenix* bragged about the Cherokees' nascent nationalism, claiming that he and his countrymen were more patriotic and devoted to constitutional government than either Henry Clay or John Randolph, two leading politicians of the day. To the supporters of the new constitution, natural law and republican rule meant that communities had the right to govern themselves as they saw fit and that such government secured their claims to land and property even if, in some cases, that right extended to people held as property as well.[25] Because citizenship hinged on participation in the new constitutional experiment, voting emerged as a right and duty "of great importance," one commentator remarked to his fellow Cherokees, "to yourselves and to your country."[26]

American citizens upset with the Adams administration's abrogation of the Treaty of Indian Springs and concerned about the Cherokees' national claims helped vote Andrew Jackson into the White House in 1828.[27] Jackson had advocated for the first peoples' expulsion from their homes for several years, and his election emboldened Georgia, Alabama, and Mississippi to take matters into their own hands. In 1828, for example, the government of Georgia extended state law over land occupied by the Cherokees, and after June 1, 1830, over the Cherokees themselves in order to nullify their "laws, usages, and customs." The governments of Alabama and Mississippi followed suit and extended their legal systems over land owned by the Creeks, Choctaws, and Chickasaws.[28] Jackson's administration supported the passage of such measures in spite of their contravention of federal laws and treaties. To smooth over any jurisdictional difficulties, secretary of war John Eaton cautioned the Cherokees that the Declaration of Independence granted the states inviolable sovereignty and that the Constitution also mandated complete state sovereignty. No amount of protest by indigenous leaders, the secretary promised, could overcome their peoples' lack of sovereignty and their irredeemable possession of so-called savage habits.[29] As Andrew Jackson, calling himself the "Great Father," put it to the Creeks, "My children listen, my white children in Alabama, have extended their law over your country. If you remain in it, you must be subject to that law."[30]

Creeks quickly invoked a federalist conception of both their treaty rights and Alabama's sovereignty as a state to argue against the legislation. In a letter sent to the editor of the *Montgomery Journal*, one group of Creek leaders relied upon the security of their treaties with the United States to guarantee their possession of their land. They also admonished their audience. "You understand how to appreciate free principles," they hoped, "and according to your honest conception of such laws, you will deal out to us all the rights and privileges that we are entitled to."[31] Leaders like Opothle Yoholo and Tukabatchee Mico, who sought their own changes to Creek government to safeguard their land, further petitioned Congress to uphold the promises that the federal government had made to them in the treaties and to not leave them, the chiefs implored, "to the rigorous management of any State disposed to fatten on the ruins of our natural and civil rights."[32] Drawing further on American political rhetoric and the touchy politics of the South's "peculiar institution," the leaders contrasted their birthright in freedom with the "slavery" to which the Alabama government had condemned them.[33]

With their expulsion from Alabama imminent, Creek leaders moved from a general consideration of their treaty rights to a more pointed assertion of federal supremacy over the state that threatened their lives. Surrounded by enemies, they turned to their archives. Their only recourse outside of a suicidal rebellion was to claim federal protection as stipulated by treaties reaching back to what they called the "Old British War."[34] On the basis of their reading of American political history, Creek leaders argued, in opposition to Alabama's leading men, that Alabama derived its sovereignty from the federal government and the Constitution, and that the state's rights were therefore subordinate to federal laws and treaties. They were also aware of the more visceral sensibilities that informed the hearts and minds of those voters who coveted their land. "We have never been slaves; we have been born free," the chiefs argued, "for what of our services to you are we condemned to slavery?"[35] Rarely did anyone within southern society force its citizens to own up in a self-conscious way to their culpability in reproducing daily a system that enslaved and wrecked millions of peoples' lives, but these Creek leaders did and in ways that had nothing to do with abolitionism.

In Mississippi, the Colberts, who as owners of cotton plantations, stores, inns, and large numbers of slaves were by far the most powerful Chickasaw family—juggled respect for older traditions with a centralizing imperative in government. They tried to defend their peoples' claim to the northern part of the state, but at the same time, they had to face off staunch Chickasaw opposition to their power as well as the many federal agents who sought constantly to lure them into land cessions.[36] Choctaw leaders Greenwood LeFlore, whose thirty-two slaves worked his vast cotton fields and staffed his other entrepreneurial endeavors, and David Folsom, whose ten slaves worked his more modest holdings, went one step further than the Creeks and the Chickasaws, and, like the Cherokee government with which LeFlore had previously corresponded, committed to paper a series of laws that transformed the loose confederacy of chiefs, clans, towns, and districts that Europeans and Euro-Americans had for two centuries called the "Choctaw Nation" into a more unified polity under the guidance of an elected council and chief.[37] After the drafting of the Choctaw constitution, a federal agent remarked to the head of the Office of Indian Affairs: "This nation are so completely governed or under the influence of three men who have a purty good knowledge of the Laws of nations."[38] That "purty good knowledge" was dangerous, the agent knew, because it gave the lie to the government's constant talk of first peoples being nothing more than wandering savages. Even the primary opponent of LeFlore and Folsom's reforms, an aged war leader named Mushulatubbee, whose ten slaves worked his thirty acres of corn and cotton, drew on American political rhetoric to buttress his opposition to their new government. Proudly displaying a portrait of Andrew Jackson in his home, the chief went Old Hickory one better and denounced the "despotic" opponents who imperiled his "Republican party."[39]

Such uses of the language of liberty and slavery supplanted the language of savagery as the dominant discourse around which first and second peoples engaged and debated the former's political rights and occupancy of the land and the latter's treaty obligations and conflicting state and federal jurisdictions. Rather than concede the ground, however, Georgia, Alabama, and Mississippi struck back in an effort to erase such presumptuous challenges. Emboldened by Jackson's support for the state law extension measures and by the passage of the federal Indian Removal Act in May 1830, which provided funds for the negotiation of the treaties that would enable the United States to expel the people from their homelands, the governments of Georgia, Alabama, and Mississippi initiated another round of state laws to harass the nations out of existence. "All experience has shown," a Georgia statehouse report concluded, "that the association of the white man with the red has generally, if not uniformly, proved injurious to both."[40] To this end the state assembly passed a broader state law extension act. While Cherokees would still come under Georgia law on June 1, 1830, the new act nullified all Cherokee laws, prevented Cherokees from citing their own laws in cases before Georgia courts, and prohibited anyone from either hindering Cherokees from leaving Georgia or from preventing leaders from ceding land.[41] The Georgia assembly thus drew closer together the politics of states' rights and "Indian" removal and took active steps to expel the people Governor Troup had considered a few years before to be caught hopelessly between "whites" and "blacks." "The common conceived opinion," one Cherokee replied, "that mankind throughout the world in similar circumstances are alike, is true."[42]

Alabama followed Georgia's lead. In the face of assertions of sovereignty by Cherokees and Creeks, Congressman Samuel Mardis declared that "the novel spectacle of two sovereigns making law for the government of the same people" had to come to an end. A house committee concluded that "the State of Alabama has an undoubted right, as a sovereign State, to enact laws for the government of all her citizens, no matter whether they be white, red or black."[43] Another law extension measure over Creek and Cherokee land followed which abolished indigenous laws and customs, and at the urging of Governor Gabriel Moore, also extended to Creeks and Cherokees the rights to offer testimony in court cases and record wills and bills of sale just like "white persons." Moore hoped such concessions would forestall hostilities.[44] Indeed, one Creek delegation that visited secretary of war Lewis Cass in Washington requested that such provisions be inserted in a recent treaty "placing us on an equal footing with our white brethren" to secure federal protection in the face of state laws passed without their consent.[45] Such talk of enfranchisement, however, flew in the face of the larger question over who would prevail, and for the citizens of Alabama, that was never an open question. "That any exercise of jurisdiction on the part of the United States . . . over any portion of the territory aforesaid, in the possession of any Indian tribe," the authors of one resolution asserted, "is an usurpation of power on the part of the United States."[46]

Like Georgia and Alabama, the Mississippi state assembly revisited the issue of state law extension after the passage of the Indian Removal Act. Not only did the Choctaws' and Chickasaws' possession of land inhibit the state's economy, most politicians agreed, but their efforts to organize politically in response to state law extension meant that Mississippi would be caught in a complex jurisdictional conflict between the federal government and a Choctaw government that claimed to be sovereign. Such a state of things was, Governor Gerard Brandon believed, not to be tolerated. "The present time," he proclaimed, "is a most favorable epoch to press the subject, and claim from the government of the United States a speedy extinguishment of their title within our boundary."[47]

Choctaws spoke forcibly against President Jackson, his supporters, and their efforts to end the Choctaws' political experiment. One Choctaw, for example, wrote to Elias Boudinot, the editor of the *Cherokee Phoenix*, that "it seems to me the most goading piece of injustice that ever was implicated on any *free* people."[48] Another claimed that the state could not extend its laws without the Choctaws' consent, just as Americans had once claimed against the British Crown that there could be "no taxation without representation." "He is always talking about his red children," another man wrote of President Jackson, "and how he loved them, and wished to see them prosper and become a great people, [but] at the very same time he is trying to cheat us out of our lands."[49] Others went further. James McDonald, a Choctaw who had studied law under Supreme Court justice John McLean, ran for the state legislature in the hopes of salvaging something for his people. Mushulatubbee also stumped for the state congress in an attempt to exert some influence on the dismantling of the nation. He pledged to the crowds of voters who gathered to hear him speak, "If you vote for me I will serve you." Neither McDonald nor

Mushulatubbee, however, polled a majority, and while McDonald took his own life in despair, old Mushulatubbee initiated secret correspondence with the government to seek the most lucrative deal he could before leaving the state.[50]

In an effort to find broader support, such leaders also turned north, where at the very least, predictions of their own enslavement would find a more receptive audience, no matter their own implication in slavery's dark tangle. Cherokee planters John Ross, who owned nineteen slaves, and John Ridge, who held twenty-one, composed letters for northern newspapers to assert across the free states "that all men are by nature equal." Playing his hand even more boldly, Ridge assured citizens of Pennsylvania that Cherokees "have only practiced the lessons of [President] Washington."[51] Ridge did not write idly. Pennsylvania was an important state in Jackson's Democratic coalition, and one party man wrote to Jackson's friend Felix Grundy that agitation over the Cherokee question in the Keystone State was undermining Jackson's support.[52]

Taken together, the multiple uses to which leaders put the language of liberty and slavery constituted a powerful tool for the organization of new kinds of Native societies, a tool every bit as important as either the gun, the loom, or the plow. Moreover, the language of liberty and slavery gave such leaders a means to articulate and defend their national interests that was at the same time consonant with and a part of broader currents of American political discourse. By the early 1830s, however, it had in some ways run its course. When confronted with Native leaders like John Ross and Greenwood LeFlore, who were conversant in the politics of "civilization," not to mention adept at market economics, slave ownership, and Christian piety, federal and state leaders simply could not countenance the extension of political rights to people they increasingly understood to be racially, as opposed to culturally, inferior. Accepting Cherokee assertions that they were indeed a hardworking, sturdy, and respectable people, for example, Georgia governor George Gilmer nevertheless stated to one Cherokee correspondent that Native people would never "associate upon an equality with our own people."[53]

Conversations run in as many directions as there are speakers. Creeks, Cherokees, Choctaws, and Chickasaws appropriated Anglo-American concepts that informed their own consideration of Native government and sovereignty. By the same token, they engaged American political discourse in ways that forced citizens to confront the substantial gap between their own rhetoric and practice and to change the terms by which they defined American society and citizenship. In so doing, they also forced them to change their conception of first peoples, from one premised on the belief that they were malleable beings who could change their ways to comport with "civilization," to one that presupposed that, by dint of their essential human condition, they were racially and therefore permanently inferior. In the end, the first peoples lost the debate and the battle, and their expulsion from their homes, along with the enslaved men, women, and children they owned, caused them all great sadness and terrible loss of life.

The federal government expelled the Choctaws from Mississippi in the three years following the conclusion of the 1830 Treaty of Dancing Rabbit Creek. Subsequent treaties with the Creeks and Chickasaws in 1832 and with the Cherokees in 1835 secured their expulsions as well.[54] Federal agents kept no systematic records of the horrors, so it is difficult to ascertain how many people died during the expulsions owing to hard winter weather, disease, and substandard supplies of food and clothing. Historian Donna Akers has proposed that nearly a third of removed Choctaws, a total of perhaps five thousand people, perished. Demographer Russell Thornton has accepted the tally of four thousand Cherokee deaths, one-quarter of the total number of Cherokees expelled. Thornton also posed two other important questions. First, how many people might have lived had removal not happened? And second, how many babies were not born because their potential parents had either perished during the expulsions or were never born because of their own parents' deaths? In terms of this *total* Cherokee population loss, Thornton arrived at a figure of ten thousand men and women who would have lived or been born in the first generation had removal not occurred. One can imagine how many thousands of Cherokees are not standing today because of those dark days and awful events. Such death tolls, Akers has argued, must also be understood in the context of the loss of land. Indeed, Akers has demonstrated that for Choctaws, separation from their homeland "meant death," and Choctaw conceptions of the West as a place "where spirits unable to reach the afterworld roamed forever" only compounded their misery, sense of loss, and despair for the future.[55]

For the non-Native slaveholders of Georgia, Alabama, and Mississippi, however, the expulsions, the deaths, and the despair augured a new beginning for them and the society they sought to build, "the dawn of an era . . . when . . . this state would emerge from obscurity, and justifiably assume an equal character with her sister states of the Union," as the authors of one Mississippi House of Representatives memorial put it.[56] In addition to the hard fight for equality with the older states won by young states like Alabama and Mississippi and the full possession of their chartered limits that they now enjoyed, the expulsions had also ensured that freedom and slavery were, at least in principle, contiguous with whiteness and blackness. No longer would "Indians" challenge the racial verities that were so dear to Jackson, Troup, Murphy, and most southern politicians and citizens and so essential to constructing the society that they and the voters who had put them in office had all chosen to imagine and enact. Such achievements, however, had come at a steep human price, and the challenge for those who had benefited from the expulsions was to invent a past that could comport with the future they were making for themselves and the people they enslaved.[57] "What good man," President Jackson asked in the address that opened his second term as president, two years after the expulsions had begun, "would prefer a country covered with forests and ranged by a few thousand savages to our extensive Republic, studded with cities, towns, and prosperous farms, embellished with all the improvements which art can devise or industry execute, occupied by more than 12,000,000 happy people, and filled with all the blessings of liberty, civilization, and religion?"[58]

But for the people who attempted to resist their destruction, with language rather than with lead and steel, there was no glory. No blessings. Just hunger and cold, the bloody hack of tuberculosis, the

gutting incontinence of dysentery, and the deaths of generations untold. Such horrors left their scars on the nation that had undertaken
the expulsions as well, and in ways that become clearer as time pass-
es. By resisting the invasion of their homes and the dispossession of
their lands, while at the same time defining more sharply their difference from the "black people" they owned, leaders like John Ross and
Greenwood LeFlore forced, in their own way, the U.S. government
and the governments of Georgia, Alabama, and Mississippi to shift
their idea of the possibilities of humanity from the mutability of culture to the indelibility of race. Washington's and Jefferson's calls for
first peoples to change their ways and adopt the practices characteristic of Anglo-American life in order to enter the new republic's body
politic ended because such men could no longer be called "untutored
savages." As several state politicians, and by extension their voters, indicated, it no longer mattered if Cherokees became what policy makers called "civilized," because they had become in the minds of such
men permanently and unalterably inferior to those who claimed to
be "white." Such a situation left first peoples with no way out but to
leave their homes and land and ancestors, sometimes at gunpoint, for
uncertain futures in the "Indian Territory" that the federal government had reserved for them on the other side of the Mississippi River.

What they proved in their defeat, however, was that the empire of
liberty had no room for the people who had been here all along, and
who had welcomed their forebears to these shores, no matter the earlier promises made by Washington, Jefferson, and Monroe to respect
if not accept them. In the bigger picture, both sides lost, just in different ways and over different scales of time. The South's first peoples'
uses of the language of liberty and slavery helped to harden American
political thought, to encourage the valorization of "whiteness," and
to justify the defense of a biracial slave society. The unwillingness of
the state and federal governments to hear and to consider the nations'
pleas and to accord them their due humanity blocked the old clear and
white paths that had for so long bound the people to one another, and
set in motion the opening of those crooked red paths that would take
the nation to Fort Sumter, Gettysburg, Birmingham, and Wounded

Knee, twice. Even Vietnam.[59] Maybe even Iraq and Afghanistan, too, because the story seems to continue to unfold wherever the United States encounter others whom they name tribal, wandering, and savage but who, in response, ably adapt the language of liberty and slavery to resist what they too perceive to be their subjugation and dispossession.

Notes

1. James Taylor Carson, *Making an Atlantic World: Circles, Paths, and Stories from the Colonial South* (Knoxville: University of Tennessee Press, 2007), 82–83; Claudio Saunt, *A New Order of Things: Property, Power, and the Transformation of the Creek Indians, 1733–1816* (Cambridge: Cambridge University Press, 1999), 11–17; "Talk of the Cherokees to Gov. James Glen," November 14, 1751, in *Colonial Records of South Carolina: Documents Relating to Indian Affairs, May 21, 1750–August 7, 1754*, ed. William L. McDowell Jr. (Columbia: South Carolina Archives Department, 1958), 1:175; "Talk of the Upper Creeks to Gov. James Glen," 1752, in *Colonial Records*, 1:224; "Talk of the Chickasaws to 'The King of Carolina and his beloved men,'" April 5, 1756, *Colonial Records*, 2:110; "Original Papers Concerning the Hopewell Treaties, 1785–86," January 3 and 5, 1786, 14 U 82, 87, 90, Lyman Draper Collection, Western History Collection, University of Oklahoma, Norman.

2. Carson, *Making an Atlantic World*; Joseph M. Hall Jr., *Zamumo's Gifts: Indian-European Exchange in the Colonial Southeast* (Philadelphia: University of Pennsylvania Press, 2009); Robert Paulett, *An Empire of Small Places: Mapping the Southeastern Anglo-Indian Trade, 1732–1795* (Athens: University of Georgia Press, 2012).

3. Peter H. Wood, "The Changing Population of the Colonial South: An Overview by Race and Region, 1685–1790," in *Powhatan's Mantle: Indians in the Colonial Southeast*, ed. Peter H. Wood, Gregory A. Waselkov, and M. Thomas Hatley (Lincoln: University of Nebraska Press, 1989), 38; Ben J. Wattenberg, ed., *Statistical History of the United States from Colonial Times to the Present* (New York: Basic Books, 1976), 24, 26, 30.

4. Theda Perdue, *Slavery and the Evolution of Cherokee Society, 1540–1866* (Knoxville: University of Tennessee Press, 1979), 57–59; William G. McLoughlin, *Cherokee Renascence in the New Republic* (Princeton NJ: Princeton University Press, 1986), 396.

5. Cynthia Cumfer, *Separate Peoples, One Land: The Minds of Cherokees, Blacks, and Whites on the Tennessee Frontier* (Chapel Hill: University of North Carolina Press, 2007), 102–3; *Cherokee Phoenix*, February 21, 1828; and McLoughlin, *Cherokee Renascence*, 396–401.

6. Winthrop D. Jordan, *The White Man's Burden: Historical Origins of Racism in the United States* (New York: Oxford University Press, 1974), 3–25, 50–56; 87–106, 194–204; William Stanton, *The Leopard's Spots: Scientific Attitudes toward Race in America, 1815–1859* (Chicago: University of Chicago Press, 1966); Martin S. Staum, *Labeling People: French Scholars on Society, Race, and Empire, 1815–1848* (Kingston ON: McGill-Queen's University Press, 2003); James Taylor Carson, *Searching for the Bright Path: The Mississippi Choctaws from Prehistory to Removal* (Lincoln: University of Nebraska Press, 1999), 80; Arrell M. Gibson, *The Chickasaws* (Norman: University of Oklahoma Press, 1971), 163; Robbie Ethridge, *From Chicaza to Chickasaw: The European Invasion and the Transformation of the Mississippian World, 1540–1715* (Chapel Hill: University of North Carolina Press, 2010); 194–231; Fay A. Yarbrough, *Race and the Cherokee Nation: Sovereignty in the Nineteenth Century* (Philadelphia: University of Pennsylvania Press, 2008), 151n13.

7. Perdue, *Slavery*, 57–59; Tiya Miles, *Ties that Bind: The Story of an Afro-Cherokee Family in Slavery and Freedom* (Berkeley: University of California Press, 2005), 4, 127–28; Yarbrough, *Race and the Cherokee Nation*, 5, 9, 39–48; Christina Snyder, *Slavery in Indian Country: The Changing Face of Captivity in Early America* (Cambridge MA: Harvard University Press, 2010), 193, 202, 210.

8. Jack Goody, *The Logic of Writing and the Organization of Society* (Cambridge: Cambridge University Press, 1986), 172–77; Carlo Sini, *Ethics of Writing*, trans. Silvia Benso and Brian Schroeder (Albany: SUNY Press, 2009), 19–22, 56–63.

9. Richard Terdiman, *Discourse/Counter-Discourse: The Theory and Practice of Symbolic Resistance in Nineteenth-Century France* (Ithaca NY: Cornell University Press, 1985), 13–14 and 35–27; Alan Sinfield, *Faultlines: Cultural Materialism and the Politics of Dissident Reading* (Oxford: Clarendon Press, 1992), 47.

10. Anuradha Dingwaney Needham, *Using the Master's Tools: Resistance and the Literature of the African and South-Asian Diasporas* (New York: St. Martin's Press, 2000), 2–3; Benita Perry, "Resistance Theory/Theorising Resistance, or Two Cheers for Nativism," in *Colonial Discourse/Postcolonial Theory*, ed. Francis Barker, Peter Hulme, and Margaret Sversen (Manchester: Manchester University Press, 1994), 176, 178.

11. Theda Perdue, *Cherokee Women: Gender and Culture Change, 1700–1835* (Lincoln: University of Nebraska Press, 1998), 113; Saunt, *New Order*, 188–204.

12. Bernard S. Cohn, *An Anthropologist among the Historians and Other Essays* (Oxford: Oxford University Press, 1987), 44.

13. Snyder, *Slavery in Indian Country*, 187; *Journal of the Senate of the State of Mississippi at Their Third Session of the General Assembly* (Natchez: Richard Langdon, 1820), 8, 18–19.

14. Michael Green, *Politics of Indian Removal: Creek Government and Society in Crisis* (Lincoln: University of Nebraska Press, 1982), 81–102.

15. George Troup to John C. Calhoun, February 28, 1824, M234, reel 7, Cherokee Agency, Letters Received, 1824–1881, Correspondence of the Office of Indian Affairs, Record Group 75, Bureau of Indian Affairs, National Archives, Washington DC; *Journal of the House of Representatives of the State of Georgia* (Milledgeville: Camak and Ragland, 1826), 10.

16. *Augusta (GA) Constitutionalist*, June 14, 1825. Emphasis in original.

17. Senate Resolution, December 8, 1826, *Acts of the General Assembly of the State of Georgia* (Milledgeville: Camak and Ragland, 1826), 233.

18. *Journal of the Senate of the State of Alabama* (Cahawba: William B. Allen, 1826), 128–30.

19. "Constitution of the Cherokee Nation," July 1827, *Cherokee Phoenix*, February 21, 1828; John Ross and Major Ridge to Alexander Gray, John Cocke, and George Davidson, September 27, 1827, *Cherokee Phoenix*, May 21, 1828.

20. Senate Resolution, December 19, 1827, *Acts of the General Assembly of the State of Georgia* (Milledgeville: Camak and Ragland, 1826), 241–48.

21. "Message of the Principal Chiefs of the Cherokee Nation," October 13, 1828, *Cherokee Phoenix*, October 22, 1828.

22. *Cherokee Phoenix and Indian Advocate*, May 21, 1828, and as quoted, *Cherokee Phoenix and Indian Advocate*, June 17, 1829.

23. *Cherokee Phoenix and Indian Advocate*, May 19, 1832; Cumfer, *Separate Peoples*, 86.

24. *Cherokee Phoenix and Indian Advocate*, February 11, 1832.

25. *Cherokee Phoenix and Indian Advocate*, August 25, 1832.

26. *Cherokee Phoenix and Indian Advocate*, May 6, 1828.

27. Ronald Satz, *American Indian Policy in the Jacksonian Era* (Lincoln: University of Nebraska Press, 1975), 11; Anthony Gene Carey, *Parties, Slavery, and the Union in Antebellum Georgia* (Athens: University of Georgia Press, 1997), 23–24; and J. Mills Thornton III, *Power and Politics in a Slave Society: Alabama, 1800–1860* (Baton Rouge: Louisiana State University Press, 1978), 22–24.

28. Carey, *Parties, Slavery, and the Union*, 24; "An act to add the territory lying within the limits of this state, and occupied by the Cherokee Indians, to the counties of Carroll, DeKalb, Gwinnett, Hall and Habersham; and to extend the laws of this state over the same, and for other purposes," *Acts of the General Assembly of the State of Georgia* (Milledgeville: Camak and Ragland, 1829), 88–89; "An act to extend legal process into that part of this state, now occupied by the Chickasaw and Choctaw tribes of Indians," *Laws of the State of Mississippi Passed at the Twelfth Session of the General Assembly* (Jackson: Peter Isler, 1829), 81–83; and "An act to extend the jurisdiction of the state of Alabama over the Creek nation," *Acts Passed at the Tenth Annual Session of the*

General Assembly of the State of Alabama (Tuscaloosa: McGuire, Henry and Mc-Guire, 1829).

29. John Eaton to Edward Gunter and William Coody, April 18, 1829, *Cherokee Phoenix*, June 17, 1829; Report of the Secretary of War, November 30, 1829, *Banner of the Constitution* 1 (December 19, 1829): 17; John Eaton to William Ward, August 2, 1830, *Cherokee Phoenix*, October 16, 1830.

30. Andrew Jackson to the Creeks, March 23, 1829, *Cherokee Phoenix*, June 17, 1829.

31. *Charleston Mercury* (from *Montgomery Journal*), August 25, 1829.

32. Green, *Politics of Indian Removal*, 38–39; *Cherokee Phoenix and Indian Advocate*, March 17, 1830.

33. *Cherokee Phoenix and Indian Advocate*, March 10, 1832.

34. Tuskenehahaw to Andrew Jackson, May 21, 1831, reel 222, and Neah Micco and Tuskenehahaw to Lewis Cass, December 20, 1832, reel 222, M234, Cherokee Agency, Letters Received, 1824–1881, Correspondence of the Office of Indian Affairs, Record Group 75, Bureau of Indian Affairs, National Archives, Washington DC.

35. Memorial to the House of Representatives, January 24, 1832, *Cherokee Phoenix*, March 10, 1832.

36. Gibson, *Chickasaws*, 99–102, 122–30, 137–41.

37. Carson, *Bright Path*, chs. 5 and 7.

38. Carson, *Bright Path*, 80; William Ward to Peter Porter, October 11, 1828, reel 169, M234, Choctaw Agency, Letters Received, Correspondence of the Office of Indian Affairs, Record Group 75, Bureau of Indian Affairs, National Archives, Washington DC.

39. "Chiefs, Captains, and Warriors of the Southeastern and Northern Districts to John Eaton," June 2, 1830, M234, reel 169, Choctaw Agency, Record Group 75, Bureau of Indian Affairs, National Archives, Washington DC.

40. House of Representatives Resolution, December 12, 1829, *Acts of the General Assembly of the State of Georgia* (Milledgeville: Camak and Ragland, 1830), 267.

41. "An act to add territory lying within the chartered limits of Georgia, and now in the occupancy of the Cherokee Indians," *Acts of the General Assembly of the State of Georgia* (Milledgeville: Camak and Ragland, 1830), 98–101.

42. *Cherokee Phoenix and Indian Advocate*, April 25, 1832.

43. *Journal of the House of Representatives of the State of Alabama* (Tuscaloosa: Wiley, McGuire and Henry, 1831), 43, 93–95.

44. "An act to extend the jurisdiction of the state of Alabama over the territory according to the geographical boundaries within the limits of said state," *Acts Passed at the Thirteenth Annual Session of the General Assembly of the State of*

Alabama (Tuscaloosa: Wiley, McGuire and Henry, 1832), 7–8; *Journal of the Senate of the State of Alabama* (Tuscaloosa: Wiley, McGuire and Henry, 1831), 13.

45. Creek Delegation to Lewis Cass, March 19, 1832, M234, reel 223, Creek Agency, Letters Received, 1832–33, Correspondence of the Office of Indian Affairs, Bureau of Indian Affairs, Record Group 75, National Archives, Washington DC.

46. Joint Resolution, December 31, 1831, *Acts Passed at the Thirteenth Annual Session of the General Assembly of the State of Alabama* (Tuscaloosa: Wiley, McGuire and Henry, 1832).

47. *Journal of the Senate of the State of Mississippi at Their Twelfth Session* (Jackson: Peter Isler, 1829), 9.

48. *Cherokee Phoenix*, March 24, 1830. Emphasis in original.

49. *The Natchez*, February 13, 1830.

50. *Niles' Weekly Register* 38 (August 21, 1830): 457–58; 38 (June 26, 1830): 327; 38 (July 10, 1830): 362–63; and James McDonald to Alexander McKee, March 30, 1831, box 1, folder 22, Peter Perkins Pitchlynn Papers, Western History Collections, University of Oklahoma, Norman.

51. Perdue, *Slavery*, 59; John Ridge to Elliot Cresson, February 6, 1831, *Poulson's American Daily Advertiser*, cited in *Cherokee Phoenix*, April 16, 1831.

52. T. Hartly Crawford to Felix Grundy, July 1, 1830, Felix Grundy Papers, Southern Historical Collection, University of North Carolina, Chapel Hill.

53. George Gilmer to John Rogers, March 10, 1831, Governor George Rockingham Gilmer's Letterbook, November 1829–June 1831, *Microfilm Collection of Early State Records*, compiled by William Sumner Jackson (Washington DC: Library of Congress, 1950), reel 1388, fr. 248.

54. Francis Paul Prucha, *The Great Father: The United States Government and the American Indians* (Lincoln: University of Nebraska Press, 1984), 222, 226; Robert Remini, *The Legacy of Andrew Jackson: Essays on Democracy, Indian Removal, and Slavery* (Baton Rouge: Louisiana State University Press, 1988), 75; Carson, *Searching for the Bright Path*, 123.

55. Russell Thornton, "The Demography of the Trail of Tears Period: A New Estimate of Cherokee Population Losses," in *Cherokee Removal: Before and After*, ed. William L. Anderson (Athens: University of Georgia Press, 1991), 86, 91–93; Donna L. Akers, "Removing the Heart of the Choctaw People: Indian Removal from a Native Perspective," *American Indian Culture and Research Journal* 23 (1999): 66–67, 69, 72.

56. *Journal of the House of Representatives of the State of Mississippi, at Their Sixteenth Session, Held in the Town of Jackson* (Jackson: Peter Isler, 1833), 141.

57. James Taylor Carson, "'The Obituary of Nations': Ethnic Cleansing, Memory, and the Origins of the Old South," *Southern Cultures* 14 (2008): 6–31.

58. As quoted in Reginald Horsman, *Race and Manifest Destiny: The Origins of American Racial Anglo-Saxonism* (Cambridge MA: Harvard University Press, 1981), 202.

59. Richard Drinnon, *Facing West: The Metaphysics of Indian-Hating and Empire Building* (Minneapolis: University of Minnesota Press, 1980).

| Chapter 7

Resistance and Removal
Yaqui and Navajo Identities in the Southwest Borderlands

Claudia B. Haake

In the southwestern borderlands, two nation-states, Mexico and the United States of America, sought to remove Native peoples from their lands in order to gain control of and access to those lands themselves, as well as to contain the threat Native Americans posed in their perception. Removal and displacement, even if at times only temporary, impacted Native Americans in a number of ways. Among other things, Native resistance to policies such as removal, as well as the will to retain and/or return to their own lands from an enforced diaspora, contributed significantly to shaping Native identities in the southwestern borderlands, as the study of the Navajos and Yaquis and their interaction with their respective colonial governments demonstrates. In the case of the Navajos, removal and exile may actually have helped to create a larger tribal or national identity that may have made them stronger in their dealings with the United States government. For the Yaquis, exile posed a serious challenge to their communal identity and especially to the spirit of resistance among those exiled.

The area today referred to as the U.S. Southwest was for the longest time under Spanish and later Mexican rule but came under U.S. control in the middle of the nineteenth century. At times this new border split Native territories and hindered indigenous movement, while at other times Native populations used this semipermeable new line to escape, at least temporarily, from the treatment that the governments on both sides of the border saw fit to level against them. Even though the rhetoric of benevolence toward Native Americans in the United States might suggest otherwise, the national Indian policies of Mexico and the United States differed little in their ultimate objective, the breaking up of tribes within their national borders.[1] The impact of the desire to do so is exemplified by the Navajos, who through the reordering of the Southwest from the late 1840s found themselves within the territorial boundaries of the United States, and by the Yaquis, who, after going back and forth across the border between the countries, eventually came to have populations on both sides of it. Both the Navajos and the Yaquis experienced mass dislocations in the nineteenth century, initiated by the national governments of the country they lived in. In the United States these removals were part of a national policy program known as "Indian Removal," which claimed to be for the benefit and protection of Natives who were to become "civilized" in this way. In Mexico these dislocations were conducted in a more impromptu manner and not as a nationwide policy. The goal of Mexico and the United States in removing the Yaquis and the Navajos was the "pacification" and development of the areas occupied by the two tribes, as well as redistribution of resources such as land in favor of nonindigenous settlers. Native Americans were seen as obstacles in such development. Indigeneity was negatively defined, as neither the Navajos nor the Yaquis were willing to conform to the norms of the nonindigenous members of the imagined communities that were the United States and Mexico. Consequently, both the United States and Mexico sought to break up and relocate the tribal communities that were considered to be in the way of national progress.

This approach succeeded neither for the Navajos in the United States nor for the Yaquis in Mexico. In both cases, the Native group's collective identity was forged by resistance to the imposition of alien rule over their territory. It was also forged, following defeat, especially for the Navajos, by the effort to negotiate with the new rulers for their interests as a group. Yet despite considerable similarities, there were also significant differences in the experiences of Navajos and Yaquis

vis-à-vis the states they resided in. These contributed to the success
with which they could fight against state policies and for their land
and identity. In the United States, a rhetoric of law and benevolence
toward indigenous peoples required the authorities to at least superficially conform to certain standards. At times Native Americans like
the Navajos managed to use this to their advantage, as they did in negotiations over land. In Mexico, such a discourse was largely absent.
Its government was thus able to devise a tailor-made removal or deportation program for the Yaquis. Unlike in the United States, Mexican officials were not constrained by national laws or policies and also
did not feel bound to live up to certain self-devised standards of benevolence that were proclaimed to be at the root of U.S. Indian policy. This afforded the Yaquis less room to maneuver in the dealings
with the state, even though the state eventually came to pass off the
Yaquis' removal as a benevolent gesture because it permitted the Indians to live rather than killing them outright. Furthermore, while
the Yaquis were valued as excellent laborers in Mexico, this advantage
turned into a disadvantage when the Mexican state decided to exploit
their labor force in Yucatán in Mexico's south rather than in their native Sonora in the north. This, in addition to outsiders' desire for their
fertile lands, sealed the Yaquis' fate. However, the United States attached no value at all to Navajo labor or even to Navajo lands, which
were considered to be of poor quality. Once their feared raiding had
ceased, the Navajos stopped being a priority, and the state was reluctant to incur any more expenses on their account. As a consequence,
the Navajos, after a few years in exile, found themselves in a better
bargaining position than the Yaquis. For both tribes, however, the experiences of removal and exile and their sustained resistance shaped
and reshaped identity.

The Navajos in Exile

The first Europeans the Navajos encountered were Spaniards who
brought horses and sheep, which were to become very important to
the Navajo way of life. The Navajos, who live in the Four Corners region of today's United States and refer to themselves as Dinés, were

not a unified people at the time of first contacts with Europeans, and even much later on many of their political units could not be bound by just one agreement, something that was to contribute to their problems with the U.S. government.[2] Instead, there were many different group identities mainly based on kinship, without an overarching tribal or national one. Navajo economy was diversified, and they depended on stock raising, hunting, and gathering, as well as on raiding. Raiding increased in the face of European expansion attempts, and during the Mexican period, from 1821 to 1846, Mexican officials were unable to enforce regulations on the Navajos.

Yet a much stronger and more assertive colonial power than Mexico was about to appear on the scene. As historian Peter Iverson has pointed out, even prior to the Treaty of Guadalupe Hidalgo in 1848, which ended the war with Mexico, the United States had attempted to assert its authority over the Navajos in their own territory.[3] However, "the Anglo Americans who claimed the Navajo territory as a result of the Mexican war initially followed much of the same tradition as the Spanish and Mexicans and with essentially the same results," in spite of the signing of several treaties.[4] The United States built forts in an attempt to control the area, but in April 1860 the Navajos under the leadership of Manuelito and Barboncito attacked Fort Defiance with about one thousand followers. Trying to expel the Americans, they came very close to overcoming the fort's defenses. The U.S. Civil War delayed any retaliatory measures against the Navajos, but General James H. Carleton, who took command in New Mexico in 1862, soon began to plan the removal of the tribe. The army rounded up the Navajos in order to relocate them to a place called Bosque Redondo.[5] In the face of the relentless persecution and drastic measures taken against them, few Navajos managed to avoid being captured and relocated. The trek into exile came to be known as the Long Walk, even though in reality it was not just one march but many, along different routes, between August 1863 and the end of 1866.[6] Due to a lack of blankets and scarcity of food, many Navajos died even while waiting to be removed, and many also perished on the walk. Yet as Iverson has explained, even for those Dinés who, fearing themselves to be involved in a war of extermination, surrendered and went to Bosque Redondo, it "did not mean they had surrendered forever. It meant that they wanted to survive and they wanted their children to realize some kind of future."[7]

According to Carleton's vision, removal to Bosque Redondo "would help the aborigines advance into what he believed to be the superior ways of his own civilization" and there they "would become independent yeomen and eventually take their place among the American citizenry."[8] But life in the place the Navajos called Hwéeldi, which they shared with Apaches, was not as Carleton had envisaged it.[9] The land and the water were poor and there were frequent raids by the Comanches and conflicts with the Apaches. In spite of efforts at agriculture, there was rarely sufficient food for the large number of Navajos (and Apaches) confined there, and diseases prevailed. After repeated crop failures, the Indians had to be fed from army supplies that had been rejected by government inspectors as unfit for troop consumption.[10] Death rates mounted, and in November 1865 all but nine Apaches fled the reservation, taking Navajo horses with them. In the same year the Navajos also started slipping away. A national enquiry was mounted, which turned Bosque Redondo and with it the fate of the Navajos into a national issue. Furthermore, the government transferred the budgetary responsibility for Bosque Redondo to the Indian Bureau, which then claimed to be unable to support the Navajos.[11] These budgetary concerns, paired with national interest in the matter, significantly helped the Navajos' bargaining power in the ensuing negotiations.

Due mainly to these concerns, by the time General William T. Sherman and Samuel F. Tappan of the Peace Commission came to Bosque Redondo and its garrison at nearby Fort Sumner to negotiate with the Navajos, "the question had become not whether Fort Sumner would continue to hold the Navajos, but rather where the people would go."[12] The military man and the humanitarian initially sought to move the Navajos to the Indian Territory. Historian Lynn Bailey, in an early study, has argued that "the Navajo, starving, diseased, and homesick, were willing to agree to anything, so long as they would be granted their one desire," to go back to their own country.[13] However, a closer examination of the recorded speeches made during a number of talks and councils indicates that the Navajos produced sophisticated arguments intended to convince the government that it was in everyone's best interest to send them back to their own country. A sense of collective identity was forged among the Navajos because of their forced migration and exile as well as a realization that they would always be held collectively accountable for any so-called transgressions and that their only chance to return consisted of promising that all Navajos would do better in the future. Yet while Navajo negotiation techniques and behavior reflected this awareness, they still shrewdly bargained to get as many concessions as possible out of the government representatives.

In order to persuade the government to consider their demands, the exiled Navajos claimed to appreciate what the federal government had done for them. At one council, an unidentified Navajo speaker claimed to value the good intentions of the U.S. government by saying that the Dinés "believe the Great Father and his people are our good friends." Probably bending the facts more than a bit, he claimed they had plenty to eat and to wear and that Bosque Redondo "is the best place for us we know outside of our own Country." He said that although the federal government had expected them to "become so attached to the spot [Bosque Redondo] as to be unwilling to leave it," this had never happened. Carleton, the Navajo speaker also recalled, "told us we would be happy and contented here and we are not." While hinting at their discontent without openly blaming the government or even Carleton for their misery in exile, the Navajo also took pains to emphasize their compliance, assuring "the Great Father we will obey him." Gesturing toward the reasons given to them for their removal, the Navajo representative acknowledged that they had "done wrong but we have learned better and if allowed to return to our Mountain homes will behave ourselves well." In this story, the exiled Navajos emerge as a people wronged.[14]

In spite of the strong emphasis on their wish to return home, in this council the efforts the Navajos had made at Bosque Redondo were given prominence. The speaker emphasized their work, declaring that

"the Great Father has done well by us and we are willing to work,"
and proudly stated that they had learned to use the tools and imple-
ments they had been given.[15] Without ever clearly saying so, he thus
absolved the Navajos from any guilt for the failure of the resettlement
experiment while subtly yet firmly laying it at the feet of the government and its agents. According to the speaker, the tribe was still willing to continue to follow the government's bidding. He affirmed that
"if the Government wants us to remain here we will do so and do the
best we can" but he also made it very clear what they really wanted
by immediately adding that they could not "be as contented as we
would be in our old homes."[16] He thus emphasized the obedience of
the tribe, which the United States government had for so long sought
in vain, especially when it came to raiding, but which the exiled Dinés must have recognized as an essential prerequisite for permission
to return home. In an often quoted and poetic statement, the spokesman went on to illustrate the Dinés' relationship to the land through
analogies with the animal kingdom: "Cage the Badger and he will try
to break from his prison and regain his native hole—chain the Eagle
to the ground—he will strive to gain his freedom and though he fails
will lift his head and look up to the sky which is his home—and we
want to return to our Mountains and plains where we used to plant
corn wheat Beans Pepper Melons Onions."[17] This beautiful analogy,
which in a frequently omitted part at the end also emphasized the
desire for a peaceful agricultural existence—the proclaimed goal of
removal and Bosque Redondo—has often obscured the tribe's other accomplished arguments that may have influenced U.S. negotiators into agreeing that it would be best to send the tribe back home.[18]

    After years in exile, in which they had encountered many officials,
the Navajos knew full well the type of argument white people in governmental employ tended to respond to. Therefore, the speaker provided the government agents with practical reasons to let the tribe
return to their old homes. The high mortality was foremost among
those: "In our country our people *die* but here whole families die—if
we remain here we will all die very soon."[19] In the minds of the Navajos, the high death rate in exile was a "divine act of the Great Spirit,"

as "the Great Spirit never intended we should be removed to this side of the Rio Grande and we would be glad to return."[20] After first adopting a conciliatory strategy emphasizing their obedience and goodwill, then supplying practical reasons for sending them back home, the speaker proceeded to make demands on behalf of the tribe. "Without protection from the Utahs who are our enemies," he stated, "we would not care to go back."[21] Maybe the Dinés would have promised anything in order to be permitted to return home, yet that did not mean they would not try to get the best possible deal for themselves. By means of a shrewd argument that implied Navajo innocence and governmental guilt about the failure of Bosque Redondo, and by stopping short of making this claim explicit so as not to put the agents on the defensive, the Navajos exiles did their best to secure a return home as much as possible on their own conditions. They managed to construct a subtle argument that influenced the government agents quite possibly without their ever realizing they were being manipulated.

In a subsequent meeting the Navajo headmen again took a similar approach. In making further demands, the headmen provided practical explanations for why Bosque Redondo was failing in spite of their own persistent efforts. At this gathering on July 15, 1868, at Fort Sumner, the post at the Bosque Redondo reservation, it was mostly Herrera and Ganado Mucho who spoke on behalf of the tribe. Herrera, while supplying plenty of reasons for why it was in the government's best interest to let the Dinés go back home, began his speech with a demand to have their herds restored. He neatly linked this request to the problem of feeding the tribe and the hunger that prevailed at Bosque Redondo as well as to the depredations by the Comanches who, he explains, "will come here and steal our stock." He then went on to outline exactly why it would be in the government's best interest to let the Dinés go back home, emphasizing the bad quality of the water as well as monetary reasons, something he must have known to be of high importance to the United States. He explained that he knew government had spent a lot of money on them but said it was hardly enough to support them. In an astute analysis of governmental preoccupations, he suggested that it would be better for everyone involved if the Navajos were to be allowed to return "rather than the Government should lose so much money." In their own country, he argued, they would have plenty while "now we have nothing."[22]

Herrera took great care trying to anticipate any counterarguments, explaining "that the Government will give us presents, and do as they can for us, but we think the Government is losing money but on account of keeping us here." This, he implied, was something that could be avoided by sending the Dinés back home and without jeopardizing any advancements in the realm of civilization they had made at Bosque Redondo. Neatly reducing the issue to the essentials, Herrera argued that "we are all the time thinking of our old Country and we believe if the Government will put us back in our old Country they could have us the same there as here and they could work us the same there as here." He thus made it clear that sending them back home would not be a compromise but rather a way for the U.S. government to have everything and at the same time make the Navajos happy. "We would be better satisfied if the Government could find us a hatchet and a hoe and send us back to our Country, they would not have so much money to expend on us."[23]

In addition, Herrera promised that in their own country "we will have no complaints to make" because they would have sufficient food once again and would be able to defend themselves against their enemies, thus arguing that a return home would solve the problems that ailed them most at Bosque Redondo. At the same time he made clear the futility of what they were doing in their current exile when he said that they "have enough land and it is good land but it is not ours. We are cultivating the lands of the Comanches." Crucially, in his eyes, the fact that they were on the lands of other Indians doomed the Bosque Redondo experiment, as the Navajos' "best men are those who have been killed by the Comanches" when they went out to look for lost stock. This situation was something they had not been warned of; to the contrary, when they came there they were "told that no enemies would interfere with us." Instead, they found that "every day we are molested." Herrera concluded that this insecurity contributed to their longing for home: "I am thinking more about my old Country than

ever before because there I could secure myself from the enemies."
Herrera explained that the Comanches thought they had a right to
come there and kill them: "they told us the land belonged to them,
the water belonged to them, the hunting ground belonged to them,
the wood belonged to them." He believed this to be true "because they
(the Comanches) come in here every day and steal our stock." It was
clear to him that "this land don't belong to us and now our enemies
can come here and kill us."[24]

In Herrera's view, even though the Navajos had amply shown their
goodwill in trying to make the experiment at Bosque Redondo work,
they could never be successful. Still, he took pains to emphasize all the
work they had done and how obedient they had been ever since coming to Fort Sumner, and also that the Apaches had been much less so.
"Notwithstanding the Cold and Heat we have worked," he pointed
out, and he promised that they would continue to do so, "but poor as
we are we would rather go back to our own Country."[25] Although the
wish to go home was central, being permitted to return was not all
he asked for. Herrera also wanted "the soldiers to go with me" to protect the Dinés on their journey home.[26] He indicated that upon their
return they "want to have all the 'Herd' we had before we left our old
Country."[27] He also while suggested that once safely back home they
would be able to defend themselves against their enemies.[28] Far from
promising anything just to be able to return home, Herrera gave the
impression of knowing exactly what he wanted for the tribe. Going
home was not enough unless his people would be safe there and able
to make a living.

At the same meeting, Ganado Mucho made similar arguments, focusing on the Navajos' enemies, loss, death, water, and diseases. He
concluded that they had to return to their old homes to address these
issues, promising good behavior in the same breath that he listed the
various problems: "We think we were born to live in our old Country.
Disease is more prevalent here than there. The water does not suit us
here. We think we were not born to live here. We would not commit
depredations there."[29] Ganado Mucho stuck to the formula of pair-
ing subtle condemnations with assurances. He went on to talk about

the shortcomings of their current residence in comparison with their former one and about how they would continue to work once back home. "The land here will never be as good as in our own country. The Government does not supply us with wood and we had plenty there. If the Government would put us on a reservation in our own Country and keep us the same as here, the Government would see how we would work."[30] However, even these assurances contained implicit demands for support: "We will never do bad anymore. We want to go back there and be kept there, the same as we are kept here."[31] Without resorting to a clear threat, Ganado Mucho made sure the government agents knew exactly what to expect should they not acquiesce to Navajos demands: "We don't want to run away from here. We want Government to take us there and give us such a reservation as we have here."[32] Clearly, the government's noncompliance with their requests would bring the Dinés' disobedience in the form of flight. This, as the government would have known, was not an empty threat, as the garrison at Fort Sumner was understrength and could not patrol the reservation.[33] This task instead fell to the Navajos.[34] William Haas Moore has speculated that "Navajo leaders . . . knew this and dealt with authorities from a position of limited strength."[35]

The negotiations continued in September 1867 and involved a delegation of eleven Navajos. They wasted no time in trying to determine "what you did with the talk you had with us last year" and to reiterate their grievances. Again they stated that they "don't think we have a right to occupy any other land," and they listed the foods they used to have prior to removal. They claimed that the bacon fed to them in their exile made them sick and that "the land is bad and the water is very bad." When questioned if any of them thought Bosque Redondo was a good place, they responded that "some of our people did but since then they are all dissatisfied because the land is poor, water bad, and no wood." Once again they hinted at their failed but nonetheless determined efforts, saying that they did not think they could raise wheat there. They also complained about the cold and the problems it brought, declaring that they had to walk eighteen miles to get wood and that they had no burros or carts to transport it. This was very hard and time-consuming work; they had to "start early in the morning at day break and don't get back until night." Furthermore, "some . . . die on the road with the load they carry." They especially feared the coming winter, as they did not know where to go in order to obtain wood. They endured exposure and suffered from frozen body parts because they had received only one poor-quality blanket each the previous October.[36]

During the meeting it also emerged that other issues aggravated the situation. The Indian delegates were especially critical of the water, which was salty, bad-tasting, and, they said, "some of our children die from its effects." Moreover, in Navajo opinion, the water was responsible for even more evils: "the water we think infects the land." Unsurprisingly, under these circumstances the death rates being reported were staggering. They informed General Sherman and Superintendent Tappan of five to eight deaths per day and told them that "the greater half have died here." The hospital was not much help, as "few go there even if sick. The medicine kills them, they are afraid of it. We prefer our own medicine men." They claimed that their own medicine men did not kill even if they could not cure. In the light of this, the conclusion that "none are contented" was obvious.[37]

Still, the Navajos remained conciliatory, promising that "if sent back we will keep the peace" and that the former difficulties they had with the government were "not the fault of the entire tribe" but "the fault of the bad men." They went on to clarify that "we had bad men and we did wrong defending them" but promised they would deliver them to the authorities in the future, something they made good on soon after. The tribe thus made it clear that while they owned up to what they referred to as their wrongs, they made sure to place the blame on just a few Dinés. However, they also acknowledged some culpability for what had taken place by admitting that they had done wrong to defend the culprits. The speakers went on to conclude that "if we had obeyed you we would not have lost all our property, we would not have been thus punished, humiliated, and corrected by soldiers."[38]

In order to secure their return home, the exiled Dinés, in response to governmental demands, seemed willing not only to admit to a share

of the blame but also to make promises for the entire tribe, as requested by General Sherman in the negotiations.[39] This may have contributed to the emergence of their national consciousness and communal
Navajo identity. In requests as in promises, a new sense of communal
identity is tangible. It was necessary for the Navajos to think like this
to be able to make and keep such promises.

In spite of making some concessions in order to secure permission
to return home, the Navajos very skillfully and subtly suggested that
the government carry at least part of the blame for the situation they
encountered in exile. They told government negotiators that it was in
the best interest of everyone involved to allow the Dinés to return. Far
from promising just anything to secure their goals, they were adroit-
ly negotiating in order to secure as many of their demands as possible. And they made sure that, in spite of all the tactical manipulation,
the government's agents knew exactly what they wanted. Their diplomatic skills in tapping into the government's concern that the Dinés be self-sufficient again may have helped them avoid being sent to
Indian Territory, and may even have contributed to securing them a
permanent reservation in their old home.[40] General Sherman seems
to have been sympathetic to the Navajos.[41] After all, at this stage it
was not a question of whether the Navajos were to leave Bosque Redondo but merely one of where they would go. Also, the fact that the
place they so desperately wanted to go back to was made up of lands
generally deemed undesirable would have also worked in their favor.

Historian Peter Iverson sees the return to a reservation with defined boundaries after a period of shared suffering as the beginning
of the Navajo Nation, an entity based on a shared Navajo identity.[42]
Judging by statements made by the exiled Navajos, the seeds for this
identity were present even prior to the return of the Dinés. The negotiations between the Dinés and U.S. government agents show not
only how much they yearned to return to their old homes but also
how insistent they were on what was most important to them, those
things that constituted home. Their emerging identity as Navajo Indians and as a unified nation was closely tied to their way of life, and
thus, they sought to preserve as much of this as possible. Their skillful

negotiations may have helped the Dinés to preserve at least the possibility of returning to their stock raising, hunting, and gathering, though not to their old raiding habits, which they realized had contributed to the decision to remove them. And undoubtedly, for those who had suffered so much in exile at Bosque Redondo, their old way of life had assumed a new meaning. Home had come to be associated with safety, and safety needed stability. Governmental pressure and demands had made it clear that these conditions could only be reached if the entire tribe abided by certain rules and conditions. Through the experience of exile, the memory of home, and also in response to governmental pressure, an increased sense of community developed among the Navajos.

The Navajos at Home

The Treaty of 1868 afforded the Dinés a reservation of 3.5 million acres back in their old homelands. While this was smaller than the area they had laid claim to prior to their removal, it was nonetheless a considerable achievement to avoid being sent to Indian Territory. However, they received less land per capita than any other tribe that signed a treaty in 1868. Because of their labors at Bosque Redondo, they were deemed ready to become agriculturalists and thus were understood to be needing less land.[43]

Once returned home, the Dinés remained conscious of the factors that had forced them into exile and were keen to avoid repeating this experience. Their interactions with the government mostly centered on Navajo thieves, reservation boundaries, treaty clauses, conflicts with the Apaches, and issues surrounding agents and interpreters. When talking to the government, the Dinés often returned to the negotiating tactics they had used so successfully before. Again they subtly blamed the government for what went wrong while at the same time expressing their thanks for what it had done for them. Once again they strove to supply practical reasons for their demands and especially for needing more land. But it is unlikely that the government would have acceded had it not been for its poor opinion of the lands sought by the Navajos.[44] As Iverson has contended, "their ability to remain and, indeed, expand their territory can be explained primarily in terms of the value the U.S. government placed on their high desert terrain."[45] The Dinés suggested that an increase of Navajo lands was the best solution all around, as it would allow them to feed themselves and thus save the U.S. government further expenses while not requiring it to sacrifice any lands of value in the process.[46]

Soon after their return, the Navajos found themselves confronted with problems similar to those that had led to their removal, such as accusations of thievery and raiding. The nineteen Diné representatives at an 1872 peace council undoubtedly recognized the danger of history repeating itself. Juaro, who spoke first, thus moved straightaway to reassure the governmental representatives of the Navajos' wish for peace, stating that his "people want to have peace with everybody." He explained that "when we were at war we lost many of our people, and now we wish to live at peace here in our country." He then indicated that they did all they could to keep the peace, confessing that "there are bad people among us, as among all others, but when they commit depredations we do all we can to hunt them down." While pinning the problem on a few bad people, he outlined the solution and pointed to the universality of the issue. Juaro also expressed the desire to leave the past behind and start afresh by pronouncing that the events of the past were "all forgotten now; we can go about the country in peace."[47]

Manuelito, who spoke next and for all the chiefs present, began by commenting on recent troubles between Navajos and Apaches, indicating that he thought General Oliver O. Howard, who was present at the talks, could regulate matters between the two tribes. He took the opportunity to turn these potentially negative issues into a tactical advantage for the Dinés by indicating how far they had come, stating that formerly "the Navajo did not believe in it [peace] but now they do," and also emphasizing their readiness for talks.[48] At the same time he pleaded for some leniency, emphasizing their continued difference from the Americans: "We are not the same as Americans, their regulations are different; we can't have the same regulations as Americans, and we cannot accomplish things so quickly."[49] However, he also illustrated the Dinés' commitment through a tale of horses returned to the Apaches, thus emphasizing how much progress they had made.

Manuelito reiterated that there were good as well as bad people among the Navajos, an argument they had already used successfully while at Bosque Redondo when negotiating for their return to their lands. Probably only too aware of government impatience, he hinted at possibly asking the United States for help in addressing depredations in the future. He promised that "if we cannot accomplish it we will call the president for help," and that he could not "do it all myself, but I want to do all I possibly can." Subtly stalling, Manuelito reserved the right to deal with the issue without resorting to bluntly telling the agents to stay out of Diné affairs. And just as in previous negotiations, he sought to secure the government's goodwill for the tribe by saying he did "not wish that the whole people should be distrusted or ill treated on account of the thieves." He reiterated their commitment to the United States but also hinted at his foremost preoccupation, the land: "Now that we are together with the Americans, and for the sake of one thief I do not want to separate again." Manuelito was well aware that the behavior of one could be held against all if it suited the government's objectives, stating that "I don't want the thieves to take our land away; we want to remain here." He also appeared determined not to be parted from his lands again, indicating that to remain there was his prime concern.[50]

Land remained foremost in any negotiations between the Dinés and the U.S. government. In a letter sent by the Navajos to commissioner of Indian affairs Edward P. Smith in December of the next year, the issue of reservation boundaries was the main concern.[51] Here the "Chiefs and Principal Men of the Navajo Nation" asked that agent William F. M. Arny be authorized to take a delegation to Washington, possibly because past dealings with the government had shown them that it was best to negotiate in person to get the right as well as timely results. They explained that they wanted "to consult with the Government in reference to a change of the boundaries of our reservation and matters connected with the treaty of 1868" and that for this purpose they sought to send fifteen Navajos and two interpreters to Washington.[52] The matter was of sufficient importance to them to suggest that the expenses be deducted from their annuities: "if we can see the Great Father and talk with him and . . . explain to him our wants that it will be so much good to us that we can pay the expenses to go."[53] The signatories, including Ganado Mucho, indicated that it was important they be back in time for planting, thus making it clear that for practical reasons they needed to go and discuss the issue soon but also emphasizing their civilized and productive lifestyle.

Another letter, dated February 11, 1874, reiterated the request to send a delegation even though the Dinés had been informed through a letter read out to them by their agent that the money would not be available until July 1, 1874.[54] They expressed the desire to talk about the boundaries of the reservation, as the relevant treaty article had not been explained to them.[55] Just as in previous negotiations they confidently made suggestions, probably suspecting that the government would not on its own accord find a solution that would be to their liking. Therefore, they asked for their treaty to be "so modified as to give us lands south of the present reservation in lieu of lands we are willing to relinquish."[56] Again, several practical concerns, such as the Dinés' intended self-sufficiency for budgetary reasons and whites' poor estimation of their lands, probably made sure their arguments fell onto fertile grounds.

The government acceded to this request. The Articles of Agreement of 1874 between the Navajo Nation and the United States relinquished a portion of the reservation granted them through the Treaty of 1868 but also stipulated that land be given to the Dinés in return. Discussions about the borders of the reservation resumed at a council meeting in May 1879, called by Manuelito, who, according to Ganado Mucho, spoke for all of them.[57] And once again Manuelito resorted to the formula that had worked so well for the Dinés before. He supplied practical reasons why the Navajos needed to increase their land base, also implying that part of this need arose out of their adherence to advice given by government agents, for which he still expressed the tribe's thankfulness. He began by articulating the Navajos' feelings about the extent of their land base, saying "this place where they live, the limited amount of land, makes them feel bad, because it is so small."[58] He elaborated on the reasons why they felt the need for more land, while also countering at least one possible objection by clarifying that "the Americans think this Reservation is large enough but it is not so; in the summertime it is so but in the winter it is impossible to keep their sheep upon it, they would all die."[59] He thus highlighted the need for more land by pointing to its quality, something the government would have understood, as the general perception of Navajo lands was that they were very poor.

To explain why the Dinés had so many animals that they needed an extension of the reservation boundaries, Manuelito recalled the negotiations of the treaty of 1868, and specifically the advice they had received from General Sherman. "General Sherman and the agent," Manuelito remembered, "gave them advice to get more stock, and now they have plenty and no place to keep them." Lest the government's agents think them foolish for following a bad suggestion, he then explained that "they took the advice believing that more land would be given them to extend themselves," yet this had not been the case. Manuelito later hastened to emphasize how grateful the Dinés still were to the government, saying that they were "very happy now because they have all kinds of animals and are thankful to the Americans for their good advice." Thus taking great care not to offend, Manuelito still made it very clear that the one solution that could be relied upon to fix the problem was the extension of the reservation so that there would be sufficient feed for all the animals even in winter. The animals, he argued, in turn provided the Navajos with much-needed sustenance, as "they have but little and are hearty eaters."[60]

After thus having argued the Dinés' need for more land, Manuelito reiterated their demands, stating that "he wants an extension on every side." He directed his plea to the top, saying "the President is very good but he ought to consider what they are asking." At the same time, Manuelito bemoaned the unresponsiveness of the government to the Navajos' repeated letters complaining that they had been promised extensions of their reservation on all sides but had never got them. Several times he implied that he would prefer to go to Washington and talk in person rather than having to depend on an agent to write a letter for the tribe. He emphasized their reliance on their agent, as the Navajos were "like blind men + don't know anything." Statements such as this went a certain way to make the Navajos look unthreatening or even submissive.[61]

Manuelito's subtle and sophisticated argument did not stop with passing off the Navajos as unthreatening to and reliant on the government. Instead, he took the opportunity to further strengthen his case by emphasizing the virtues of the tribe. He contended that "160 acres is not enough for one man," insisting "a little dwarf would work that; a strong man could work a great deal more."[62] He took pains to draw attention to their progress, stating that "they have done well since the agency has been here."[63] He also discussed possible locations for a school, again emphasizing their progress toward civilization that the government claimed to pursue through its removal policy. He then twice reiterated an old winning argument, promising self-sufficiency and thus fewer expenses for the government because the Navajos could "make their own living if they can have more land."[64] Following Manuelito's lead, Ganado Mucho subsequently argued that "they have done all they promised and should have have [sic] what they ask for."[65]

Similar arguments were used in talks held at Fort Defiance over three days in December 1880. This time around, several of the speakers for the Navajos stressed their progress, possibly in an attempt to justify and strengthen their demands for tools and equipment. Ganado Mucho argued that now that the Navajos knew how to plow, they required wide hoes, shovels, and spades, and he ended his speech by asking for a windmill, a home, and a wagon "that he may live like a white man." In spite of this focus on "civilized" agriculture, two of the speakers, including Manuelito, again asked for an increase in their landholdings. They stressed that the lands they sought were of no value to the Americans, as it was "ground that neither Americans or Mexicans can use" but which the Navajos could utilize for grazing.[66]

While they were not given all the land they asked for, the Navajos received five additions to their reservation between 1878 and 1886, and they still stood to gain a few more minor ones later on.[67] This is especially significant compared with the major land losses suffered by other Native Americans during the same period when removal and allotment cost them vast acreages. And while this outcome in part may have been due to the poor opinion that Americans had of Navajo lands, the Navajos' negotiation skills and tactics were still nothing short of remarkable. They created a rhetoric that told the government officials what they wanted to hear and were able to understand, while at the same time subtly implicating the United States in all that had gone wrong. Navajo guilt, while acknowledged and paired with promises and reassurances, was minimized. In this manner the Diné negotiators, often led by Manuelito, managed to suggest to the government's agents that it would be a good idea for everyone involved to give the Navajos the land they asked for because it would address all the problems that came up in the negotiations.

As Iverson has indicated, exile and suffering were the beginning of the modern Navajo nation and identity. This is visible in the negotiations at Bosque Redondo as well as later on, when the Diné negotiators entered into talks for all those in exile or even for all Navajos. While at times different groups are still mentioned, all the negotiations are conducted for the entire tribe.[68] A common identity had begun to emerge that enabled the Navajos to meet some of the demands of the federal government. It also formed the basis of the modern Navajo Nation.

The Yaquis at Home

The experience of the Yaquis in the section of the Southwest that remained part of Mexico was not all that dissimilar to that of the Navajos in the United States. They too experienced removal and the eventual return to their homelands. And even prior to their removal and return home the Yaquis' history showed many parallels to that of the Navajos, as they also had not been willing to accede to governmental domination over them.[69]

Over centuries, the Sonoran Yaquis' behavior can best be described as nonconformist. This had been the case since their first contacts with Europeans in the early sixteenth century. When they felt the situation called for it, the Yaquis always seemed willing to rise up for their de-mands. The Yaquis, who refer to themselves as Yoemes, thus achieved something of a balance between the demands of the state and the *veci-nos*, the nonindigenous citizens of the area, and their own aims and goals. The success with which they did this was to contribute to the deportation and forced exile of a significant number of Yaquis to Yu-catán, where their will to continue their resistance would be sorely tested.[70] This became especially obvious in the few legal cases the ex-iled Yoemes were involved with in the Yucatán peninsula and which reflected their continued attachment to their homeland and tribal community, but also the toll deportation had taken on them and their will to resist.

The nineteenth century alone saw two major Yaqui uprisings, one under Juan Banderas, the other led by a Yaqui known as Cajeme. These uprisings shared similar goals, with the leaders insisting on keeping the land exclusively to the tribe while generally accepting work and trade interactions with the outside world. Thus the "Yaqui tradition of not isolating themselves entirely from the outside world, while claiming the right to autonomy," as historian Evelyn Hu-DeHart has observed, created something like a state within a state.[71] This was unacceptable to the Porfiristas, the government under Porfirio Díaz. They attempt-ed to crush the Yoemes by military means, ultimately intending to colonize and develop Yaqui lands. Working toward this goal, the Por-firistas declared the lands vacant in the 1880s, and when the Yaquis were unable to produce recorded titles for their lands, the tracts were surveyed and sold.[72] Up to that time, Yaqui resistance, paired with a need for Yaqui labor, had allowed the tribe an impressive degree of maneuverability in their dealings with the Mexican state and the re-gional Sonoran government. This maneuverability had enabled them to keep at least part of their lands free of non-Yaquis. They would not accept such land losses and intrusions as the new land decrees brought.

The ensuing Yaqui wars under the leadership of Cajeme lasted twelve years in spite of the serious involvement of federal forces. The diffi-cult terrain and the climate worked in favor of the Yoemes, and their status as an important labor force may have helped, at least initially, to save them from more severe measures. As the war went on, the Yo-emes' reputation suffered, and local newspapers portrayed the tribe as "enemigos de la civilización y el trabajo" (enemies of civilization and work).[73] To the great disappointment of the government, even af-ter the defeat and death of Cajeme in 1887 the resistance of the Yaqui tribe remained unbroken. Hit-and-run attacks then became the prev-alent form of combat. Those Yoemes who worked outside their tra-ditional territory now more than ever functioned as support for the resistance of the so-called *broncos*, the active rebels. Although only a minority was actively involved in the fighting, almost every Yaqui had a part in this struggle. The so-called *pacíficos* or *mansos* supported the *broncos* and made it hard, if not impossible, for the Mexican forces to overcome the armed resistance fueled by the "peaceful" members of the tribe. The rebels went to the haciendas to rest and recharge while workers took their part in the fighting. This constant exchange pre-vented the military from effectively isolating the rebels. After several unsuccessful attempts to do so, the Sonoran and federal governments arrived at deportation as the only option left to them short of out-right killing all the Yaquis, which would have been deemed a waste of their valuable labor.

Deportations had been tentatively pioneered in a previous cam-paign against Juan Banderas and were now reintroduced.[74] At first this method was adopted partly due to commercial interests from the United States and only used on a very small scale. Eventually these in-terests inspired the Mexican government to take more drastic steps to rid itself of the "Yaqui nuisance" and open up the way for commer-cial agricultural development of the area. At first, the Yoemes had been convenient because they supplied cheap labor not only for ex-panding agriculture but also for mines, railroads, and industries. But the growing need for labor on the Yucatecan henequen (sisal) plan-tations conflicted with the demand for a Yaqui workforce in Sono-ra. The Sonoran hacendados had been disposed to accept the latent threat posed by the Yaquis in exchange for their labor, and until that point the federal and regional governments had also agreed to this trade-off. Yet with the rise of demand for cheap labor in Yucatán it was no longer necessary to accept such compromises. Several goals could be met through the implementation of just one measure, deportation. While groups of so-called prisoners of war were removed from Sonora, it was individual workers who arrived in Yucatán, usually already slated for a particular plantation. Their work reputation had turned against the Yaquis, and Sonoran labor needs were considered secondary to those of Yucatán.

Yet even the draconian policy of deporting the Yoemes did not immediately bring forth all the desired results. The rebels still kept up their resistance. Their attempts to obtain peace repeatedly failed because they still insisted on many of their traditional demands, like having their territory to themselves. Yet the deportations took their toll on the Yaquis, as a letter from 1904 shows. In it the Yaquis complained to state governor Rafael Izábal that troops killed them even though they were born in Sonora ("aunque Seamos nacidos aqui En Sonora").[75] This letter by the "Nueve Capitanes," nine Yaqui captains, also reflects the Yaquis' strong attachment to their land and the complex function of land in Yaqui society.[76] Signaling their attachment, they stated that they were in Sonora because that was where they were from ("porque Somos de aqui"), not because they wanted to fight.[77] The Yoemes, whose identity seems to have been tied to the land, obviously felt that being native to the area gave them rights, and they specifically objected to the killing of persons who did not even carry weapons ("sinque Tenga arma").[78] In the letter they also complained about hangings and said that they did not know why and for what they were to blame, "no Sabemos que culpa tenemos."[79] In this letter, the Nueve Capitanes also stated that the rebellion was taking place only at the river and not in the countryside, presumably to convince the military to spare the *mansos*, as they were so crucial to the rebellion.[80] They generally expressed concern for the Yoemes working outside their territory, which the Yaquis called the Yaquimi. Apparently, many of them feared the relentless persecution by governmental forces, and in particular, hanging. In a deft move designed to trigger the fears of Sonoran hacendados, the men also voiced their fear for the Sonoran harvest, which they claimed was going to be lost without

Yaqui labor. This argument was also used in a letter to the *vecinos*, the local landholders, on the same day, probably echoing and feeding fears the *hacendados* had anyway while at the same time proving the Yaquis' awareness of their main advantage.[81] In this letter the Yoemes insisted that they did not know what they had done wrong and that they had always kept their word. They showed themselves desirous of a "Santa Paz," a holy peace, and hence they implored the recipients of the letter to "do them the favor" with "El Señor Precidente." The letter seems to suggest that the Yaquis, being from Yaquimi, considered themselves to be involved in a defensive war against the Mexican government and that they saw this defense as their right.

In spite of an obvious desire to make peace, if on their own conditions, the rebels still held out and kept up their steadfast resistance. In another letter to the government they warned and even threatened the officials in question not to come to the river (Yaqui).[82] In their attempts to evade capture they roamed an even wider area than before and actively used the U.S. border to escape persecution by going there to hide and to obtain weapons. Until stricter border patrols were put in place the Yaquis were able to use the new borderline to their advantage. Raids and plunder sustained them along with what the *mansos*—who by then were severely restricted through various government measures—could muster. The efforts to subjugate the Yaquis were redoubled as a consequence of the failure of the earlier peace negotiations. Vice President Ramón Corral, himself a Sonoran, had actively encouraged this step, as had President Díaz by then, because the deportation of the Yaquis would not threaten but support his goal of modernization. In short, the deportations made Yaqui labor available outside Sonora while at the same time opening up the Yoemes' territory for colonization. And the deportations affected the Yaquis severely.

The drawn-out peace negotiations led by Luis Bule, one of the rebel leaders, indicate just how disruptive the campaign had become for the Yoemes as a community. In May 1908 government representatives met with the rebel chieftain to explain their conditions.[83] They required complete submission and disarmament. In return they promised necessities like food and clothing and offered the Yaquis permission to keep a few hunting weapons. Bule was also expected to convince the other rebel leaders to surrender. For his part, the Yaqui leader asked for the return of the Yoemes who had been deported to Yucatán, and he refused to accept any of the proposed conditions. Instead, he wanted time to gather the *parientes*, the other members of the tribe. But Bule, under extreme pressure from the government, could not convince his fellow Yaquis to surrender, and thus the deadline to turn over the weapons could not be met. The negotiations dragged on, with the Yoemes insisting on keeping their arms and also maintaining their religious ceremonies and practices. Furthermore, they required guarantees for their lives and for the return of the deported *parientes*.[84] However, in return for such assurances the government wanted the complete submission of the Yaquis and would permit only a few of them to keep their weapons. They were also told that the return of the deportees depended entirely on the conduct of the Sonoran Yaquis. The government refused to make any further concessions. In spite of this, in January 1909, Luis Bule and some 180 rebels agreed to the government's peace conditions and were disarmed. Possibly because the deportees to Yucatán remained unmentioned, not all Yoeme rebels actually surrendered, and some quite literally stuck to their guns. Thus the repeated failure of the negotiations, the problems of representation and decision making, as well as the evident fragmentation, illustrate just how much strain the military campaign and the deportations had put on the tribe.

The deportations themselves reached a peak around 1908. Generally, detention of the Yoemes was followed initially by their transfer into special camps or by imprisonment. They were then shipped by boat from Guaymas down the coast and marched or ferried by train across the width of Mexico in order to again be shipped, this time to Yucatán, their final destination. The trip took between two and four weeks, not including the time the Yoemes spent awaiting their fate while being held in Sonora. While the exact number of deportees is hard to determine, it appears that between one-fourth and one-half of the tribe was deported from Sonora.[85]

In July 1908, when the peace negotiations had failed, the secretary of war made it known to the Yaquis that for every rebel attack, five hundred of them would be deported to Yucatán.[86] This was to be communicated to the *mansos*, the peaceful members of the tribe, who were to relate the news to the rebels. In spite of this threat, the massive embarkations of Yaquis stopped abruptly at the end of July, though smaller numbers continued to be deported. There were still prices on the heads of the Yaquis, but by the end of the month the so-called concentration of *mansos* or *pacíficos* was considered to be complete. With this, governmental efforts finally seemed to have achieved the desired result. Several rebel factions had made peace with the government and even allowed themselves to be recruited to pursue those Yoemes still in rebellion. Yet while the resistance had undoubtedly diminished, it nevertheless survived, even if it was kept up by only one rebel faction under the leadership of Luis Espinosa. Hu-DeHart has observed that "had it not been for the Mexican Revolution which terminated the Díaz regime in 1911, it might have succeeded in isolating the Espinosa faction from the rest of the Yaqui people, ultimately destroying it."[87] The remnants of the resistance were saved by the outbreak of the Mexican Revolution, which brought successive leadership changes in the Mexican government and shifted the focus away from the Yaquis.

In these conflicts, the Yaquis proved that they considered themselves to be outside the social hierarchy envisioned by the government. They were carving their own political identity in relation to, but not dependent on, the Mexican government. It became evident, for instance through the statement by the Nueve Capitanes, that they considered the Yaqui River country to be theirs, and they argued that being from that country bestowed certain rights upon them that the Mexican government could not infringe. They also steadfastly resisted attempts at incorporation and usurpation of their lands. The latter resistance did not meet with complete success, and there were some land losses and encroachment. However, the Yaquis retained something like an autonomous space, both in a metaphorical way—their separateness and autonomy, and also in a very tangible, practical way—the territory they themselves called Yaquimi. They managed to do so even in the face of the massive military intervention and the deportations.

The Yaquis in Exile

Even though active resistance never completely ceased in Sonora, it was lacking among those Yoemes deported to Yucatán. Yucatecan government records rarely mention the Yoemes, and when they do it is mostly in cases of them having contracted yellow fever.[88] Apart from those instances, Yaquis appear in a only few court cases. None of them supply any evidence about active Yaqui resistance in Yucatán. Yet it is these court cases that speak volumes about the life of the deported Yoemes. They tell the Yucatecan tale most clearly and help to explain the lack of active resistance there, as they paint a picture of a people uprooted and isolated in forced exile, turning to, as well as on, one another and to alcohol for solace, all in an attempt to preserve a bit of "Yaquiness" far from their homelands.[89]

The court cases show the striking isolation that affected the Yoemes in Yucatán. In the case against Octaviano Bacasena, an eighteen-year-old hacienda worker, (almost) everyone involved was Yoeme, testifying to the limited contacts among exiled Yoemes and other plantation workers.[90] Bacasena was intoxicated when he attacked Augustín Matos, with whom he had been drinking, with a bottle. It was for the injuries inflicted upon Matos that Bacasena found himself in court. The presence of alcohol in the conflicts occurring among the Yaquis indicated a pattern that can be found repeatedly in the Yucatecan court cases involving exiled Yaquis.[91] As Allen Wells and Gilbert Joseph, authors of *Summer of Discontent, Seasons of Upheaval*, have determined, "Alcohol was . . . the principal release for resident peons; its ready availability in the hacienda stores indicates that, on another level, *henequeneros* appreciated its value as a mechanism of social control."[92] As the example of Bacasena and Matos shows, this tactic was paying off. It managed to turn the Yaquis against each other and thus potentially kept them from mounting an organized resistance in exile.

The fight between Bacasena and Matos was not an isolated occurrence. Not infrequently, exiled Yaquis got intoxicated and violent, directing the violence against one another because they mostly interacted with other Yoemes.[93] Another such case of alcohol-fueled violence among Yaquis was that of the "jornalero yaqui" Miguel Buitimea, who had been attacked by his compatriot Fidencio Alvarado Fodo.[94] Alvarado was reported to have said, "Voy a chingar al yaqüi, voy a matarlo," threatening to "screw" and kill "the Yaqui." The victim, Buitimea, believed Alvarado to have been fed up with the work for a while ("disgustado por trabajo"). The ensuing fight culminated in Buitimea having the tip of his nose bitten off by Alvarado. Such cases illustrate how patterns of violence fueled by alcohol and/or frustration dominated the life of Yaquis in Yucatecan exile. At other times in the small communities in exile, violence could arise even without the aid of alcohol, for instance through jealousy.

Jealousy, not alcohol, seems to have been the central factor in the case of Francisca Loor Ségua, who in June 1908 received a sentence of sixty-nine days in jail.[95] A native of Hermosillo in Sonora, Francisca lived on the hacienda Tanil where she did "female work," which, as anthropologist Raquel Padilla has argued, most likely afforded her at least some contact with non-Yaquis.[96] Francisca, married and in her early forties, was accused of harming the wife of José María Mendoza. In the court proceedings a veritable drama of love, hate, and jealousy between these exiled Yoemes unfolded. The victim, Luz Yoqihua, reported that Francisca had come to her house and had attacked her with a chisel. Francisca herself readily admitted to the attack and explained that it had been in revenge for a beating she herself had received from her husband the week before. He had been having an affair with Luz Yoqihua, and Francisca took the opportunity, when she knew Luz to be home alone, "to give her what she deserved." Luz's wounds were not very grave, but what really must have angered Francisca was that Luz was suffering from a venereal disease that Francisca's husband had contracted through her and passed on to his wife. In this case, as in most others, Yaquis seem to have mainly interacted with other Yoemes.

Such stories of jealousy among the exiles were probably not rare occurrences, even though few of them have been recorded in the Yucatecan state archives. The hacendados oversaw the administration of justice because "by law, the latter were in charge of maintaining 'peace and order,' and of sanctioning minor offenses with, for instance, arrest and corporal punishment," as anthropologist Wolfgang Gabbert has pointed out.[97] This meant that generally such matters would have been dealt with on the plantations themselves, and few plantation records survived the revolution. Yet the similarities in the few officially recorded cases are still striking, centering on alcohol, isolationism among the Yaquis, and the wish to preserve their separate identity.

Most of these elements became sadly obvious in the court case against María de la Luz Flores during January 1912. The defendant, known as Luz, was a thirty-year-old widow originally from Sonora. She had been living with the victim, Juan Fierros, for seven years. Juan was twenty-six, unmarried, and also from Sonora. Four large wounds had been inflicted upon him, and when questioned, he blamed his spouse for causing them while in a state of intoxication. Luz, who had been drinking with a Yaqui friend, Flora Velazco, insisted she had no idea who had attacked and wounded Juan because she had been very inebriated and could not remember anything.[98] Although several witnesses, all of them Yaquis, were questioned, no one could or would shed any more light on the matter. But when Luz was interrogated for the second time, she revealed that a few days prior to the incident, Juan had hurt her in an attempt to kill her with a knife. Later on, both Juan and Luz seem to have agreed that he had only really wanted to scare her. She also reported that Juan had threatened to leave her and go back home, "á su tierra," by himself. He had told her he did not want to be with her anymore. She explained that she always got very sad when drunk, cried, and remembered the children she had been forced to leave behind in Hermosillo and the one child who had died. This, along with the physical and emotional pain Juan had caused her, had finally brought her to the brink, and emboldened by her intoxication, inspired her attack on Juan when it appeared that one of the final links to her former life and identity was about to be severed.

The case of Luz and Juan illustrates that the exiled Yoemes never ceased to consider Sonora and more specifically Yaquimi to be their home. They clung to the remnants of their old identity almost to the point of self-destruction by isolating themselves and turning to alcohol. Both referred to their "tierra" as the place they wanted to go back to, yet both seemed unable to put up a coordinated fight for it, possibly due to the detrimental circumstances they encountered in exile. Because laborers were forbidden to leave the haciendas without permission, it would have been hard to establish the networks necessary for a coordinated uprising, especially as it was common practice to break up groups of deportees and even families.[99] Although active rebels had been among those deported to Yucatán, their will to resist and especially their resistance networks did not survive the move intact. However, as demonstrated at the advent of the revolution in Yucatán when many Yoemes joined the army in an effort to get back to Sonora, their fighting spirit did not simply die but rather lay dormant. Although there was no active resistance, such as revolts, evidenced in the court cases during their exile, the Yaquis' spirit remained alive, albeit latent. This dormant spirit for the time being manifested itself in the Yaquis' stubborn and at times self-destructive isolationism as well as in their attempts to hang onto as much of their former life as possible under the circumstances. The deportees had hardly any contacts with other workers on the haciendas but instead chose to remain with other Yaquis. This isolationism is confirmed by cases in which Yaquis cooperated and helped one another, and tried to maintain at least some of their traditions, such as, for instance, traditional burials.[100] It may have been due to the language barrier—as some of the Yoemes hardly spoke any Spanish, let alone Maya—or due to hacendado policies, or by their own choice, as only one case on file documents involvement of other hacienda workers with Yaquis.[101] Maybe by isolating themselves, the Yoemes somehow tried to keep up their sense of identity, which must have been severely besieged when they were deprived of their land, many of their traditions, and their larger community. At times these attempts at preserving their identities as Yaquis through isolationism also saw them turn against one another.

Luz and others had been deprived of those things the Nueve Capitanes had suggested were the basis of their rights when they were forcefully removed from the place of their birth. As anthropologist Alejandro

Figueroa has pointed out, the Yaquis in Sonora used community, land, customs, and religion, along with their resistance against the government, to help them insist on their separate identity. While they maintained this insistence in Yucatán, their resistance reemerged only with the possibility of returning to their land. Land probably gained additional importance by being tied closely to religion, customs, and even communal identity and may have been the link between all these elements, a link so powerful that when a return from distant exile seemed within reach, it managed to rekindle the seemingly extinct fighting spirit.

The will to actively resist came back when, after the outbreak of the Mexican Revolution, the Yaquis could leave the plantations, which restored their hopes to return to their native land. The move away from the haciendas also permitted them to revive ceremonies they most likely had not been able to practice on the haciendas.[102] Yet even then, there were no uprisings as such, although the Yaquis did take up arms under the command of Yucatecans. The Yaquis, as Padilla has argued, probably joined up in order to secure passage home to Sonora as well as to earn money, attempting to use Yucatecan officials to further their own goals.[103]

Due to the upheaval caused by the revolution, there is very little evidence about how many made it back to Sonora or how they managed the long journey. Some appear to have returned by ship while others seem to have walked. However, there is some evidence that the reintegration of those who had spent years in exile separated from the Yaqui communities in Sonora was not without difficulties. Furthermore, a Yaqui community in the United States that had served as a haven and had given access to supplies became a permanent one, resulting in a split of the tribe and independent Yaqui communities on both sides of the border.[104]

Resistance, Removal, and Identities in the Southwestern Borderlands

Yaquis and Navajos were challenged by the extension of the United States' sphere of influence over the Southwest in the second half of the nineteenth century. This is true even though at that time most Yaquis still lived within the territorial boundaries of Mexico. Indigenous identities in the Southwest, like those of the Navajos and Yaquis, were shaped by positive as well as negative factors, some of which have been discussed here. Land has emerged as a prime factor, especially as both Yaquis and Navajos viewed their rights as being connected to their lands. To them land, identity, and rights were linked. The Yaquis saw their right to oppose the government as coming from their being from the place they fought for, while the Navajos felt they had no right to live at Bosque Redondo because the land belonged to the Comanches. When removed from their own lands, the wish to return became a crucial factor in shaping Native identities. Community and traditions were also important elements that constituted affirmative factors in identity formation, while state policies directed toward indigenous peoples and especially removal formed negative factors.[105] Resistance against the removal policies also came to be a positive and affirmative influence on indigenous identities as the fight united them and provided shared goals, like the return to their homelands.[106] In the case of the Dinés, government policies and joint resistance of the exiled members of the tribe against those policies thus contributed to the creation of the modern Navajo Nation. Development of a shared identity was aided by the sizeable community in exile. For the Yaquis, who were broken into many separate groups with few or no contacts with other tribal members, the immediate result of the exile imposed by the removal policy was the cessation of all active resistance. The extreme and fragmented diasporas in Yucatán, by means of isolation from other plantation workers, made it impossible to sustain more than minimal efforts to retain Yaqui identity.

In spite of the sustained armed resistance and the impressive negotiation skills displayed by both Navajos and Yaquis, in the end the nation-states' policies toward them determined how much room to maneuver the Natives had. The United States' endeavors to pass off their Indian policy as well-meaning attempts to help the Natives become civilized enabled the Navajos to force the government to live up to at least some of its rhetoric once the tribe ceased to be a threat and thus a priority. And in their efforts to gain permission to go home, the exiled Navajos, who seem to have constituted the majority of the tribe and who were confined to one single reservation and thus one corner of diaspora, came

to discover some commonalities in their shared experiences and especially their mutual goal to return.[107] In contrast, the Yaquis' experience
of many extreme diasporas came close to destroying their sense of community. The Mexican state was not constrained by a clearly articulated national Indian policy or by the rhetoric of benevolence toward the
Indians, and it furthermore also sought to take over the Yaquis' fertile
lands. Deprived of both land and community, the Yaquis struggled to
maintain their identity. Prior to the exile of a large number of Yaquis,
they had been dependent for their identity on land and community as
well as on their active resistance against the Mexican state. While both
tribes clearly envisaged themselves as external to the nation-states with
whom they were engaged in extended struggles, only the Navajos, drawing on shared community experiences and the memory of the homelands, were able to forge a new identity through exile.

Notes

1. See Claudia B. Haake, *The State, Removal and Indigenous Peoples in the United States and Mexico, 1620–2000* (New York: Routledge, 2007).

2. Peter Iverson, *The Navajo Nation* (Albuquerque: University of New Mexico Press, 1981), 8.

3. See Peter Iverson, *Diné: A History of the Navajo* (Albuquerque: University
of New Mexico Press, 2002), 37.

4. Iverson, *The Navajo Nation*, 8.

5. See, for instance, Clifford Trafzer, *The Kit Carson Campaign: The Last Great
Navajo War* (Norman: University of Oklahoma Press, 1982).

6. Iverson, *Diné*, 52.

7. Iverson, *Diné*, 51. See also Jennifer Nez Denetdale, *Reclaiming Diné History: The Legacies of Navajo Chief Manuelito and Juanita* (Tucson: University of Arizona Press, 2007), 7.

8. William Haas Moore, *Chiefs, Agents and Soldiers: Conflict on the Navajo Frontier, 1868–1882* (Albuquerque: University of New Mexico Press, 1994), 3.

9. See Denetdale, *Reclaiming Diné History*, 75; Lynn R. Bailey, *Bosque Redondo: An American Concentration Camp* (Pasadena: Socio-Technical Books, 1970),
150; Lynn R. Bailey, *The Long Walk: A History of the Navajo Wars, 1846–1868* (Los
Angeles: Westernlore Press, 1964).

10. Bailey, *Bosque Redondo*, 79.

11. Moore, *Chiefs, Agents and Soldiers*, 13.

12. Iverson, *Diné*, 63.

13. Bailey, *Bosque Redondo*, 145.

14. Council with Navajos at Post Headquarters, recorded by Special Indian Commissioner J. K. Graves, probably late 1865, M234/553, National Archives and Records Administration (hereafter NARA), Riverside CA. As a general rule for names, I have used the spelling found in the sources. Where spelling varied among the documents (Spanish names especially have many variant spellings), I have favored the most common spelling.

15. Council with Navajos, M234/553, NARA.

16. Council with Navajos, probably late 1865.

17. Council with Navajos, probably late 1865.

18. It may be due to statements like this that much research has focused primarily on attachment to land. While this in undoubtedly an important issue it should not overshadow the excellent negotiation skills shown by the Navajo when fighting for their land.

19. Council with Navajos at Post Headquarters, recorded by Special Indian Commissioner J. K. Graves, probably late 1865, M234/553, NARA.

20. Council with Navajos, probably late 1865. See also Robert McPherson, *The Northern Navajo Frontier, 1860–1900: Expansion through Adversity* (Logan: Utah State University Press, 2001), 25, for ties between geography and religion.

21. Council with Navajos, probably late 1865.

22. Gathering of the Head Men of the Navajo Indians at Fort Sumner, July 15, 1868, M234/554, NARA.

23. Gathering of the Head Men, July 15, 1868.

24. Gathering of the Head Men, July 15, 1868.

25. Gathering of the Head Men, July 15, 1868.

26. Gathering of the Head Men, July 15, 1868. He makes this demand even though he also emphasized the Navajos' military prowess, concluding that "when they saw we were getting the best of them we were sent here."

27. Gathering of the Head Men, July 15, 1868.

28. Gathering of the Head Men, July 15, 1868.

29. Gathering of the Head Men, July 15, 1868.

30. Gathering of the Head Men, July 15, 1868.

31. Gathering of the Head Men, July 15, 1868.

32. Gathering of the Head Men, July 15, 1868.

33. Moore, *Chiefs, Agents and Soldiers*, 6.

34. Moore, *Chiefs, Agents and Soldiers*, 11.

35. Moore, *Chiefs, Agents and Soldiers*, 6.

36. Report about meeting with delegation of eleven Navajos, September 15, 1867, M234/554, NARA.

37. Report about meeting with delegation of eleven Navajos, September 15, 1867.

38. Report about meeting with delegation of eleven Navajos, September 15, 1867.

39. See Gerald Thompson, *The Army and the Navajo: The Bosque Redondo Reservation Experiment, 1863–1868* (Tucson: University of Arizona Press, 1976), 155ff.

40. See Thompson, *The Army and the Navajo*, 149.

41. Moore, *Chiefs, Agents and Soldiers*, 21ff.

42. Iverson, *The Navajo Nation*, 10.

43. See Moore, *Chiefs, Agents and Soldiers*, 28.

44. Richard White, *The Roots of Dependency: Subsistence, Environment, and Social Change among the Choctaws, Pawnees, and Navajos* (Lincoln: University of Nebraska Press, 1983), 215.

45. Iverson, *The Navajo Nation*, 11.

46. For expense figures see Thompson, *The Army and the Navajo*, 72.

47. Report of a Peace Council with Navajo Indians (1872), M234/559, NARA. In addition to the nineteen Navajo representatives, including Juaro, Largo, Manuelito (all identified as principal chiefs), there were also about one hundred subchiefs and principal men.

48. Report of a Peace Council (1872).

49. Report of a Peace Council (1872).

50. Report of a Peace Council (1872).

51. Letter from various Navajos to CIA Edward P. Smith, December 29, 1873, M234/562, NARA.

52. Letter, Navajos to Smith, December 29, 1873.

53. Letter, Navajos to Smith, December 29, 1873.

54. Letter, Navajos to Commissioner of Indian Affairs Edward P. Smith, February 11, 1874, M234/562, NARA.

55. Letter, Navajos to Smith, February 11, 1874.

56. Letter, Navajos to Smith, February 11, 1874.

57. Council minutes, May 21, 1879, M234/576, NARA. The council seems to have been designed to persuade the agent to write a letter to Washington.

58. Council minutes, May 21, 1879.

59. Council minutes, May 21, 1879.

60. Council minutes, May 21, 1879.

61. Council minutes, May 21, 1879.

62. Council minutes, May 21, 1879.

63. Council minutes, May 21, 1879.

64. Council minutes, May 21, 1879. See also Thompson, *The Army and the Navajo*, 72.

65. Council minutes, May 21, 1879.

66. Meeting from December 14 to 16, 1880(?), with Navajo chiefs at Fort Defiance, M234/580, NARA.

67. White, *The Roots of Dependency*, 216.

68. This is at least true for all the negotiations recorded in the Bureau of Indian Affairs files.

69. Parts of the following are based on Haake, *The State, Removal and Indigenous Peoples*, and Claudia B. Haake, "Breaking the Bonds of People and Land," in *Removing Peoples: Forced Migration in the Modern World*, ed. Richard Bessel and Claudia Haake (New York: Oxford University Press, 2009), 79–105.

70. Some Yaquis were also deported to Oaxaca.

71. Evelyn Hu-De Hart, "Peasant Rebellion in the Northwest: The Yaqui Indians of Sonora, 1740–1976," in *Riot, Rebellion, and Revolution*, ed. Friedrich Katz (Princeton NJ: Princeton University Press, 1988), 160.

72. Shelley Bowen Hatfield, *Chasing Shadows: Indians along the United States—Mexico Border, 1876–1911* (Albuquerque: University of New Mexico Press, 1998), 7.

73. Quote taken from a letter of the Secretario del Estado to the Prefecto de Guaymas, April 23, 1903. Tomo 1794 (1903), Archivo Histórico General del Estado de Sonora (hereafter AHGES).

74. Evelyn Hu-DeHart, *Yaqui Resistance and Survival: The Struggle for Land and Autonomy, 1821–1910* (Madison: University of Wisconsin Press, 1984), 29.

75. "Even though we have been born here in Sonora" [C.H.], typed copy of a letter dated April 25, 1904, presumably from the Nueve Capitanes and directed to the government. Tomo 1881 (1904), AHGES.

76. María Eugenia Olivarría, *Cruces, Flores y Serpientes: Simbolismo y vida ritual yaquis* (México D.F.: Universidad Autónoma Metropolitana, 2003).

77. "Because we are from here" [C.H.], typed copy of a letter dated April 25, 1904, presumably from the Nueve Capitanes and directed to the government. Tomo 1881 (1904), AHGES.

78. "Even though they are not armed" [C.H.], Tomo 1881 (1904), AHGES.

79. "We don't know what blame we carry" [C.H.], Tomo 1881 (1904), AHGES.

80. See Tomo 1881 (1904), AHGES.

81. See Tomo 1881 (1904), AHGES.

82. Letter, May 5, 1904 (typed copy), Tomo 1881 (1904), AHGES.

83. See Tomo 2315 (1908), AHGES.

84. Tomo 2316 (1908), AHGES. See also Centro de Estudios de Historia Mexicana (CONDUMEX), Colección Ramón Corral, Carpeta 1/3, Legajo 4. (Letter from Alberto Cubillas, Secretario, to Ramón Corral, May 4, 1908).

85. See Haake, *The State, Removal and Indigenous Peoples*, 134, for a detailed discussion of the number of deportees.

86. See Tomo 2315 (1908), AHGES.

87. Hu-DeHart, *Yaqui Resistance and Survival*, 197.

88. At the time, the state of Yucatán was engaged in a fierce battle against yellow fever, which is spread by mosquitoes. For reasons connected to the attempts to eradicate the disease, records were kept about those having been diagnosed with it. These records contained, for instance, information about a person's movements before coming to Yucatán.

89. As a general rule, I have used the spelling found in the Yucatecan sources. Where spelling varied among the documents, I have favored the most common spelling. More often than not, the Yaqui names found in the court documents are corruptions of Sonoran names, which must have sounded very alien to Yucatecan ears more accustomed to Mayan names.

90. Fondo Justicia, 1908, Caja 704, Archivi General del Esatado de Yucatán (hereafter AGEY).

91. See also Allen Wells and Gilbert M. Joseph, *Summer of Discontent, Seasons of Upheaval: Elite Politics and Rural Insurgency in Yucatan, 1876–1915* (Stanford CA: Stanford University Press, 1996), 170.

92. Wells and Joseph: *Summer of Discontent, Seasons of Upheaval*, 169.

93. See Haake, *The State, Removal and Indigenous Peoples*.

94. Fondo Justicia, 1912, Caja 870, AGEY. The documents are in part badly damaged by water and fungi. No other case mentions the word Yaqui as many times as this one.

95. Fondo Justicia, 1908, Caja 704, AGEY. There seems to be some confusion about the names of those involved, probably because the typical Yaqui names sounded more than strange to Yucatecan ears. First, the defendant was referred to as Francisca Flores until she explicitly stated her name to be Francisca Loor Ségua. In the Yaquis' language, "sewa" means flower, and so does "loor." So it is possible that the confusion stemmed from a mere repetition of her name on the part of Francisca, once in Yaqui and once in Spanish.

96. See Raquel Padilla Ramos, *Progreso y Libertad: Los Yaquis en la Víspera de la Repatriación* (tésis de maestría, Universidad Autónoma de Yucatána, Mérida), 133–87. See also Jane Holden Kelley, *Yaqui Women: Contemporary Life Histories* (Lincoln: University of Nebraska Press, 1978), 126–53, 154–96.

97. Wolfgang Gabbert, *Becoming Maya: Ethnicity and Social Inequality in Yucatán since 1500* (Tucson: University of Arizona Press, 2004), 44.

98. Fondo Justicia, 1912, Caja 881, AGEY.

99. See Gabbert, *Becoming Maya*, 44. Furthermore, special living arrangements sometimes were in place, especially for unmarried workers. See also Gilbert M. Joseph, "Rethinking Mexican Revolutionary Mobilization: Yucatán's Seasons of Upheaval, 1909–1915," in *Everyday Forms of State Formation: Revolution and the Negotiation of Rule in Modern Mexico*, ed. Gilbert M. Joseph and Daniel Nugent (Durham NC: Duke University Press, 1994), 158; Wells and Joseph, *Summer of Discontent, Seasons of Upheaval*, 169.

100. See Kelley, *Yaqui Women*, especially 136.

101. See Fondo Justicia, 1911, Cajas 833, AGEY.

102. See Padilla, *Progreso y Libertad*, primarily 90–132. See also Kelley, *Yaqui Women*, 126–53 and 154–96 (chapters on Chepa Moreno and Dominga Martínez).

103. See Padilla, *Progreso y Libertad*, primarily 133–87. See also Haake, *The State, Removal and Indigenous Peoples*.

104. Some Yaquis remained in the United States. See, for instance, Edward H. Spicer, *People of Pascua* (Tucson: University of Arizona Press, 1988).

105. See Bessel and Haake, *Removing Peoples*.

106. This is not to say that the experience was in any way positive or beneficial.

107. This, however, did not mean that this identity remained unchallenged by those Navajos who had managed to escape removal and had remained on their lands.

Chapter 8

Progressivism and Native American Self-Expression in the Late Nineteenth and Early Twentieth Century

Joy Porter

The key theme of this chapter is to argue that thinking about Native American Indian life in the early decades of the twentieth century requires a special awareness, a sense that conventional ideas about the dimensions of ethnic protest and resistance are inadequate because of the almost overwhelming onslaught of cultural attack many Native peoples faced at this time. We need to broaden our conceptual approach when we consider this period so as to fully encompass the spectrum of Native responses to unprecedented change. These ranged from seemingly uncomplex structural and cultural assimilation to aggressive resistance to the imposition of WASP ways and the great variety of lived experience between those two poles. By broadening our analysis so as to make indigenous *persistence* by any means as important as *resistance*, however recognized, we have much to gain. By necessity this chapter will explore this theme primarily through political and literary expressions of Indian identity since these present a rich record of written material for analysis. However, as later sections will make clear, such a focus ignores the bulk of Indian peoples who did not leave such records. It is hoped that these unwritten histories will increasingly come to the fore in future decades.

Because the survival of Indian peoples in the early decades of the twentieth century was by no means guaranteed, we need to think of the fundamental unit of Indian resistance as being Indian persistence in

any form. Indian resistance (to physical attack, environmental degradation, urbanization, forced migration, disease, and individual and cultural denigration) required survival first and the maintenance, often against
terrific odds, of the web of social, familial, political, and cultural plat-
forms that make such resistance possible. This was work done by women
as much as by men, and by Native peoples in an extremely diverse fashion, in communal groups, as families, and as individuals. If we reorient
our thinking so as to view Indian survival as protest in this period, it allows us to unearth much forgotten history and it makes it possible to
see Indian peoples as part of, rather than discrete from, the larger and
more familiar trends of the time. It moves the field beyond the customary textbook emphasis upon Indian heroes who resisted non-Indian encroachment in ways triumphalist non-Indian culture tends to recognize
(usually through "doomed" physical resistance) and it brings to the fore
a vast new hinterland of forms of Indian response that are as complex as
they are rewarding to comprehend. It also removes any tendency to ig-
nore these often dark years in Indian life altogether or to sideline those
who did assimilate during the Progressive Era as "sellouts" or as unwor-
thy oppositional characters in the great story of the American past.

Today, as the globe shrinks and indigenous peoples, particularly
the forest dwellers of South America, face threats to their survival in
many ways comparable to those faced by indigenous Americans in the
decades prior to the turn of the twentieth century, this intellectual re-
orientation is more important than ever. If we are to understand the
complexity of indigenous processes and responses to cultural engulf-
ment, we need to look afresh at what it meant to rebuild Indian culture at the darkest point before what we can now see, with hindsight,
was a new indigenous dawn. We must retain a fundamental awareness that the expression of Indian identity in the Progressive Era was
circumscribed by the imperative to protect Indian assets, homelands,
and resources in order to survive.

Without doubt, the years surrounding 1900 were dark for the majority of Native peoples. During the preceding decades, the drive to enforce conformity to often contradictory non-Indian norms had been

searingly acute. It was combined with repeated and erroneous national reiterations that those Indian peoples who survived were "remnants" and vestiges of a "doomed race." The cruelty of the frontier populations pushing west, backed by the military, made the idea of allotting Indian lands in severalty seem like a positive solution to what those living in cities in the East thought of as a difficult but essentially short-term "Indian" problem. The resulting 1887 Dawes Act, a "mighty, pulverizing engine," as President Theodore Roosevelt described it, attacked one of the most powerful mainstays of tribal identity—communal ownership of land underpinned by Indian understandings of the life of the spirit. Admittedly, prior treaties had allowed for a degree of subdivision and allotment since the 1850s, but this new General Allotment Act, or Dawes Act, extended it to most but not all Indian reservations.[1] Its initial formulation allowed for a twenty-five-year "trust" period during which the Indian allottee was to remain under federal supervision until receiving legal title and citizenship. By 1906, however, the Burke Act permitted the Indian Office discretion to grant fee title in response to individual applications. Then, in 1910, Congress authorized "forced fees" whereby title could be awarded with or without the consent of the allottee. The result was another land grab such that Indians in what would later be the lower forty-eight states lost two out of every three acres they held prior to 1887.

A number of Indian figures of the time, such as the Santee Sioux lecturer, author, and physician Dr. Charles A. Eastman (Ohiyesa) and the Paiute writer Sarah Winnemucca (Thocmentony, or Shell Flower), thought the 1887 Dawes Act would foster Indian independence and give Indians citizenship, but its effect was to take Indian land out of tribal ownership and to plunge Indian peoples further into economic dependence on the federal government. Land, with its multiple social, spiritual, and resource significance, was and remains central to how a great many indigenous peoples express a sense of self. The attack upon Indian land in this period was an attack upon Indian identity, since the two were, and for a great many remain, inextricably linked.

In the West, Indian communities had responded to the onslaught of disease, attack, enforced hunger, forced displacement, and confinement within reservation lands with the Ghost Dance movement, an attempt

to restore some of the spiritual, political, and social balance that had
been lost. The brutality of the 1890 Wounded Knee massacre that sent
the movement further underground was an especially low point in what
has been an ongoing story of utter cultural incomprehension by non-
Indians when faced with expressions of Native spirituality. Meanwhile,
the new disciplines of anthropology and museology continued the work
of attempting to "salvage" Indian culture and its spiritual accoutrements
for triumphalist display in public museums. Government forces out-
lawed Indian dances and practices such as potlatch, with its enjoyment
of giving, and from a non-Indian perspective, wanton waste of time and
disregard for private property. Prohibitions against the potlatch, Sun
Dance, and peyote faith were not to be rescinded until the late 1950s.

As the nineteenth century closed, the overwhelming impetus was
for the United States to construct and maintain a culturally uniform
nation-state through interlinked programs of Christian missionizing,
philanthropic eradication of "savagery," and myriad active processes of "civilization." Prior generations had suffered from the regimen-
tation, cultural alienation, violence, and soullessness of the Indian
boarding school movement but had also benefited from the forms of
pan-Indian consciousness and language they generated as well as from
whatever positive attributes they provided for accessing the non-Indian
world. Successive generations, however, left Indian schools profoundly adrift from their communities and with aspirations mainstream society was unwilling to fulfill. By 1920, 6 percent of Indians would live
in urban environments, many experiencing geographical, educational, and cultural alienation. Detached from a meaningful community
context and blocked in their efforts to assimilate to the dominant society, a number of Indian people adopted a "satellite" relationship to
their reservation homelands. They visited sporadically, often prompted by the need to make use of indigenous and/or mainstream health-
care, but were prevented structurally from being able to fully express
the collective or individual Indian identity they might have preferred.

Thus, Progressive Era Native peoples often found themselves be-
reft of traditions or living with their traditions in abeyance. They were
survivors of centuries of wars of extermination, the latest episodes of

which had occurred in the preceding decades during what textbooks euphemistically call "westward expansion." Indian peoples in the early twentieth century were thus at the forefront of processes connected to modernity that were characterized by a profound reorganization of time and space. They were both victims and active constituents of modernity. Like many peoples across the globe, including many of America's immigrants, Indian peoples were being forced to rapidly reconcile life in a posttraditional world. As contemporary scholars remind us, this meant grappling with a chief characteristic of the modern condition—doubt, and its impact upon personal identity.[2] It is also worth recognizing in this context that many Indian peoples were themselves products of generations of rapid change. After all, Progressive Era Indians were the survivors of a globally unprecedented and almost continentally overwhelming biological attack upon their ethnic group by European pathogens. As the Cherokee demographer Russell Thornton observes, in the United States alone, the Indian population "decreased from 5+ million in 1492 to about 250,000 in the decade from 1890 to 1900. . . . Such a population decline implies not only that some 5 million American Indians died during the 400 years but that, in fact, many times the approximate figure of 5 million died, as new but ever numerically smaller generations of American Indians were born, lived and died."[3] This legacy of conquest should never be detached from any serious consideration of Indian identity at this critical juncture when Indian population figures finally start to recover.

The Limits of Assimilation

Progressive Era Indian peoples were the generations forced to realize the limitations of what Frederick Hoxie called the nation's "final promise" of assimilation. The post–Civil War years had been characterized by a self-serving desire to dismantle tribal coherence and an elaborate program designed to incorporate Indians as individuals into the nation. By the 1920s, reformers, intellectuals, "friends," and policy makers responded to pressure from Western politicians and eschewed guarantees of Indian equality and talk about Indian transformation. Clearly, the nation's culture, society, and institutions were not capable of fully accepting the Indian presence. And when American Indians were incorporated into American society, it was on the bottom rungs of that society. Indian peoples found themselves positioned on the periphery of American political culture, being allowed only partial inclusion at a time when the segregation of blacks was common practice, and immigrants from Japan and southern and eastern Europe were viewed with intense suspicion. Indian schools, for example, were not designed to encourage integration; rather, they focused on fitting Indian peoples for their peripheral social and economic status. They were, as Hoxie put it, "schools for dependent people."[4] Like the black Americans preached to by Booker T. Washington, Indians were advised to make peace with what non-Indians supposed were their racial (in)abilities and to accept manual labor as their lot. As the Board of Indian Commissioners announced in 1898, while a few Native Americans "might push their way into professional life . . . the great majority must win their living by manual labor."[5] In this sense, government officials sought to encourage Native peoples to accept roles as proletarian workers rather than thinkers, an identity other colonizing governments such as Australia's tried to foster among their Native peoples, too.

All this occurred during a period of profound change in America. Change was evident not just in terms of technological developments and steady industrialization but also in terms of how Americans thought about themselves and their future as a nation. As the twentieth century dawned, the internal American frontier had disappeared, or so renowned commentators such as the young historian Frederick Jackson Turner told their audiences. What replaced it was a potential transoceanic empire following the 1898 war with Spain. None of this necessarily made Americans feel easy about the future. The grimness of labor conditions had led to the emergence of a new internal union, the "Wobblies," and to a new "muckraking" voice in American newspapers bemoaning domestic social and industrial conditions. The flip side of a speeding economy experiencing the full force of industrialized capitalism and unprecedented levels of immigration was a demand from native-born citizens for immigration to be controlled, and at the same time, for social justice to be some-how secured. What to do with an ever-burgeoning immigrant influx was much more important to most Americans than the numerical-ly less significant problem of somehow incorporating Indian popu-lations. Indian numbers remained in the low hundreds of thousands as the early decades of the twentieth century progressed, but immi-grant numbers truly threatened to overwhelm. The peak decade for immigration was 1900–1910, but over 1 million immigrants arrived in 1920 alone. Congress responded to early twentieth-century immigra-tion by creating the Dillingham Commission in 1907. The commis-sion concluded that these "new" immigrants were racially inferior to the old-stock European colonizers of the past. Such perceptions fos-tered a fear of contagion or national depreciation within the United States that resulted in concerted efforts to enforce complete assimi-lation. President Theodore Roosevelt explicitly stated that there was "no room for the hyphen in our citizenship." He saw the hybrid as an internal disease and advised the nation, "We must shun as we would shun the plague all efforts to make us separate nationalities. We must all of us be Americans, and nothing but Americans."[6]

As has happened repeatedly in relations between Indians and non-Indians, aspects of non-Indians' concerns and anxieties were project-ed onto Indian communities. Fears about sexual freedom and family disintegration are a good example. Profound change in social and sex-ual mores saw the divorce rate multiply 2,000 percent between 1867 and 1929, with one in six marriages ending in divorce by the end of the twenties.[7] In 1920, when reformers and government officials looked at Indian dances, such as those practiced at the Hopi Indian Reservation in Oraibi, Arizona, they saw a reflection of all the immorality and sex-ual threats to family life they perceived within their own societies and made moves to stamp them out.[8] Indian "paganism," like black Amer-ican culture during the Jazz Age, was wholly misunderstood and seen as a contagion capable of dragging white society "back" to some pri-mal, highly sexual, and socially libertine stage. Such thinking char-acterized an age when experts were increasingly revered. The expert opinion on Indians was that they were irrevocably trapped in a prior stage of development through which the bulk of the American people, especially the white Anglo-Saxon elite, had already triumphantly passed. In this respect, the legacy of anthropologist Lewis Henry Morgan's thinking was strong, and the dominant non-Indian culture comforted itself with the idea that Indian peoples, like other "backward" classes, ethnicities, colors, and nationalities, were unlikely to catch up. If, as Morgan suggested, all societies by necessity gradually evolved through inevitable stages of savagery, barbarism, and civilization, then Indian peoples, still deemed savage in political form, social conditions, and religious life, were destined to lag behind. From this perspective, the imposition of WASP values and the displacement of indigenous practices seemed positive, beneficial, and philanthropic.

Of course, this theoretical emphasis upon evolutionary gradualism by experts and intellectuals flew in the face of the impetus behind the Dawes Act, which was explicitly intended to convert Indian peoples to settled agriculture and individualism in just one generation. However, few powerful voices queried the logic behind such an invidious and cynically self-serving piece of legislation. It was to succeed primarily in assimilating great swaths of Indian land to white ownership rather than Indians themselves to non-Indian society. The end of the nineteenth century saw strong advocacy of cultural relativism and promulgation of the idea by the anthropologist Franz Boas that cultures were adapted to the specifics of their environment and geography.[9] Nevertheless, Morgan's thinking still retained great currency well into the Progressive Era. In this period as in no other, Native American identity formation and its meaning were shaped, reshaped, and articulated by competing and oppressive colonial voices and forces.

At the turn of the century, indigenous Americans knew well that they were in for a long fight. While it might be reassuring to think otherwise and to view federal Indian policy as a swinging pendulum that was about to lurch toward a renunciation of assimilation in the 1930s, in fact, as Russel Lawrence Barsh has shown, Indian policy was characterized by a continuity of effect, at least as far as land and resources were concerned.[10] Gradual integration and assimilation of Indians was to remain the overarching policy for much of the twentieth century. Furthermore, the focus of the federal government's Indian policy made it questionable whether an intelligent and capable Indian individual could succeed when confronted with the great wall of racial thinking that ignored the importance of Native American heritage in the articulation of an early twentieth-century Indian identity.

I am not suggesting that life was disproportionately difficult for young Indian intellectuals in the early years of the twentieth century in comparison with the restrictions and prejudices imposed on the bulk of Native peoples, but those indigenous people who saw themselves as natural leaders beyond the confines of reservations certainly faced specific historic challenges that to date have not been fully appreciated. They were often mixed-blooded in an era that disparaged mixedness and instead revered the "authentic" and frightened itself with stories about deceit and imposters. At the point when a gradually secularizing America first began to suspect that there might in fact be "no clear core of self," the only version of Indianness the dominant culture would countenance was one that was primitivist and tribal in a way that was not coeval with the contemporary world.[11] It had to be a form of Indianness that reassured modern Americans living in an overcivilized world that *something* real existed. At this point, when settler America had successfully made its home upon almost all available Indian land, it increasingly looked to the very peoples it had displaced to assuage the feelings of spiritual homelessness that accompanied its triumph. The bourgeoisie wanted to be injected with renewed vigor through contact with the simple, with the soil and with the kind of immediacy of experience they associated with childhood and with those deemed to embody "the childhood of the race." These antimodern longings were, as T. J. Jackson Lears pointed out, a symptom of the "therapeutic world view" adopted by the dominant classes of the age, impulses in themselves easily absorbed by the larger, overarching impulses of bureaucratic corporatism.[12]

Whether the Progressive Era is viewed as a time of pragmatic philosophy (James T. Kloppenberg), cosmopolitan activism (Daniel T. Rodgers), or agrarian political action (Elizabeth Sanders), it is difficult to see where aspiring middle-class Native American concerns might reasonably have fitted.[13] The Progressive Era was a time of shifting and sometimes contradictory coalitions into which Indian interests did not always easily slot. Middle-class Americans in the Progressive Era wrote and talked much about abandoning self-interest and instead "associating" so as to bring about positive social change. They also talked a lot about wielding the power of the state for good, but it was difficult to see how specific Indian claims for redress, and the imperatives of Indian communities for basic provision in terms of health-care, subsistence, and autonomy, fitted into such rhetoric.[14]

How was the new cadre of middle-class Indian leadership going to articulate a Progressive Era Native American identity when, especial-ly during the interwar years, American intellectuals emphasized the superiority of "traditional" Indian cultures in relation to the artifici-ality of consumerism in Euro-American culture? This was a difficult question, made even more problematic after the horrors of Verdun and the Somme made it harder to blithely label American Indians as uniquely "barbaric." Surely also, America's first nations deserved the same freedom of self-determination that President Woodrow Wilson claimed the United States had fought to defend abroad? Concurrent to these historical developments was the resurgence of popular imag-ery that emphasized a romantic vision of painted Indians as passive, an imagery that belittled Indian communities and their need for the basics—survival space, sanitation, and a means of subsistence. Now Indians, especially those who had escaped the worst of assimilation in the Southwest, were praised for the very things for which Indian peoples had once been condemned. They were held up as having what American culture had lost—cohesion, community, a primitive com-munion with nature, and spiritual peace. As has happened repeatedly in American history, when Progressive Era Americans and especially cultural elites felt under threat, they looked to Indians for answers. It happened again in the 1940s, 1960s, and 1990s. As Philip Deloria puts it, "Whenever white Americans have confronted crises of identity, some of them have inevitably turned to Indians."[15]

An inconsistent approach to Indian affairs and contradictory per-ceptions of Native Americans was a product of the First World War shattering the Euro-American consensus about the probity of forced assimilation. While Christianity continued to be enforced in Indian boarding schools during the early twentieth century, practical change in federal Indian policy did not emerge until after the 1928 Meriam Report and the reign of John Collier as commissioner of Indian affairs in the New Deal years.[16] In this changing social and political milieu, Indian spokespeople were repeatedly called upon to condemn the supposed iniquity of the Indian "peyote cult" and its alleged association with Indian sexual depravity. Zitkala Ša (Gertrude Simmons Bonnin) and Charles Eastman were among the best-known Indian leaders to speak out on Native American issues. Zitkala Ša, normally sympathetic to calls for Indian self-determination, spoke out against peyote. In 1916 she wrote that "the human system, disabled with dope, is no receptacle for the jewels of education and civilization. The Indian is no exception."[17]

The decade following 1915 saw a groundswell of support for Indian peoples that successfully halted plans of the Bureau of Indian Affairs to suppress Indian dances in a blanket fashion. Intolerance, however, was still a daily reality for the bulk of Indian peoples, especially on reservations where Christian values tended to dominate well into the 1930s. For example, Americans were surprised by American Indian support for the First World War effort. Ten thousand joined the U.S. army for conflict overseas, two thousand more joined the navy, millions of Indian dollars were spent on war bonds, and reports reached home of the bravery of Joseph Oklahombi (Choctaw) in the trenches. This bolstered efforts to secure universal Indian citizenship, which came in 1924, but even when achieved it was not to have the kind of transformative effect that Indian and non-Indian Progressive Era reformers hoped. Even when a significant number of Indians had citizenship and the right to vote, most Native Americans remained reticent or unprepared to participate in civic life for fear of losing their property rights.

The Society of American Indians

Progressive Era Indians were thus caught up in a period of unique crisis and transformation. Some change was small but in its own way indicative and meaningful. For example, Indian peoples literally gained

a human face in popular culture when in 1913 James Earle Fraser's buffalo nickel actually showed a recognizably Indian face on U.S coinage.
The earlier "Indian head" penny and 1907 ten-dollar coin had been
modeled on a white man's head. Other, wider changes seemed truly momentous. The new generation of assimilated Indian leadership
who found an outlet in the Society of American Indians (SAI) from
1910 until around 1923 certainly felt that the Progressive Era was a time
of unprecedented opportunity for themselves and for the Indian con-
stituencies to which they were linked. These "red progressives" were
a secular cross-tribal group that seized the chance to push for national reform at a time when it appeared that minority leadership had a
golden opportunity to initiate and direct change in government policy. Its agenda was comparable to that of other groups formed to further "race" interests, such as the NAACP (the National Association for
the Advancement of Colored People). Like the NAACP, the SAI campaigned for legal and political recognition of its people and spread the
word through its own journal. Drawing on a long history of intertribal confederacy, the SAI developed alongside the religious intertribalism
of the peyote faith and its organizational body, the Native American
Church, but eventually was to be eclipsed by the city-based fraternal intertribalism that crystallized during the 1920s. In retrospect, the Alaskan
Native Brotherhood and Alaskan Native Sisterhood, founded in 1912,
which also focused on acculturation and rights, proved longer lasting.

The SAI, however, was unique in that although it enjoyed white support, American Indians ran it. It was, as one society publication put it,
an association "of Indians, by Indians, and for Indians."[18] While for a
time at the height of progressive thinking it marshaled the energies of
a great many of the nation's foremost Indian intellectuals, including
Charles Eastman, Zitkala Ša, and the Seneca-Iroquois archaeologist
and ethnologist Arthur Caswell Parker, it was always a complement
to the non-Indian reform organizations. After all, it shared their basic agenda: final detribalization and the individual absorption of Indians into American society as patriotic citizens.

SAI members who worked toward these goals included prominent
individuals from education and established professionals from law,

medicine, government, and the church. People with connections to Indian communities since childhood such as the anthropologist Frank Speck and those like the Tuscarora linguist and ethnologist J. N. B. Hewitt, who were proud of their Indian extraction, were also SAI members. Other foundational figures included the Winnebago lawyer Henry Roe Cloud, the lawyer of Omaha extraction Thomas L. Sloan, the Peoria BIA supervisor of employment Charles E. Daganett, and the Arapaho Episcopal minister Rev. Sherman Coolidge.

Although SAI leadership made rhetorical claims to being a "representational government" for Indian peoples, in truth a representative intertribal confederation was impossible at that time. The SAI was "pan-Indian" only in the sense that it expressed an aspiration for, and the notion of, the political union of all Indians. What really united the group from the outset was an educational history within eastern Indian boarding schools rather than any clearly delineated project to represent the concerns of the majority of Indian peoples, however defined. The group's concern to foreground the idea of an intertribal Indian "race" was in itself a symptom of the social evolutionary thinking characteristic of most of their backgrounds. In practice, the SAI found itself unable to ever fully resolve the distinction between Indian tribal identity and some kind of pan-Indian "race-consciousness." Like Progressive Era African Americans, Native American intellectuals were deeply divided over issues surrounding assimilation and self-determination. Yavapai activist Carlos Montezuma, for example, caused untold ructions within the SAI over his resistance to any official BIA influence, and the BIA returned the favor, characterizing Montezuma and his associates as bolsheviks.[19]

A number of the SAI's leading lights were also ambivalent about their involvement. Arthur Parker, a figure of great importance to the development of the SAI, knew from the outset that his participation would alienate him from his own people. As he put it, "The Seneca of a certain class will think that I am working to make citizens of them and this they have protested for 60 years. They wish to remain as they are, and today the percentage of adult illiteracy in New York among the Indians is greater than in Oklahoma. In a movement of this kind

I am injuring myself in a field which must be my life's work. Someone must sacrifice however before any good can ever be done."[20] Here
we glimpse the rhetoric of the time, both the public service ideal and
romantic individualism. In the words of the better-known WASP reformer Jane Addams, Parker had fully adopted the "social ethic." His
SAI letters and writings were grounded in a newly popular belief that
all individuals were capable of remaking both themselves and their
culture. Like so many others involved in the bureaucratization and
professionalization processes of the progressive years, he felt able to
claim a moral benefit to his own activities and to those of his group.

A key component of the SAI's agenda was to educate non-Indians
about Indian potential. Partly as a rebuff to the success of Buffalo Bill's
Wild West shows, which had enjoyed great notoriety since 1893, SAI
sponsored a national Indian day. It was designed to associate the Indian with the great outdoors, to invoke a glorious Indian past, and
to bring together Indians and whites in patriotic celebration. It was
sporadically observed, but it spoke to a wider concern of Parker's and
others about how, in order to be Indian in the modern world, Indians had to "play Indian in order to be Indian."[21] For the same reason,
Parker wrote as SAI secretary several times to the BIA commissioner
criticizing the use of the word "squaw" by Indian school superintendents, a practice he described as "bad form." Perhaps the highlight of
SAI cohesion and achievement came in 1913 with the group's "Denver
platform." A reasonable minority of reservation Indians participated
in the organizational conference, with numbers peaking at over two
hundred, mostly delegates from Oklahoma, Montana, South Dakota, Nebraska, and New York. The platform included support for the
Carter Code Bill to define Indian status, support for an amended Ste-
phens Bill asking for the admission of Indian tribal claims directly to
the federal courts of claims, and demands for "the complete reorganization of the Indian school system." This was an agenda well ahead
of its time, antedating reforms of the twenties, thirties, and forties,
respectively.

Yet the SAI was to gradually lose cohesion as members like Parker
became more strident in their demands that fellow Indians instantly

assimilate. At points as SAI president, Parker went beyond social reform rhetoric and veered toward eugenicist thinking. Frustrated by
SAI internal wrangling and factionalism over the BIA and "the peyote
poison," his SAI involvement taught him how detached his thinking
and agenda were from that of the bulk of Indian peoples. Indian affairs
were riven with graft and corruption, and as he put it, SAI membership was "composed of persons whose interests are linked perhaps in
some way directly or indirectly with the men we may attack."[22] When
war came he readily threw himself into recruitment and service in the
New York State National Guard. Eventually around fifteen thousand
Indians from across the nation fought in the First World War, with a
significant number of Indian women serving in relief organizations
like the Red Cross. Parker was of course delighted when a 1919 act was
passed that gave citizenship to all Indian veterans. Like a number of
SAI members, by this stage he was increasingly turning his reform focus inward, toward his own Seneca-Iroquois people, advising them to
demand exception from the very legislation he had advocated as appropriate for Indians nationally within the SAI. He even specifically
suggested that they maintain their sovereign status by independently declaring war on Germany and Austria-Hungary.

The SAI ended a sorry mess, and Parker's ultimate disillusionment
about its impact was shared by many of his peers. He went from being
an advocate of integration, assimilation, and amalgamation for European immigrants and Native Americans in 1916, to a general advocate
for exclusion and the preservation of the white race in 1922. The new
science, eugenics, provided theoretical support for his fresh perspective, even though it disapproved of exactly the kind of intermarriage
across cultures that characterized his own family background and
that of many SAI members. The SAI left him angry and disappointed
with his own "race" and a vociferous advocate of the kind of mainstream hostility toward minorities that was rife during the "tribal
twenties."[23] In contrast to the thrusting assimilation advocated by the
SAI, the kinds of Indian organizations that rose to prominence in the
1920s, such as the Indian Rights Association and the American Indian

Defense Association, instead would unite around John Collier's idealistic southwestern vision of the Indian contribution to American life.

The SAI achieved nothing in terms of practical legislative change, and both its sphere of influence and its constituency were limited and ill defined from the outset. It was run by and for the emerging educated Indian middle class, and they were unable to garner either the funds or the broad-based support needed to renegotiate the Indian position within American society. As Parker gradually realized, "race leadership" on the terms advocated by SAI members was neither wanted nor understood by most Indians or their communities; neither was it desired by the dominant Euro-American society. Instead, it was the image of the painted and feathered Indian that America was to remain most comfortable with. Even when significant legislative reform did eventually come in the mid-1930s with Roosevelt's New Deal, it took as its model a primitive version of Indian culture. As Parker put it with considerable acuity in 1920, describing the dominant society's resistance to accepting Indians as coeval with modernizing America: "To the white man an Indian is only an Indian if dressed in feathers and buckskins. The white man is a queer mixture of inconsistencies and he likes to view men and things in the light of his preconceived notions. He may agree that everything in the world changes, but he does not want to know that the Indian changes with the world."[24]

Literary Voices

In recent years, the field of Native American studies has paid more attention to how Indian identities were expressed through literature in the Progressive Era than to how it was expressed via the messy and problematic arena of Indian-authored political organization. One voice that has recently garnered attention was that of Simon Pokagon, the son of Leopold, chief of the Pokagon band of Potawatomis. He published *O-gi-mäw-kee Mit-I-gwä-ki*, or *Queen of the Woods*, with a collaborator in 1899. The novel conjured up the lost Edenic past of the Potawatomis and cried out against the vice of alcohol that had destroyed so many Indian families. The hero, also named Simon, at one stage abandons "civilized" society for the life of the forest, but the story ends in tragedy.

It is worth thinking of Pokagon's writings in the larger context of the fact that Indian landholdings were at an all-time low in the Progressive Era, having gone from 138 million acres in 1887 to 48 million acres, much of it desert, in 1934, when the policy was to change. At a time when mainstream America was slowly waking up to the costs of its extractive industries and of the exploitation of American land, Indian spokespeople such as Pokagon made strong claims for Indians as ecological exemplars. In his 1893 *Red Man's Greeting* to the World's Columbian Exposition in Chicago, he spoke of early America full of game and fish: "All were provided by the Great Spirit for our use: we destroyed none except for food and dress, had plenty and were contented and happy."[25] Pokagon's work highlights a much-discussed and ongoing issue in the expression of Indian identity through literature: to what extent is it mediated or even constructed by preconceived notions about what is "Indian"? To what extent is Indian literature dictated to by the concerns of the dominant culture and its nostalgic desire for a lost American past where tribalism, community, and nature held sway? Is Indian literature "managed exoticism"?—to use the phrase that Louis Owens, one of the foremost Indian intellectuals of recent years, notoriously applied to the Pulitzer Prize—winning novel by the Kiowa writer N. Scott Momaday.

Irrespective of this issue, it is entirely positive that so much early Native American Indian literature is now gaining profile. It is also significant that a number of Progressive Era literary Indian women's voices have begun to receive the attention they deserve. One of the strongest is that of the Canadian Mohawk Emily Pauline Johnson. She achieved critical and popular acclaim for her poetry and performances during her lifetime throughout North America and the United Kingdom. She published short stories in relatively large circulation journals such as *Mother's Magazine* and *Boy's World*. The bulk of her fiction was collected in two posthumous volumes, *The Moccasin Maker* (1913) and *The Shagganappi* (1913). In keeping with the fashion of the time, her work tended to focus on the sentimental theme of women triumphing against great odds. It also dealt with powerful issues such as non-Indian hypocrisy, mixed-blood female experiences, and the transcendent power of mother love.

SAI member Zitkala Ša, like Johnson, had a career as a creative writer and spokesperson for indigenous Americans. Her most noteworthy book was *American Indian Stories* (1921), which drew upon her work with the Dakota language and oral traditions. Among much else, Zitkala Ša's work spoke to the injustices of life for Native peoples at missionary schools and articulated Dakota notions of justice, harmony, and kinship. Another important early twentieth-century Indian female novelist was the Colville writer Christine Quintasket, or Mourning Dove, who published *Cogewea, the Half-Blood* in 1927. There is much from the popular Western in the novel but also a series of profound comments on the true meaning of cultural sovereignty, the power of oral traditions, and the personal and political ramifications of a mixed-blood identity.

While women's writing was significant in this period, the most widely read and controversial Native writers were men. Like Zitkala Ša, Charles Eastman was a political figure and a writer of Sioux extraction. Eastman wrote many mostly nonfiction books in collaboration with his wife, Elaine Goodale Eastman. A significant proportion of Eastman's work reinterpreted Indian stories for children, a phenomenon publishers of the time were especially attracted to, and which other figures like Arthur Parker capitalized upon, too. Such writing reflected the age's determination to see Indian spirituality, and indeed Indian cultures, as childlike. Indian spiritual narratives were perceived as an infant version of the more sophisticated lessons advanced (white) American society might wish to remind itself of or teach to its young. However, the Eastmans' work still endeavored to portray a Dakota and/or Sioux outlook on the world and its history in books such as *Red Hunters and the Animal People* (1904) and *Old Indian Days* (1907).

A second figure, Sylvester Clark Long Lance (1890–1932), of Lumbee extraction, used his wit and intelligence to dance across the color line and tell a version of his life story in *Long Lance* (1928). A "mixed blood," he was deemed a "colored" in early life, as were all Africans and Indians throughout the South at the time. Yet Long Lance ensured he got admitted as a Cherokee to Carlisle Indian School and later to West Point, which excluded African Americans. *Long Lance* was

much praised by the antimodern elite including Ernest Thompson
Seton and Paul Radin, and its hero was able to perform to great popular acclaim in full Indian regalia throughout the country.

Long Lance became the toast of both Hollywood and New York in
the 1920s. Tragically, his life ended in suicide when he was only forty-
one years old. It is commonly held that the undeniable pressure of
keeping up his preferred, constructed identity as an "authentic" Indian was what caused him to take his life. If so, he joins a long list of
high-functioning Native peoples over time who found the stress of
forging and maintaining a mixed-blood identity unsustainable. The
problem remains not with those who have benefited from having multiple heritages but with the wider society at large, which persists in
recognizing only a very limited number of ways of expressing Indian
identity. A racial identity, as the sociologist Joane Nagel reminds us,
is "both optional and mandatory."[26] We may choose to express ourselves in a variety of ways, but it is too often the larger society that dictates whether that expression has legitimacy. Long Lance performed
what Wernor Sollors dubbed "ethnic transvestism" by assuming the
identity of his own fictional character.[27] He performed a self that allowed him more scope than the racially imposed identities available
to him as a black American. His history illustrates how significant
performance is to modernity and the risks that accompany the individual's adoption of a fluid sense of self.

Conclusion

If we are to agree with Russel Barsh, one of the more exciting recent
commentators on Indian life in the Progressive Era, the contours
of what it was possible for Indian individuals and communities to
achieve for the first half of the twentieth century were mapped out
in the Progressive Era by federal bureaucrats. When the newly elected president Wilson asked the ex-Princeton professor and New York
progressive reformer Arthur C. Luddington to reassess Indian policy,
Luddington mapped out the future: a period of training for citizenship, then a period of local self-government, and inevitably, a period
when Indians would be allowed to deal with non-Indian civilization

by themselves. John Collier and his New Deal coalition had this view, too. Collier did not so much inaugurate an Indian "New Deal" as roll out the next stage, or a new variant of an established program of integration. After all, as Collier would do subsequently, Luddington drew heavily on British ideas about how colonized peoples might be dealt with. The American approach to indigenous peoples was by no means unique within global history in terms of its violent disregard for cultural difference or its patriarchal understanding of progress. Both Collier and Luddington shared a conviction that it was in the best interest of Indian communities to have key aspects of their political institutions undermined. Barsh has perhaps justifiably been accused of making too much of Luddington's input, but his general point, that twentieth-century Indian policy evinces greater continuity than change, holds true.[28]

If we are to understand the complexities of life for Progressive Era Indians, we need take on board this larger context and the weight of cultural hegemony impacting upon Indian lives. We need to be alert to the limits placed on who and what could be heard and acknowledged in this era of acute racist hauteur toward Indian peoples, who in spite of all evidence to the contrary, were seen as backward, childlike, and in need of uplift and training so as to ultimately mirror non-Indian culture. Sometimes simultaneously they were also seen as custodians of moral, environmental, and community values that the mainstream society increasingly cherished with all the white heat of nostalgia for things recently lost. What was rarely addressed was the obvious, the need for Indian peoples to regain control over their resources so that they might survive and prosper. In essence, what was acceptable in terms of the expression of Indian identity in this period served to obscure what really mattered in Indian Country. What mattered was the absence of opportunity, the hypocrisy of the drive for assimilation, and the glaring need for a restoration of Indian lands and means of subsistence.

For all these reasons, the progressive figures we have heard most about in this chapter are not necessarily the most important in terms of how the web of connections that sustained Indian cultures was maintained against terrific odds. Understudied figures include the tribal leaders who worked to preserve the integrity of their communities, who used every means possible in their relations with federal and state officials to secure the best interests of their people. Here I include, for example, intertribal groups such as the Black Hills Treaty Council and men like Crow leader Robert Yellowtail. Progressive Era women's voices are also particularly absent, largely because of conventional history's reliance upon the written word. Even so, new research continues to bring to light unique figures such as the Penobscot performer Lucy Nicolar (1882–1969) and the Tewa potter Maria Montoya Martinez (1887–1980). In order to continue to reveal the color and texture of Progressive Era Indian life, we need to remain alert to the perils of the tendency to see indigenous or colonized peoples as most authentic when they are least engaged with all things Euro-American. As the historian Arif Dirlik has pointed out, doing so denies the experience of indigenous peoples in time.[29] It denies the necessary complexity of their active responses to what were often insurmountable challenges to the full expression of indigenous identity. We must always remember that survival, whether it is achieved within or away from non-Indian culture, was the primary act of resistance of all those indigenous Americans who lived through that historical turning point for indigenous America, the Progressive Era.

Notes

1. Dawes Act legislation excluded the Five Civilized Tribes, an area in Nebraska, several other groups in Indian Territory, and the New York Senecas.

2. See Anthony Giddens, *Modernity and Self-Identity: Self and Society in the Late Modern Age* (Stanford CA: Stanford University Press, 1991), 2, 3, 6.

3. Russell Thornton, *American Indian Holocaust and Survival: A Population History since 1492* (Norman: University of Oklahoma Press), 1987, 43. For a discussion of the wider debate over Indian population decline up to 1900, see Joy Porter, "Population Matters in Native America," in *America's Americans: Population Issues in U.S. Society and Politics*, ed. Philip Davies and Iwan Morgan (London: Institute for the Study of the Americas, University of London, School of Advanced Study, 2007), 31–49.

4. See Frederick Hoxie, *A Final Promise: The Campaign to Assimilate the Indians, 1880–1920* (Cambridge: Cambridge University Press, 1984), 189.

5. Annual Report of the U.S. Commissioner of Indian Affairs, 1898, 1096, Record Group 75, National Archives and Records Administration, Washington DC.

6. Theodore Roosevelt in Herman Hagedorn, *Americanism of Theodore Roosevelt* (Cambridge MA: Houghton Mifflin, 1923).

7. William L. O'Neill, *Divorce in the Progressive Era* (New Haven CT: Yale University Press, 1967), 3, 33–63.

8. Margaret D. Jacobs, "Making Savages of Us All: White Women, Pueblo Indians, and the Controversy over Indian Dances in the 1920s," *Frontiers: A Journal of Women Studies* 17, no. 3 (1996): 178–209.

9. Franz Boas, *The Shaping of American Anthropology* (New York: Basic Books, 1974).

10. Russel Lawrence Barsh, "Indian Resources and the National Economy: Business Cycles and Policy Cycles," in *Native Americans and Public Policy*, ed. Fremont J. Lyden and Lyman H. Letgers (Pittsburgh: Pittsburgh University Press, 1992), 87–109.

11. David Riesman, with Nathan Glazer and Reuel Denney, *The Lonely Crowd: A Study of the Changing American Character*, 3rd ed. rev. (New Haven CT: Yale University Press, 1969), 157.

12. T. J. Jackson Lears, *No Place of Grace: Antimodernism and the Transformation of American Culture, 1880–1920* (Chicago: University of Chicago, 1981), xix.

13. James T. Kloppenberg, *Uncertain Victory: Social Democracy and Progressivism in European and American Thought, 1870–1920* (New York: Oxford University Press, 1986); Daniel T. Rodgers, *Atlantic Crossings: Social Politics in a Progressive Age* (Cambridge MA: Harvard University Press, 1998); Elizabeth Sanders, *Roots of Reform: Farmers, Workers, and the American State, 1877–1917* (Chicago: University of Chicago Press, 1999).

14. Michael McGerr, *A Fierce Discontent: The Rise and Fall of the Progressive Movement in America, 1870–1920* (New York: Free Press, 2003), 67.

15. Philip J. Deloria, *Playing Indian* (New Haven CT: Yale University Press, 1998), 156.

16. Lewis Meriam, Ray A. Brown, Henry Roe Cloud, Edward Everett Dale, Emma Duke, Herbert R. Edwards, Fayette Avery McKenzie, Mary Louise Mark, W. Carson Ryan Jr., and William J. Spillman, *The Problem of Indian Administration* (Baltimore: Johns Hopkins University Press, 1928).

17. Zitkala Ša, *American Indian Stories, Legends, and Other Writings* (New York: Penguin, 2003), 241.

18. Quoted in Joy Porter, *To Be Indian: The Life of Iroquois-Seneca Arthur Caswell Parker* (Norman: University of Oklahoma, 2001), 92.

19. See Peter Iverson, *Carlos Montezuma and the Changing World of American Indians* (Albuquerque: University of New Mexico Press, 1982).

20. Quoted in Porter, *To Be Indian*, 102.

21. Parker quoted in Hazel Hertzberg, *The Search for an American Indian Identity: Modern Pan-Indian Movements* (Syracuse NY: Syracuse University Press, 1971), 59.

22. Quoted in Porter, *To Be Indian*, 120, 123.

23. John Higham, *Strangers in the Land: Patterns of American Nativism, 1860–1925* (New Brunswick NJ: Rutgers University Press, 1955).

24. Quoted in Porter, *To Be Indian*, 142.

25. Simon Pokagon, "The Future of the Red Man," *Forum* 23 (1896): 693–708.

26. Joane Nagel, "Constructing Ethnicity: Creating and Recreating Ethnic Identity and Culture," in *New Tribalisms: The Resurgence of Race and Ethnicity*, ed. Michael W. Hughey (New York: New York University Press, 1998), 237–72.

27. Werner Sollors, *Beyond Ethnicity: Consent and Descent in American Culture* (New York: Oxford University Press, 1987).

28. The most insightful critique of Barsh's thesis is Donald L. Parman, "Probing an Intellectual Quagmire," *American Indian Quarterly* 15, no. 1 (1991): 45–47.

29. Arif Dirlik, *Postmodernity's Histories: The Past as Legacy and Project* (Lanham MD: Rowman and Littlefield, 1999), 183–84.

| Chapter 9

Mixed-Descent Indian Identity and Assimilation Policy

Katherine Ellinghaus

In 1937 Amanda M. Thompson was one of many Native Americans who wrote to the U.S. government in the wake of the 1934 Indian Reorganization Act to ask to be recognized as an Indian. Thompson addressed her letter to Eleanor Roosevelt in the familiar tone that pervaded so much of the correspondence that Roosevelt received:

> Well dear friend just a few lines to let you hear from me I am in the hospital in Springfield with creeping peralises [*sic*] I sure suffer. . . . Mrs Roosevelt I want you to do a favor for me and I heard they had reopened the Indian Role [*sic*] if they do please put my name on the Role. I am half Indian.[1]

Thompson was mistaken when she thought that the government had reopened the rolls on which tribal members were listed. There was a section of the 1934 act that allowed Indians of "one half or more Indian blood" to register officially as Indians and become eligible for some small government programs, but the tribal rolls had long been closed. Nevertheless, in the years following the 1934 act, which officially ended the assimilation period, many Indians, like Thompson, wrote to the government asking to be recognized as Indians. Extensive correspondence of this kind is now collected in a series of boxes held in the National Archives in Washington DC.

The assimilation period had tragic consequences for Native Americans, something that has been deservedly well rehearsed by historians. The years after the Dawes Act of 1887, which divided reservations into individually owned allotments, saw a staggering loss of land, and the parallel emphasis on Christianization and education resulted in thousands of Native American children suffering the harsh process of acculturation in boarding schools. But there was another consequence of this period that has not been fully recognized: how many Indians of mixed descent were denied officially recognized Indian status as a consequence of the policies of enrollment and allotment. Eva Marie Garroutte calls these unsung victims of the assimilation period and their relatives "outalucks, people of Indian ancestry who are nevertheless unable to negotiate their identity as Indians within the available legal definitions."[2]

Mixed-descent Indians were not, as a whole, treated separately by the legislation of the assimilation period. Nor was there an official definition of Indian status that excluded them.[3] But because the Dawes Act required each Indian community to be enumerated before its land was divided into allotments, the status of "Indian" very quickly became something that could be measured. The most common gauge of who was an Indian was their "blood," and scholars such as Melissa Meyer, Devon Mihesuah, Circe Sturm, Theda Purdue, and Bonita Lawrence have explored in detail how blood has defined and complicated Indian identity up to the present day.[4] The discourse of blood saw racial identity as residing somehow in a person's body. Children of mixed descent were seen as receiving an equal mixture of each parent's ethnicity; thus, for example, a white mother and an Indian father of full descent would create a "half-blood" child. When men and women of mixed descent had their own children, things became more complicated. In an increasingly complex framework, Indian ancestry was measured in fractions of blood—half, quarter, even five thirty-seconds.

The discourse of blood carried with it the assumption that Indians of mixed descent had their own recognizable characteristics. Indians with white ancestry were seen as more intelligent and more acculturated. They were often assumed to be cultural brokers or interpreters who were able to exploit Indians of full descent with their talents.[5] Indians with black ancestry, on the other hand, were subjected to similarly intense racism to that reserved for African Americans at this time, as scholars such as Claudio Saunt, Celia Naylor, Ann McMullen, and Circe Sturm have shown.[6] Even some Indian communities, in sync with the broader American population, showed a clear racial bias against Indians of African American descent.[7] Indians of mixed descent of either white or black ancestry were not perceived as being as "authentic" as their full-descent relatives, the "real" Indians.

Consequently, Indians of mixed descent were often seen as being ineligible for enrollment and allotment, and if they were allotted they were more likely to be declared "competent," a status that released their lands from government protections and left them open to exploitation. If their names were left off the rolls they often were unable to get them reinstated. The actual bureaucratic processes of allotment were enormously intricate, and contributed to many Indians of mixed descent being left out of the process. Although every tribe was enrolled slightly differently, the Office of Indian Affairs generally sent a commission made up of at least several, sometimes many more, public servants. These men used tribal rolls when they were available and traveled around the area conducting face-to-face interviews, usually in tents, with potential enrollees. Face-to-face interviews also allowed public servants to let their racial biases and assumptions affect their work. These biases dealt with skin color, what an "Indian" looked like, and assumptions about how people of mixed and full descent lived. Thus, as Felix Cohen wrote in 1945, "Though a white man cannot by association become an Indian . . . an Indian may, nevertheless, under some circumstances, lose his identity as an Indian."[8] Indians of mixed descent were left off tribal rolls, called "colored" or "white" or even "black" rather than Indian, and if they were successful in gaining an allotment were declared legally "competent" so their lands were no longer protected from sale or mortgage to greedy whites.[9]

But many Indians of mixed descent, just like Amanda Thompson, still thought of themselves as Indians and had an interest in being recognized as such. Histories of this period often focus on so-called real Indians, those of "full descent" with strong ties to their tribal community. By contrast, according to Hertha D. Sweet Wong, a "key focus in twentieth-century Native American autobiography, as in fiction, has been Native identity. Is a Native American defined by blood quantum, cultural involvement, community recognition, self-identification, or residence?"[10] In this chapter I attempt to reconcile these two different foci, offering a historical explanation as to why Indian identity in the twentieth and twenty-first centuries is so contested, and then, using three case studies, freeing some of those "outaluck" voices from the archives to tell the story of the tangled web of legislation and localized particularities that led to the disenfranchisement of mixed-descent Native Americans from Indian status. These examples, spanning the continental United States and different Indian nations, demonstrate the difficulties Native Americans faced in defining and defending a sense of indigenous identity in an age when government was attempting to prescribe who was and was not Native American.

It is certainly not the case, as might be expected from the historical silences about them, that this group of people were excluded from the archives. Quite the contrary, as the government's main concern was to enumerate and define the Indian population, many of the letters in the files are from people negotiating their way through that process. The cases discussed below are not about well-known people, nor are their appearances in the archives out of the ordinary. They are simply instances when, despite there being no law or policy outright denying mixed-descent Indians' enrollment, some individuals lost their chance to be officially recognized as Indian. These are moments when a branch of the "outaluck" Indian family tree was created, three small turning points in history when the current problems with Indian identity came into being.

Mary Jane Moran

In 1889 the "Chippewa Commission" was established to enroll and allot the indigenous nations of Minnesota. Mixed-descent Anishinaabeg were not explicitly excluded from the possibility of being officially recognized as "Chippewa" and receiving a piece of land. But as the process of enrollment and allotment proceeded, and the inhabitants of Minnesota scrambled to get the best land, the commission began to believe that Anishinaabeg of mixed descent were taking advantage of the system of allotment to the detriment of "real" full-descent Anishinaabeg. In December 1891 the commissioner of Indian affairs, Thomas J. Morgan, wrote to the Chippewa Commission chairman to warn him that, while it was the "plain duty of the commission to hear as carefully and thoroughly as possible each case where there is a contest as to whether an Indian should be enrolled or not . . . great pressure will probably be brought to bear by claimants who have no bona fide rights to enrollment."[11] Some Anishinaabeg had similar concerns, but their overall objective was that they would be the ones to decide who belonged to their community.[12] The commission agreed. "The mixed bloods . . . acknowledged as belonging to your tribe will be treated the same as yourselves," Commissioner Rice promised the Mille Lacs. "If there are any others who apply to be admitted . . . and you object, the matter will be referred to Washington."[13]

Nevertheless, over the next decade, policies were developed that allowed for the disqualification of mixed-descent Anishinaabeg because of their lack of tribal involvement, their failure to live inside tribal boundaries, or their intermarriage outside the tribe. Then in 1895, the U.S. assistant attorney general officially defined a "Chippewa Indian" as someone who was of "Chippewa Indian blood," had "a recognized connection with one of the bands of Chippewa Indians in the State of Minnesota," had been a resident of Minnesota when the 1889 act was passed, and lived on one of the Chippewa reservations "with the bona fide intention of making it his permanent home."[14] The power to determine Anishinaabe membership was now in the hands of the U.S. government.

So when Mary Jane Moran presented herself to the commission on October 18, 1899, and asked for herself and her sister to be enrolled on the basis that their mother and father were both "mixed-blood Chippewa," she did not receive a sympathetic hearing. She was asked why her parents had not attempted to be enrolled in the early stages of the commission's work. She did not know, but she did recall that six years earlier they had tried but failed to get their "rights." Peter Leith, an "enrolled Chippewa" who had been raised with Mary's father, testified that at the time the rolls were open, Mary's father, an ex-soldier, "was trying to get a pension and had no chance to attend" the commission's hearings. Other witnesses testified that they knew her family, but not Mary herself. Joseph Bellanger, an eighty-three-year-old Chippewa man who was present at many such hearings, perhaps as an interpreter or assistant, testified that Mary's parents lived "right among" the Indians, but he did not know Mary herself. Chief May zhuc ke ge shig said he did not know Mary personally but that his "wife's mother [had told him that] the parents of Mrs Moran were Chippewa" and that the "Grandmother of Mrs Moran was a cousin of my mother in law."

The commission called the evidence from Bellanger and May zhuc ke ge shig "about as vague and indiffinate [sic] as it well could be."[15] Nor did the commission recognize the difficulty the family had had in enrolling or that their move to St. Paul (where they had been living self-sufficiently as assimilation policy ultimately asked of them) might have made it difficult for them to find tribal members who knew them directly. But that was not as damning as the fact that Mary's family had lived in St. Paul at the same time that the Chippewa Commission had begun its work enumerating the tribe. "[T]hose petitioners and their parents were almost neighbours to Chairman Rice," the decision stated, "and that would have been the time for them to have presented their claims. They have however, waited ten years." Although the commission admitted that the family "may have vested rights which courts may recognized upon proper showing," they were not convinced that the testimony produced was "sufficient to warrant" enrolling the two sisters.[16] Thus, this family, whose neighbors and relatives had made it onto the rolls, was no longer officially Anishinaabe. They were stripped of their Anishinaabe status by administrative bungling and the belief that mixed-descent Indians who had lived off the reservation had no right to the dwindling tribal resources. In only ten years, the commission had broken its promise to the Anishinaabeg that they would have final say about who was on their rolls. Instead, a definition of Anishinaabe status based on blood now aided the commission in ensuring the ineligibility of as many Anishinaabeg from enrollment as possible, and thus more Anishinaabe land declared surplus and ultimately opened to white ownership.

Charles Eastman and Fannie Rodgers

Seven years later, in 1906, in Indian Territory, the children of Charles Eastman, a citizen of the Chickasaw nation who was officially regarded as being "half" Chickasaw, and Fannie Rodgers, an African American "Chickasaw freedman," presented themselves to the Dawes Commission. They wished to transfer their names, and the names of their children, from the Chickasaw "freedman roll" to the "roll of citizens by blood."

With their Chickasaw descent, this should have been well within their rights. In 1893 Congress had put together the Dawes Commission and sent them to Indian Territory to convince the Five Nations, who had been exempted from the 1887 General Allotment (Dawes) Act, to submit to the allotment process. In 1898, this task completed, the Curtis Bill authorized the Dawes Commission to begin the process of allotment. The commission began compiling lists of Indian citizens, basing their lists somewhat on the tribes' own records but also requiring individuals to report to the commission for face-to-face interviews. These interviews, Paul Spruhan has pointed out, were the first occasion on which the U.S. government applied the concept of "blood quantum on a large scale." The Dawes Commission created separate rolls for "Indians by blood," intermarried white citizens, and ex-slaves or "freedmen." The commission also recorded a blood quantum for each person, often making fast and unsupported assumptions. Spruhan notes that "the commission . . . apparently counted only the blood of the mother's tribe for persons with fathers from a different Indian nation, and failed to record any Indian blood at all for many of African and Indian ancestry, whom the Commission listed on the 'Freedmen' rolls."[17]

Being on the "freedman roll" entitled the Eastmans to allotment and membership in the tribe, but it also placed them in a lesser social category. A year later, Oklahoma entered statehood with a constitution that contained a series of Jim Crow laws. It segregated public schools, and the legislature later added laws that segregated an assortment of public institutions and instituted a literacy test and grandfather clause to disenfranchise African Americans.[18] From social, legal, and economic perspectives in Indian Territory at this time, Native American status was far preferable to African American. Being on the Chickasaw blood roll was also more secure. Joseph W. Howell, who investigated the commission's work in 1909, reported that "freedmen . . . were accorded but little, if any, protection by the law."[19]

A lawyer for the Choctaw and Chickasaw tribes opposed the Eastman's enrollment. The Chickasaws themselves had laws to discourage intermarriage, and the Dawes Commission followed the tribal practice of having the children adopt their mother's status when it enrolled as freedmen people who had Indian parentage.[20] Choctaw and Chickasaw freedmen formed associations and hired lawyers to gain their rights. In 1905 a long-running case, that of brothers Joe and Dillard Perry, was finally decided by the Department of Interior, establishing the rights of children of mixed freedman and Chickasaw parentage to transfer their names from the freedman roll to the blood roll. The assistant attorney general of the Department of the Interior declared that children should be able to elect to enroll with one parent or the other. This opened the door to many similar cases, of which the Eastman family was just one.[21] The cases hinged, as the Joe and Dillard Perry case had, on proving that the applicant had applied for enrolment as a citizen by blood by the deadline of December 25, 1902.[22]

Fannie had enrolled her children in 1896 and reported that when she went in front of the Dawes Commission they "laughed but did not say anything else" when she told them that Charles Eastman "was a half blood Indian [and] that she was not married to this Indian." Perhaps the de facto nature of their relationship was enough for the Dawes Commission to discount the children's "1/4 Chickasaw blood," which should have been enough for them to get on the roll. Fannie testified that there was no doubt that Charles was the children's father. She said in her statement that "Charles Eastman helped to support these children until Ada (the child that is dead) was fifteen years old, that he was the father of my children was not secret, I never heard of him denying being the father, and I have heard him publicly say that they were his children, and that [I] knows that they are his children and no one else."[23] Frank Eastman, one of Fannie and Charles's sons, was cross-examined by a lawyer who wanted to make the point that Frank had been happy to receive an allotment as a freedman in 1903. But despite this and the intimations that the children were illegitimate and that their parentage was suspect, it was the complex nature of the Joe and Dillard Perry precedent that sounded the death knell for the Eastmans' hopes of having their Chickasaw heritage officially recognized. The Eastmans' application was denied because it had not been made prior to December 25, 1902. The Eastmans missed out nominally because of a mixture of complicated laws, but visible in the wings of these official explanations and decisions were the same racial divisions that plagued the rest of the nation. This discrimination worked in the U.S. government's favor. The more people who were seen as African American and therefore not having the status of Native Americans, the fewer Indians there were to allot land to. The discourse of blood was convenient to the broader colonial goal of land removal.

The Beverleys and the Adcocks

Even in states where land was not the issue, racial hierarchies worked to disenfranchise people of their status as Indians. In Jim Crow Virginia in the 1920s, 1930s, and early 1940s the Rappahannock, Chickahominy, Pamunkey and Mattaponi Indians found themselves reclassified as "colored" by government officials. During this period the white population of Virginia had channeled its anxieties about the state's diverse population into the 1924 Racial Integrity Act. This piece of legislation prohibited whites from marrying anyone save another white. The act defined a white person as one "who has no trace whatsoever of any blood other than Caucasian," leaving blackness to be defined according to the infamous "one-drop rule." One exception was made to this definition of "white." In recognition of the many elite Virginian families who claimed descent from the "Indian princess" Pocahontas and the white settler John Rolfe, the bill included the "Pocahontas exception," which stated that persons "who have less than one sixty-fourth of the blood of an American Indian and have no other non-Caucasic blood shall be deemed as white persons."[24]

A man called Walter A. Plecker was in charge of the Bureau of Vital Statistics, and during his long reign (from 1924 to 1946), he did everything in his power to recategorize the Virginia Indians neatly into the African American population. Plecker claimed, on the basis of historical evidence of intermarriage between the Virginia Indians and slaves in the seventeenth, eighteenth, and early nineteenth centuries, that there were no Virginia Indians that did not have at least "one drop" of African American blood. Under the 1924 act, therefore, they were technically "colored." If Plecker was wrong, then the ironic possibility existed that people with only a small amount of Indian ancestry could claim to be white under the Pocahontas exception. Plecker referred to this as the "Indian route" to whiteness.[25] Plecker used his position as registrar of the Bureau of Vital Statistics to make sure that, officially at least, the Virginia Indians were registered as "colored" on state documents such as birth, death, and marriage certificates. He wrote to local courts and registrars warning them about the threat of the Indian population. He also contacted doctors and midwives to make sure that birth certificates gave the race of the child as "mixed," "colored," and certainly not as "white." If they were uncertain, they should "use an interrogation mark (?) and write us privately."[26] In the Jim Crow South, where the black/white dichotomy was the salient racial issue, the Virginia Indians were thus classified as "colored" by the government officials in charge of keeping track of racial identity and metaphorically blackened by the discourse of blood.

Plecker targeted particular families. In 1929 and 1930, for example, Plecker changed the official recognition of the Adcock and Beverley families from "Indian" to "colored." In October 1929 Plecker wrote to Pal S. Beverley detailing the extensive work he had put into locating African American ancestry in Beverley's family history. He had made the effort because, he said quite openly, "of your constant agitation of the question that you are a white man." In previous correspondence Plecker had asked Beverley for the names of his father, grandfather, and his grandfather's mother. "Just as I expected," wrote Plecker, "you declined to give the information, but I did not expect you to come down quite as hard upon your mother as you did when you say that you do not know who your father was." Using the names on Beverley's marriage certificate, Plecker did research on Beverley's mother's death certificate, the marriage license of his father, the "tax books in the State library," a list of "free negroes over 12 years of age in Amherst County in 1861," and census records, and included in the letter a detailed rundown of the many times in these records that people with the "Beverley" surname were recorded as "negro," "colored," or "free issue." "In consideration of the above evidence secured from our old records, from tax books, from U.S. census reports, and from the positive knowledge of old persons now living," Plecker wrote, "I am notifying you finally that you can have no other rating in our office under the Act of 1924 than that of a mulatto or colored man, regardless of your personal appearance, voting list, or statements which any persons may make to petitions on your behalf. . . . Any further effort to register yourself or your family in our office as white is . . . a felony."[27]

In January 1930 Plecker wrote to local registrars in Amherst County to warn them that the heads of the Beverley and Adcock families had been making "strong efforts to secure registration in our office as white." Plecker instructed the registrars to "handle this situation with firmness" and to refuse their applications to register. "It would be an overwhelming disaster for Amherst County if from eight to ten hundred of these mixed breeds as a body enter the white race."[28]

Neither the Adcock nor Beverley family was willing to pay heed to these administrative threats. William Adcock wrote to Plecker in October 1929 stating, "We have decided to lose the last drop of blood we have in us before we will be classed as colored," prompting an identical letter from Plecker to the one he wrote Beverley, detailing what Plecker viewed as the Adcock family history, and concluding with warnings about the felonious nature of attempting to register incorrectly as white or marrying outside the colored race.[29]

But it did not end there. In 1935 the Beverley family changed their name by order of the court to "Birch," the maiden name of a woman in the family with undisputed white status.[30] Nor did the Adcock family give up. At least one more time, a member of the family tried to lodge a birth, death, or marriage certificate with her classification as "Indian." It was refused.[31] Although Plecker's reign is now seen as a particularly shameful part of Virginian history, his efforts had long-lasting effects on people's lives and the lives of their descendants, demonstrating that his methods were a radical expression of a popular feeling that mixed-descent Indians should be redefined as not truly "Indian." His zealous efforts to protect Virginian "whiteness" from any possible impurities speaks directly to the important role racial biology played in the hierarchies of the early twentieth century.

Conclusion

In the Bureau of Indian Affairs records held in the National Archives and Records Administration in Washington DC, the files kept on the subject "Enrollment—Citizenship—Degree of Indian Blood" take up hundreds of boxes. In these boxes are thousands of letters from Indians of mixed descent who contacted the Bureau of Indian Affairs once the majority of allotments had been made in the hope that they might still be able to be enrolled. In October 1902 C. F. Larrabee, the acting commissioner of Indian affairs, wrote to Nannie Stell of Paris, Texas: "Madam: You say you know that you have Indian blood but do not know how you will be able to prove it. In reply you are advised that the possession of Indian blood was not of itself sufficient to entitle anyone to rights in the Indian Territory. . . . You are further advised that the time within which application for enrollment could have been made has long since expired."[32] Mrs. R. L. Miller of Roscoe, Texas, wrote to the commissioner to ask "why it is that all the rest of the Indians are getting the pay and I can't? Is it because I can't remember anything about my people or not?"[33] Judd Yelland, a judge from Escanaba, Michigan, wrote to the Department of the Interior on behalf of George Sharkey, who "claims that he is entitled to some kind of compensation from the government and that his name was stricken from the list for some reason unknown to himself." The office sent a reply informing Yelland and Sharkey that some "mixed bloods" were struck from the Ottawa and Chippewa rolls "as were declared by the chiefs to be not entitled to [be] enrolled," that all the funds and land had been distributed, and there was "no way under existing law by which any person who failed to be enrolled as indicated can now be granted any relief."[34]

The process of enrollment resulted in many such cases of people who missed out on official recognition as Indian through a mix of administrative confusion, missed deadlines, snap decisions by public servants, personal endeavors by individuals such as Plecker, or racial discourses that saw Indians of mixed descent as inauthentic. In some cases Indians of mixed descent were not only struggling with the U.S. government's opinions about their status, they were also up against the very nations they wished to become part of. Enrollment and allotment imposed settler discourses about blood and race onto Indian tribes as they simultaneously placed them in enormous and threatening upheaval. People with no Indian ancestry wrongly claimed tribal membership in order to get land, tribal funds, or whatever personal satisfaction was to be gained from playing the role of "Indian."[35] It is little wonder that many tribes responded by closing ranks, and made efforts to reserve tribal resources for an "inner circle" whose ancestry was not called into question.

In this climate it was difficult for people of mixed Indian descent to claim official Indian status. Not only did the U.S. and tribal governments place the burden of proof on mixed-descent Indians hoping to be recognized as Indian, but applicants also had to endure extraordinary interference in their lives. Whether it be the traumatic experience of convincing strangers in a public setting about the paternity of her children, or receiving threatening and personal correspondence from a powerful government official, assimilation policy allowed for significant intervention into the personal lives of mixed-descent Indians in the name of bureaucracy.

This history has very clear implications in the present day. Just as the Office of Indian Affairs did for the writers of letters in General Services File 53, the Bureau of Indian Affairs website currently fends off people with the mistaken impression that the bureau can help them find information about their Indian ancestry: "When people believe they may be of American Indian ancestry, they immediately write or telephone the nearest Bureau of Indian Affairs . . . office for information. That is not the best place to start. Many people think that the BIA retrieves genealogical information from a massive national Indian registry or comprehensive computer database. *This is not true.*"[36] Since the 1980s, there has been a much-reported and increased tendency for people of Indian descent to identify themselves as Indian in census counts. Between 1970 and 1990, despite a low Indian birthrate, the federal census reported an increase of 259 percent in the American Indian population.[37] Joane Nagel argues that the "dramatic twentieth-century rebound in the Indian population . . . is not simply a tale of high birth rates or the discovery of forgotten enclaves of native peoples."[38] What remains, Nagel says, "is the stuff out of which ethnic constructions are made—shifts in self-definition, changes in ethnic identification, ethnic and racial switching and fluidity in the boundaries surrounding Indian ethnicity."[39]

The boundaries of Indian ethnicity were fluid but they were also, for some, insurmountable. Popular discourse often hints or states outright that people who suddenly "discover" their Indian ancestry are figures of fun who are simply jumping on the bandwagon of indigenous identity now that it has gained some kind of postcolonial cachet. The popularity of claiming descent from Powhatan "Princess" Pocahontas is well known.[40] But considering the history outlined above, we might offer another perspective on these social phenomena. How many such people were victims of the U.S. government's efforts to enroll, allot, and enumerate Indian nations, and in so doing set in stone an understanding of Indian status that disadvantaged those of mixed Indian descent?

In 1919 the Office of Indian Affairs wrote to Mr. M. S. Curtis of Tunica, Mississippi, in reply to his letter claiming Indian benefits on the basis of his descent from Pocahontas. Whether Mr. Curtis was really a descendant or not, the Office of Indian Affairs reply might have been addressed to a great many Indians of mixed descent: "You are advised that the Indian tribe in Virginia to which Pocahontas belonged long since became merged into the body politic, and the descendants thereof are citizens of the United States and of the respective States in which they may reside. There are no lands or funds held by the Government for such descendants, nor are there any funds available from which they could be granted any relief."[41] Besides articulating a well-deserved rejection of a ridiculous request, the letter also conveyed the idea that mixed-descent Indians were essentially undeserving of Indian status. It is impossible to know which of the two groups—deserving, unenrolled Indians of mixed descent or unethical imposters—were more numerous. But both certainly existed. And the existence of the latter should not blind historians to the experiences of people who but for the flick of an official's pen would have been designated Indian.

Notes

1. Mrs. Amanda M. Thompson to Mrs. Franklin D. Roosevelt, September 13, 1937, Box 1, E616 Applications and Other Records Relating to Registrations Under the Indian Reorganization Act of 1934, Record Group (RG) 75, National Archives and Records Administration (NARA), Washington DC.

2. Eva Marie Garroutte, *Real Indians: Identity and the Survival of Native America* (Berkeley: University of California Press, 2003), 14.

3. The section in the Code of Federal Regulations that implemented the General Allotment Act simply required an applicant for allotment to show that "he is a recognized member of an Indian tribe or is entitled to be so recognized. Such qualifications may be shown by the laws and usages of the tribe." The regulations directly stated that the "possession of Indian blood, not accompanied by tribal affiliation or relationship, does not entitle a person to an allotment." "Qualifications of Applicants," Code of Federal Regulations, Title 43, Pt. 2531.1 (1887).

4. See, in particular, Thomas Biolsi, "The Birth of the Reservation: Making the Modern Individual among the Lakota," *American Ethnologist* 22, no. 1 (1995): 28–53; Ward Churchill, "The Crucible of American Indian Identity: Native Tradition versus Colonial Imposition in Postconquest North America," in *Contemporary Native American Cultural Issues*, ed. Duane Champagne (Walnut Creek CA: AltaMira Press, 1999), 39–68; E. J. Dickson-Gilmore, *"Iati-Onkwehonwe*: Blood Quantum, Membership, and the Politics of Exclusion in Kahnawake," *Citizenship Studies* 3, no. 1 (1999): 27–43; Garroutte, *Real Indians*; James F. Hamill, "Show Me Your CDIB: Blood Quantum and Indian Identity among Indian People of Oklahoma," *American Behavioral Scientist* 47, no. 3 (2003): 267–82; M. Annette Jaimes, "Federal Indian Identification Policy: A Usurpation of Indigenous Sovereignty in

North America," in *The State of Native America: Genocide, Colonization, and Resistance*, ed. M. Annette Jaimes (Boston: South End Press, 1992), 123–38; Bonita Lawrence, *"Real" Indians and Others: Mixed-Blood Urban Native Peoples and Indigenous Nationhood* (Lincoln: University of Nebraska Press, 2004); Melissa Meyer, "American Indian Blood Quantum Requirements: Blood is Thicker Than Family," in *Over the Edge: Remapping the American West*, ed. Valerie Matsumoto and Blake Allmendinger (Berkeley: University of California Press, 1999), 231–49; Devon A. Mihesuah, "American Indian Identities: Issues of Individual Choice and Development," in Champagne, *Contemporary Native American Cultural Issues*, 13–38; Theda Perdue, *"Mixed Blood" Indians: Racial Construction in the Early South*, Mercer University Lamar Memorial Lectures No. 45 (Athens: University of Georgia Press, 2003), and "Race and Culture: Writing the Ethnohistory of the Early South," *Ethnohistory* 51, no. 4 (2004): 701–23; Audra Simpson, "Paths toward a Mohawk Nation: Narratives of Citizenship and Nationhood in Kahnawake," in *Political Theory and the Rights of Indigenous Peoples*, ed. Duncan Ivison, Paul Patton, and Will Sanders (New York: Cambridge University Press, 2000), 113–36; Pauline Turner Strong and Barrick Van Winkle, "'Indian Blood': Reflections on the Reckoning and Refiguring of Native North American Identity," *Cultural Anthropology* 11, no. 4 (1996): 547–76; Circe Sturm, *Blood Politics: Race, Culture, and Identity in the Cherokee Nation* (Berkeley: University of California Press, 2002); Hilary N. Weaver, "Indigenous Identity: What Is It, and Who *Really* Has It?" *American Indian Quarterly* 25, no. 2 (2001): 240–55; and Rose Cuison Villazor, "Blood Quantum Land Laws and the Race Versus Political Identity Dilemma," *California Law Review* 96, no. 3 (2008): 801–37.

5. See, for example, Brian C. Hosmer, "Reflections on Indian Cultural 'Brokers': Reginald Oshkosh, Mitchell Oshkenaniew, and the Politics of Menominee Lumbering," *Ethnohistory* 44, no. 3 (1997): 493–509; and Terry P. Wilson, "Blood Quantum: Native American Mixed Bloods," in *Racially Mixed People in America*, ed. Maria P. P. Root (Newbury Park CA: Sage Publications, 1992), 119.

6. See Tiya Miles and Sharon P. Holland, eds., *Crossing Waters, Crossing Worlds: The African Diaspora in Indian Country* (Durham NC: Duke University Press, 2006); Katja May, *African Americans and Native Americans in the Creek and Cherokee Nations, 1830s–1920s* (New York: Garland Publishing, 1996); Ann McMullen, "Blood and Culture: Negotiating Race in Twentieth-Century Native New England," in *Confounding the Color Line: The Indian-Black Experience in North America*, ed. James F. Brooks (Lincoln: University of Nebraska Press, 2002), 261–91; Tiya Miles, *Ties that Bind: The Story of an Afro-Cherokee Family in Slavery and Freedom* (Berkeley: University of California Press, 2005); Claudio Saunt, *Black, White, and Indian: Race and the Unmaking of an American Family* (New York:

Oxford University Press, 2005); Celia E. Naylor, *African Cherokees in Indian Territory: From Chattel to Citizens* (Chapel Hill: University of North Carolina Press, 2008); Sturm, *Blood Politics*.

7. Circe Sturm, "Blood Politics, Racial Classification, and Cherokee National Identity: The Trials and Tribulations of the Cherokee Freedmen," in *Confounding the Color Line: The Indian-Black Experience in North America*, ed. James. F. Brooks (Lincoln: University of Nebraska Press, 2002), 224.

8. Felix Cohen, *Handbook of Federal Indian Law* (Washington DC: U.S. Department of the Interior, 1945), 3.

9. Fee patents, also known as certificates of competency, were awarded to individual Indians who were designated "competent," and allowed them to sell, lease, or mortgage their allotted land without interference from the Office of Indian Affairs. This most often resulted in sale or lease to exploitative whites, and led to an overall enormous loss of Indian land. Awarding competency preferentially to Indians of mixed descent became a deliberate policy until 1917—but before that date it was a tendency of competency commissions to assume that Indians of mixed descent were more acculturated and thus more likely to be "competent." For more on competency, see Janet A. McDonnell, *The Dispossession of the American Indian, 1887–1934* (Bloomington: Indiana University Press, 1991).

10. Hertha D. Sweet Wong, "Native American Life Writing," in *The Cambridge Companion to Native American Literature*, ed. Joy Porter and Kenneth M. Roemer (Cambridge: Cambridge University Press, 2005), 135.

11. T. J. Morgan to D. S. Hall, December 10, 1891, E1297, Chippewa Commission Records, RG 75, NARA, Chicago.

12. One chief expressed the concern of the Anishinaabeg that their lands be protected from the "great many . . . Indians, half-breeds, and whites" that had "come only on account of the land, with their ears open to listen to anything that will give them a chance to get an allotment made in the pine," the richest lands on the reservation. U.S. Congress, House, *Final Report of the United States Chippewa Commission, December 26, 1889, Presidential Message on Relief of Chippewa Indians of Minnesota*, 51st Cong., 1st sess., 1890, 102.

13. U.S. Congress, House, *Final Report*, 170.

14. U.S. Congress, House, *Annual Report of the Commissioner of Indian Affairs, 1895* (Washington DC: Government Printing Office, 1896), 29.

15. E1303 Proceedings in Enrollment Cases, 1897–1899, Chippewa Commission Records, RG 75, NARA, Chicago.

16. E1303 Proceedings in Enrollment Cases, 1897–1899.

17. Paul Spruhan, "A Legal History of Blood Quantum in Federal Indian Law to 1935," *South Dakota Law Review* 51, no. 1 (2006): 39–40.

18. *Encyclopedia of the Great Plains*, ed. David J. Wishart (Lincoln: Center for Great Plains Studies, University of Nebraska Press, 2004), 454.

19. Joseph W. Howell, *Report Relating to the Enrollment of Citizens and Freedmen of the Five Civilized Tribes, to the Secretary of the Interior, March 3, 1909*, 23, 65, 73, Choctaw Removal Records, RG 75, NARA, Washington DC.

20. Kent Carter, *The Dawes Commission and the Allotment of the Five Civilized Tribes* (Orem UT: Ancestry.com, 1999), 71.

21. Ariela Gross, *What Blood Won't Tell: A History of Race on Trial in America* (Cambridge MA: Harvard University Press, 2008), 161.

22. Gross, *What Blood Won't Tell*, 161; Carter, *The Dawes Commission*, 93.

23. Folder 2, E90C Applications to Change from Freedmen to by Blood (Joe and Dillard Perry), Records Relating to Enrollment, Records of the Commission to the Five Civilized Tribes, RG 75, Bureau of Indian Affairs, NARA, Fort Worth.

24. Copy of 1924 act reprinted in Bureau of Vital Statistics, Virginia State Board of Health, *Eugenics in Relation to the New Family and the Law on Racial Integrity* (Richmond VA: David Bottom, Supt. Public Printing, 1924).

25. W. A. Plecker to H. D. Kissenger, May 17, 1939, Box 56, MSS 7284, John Powell Papers, Alderman Library, University of Virginia, Charlottesville.

26. W. A. Plecker to Physicians of Virginia, June 1924, and W. A. Plecker to Mr. V. W. Davis, May 13, 1924, Clerk's Correspondence (A. T. Shields), Library of Virginia, Richmond.

27. W. A. Plecker to Pal S. Beverley, October 22, 1929, Rockbridge County Court Records. This correspondence makes it appear that the Beverley and Adcock families were trying to be seen as "white," but this might not have been the case. From Plecker's perspective there were only two possibilities: white or "colored"; "Indian" was not a possibility.

28. W. A. Plecker to Local Registrars, Amherst County, VA, January 8, 1930, Rockbridge County Court Records, Box 1, Clerk's Correspondence (A. T. Shields), Library of Virginia.

29. W. A. Plecker to William T. Adcock, Amherst VA, January 7, 1930, Rockbridge County Court Records, Box 1, Clerk's Correspondence (A. T. Shields), Library of Virginia.

30. W. A. Plecker to A. T. Shields, September 26, 1935, Rockbridge County Court Records, Box 1 Clerk's Correspondence (A. T. Shields), Library of Virginia.

31. W. A. Plecker to Miss Hallie Adcock, Monroe VA, February 16, 1942, Box 56, MSS 7284, John Powell Papers, Alderman Library, University of Virginia, Charlottesville.

32. C. F. Larrabee, Acting Commissioner, to Nannie Stell, Paris TX, October 25, 1907, 82462/07, Box 204, General Services File 53, Enrollment—Citizenship—

Degree of Indian Blood, Central Classified Files 1907–1939, RG 75, NARA, Washington DC.

33. Mrs. R. L. Miller, Roscoe TX, to Mr. Cato Sells, May 8, 1914, 7403/17, Box 204, General Services File 53, Enrollment—Citizenship—Degree of Indian Blood, Central Classified Files 1907–1939, RG 75, NARA, Washington DC.

34. Judd Yelland, Judge, Escanaba, Michigan, to Indian Agent, Interior Department, February 7, 1917, and C. F. Hawke, Chief Clerk, to Judd Yelland, February 26, 1917, 13897/17, Box 218, General Services File 53, Enrollment—Citizenship—Degree of Indian Blood, Central Classified Files 1907–1939, RG 75, NARA, Washington DC.

35. Rayna Green, "The Tribe Called Wannabee: Playing Indian in America and Europe," *Folklore* 99, no. 1 (1988): 30–55.

36. Office of Public Affairs, *Guide to Tracing Your American Indian Ancestry* (Washington: U.S. Department of the Interior, n.d.), available at http://www.doi .gov/bia/docs/TracingIndianAncestry508compliant.pdf (accessed July 16, 2009).

37. David Hollinger, "Amalgamation and Hypodescent: The Question of Ethnoracial Mixture in the History of the United States," *American Historical Review* 108, no. 5 (December 2003): 1368. R. David Edmunds has also argued that the popularity of claiming Indian ancestry needs further study. R. David Edmunds, "Native Americans, New Voices: American Indian History, 1895–1995," *American Historical Review* 100, no. 3 (1995): 734. For a detailed statistical analysis, see Jeffrey Passel and Patricia A. Berman, "Quality of the 1980 Census Data for American Indians," *Social Biology* 33 (1986): 163–83. For a discussion of the problems inherent in defining American Indian identity on the basis of census data, with particular reference to the difference between the statistics produced by questions that asked respondents to identify their "race" and their "ancestry," respectively, see C. Matthew Snipp, "Who Are American Indians? Some Observations about the Perils and Pitfalls of Data for Race and Ethnicity," *Population Research and Policy Review* 5 (1986): 237–52.

38. Joane Nagel, *American Indian Ethnic Renewal: Red Power and the Resurgence of Identity and Culture* (New York: Oxford University Press, 1996), 9–10.

39. Nagel, *American Indian Ethnic Renewal*, 94.

40. See, for example, Robert S. Tilton, *Pocahontas: The Evolution of an American Narrative* (New York: Cambridge University Press, 1994), and Stuart E. Brown Jr., Lorraine F. Myers, and Eileen M. Chappel, *Pocahontas' Descendants: Supplement* (Berryville VA: Pocahontas Foundation, 1987).

41. C. F. Hawke, Chief Clerk, to Mr. M. S. Curtis, Tunica MS, February 14, 1919, 11380/19, Box 221, General Services File 53, Enrollment—Citizenship—Degree of Indian Blood, Central Classified Files 1907–1939, RG 75, NARA, Washington DC.

| Chapter 10

"All Go to the Hop Fields"
The Role of Migratory and Wage Labor in the Preservation of
Indigenous Pacific Northwest Culture

Vera Parham

In September 1903 the *Puyallup Valley Tribune* carried three columns
of front-page articles featuring the hop-picking season in Washington State's Puyallup Valley. The article in the first column described
the incredibly rich soil and harvest as well as the rich profits that
would be made that year by hop growers. The article in the third column discussed the international hop market and competition faced
by Puyallup hop-field owners. The center-column article was almost
entirely devoted to examining the lives of the Native American hop
pickers, who migrated from all over the region to make up a dominant portion of the labor force on the farms each season. The article marveled at the business acumen and success of the indigenous
pickers, extolling their quality work ethic and financial resourceful-
ness. Moreover, readers were encouraged to travel to the Puyallup
hop fields where they were assured of a glimpse of the traditional
lifestyles of Pacific Northwest Native Americans. Like other Pacific
Northwest newspaper articles written between the late nineteenth
and early twentieth century on the subject of Native American workers, this article clearly demonstrates that the migratory labor practices of indigenous workers did not hinder but instead helped them
to retain some of their traditional lifestyles and culture in a rapidly
changing world.

Before I launch into the history of Native American labor on the hop fields, I want to define and dismantle a few specific concepts that appear throughout this work, including wage labor, the authenticity of identity, and the concept of diaspora. These three terms—labor, identity, and diaspora—come together to create a new paradigm with which to view indigenous history in the Pacific Northwest. Wage labor, notably migratory wage labor, supported a diasporic identity, which in turn protected a regional Indian identity that assimilationist policies were attempting to stamp out. Studying the diaspora of wage labor within the Pacific Northwest Native American community challenges the "conceptual limits imposed by national and ethnic/racial boundaries" and promotes new methods with which to address Native American history.[1]

"Diaspora" is not often used to describe the Native American experience, but the concept of diaspora captures the complex, shifting Native American identity of the region better than "tribe" or "region" or "work." This is because diaspora implies cultural construction and a state in flux, not one of permanence. A diaspora represents loss and retention, people who have lost their homelands but who have maintained an ethnic identity. It illustrates agency over passivity, promoting the idea that indigenous identity survives colonial legal and cultural impositions and land loss though selective adaptation. A simple definition of a diaspora is the creation of a home away from home as well as the connections a community of people maintain over distance. These connections can take the form of circulating people, money, and goods, and are maintained by transportation (railroads and canoes in this case) and by the availability of seasonal labor that promotes the movement away from and return to a homeland.[2] Diaspora includes some sense of isolation and belief in separation from the majority society. Diasporic people constantly struggle to maintain their culture in the face of a repressive force. Diaspora also implies a power relationship, one in which a people have been forced from their homelands. In this sense it creates a hierarchy between colonizer and colonized. Within that hierarchy lies the assumption by colonial powers that the colonized must be assimilated to their superior ways. By retaining a tie to homeland and identity, a diaspora struggles against that hierarchy and assumption of cultural dominance. Native American laborers in the Pacific Northwest do not technically fit all aspects of the definition of diaspora, as they often maintained small portions of their ancestral homelands, though they generally lost much more than they maintained. No matter how little or how much they maintained, association with the land, directly or via diaspora, is a key symbol to express ethnic identity. Maintenance of a diaspora also implies the maintenance of culture, though that culture is fluid and relies on circuits of social and economic ties. To this end, migratory wage labor supported an indigenous Pacific Northwest diasporic community.

The suggestion that participation in wage labor and the capitalist economy allowed Native Americans of the nineteenth and twentieth centuries to maintain their culture and traditions would have seemed preposterous to most twentieth-century scholars. As historian Daniel Usner observes, "The popular notion that American Indians have not participated in the economy as wage laborers is deeply embedded in American consciousness."[3] In North America, histories of labor (especially organized labor) have long been the purview of white male workers.[4] Some histories have included immigrant laborers, African Americans, or women, but few, if any, have acknowledged the important role Native American employees played in agricultural and industrial fields throughout the nineteenth and twentieth centuries. Studies of North American Indian economic life seemed to view Native American society as completely separate from the rest of American life, their indigenous practices the binary opposite of American capitalism. The notion that Native Americans were economically ignorant and inferior to colonizing Europeans was even used as justification for colonization in itself. Many early anthropologists like Franz Boas and Alfred Kroeber, and nineteenth-century historians such as Francis Parkman, imposed on Native Americans an identity and history in which few indigenous people could be viewed as authentic. The tension in this real versus imposed history stems from the fact that the general public (and often historians) assumed that Native American culture was a static and dying entity, rooted in the land.[5] Anthropologists and historians long emphasized the notion that any adoption

of European colonial modes of life or labor automatically discount-
ed ties to an authentic Indian identity.

Such beliefs persisted into the twentieth century in spite of the fact
that access to the wage labor system was often essential for the survival of Native American people. For a generation of historians, authenticity in Native American life meant the practice of entrenched
customs. "Real Indians" ceased to exist when they donned slacks and
cotton skirts and headed off to pick hops for daily pay. Yet the survival of indigenous people of the Pacific Northwest depended, for better
or for worse, on their ability to adapt to the new world created by the
Anglo-American settlers. In an effort to maintain sovereignty in a colonial world, indigenous people across North America sought to com-
bine traditional and foreign culture, labor, and agricultural practices.

The desire of indigenous people to join the Anglicized labor force
was more often a symptom of losing conventional forms of subsistence, land, and resources due to colonization than it was a desire for
assimilation. However, for some laborers, working for wages was a
means to establish equality with foreign powers, freeing them from
colonial status and earning them a unique avenue to recover sovereignty. For example, wage labor offered a way to maintain established
practices like the potlatch (a celebration loosely intended to maintain
alliances and redistribute resources). Because those Native Americans
with better jobs and higher wages could distribute more gifts to their
potlatch guests, wage labor reinforced traditional social structures.
By assuming that Native Americans turned to wage labor simply because they had no other options, some historians place too much emphasis on the belief that indigenous people lived in constant reaction
to white society. They deemphasize the ability of Native American
people to make their own choices and to develop their own sense of
identity despite the limited economic opportunities left to them by
encroaching settlers.

This notion of static authenticity plagues Native American histories in the Pacific Northwest, a place where identity was and is quite
fluid. Identities were not simply either Indian or American, either Salish or hops picker, either domestic worker or well-known daughter of

a powerful chief. Identity for Pacific Northwest Native Americans was
not nearly as fixed and rigid as European systems of scientific class and
status were. There was always potential for identities to shift across
place and time. Culture was accretive. Assertion of identity was situationally based on desires and demands. Individuals made "practical
choices based on what was at the time self-evident" or the most effective strategy of the moment.[6] Older identities became tools—compasses
for navigating the new Anglo-American world. Long before the Europeans' arrival, Native Americans in the Pacific Northwest had adopted
means of constituting identity based upon "others," due in large part
to the interactions of the many diverse peoples in the region. Contacts through trade and marriage widened the worldview of Pacific
Northwest Native Americans while at the same time strengthening
the individual's sense of place and self. However, Europeans brought
more dramatic changes, and indigenous people were forced to create
more substantial reconstitutions of self-identity, which were then vali-
dated through group identity. Native Americans in the Pacific Northwest took careful measure of their environments and neighbors. From
there, they crafted group and individual identities that allowed them
to survive and resist the new economic world introduced by European and American settlers.

With that said, it is important to elucidate the term "traditional"
due to its complex connotations. In American Indian history, "tradition" or "traditional" can be a loaded term. It is often used to justify
an inferior social status for American Indians who did not assimilate
or "conform" to modernity. "Traditional" is a general term, implying
a set mode of action rooted in history and repetition. But what is considered traditional is fluid, morphs over time, and is a social construction. Tradition is not the "unwavering reproduction of the past," it is
the constant evaluation of meaning.[7] For most cultures, traditional
simply connotes significance. It is an important piece of culture, either
material or intellectual, that provides a link to the past. Traditional
identities, patterns, or landscapes are not permanent, though they represent something of permanence. By practicing traditions, individuals
lay claim to a group identity and authenticity and maintain history.

Native Americans in the Pacific Northwest used migratory labor not only to maintain accepted lifestyles but also to organize and pressure the colonial powers of the capitalist workforce into acknowledging Native American rights. While smaller in numbers, Native Americans were always part of the labor force, but because they rarely organized as a distinct ethnic group, it has been assumed that they did not organize. In the Pacific Northwest, the Native American labor population shattered those generalizations by proving not only that the indigenous local and migrant laborers were the majority of the workforce for decades, they were also willing to organize union-style strikes and work stoppages, even without a union.[8] These actions were taken in order to maintain desirable working conditions, which included maintaining their own camps in which to practice and protect accustomed lifestyles. Native American wage employees refused to be overwhelmed by economic transformations.

Before focusing on the introduction of wage labor in the Pacific Northwest, and more specifically, on labor in the hop fields, which grew in importance in the 1880s, it is necessary to briefly address some traditional systems of labor and historic economics in order to recognize the changes that wage labor brought to the region.[9] The Pacific Northwest is bordered by the Pacific Ocean, and powerful rivers crisscross the land. Water and fish were at the heart of Pacific Northwest life and culture for hundreds of years. The collection, processing, and trading of fish (most notably salmon) was the center of economic life and labor for many Pacific Northwest Native Americans. Large tribes such as the Snoqualmies and the Chinooks that were spread across numerous villages, as well as the smaller communities such as the Squaxins and the Quileutes, relied on aquatic resources for food and goods to barter. Tribes and nations took their names from the locations of their villages, which were generally organized around watersheds, illustrating the importance of the aquatic resource.[10]

As well as shaping attitudes toward resources, fishing has played an important role in shaping the economy of the Pacific Northwest, bringing divergent groups together through trade and generating great wealth.[11] It has also shaped culture through various ceremonial practices including songs, stories, and dances intended to honor the salmon.[12] Stories and ceremonies helped foster community and a cohesive identity. Group activity was the norm, and communities lived together in close-knit conditions in order to create stronger social bonds. One specific ceremony intended to create strong social bonds was the potlatch. A potlatch was held to celebrate any number of occasions, from a marriage to a naming, from a successful hunt to a death. At a potlatch, tribal members and neighbors were invited to share in a feast and the distribution of gifts. Thus, the potlatch was loosely indented to maintain alliances and redistribute resources. The social unity created out of this system of community living helped the various Northwest tribes maintain a sense of unique identity and culture throughout the nineteenth and twentieth centuries.[13]

The fish, the land, and the waterways were not owned outright as they were in Anglo-American society. Instead, specific families, the upper classes of society, controlled rights to land and access to fishing, gathering, and hunting grounds. Lands controlled by specific families or tribes could spread across miles. This meant that the seasonal rounds of gathering resources took both tribes and individuals across others lands. Rights of access were considered sacred because they had been passed to the family by an ancient powerful being. Because these rights were inherited, the family who controlled the rights was required to protect and utilize the resources available or their rights would be forfeit.[14] These rights fostered a stratified society in which elites controlled natural resources via their spiritual strength or wealth.

Gathering fish and other resources was seasonal. Labor-intensive fishing was practiced in the early summer and some fishing in the winter. The fish were processed for storage, and the surplus allowed Pacific Northwest Native Americans several months out of the year to devote to creative and artistic pursuits. Even though many tribes shared the common characteristic of reliance on fish as their prime resource, each tribe retained its own identity. A very diverse place, the Puget Sound region has been home to numerous cultures, languages, and lifestyles.[15] Even before contact with Anglo-Americans, the people of the Pacific Northwest were accustomed to dealing with outsiders and incorporating them into their societies. Marriage and kinship crossed boundaries of class and tribe, and the incorporation of new members through marriage into a community meant the ability of peoples to share and utilize one another's resources.[16] In other words, kinship was at the core of the indigenous economy and intermarriage was the glue that held the Pacific Northwest region together.[17] Partly due to the flexibility of their social structures and intermarriage, the shared tradition of the potlatch, the importance of trade networks and economic ties, their seasonal patterns of labor and migration that regularly took them through neighboring countries, and the unifying force of fishing on their cultures, these numerous peoples lived together in relative peace.

Surprisingly, the concept of wage labor was not new to Native Americans in the Pacific Northwest. Perhaps this is one aspect that can help explain the success of indigenous peoples in the region and their adaptation to and participation in the capitalist labor market. Even before the introduction of Anglo-American concepts of wage labor, Coast Salish and inland Salish used wage labor in times of great abundance. Friends, neighbors, or even strangers could be hired to join the family crew, especially in families that controlled larger tracts of fishing sites but did not have the labor to gather all the fish in high run times.[18] Food, goods, or shell currency were all forms of payment. This extra capital could then be spent hosting large potlatches or for services like building or healing/medical help.[19] Payment was not just for labor; it was also granted for favors like the delivery of food or gifts.[20]

Working for colonists and incorporation into a global labor market started with the arrival of the first fur traders. While it did little to fundamentally alter their lifestyles, the fur trade, begun in the early 1800s, introduced the beginning of major change into the economic and cultural life of Pacific Northwest Native Americans. Fur-trade posts relied on the local indigenous population mainly for fish and supplies. The earliest fur traders, from the British Hudson's Bay Company and the American Pacific Fur Company, simply integrated themselves into the Indian trade networks that were already in place. Much of the hired labor used to build the forts and hunt for

furs came from imported Iroquois/Haudenosaunees and other eastern tribesmen, Native Hawaiians, and immigrants from the United
Kingdom. Unlike the fur-trade experience of tribes in the regions farther east, the relationship with English and American companies did
not create a dependency status for Pacific Northwest Native Americans. They maintained fishing methods and did not become reliant
on European guns or goods. The merchandise these companies provided, like blankets, did not displace the indigenous economy but
was incorporated into it, like the potlatch. The introduction of these
items did reinforce the social divisions between some Salish peoples,
allowing the elites to gather more goods for redistribution, thus so-
lidifying their position.

    The first major party of American settlers to come to Puget Sound
was the Denny Party in 1851. On the shores of Low Point in the sound,
Denny and his companions met Chief Seeathl (Seattle) and his men
from the Suquamish and Duwamish. Seeathl and his men greeted the
migrants and began helping them to build their lodgings for the price
of food and bread, already proving their knowledge of wage labor and
its importance to white society.[21] Although they laid the groundwork
for future Anglo-American settlement, which would radically alter
land use and usurp indigenous resources, these early settlers did little to seriously impede the accustomed lifestyles of the people of the
region. Early settlers, however, brought contagion to the land. The
once thriving indigenous population continued to fall in dramatic
numbers because of foreign diseases.[22]

    The most serious blow to Native American sovereignty and culture
in the region came with the Oregon Donation Act of 1850. The United States allowed its citizens to claim lands in Oregon and Washington, even though it had yet to acquire title to those lands from their
Native American "owners." These new settlers demanded the government treat with the indigenous population in order to divest them of
their remaining lands and confine them to reservations. In just over
a year, territorial governor Isaac Stevens cajoled, coerced, bribed, gift-
ed, and threatened his way into ten treaties with many of the local
tribes. The treaty councils were often hotly contested, and in the end,

Stevens, under tribal pressure, preserved more Native American land for the treaty signatories than the expanding settler population wished.

For the federal government, reservations and centralized settlement were seen as a method to incorporate Native Americans into the wage economy and foster assimilation. On the other hand, wages became a way to support traditional lifestyles because migratory labor helped maintain conventional forms of movement. During the treaty era, as the federal government struggled to place titles and labels on Pacific Northwest Native American people in order to manage treaty negotiations, the idea of territories or boundaries drawn on land became significant. To claim an identity, and thus the treaty rights that came with it, an individual or group had to claim a tie to a specific portion of land. Diasporic identities therefore became significant in the post–treaty era because they allowed Pacific Northwest Native American people to maintain ties to specific groups, even if they had no "claim" (in the eyes of the government) on specific land.

Faced with the prospect of losing wages from the imposition of the reservation system, many Native Americans either refused to move to the impoverished marginal lands or refused to stay on the reservation. Even after the treaties were signed and the reservations created in the 1850s, most Pacific Northwest Native Americans still followed seasonal migrations. They moved from city to country to reservation to find supplemental wage labor. In an 1858 report to Congress on the conditions in Indian country in Washington Territory, Bureau of Indian Affairs special agent J. Ross Browne admitted that "the Sound Indians can not be made to understand why government should take their country away from them and then compel them to work for a living. They say government deprived them of their natural heritage. . . . If they work, they must be paid for it."[23] Local Indians preserved old migration practices in order to follow productive labor areas rather than engage in farming or ranching or remain on reservation lands. To Browne's chagrin, trade went on as usual, since it meant the Washington Indians were not confined to reservations and were in regular contact with old British trading partners and local Americans.[24] The ability of Pacific Northwest Native Americans to maintain their place in the Anglo-American wage economy while maintaining a land base created visibility. In other words, Native Americans in the Pacific Northwest remained a constant presence. The federal government and Bureau of Indian Affairs could not simply hope that Pacific Northwest Native American people would fade away on distant reservations or become completely acculturated into urban Anglo-American society. Working for pay did not mean that Pacific Northwest Native Americans were giving up their culture, because in reality the wages allowed them to retain cultural practices and survive in a capitalist world.

By the 1860s, working for wages was a regular part of the Indian economy. Jobs taken were broad and varied. They included domestic labor, logging, fishing, construction, police work, coal mining, cannery work, and agricultural labor. Native Americans worked "not only as unskilled laborers but as expert fisherman and lumbermen, as foremen, and in other positions of responsibility."[25] Jerry Meeker, a local Native American of mixed tribal heritage is a good example of the broad range of jobs Native Americans found themselves employed in. Beginning in 1882, he worked as a farmer, carpenter, policeman, school employee, and real estate broker.[26] Not all labor opportunities in the Pacific Northwest called for workers to migrate to and from the fields of employment, but those in agriculture, construction, cannery work, and fishing did. Maintaining migrations ensured a flow of information and infusion of energy on the reservations as well as the preservation of a distinct region, the reservation, in which to preserve culture and tradition. Other methods of incorporating wage labor with established patterns of movement included selling goods like baskets and chopped wood by canoe in various settlements and employment as hunting or fishing guides.[27]

Even with all this variety, the largest economic resource for Pacific Northwest Native Americans remained in the oceans and rivers. Throughout the nineteenth century, fishing was centrally important to the economy and culture of Pacific Northwest Native Americans.[28] And the fishing industry in the Pacific Northwest allowed Native Americans to retain an incredibly important aspect of their society in a changing economy. Tribes like the Makahs on the ocean and the Puyallups on the sound still used traditional methods of catching fish with nets and spears. They also retained important rituals, like the first salmon ceremony to bless the harvest of fish. Because fishing was historically a deeply ingrained spiritual and economic activity, the ability to fish and make money from doing it allowed Pacific Northwest Indians to participate in the new Anglo-American economy without having to undergo assimilation into Anglo-American culture. The constant movement required by salmon fishing, following the runs of salmon from ocean to river and back, rewarded many Puget Sound Indians with a level of freedom and independence from the oversight of Indian agents not enjoyed by those on reservations. One agent noted the fishermen and -women were "more independent and show less inclination to cultivate their land."[29]

While fish were still used as a trade commodity, they became important as an item for sale. From the 1870s on, Pacific Northwest Native American fishermen and -women sold their catches to canneries that sprang up across the region. Indian men found employment on fishing boats, working as deck hands and as seal, whale, or otter hunters. Trips aboard American and British trading, lumber, and fishing vessels as sailors and crew gave local Native Americans the ability to earn cash and to see the world. Several men became expert navigators on the ships that employed them.[30] And as Native Americans continued to work on ships, they advanced to more skilled and higher-paying positions.[31]

Native Americans in the Pacific Northwest incorporated the wage economy into social and economic activities in innovative ways. Native shamans and healers worked for wages, thereby incorporating cash into traditional social activities. John Fornsby made over one hundred dollars for singing one guarding power song to help heal a sick man.[32] He recalled another shaman working in the hop fields who "made money fast" by healing hop pickers.[33] The new widespread Native American participation in the cash economy and wage labor of the 1890s supported and augmented older traditions such as the potlatch, which marked weddings, religious holidays, or simply a gathering of friends and family.[34] Fornsby recalled his father's potlatches near the end of the nineteenth century. Instead of giving away gifts at his potlatches, he gave away cash, transforming an old custom into part of the cash economy and thus revalidating its significance. Between himself and his brothers, Fornsby's father gave away six hundred dollars at one time.[35]

Wages were not just for the support of the individual. Wages were used to maintain social cohesion. Individuals or families in the community could be strategically deployed in various fields, farms, or factories and the wages divided among the family or distributed via potlatch. This allowed various family members freedom from the drudgery of a "day job" and time to focus on conventional crafts such as canoe carving, basket weaving, or the creation of ceremonial or religious objects. Access to shared wages also helped to solidify group identity. Benefits that wages provided, like housing and transportation, were dispersed through close "identity" lines. Families or tribal members who shared a group identity could lay claim to these benefits, as they had been able to do for hundreds of years around the sound.

By far the most significant and popular form of migratory employment that took Pacific Northwest Native Americans from reservations into the heart of the capitalist economy was working in the hop fields. In years when salmon runs were lean or resources hard to come by, hop picking was an important source of employment for Pacific Northwest Native Americans. The pay from a season of picking hops could support a family for almost an entire year. Wages were very good, and "experts among them make as high as three dollars a day in some cases."[36] The hop fields became an important place where Native Americans could participate in the wage labor market without giving up their historic lifestyle. They were able to set up camps and engage in culturally unifying behaviors like fishing for subsistence, speaking their native language, practicing their own religion, and using familiar methods of transportation. Hop picking gave them freedom, which nurtured the traditional social fluidity and interaction that marked their earlier history. Hop picking was such a popular occupation for Native Americans that it became a regular part of the seasonal round of labor. As the hop-field owner Ezra Meeker observed, "Often a month is occupied in making the trip, leisurely working their way, camping here and there to hunt or fish, as their inclination prompts."[37] As Native Americans from across the region migrated to and from the hop fields, they stopped in cities en route to sell their crafts and wares. They also visited various usual and accustomed fishing and hunting grounds.[38] Marriages were celebrated across tribal lines and new "alliances" were forged as "all, little and big, young and old, go to the hop fields."[39]

Hops, cultivated as a perennial since the eighth century, are used to flavor and provide stability to beer. The Pacific Northwest's rich soil and moderate climate proved perfect for growing hops. In 1882 the Hops Grower's Association was incorporated in Seattle.[40] They would later own and cultivate hops on over three hundred acres of land. In 1883 John Claussen and Edward Sweeny built the first brewery in the Duwamish region. Their Rainier brand of beer was instantly popular and relied on hops grown in local fields.[41] Farms spread all around the sound initially, and later into eastern Washington. In a good season hops are an incredibly profitable crop with a relatively low overhead, making hop farms a popular endeavor for new and old immigrants to the region. The main marketing center for hops was located in Puyallup, where Ezra Meeker built his farm, the Puyallup Hop Company. By the 1880s, Meeker and his fellow farm owners employed approximately three thousand Native Americans per season.[42] Hop cultivation continued to spread east of the Cascades into the Yakima Moxee Valley region, and by 1888 over two thousand acres of land in the Washington area were under cultivation.[43]

Hops are female flower clusters and are quite small, resembling a pine cone. They come in several different grades, with fancy to choice hops valued highest. The buds are extremely sensitive to heat or cold, wind or rain, and must be closely monitored year round. Hop fields are arranged like vineyards. Hops grow as a vine, trailing up or down long poles. Over the years hop growers experimented with tall or short poles to encourage hop growth. Hundreds of hop buds grow on a vine, and picking the buds is an exact science. Buds that are thrown into the mix with leaves or stems attached have to be cleaned again. Pickers can move up and down rows of vines or even sit in one spot all day long if they place themselves in front of a particularly healthy plant. An experienced picker could quickly strip a vine and fill several baskets or bins a day with the ripe hop buds.

Native American workers came to the hop fields by wagon, on foot, on horseback, via train, or by canoe. The Duwamish, Puyallup, Yakama, Spokane, Sammamish, and Lummi represent just a few of the numerous tribes to arrive from points in Washington State. Tlingits and Haidas from Alaska and Canada spent several months winding their way down the coast in large family canoes to migrate to the hop fields. Local Anglos commented on the hundred of canoes that made the journey every picking season.[44] In 1882 over twenty-five hundred Pacific Northwest Native Americans came to the Puyallup Valley alone.[45] In 1885 six thousand Native Americans, almost one-fourth of the entire British Columbia Native American population, came from Canada to work in the hop fields.[46] The famous Klallam leader Prince of Wales recalled the hop-picking season and the vast number of Native Americans who arrived from far and wide. "Their canoes . . . were hauled up on the beaches below Point Hudson by the hundreds, and for several weeks our people made good money picking hops."[47] In 1878 so many Native American pickers arrived in Sumner, Washington, for the picking season that nervous whites ordered a military company of sixty-four men to the area to "preserve the peace."[48] No conflicts ever broke out between the military and the hop pickers.

Field owners considered Indian pickers "fast reliable workers" and eagerly sought them out.[49] Field owners and overseers claimed "they are our best pickers."[50] They worked with diligence and expertise, filling endless baskets with the highest-quality hops. This desire for Native American laborers is an interesting counterpoint to the popular racial stereotype in the nineteenth and twentieth centuries that Native Americans were lazy and did no labor. In 1836 anthropologist Albert Gallatin famously claimed, "The Indian disappears before the white man, simply because he will not work."[51] Yet Native American workers picked from dawn to dusk. They were known as incredibly thorough and dependable. And as long as there were enough Indian employees to be had, few others could find work in the fields.[52] An article published in the *Washington Standard* in 1877 highlighted both the power of Native American workers to create a desirable work environment as well as the nineteenth-century's widespread anti-Chinese sentiment. This was due in part to concerns about cheap labor undercutting wages, growing American nationalism, and apprehension about increasing immigration from non-European countries. The author of the article noted with some satisfaction that "while Chinamen receive ninety cents a day for picking hops on the Puyallup [farm], Indians demand and receive $2.50 a day."[53] Native Americans used their ethnic identity as leverage against what they viewed as an invading foreign workforce. In one notorious affair, on September 7, 1885, several Native American and Anglo workers banded together to violently chase off Chinese workers on the Wold Brothers farm. The attack killed three of the Chinese workers, but when the perpetrators were brought to trial, they all were acquitted.[54] Hop picking had so melded with the indigenous identities of the day that the field of employment appeared an almost exclusively Native American one.

Indian hop workers were in such demand by field owners that the owners would go to exceptional lengths to attract them. In Yakima, one field owner built a sweat bath for his Native workers while another built a movie theater.[55] Some field owners sought out specific families due to their work ethic and nurtured long-term relationships with them. For instance, year after year, owner William Lane invited George and Mary Stiltamult back to his farm and offered them continual cash bonuses to return.[56] Many field owners even paid the transportation costs for Native American workers from areas like British Columbia, Alaska, or across the Cascade Mountains.[57]

Problems with sanitation and disease in the hop fields created serious health risks, due to the sudden influx of hundreds of people at a work site. Consequently, some owners used cleaner conditions to draw in workers.[58] A number of field owners, in a bid to attract workers, tried to control the spread of diseases like typhoid and dysentery, and some built larger, cleaner living quarters. However, most hop-field owners simply relied on their pocketbooks to fill the fields. Field owners were not above raiding another field's workforce. Owners were sometimes seen in other owners' yards, attempting to entice workers away with higher wages; it was a pickers' market and workers were not held to most fields by contract. As a result, workers went wherever the wages were highest in any part of the season.[59] In 1877 a grower named Allen Miller lost his entire workforce to a higher bidder.[60] While contracts were not common, they could be used to entice workers with promises of bonuses if they stayed until the end of the season. Other temptations were used as well, with one grower apparently throwing a large beer fest at the end of the season as an incentive.[61]

As fields spread across Washington and the demand for labor grew, American Indians began to realize their superior position in the industry. Because hops are a delicate crop and their lifespan on the vine is short, growers were forced to hire as many hands as possible in the picking season. Field owners anxiously planned and strategized to ensure they had enough laborers. If not, the loss in profits was astounding. In 1887 the governor of Washington Territory noted that the supply of labor was much smaller than the demand. During that year, wages correspondingly went up.[62] According to employer Ezra Meeker, "The Indians are quick to perceive the situation and ready to profit by the anxiety of growers and to drive the best bargain possible. They are masters of the situation."[63]

Hop fields became places of permanent new settlements for some Indian people. For communities who had been migrating from labor camps to reservations in recent decades, this was quite unusual. Several Snoqualmies relocated to Lake Sammamish to work the hop fields there. These families built individual cabins, instead of living in tents as usual. They also constructed one sizeable traditional longhouse in which ceremonies and gatherings were celebrated.[64] While still practicing seasonal hunting, fishing, and gathering, the Snoqualmies established a new community at the lake, combining traditional fishing and gathering methods with wage labor. The ability to transform business or work space into indigenous space created a sense of self-determination unavailable on the reservation. Hop-field owners had no vested interest in assimilating Native American workers. In fact, it seems many believed assimilation would destroy the very qualities that made them such sought-after employees. And so, field owners encouraged this creation of Native space. Language retention was another important aspect of culture preserved by the creation of indigenous space on the hop fields. Unlike the life imposed on Indians on the reservations and in the Anglo schools throughout the Pacific Northwest, where watchful Indian agents and missionaries promoted assimilation by forbidding the use of indigenous languages, the migratory, wage-laboring Native Americans were allowed to speak their own tongue. They were surrounded by other language speakers who understood them, and field owners encouraged this communication in order to encourage higher work standards. Happy workers equaled better workers.

Hop fields also became a "meeting ground" between Anglos and Indians. Tourists traveled to the fields to meet "real" Native Americans as well as to escape the city and to enjoy the benefits of nature. Along with this idealized trip to the great outdoors, popular throughout the nineteenth century and promoted by hop-field owners, what tourists hoped to see was a "romanticized" version of the rustic, nature-oriented Native American. The Native American represented freedom from the constraints of settled society, and hop fields were an escape from the drudgery of urban living. Magazine and newspapers both waxed poetic about the idyllic scene of hard-working, lively, and jovial indigenous people.[65] Some tourists seemed disappointed by the trouser-wearing modern Native Americans they encountered. Yet tourists still had access to a market to purchase "authentic" Indian goods.[66] The Anglo demand for Native American baskets, carvings, and blankets encouraged the survival of these traditional skills and fostered a meaningful way to make a living.

It is difficult to pinpoint the importance of material culture in the retention of cultural identity. Is it a manifestation of culture or a carrier of culture? Either way, without the introduction of a currency value to many handcrafted items, the ability to make those items may have been lost as individuals struggling to make a wage turned away from the delicate and time-consuming work of craft creation. Tourists also waited for the returning Native Americans in Seattle. Hop pickers, fresh from the fields, would "line the sidewalks, the women displaying some of the finest needlework and beadwork, blankets and baskets one ever saw."[67] The Native American sellers were shrewd businessmen and -women, striking hard bargains and taking advantage of tourists from the East, whom they recognized by their accents.[68] They may have been playing up to white expectations, but the basket sellers found an outlet to express their identity by bridging customs with capitalist opportunity. When the picking season ended, hop pickers used their wages in the cities they passed through as they returned home. They purchased a wide variety of items—axes, clothing, farm equipment, staples such as flour and sugar. For shopkeepers in Seattle, the arrival of so many Native Americans flush with wages from the fields was a very welcome sight. Native people spent money on goods for maintenance, potlatches, and pleasure, and "between . . . calls going and returning they will leave several thousand dollars in Seattle."[69]

Working in the hop fields opened the door to another lucrative employment option for Native Americans—posing for pictures. Tourists arrived to view the picking and the pickers and were constantly taking photographs. To many, viewing Native Americans at work smacks of exploitation and spectacle, but savvy workers soon realized that they could charge exorbitant sums for posing for these pictures. They worked within the framework imposed by colonial whites to make extra cash and to promote their lifestyle. Even anthropologists were forced to pay for photos.[70] Although anthropology was still an emerging academic field in the late nineteenth century, anthropologists like Franz Boas and Edward Curtis rushed to gather information and photographs of what they perceived to be the last vestiges of real Indian life.

Due to the increasing sense of the "closing of the West," tourists became more interested in photographing the indigenous workers as time passed. Tourists believed they were capturing images of "authentic" Native Americans in an age when the people they were photographing were supposedly "passing from the scene." It was a process of romanticization and nostalgia in an America that began to turn away from modernity and look to a mostly fabricated rustic past for inspiration. Rather ironically, all these people seemed unaware of the fact that Native Americans had long been adapting to the changes brought about by contact with Europeans. Despite these adaptations that might have made them seem less "authentic" to tourists and anthropologists photographing and studying them, they had withstood the onslaught of post-European contact and maintained a claim to their own identity in the changing world that threatened to engulf them. In some cases the imagery of Indian hop pickers or basket sellers in the fields was viewed with pity or scorn by a public who equated migratory labor with poverty. But the skills in negotiating high prices for goods and images belie the Anglo-American notion of an antiquated culture.

Thanks to the tourists who came to the area to view Native peoples working in the hop fields, as well as to those who came to enjoy hunting and fishing pursuits, yet another source of income became available to Native Americans. They not only could pose for photographs for curious tourists but also could earn money by serving as guides for those who wanted "authentic" Native fishing and hunting experiences. This helped Native Americans maintain regional traditions because they preserved ancient knowledge of tribal and familial hunting and fishing grounds. "Local knowledge and specialized skills were thereby adapted to changing economic circumstances."[71] Native American hunting guides may have reinforced Anglo-American notions of Indians tied to nature, but they also contributed to livelihood and survival. In the hop fields, tourists and anthropologists encouraged historic practices and helped secure indigenous fishermen and hunters access to their usual and accustomed lands that might otherwise have been closed to them.

An additional benefit to hop-field employment was the amount of leisure time the work afforded. Workers did not follow a clock. They did not have an overseer or floor manager policing their efforts. Even on farms where there was an overseer, Indian pickers were left to their own devices because of their strong work ethic. Individuals completed work at their own pace, and working as families and as extended families intensified how many hops a family could pick and how clean (leaf-free) those hops were. By the time the day was half over, many families had enough bins of hops filled to provide a solid earning for that day. The rest of the day could be spent seeking other sources of income, or in creating baskets, canoes, or boxes. Workers were often paid by the number of boxes of hops they filled; thus, many Native American laborers picked all day long in order to make as much money as possible. But the amount of work completed was up to the individual, and for many Native workers, the work did not take all day and was not considered particularly strenuous or dangerous. Families often worked as a team, picking hops, filling the box, and taking a break while a child or sibling moved in to take over the work. Working as a team helped maintain family unity and traditional social structures organized around collective production and distribution. Hop-field employees recalled having plenty of time to socialize and have fun.[72] For Native Americans, the socializing included visiting friends and family, as well as gambling at the local Puyallup racetrack, which also attracted Anglos.[73] Another popular pastime was canoe racing, which was generally done to celebrate the closing of the picking season.

Throughout the years of hop picking, trade between tribes was an integral part of Indian life in the hop fields, illustrating Pacific Northwest Native Americans' ability to blend their historic activities with the changes that were imposed on their culture. Traditional kinship networks provided the basis for systems of exchange and trade in the hop-field camps. Anglo wages supported an Indian economy that was based on historically developed social ties. Native ingenuity led to the hop fields becoming places where one could find anything one wanted. Some families even brought horses to sell.[74] Because of the trade, the fields also became a place to prove one's business acumen and prowess. Potlatches were celebrated at the hop fields, and most fields hosted a large potlatch to celebrate the closing of the picking season. In 1899 Arthur Clah noted a feast he attended on the Hayes hop farm with about one hundred other attendees.

One of the most important changes the hop fields encouraged was the growing idea of intertribalism, or "pan-Indianism," in the Pacific Northwest. In the past, the ability of Puget Sound Native Americans to cross tribal lines to find marriage partners and create shared resources through marriage alliances built a smaller version of intertribalism. In the 1880s and 1890s, the new influx of Native Americans from British Columbia and Alaska into the fields fostered a new sense of broader identity for some people. Old rivalries (mainly between northern and southern tribes) still flourished in the fields. However, for many, the new introduction to different people helped spark an interest in a broader national Native American community.[75] Mass media and greater community fostered this sense of "Indianness," as newspapers sprang up to unify this community. In 1922 the *Real American* began publication in Hoquiam, Washington. The paper, written and edited by an all-Indian staff, advanced a pan-Indian agenda by sharing news from across Indian country and promoting unifying events and get-togethers. A working class or union consciousness tended to exclude those who refused to relinquish their unique ethnic identity. Joining in pan-tribal solidarity was a tool to maintain Native American identity in a capitalist society.

In 1894 a powerful new form of Indian protest and solidarity building took shape on the hop fields in the Moxee Valley near the city of Yakima, Washington, when SoHappy and Columbia Jack, both Yakama Indians from the Yakama Reservation, organized a work stoppage to demand higher wages. The strike was a tool to assert the workers' independence and control over the work process. As only Native American workers joined in the strike, it also illustrated cultural identity and community. William Ker, owner of the hop field, detailed the strike's events in a story that appeared in the *Northwest Magazine*. According to Ker, Native American hop pickers, mainly from eastern Washington and mostly from off the reservation, were encouraged by SoHappy and Columbia Jack to stop picking hops until their demands were met. The key demand was for twenty-five cents more per box of hops than the price initially agreed upon. Despite despairing the fate of his crop, which would die if unpicked, Ker at first refused to negotiate when he arrived at SoHappy's camp.[76] After hearing Ker's initial refusal, So-Happy simply told the unbending Ker that the matter of labor was up to the women, whom Ker would not negotiate with, and strode away. When Ker approached SoHappy a few days later with a much higher offer of $1.12 per box, SoHappy accepted the offer and the strike ended. The "gentle squeeze" of work stoppages and slowing production at the height of the picking season paid off, and their demands were met.[77] The indigenous workers won a major victory, and field owner Ker learned about the power of effectively united Native Americans.[78]

The 1894 strike led by SoHappy and Columbia Jack is the best-documented Native American work stoppage, but at least two other successful strikes in the Snoqualmie Valley were also recorded, the first one taking place in 1877 and the second in 1903.[79] While very little information survives on the 1877 strike, the 1903 strike by hop pickers on the Overlake farm began when Indian workers protested oversized hop-picking boxes. The strike, at the height of the picking season, lasted only one day before the workers returned to the fields with smaller boxes. Victory was due to both the tenacity of the strikers and the field owner's desperation to save his crops.[80] It is unknown how widespread participation in these strikes was or if any farm laborers other than the Native American pickers were involved in them. Nevertheless, it is clear that work stoppages became an important tool for displaced indigenous workers to use when resisting what they felt was mistreatment by colonial employers.

In 1915 Joe Shell, Indian agent and "farmer in charge" on the Swinomish reservation, wrote to Tulalip Indian Agency superintendent Charles Buchanan summing up the role of the wage economy in the lives of Pacific Northwest Native Americans: "It seems that soon after the first of June, the majority, in fact nearly all of these Indians, will leave the reservation to work in the canneries or hopfields. . . . I am not surprised that the Indian consigns his garden patch to oblivion and goes to the cannery or hopfield where he is assured of fair pay; where he knows he will meet his friends and relatives; and where he has actual monetary evidence of the results of his weeks work."[81] Quite simply, participation in the new capitalist economy of the nineteenth and twentieth centuries meant that the indigenous inhabitants of the region could maintain some of their autonomy and a connection to their homelands in a world dominated by forces outside their control. Working for wages and migratory labor did not magically protect indigenous culture and identity, but in a world of limited options, where each passing year seemed to provide new disadvantages to Indian people, wage labor was an adaptive strategy for survival. In the words of Daniel Usner, "American Indian engagement with commerce through numerous means, over a long span of time, has consistently defied the narrow choices that observers insisted upon seeing."[82] Wage labor may not have been an ideal tool to maintain autonomy, but it supported a diasporic community attempting to conserve their identity.

Oftentimes, the story of the original indigenous inhabitants of the Americas becomes obscured by a national mythology of American history or it becomes trapped between the dialectic of tradition versus modernity. Perhaps it is because Native peoples did not easily assimilate into the standard depiction of American individualism and economic development that they simply vanish from many of our history books. However, there are some historians who believe that a completely accurate history of the Pacific Northwest still remains to be fully explored and recorded. One reason for that may be the conundrum of why it is that even though Northwest Native Americans appeared to engage in some of the same economic behaviors as immigrating Europeans and Anglo-American settlers, and appeared to share some similar ideologies, they seemed to have very differing beliefs about such things as the use of the region's natural resources. For both American Indians and Anglos, acquiring rights to land and resources, as well as acquiring wealth through trade, was a powerful goal, but their reasons for pursuing that goal were quite dissimilar. Anglos generally desired capitalist gain, whereas Native Americans primarily appeared to have been seeking spiritual powers as well as maintaining social status.

Part of the reason Native Americans resisted and survived Anglo encroachment may have been their ability to advantageously capitalize on the similarities they shared with Anglos. They did so in order to remain

free to practice the important spiritual traditions that guided their economic transactions, use of resources, social relationships, and all other
aspects of their lives. Traditional subsistence practices like fishing were
no longer the primary means of survival. By the twentieth century, primary subsistence came from wages. However, activities like fishing still
retained their spiritual and ritual significance, which made protecting
those practices a sacred duty. As Colleen O'Neill explains, "American
Indians in the twentieth century blended their modern and traditional
worlds as a matter of course and in the process redefined those categories in ways that made sense to them."[83] They created meaning for themselves by reinventing customs and traditions and adapting to change
with continuity. Historian Coll Thrush illustrates this idea in his discussion of the foundations of the city of Seattle: "Seattle was dominated by
indigenous people, who made it their own, using the new proto-urban
venue, with its connections to new trade networks, new forms of political and spiritual power, and new audiences, to enact and even enhance
economic, political, religious, and social traditions."[84] Relying on seasonal labor was a risk in a fluctuating capitalist economy, but it was a risk
well worth taking when it protected access to traditional lands, fishing
grounds, social circles, and seasonal paths of migration.

For Pacific Northwest Native Americans, flexibility and adaptability were the keys to surviving the European colonial experience. When
European powers took their lands and encroached on their fishing and
hunting grounds, Native Americans took to other seasonal forms of
employment, like work in the hop fields or canneries, which compli-
mented their customary migrations and allowed them to retain their
independence. Sovereignty is individual and so the ability to maintain
individual choices in lifestyle without government regulation promoted sovereignty. The shared space in the fields for Native Americans all
across the Pacific Northwest helped facilitate a growing awareness of
"nationhood" and a collective consciousness. This consciousness was
rooted in the shared sense of struggle against colonial rule retained
by a people whose individual identities were rooted in history and
tradition and who would use any tool necessary to survive as individuals and as a community in a rapidly changing capitalist world. All

cultural identities transform, change, and mutate over time and all are historically constructed, shaped by the events of the larger world. Seasonal labor therefore became a part of Pacific Northwest Native American life, but it did not replace it.

Notes

1. Smadar Lavie and Ted Swedenburg, eds., *Displacement, Diaspora, and Geographies of Identity* (Durham NC: Duke University Press, 1996), 14.

2. James Clifford, *Routes: Travel and Translation in the Late Twentieth Century* (Cambridge MA: Harvard University Press, 1997), 246.

3. Daniel H. Usner Jr., *Indian Work: Language and Livelihood in Native American History* (Cambridge MA: Harvard University Press, 2009), 4.

4. In her essay "Labor Struggles: Gender, Ethnicity, and the New Migration" in *Cultural Diversity in the United States* (Westport CT: Bergin and Garvey, 1997), June Nash argues that unions were a force for assimilation, not just solidarity. Ethnic minorities were often excluded from union membership, but many also refused to join because they did not wish to subsume their ethnic identity under that of the union.

5. An excellent work on the idea of the vanishing Native American is Brian W. Dipple's *The Vanishing American: White Attitudes and U.S. Policy* (Middleton CT: Wesleyan University Press, 1982).

6. David Boeri, *People of the Ice Whale: Eskimos, White Men, and the Whale* (New York: E. P. Dutton, 1983), quoted in Usner, *Indian Work*, 14.

7. Paige Raibmon, *Authentic Indians: Episodes of Encounter from the Late-Nineteenth-Century Northwest Coast* (Durham NC: Duke University Press, 2005), 13.

8. Technically, the right to organize was illegal until 1934, when the federal government via the National Labor Relations Board recognized unions' rights to exist.

9. There are a number of interesting studies on the adaptations and changes made by Pacific Northwest indigenous cultures before European contact, including Jerome Cybulski's "Culture Change, Demographic History, and Health and Disease on the Northwest Coast," in *In the Wake of Contact: Biological Responses to Conquest*, ed. Clark Larsen and George Milner (New York: Wiley and Sons, 1994).

10. Coll Thrush, *Native Seattle: Stores from the Crossing Over Place* (Seattle: University of Washington Press, 2007), 23. For example, the Duwamish (located near present-day Seattle) are "the inside river people" and "the people of the inside place." The Suquamish (located on the Puget Sound) are the "people on the clear salt water."

11. A common phrase Pacific Northwest Indians use to describe fishing is "When the tide goes out, the table is set." In Charles Wilkinson, *Messages from Frank's Landing: A Story of Salmon, Treaties, and the Indian Way* (Seattle: University of Washington Press, 2000), 22.

12. Most tribes celebrated a form of the first salmon ceremony in which the first salmon of the season was ritually caught and honored. Fay G. Cohen, *Treaties on Trial: The Continuing Controversy over Northwest Indian Fishing Rights*, a report prepared for the American Friends Service Committee (Seattle: University of Washington Press, 1986.) Other tribes call the ceremony Salmon Days, and the celebration goes on for around a week. In Lawney Reyes, *White Grizzly Bear's Legacy: Learning to Be Indian* (Seattle: University of Washington Press, 2002).

13. Pamela Amoss in Raymond D. Fogelson and Richard N. Adams, eds., *The Anthropology of Power: Ethnographic Studies from Asia, Oceania, and the New World* (New York: Academic Press, 1977), 132.

14. Alice B. Kehoe, *North American Indians: A Comprehensive Account*, 2nd ed. (Upper Saddle River NJ: Prentice Hall, 1992), 435.

15. One hundred and twenty-four different villages or group identities were recorded for the Puget Sound by 1941. Marian W. Smith, "The Coast Salish of Puget Sound," *American Anthropologist* 43 (1941): 203.

16. Alexandra Harmon, *Indians in the Making: Ethnic Relations and Indian Identities around Puget Sound* (Berkeley: University of California Press, 1999), 8.

17. John Fornsby, a Skagit born in 1855, recalled how many different tribal affiliations were represented literally under one roof in his home village of Sikwigwilts. In his family's longhouse there were Skagits, Lummis, Nookachamps, Snohomish, Lower Skagits, and a former Native American slave (tribal affiliation unknown) who had married the head of the family. Fornsby in Marian W. Smith, *Indians of the Urban Northwest* (New York: Columbia University Press, 1949), 293.

18. Allan Richardson in Nancy M. Williams and Eugene S. Hunn eds., *Resource Managers: North American and Australian Hunter Gathers* (Canberra: Australian Institute of Aboriginal Studies with permission from American Association for the Advancement of Science, 1986), 102.

19. Ram Raj Prasad Singh, *Aboriginal Economic System of the Olympic Peninsula Indians, Western Washington: Sacramento Anthropological Society Paper 4* (Sacramento CA: Sacramento Anthropological Society, Sacramento State College, 1966), 63.

20. Wayne Suttles, *Coast Salish Essays* (Seattle: University of Washington Press, 1987), 19.

21. Thrush, *Native Seattle*, 28–29.

22. For a good look at the statistics on the number of Native Americans in North America killed by foreign disease, see Richard White, *"It's Your Misfortune*

and None of My Own": A New History of the American West (Norman: University of Oklahoma Press, 1993), 18–21.

23. J. Ross Browne in *Letter from the Secretary of the Interior, Transmitting, in Compliance with the Resolution of the House of Representatives of the 19th Instant, the Report of J. Ross Brown, Special Agent, on the Subject of Indian Affairs in the Territories of Oregon and Washington*, 35th Cong., 1st sess., House of Representatives, Ex. Doc. 39, January 23, 1858, 6.

24. J. Ross Browne, *Letter*, 14.

25. Fornsby in Smith, *Indians of the Urban Northwest*, 6.

26. Harmon, *Indians in the Making*, 170.

27. Kenneth D. Tollerfson, "The Political Survival of Landless Puget Sound Indians," *American Indian Quarterly* 16, no. 2 (1992): 217.

28. Daniel L. Boxberger, "In and Out of the Labor Force: The Lummi Indians and the Development of the Commercial Fishery of North Puget Sound, 1880–1900," *Ethnohistory* 35 (1988): 169.

29. Lummi Indian Agent, 1891, quoted in Boxberger, "In and Out of the Labor Force," 171.

30. *Report of the Governor of Washington Territory* (Washington DC: U.S. Government Printing Office, 1889), 35.

31. Russel Lawrence Barsh, "Puget Sound Indian Demography, 1900–1920: Migration and Economic Integration," *Ethnohistory* 43 (1996): 83.

32. Barsh, "Puget Sound Indian Demography," 327.

33. Barsh, "Puget Sound Indian Demography," 330.

34. The *Seattle Post Intelligencer* celebrated the size of a potlatch in 1907 held in Auburn to honor one of Chief Seeathl's descendants. According to the paper, over two hundred friends and family gathered on "John Seattle's" farm to honor the memory of his son in traditional fashion. The paper lauded another potlatch in the same year near Olympia. The potlatch was hosted by "Mud Bay Sam" and drew Native Americans from all over the Pacific Northwest, including such notables as Alice Bill James, who recently had hosted a large potlatch of her own, and Jim Tobin, identified as the "oyster baron" of Mud Bay.

35. Fornsby in Smith, *Indians of the Urban Northwest*, 316.

36. The average non-Indian picker generally made about $1.50 per day. Ezra Meeker, *Hop Culture in the United States: Being a Practical Treatise on Hop Growing in Washington Territory from the Cutting to the Bale* (Puyallup WA: E. Meeker & Co., 1883), 18.

37. Meeker, *Hop Culture in the United States*, 18.

38. Raibmon, *Authentic Indians*, 99.

39. Lummi Indian Agent, 1895, in Boxberger, "In and Out of the Labor Force," 171.

40. Ada S. Hill, *A History of the Snoqualmie Valley* (Olympia: Washington State Library, 1970), 56.

41. HistoryLink.org, the Online Encyclopedia of Washington State History, "Turning Point 15: Seattle's Other Birthplace: From Hop Field to Boeing Field," http://www.historylink.org/essays/output.cfm?file_id=3579 (accessed February 8, 2007).

42. Michael A. Tomlan, *Tinged with Gold: Hop Culture in the United States* (Athens: University of Georgia Press, 1992), 34.

43. Raibmon, *Authentic Indians*, 76.

44. Mrs. Clara A. McDiarmid, "Our Neighbors the Alaskan Women," in *The Congress of Women: Held in the Woman's Building, World's Columbian Exposition, Chicago, U.S.A., 1893* (Chicago: Monarch Book Co., 1894), 723–26.

45. Meeker, *Hop Culture in the United States*, 18.

46. Paige Raibmon, *Authentic Indians*, 79.

47. Prince of Wales interview in Jerry Gorsline, ed., *Shadows of Our Ancestors: Readings in the History of Klallam-White Relations* (Port Townsend WA: Empty Bowl, 1992), 216.

48. *Washington Standard*, August 17, 1878, 4.

49. Otis W. Freeman, "Hop Industry of the Pacific Coast States," *Economic Geography* 12, no. 2 (1936): 157.

50. Ninetta Eames, "In Hop Picking Time," *The Cosmopolitan, a Monthly Magazine*, November 1893, 3.

51. Albert Gallatin, *A Synopsis of the Indian Tribes within the United States East of the Rocky Mountains, and in the British and Russian Possessions in North America* (Merchantville NJ: Evolution Publishing, 2008), 154.

52. Eames, "In Hop Picking Time," 3.

53. *Washington Standard*, September 15, 1877, 1.

54. "George W. Tibbetts' account" in HistoryLink.org, "White and Indian Hop Pickers Attack Chinese in Squak Issaquah on September 7, 1885,"http://historylink.org/essays/output.cfm?file_id=2746 (accessed February 8, 2007).

55. Paul H. Landis, "The Hop Industry, a Social and Economic Problem," *Economic Geography* 15, no. 1 (1939): 91.

56. Paige Raibmon, "The Practice of Everyday Colonialism," 34.

57. Landis, "The Hop Industry," 91.

58. Landis, "The Hop Industry," 91.

59. Landis, "The Hop Industry," 92.

60. *Washington Standard*, September 15, 1877, 2.

61. Landis, "The Hop Industry," 92.

62. *Report of the Governor of Washington Territory*, 33.

63. Meeker, *Hop Culture in the United States*, 20.

64. Tollerfson, "The Political Survival of Landless Puget Sound Indians," 218.

65. Eames, "In Hop Picking Time," 1, 16.

66. Raibmon, *Authentic Indians*, 91.

67. Seattle pioneer reminiscence in Paige Raibmon, "The Practice of Everyday Colonialism: Indigenous Women at Work in the Hop Fields and Tourist Industry of Puget Sound," *Labor: Studies in Working-Class History of the Americas* 3, no. 3 (2006): 37.

68. Raibmon, *Authentic Indians*, 96.

69. From the *Seattle Daily Intelligencer* in Thrush, *Native Seattle*, 108.

70. Raibmon, *Authentic Indians*, 91.

71. Usner, *Indian Work*, 6.

72. Minnie Lingreen and Priscilla Tiller, *Hop Cultivation in Lewis County, Washington, 1888–1940: A Study in Land Use Determinants* (Centralia WA: Washington State Commission for the Humanities, 1981), 22.

73. Hill, *A History of the Snoqualmie Valley*, 58.

74. Tomlan, *Tinged with Gold*, 132.

75. Fornsby in Raibmon, *Authentic Indians*, 110.

76. William Ker, "A Siwash Strike on the Yakima," *Northwest Magazine* 12, no. 8 (August 1894).

77. John Brown and Robert Ruby, *Indians of the Pacific Northwest* (Norman: University of Oklahoma Press, 1981), 180.

78. Ker, in "A Siwash Strike on the Yakima."

79. Raibmon, *Authentic Indians*, 87.

80. Raibmon, *Authentic Indians*, 88.

81. Joe L. Shell in Barsh, "Puget Sound Indian Demography," 69.

82. Usner, *Indian Work*, 146.

83. Colleen O'Neill, "Rethinking Modernity and the Discourse of Development," in *Native Pathways: American Indian Culture and Economic Development in the Twentieth Century*, ed. Brian C. Hosmer, Colleen O'Neill, and Donald L. Fixico (Boulder: University Press of Colorado, 2004), 3.

84. Thrush, *Native Seattle*, 42.

Part 3

Twentieth-Century Reflections on
Indigenous and Pan-Indian Identities

| Chapter 11

Tribal Institution Building in the Twentieth Century

Duane Champagne

The patterns of institutional change among American Indian reservation communities are diverse and complex. The complexity continues
to reflect the cultural and social diversity of American Indian nations
that preexisted before Europeans came to establish the North American colonies. Western contact has been a powerful force placing great
demands on Indian nations to change their worldview, culture, political organization, and economy along patterns similar and compatible
with the development of Western and global political, economic, and
cultural institutions. Nevertheless, nowhere have indigenous nations
merely accepted Western cultures and consensually entered into modern nation-states. Indigenous peoples want to participate in nation-states
but at the same time retain indigenous identities, culture, social organization, land, and political, economic, and cultural autonomy. American Indians have selectively adopted technological and social-cultural
change while seeking to retain indigenous identities and commitments
to specific tribal communities. American Indians, and indigenous peoples in general, want to engage the contemporary world but want to
meet contemporary social, political, and economic challenges with approaches that reflect their own specific tribal values and social relations.

Indigenous peoples and nation-states contested the very foundations of social and cultural organizations, a reflection of fundamental

differences in the social construction of society, identity, and culture. Relations between indigenous peoples and nations-states are fundamentally a struggle between two different interpretations of society. The goals of nation-states are to create allegiances and cultural consensus around shared values and institutions. Indigenous communities, unlike racial or ethnic groups, have their own institutional orders and long-term political commitments. Indigenous communities are not parties to the U.S. constitution, and members were not citizens until 1924, and then by legislative act and not by their universal consent. Contemporary modernizing nation-states actively work to establish a common national culture among its citizenry. Indigenous claims to political and cultural autonomy, and their rights to carry on their own social and political orders, are often ignored and overpowered. U.S. policy toward Indians, despite recent movement toward self-determination, has been largely focused on assimilation and inclusion. Policies of assimilation encourage indigenous peoples to adopt and internalize American values, culture, and institutions. Inclusion as a citizen in the United States requires indigenous peoples to actively participate in American political and social life while abandoning tribal political identities, cultures, and institutions.

Studying institution building among U.S. tribal communities presents a series of conceptual issues. Institutions are enduring normative relations that have general consensual support among the large majority of the engaged community.[1] This is a critical point, since much of U.S. policy toward American Indians during the twentieth century was not based on consensual agreements or understandings. Institutions that are maintained by external force or external funds are inherently unstable and will dissolve when the force or funding is withdrawn. When community members do not have a cultural or normative or material investment in an institutional relation, then they do not have strong motivations to uphold and adhere to that specific institutional complex. Indian history recounts several cases where constitutional governments or programs were introduced into tribal communities but were not upheld or sustained by the community.[2] Therefore, enduring and sustained institutions must have the consensual support of the community. The general absence of consent creates suspicion about the enduring and internalized character of externally developed institutional projects that are not developed with the collaboration of Indian communities. Most Indian policies until the 1970s did not gain consent from Indian communities, and therefore we would expect that such innovations were not sustainable unless backed by continuous force or material resources. Change of this nature might be called coerced institutional change.[3] When institutional change is supported through agreement and consensual processes, then we can say that it is consensual institutional change. Both consensual and coercive institutional change play major roles in understanding patterns of change in American Indian communities during the twentieth century.

Consensual and Coercive Institution Building

The form of institution building we are seeking to understand is the consensual change that has occurred in Indian country and that has captured the commitments of tribal communities and is sustained by community values and worldviews. The institutions of precontact tribal communities were sustained by tribal consent. All human communities, including Indian communities, contend the institutional arrangements of their society and culture. Not all people agree on every issue, and through discussion and ultimate consensus, new or modified arrangements are introduced. The instances when tribal community members do not agree on the exact nature of traditional institutions are to be expected, and through discussions those traditional institutions are modified. Many new year ceremonies, like the Sun Dance or the Green Corn ceremonies, legitimized change that occurred over the past year since the last ceremony. American Indians confront U.S. society and policy from the point of view of their own specific tribal institutional orders. However, much of U.S. assimilation policy is designed to induce American Indians to internalize Western worldviews and accept U.S. citizenship, or adopt institutions that are culturally compatible with U.S. political and economic institutions.

The purpose of this chapter is to examine the processes of institutional change among tribal communities during the twentieth century. The interplay of both coercive and consensual institutional change is key to understanding patterns of institutional change among U.S. Indian nations. In order to track institutional change through the twentieth century it is useful to identify several concrete institutions and follow the patterns, and to the extent possible, comment on the causes of change. This can be done by focusing on key twentieth-century concepts such as citizenship, market economy, the organization of political government, political community, worldviews, and identity.

Citizenship or membership is a major issue for nation-states and tribal communities. In the United States, citizenship implies that an individual has taken up the obligations and benefits of a member of the national political community or nation. During the twentieth century tribal communities gained control over tribal membership and negotiated with the U.S. government their status as U.S. citizens and tribal members.

Markets are social constructions; they need cooperation, rules, trust, and a shared understanding of the purpose and goals of exchange. The markets that are significant for us are capitalist markets, where land, labor, and capital are used to produce goods for a marketplace. Traditional Indian communities traded and exchanged but generally produced for local or family consumption, and provided limited consumption for tribal and ceremonial needs. The traditional Indian labor ethic is often called a subsistence form of economy. During the twentieth century, Indian tribes are in contact with and engaged in market relations and in some cases carry on active subsistence economies.

U.S. political organization is a representative constitutional democracy based on separation of powers and a supporting political community. Traditional indigenous political arrangements throughout North America were decentralized, often without a central chief or council, but composed of confederations or coalitions of bands, lineages, clans, or villages.[4] During the twentieth century, many tribal communities were induced by the federal government to take on constitutional governments, but many retained significant aspects of traditional forms of sociopolitical organization.

The political community of the United States is the body of citizens. The body of politically active citizens and organizations is often called U.S. civil society. Since there was much emphasis on developing constitutional political forms during the twentieth century, a question arises about whether the formation of individualistic and committed citizens is a prerequisite to support constitutional political governments in the U.S. model? Do such national forms of political mobilization emerge among tribal communities in support of constitutional governments?

U.S. worldviews are Christian, in general, and U.S. institutions are of Protestant origin. Secular worldviews, scientific orientations, and pluralistic and inclusive worldviews are also apparent among tribal members during the twentieth century. U.S. indigenous worldviews in traditional times are very specific to the tribal community. Most indigenous communities had their own creation stories, ceremonial cycles, and accompanying beliefs and values. U.S. worldviews emphasized domination of the earth, sacredness of the individual soul, and otherworldliness, or the view that the only true salvation is in the next world, not in the secular this-world. The many different indigenous worldviews tend to emphasize sacred this-world, balanced and respectful relations with the powers of the universe, and respect for rather than domination of the earth.

Tribal identities originally were closely intertwined with kinship groups and locality, which are often defined or supported by religious and ceremonial teachings. Each Indian nation has its unique institutional and cultural arrangements and therefore each nation has a unique social, political, and cultural identity as a group and as individuals.

The diversity of institutional change found among American Indian nations reflects not only the continuity of many diverse traditional identities and social orders, but also the diversity of relations with U.S. policy, market relations or economic marginalization, and external cultural influences. The major patterns of change fostered by U.S. nation-state policies have been both assimilative and inclusive. Strong nation-states want to organize their citizens around common values and create common ground in the political and economic spheres of society. While inclusive and assimilative policies have been useful for racial and ethnic groups, they have been antithetical to Indian nations, who have their own common cultural grounds and sociopolitical orders that predate the formation of contemporary nation-states. Indian peoples want to preserve their own cultures, land, identities, and political autonomy, and do not share with nation-state cultures common values, understandings about human philosophy, similar views of human nature, and the primary goals and values of life. Indian peoples did not share common political or cultural ground or government organizational forms with the U.S. nation-state. The continuous contention over moral order, political relations, economic participation, and worldviews underscores the ongoing conflict among indigenous peoples and nation-states.

U.S. nation-state policies of assimilation and inclusion work at two levels, the nation and the individual. Individual Indian people attend schools that provide a predominantly Western worldview, and are at best designed to introduce new values and national commitments. Since the boarding-school days of the late nineteenth century, Indian individuals have been encouraged to abandon their own cultures and accept Western religions, science, political theory, and social-economic life. Many individuals have done so; many have left tribal communities, while others have remained in reservation communities, although often with little understanding of their own cultures and histories. Tribal identities became more mixed, as social participation, language, and kinship ties became less important as identity markers for many boarding-school students, many of whom became at least nominal Christians. The Office of Indian Affairs imposed tribal membership rules based on descent and blood quantum. Tribal membership, in the eyes of many, became increasingly racial and legal, and less based on tribal cultural commitments, knowledge, or participation.

Policies of assimilation and inclusion also address changing tribal institutions into forms more compatible, perhaps more functional, in U.S. political and economic life. Hence the emphasis on constitutional government forms and political individualism. The relations of institutional and individual policy change are interrelated. The world of nation-states and globalization fostered internal cultural and political diversity within tribal nations, which in many cases created tribal groupings that did not share common political and cultural ground as in traditional or precontact times. The multicultural diversity and identities of contemporary reservation communities combined with the decentralized and autonomous political traditions of villages, families, clans, and bands tended to increase cultural and political competition within tribal nations.

The clash between U.S. Indian communities and the Indian policies of the twentieth century were not solely about resources, or political or cultural marginalization, but also about differences in social order, identity, and values. American goals and values required Indians to remake or totally transform their personalities and communities so that they could join in the benefits of the U.S. economy and political freedoms.[5] Tribal community members and communities were often willing to accept U.S. political citizenship and economic opportunities, but not at the expense of giving up their Indian tribal identities and their traditions and values. The primary struggle between the nation-state and indigenous peoples was over different ways of life, different political systems, and different ways to understand and approach the world. The nation-state wants to remake Indian communities and individuals for its own purposes and in its image, while many indigenous peoples want to preserve their identities, territory, ways of life, and have the capability and options to approach the future in ways that are informed by their own beliefs, social orders, and ways.

The issues that I explore are aimed at understanding the patterns of institutional change among American Indian nations during the twentieth century. In what ways did U.S. policy for Indians foster coercive and/or consensual change? What were the patterns of citizenship, market economy, political government, and worldviews and identities that emerged among U.S. Indian nations? There are many ways to look at institutional change, but I will limit the discussion to an overview of the several institutions mentioned above for lack of space to cover the processes in the historical and ethnographic detail they deserve. If one takes the perspective that there are over 560 federally recognized Indian nations in the United States and another 300

Indian communities seeking federal recognition, then the empirical task of understanding and documenting the processes of institutional change is daunting, and at this time impossible to manage systematically. Here I will make some generalizations about the patterns of institutional change that may serve as conceptual or theoretical positions upon which case and comparative studies may be constructed. There are several goals for the chapter. One is to set out a framework for understanding the types and patterns of institutional change that have occurred among U.S. Indian nations. A second goal is to understand the conditions that foster patterns of consensual institutional change among Indian nations. What conditions foster consensual institutional change among Indian nations, and what are the future prospects for consensual institutional change?

The patterns of institutional change that emerged among Indian nations during the twentieth century were the result of an interplay of external coercive Indian policies, often aimed at complete transformation and elimination of tribal communities, and Indian efforts at maintaining their institutional orders or adapting to the new conditions by consensually changing their institutional relations. By coercive Indian policies, we do not necessarily mean to imply that the policies were designed to do harm to Indian nations. Quite the contrary, most Indian policies were designed to help Indian communities but were framed within U.S. cultural goals and values and often imposed without consent or full discussion with tribal communities. The absence of shared values or consensual institutional relations between the United States and Indian nations creates situations where policies were informed by the values of U.S. society but were not compatible with the values and cultures of Indian nations. Therefore policies were imposed on tribal communities to which they did not agree or give consent, and to which their values and goals moved them in other cultural and institutional directions. Especially during the first seventy years of the twentieth century, tribal communities had limited ability to affect the formulation of policies that were presented to Indian nations.

The twentieth century can be divided into several periods that illustrate differing patterns of institutional change for U.S. indigenous nations. The period from 1900 to 1932 saw a form of termination and transformation policy where external coercive policies predominated, and consequently very little consensual institutional change occurred among Indian nations. The New Deal period, 1933 to 1945, was predominated by externally coercive government policies in support of increased tribal government and economic autonomy and development, but there was little Indian consensus in support of the policies and proposed patterns of institutional building. The 1946 to 1969 period was a termination period designed to dismantle tribal communities and offer full citizenship in the United States. There was little support or emphasis on consensual tribal institutional building. The self-determination period from 1970 to 2000 included mixed forms of consensual and coercive institution-building patterns. For the policy periods of the twentieth century, I describe patterns of change among the institutions of citizenship, political government, economic market relations, national political community, worldview, and identity. The combination of institutional change patterns help to account for the state of Indian nations during the twentieth century.

Reservations as Total Institutions

Each colonial period has a particular pattern of political and economic change.[6] One way to look at colonial relations is to determine the degree of external control exerted over indigenous peoples and to consider to what extent indigenous peoples have the power and opportunities to make their own institutional accommodations to changing political, economic, and cultural relations. Consensual institution building will depend on the ability of indigenous communities to have the power, resources, and opportunities to express their goals and values. The degree to which indigenous communities have political, economic, and cultural autonomy will play a central role in the capacity to make enduring self-directed institutional change.[7]

By the end of the nineteenth century, most federally recognized American Indian nations were gathered onto reservations and were under extensive control by the Office of Indian Affairs. While on reservations, Indian persons were not U.S. citizens. They maintained political

government but were discouraged from carrying on their own languages, cultures, and ceremonial activities. The forces of change were largely external and focused on education and Christianization, with an
emphasis on ultimately dismantling tribal communities and transfer-
ring to U.S. citizenship.[8] Economic self-sufficiency was to be obtained
as Indians became farmers with individual land allotments and with-
drew from reservation territories. During the late nineteenth century, tribal nations were not in position to make independent political
choices nor did they have resources to support institutional change informed by their own worldviews, values, or interests. By the turn of the
nineteenth century, the Office of Indian Affairs gained considerable
control over every facet of Indian reservation life. The model of reservation administration was taken from the California Indian missions,
which were considered by U.S. officials to have been economically sustainable. These missions established strong control over everyday Indian life and encouraged labor and Christian religion. Early reservations
were total institutions and provided tribal communities, leadership,
and governments with few independent choices.[9] Tribal membership
was defined by the Office of Indian Affairs' rules and regulations and
supported by U.S. law and policy. While traditional and holistic community identities persisted in many Indian communities, legal and
blood quantum definitions of Indian identity persisted in American
government and national relations.

The U.S. policies of the early twentieth century aimed at remaking
Indian communities along the lines of American society. Measured
against Christian ideas of morality and religious thought, and new
ideas of progress and social evolution, Indian communities were considered backward and primitive, maintaining archaic social control
over their populations. During the late nineteenth and early twentieth centuries, under Indian policy aimed at dismantling tribal communities, children were sent to boarding schools, land was allotted
into small plots, and reservation residents were encouraged to take
up farming. Indians were not citizens of the United States, but those
able to secure an allotment and demonstrate competence in farming
and self-support were invited to abandon tribal identity and tribal

membership in order to take up U.S. citizenship. U.S. policy and Office of Indian Affairs officials dictated patterns of change. The emphasis on external control and management of Indian communities
did not promote institutional change that was informed by tribal social order or culture. Indian reservations and communities were seen
as transient entities, and little was invested in their continuity or further development. Under such conditions there were few openings
for tribal leaders or communities to choose their own paths for social and cultural change. One would expect very little self-directed
or consensual institutional change that embodied tribal worldviews,
values, or interests.

Since explicit change was measured primarily as adoption of the U.S.
sociopolitical model, the period saw very little collective community
change. Many communities operated under tribal government forms,
but often they were not compliant or willing to make economic decisions such as signing contracts for the sale of coal, oil, or land rent-
als. In many cases, the main political institutional change during this
period was the formation of tribal business councils, which were creations of officials of the Office of Indian Affairs. Often, federal agents
appointed the leaders to the tribal business councils, and their primary focus in the early years was to represent their reservation communities as a legal body. Other tribes wrote constitutions or political
bylaws under guidance of the Office of Indian Affairs, but both the early constitutions and business councils were instruments for transacting
business with the government. Some communities, like the pueblos,
maintained traditional forms of government. The new constitutions
or business councils did not require formation of a new form of body
politic, or political nations, since at this time the tribal governments
generally were under direct administration of the Office of Indian Affairs. The business councils bypassed traditional governments, leaders,
and the kinship networks that supported the tribal political confederations of decentralized villages, bands, lineages, or clans. The new political forms were largely served by the interests and values of external
policy and generally were not affirmed by consensus among the tribal community. Traditional tribal community and governments were

underserved, if not ignored. The main form of resistance came in by way of maintaining language, identity, kinship relations, continuing underground ceremonial life, and not wholly taking up the new program of assimilative change and inclusion into U.S. society.

During the first decades of the twentieth century, the Office of Indian Affairs offered resources to build agriculture and grazing production among many tribal communities. By the 1920s, many reservation tribal members achieved economically self-sufficient farms, although U.S. farmers leased considerable portions of irrigated Indian land and also benefited from government programs on Indian reservations.[10] The Great Depression and dust bowl, however, greatly inhibited continued development of reservation agriculture and husbandry.

After boarding-school experiences, some Indian students decided not to return to reservations and sought livelihoods in the U.S. economy. The education of Indian children as well as the draw of the overheated U.S. economy during the early 1920s created incentives to move to urban areas where many Indians found work. The migration of Indian families to urban areas conformed to the policies of dismantling tribal communities and governments. Other Indian boarding-school students returned to their communities, but now trained in American school knowledge and Christian religion, they were no longer deeply embedded in their traditional cultures and knowledge. Yet they were often not trained to make a livelihood in U.S. society. The boarding-school education of generations of Indian students tended to create individuals who were alienated from their traditions and formed a new group of culturally informed individuals whose identities focused on legal tribal membership, not on cultural relations. The cultural composition of Indian communities became more multicultural with the growth of diverse identities. The new identities and communities began to include individuals with mixed knowledge and identities of tribal understandings and many American and Christian beliefs. Since U.S. Indian policy did not hold out any promise for the future of tribal identity, community, or government continuity in the long run, many Indian parents advised their children to take up the English language and accept work and life in the American style. While the pattern varied from community to community, many communities started on a path or continued a path of cultural demographic change where tribal members who were carriers of American and Christian worldviews and culture eventually outnumbered those who adhered to more traditional tribal community and political forms. The mixed identities on reservations often defined cultural and political competition and produced resistance to change from the more traditional community members, while tribal members who carried American values were more accepting of change introduced by U.S. policies. When a majority of tribal members agreed with U.S. policy goals and plans, then policy changes were not coercive. Often a minority continued to resist change, and the internal diversity of tribal identities and views were difficult to reconcile.

Until 1924, many American Indians were not citizens of the United States. Land allottees could become American citizens if they demonstrated competence and economic self-sufficiency. Tribal membership was based largely on treaty relations and censuses associated with treaty agreements, or in later years legislation, especially records of land allotments. The Indian Citizenship Act of 1924 granted Indians rights as U.S. citizens, but allowed tribal members to retain rights to tribal property.[11] Traditional tribal membership and identity were based on kinship ties, where individuals belonged to a lineage, village, land, or band. While some Indian individuals and tribal communities lobbied for U.S. citizenship, others did not. The Indian Citizenship Act did not require Indians to take an oath of allegiance to the United States, and Indians were not given the opportunity to accept or reject U.S. citizenship. Indians became U.S. citizens not by consent; a form of dual citizenship emerged in which tribal members were both U.S. citizens and members of a tribal community.

The first several decades of the twentieth century was a period of external and coercive institutional change. Indian communities did not have autonomous political power, economic resources, or a culturally supportive U.S. government or cultural environment to engage in tribally informed consensual institutional building. Major forms of change such as education, tribal constitutions, business committees, allotment, economic training, and citizenship were designed to dismantle tribal communities and cultures and invite Indian people to accept and participate in American society. The supportive conditions for consensual institutional change were not available to tribal communities. Tribal identities became more diverse, and there was less internal agreement or articulation about future community strategies.

The Indian New Deal

The Indian New Deal (1933–45) is generally considered a bright spot in the philosophy and implementation of federal Indian policy. President Franklin Roosevelt emphasized that Indian communities were not doing well by economic, health, education, and other standards of well-being. The president supported legislation intended to recognize local tribal governments and invited tribal leaders and communities to collaborate in development of solutions to the social and economic problems confronting tribal reservation communities. The Indian policy during the first three decades of the century, which Roosevelt characterized as paternalistic, did not invite tribal participation in solutions to issues confronting reservation communities. The president invited greater consensual change and administration.[12] Indian New Deal legislation, the Indian Reorganization Act of 1934 (IRA), ended the allotment and associated loss of Indian land, provided mechanisms for limited recovery of land for tribal communities, proposed economic development funding, and suggested strengthening new constitutional tribal governments and economic corporations.

The Office of Indian Affairs, led by Commissioner John Collier, started a campaign to reorganize tribal governments. Tribal communities were allowed to vote on whether they would accept or reject a proposed constitutional government under the IRA. Over one hundred tribal communities eventually accepted IRA government forms, while many others were induced to take up bylaws. The new governments bypassed traditional political forms and governments. In some cases, tribal communities voted in favor of IRA governments because they looked more democratic than the business councils that were often lead by federal appointees and overrepresented by Indian cattle ranchers, who were generally a small portion of the community. The proposed new IRA governments introduced electoral representative government and executive and legislative branches. Usually the tribal chair or president did not have the power to vote except in case of a tie among the tribal council. The tribal councils were directly elected by districts, which sometimes represented traditional tribal groupings. Most IRA governments did not have judiciary branches, and if they did, they were often subordinate to the tribal council. The tribal councils could be controlled by a majority, which often left no checks and balances to weigh against a majority coalition. Representative government, majority rule, and individual membership were often new to tribal communities, and were often alien to the decentralized, consensual, and autonomous political processes of tribal confederations.[13]

The IRA constitutional governments were often mismatched with tribal social and political institutions. Traditional forms of social and political power were bypassed, and the new form of government concentrated and centralized power and decision making in ways that were not common among tribal communities. There was much controversy about many of the elections ratifying the new constitutions. In some cases, government officials accepted relatively small turnouts of voters and counted those who did not vote as votes in favor of constitutional reform. In many tribal communities, nonparticipation is usually seen as a negative vote. Some scholars point out that in some decentralized tribal communities, the IRA governments provided pathways to stronger and more stable governments.[14] In other cases, IRA governments led to continuing controversies over the legitimacy of the government, as among the Hopi and many Lakota communities.[15] Tribal communities did not first create or form political nations composed of citizenships before considering the IRA and other constitutional forms. Rather, tribal social and political organization was ignored and assigned to the background. A new tribal citizen was expected to behave as an individual and not as a member of a kinship group, village, or clan.

Some Department of Interior anthropologists objected to the IRA constitutional governments on the grounds that they were not

compatible with Indian political culture or organization. The Office of
Indian Affairs ignored the complaints of anthropologists and worked
quickly to revise as many tribal governments as they could. After the
Indian New Deal, the organization of tribal governments varied according to IRA constitutions, non-IRA constitutions, bylaws, federal
rules, and traditional governments. Most tribal governments had few
independent resources and were greatly constrained by Office of Indian Affairs rules and regulations; to a large extent, tribal governments
remained appendages to the Indian Affairs bureaucracy.

The conditions of the depression and the emergence of the Second
World War greatly limited the resources that the Indian New Deal
could muster, and they curtailed its policy impact. By the middle 1930s,
members of Congress were turning against the Indian New Deal and
began favoring the elimination of tribal reservations and the incorporation of tribal members as full U.S. citizens. Indian boarding-school
education continued, and by now multiple generations of some families were schooled in Christian boarding schools. Economic conditions on most reservations were extremely difficult, and New Deal
programs helped employ many tribal members, who built roads and
buildings on Indian reservations. During the Second World War, the
Office of Indian Affairs also tried to foster reservation jobs and economic development by hosting Japanese American internment camps
on Indian reservations. The plan, however, did not have a significant
sustained economic affect. Many Indian tribal members served in
the armed forces, and others migrated to urban areas to participate
in the economic support for the war. Many Indian tribal members
gained considerable knowledge and experience with the non-Indian
world. Tribal communities became demographically more culturally
diverse, with both traditional and American worldviews represented.

In terms of tribal-wide consensual institution building, the New
Deal did not inspire the intended participation and empowerment
from tribal communities. Where tribal communities were led by a
majority of community members who carried American values, then
there was a tendency for more acceptance of New Deal institutional reform. However, New Deal policies did not provide the more traditional

communities and tribal members with an alternative, except rejection of New Deal proposals. The New Deal proposal for institutional change, mainly in government organization, presented communities with an either/or ultimatum and actively encouraged tribal communities to accept the new governments and economic corporations. The option to form tribal economic corporations was taken up by only a few tribal communities.

The proposals did not originate in the tribal communities, and there was not enough input, empowerment, or time given to tribal communities to make alternative proposals. Consequently, the New Deal proposals exacerbated existing cultural divides within multicultural communities that had multiple and antagonistic identities and worldviews offering different perspectives on institutional order and future possibilities. The absence of broad community support tended to restrict the effectiveness of many New Deal constitutional governments.[16]

The new constitutional governments were constructed with some participation and cooperation from the tribal communities, but their conception, purpose, and implementation were largely in the U.S. political tradition. As effective tools of tribal government, the new constitutions had inherent limitations, and the governments worked with few independent resources and in many cases did not have strong support from the tribal community. The lack of resources, and a relatively hostile congressional political environment, worked against full and timely implementation of the Indian New Deal vision. Tribal communities did not command enough independent economic resources nor was there a policy or political context that would have enabled them to develop self-directed consensual institutional governments. Perhaps the most explicit try came from the Navajo Nation, which in the middle 1930s held a constitutional convention to adopt an IRA constitution that was rejected by the Department of the Interior. A set of organic political documents, the "Rules of 1938," were dictated to the Navajos, and remains their fundamental political document.[17] In the Navajo case, political identities remained tied to about 110 local communities that were organized in the 1920s into "chapters." Navajo political relations were strongly influenced by the traditional, decentralized, local chapters that struggled to organize resistance to government policies such as federal restrictions on sheep herd size, and worked to restore political power and authority within a government structure that did not recognize them.

Termination and Dual Citizenship

When President Roosevelt died on April 12, 1945, his successor Harry Truman did not share his ideas about the Indian New Deal. Instead Truman supported the views of former president Herbert Hoover. Hoover was willing to protect Indian land but objected to the expense and administrative attention given to Indian reservation communities. Instead of supporting Indian local government, the Hoover administration (1929–33) added additional funds for the education of American Indians, with the intention of providing training and opportunities for Indians to leave reservations and become U.S. citizens. Truman followed the same plan, which we know today as termination policy, a reference to the severing of the government-to-government relations between the federal government and Indian nations. Indians were invited to accept the benefits of U.S. citizenship and share the opportunities of the U.S. economy and society. Truman believed that Indians on reservations were second-class citizens and had limited futures there.[18] The termination plan underlies Indian policy from 1945 thru 1969.

While Presidents Truman and Eisenhower were not personally active in the termination policy, members of Congress became impatient during the early 1950s, and the policy of termination was advanced through legislative acts of Congress.[19] Specific reservation tribal communities, such as Turtle Mountain, the Menominee, Klamath, and others, initially were selected for termination because they were promising candidates for developing economic self-sufficiency. As time went on, tribal communities were selected regardless of future collective economic prospects, as many communities were dismantled, the assets divided among the tribal members, the tribal government dissolved, and the tribal members became full U.S. citizens. Some tribal communities fought termination through their state congressional delegations and thus escaped termination acts. About 110 tribal communities were eventually terminated; about forty-two were small tribal communities from northern California.

Tribal communities objected to the new termination policy since it broke treaty and other agreements and threatened to dissolve tribal communities. The threat of termination helped foster the development of a strong national lobbying organization named the National Congress of American Indians (NCAI). NCAI was formed in 1944 and was the result of efforts by tribal leaders over many years to form a national Indian political group capable of influencing the federal government. The NCAI was formed very much like a traditional tribal confederation. The sovereignty of each nation was preserved in the organization. Each Indian nation participating in the NCAI was federally recognized and voted in NCAI proceedings, based only to a small degree on tribal population.[20] The NCAI was eventually effective in mobilizing state congressional delegations in support for ending termination legislation. NCAI leaders argued that federal termination policy left states and local government to support impoverished tribal members.

Indian leaders also argued that while they affirmed and wanted full U.S. citizenship, they did not want to give up tribal governments, communities, and cultures, and the government-to-government relations outlined in treaty and law. Indians affirmed the dual citizenship of the Indian Citizenship Act, which maintained that Indians need not surrender rights to tribal land. NCAI gathered collective national political interests in Indian country. The organization of NCAI preserved the principle of tribal identity and sovereignty while creating a platform of tribal communities and leaders to engage in the U.S. legislative and political process. Tribal community and local identities were preserved within a supratribal collectivity organized to represent tribal interests within U.S. political institutions. During the 1950s, however, tribal communities reacted to a common political threat carried by the termination policy. The Indian communities did not submerge their political rights or identity in the NCAI or any other national organization, but many tribes had common interests in national representation. After surviving the common threat of termination, tribal

communities struggled to redefine Indian policy in a way that preserved tribal governments and communities.

NCAI successes in stopping passage of termination acts catapult-
ed NCAI into a central role in national Indian politics. Tribal leaders,
since the beginning of the U.S. government in the late 1700s, traveled
to Washington and met with presidents and government officials. The
tradition of Indian leaders traveling to Washington was a means for
them to present tribal issues before the federal government and to negotiate agreements. NCAI created a platform of legislative lobbying
in Congress, as access to U.S. presidents became rarer, although presidents started to meet with the NCAI as a group. The active lobbying
and legislative campaigning by NCAI and tribal leaders mark the entry of collective Indian political organization into U.S. civil society.
American Indians began to organize nationally as a legislative interest group and to actively engage the U.S. legislative political process.

In the early 1960s, Indian students, activists, and leaders wanted
to move Indian policy in new directions that gave greater support
and recognition to tribal culture, land rights, and autonomous tribal government. The Kennedy and Johnson administrations, however,
did not move to acknowledge or support American Indian political
rights. Instead, both administrations offered antipoverty funds as well
as programs designed to foster greater civil rights and economic opportunities in U.S. society. The antipoverty programs were passed
directly to tribal governments, bypassing the Bureau of Indian Affairs (BIA), the old Office of Indian Affairs. Starting in the mid-1960s,
many tribal communities enjoyed direct access to government grants
and programs, and could establish direct relations with government
agencies. Access to multiple funding agencies created greater opportunities and less control and reliance on the BIA. Direct funding and
more funding created more resources and greater local administrative control. The flow of funding and resources for overhead administration created significant resources for many tribal governments,
who previously had few or no resources for government activities.
Tribal governments became more powerful, controlled personnel and
grant resources, and created more interest, competition, and leadership

among tribal members. Many tribal governments were moribund before the mid-1960s. They were without power or resources and often merely rubber-stamped proposals made by BIA officials. While still dependent on BIA administration and funds, many tribal governments gained a greater degree of autonomy by working with several federal funding agencies.[21]

Nevertheless, tribal government administrations remained almost wholly dependent on federal funding. Tribal bureaucracies for government service delivery expanded considerably. Few tribal governments, however, at this time actively sought to rewrite their constitutions or seek greater political autonomy. Tribal governments became service centers for tribal communities. There was little autonomous economic development and therefore few autonomous resources for consensual institutional change. Some tribes had income from forestry, land rents, or minerals, but most of this activity was managed and controlled by the BIA. With few individual or tribal market enterprises and consequently few independent economic resources, few tribal governments pursued political reorganization to create more efficient constitutions or to recover political institutions more congruent with traditional worldviews, values, and community organization. Nor did politically mobilized nations of Indian citizens emerge demanding stronger, more effective, and culturally congruent political institutions or processes. In most tribal reservation communities, many tribal citizens and the tribal government were predominantly dependent on federal funding, and therefore had little incentive or opportunity to change government-supported tribal bureaucracies.

Self-Determination

In the summer of 1970, President Richard Nixon presented a new Indian policy to Congress. He made many innovative changes and set the tone for future self-determination policy. Nixon asked Congress to rescind termination policy, and Congress did so. He stated that the obligation of the federal government was not support for disadvantaged citizens, but rather was to be pursued on the basis of treaty agreements and government-to-government relations. Nixon was the first president of the twentieth century to recognize the rights of American Indians, and he enshrined them in U.S. Indian policy.[22] The president went on to say that federal programs should support the self-determination of tribal governments, and he advocated that tribal governments should contract federal services and administer them. He took the subcontracting example from the successful management of federal programs carried out by the Zuni tribe and others.[23] The self-determination policy was the result of much rethinking of tribal policy and activism by Indian groups, leaders, and the NCAI during the 1960s. Nixon was vice president during the Eisenhower administration, and he rejected the termination policy of that era. The subcontracting model was enacted by Congress into the Self-Determination and Education Act of 1975, also known as Public Law 93–638. The self-determination policy formalized into law the access to federal programs that emerged during the 1960s. Now tribal governments or organizations by law could subcontract government programs and manage them under their own tribal government administrations. Self-determination became defined as the ability to subcontract and manage federal programs, but it did not induce tribal communities or governments to reorganize.

Over time the self-determination policy created an informal fourth branch in U.S. government. The constitution sets out state and federal relations, and states delegated powers to county and municipal governments. Treaties, congressional acts, executive orders, and court decisions set out a fourth federal level composed of tribal governments. Self-determination policy was a method for delivering federal funds and support to tribal governments. Tribal government as a fourth entity in U.S. government, however, was not formally recognized and was contingent on congressional acts.

In the 1978 court case *Santa Clara Pueblo v. Martinez* the court ruled that the federal government did not have jurisdiction over tribal membership rules.[24] For many years, the BIA had managed tribal membership rolls and had often specified membership rules. In the *Santa Clara Pueblo* case, the judges determined that tribes retained the right to define membership, and traditional rules of kinship members could serve as membership criteria. Tribal communities recovered the power to determine group membership while at the same time retaining U.S. citizenship. Dual citizenship is not without its ambiguities, but it was a result of political compromises that enabled tribal persons to retain some indigenous rights and enjoy many of the rights of U.S. citizens. Tribal law prevails for Indians living on the reservation, while U.S. law prevails for tribal members when living off the reservation.[25]

Until the 1990s, very few tribal communities had significant or sustained experience with market enterprise. By the 2000 census about two-thirds of the Indian population were living in urban areas. Many tribal members moved to urban areas in search of work. Most were trained to engage in wage labor. Over time, many worked for businesses, and many began to own small businesses. By the early 1990s, perhaps as many as 100,000 Indians were engaged in primarily small businesses, and by 2005, about 206,000 Indian entrepreneurs were active.[26] While the data do not say where all the Indian entrepreneurs are working, most likely most are living in urban areas. With tribal governments, courts, and laws that are unfamiliar with supporting individual businesses, few reservations governments have created the legal and cultural conditions supportive of individually owned private economic enterprise. In recent decades, there is more talk about promoting Indian businesses on reservations. Self-determination is seen as more realizable where local market enterprises can create wealth and provide jobs for tribal members. Most tribal governments, however, remain tied to the self-determination subcontracting and to federal programs. Some communities have developed profitable tribal corporations that also support tribal government and community goals and culture. The Mississippi Choctaws have many businesses that provide significant economic support to the community. There are twelve Alaska Native Corporations and a couple hundred Alaskan Native village corporations. Some have become very profitable for their tribal community shareholders by working on national markets and providing services.[27]

Gaming, however, above all else has provided significant amounts of capital to tribal communities. The right to game was fought for in U.S. courts by tribal governments, and was not part of a government economic development plan. Several court cases clarified the right to game as part of the inherent sovereignty of tribal governments. Nevertheless, by law the tribes must negotiate with state governments to make compacts about how gaming will be managed. The gaming compacts are government-to-government agreements and mark state recognition of tribal government powers.[28] Some gaming tribes, perhaps about thirty out of more than three hundred tribal gaming communities, have made significant amounts of money. With significant cash flows, tribal casinos redistribute 70 percent of the profit for community programs or direct per capita payments.[29] Along with significant access to capital, some tribal governments enjoy political recognition and political access.[30]

Despite greater political and economic power and successful gaming enterprise, many gaming communities have not significantly restructured their governments or political communities.[31] This is seen quite clearly throughout most of southern California, where locations near the large cities of San Diego and Los Angeles have made many tribal gaming establishments very profitable. Nevertheless, most southern California tribal governments are based on general councils where all adults can attend and vote on issues. The general councils have plenary powers, and although tribal councils or business councils are elected, all major decisions must pass a vote of the general councils. The general councils are composed of families or clans that have long-standing traditional origins. The general council is a tradition among the southern California Indian communities that had ceremonial significance in the form of a kin-based ceremonial house and kin-based political and spiritual leadership. The general council embedded in the ceremonial house also made social and political decisions. Contemporary southern California tribal governments are a community, government, or corporation, depending on the context and issue. A confederation of Indian families owns and manages multimillion-dollar tribal casinos, and many do quite well. Success at capitalist-style gaming enterprise and significant amounts of private and community wealth have not induced the southern California tribes to reform their governments by creating representative constitutional governments or an associated body politic of individualistic citizens. Left to their own devices, southern California tribes prefer to maintain their family- or clan-based communities and governments.[32]

The trend toward greater education and the continued emphasis on American subject matter has created multicultural tribal communities composed of multiple worldviews and religious orientations. How a community decides to form a government will depend on the distribution of values and consensus within the community. A critical issue may arise when the majority of the Indian tribal members no longer practice traditional culture and carry nontraditional or Western beliefs. Since most tribal communities are now organized by majority rule, the belief systems with the greatest share of the community demography will prevail. Consequently, it is possible to have Indian nations where most of the tribal members no longer share significant tribal customs or beliefs. Persons of Indian descent, but who do not participate in their tribal community and culture, may be called "ethnic Indians." Tribes with majority or significant ethnic Indian tribal members may be more agreeable to accepting American economic, political, and cultural institutions. Some tribal communities are extremely vigilant about the community and cultural commitments of their members. Persons from the Cochiti Pueblo must participate in ceremonies and clan moieties. If they fail to participate, they are relegated to nonvoting status.[33] Other communities want to keep voting powers local and do not grant voting rights to tribal members who have left to live in urban areas. In other cases where ethnic Indian tribal members are a majority, off-reservation voting is allowed, and ethnic tribal members can dominate the tribal community. Often when there is an ethnic tribal majority, more traditional members form a vocal but powerless minority. There is a trend toward greater identification among ethnic Indian individuals, such that there are more individuals who identify as having Indian ancestry than there are Indian individuals who are active within a tribal community.

Comments

The first seventy years of the twentieth century were dominated by U.S. policies that introduced coercive institutional forms into Indian country. These policies were aimed at transforming or dismantling Indian tribal governments and encouraged Indian assimilation of American worldviews and acceptance of full U.S. citizenship while abandoning tribal status and identity. Tribal communities resisted full assimilation and were willing to negotiate and affirm dual-citizenship status. Tribal communities regained the power to determine their own tribal membership. During the 1970s, Congress recalled termination policy. The working out of dual-citizenship relations preserved tribal membership and rights. Canada has worked out a similar pattern of dual citizenship with its indigenous communities.[34] Throughout most of the world, indigenous communities are not recognized political entities by their surrounding nation-states, and indigenous peoples are granted citizenship in the nation-state. Granting citizenship to indigenous peoples without first gaining their consent to participate in the nation-state on their own terms and without preserving local political and cultural autonomy and rights was a means to avoid recognizing indigenous rights. The pragmatic political solution of dual citizenship may be a model for other nation-states to adopt if they move in the direction of recognizing indigenous communities as political and cultural entities.

During the last two decades of the twentieth century, funding for tribal communities declined in real terms, the federal courts became more conservative, and the executive branch less active. Much of the vision and activism for institutional change comes from tribal communities who are pursuing greater sovereignty, renewal of culture, and economic development. The mobilization of tribal communities during the 1950s against the threat of termination had a long-term effect on tribal communities and predisposed them to take on consensual institution-building projects. Federal government agencies gave only lip service to tribal nation-building efforts and provided limited resources, legal context, or shared values and goals for building tribal communities within their own worldviews. The shared goals of preserving tribal sovereignty, dual citizenship, and treaty rights created common goals and political unity within many tribal communities. Although tribal members within their communities still debate the details of institution building, there is much contemporary consensus that tribal nations are here to stay and that tribal members must have primary say in the direction, implementation, and future of their own lives and institutions. Indian identities remain primarily tribal and local, but contemporary identities are now armed with the language of treaty rights, self-government, tribal sovereignty, and international recognition through the Declaration on the Rights of Indigenous Peoples and the United Nations Permanent Forum on Indigenous Issues. The collective indigenous rights movement in recent decades has strengthened and empowered local tribal identities and has contributed to mobilization toward consensual institutional change aimed at regaining sustained economic, political, and cultural autonomy for indigenous peoples.[35]

Through most of the century Indians participated in the market mainly as farmers, workers, and sellers of natural resources. Significant Indian entrepreneurship arose by the 1990s, but most individual entrepreneurship was concentrated in urban areas. Tribal corporations, Alaska Native Corporations, and gaming casinos gained significant footholds as profit-making enterprises. Collective tribal business enterprises are preferred in many tribal communities because the profits are shared and redistributed for community benefit. Nevertheless, the market participation and income varies considerably in Indian Country, and most tribal communities so far have not enjoyed significant success in market enterprises. A quarter of tribal people in the United States continue to live below the poverty line.[36]

The organization of tribal governments has been a primary policy concern throughout the twentieth century. The policy efforts to dismantle tribal governments stifled any consensual political institution building for most tribal communities. IRA and other constitutional tribal governments were underfunded and lacked power outside the administrative arm of the Office of Indian Affairs. The self-determination policy created contract mechanisms for tribal governments to assume management of social services and other programs. Tribal governments benefited greatly from the new programs, by means of greater control over administrative resources, personnel, and programs. Nevertheless, the self-determination contracting strategy led to tribal government administration of government service programs, and not toward greater economic self-sufficiency or greater government efficiency and cultural relevance. The self-determination policy reaffirmed the treaty and legal basis of the government-to-government relations between Indian tribal governments and the federal government. Tribal governments sometimes have status like states and form a fourth government entity parallel to the federal, state, and county-municipal relations. The relation of tribal governments to the federal government does not have constitutional status, and Congress more than once has tried to dissolve tribal governments. Federal-government-to-Indian-government relations remain vulnerable to congressional or American politics.[37]

Tribal constitutional governments were generally created by outside forces and values and during the self-determination period were supported by outside programs and resources. There is currently much talk about constitutional reform and some very interesting cases of constitutional reorganization, for example among the Mississippi Choctaws, Osages, Citizen Band Potawatomis, and others.[38] While tribal communities have been mobilized to preserve tribal rights and sovereignty, they have not often mobilized as nations of citizens to form representative constitutional governments. Many tribal communities are mobilized to preserve indigenous culture and political autonomy, but they often want to live in communities that are expressions of their own values and institutional traditions. Some of the successful gaming communities have the greatest opportunities for consensual institutional change, such as forming or reforming constitutional governments. Nevertheless, the Pequots and most southern California Indian gaming communities do not have constitutional governments. Instead they rely on family relations and general councils to manage their community, economic, and political issues.[39] The kin-based communities and governments of the highly profitable gaming communities are not predicted by current theories of economic or political development. These tribes are using traditional forms of social and political organization to manage highly successful profit-making enterprises. The economic success and opportunity have not necessarily fostered political reform or reorganization away from kin-based general councils composed of adult members. The body politic is formed by coalitions or confederations of families, lineages, or clans, and has more traditional kinship identities and relations than a national community composed of individual citizens.

Education has been a powerful force for introducing new worldviews and values into tribal communities during the twentieth century. While education is necessary for tribal communities, the emphasis on Western culture and skills did not introduce tribal culture, history, or information about tribal political and social processes. At the end of the twentieth century, few Indian children were taught the history of their communities or the operations, powers, or rights of their tribal governments. During the 1970s, many tribal communities regained control over reservation schools with self-determination contracts, but the cultural foundations of education curriculum did not change significantly. Indian studies materials are available in college courses, but rarely in K–12 courses. Boarding schools did not permit talking in Indian languages. Indian children needed to learn to read and write in English, but there was no sound reason to suppress tribal language and culture, thereby limiting the possibilities of children gaining language and cultural skills. Supporting the use of tribal languages would have helped preserve Indian languages and culture. Tribal communities have moved to regain control over reservation education through development of tribally controlled community colleges, language education programs, tribally controlled K–12 schools, and greater emphasis on recovering tribal culture and community. Tribal communities are deeply concerned about the education of their children and want to balance tribal teachings and general education. Nevertheless, American education remains a powerful tool for cultural assimilation, and not necessarily a tool for gaining multicultural knowledge or skills. The American-centric cultural education provided to Indian students often leaves them with few ties to their tribal histories, cultures, or communities.

For most of the twentieth century, the prospects for consensual tribal institution building were limited. There were few possibilities during the first seventy years when policies of dismantling or constitution building were largely created and supported by external government sources and values. Since tribal governments were seen as temporary, there were no long-term investments in their future. Tribal communities had few autonomous resources and worked under federal bureaucratic controls; U.S. Indian policy did not support stronger and more independent tribal governments. The self-determination period provided program resources, strengthened tribal governments organizationally and financially, and created some autonomy from BIA controls. Nevertheless, federal program rules and regulations prevailed, and tribal government remained heavily dependent on federal programs and funding. Greater possibilities for consensual institution building emerged during the 1990s, when many tribal communities benefit from gaming establishments. The combination of significant and autonomous resources, a community mobilized to protect tribal sovereignty, and the availability of the U.S. constitutional model would appear to lay the foundation for significant economic and political innovation. In some cases that was true, but in southern California and among the Pequots and others, the tribal communities retained traditional kinship identities and governed in traditional institutional frameworks of a general council of families. Most tribal communities continue to have limited resources and opportunities for consensual institution building.[40] The patterns of institution building or institutional continuity will continue to be diverse, depending on the cultural demography of the tribal community, the continuity of traditional tribal social-cultural arrangements, economic self-sufficiency, and a supportive legal and policy context. Many communities will choose to retain tribal social and cultural institutions and governments while engaging in markets and working with contemporary federal, state, and local governments.

Notes

1. Changkuk Jung, "Political Institutions, Social Trust, and the Inequality Trap" (paper presented at the Sixty-Seventh Annual National Conference of the Midwest Political Science Association, Chicago, 2009), abstract; Ugo M. Amoretti, "Introduction: Federalism and Territorial Cleavages," in *Federalism*

and Territorial Cleavages, ed. Ugo M. Amorettie and Nancy Bermeo (Baltimore: John Hopkins University Press, 2004), 10–15; Arend Lijphart, *Patterns of Democracy: Government Forms and Performance in Thirty-Six Countries* (New Haven CT: Yale University Press, 1999), 300–08.

2. Angie Debo, *The Road to Disappearance: A History of the Creek Indians* (Norman: University of Oklahoma Press, 1984), 141–69; Duane Champagne, *Social Order and Political Change: Constitutional Governments among the Cherokee, the Choctaw, the Chickasaw, and the Creek* (Stanford CA: Stanford University Press, 1992), 56–57, 72, 202–3, 73–75; William W. Newcomb, "The Culture and Acculturation of the Delaware Indians," in *Anthropological Papers* (Ann Arbor MI: Museum of Anthropology of Michigan, 1956), 95–104; C. A. Weslager, *The Delaware Indians* (New Brunswick NJ: Rutgers University Press, 1972), 419.

3. John R. Commons, "A Sociological View of Sovereignty," *American Journal of Sociology* 5, no. 3 (1899): 350–53; Douglas Cecil North, *Institutions, Institutional Change, and Economic Performance* (Cambridge: Cambridge University Press, 1990), 13; John R. Hepburn and Ann E. Crepin, "Relationship Strategies in a Coercive Institution: A Study of Dependence among Prison Guards," *Journal of Social and Personal Relationships* 1, no. 2 (1984): 139.

4. Harold Driver, "Excerpts from the Writings of A. L. Kroeber on Land Use and Political Organization of California Indians with Comments by Harold E. Driver," in *A. L. Kroeber Papers, 1869–1962*, BANC 2049 (Berkeley: Bancroft Library, University of California, 1953), 11; A. L. Kroeber, "Nature of Land-Holding Group," in *A. L. Kroeber Papers*, 1–18.

5. Herbert Hoover, *The Memoirs of Herbert Hoover: The Cabinet and the Presidency, 1920–1933* (New York: Macmillan, 1952), 318.

6. "Total institution" was a concept that Erving Goffman used to compare similarities among prisons, mental hospitals, monasteries, and other institutions. See Gerald L. Klerman, "Behavior Control and the Limits of Reform: The Hope and Fear of New Technologies in Total Institutions," *Hastings Center Report* 5, no. 5 (1975): 40.

7. See, for example, Stephen Cornell and Joseph P. Kalt, "Sovereignty and Nation Building: The Development Challenge in Indian Country Today," *American Indian Culture and Research Journal* 22, no. 3 (1998): 187–214; Ron Trosper, "Mind Sets and Economic Development on Indian Reservations," in *What Can Tribes Do? Strategies and Institutions in American Indian Economic Development*, ed. Stephen Cornell and Joseph P. Kalt (Los Angeles: UCLA American Indian Studies Center, 1992), 303–33; Dean Howard Smith, *Modern Tribal Development: Paths to Self-Sufficiency and Cultural Integrity in Indian Country* (Walnut Creek CA: AltaMira Press, 2000).

8. Robert V. Dumont and Murray L. Wax, "Cherokee School Society and the Intercultural Classroom," *Human Organization* 28, no. 3 (1969): 217–26.

9. Paul Kariya, "The Department of Indians Affairs and Northern Development: The Culture-Building Process within an Institution," in *Place/Culture/Representation*, ed. James S. Duncan and David Ley (New York: Routledge, 1993), 188.

10. United States Interior Department, *Annual Reports of the Interior Department for the Fiscal Year Ended June 30, 1920* (Washington DC: Government Printing Office, 1920), 64, 77; James A. Vlasich, *Pueblo Indian Agriculture* (Albuquerque: University of New Mexico Press, 2005), 160–75; Leonard A. Carlson, "The Economics and Politics of Irrigation Projects on Indian Reservations, 1900–1940," in *The Other Side of the Frontier: Economic Explorations into Native American History*, ed. Linda Barrington (Boulder CO: Westview Press, 1999), 235–36.

11. Charles J. Kappler, ed., *Indian Affairs: Laws and Treaties* (Washington DC: Government Printing Office, 1929), 4:1165–66.

12. Samuel I. Rosenman, ed., *The Public Papers and Addresses of Franklin D. Roosevelt: The Crisis Years* (New York: Random House, 1938), 2:63, 202–3.

13. Duane Champagne, "American Bureaucratization and Tribal Governments: Problems of Institutionalization at the Community Level," in *Occasional Papers in Curriculum Series* (Chicago: Newberry Library, 1987), 176–77.

14. Wilcomb E. Washburn, *Against the Anthropological Grain* (New Brunswick NJ: Transaction Publishers, 1998), 17–30, 63–68.

15. Thomas Biolsi, *Organizing the Lakota: The Political Economy of the New Deal on the Pine Ridge and Rosebud Reservations* (Tucson: University of Arizona Press, 1998); Washburn, *Against the Anthropological Grain*, 17–30, 63–68; Richard O. Clemmer, *Roads in the Sky: The Hopi Indians in a Century of Change* (Boulder CO: Westview Press, 1995), 144–61.

16. Biolsi, *Organizing the Lakota*; Clemmer, *Roads in the Sky*; Graham D. Taylor, *The New Deal and American Indian Tribalism: The Administration of the Indian Reorganization Act, 1934–45* (Lincoln: University of Nebraska Press, 1980), xi–xiii, 139–50.

17. David Eugene Wilkins, *The Navajo Political Experience* (Lanham MD: Rowman and Littlefield, 2003), 39, 85–87, 102–6, 210; R. W. Young, *A Political History of the Navajo Tribe* (Tsaile AZ: Navajo Community College Press, 1978), 114–18.

18. Donald McCoy, *The Presidency of Harry S. Truman* (Lawrence: University Press of Kansas, 1984), 296; Richard S. Kirkendall, ed., *The Harry S. Truman Encyclopedia* (Boston: G. K. Hall, 1989), 47, 172.

19. Duane Champagne, "From Full Citizen to Self-Determination: 1930–75," in *American Indians/American Presidents: A History*, ed. Clifford E. Trafzer (New York: HarperCollins, 2009), 144–83.

20. National Congress of American Indians, "NCAI History," NCAI, http://www.ncai.org/?8.

21. Kevin K. Washburn, "Tribal Self-Determination at the Cross Roads," *Connecticut Law Review* 38, no. 4 (2006): 777–96.

22. Richard Nixon, *Public Papers of the Presidents of the United States: Richard M. Nixon, 1970* (Washington DC: U.S. Government Printing Office, 1971), 565–67.

23. Richard Hart and Calbert Seciwa T. J. Ferguson, "Twentieth Century Zuni Political and Economic Development in Relation to Federal Policy," in *Public Policy Impacts on American Indian Economic Development*, ed. C. Matthew Snipp and Carol Ward (Albuquerque: Institute of American Indian Development, University of New Mexico, 1988), 113–44.

24. *Santa Clara Pueblo v. Martinez*, 436 U.S. 49 (1978).

25. Duane Champagne, *Notes from the Center of Turtle Island* (Lanham MD: AltaMira Press, 2010), 63–82; Richard B. Collins, "Indian Consent to American Government," *Arizona Law Review* 31 (1989): 365–421.

26. U.S. Census Bureau, "Minority Groups Increasing Business Ownership at Higher Rate than National Average, Census Bureau Reports" (Washington DC: U.S. Department of Commerce, 2005). See also Duane Champagne, "Tribal Capitalism and Native Capitalists: Multiple Pathways of Native Economy," in *Native Pathways: American Indian Economic Development and Culture in the Twentieth Century*, ed. Brian Hosmer and Colleen O'Neill (Boulder: University Press of Colorado, 2004), 308–29.

27. Stephen Cornell and Joseph Kalt, "Where's the Glue: Institutional and Cultural Foundations of American Indian Economic Development," *Journal of Socio-Economics* 29, no. 5 (2000): 443–70; Duane Champagne and Carole Goldberg, "Federal Contracting Support for Alaska Natives' Integration into the Market Economy," in *Diversifying Native Economies: Oversight Hearings before the Committee on Natural Resources, U.S. House of Representatives, 110th Congress, First Session, September 19, 2007*, Serial No. 110–44 (Washington DC: U.S. Government Printing Office, 2008), 99–105.

28. Carole Goldberg and Duane Champagne, "Ramona Redeemed?: The Rise of Tribal Political Power in California," *Wicazo Sa Review* 17 (2002): 43–64.

29. Naomi Mezey, "The Distribution of Wealth, Sovereignty, and Culture through Gaming," *Stanford Law Journal* 38, no. 3 (1996): 711–37.

30. Joseph Jorgensen, "Gaming and Recent American Indian Economic Development," *American Indian Culture and Research Journal* 22, no. 3 (1998): 162–69; Kate Spilde Contreras, "Cultivating New Opportunities: Tribal Government Gaming on the Pechanga Reservation," *American Behavioral Scientist* 50, no. 3 (2006): 1–38; Center for California Native Nations, "An Impact Analysis of Tribal

Government Gaming in California" (Riverside: Center for California Native Nations, University of California, Riverside, January 2006); Goldberg and Champagne, "Ramona Redeemed?," 43–64.

31. Kevin K. Washburn, "Recurring Problems in Indian Gaming," *Wyoming Law Review* 1, no. 1 (2001): 427–44.

32. Clifford E. Trafzer, *The People of San Manuel* (Patton CA: San Manuel Band of Mission Indians, 2002), 128–41. Some of the southern California tribes that maintain general councils as centrally powerful in the tribal government are the San Manuel Band of Mission Indians, Pala Band of Mission Indians, Pauma Band of Mission Indians, Rincon Luiseño Band of Mission Indians, Soboba Band of Mission Indians, Santa Ynez Band of Mission Indians, San Pasqual Band of Mission Indians, and others. Some tribes like the Viejas Band of Mission Indians and Pechanga Band of Mission Indians have general councils that are responsible primarily for land issues, and elect tribal council to manage day-to-day issues and operations. Others tribes like the Agua Caliente Band of Cahuilla Indians and the Morongo Band of Mission Indians have constitutional governments that recognize the general council as the body politic of the government. See http://www.cnr.berkeley.edu /classes/espm-50/11california.pdf; Contreras, "Cultivating New Opportunities," 1–38.

33. Regis Pecos, personal communication with author, Tucson AZ, August 23, 2009; Cochiti Pueblo Government, "Pueblo Government," http://www .puebldecochiti.org/government.html.

34. Paul L. A. H. Chartrand, "Citizenship Rights and Aboriginal Rights in Canada: From 'Citizens Plus' to 'Citizens Plural,'" in *The Ties That Bind: Accommodating Diversity in Canada and the European Union*, ed. John Erik Fossum, Johanne Poirier, and Paul Magnette (Brussels: Peter Lange, 2009), 129–54.

35. Duane Champagne, "The Indigenous Peoples Movement: Theory, Policy, and Practice," *Kalfou: A Journal of Comparative and Relational Ethnic Studies* 1, no. 1 (2010): 77–93.

36. U.S. Department of Commerce, U.S. Census Bureau, "Income Climbs, Poverty Stabilizes, Uninsured Rates Increase," *U.S. Census Bureau News*, Washington DC, 2006.

37. Collins, "Indian Consent," 365–421; Champagne, *Notes from the Center of Turtle Island*, 127–85; Mary Christina Wood, "Indian Land and the Promise of Native Sovereignty: The Trust Doctrine Revisited," *Utah Law Review* 13 (1994): 1471–1514.

38. "Osage Nation Governmental Reform Initiative," in *2008 Honoring Nations*, ed. Harvard Project on American Indian Economic Development (Cambridge MA: Harvard Project on American Indian Economic Development, 2008), 18–23; Eric David Lemont, ed., *American Indian Constitutional Reform and the Building of Native Nations* (Austin: University of Texas Press, 2006).

39. Laurence M. Hauptman, "A Review of Jeff Benedict's 'Without Reservation: The Making of America's Most Powerful Indian Tribe and Foxwoods, the World's Largest Casino,'" *National Indian Gaming Association*, http://www.indiangaming.org/library/articles/novel-attack.shtml (accessed November 19, 2011).

40. Kathryn R. L. Rand, "There Are No Pequots on the Plains: Assessing the Success of Indian Gaming," *Chapman Law Review* 5 (2002): 47–86.

Chapter 12

Disease and the "Other"
The Role of Medical Imperialism in Oceania

Kerri A. Inglis

When Euro-Americans ventured into the Pacific Ocean in the eighteenth and nineteenth centuries, they brought with them many tools of colonization and imperialism—capitalism, religion, education, European legal constructs—yet some of the more significant instruments of hegemony were western concepts of disease and medicine.[1] By the early 1800s, foreigners to Oceania not only sought to control indigenous bodies through western medical treatment(s), which were themselves undergoing a process of change, but also to use medical knowledge to control one of the most fundamental aspects of life—one's bodily well-being. Moreover, the dissemination and application of foreign concepts of health, disease, and medicine altered indigenous peoples' self-perceptions. In sum, the emergence of foreign diseases and depopulation, and the introduction of western medicine, revealed itself in the political dominance over indigenous populations.[2]

Colonizers used western medical systems and infectious disease experiences on/in indigenous bodies to differentiate between "self" and "other" within the colonial encounter. Indigenous medical concepts of health, disease, and medicine were portrayed as uncivilized, naïve, and harmful; western concepts of health, disease, and medicine, in contrast, were accepted as civilized, sophisticated, and beneficial, thus assisting in the colonization process, ultimately constituting a form of cultural imperialism that had historical implications for indigenous peoples' relations with one another in individual, family, and social contexts. There are many examples of western medicine being used to control indigenous bodies—quarantine, vaccination, health inspections, and other imposed public health policies; blood quantum policies; and challenges to the authority of indigenous medical knowledge and practitioners—all of which ultimately contributed to the *commoditization* of the indigenous body through a medical or scientific view of identity.

This chapter argues that disease and medical experiences were a critical component of Euro-American imperialism and influenced the construction of identity throughout the Pacific. I analyze the historical significance of disease in the construction of colonial forms of knowledge and indigenous identity in American-controlled Hawai'i and Guam. An examination of the ideological and administrative mechanisms by which western systems of knowledge and power extended themselves into and over indigenous bodies within the context of imperial medical practices reveals the importance of medicine in colonial contexts. Infectious disease experiences and the implementation of colonizers' public health policies led to the healthy indigenous population looking upon those with disease (within their own population) as a cultural "other." In other words, western concepts of disease and medicine had a significant impact on indigenous consciousness.

Historians, Colonialism, and Medicine

While the role of disease and medicine in world history is receiving increased scholarly analysis (especially in terms of depopulation models and settler colonial expansion), the role of disease and medicine in Pacific history has not attracted as much attention. Additionally, little has been said about the long-term effects of western public health and medical policies on the perceptions of the colonized. David Arnold's edited volume *Imperial Medicine and Indigenous Societies* engaged this important point of discussion in 1988. Arnold asserted that research "identifying disease and medicine as a site of contact, conflict and possible eventual convergence between western rulers and indigenous peoples" will help to "demonstrate the centrality of disease and medicine to any understanding of imperial rule."[3] Further, Arnold points to the "instrumentality" of disease and medicine in the process of imperialism, arguing that scholars are beginning to view "medicine and disease as describing a relationship of power and authority between rulers and ruled and between colonialism's constituent parts."[4] With the exception of Warwick Anderson's recent work, the significance of Oceania in this history remains underdeveloped.

As biomedicine developed in the nineteenth century, doctors trained in European medical schools often traveled to the expanding reaches of the colonized world. While specific debates over theories of disease and treatment continued, the status and authority of biomedicine grew, both in Euro-American centers and in peripheral communities. Developments in bacteriology were especially significant in establishing scientific medicine as primary, the work of Louis Pasteur and Robert Koch (1860s–1880s) being most influential. The combination of these significant developments in biomedicine and the experiences of Euro-Americans in lands and environments new to them led to the development of what came to be known as "tropical medicine"—which by the late 1890s was at the pinnacle of the western medical profession.[5]

Just as missionaries often brought western education to indigenous populations and served as "the cutting edge of colonization," it can also be argued that the many medical missionaries who represented the West likewise served as a colonizing force.[6] Occasionally, physicians came to Oceania as ship's surgeons, intermittently providing services on shore for foreign settlers, but it was the missions who sent physicians to settle in the various islands as part of their larger objective to administer to the needs of the indigenous populations. The Protestant missions in particular sent couples and families together to the Pacific. Members of the mission included teachers, printers, blacksmiths, and physicians, all of whom promoted western ways of life along with their gospel. Medical missionaries came into the Pacific largely with the belief that their culture and beliefs were superior to those of other peoples. They zealously worked to replace indigenous medical systems with western practices. Indeed, many scholars have noted that one of the fundamental tenants of western culture, monotheism, led missionaries to emphasize that there was only one "correct" approach to religion, education, politics, or medicine.[7] So, as western medicine was introduced to indigenous societies, it was often presented as superior to any indigenous knowledge of the body, health, or disease, and was expected to be accepted as such.

John Miles's *Infectious Diseases: Colonising the Pacific?* examines the introduction of human pathogens among Pacific Islander populations during the eighteenth and nineteenth centuries. Miles tries to determine which diseases were present in Oceania prior to European arrivals and which diseases Europeans introduced.[8] He hints at the role that disease may have played in colonizing efforts but does so mainly from the perspective of depopulation and its effects (significant in and of itself). There is no doubt that Euro-American expansionism and settler colonialism into the Pacific allowed for the movement of people and pathogens in ways that influenced islander demographics in the most tragic sense. But there is more to the story when we consider not just the effect of disease on island populations but the corresponding influence of western medicine as well.

A small number of scholars are turning their attention to this type of analysis. In the journal for the *Society for the Social History of Medicine*, for example, Shula Marks's 1997 presidential address asked, "What is Colonial about Colonial Medicine?"[9] Acknowledging that much of the work done in the history of colonial medicine in the early twentieth century privileged "the triumph of science and sewers over savagery and superstition," Marks outlined the discipline's transition to a new emphasis on social history. Similarly, Charles Rosenberg asserts that since the 1970s, professional historians of medicine have been most influenced by "the way disease definitions and hypothetical etiologies can serve as tools of social control, as labels for deviance, and as a rationale for the legitimation of status relationships."[10] Marks confirms that "in many ways this emphasis in colonial medicine is not entirely surprising. After all, the colonial context provides a particularly fertile ground for exploring the relationship of medicine and its discourses to issues of colonial power and control."[11] Marks also argues that by the end of the 1800s, ideas about racial difference and social Darwinism led to increasing anxiety about the role of imperialism and its threat to the metropole, resulting in an emphasis on protecting the colonizing population in faraway lands as well as the population of the homeland.

In their influential collection on the history of imperial medicine, *Disease, Medicine, and Empire*, Roy MacLeod and Milton Lewis examine the use of medicine as an instrument of empire and as an imperializing cultural force. Their contributors explore the use of western medicine overseas in various colonies, whether they were established by conquest, occupation, or settlement.[12] But room remains to push the analysis of this instrument of empire. For instance, the responses of indigenous peoples to western medicine and all that it entailed were very complex—and the various levels and forms of acceptance, accommodation, adaptation, and resistance also provide meaningful research questions. To add to that complexity, it should also be noted that despite the role of western medicine in the colonizing process, "colonized peoples also engaged in a complex set of contestations, negotiations and adaptations in their encounter with western biomedicine. And while by the late nineteenth century Western medical practitioners had come to believe in the single 'universalizable truth' of their own understanding of health care, and to show little tolerance for alternatives, non-Western medicine . . . showed itself far more tolerant and accepting of new ideas."[13]

A more recent volume in the history of imperial medicine includes works that examine the role of biomedicine in the colonial/imperialistic contexts of Egypt, India, South America, Latin America, (South) Africa, China, and Vietnam, but not Oceania. The emphasis of this work is on the coevolutionary relationship between biomedicine and colonialism. This research reinforces the understanding that "colonial expansions provided new territories for European-based biomedicine, while medicine also rendered colonialism possible, facilitating provision and maintenance of healthy workforces, protecting colonists from the pathogens of the new territory, and drawing colonized populations into colonial institutions."[14] But the emphasis is on the empowerment of the colonizer (through maintaining their health) rather than on the effect and consequences of western medicine (practice and ideas) on indigenous bodies and culture. Certainly, tropical medicine made Euro-American expansionism possible, but as a result of colonial medicine facilitating imperialism, the intersection of colonialism and medicine is imbued with the hegemonic power of one group over another (with or without their consent), and as such, "colonial powers became paradigmatic examples of hierarchy along racial, ethnic, religious, and gender lines."[15]

Cultural imperialism—the imposition of a foreign viewpoint or worldview by one group of people onto another—can play an important role in a colonizer's assertion of political hegemony over a colonized population, but it can also be just as significant in settings of informal imperialism. Cultural imperialism sometimes precedes formal imperialism and often lingers after the processes of political decolonization have concluded. For example, in her discussion of how Papuans viewed themselves as "inferior" to the "superior white man" under British imperial rule prior to the Second World War, Judith Bennett argues that the "colonization of the consciousness was the worst feature of the colonial experience" because of its long-lasting affects on identity and self-perception.[16] Thus, while most studies feature the resultant imperial success of the disease experience and depopulation in colonial settings, it is time to examine the critical role colonial medicine played in gaining control over colonized bodies and minds. The colonizers' control of the colonized body through medicine and public health policies facilitated a process that altered not only how indigenous people viewed themselves but also how they viewed others with disease.

The colonial control of indigenous bodies relied heavily on the epistemologies of western medical knowledge. By the latter half of the nineteenth century, the study of race and disease was of particular concern to European and Euro-American colonial powers. The historian Alfred W. Crosby famously highlighted the importance of disease to the colonial experience and argued that biological determinism explained the success of "the establishment of European crops, animals and diseases at the expense of native flora, fauna and peoples" across the globe.[17] This colonial expansionism was accompanied by western forms of political, economic, social, and cultural imperialism. Further, moments of political colonization were often followed by efforts at assimilation—most especially through religion, education, and medicine, as these three intertwined factors represented one's beliefs, thoughts, and body. Commenting on the relationship between political power and the role of medicine, Arnold asserts that "recourse to state power to enforce sanitary and health measures (as in Victorian Britain) gave the medical profession unprecedented authority in public life and affairs of state, and this was quickly reflected in Europe's overseas possessions too."[18] Medical hegemony and feelings of racial superiority were often reinforced following epidemics, prompting coordinated legislative responses from imperial authorities that gave medical physicians key roles in colonial governance. A good example of this occurred during the plague epidemic in Honolulu between 1898 and 1900. A joint resolution for annexation of the islands by the United States was passed in 1898, but the islands would not become an official territory of the United States until 1900. Therefore, during the plague, three Board of Health physicians of the Republic of Hawai'i (an extension of the group who overthrew the Hawaiian monarchy) became "the government" during the outbreak and ruled with the aid of martial law.[19]

As tropical medicine developed, it gave "scientific credence to the idea of a tropical world as a primitive and dangerous environment in contradistinction to an increasingly safe and sanitised temperate world."[20] Thus it served to further the racial distinction between the European "self" and the indigenous "other" by demonstrating how disease "became part of the wider condemnation of [indigenous societies]" and "medicine became a hallmark of the racial pride and technological assurance that underpinned the 'new imperialism' of the late nineteenth century."[21] As Euro-Americans searched for rational scientific ways of administering colonial rule, they depicted indigenous medical systems as unscientific and irrational, while they portrayed western medicine as scientific and objective. Even though

Euro-Americans made use of locally available medicines in their various "frontiers," at least one scholar contends that "during the course
of the nineteenth century, however, Europe took a radical step away
from medical pluralism. A growing conviction of the unique ratio-
nality and superior efficacy of western medicine began to possess European doctors and lay men alike."[22] The diseases that attracted the
most attention from western physicians in the tropics were those that
threatened Euro-American lives in colonial settings. In the context
of American colonialism in the Pacific, western medicine's focus on
bacteriology and microbial outbreaks had clear social, cultural, and
economic significance to colonial expansion and governance in the
Pacific. As imperial regimes developed, so too did the belief that all
health problems could be resolved through science.

Douglas Haynes makes a similar point in relation to British imperialism and Victorian-era medicine. Haynes wrote that "the image of
the helpless tropical inhabitant and the resourceful European representative of medical science presumes a natural hierarchy of power
and authority based on universal principles of knowledge. Of course,
this presumption is both paternalistic and self-serving."[23] While imperial medicine was once viewed as unproblematic and one of the
"blessings" of colonialism, historians have recognized that "medical
intervention impinged directly upon the lives of the people, assuming an unprecedented right (in the name of medical science) over the
health and over the bodies of its subjects."[24] But this influence over
indigenous bodies went beyond medical intervention within indigenous communities when colonial medicine was used "to provide a
'naturalized' and pathologized account of those subjects" furthering
the colonizers' agenda.[25]

The view of western medicine as one of the "gifts of civilization"
was used to justify Euro-American imperialism throughout the colonized world. It was once a prominent theme in histories of medicine.[26]
More recently, critics of imperialism have recognized that both initial
and ongoing encounters with disease as well as western forms of medical colonialism were "a major health hazard for indigenous peoples."[27]
The demographic impact of epidemics on indigenous populations

continues to be debated, but regardless of the extremes "it still seems likely that the scale and intensity of European intervention in the period from the late eighteenth to the early twentieth centuries had a massive, and possibly unprecedented, epidemiological and environmental impact on the peoples of Africa, Asia and Oceania."[28] Thus both the diseases introduced by foreigners into indigenous populations and the foreign medicine that so many extolled as having the capacity to reverse the depopulation trend can be listed among the "tools of empire" that enabled Euro-American expansionism.[29] Throughout the colonized world, Euro-Americans used western medicine as a form of social control, although they did this in a way that emphasized how medical knowledge contributed to the humanitarian zeal of colonial rule and redeemed the blighted body of the indigenous "savage."[30]

Many measures that were introduced in the Pacific during the nineteenth and early twentieth centuries were done so in the name of public health. However, these measures had more to do with concerns about the health of westerners than with the health of the islanders. Colonizers thus privileged the health of foreigners over the health of indigenous populations. As bacteriological research began to reveal how diseases were transmitted from one host to another, disease came to be identified less with the environment and more with living "native reservoirs" of disease.[31] Separation (confinement or quarantine) from such reservoirs was the only proven method of prevention, thus the most often prescribed "treatment." As western medicine increased in prominence in the list of benefits that western civilization saw itself bestowing upon the rest of the world, it also became one of the most intrusive mechanisms exercising power over indigenous bodies and knowledge systems. Further, some colonial governments trained islanders to work in the medical field—assisting western physicians, reporting on epidemics, or patrolling for those with disease.[32] This participation in and inclusion of western biomedicine (and all its cultural baggage) often led indigenous societies to begin to see a "new" difference between the *self* and the *other* within their own society. These differences were based on new conceptions of "disease," as the histories of disease in both Guam and Hawai'i demonstrate.

Medical Imperialism in Hawai'i and Guam

At the end of the nineteenth century both Guam and Hawai'i became U.S. colonies. The United States acquired Guam as a result of
the Spanish-American War in 1898. The Hawaiian monarchy was ille-
gally overthrown in 1893 by a group of business elite and subsequently
"annexed" by a joint resolution of the U.S. Congress in 1898. American control of these island nations "marked the United States' formal
commitment to imperial expansion in the Pacific."[33] American presence in the islands contributed to the colonization of the islanders'
consciousness in both Hawai'i and Guam. Their histories of health,
disease, and medicine illustrate this clearly—and most strikingly in
their respective histories with leprosy, or Hansen's disease. As with
many other parts of the colonized world, the indigenous peoples of
Guam and Hawai'i had to deal with the introduction of foreign diseases that decimated their populations and challenged their worldviews.

The introduction of foreign diseases and subsequent attempts to
deal with epidemics led to an abundance of theories about why indigenous populations were more susceptible to these infections than
Euro-Americans. Neither immunity nor germ theory were understood during this time, and the temptation to blame those suffering from these epidemics as being responsible for that susceptibility
dominated colonial medical discourse. As more and more epidemic
diseases became associated with indigenous populations, social Dar-
winian ideas about Euro-American superiority were clarified; indigenous populations, in contrast, were considered racially inferior. Such
associations were reinforced through experiences with epidemic diseases and ultimately saturated the indigenous consciousness. Thus the
indigenous individuals who accepted perceptions that disease and in-
feriority were linked used this knowledge to differentiate between the
strong and healthy *self*, and the weak and diseased *other*.

The tendency to view people of the same ethnicity as "other" because of disease was a profound development. In his examination of
Samoan medical systems, sociologist Cluny Macpherson illustrates
the paradigmatic transformation of an indigenous knowledge system

into a hybrid of traditional and western systems. Just as significantly, Macpherson demonstrates that changes in belief preceded change in practice.[34] That is, once indigenous societies began "practicing" western medicine, it became likely that western medicine had been culturally accepted, further offering the opportunity to differentiate between "self" and "other" within the indigenous community because of disease experience(s).

As the following case studies of Hawai'i and Guam demonstrate, the *self* and *other* dichotomy that developed as a result of disease experiences can be attributed to quarantine policies not previously experienced by these indigenous societies (especially as occurred under the colonizer with leprosy), objectification of patients, and the criminalization of those with disease.[35]

Guam

The island of Guam is the southernmost of the Mariana Islands in the western Pacific. It has a rich history of indigenous culture, encounters with foreigners, colonization, and resistance. Ferdinand Magellan was the first European explorer to visit the Chamorro people of the Marianas when he arrived with his fleet at Guam in 1521. As the Spanish galleons later established themselves and their trade routes across the Pacific, the Marianas were formally colonized by the Spanish in 1668 with the establishment on Guam of the first European settlement in the Pacific. During the Spanish-Chamorro Wars that lasted from 1670 to 1700, the indigenous Chamorro population dropped from seventy thousand (as reported by Jesuit missionaries in 1668) to less than four thousand in 1710 (according to Spanish accounts). While the conflict accounted for many losses, most historians agree that most of the Chamorro depopulation occurred because of foreign infections. As the eighteenth and nineteenth centuries progressed, conditions were conducive to the spread of disease, and several epidemics struck the Chamorro population—including leprosy, smallpox, measles, whooping cough, and influenza. By the end of the 1800s, the overall population of Guam began to increase, but by then it was one of mixed Chamorro, Filipino, and Spanish ancestry.

After more than two centuries of Spanish colonization, the United States claimed political control of Guam following the end of the Spanish-American War in 1898. The United States proclaimed the entire island to be the "Naval Station of Guam" while Spain sold the remaining Mariana Islands to Germany. Germany controlled the Marianas until after the First World War. Thereafter, Japan remained in control until the Second World War, before the United States defeated Japanese forces in the islands. But as Pacific historian Anne Perez Hattori asserts, "for the Chamorro people the most profound change occurred in 1898, when the United States claimed Guam alone as a spoil of war, beginning an estrangement of Guam from the rest of the Mariana Islands that continues to this day."[36] The U.S. Navy took control of all civil and military affairs on the island throughout the administration of thirty-two different naval governors from 1898 to 1941—all of whom addressed issues of health and hygiene as primary. The naval governors often stated the "twin goals of protecting both the native Chamorros and their military personnel" and placed more emphasis on one or the other depending upon any particular medical concerns at the time. In the context of discussions around the topic of health and the Chamorro people, Hattori notes, "Portraying them as sometimes wretched, sometimes decent, these elastic representations of the indigenous people could be manipulated to justify a wide range of colonial policies."[37]

The naval administration implemented a series of sanitary laws aimed at improving hygiene and preventing the spread of disease, but in so doing it also further entangled medical practices with issues of colonial power. A measles epidemic in 1913, whooping cough in 1915, and the influenza pandemic that hit Guam in 1918 (which killed approximately 6 percent of the population) had of course both a severe and significant impact on the island population.[38] But the public health policies that were developed by the naval administration have an equally significant legacy—especially as they dealt with hookworm and leprosy. Chamorro lifestyles and culture were targeted by campaigns to eradicate one (hookworm) by focusing on schoolchildren and to stop the spread of the other (leprosy) by exiling those who contracted it. Moreover, "through hospitalization and treatment, and through intensive

and extensive education campaigns, the navy attempted to indoctri-
nate Chamorro children in western hygienic practices and, in the process, acculturate them as compliant colonial subjects."[39]

The naval government enlisted the cooperation of Native nurses,
teachers, and a few other local employees to not only transmit colonial policies but also become the primary tool of surveillance in their
communities. The governors of Guam employed "the clinical gaze of
school administrators, teachers, doctors, nurses, and hospital corps-
men" to promote their public health policies, which served to divide
the indigenous community and further distinguish the difference
between the colonized and the colonizer. In cases of hookworm, for
instance, military personnel were only treated if diagnosed with the
parasite, whereas "navy doctors systematically administered annual
treatments to all Chamorro schoolchildren without prior diagnosis
of illness."[40] Navy patrolmen were given the power to arrest and fine
those who had violated sanitary codes.[41] As medical duties were continually divided between the department of health and the police department, the policies surrounding health and hygiene soon came to
be viewed "in terms of the charitable activities of the military and the
criminal activities of the Chamorros."[42] Executive orders allowed for
entire towns to be inspected once a week and expected inspectors to
report in writing "the result of the inspection to the Governor" and
"the names and residences of those delinquent in observing this order."[43] Thus it is not surprising that there were many reports of Chamorros evading authorities, hiding out, or otherwise finding ways to
elude health inspectors and medical officers.

Patients in Guam with Hansen's disease were first quarantined in
the village of Tumon and later sent to Culion in the Philippines. The
Chamorros had two terms for Hansen's disease, both of which were
Spanish transliterations for the word "leprosy," but only one indigenous term for the disease—*atektok*—existed. Hattori explains that *atektok* is "translated as 'to hug each other'" and postulates that "while
the etymological roots of this word are uncertain, perhaps this particular meaning reflects a sense of needing to nurture and embrace
the sick person. Patients, particularly in the later stages of the disease,

frequently require the physical assistance of others, and this definition of *atektok* may reflect an awareness of these needs. Beyond its
layers of literal and metaphorical definition, the term reveals Chamorro attitudes of acknowledgment and assistance for those unfortu-
nates rendered infirm."[44]

As we will also see in the history of Hawai'i, Guam's leprosy patients
were treated more as inmates than as patients, prompting one scholar
to observe that "perhaps the best examples on Guam of criminalizing
health care in the interests of colonialism and military power are found
in the policies toward Hansen's disease."[45] The description offered by
senior medical officer C. P. Kindleberger in 1912 details how Hansen's
disease patients were "surrounded by a high barbed wire fence except
on the ocean side and two native guards are employed for the purpose
of preventing the lepers or their relatives from leaving or entering the
grounds. In addition to these precautions iron bars have been placed
upon the windows of the houses occupied by lepers and padlocks upon
the doors. At nine p.m. every night each leper is locked in his house
by the Superintendent of the 'Colony.'"[46] This level of monitoring was
perhaps a function of naval administration at a time when military involvement in medical policy making was "one of [the] most striking
and significant features" of the colonial era.[47] Yet as the apprehension
and exile of Hansen's disease patients on Guam was largely carried
out by the U.S. military, and in one decade alone "navy officials confined nearly 2 percent of the population," the result was to stigmatize
Chamorros "as diseased and dangerous" while demonstrating the navy's "authoritarian powers."[48] Furthermore, the confinement of leprosy patients created conflict between military concerns for their own
health and "Chamorro concerns for the interests of the patients, not
merely as individuals but as members of extended family groups."[49]

U.S. naval public health laws in Guam, and the Chamorro response
to those regulations, reflect a history of adaptation, accommodation,
acceptance, and resistance. Perhaps due to difficulties in dealing with
Chamorro resistance to the navy's policies concerning Hansen's disease, officials recommended sending patients to the colony at Culion.
For twelve years, "any Chamorro diagnosed with Hansen's disease"

was transported to Culion. As of 1924, no new patients were sent to Culion, but those already there were not permitted to return to Guam.

There is very little documentation of the personal experiences of those who contracted Hansen's disease or the effect that policies concerning leprosy had on the Chamorro people. But in Anne Hattori's *Colonial Dis-Ease*, she recounts an interview she conducted with a descendent of a patient sent to Culion:

> Antonio Unpingco . . . recalled that once his grandfather left for Culion he was never heard from again. Though this was likely due in part to the limited literacy of most Chamorros in the early twentieth century, Unpingco believes that his grandfather's sense of *mamahlao* (shame) was also a factor. Because of the navy's view of the Hansen's disease patients as dangerous outcasts, and their relatives as medically suspect, Unpingco reflected that it would have been understandable for his grandfather to feel *mamahlao* for the embarrassment and trauma caused his wife, children, and other family members as a result of his illness.[50]

The transition of the Chamorro perception of a disease such as leprosy from *atektok* (to hug each other) to one cloaked in *mamahlao* (shame) speaks perhaps to the lasting power and influence of the naval regulations on the indigenous population. Chamorros seemingly adopted these western concepts to the extent that they were willing to convey these perceptions onto themselves, demonstrating the degree to which they have been accepted. Moreover, from 1898 to 1941, policies that included a variety of intrusive and severe laws, and the means of their regulation, created division and distrust, with the naval administration and sometimes within the Chamorro community as well.[51]

Hawai'i

Even before a group of elite businessmen overthrew the Hawaiian Kingdom in 1893 (setting the stage for the U.S. "annexation" of the island nation in 1898), there was a strong western influence on the Native Hawaiian population. This influence can be seen in the kingdom's

dealings with foreign diseases, most notably in its experience with leprosy. While cases of leprosy are known to have existed in the islands
as early as the 1820s, it was not until the 1860s that the disease was of
great concern to kingdom officials. Subsequently, an "Act to Prevent
the Spread of Leprosy" was passed in 1865, which began the removal of men, women, and children from their families and home communities to live and die in exile on a small peninsula on the northern
coast of the island of Molokai. This was not the first time that quarantine was used to deal with epidemics of foreign disease in Hawai'i.
Quarantine was the only proven method of disease prevention at that
time.[52] Yet the enactment of the quarantine policy had many social,
cultural, economic, and political consequences. Approximately five
thousand persons diagnosed with leprosy were separated from their
loved ones between 1865 and 1900.[53] A hospital for the treatment of
mild cases was established near the seashore of Honolulu (the Kali-
hi Hospital) and a settlement for advanced cases was set apart on the
Kalaupapa peninsula on Molokai. With the features of a natural prison (surrounded by steep cliffs and treacherous ocean), the peninsula
soon gained a reputation as a "living tomb," and from the early years
conditions at the settlement were a source of controversy. Horror stories of what life was like on Kalaupapa spread, prompting families to
hide loved ones who had contracted the disease.

It is telling that among the several names Native Hawaiians had
for the disease, none spoke of what the infection does to ones body.
Instead, the most common name for the disease by the late nineteenth century was *ma'i ho'oka'awale 'ohana*, or "the disease that sep-
arates families." Hawaiians had little to no fear or disgust of leprosy
or of those who had it. Their fear, however, was inspired by compul-
sory banishment to Kalaupapa, the public health officials who sought
to send them to Kalaupapa, and their treatment by a fearful foreign
community that shared power with, and greatly influenced, the Hawaiian monarchy. Native Hawaiians continually petitioned the legislature to create leprosy hospitals on each island, but the overthrow of
the monarchy in 1893 put an end to any Native control. As Hawaiian
residents of American descent were lobbying for annexation, leprosy

was increasingly identified as a Native disease, and the disease was increasingly linked with alleged Hawaiian immorality. With statements that leprosy was caused by Hawaiian licentiousness came the belief that whites who adopted Native customs or lived too close to Hawaiians were in danger of contracting the disease.[54] Then, when the Norwegian bacteriologist Gerhard Henrik Armauer Hansen discovered the bacterium that causes leprosy, foreigners' fears of contagion were heightened. By the late 1880s the segregation of leprosy patients was enforced more strictly. Hawaiians were viewed as a weak and dying race, and those with the stigma of leprosy were to be entirely outcast, lest all of Hawai'i become a "leprous population."[55]

Throughout the history of the Kalaupapa settlement and ever since the 1865 Act to Prevent the Spread of Leprosy, victims of the disease were treated more like criminals than patients. Public health measures were used as instruments of colonial authority. In particular, authorities viewed segregation as a way to protect the "civilized" from the diseased. According to one physician in the 1890s, "every leper is a possible source of danger."[56] European anxieties about leprosy were also fueled by apparent indifference of Hawaiians to the disease and by Hawaiians' resistance to segregation. Hawaiians were prepared to shelter and care for those with the disease and were willing to be *kōkua* (helpers) to those sent to Kalaupapa. The sexualization of leprosy (some theorized that it was the fourth stage of syphilis) further projected these deep anxieties. Though long absent from most of Europe, with the spread of western imperialism leprosy now threatened to return.[57] Moreover, leprosy offered rich metaphoric possibilities for expressing the innate corruption of indigenous culture, justifying further western domination.

Fundamental to the differences between Native Hawaiian and Euro-American views on health and disease were indigenous perspectives on the body. In the late nineteenth century, the Hawaiian view of the body and disease was intertwined with particular Hawaiian views of the self in relation to collectivity and cosmology. First and foremost, all Hawaiians believed they were connected to the land, as children are connected to parents, in the belief that *Wakea* (Sky Father) and

Papa (Earth Mother) gave mystical birth to the islands and human birth to their descendants.[58] Thus, *Papahanaumoku*—she who births the islands—was understood as the mother of all humans. Hawaiian cosmology connected the land and people as family, therefore caring for the land and concern for family were linked. Hawaiians believed that the earth was a living entity (embodying *mana*) and that Hawaiians had a relationship and a connection to that life force. This view held that good health was the reward of respect for the *kapu* (which often included the ethics of caring for the land), reverence for the gods, and integrity, expressed in their relationships with family and neighbors. Native Hawaiians also recognized a dualism of complementary opposites in their cosmology. These dualities required *pono* (balance and harmony) and *mana* (power) to maintain these *pono* relationships.[59] Disease was understood to be the result of losing *mana*, either through offending an *amakua* (ancestral god) or breaking a *kapu*. Restoring *mana* would restore health and well-being.

For most Native Hawaiians, leprosy was no different than any of the other foreign infections that were introduced to the islands. Most of the introduced diseases contributed to depopulation (syphilis, tuberculosis, influenza), and many of these foreign infections affected the skin (measles, smallpox), but leprosy came with western stigmas attached to it. It also had a slow pathology, giving the community time to offer meaning to the disease and its consequences.[60] As the policies to stop the spread of leprosy were enacted, many Hawaiians resisted the segregation law and refused to separate themselves from those with leprosy. Those with the disease often hid from the authorities, and others who opposed the roundup of those with leprosy went so far as to hide their family members and friends.

For those who were exiled, they were separated physically, culturally, and emotionally by the Kalaupapa settlement. They were, in essence, isolated and imprisoned for life. Cultural and personal identities were lost. Further, a greater process of the colonization of the Hawaiian people was at work. Under the rubric of the Act to Prevent the Spread of Leprosy (the formation of a "leper" colony at Kalaupapa and the segregation of those afflicted by the disease) was a diverse array of ideological and administrative mechanisms by which an emerging system of knowledge and power extended itself into and over the Native Hawaiians.[61]

Leprosy represented not one but a variety of meanings and metaphors. The victims of this dreaded disease were treated as criminals because those in power viewed leprosy as a metaphor for all that was socially and morally wrong (according to Euro-American views) with Native Hawaiian society. For Hawaiians, the change from no fear of leprosy to a horror of the disease was not because of the disease itself, but because leprosy soon meant separation from family and society. To have leprosy meant one ran the risk of being treated as one who had sinned against society. This criminalizing of the disease not only justified western policies of treatment but also had the most profound affect on Hawaiian views of those with the disease. Thus, by the end of the nineteenth century even the Hawaiian "self" was beginning to look upon those with leprosy as the "other." The colonized Hawaiian mind now looked upon those with the disease as an "other"—Euro-American perspectives and stigmas of those with disease had altered Hawaiian cultural perceptions and were reshaping the ways indigenous peoples related to one another.

For example, Ka'ehu the Chanter, who was diagnosed with leprosy in the late 1880s, composed this autobiographical *mele* (chant/song) upon his arrest and exile to Molokai:

'Ano'e mai ana nā hoa hui	Strange when a man's neighbors
Like 'ole ka pilina mamua.	become less than acquaintances.
He 'āhiu ke 'ike mai,	Seeing me they drew away.
Ne'e a kāhi 'e noho mai,	They moved to sit elsewhere,
Kuhikuhi mai ho'i ka lima,	whispering,
He ma'i Pākē kō 'iā 'la.	and a friend pointed a finger:
	"He is a leper."
Kūlou au a hō'oiā'i'o,	I bowed my head;
Komo ka hilahila i ka houpo.	I knew it was true.
	In my heart I hugged my shame.[62]

Ka'ehu's *mele* indicates that there was a change in Native Hawaiian views toward the disease. Both fear of the disease and the "shame" of contracting it had become prevalent; fear and shame were not common sentiments prior to this time. Before the late nineteenth century, it was unusual for a Native Hawaiian to refer to another as a "leper." Imperial medical practices changed this, and the term "leper" became the nomenclature for "otherness" that reinforced the efficacy of colonial rule.

The shame referred to in Ka'ehu's *mele* was part of the stigma attached to leprosy, and it was that stigma that facilitated the shift in Hawaiian (self-)identity toward perceiving those with the disease as an "other." For those who contracted the disease, this shift is especially apparent in oral histories. In the following example, a "patient" shares his story in the 1960s, recalling his experience as a young boy around 1906:

> My father came to take me home from school. But instead of taking me to the Kalihi Receiving Station immediately like the principal said they should, my parents took me home. . . . The whole family cried, including my father. The next day my father took me downtown and bought me a new suit. . . . Even though we were poor, my father said he wanted me to be dressed nicely when I was taken to Kalihi to be declared a leper. They took my picture for the official record of the Board of Health wearing that suit of clothes. When the picture was taken, my father broke down again and cried. So, I became a leper.[63]

Recalling perhaps his most profound memory, this man takes us to the moment when everything changed for him—his life forever changed, his identity forever altered. Not only was he separated from his parents and family from that day on, but he saw that moment as the instant when he was no longer his *self*, but rather one to be stigmatized and banished because of a disease. That was the day he was "declared" and "became" a "leper"—he became the *other*. As Arnold reminds us, the disease experience is not just about microbes and mortality, it is an "experience" with social, political, economic, and cultural ramifications: "Inevitably 'man clothes his cosmos in a moral cloak,' and in every society, present as well as past, disease, especially epidemic disease, takes on a wider social, political, and cultural significance."[64]

Conclusion

When two separate systems of medical explanation came into contact (indigenous and western), and as epidemic diseases were introduced to the Pacific Islands, the western model soon dominated the indigenous views of the body, health, and disease. As a result, those who survived the epidemics were left to mourn the loss of their land (to whom they were cosmologically connected) to foreigners, to mourn the loss of their health (and what was *pono*), and specifically in the case of leprosy, to mourn the loss of their families—to be separated from their loved ones, to feel ashamed for contracting this disease, and to be treated as criminals for having the disease. The laws, rules, regulations, and policies surrounding infectious diseases, especially leprosy, in Hawai'i and Guam labeled patients as immoral and criminal. The disease marked their bodies, but public health policies imprisoned their bodies by removing them from society for a life in quarantine or exile. With their freedoms, family, and homes taken from them, so their former sense of self was lost.

In both Guam and Hawai'i this experience with foreign diseases contributed to the creation of a cultural "other" within indigenous society. In both cases, criminalizing those with disease functioned as a trigger to change the way Chamorros and Native Hawaiians saw themselves. Euro-American views invaded indigenous concepts of health and disease, much in the same way that foreign diseases had invaded, along with an emerging biomedicine. The stigma attached to leprosy (and held onto by Euro-Americans) further facilitated this indigenous transition to viewing those with disease as an "other." As time passed, Chamorros and Native Hawaiians saw this disease as little different than any of the other foreign infections that had decimated their populations (smallpox, measles, venereal diseases), and they adopted the western stigma that had been carried for centuries with this particular illness.

Foreign infectious diseases, especially leprosy, facilitated a significant aspect of cultural exchange between western colonizers and indigenous populations—as indigenous views of the body, disease, and health were subject to western views of the same, indigenous perceptions of why they suffered from disease were greatly influenced and changed by western perceptions—leaving Chamorros and Native Hawaiians to view those disease sufferers within their own indigenous population as a cultural *other* no longer part of the *self.*

Notes

1. I have not capitalized the terms "western" and "indigenous" throughout this chapter so as to refrain from promoting either as superior to the other.

2. While the medical practice I am speaking of could best be understood as "biomedicine" (as opposed to indigenous, traditional, or folk medical practices, also present in the West), it is recognized that the biomedicine of the nineteenth century was still in its developing stages, and further that even when it was "science" based, Euro-American medical practitioners came to Oceania with their unique cultural perspectives and influences. Thus I have chosen to use the term "western medicine" to denote biomedicine as introduced by Euro-Americans into the Pacific.

3. David Arnold, "Introduction: Disease, Medicine and Empire," in *Imperial Medicine and Indigenous Societies*, ed. David Arnold (Manchester: Manchester University Press, 1998), 2.

4. Arnold, "Introduction: Disease, Medicine and Empire," 2.

5. For example, see Warwick Anderson, *Colonial Pathologies: American Tropical Medicine, Race, and Hygiene in the Philippines* (Durham NC: Duke University Press, 2006), for more on the role of science and medicine in the American colonization of the Philippines.

6. Ranginui Walker, *Ka Whawai Tonu Matou = Struggle Without End* (New York: Penguin, 2004), 85.

7. Arthur Kleinman, "What Is Specific to Western Medicine?" in *Companion Encyclopedia of the History of Medicine*, vol. 1, ed. W. F. Bynum and Roy Porter (New York: Routledge, 2001), 16–18.

8. John Miles, *Infectious Diseases: Colonising the Pacific?* (Dunedin: University of Otago Press, 1997).

9. Shula Marks, "What Is Colonial about Colonial Medicine? and What Has Happened to Imperialism and Health?" *Social History of Medicine* 10, no. 2 (1997): 205–19.

10. Charles E. Rosenberg, "Introduction—Framing Disease: Illness, Society, and History," in *Framing Disease: Studies in Cultural History*, ed. C. E. Rosenberg and Janet Golden (New Brunswick NJ: Rutgers University Press, 1992), xv.

11. Marks, "What Is Colonial about Colonial Medicine?," 210.

12. Roy MacLeod and Milton Lewis, eds., *Disease, Medicine, and Empire: Perspectives on Western Medicine and the Experience of European Expansion* (New York: Routledge, 1988).

13. Marks, "What Is Colonial about Colonial Medicine?," 214.

14. Poonam Bala and Amy Kaler, "Introduction—Contested 'Ventures': Explaining Biomedicine in Colonial Contexts," in *Biomedicine as a Contested Site: Some Revelations in Imperial Contexts*, ed. Poonam Bala (New York: Rowman and Littlefield, 2009), 1.

15. Bala and Kaler, "Introduction—Contested 'Ventures,'" 2.

16. Judith A. Bennett, "Holland, Britain, and Germany in Melanesia," in *Tides of History: The Pacific Islands in the Twentieth Century*, ed. K. R. Howe, Robert C. Kiste, and Brij V. Lal (Honolulu: University of Hawai'i Press, 1994), 50.

17. Arnold, "Introduction: Disease, Medicine and Empire," 9; Alfred Crosby, *Ecological Imperialism: The Biological Expansion of Europe, 900–1900* (New York: Cambridge University Press, 1986).

18. Arnold, "Introduction: Disease, Medicine and Empire," 12.

19. See James C. Mohr, *Plague and Fire: Battling Black Death and the 1900 Burning of Honolulu's Chinatown* (New York: Oxford University Press, 2005).

20. Arnold, "Introduction: Disease, Medicine and Empire," 7.

21. Arnold, "Introduction: Disease, Medicine and Empire," 7.

22. Arnold, "Introduction: Disease, Medicine and Empire," 12. See also Michael Worboys, *Spreading Germs: Disease Theories and Medical Practice in Britain, 1865–1900* (New York: Cambridge University Press, 2000).

23. Douglas M. Haynes, *Imperial Medicine: Patrick Manson and the Conquest of Tropical Disease* (Philadelphia: University of Pennsylvania Press, 2001), 5.

24. Arnold, "Introduction: Disease, Medicine and Empire," 18.

25. Megan Vaughan, *Curing Their Ills: Colonial Power and African Illness* (Stanford CA: Stanford University Press, 1991), 25.

26. See O. A. Bushnell, *The Gifts of Civilization: Germs and Genocide in Hawai'i* (Honolulu: University of Hawai'i Press, 1993).

27. Arnold, "Introduction: Disease, Medicine, and Empire," 4.

28. Arnold, "Introduction: Disease, Medicine, and Empire," 5. See also Ned Blackhawk, *Violence over the Land: Indians and Empires in the Early American West* (Cambridge MA: Harvard University Press, 2006); Alfred A. Cave, "Genocide in the Americas," in *The Historiography of Genocide*, ed. Dan Stone (Basingstoke: Palgrave-MacMillan, 2008), 273–95; Gregory D. Smithers, "Rethinking Genocide in North America," in *Genocide (Oxford History Handbooks)*, ed. Donald Bloxham and A. Dirk Moses (Oxford: Oxford University Press, 2010), 322–41.

29. See D. R. Headrick, *Tools of Empire: Technology and European Imperialism in the Nineteenth Century* (New York: Oxford University Press, 1981).

30. David Arnold, "Medicine and Colonialism," in *Companion Encyclopedia of the History of Medicine*, ed. W. F. Bynum and Roy Porter (New York: Routledge, 1993). See also John and Jean Comaroff, *Ethnography and the Historical Imagination* (Boulder CO: Westview Press, 1992).

31. Arnold, "Introduction: Disease, Medicine and Empire," 8.

32. Stewart Firth, "Colonial Administration and the Invention of the Native," in *The Cambridge History of the Pacific Islanders*, ed. Donald Denoon (New York: Cambridge University Press, 1997), 278–80.

33. David Hanlon, "Patterns of Colonial Rule in Micronesia," in Howe, Kiste, and Lal, *Tides of History*, 110.

34. Cluny Macpherson, "Samoan Medicine," in *Healing Practices in the South Pacific*, ed. Claire D. F. Parsons (Lai'e HI: Institute for Polynesian Studies, BYU–Hawai'i Campus, 1995), 1–15.

35. Today, the accepted term for leprosy is "Hansen's disease," but as the examples I cite are from the era before this change in terminology in 1949, the name "leprosy" is generally used in reference to this disease. However, the term "leper" is considered derogatory and a painful reminder of the stigma that accompanies Hansen's disease, and as such this term is used only when historically appropriate or quoting directly from historical sources.

36. Anne Perez Hattori, *Colonial Dis-Ease: U.S. Navy Health Policies and the Chamorros of Guam, 1898–1941* (Honolulu: University of Hawai'i Press, 2004), 17–18.

37. Hattori, *Colonial Dis-Ease*, 20.

38. Robert F. Rogers, *Destiny's Landfall: A History of Guam* (Honolulu: University of Hawai'i Press, 1995), 133.

39. Hattori, *Colonial Dis-Ease*, 158.

40. Hattori, *Colonial Dis-Ease*, 21.

41. Sanitary codes in Guam, 1898–1941, included everything from policies on footwear, to lawn mowing, to the regulation of Chamorro midwives. From 1907, violations of sanitary regulations were grounds for arrest and imprisonment.

42. Hattori, *Colonial Dis-Ease*, 23.

43. Executive General Order 8, December 8, 1905, Naval Government of Guam Executive General Orders, quoted in Hattori, *Colonial Dis-Ease*, 30.

44. Hattori, *Colonial Dis-Ease*, 62–63.

45. Hattori, *Colonial Dis-Ease*, 72.

46. Kindleberger to Surgeon General, U.S. Navy, January 30, 1912. Quoted in Hattori, *Colonial Dis-Ease*, 73.

47. Arnold, "Introduction: Disease, Medicine, and Empire," 19.

48. Hattori, *Colonial Dis-Ease*, 79.

49. Hattori, *Colonial Dis-Ease*, 36.

50. Hattori, *Colonial Dis-Ease*, 86.

51. Hattori, *Colonial Dis-Ease*, 187.

52. A quarantine ordinance was passed as early as 1836.

53. From 1865 to 1969 (when the isolation policy was finally lifted) some seven thousand to eight thousand "patients" were taken to Molokai's peninsula. One medical scholar, Dr. Kekuni Blaisdell, speculates that every Native Hawaiian family has been affected by this disease.

54. Pennie Moblo, "Defamation by Disease: Leprosy, Myth and Ideology in Nineteenth Century Hawai'i" (PhD diss., University of Hawai'i, 1996), 4.

55. Prince A. Morrow, MD, "Leprosy and Hawaiian Annexation," *North American Review* (1897): 590.

56. Morrow, "Leprosy and Hawaiian Annexation," 585.

57. See J. R. Tryon, "Leprosy in the Hawaiian Islands," *American Journal of the Medical Sciences* (1883): 443–50; Henry Press Wright, *Leprosy and Its Story: Segregation and its Remedy* (London: Parker and Co., 1885).

58. Mary Kawena Pukui, E. W. Haertig, C. A. Lee, and J. F. McDermott, *Nana I Ke Kumu: Look to the Source*, vol. 2 (Honolulu: Hui Hanai, 1979).

59. See Kekuni Blaisdell, "Historical and Cultural Aspects of Native Hawaiian Health," in *Social Process in Hawai'i* 32, no. 1 (1989): 1–21; George S. Kanahele, *Kū Kanaka, Stand Tall: A Search for Hawaiian Values* (Honolulu: University of Hawai'i Press, 1986).

60. Western stigma attached to the sufferers of leprosy included the perception that persons with leprosy were unclean and immoral.

61. See David Arnold, *Colonizing the Body* (Berkeley: University of California Press, 1993).

62. "Mele a Ka'ehu ka Haku Mele (Song of the Chanter Ka'ehu)," in *The Echo of Our Song*, ed. and trans. Mary Kawena Pukui and Alfons L. Korn (Honolulu: University of Hawai'i Press, 1973), 126–29.

63. Emmett Cahill, *Yesterday at Kalaupapa* (Honolulu: Editions Ltd., 1990), 5.

64. Arnold, "Introduction: Disease, Medicine, and Empire," 7.

Chapter 13

"Why Injun Artist Me"
Acee Blue Eagle's Diasporic Performative

Bill Anthes

Many peoples was wonders why
My eyes not on a stars and sky
Sed it my fren's, he easy could
Make good lawyer, doctor, an' should
Oh, could make it lots of moneys
Fo' him it sure would be good.
I'm long years ago, use to think so
But like that, don' think it no mo'
I'm jus' don' know'd why is so
But som'thing sed nother way to go.
Maybe Great Spirit, high in a sky
He's know heap much better than I
Guess lots of it nother of man
Be Doctor, lawyer, so many can
So want me paint Indian and sacred sun
Sacred dances, games, and lot of fun
So people see for many years to com'
So that's why I'm not go like
Injun to be like white man
But paint Sacred, many pictures
Of Injun and hope it can
Be good medicine, with sacred beauty,
Like Injun Priest paint with sand.
ACEE BLUE EAGLE (1907–1959)

Fig. 13.1. "Acee Blue Eagle Wearing Feathered Headdress and Buckskin Clothing, Holding Book and Sitting Near Dog," n.d., photo reproduction. Manuscript Acee Blue Eagle Papers: Painting and Drawings by Blue Eagle, National Anthropological Archives, Smithsonian Institution, NAA INV 08773802.

Artist, celebrity, teacher, and performer Acee Blue Eagle embraced eagerly what Gerald Vizenor terms a simulation of Native American identity.[1] He was widely known for his frequent public appearances in full Plains regalia that was instantly recognizable to his white audiences (dressed up for a steamer trip from New York to England, he mugged for the cameras), and for his speeches, performances, and writing in dialect—a kind of Indian-pidgin seen in the poem above.[2] Indeed, every inch a figure of the twentieth century, Blue Eagle reveled in mass culture stereotypes and mass media itself. An erstwhile vaudeville performer and movie extra during the 1930s, Blue Eagle would in the 1950s host a children's television program in Tulsa-Muskogee, Oklahoma. Importantly for this volume, Blue Eagle was no less a product of the histories of Native displacement and diaspora and national Indian policy. Born of Creek-Scottish ancestry in Oklahoma in the year of its incorporation as the forty-sixth state in the Union, he was educated in federal boarding schools in Kansas, Oklahoma, and Virginia, as well as the Baptist-founded Bacone Indian College in Muskogee, where he was a star athlete. He later attended the University of Oklahoma. Blue Eagle was also in many ways a consummate *American* artist—as a painter, his first public commissions were murals produced under the auspices of the Works Progress Administration Federal Art Project. During the Second World War, Blue Eagle served in the Army Air Corps—stateside, as a camouflage artist, although newspaper articles reported that the famous Indian artist was looking forward to a bombing run over Berlin. A painting by Blue Eagle of a buffalo hunt sank with the USS Oklahoma in Pearl Harbor in 1941. Blue Eagle was also a *modern* artist—embodying an entrepreneurial ethos as he launched a line of mass-produced greeting cards and lent his designs to advertising campaigns.

The one-time husband of well-known Balinese dancer Devi Dja, Blue Eagle moved with as much ease between expressive media as he did across cultural boundaries. A larger than life figure—tall, handsome, and by all accounts popular with the ladies—he was admired for his considerable charisma as a storyteller and entertainer. Blue Eagle's public persona was apparently characterized by what Joseph Roach terms "It"—"the easily perceived but hard-to-define quality possessed by abnormally interesting people."[3] It seems clear that Blue Eagle saw himself in his public persona (resplendent in buckskin and feathers, orating in pidgin) as a cultural ambassador and broker between Native and non-Native worlds, even as the role he played was so clearly a simulation. In 1954, for example, a meeting was arranged between Blue Eagle and Ethiopian emperor Haile Selassie, who was traveling to Oklahoma on a diplomatic tour and wanted to meet a Native American. Selassie, upon landing in Stillwater, Oklahoma, was greeted by Blue Eagle in full regalia. Blue Eagle bestowed upon the visiting emperor the honorary title of "Great Buffalo High Chief" and presented Selassie with a "war bonnet" made from eagle feathers.[4]

While Blue Eagle fascinated audiences with his flamboyant personality, he was also revered for his art. His meticulously researched paintings of traditional Indian subjects (painted in a linear, quasi-*art deco*

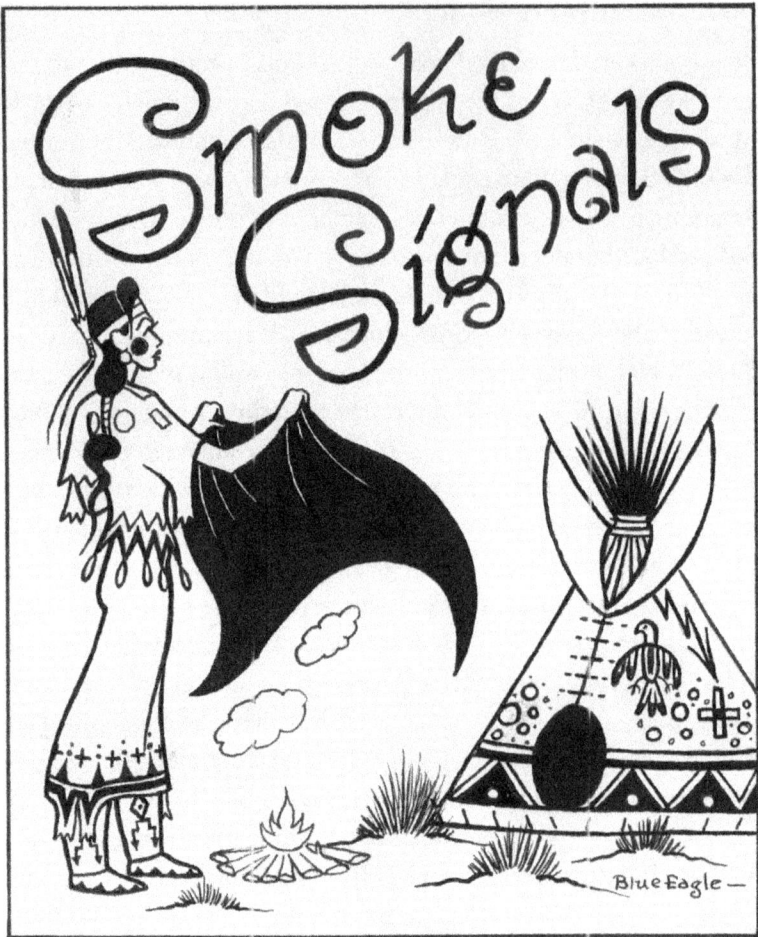

Fig. 13.2. "Smoke Signals," n.d., drawing. Manuscript Acee Blue Eagle Papers: Painting and Drawings by Blue Eagle, National Anthropological Archives, Smithsonian Institution, NAA INV 08771100.

style) were shown widely, including some of the earliest exhibitions to highlight Native American modern art in a fine art (rather than an ethnographic) context. Blue Eagle's works were included in the *Exposition of Indian Tribal Arts* at New York's Grand Central Galleries in 1930, the Los Angeles Olympics in 1932, the Century of Progress Exposition in Chicago in 1933, and at the Museum of Modern Art's groundbreaking *Indian Art of the United States* in 1941, among other venues. As an artist

Fig. 13.3. Acee Blue Eagle, "Seminole(?) Man on Horseback and Two Pheasants," n.d., painting. Manuscript Acee Blue Eagle Papers: Painting and Drawings by Blue Eagle, National Anthropological Archives, Smithsonian Institution, NAA INV 808759000.

and educator, Blue Eagle was a key figure in formalizing and institutionalizing what became known (with unintended irony) as the "Traditional Style" of Indian painting at midcentury. Blue Eagle synthesized a stylized, decorative approach to painting traditional Native American subjects, drawing from precedents such as the Kiowa school of painting developed under Oscar Jacobson at the University of Oklahoma in the 1920s and the pan-Indian "Studio Style" practiced by students at the Santa Fe Indian School in the early 1930s.[5] As was often noted in published interviews, popular newspaper and magazine profile features, and biographical sketches, Blue Eagle's paintings could be found in the collections of Emperor Selassie, as well as Adolf Hitler, Benito Mussolini, and Alfonso XIII, the exiled king of Spain, all of whom apparently met the artist personally. After the Second World War, Blue Eagle's paintings were frequent prizewinners in the Indian Annuals—the influential, national exhibitions held each year at the Philbrook Museum of Art in Tulsa, Oklahoma.

Blue Eagle was often described as America's "foremost living Indian artist." He was listed in a plethora of "Who's Who" publications—including *Who's Who of Outstanding Indians*, *Who's Who of American*

Fig. 13.4. "Close Up and Comedy of Acee Blue Eagle," n.d., newspaper clipping. Manuscript Acee Blue Eagle Papers: Painting and Drawings by Blue Eagle, National Anthropological Archives, Smithsonian Institution.

Fig. 13.5. "Blue Deer," n.d., painting. Manuscript Acee Blue Eagle Papers: Painting and Drawings by Blue Eagle, National Anthropological Archives, Smithsonian Institution, NAA INV 08773900.

Artists, Who's Who in Oklahoma, and *Who's Who in the World*—and listed in countless "halls of fame." He was an in-demand lecturer, entertaining audiences with speeches on the "Original American" and "Redman Art" in Europe, New York, and throughout the United States.

And yet today, Blue Eagle is absent from the histories of Native American art and from histories of American modernism generally. Blue Eagle remains largely unknown because his legacy has been obscured by the emergence of a school of Native American contemporary art since the 1960s that has tended to dismiss the showy persona and sentimental art of Blue Eagle and others of his generation. In 1959 Yanktonai Dakota painter Oscar Howe sent an angry letter to the Philbrook Museum in response to the disqualification of Howe's innovative abstract painting *Umine Wacipi: War and Peace Dance* from the Indian Annual on the grounds that it was "a fine painting, but not Indian." Howe retorted, "Who ever said . . . that my paintings are not in traditional Indian style has poor knowledge of Indian art indeed. There is much more to Indian art than pretty, stylized pictures."[6] Indeed, it is hard to imagine a painting more pretty or stylized than

Blue Eagle's images of leaping blue deer and coquettish Indian maidens. Following Howe's protest, Native artists began to see themselves as arbiters of Native culture, refusing to offer up simulations for non-Native audiences and producing an art embodying the new spirit of self-determination and activism. Contemporary Native American art has addressed issues specific to the history of settler colonialism in the United States and Canada—land, treaty rights, sovereignty, citizenship, and the legal fictions of identity and blood quantum.[7]

In his art and career, however, Blue Eagle may be seen to embody the ambivalent position of Native Americans in the first decades of the twentieth century—caught between white expectations and an emerging political agency that would characterize the 1960s and beyond. Of Creek ancestry and formed by the experience of displacement and loss, Blue Eagle's persona was, moreover, a diasporic performative—a savvy reinvention of self and culture that drew from then current and quite powerful images and ideas of Indianness in the context of an emerging "culture of personality" in the early twentieth century.[8]

Additionally, Blue Eagle's story is part of a larger history of Native American art in the twentieth century, as traditional arts were revived and transformed, and new forms and markets were embraced. The history of Native American art in the twentieth century is an often overlooked episode in the histories of modernism, much as the histories of Native peoples in the twentieth century have been obscured by popular and scholarly accounts of the decline in the nineteenth century of Native cultures under the heels of North American settler colonialism and manifest destiny.[9] In the late nineteenth century, few would have predicted the remarkable renaissance of Native North American cultural production that characterized the Reservation Era of the late nineteenth and early twentieth centuries. With the indigenous population at its nadir, nations and communities confined to meager slices of marginal land, and traditional cultures and languages under assault by the assimilationist policies of the Canadian and United States governments and allied Christian-missionary organizations, Native peoples responded with a remarkable and unexpected outpouring of creativity. In particular, women's arts such as textile weaving, ceramics, and beadwork blossomed, as confinement on reservations led to the codification of tribal styles as expressions of identity and pride; in the Plains, particular attention was lavished on items made for the next generation—such as elaborately decorated cradleboards, for example. Men's arts also flourished, as warrior-artists adapted a tradition of producing pictorial records of personal, community, and legendary histories to tell of their battles with federal forces and rendition to far-flung military prisons. Many of these products were made according to traditional standards for community use, but a growing number were destined for circulation in new markets eager for these intercultural aesthetic commodities. Formerly sacred arts were secularized and commercialized.[10]

As traditional arts were revived and reinvented by practitioners who often worked in collaboration with non-Native mentors and patrons, novel media including painting and sculpture were readily adopted. Moreover, with the development of new markets, traditional gender divisions in artistic practice were overturned. Art forms traditionally practiced by women, such as weaving and ceramics, were taken up by male artists in the twentieth century in the Southwest. Hosteen Klah, a Navajo *nadle* (a term used to describe individuals with the traits of both sexes—or a hermaphrodite—an honored position in traditional Navajo culture) made commercial weavings based on powerful, sacred—and potentially dangerous—sand-painting diagrams traditionally produced by male healers or singers. In the Plains, traditional distinctions between the abstract, geometric arts made by women and the narrative arts produced by men were blurred as Lakota women began to produce pictorial beadwork on clothing and other items.

The objects of Native American manufacture that have passed into Western collections have done so through a variety of channels: trade, diplomatic exchange, gift, and theft—to name just a few—each of which carries its own political and ethical baggage, and each of which itself is the outcome of generations of cross-cultural traffic. Moreover, the objects produced by Native American men and women have been understood and appreciated by non-Native consumers in several distinct modes: as curiosity, specimen, and artifact, through the lens of Indian

reform and uplift, and as art. As Janet C. Berlo and Ruth B. Phillips
write, the corpus of extant Native-made objects can be understood to
fall within one of three broad categories: precontact objects that were
recovered archaeologically; objects that have been carefully preserved
by Native communities because of their inherent sacred and power and
ceremonial efficacy; and the largest category—historic period objects,
generally nonsacred and nonceremonial (although this is a European
American distinction).[11] These modes of viewing influenced greatly the
ways in which Native-made objects have been seen and understood.

As such, Native American arts must be understood within the context of societal modernization and within histories of modernism generally. The third category cited by Berlo and Phillips—historic period
objects, often produced for trade to outside audiences—comprises "aesthetic commodities" that are "autonomous" in the sense that Theodor
Adorno and other theorists have employed the term, or that could be
said to privilege "exhibition" over "cult" (or use) value, following Walter Benjamin's often-cited discussion of the modern artwork.[12] But it
should also be noted that in contrast to the "autonomous" artwork
in these modernist models, cult value is never fully displaced in the
case of objects of Native American manufacture; their status as ex-
otic, talismanic fetishes persists. As intercultural commodities that
circulated between dispossessed indigenous peoples and settler colo-
nials, Native American artworks are always already bound up in ideas
of difference—initially notions of cultural evolution, and later, anti-
modernist agendas and cultural primitivist projects.[13]

It is also useful to understand Blue Eagle in dialogue with a previous cohort of Native American public intellectuals born a generation before Blue Eagle, in the closing years of the nineteenth century.
Historian Frederick E. Hoxie has explored the cultural work of what
he terms the "boarding school generation" of Native American elites
during the Progressive Era of the late nineteenth and early twentieth
century—a period that overlaps with the Reservation Era in Native
American history—during which a generation of Native American
youth attended boarding schools and came to understand the "great
divide" in Native American experience. Writing her autobiography

in the 1930s, Mourning Dove (Salish, 1888–1936) reflected that she was "born long enough ago to have known people who lived in the ancient way before everything started to change."[14] As Hoxie writes:

> Like thousands of her ancestors, she [Mourning Dove] experienced non-Indians, not as visitors on native land, but as a daily, conquering presence. But like few others, Mourning Dove had access to both the English language and modern technology and could therefore communicate her reactions widely. In this sense, Mourning Dove and her contemporaries were the first generation of Native Americans who could explore publicly the meaning of their predicament. Positioned as they were, between a remembered world of relative freedom and the grim realities of industrial society, people like the Colville author attempted to define ways in which their communities and their traditions might be valued in a new setting. They believed they could neither flee from white society nor contemplate an alternative world peopled only by Indians. For Mourning Dove's generation, the future depended on their ability to define and protect areas in American cultural and political life where the "ancient way" might somehow survive. Their efforts in the years between 1900 and 1930, which engaged them in fields as various as literature, anthropology, art, religion, and politics, were Native American journeys of discovery, journeys devoted to the search for a new home in a captured land.[15]

In his career, then, Blue Eagle benefited from three factors in early twentieth-century America: the pathbreaking work of the artists and public intellectuals of the boarding-school generation described by Hoxie (and by Porter, in this volume); the market-building work of artists such as the Kiowa Five in Oklahoma (with whom he would later claim an affinity/affiliation) and the Studio School/Pueblo painters of the Southwest, as well as their non-Native promoters; and the popular appeal of primitivizing performances of Indian culture and identity—feeding what Renato Rosaldo termed "imperialist nostalgia"—and coinciding with the search for a "usable past" in American culture in the years following the First World War and during the Great Depression.[16]

Acee Blue Eagle, the Most Famous Indian Artist in America

While there is some variation in biographical accounts of Blue Eagle's life, most have rehearsed in general the following: Born in 1907, the year that Oklahoma Territory and Indian Territory were merged into the state of Oklahoma, Blue Eagle was given the name Laughing Boy (Che-bon Ah-bee-la) by his parents, Solomon McIntosh and Mattie Odom. Interviewed in 1933 by the *Sooner Magazine* (published by the University of Oklahoma at Norman), Blue Eagle described his family: "My father came from a long line of Pawnee Medicine Men, and from him I learned, even before I was taught the English language, the sacred rites of the tribal Medicine Men. . . . My mother's father and her grandfather were Creek chiefs. From her I learned much about the civilized tribes before they were brought to Oklahoma from their eastern grounds."[17]

Accounts vary, however. A 1969 biographical sketch traces the artist's Creek heritage to Blue Eagle's paternal great-great-grandfather, Chillicothe "Chilli" McIntosh (1800–1885), who fought under Andrew Jackson at the Battle of New Orleans, and points to other Creek leaders of that name, including Roly McIntosh and other "members of the McIntosh clan [who] were recognized Creek chiefs."[18]

As a child he was known by the nickname Ah-Say, or Ah-See, which later became "Acee." As is typically reported in artists' biographies, he took an interest in art at an early age. An early promotional article titled "Amazing Rise to International Fame" related, "As soon as he walked, Acee traced figures in the sand at the feet of his tribal elders who simply said, 'He good tepee painter.'"[19] However, the young artist's childhood was also marked by tragedy, as his twin brother, mother, and father all died by the time he had reached the age of four, five, or six (accounts vary on this point). An orphan, the future artist was raised in western Oklahoma, possibly on the Wichita Reservation near Anadarko, by his grandparents, from whom he took the name Blue Eagle. (Accounts vary here, too, some citing maternal grandparents and others citing the paternal line.) One biographical sketch traces a lineage for the family name: "The Blue Eagles are supposed to have

Fig. 13.6. Spencer Asah, "Asah Dancing" (from the Kiowa Indian Art Portfolio), pochoir (screenprint), Fred Jones Jr. Museum of Art, University of Oklahoma, Norman, 1998.013.008. Gift of Elaine Bizzell Thompson, 1998.

been special tribesmen and to have had their name revealed to them by an omen, the falling of an albino eagle, shot by one of the braves, which fell into a crock of berry juice. Color me blue, and so it was."[20]

Like many Native youth, Blue Eagle was sent to Indian boarding schools, perhaps his first immersion in an English-speaking environment, at the age of seven. He attended Indian schools in Kansas, Oklahoma, and Virginia. He received manual training, as was also typical for Native students in the early twentieth century. He learned shoe repair, and during his senior year in 1928 he also designed the seal for the Chilocco Indian School in Oklahoma.[21] That year he enrolled in Bacone Junior College (founded by Baptists in 1880 to give Native Americans a Christian education) in Muskogee, Oklahoma. He excelled at football.

After graduation from Bacone, Blue Eagle matriculated at the University of Oklahoma, where he studied from 1931 to 1932 and where he began his art career in earnest under the guidance of Oscar B. Jacobson, who had in 1928 enrolled the first students in an Indian arts program—the famous Kiowa Five: James Auchiah (1906–1974), Spencer Asah (1905/1910–1954), Jack Hokeah (1902–1969), Stephen Mopope (1898–1974), and Monroe Tsatoke (1904–1937).[22] In 1929 Jacobsen published a limited-edition portfolio of silkscreen reproductions of their flat, brightly colored watercolor images of traditional costumes and dances.[23] The group exhibited widely, traveled and performed together as a dance troupe, and served as unofficial ambassadors of the university.[24] Blue Eagle would later claim affiliation with Jacobson's Kiowa Five, appearing occasionally with Mopope and Tsatoke. (Although Blue Eagle was not Kiowa, his attendance at the university was aided by the Kiowa educational fund, established by oilman Lew Wentz.[25]) As Blue Eagle explained to audiences who attended his lectures on Native American art: "This form of art is extremely unusual. There are only six of us in the world who can create it."[26]

As it was for the Kiowa Five, for Blue Eagle lecturing and performing were inseparable from his work as an artist. Appearing in Plains Indian regalia, his buckskin tunic and leggings, moccasins, and eagle-feather war bonnet were a link to his Pawnee heritage. As he had as a performer on stage (traveling with the Keith-Orpheum vaudeville circuit and for the Redpath Lyceum or Chautauqua during the previous decade), Blue Eagle narrated the history of Indian painting and delivered speeches in dialect.

In the summer of 1935 Blue Eagle traveled to Oxford University, where he lectured on Native American art and dance for the International Federation of Education. As an indication of Blue Eagle's notoriety, both *Time* magazine and the *New York Times* reported on the event. The *Times'* description of the spectacle Blue Eagle created on deck as he set sail for England is worth quoting at length:

> [Blue Eagle] walked up the gangway unobtrusively, like any tall, well-built, bronzed, American, to sail for Oxford University, England, where

he is to lecture on Indian arts and dances. An official of the French Line who examined the ticket became interested if he had his full tribal regalia with him. Acee Blue Eagle reported he had. Asked if he would mind putting on the costume for the photographers, the Indian went to his cabin and fifteen minutes later emerged in his full regalia with head-dress of blue and white feathers that have been handed down in his tribe since his ancestor, Chief William McIntosh, who died in 1825.

Acee Blue Eagle was besieged by autograph collectors when he appeared on the promenade deck, which was jammed with visitors. He set an example in manners for the crowd that surged around gazing at him.

After standing the siege for fifteen minutes and posing for photographers, returned to his cabin and changed back into his dark suit.[27]

Blue Eagle would note that playing Indian—keeping up the persona—was hard work. After returning from his trip, Blue Eagle was interviewed in a Washington DC newspaper, where he explained: "I got pretty tired of wearing my costume all the time and was certainly glad to get back to the United States where an Indian is allowed to wear civilian clothes."[28]

Blue Eagle's first opportunities to make a public impact with his art came when he joined the Works Progress Administration Federal Art Project in 1934. He painted numerous public murals in Oklahoma, including at post offices in Seminole and Coalgate and the Muskogee Public Library. He also completed numerous private commissions.

In 1935 Blue Eagle took a position as the founding director of the art department at his alma mater, Bacone Indian College. At Bacone, Blue Eagle's distillation of what has become known as "Traditional Indian Painting" was passed on to students including Cheyenne painter Dick West.[29] When Blue Eagle left Bacone in 1938 to pursue his career as an artist full-time, the director's position was taken over by painter Woodrow "Woody" Wilson Crumbo (Potawatomi, 1912–1989).

As Blue Eagle's career developed, he developed a theory of Native American painting—itself a hybrid practice dating to the early years of the twentieth century—that linked the modern art form to putative ancient, indigenous origins. Dressed in full regalia, Blue Eagle explained the antiquity of "Red Indian Art" to eager audiences:

We revived an old culture, and although we study other forms of art, we aim at keeping it absolutely pure and unaffected by them.

It is, however, perfect in its adaptation to European work, and in America, we have been very successful in mural work, while I myself have illustrated two books for American writers.

It is rather like Egyptian art found on tombs—we have similar figures and ceremonials and so on, in which there is always a symbolic meaning.[30]

Blue Eagle rehearsed this history in numerous public lectures, essays, and interviews. He explained that "Indian art" was expressed in every facet of Native life—"ceremonies, stately dances, and . . . prayer."[31] In Blue Eagle's primitivizing argument, Native art was racial in origin—ancient, unchanging, and rooted in the natural world: "His music, his tribal pageants, and, above all, his decorative arts are expressions of a racial consciousness that has developed through untold centuries from his close contact with nature."[32] Blue Eagle argued that the flat, stylized aesthetic of his modern art—and that of other twentieth-century Native painters—was grounded in an aesthetic tradition that was essentially Indian—which appealed to the Indian's innate sensibilities:

Two-dimensional, flat surfaces being one of the outstanding characteristics of Indian Art found in ritual sand paintings, pottery decoration, beadwork, basket weaving, painting on animal skins, etc., the modern Indian painters cling to this style with persistence, not only because it is the style of the early Indian artist and a hallmark of identification, but because two dimensions satisfy the needs of the artist, leaving things out that are not important, thereby in flat and simplicity, creating and lend [sic], a beautiful sophistication to their work. The Indians' feel for color is inherent. All of them possess a remarkable sense of color, doubtless coming from their close association with nature. The modern Indian art is a free, spontaneous expression, not hemmed in by academic isms.[33]

While they had turned to modern materials—paper, canvas, pencils, and paints—twentieth-century Indian artists worked to found a modern style based on the racialized past. Indian artists were characterized, Blue Eagle argued, by a "dogged determination to adhere to the traditional style of their antecedents, and at the same time progress, improve and grow with the times."[34]

Writing in 1938, Blue Eagle described his artistic goals as creating "a permanent record for the future," an archive for a time when Native American culture had passed from memory. He wrote:

> Inevitably, oncoming generations will arise with such questions as: What was the Native American like? What were the moods and modes that went to make up his peculiar civilization? What was his home life like? His battles, his hunts? What type of clothing did he wear? It is hoped that these paintings would be authentic answers to these questions.
>
> In view of the fact that the American Indian is making the transition from his peculiar mode of living to the modern, it is obvious that is a matter of only a short time, relatively speaking, until these questions will arise. Therefore, it is easy to see that this work will be a valuable contribution to authentic knowledge of our American history.[35]

Like other advocates for Native arts in the early twentieth century, Blue Eagle argued that the racial gift of Indian culture was a boon for Americans and for the world, even as that gift was doomed to historical oblivion: "Today the descendants of America's first artists are using modern paints and brushes to revitalize and record for the future, in art form, the cultural and domestic life of the Red Man. The mystic, ceremonial and religious phases, which constitute the only true background of this Continent. And, American culture is again richer for the Indian's contribution."[36]

In the 1950s Blue Eagle attempted to parlay his popularity as an artist and performer—and his narrative of Native origins—into a television career. "Chief Blue Eagle," a children's television show, was short-lived; it ran from September 1954 until May 1955, weekday afternoons on

KTVK in Muskogee. On the program, Blue Eagle, again in buckskin and seated in an "authentic KTVX Indian setting," told legends, introduced Western films, made crafts such as tie racks, and taught young viewers how to juggle. Drawing on a chalkboard shaped like a buffalo hide, he explained Indian sign language and other arcana. As Blue Eagle explained his hopes for the program: "It is my earnest hope to provide young folk with a good and wholesome influence—to give them, at a time when it's sorely needed, a desire for GOOD and GOOD LIVING. . . . I will teach the children the arts and crafts of my people. I will teach them the meanings of the traditional symbols of the tribes—and I will teach them the languages of the Creeks and Cherokees."[37]

Writing to a friend in his familiar dialect, Blue Eagle explained: "I teach 'em to talk Indian words! Sign language—tell 'em Indian legends—teach 'em to make *bows* and arrows!—peace pipes—war bonnets etc."[38] While the show was canceled within a year, Blue Eagle received hundred of letters from fans and from hobbyists across the country asking for information, advice, and translations of English phrases into dialect or sign language. He was happy to oblige each with a response.

By the middle of the decade, Blue Eagle was looking to expand his horizons. During this period, Blue Eagle launched a career as a commercial artist and entrepreneur. He produced a line of popular greeting cards with Paine Studios in El Paso, Texas, beginning in 1954. In 1957 Blue Eagle designed a set of eight glass tumblers and a china pattern featuring historic Oklahoma Indian leaders, which were given away as a sales promotion by the Knox Oil Company. By the late 1950s he was beginning to study sculpture, as well as ceramics and leatherwork. However, by the summer of 1959, Blue Eagle was in poor health and nearly penniless. He died on June 18 of that year of liver disease in a veterans hospital in Muskogee at the age of fifty-two.

Becoming Blue Eagle

For a generation of non-Indian Americans, Blue Eagle was an influential embodiment of Native American identity—a highly visible broker of a pan-Indian identity perhaps best symbolized by his ubiquitous

Plains regalia and eagle-feather headdress. But Blue Eagle's colorful and memorable public persona was a carefully crafted performance, which the artist honed and calibrated over the course of his career. His traditional naming and upbringing were fabricated after the fact. He was born Alex C. McIntosh in 1907 (although some printed sources give birth dates of 1909, 1910, or 1911).[39] He was born to Scottish-Creek parents in Hitchita, a small town in McIntosh County in eastern Oklahoma. Some accounts list his birthplace on the Wichita Reservation north of Anadarko in the western half of the state (possibly owing to the similar sounding words Hitchita and Wichita), which led some to assert a Wichita identity for the artist.[40]

Blue Eagle is often cited as being of Pawnee-Creek heritage, although this is also false. Shortly after the artist's death in 1959, a memorial article attempted to sort out some of the misunderstanding: "Blue Eagle apparently never disputed the accounts stating that he was Pawnee-Creek and was born at the reservation near Anadarko."[41] At other points, Blue Eagle claimed Wichita and Cherokee ancestry. These claims took on a life of their of own in press coverage of the charismatic artist. Blue Eagle never undertook to correct misinformation about his identity.

In the 1970s and 1980s Oklahoma oilman and art collector Arthur Silberman undertook extensive research into Blue Eagle's biography, conducting numerous interviews and researching the artist's genealogy. Silberman noted that Blue Eagle "considered himself 3/4 Indian and 1/4 paleface."[42] In his research notes, Silberman (who was born in 1929 in Antwerp to Jewish parents who in 1941 fled Europe for North America, and thus was no doubt sensitive to the experience of diaspora) noted: "Acee not Pawnee. Assumed Pawnee in order to legitimate use of war bonnet," in which he was often photographed.[43] Blue Eagle claimed a Plains identity to validate his use of an established iconography and regalia, which were more widely recognizable than Creek as pan-Indian markers of identity in the early to mid-twentieth century.

In the published sources, moreover, there is some disagreement whether Blue Eagle's mother or father was Creek, and who was Pawnee. Throughout his career, Blue Eagle recounted several different versions of his family lineage, listing his father, Solomon Macintosh, as Creek-Scottish, and his mother, Mattie Odom, variously as having Cherokee, Choctaw, or Pawnee as well as French and English ancestry. In his 1959 book *Oklahoma Indian Painting-Poetry*, published posthumously, Blue Eagle's biographical sketch reads: "On his father's side, he is a descendent of the McIntosh clan from which most of the Creek Chiefs came."[44] Earlier, as in the *Sooner Magazine* interview quoted above, Blue Eagle claimed the opposite.[45]

Recounting the inconsistencies in Blue Eagle's published biographies is not intended to undermine his claims to Native identity or his authority as a cultural broker in the context of mid-twentieth-century America, or to engage in a search for "authentic" origins. Rather, Blue Eagle's complicated genealogy is likely typical of Native communities in Oklahoma and elsewhere in the aftermath of Indian Removal—formed fundamentally by a history of cross-cultural traffic, mixed heritage, personal and familial loss, hybridity, and reinvention. Blue Eagle's deliberately crafted public persona was a diasporic performative—a knowing play with the recognized signs of "Indianness," loosed from their place-based origins and recast by a settler-colonial culture consumed by "imperialist nostalgia"—embodied the experience of a generation of Native Americans at midcentury, caught between official efforts at assimilation and incorporation and a voracious public hunger for nostalgic, primitivizing simulations.

Indeed, by the early years of the twentieth century, young, educated, and increasingly cosmopolitan Indians had become savvy to the strategic use of the outward signs of Indianness. Loretta Fowler describes, for example, that in 1920 a local Indian Bureau agent warned Indian commissioner Cato Sells that Cheyenne and Arapaho delegates' gifts of a ceremonial pipe and a coat to the visiting commissioner were a calculated ploy for sympathy, and that his Indian charges often exploited "so-called chiefs" as "instruments and tools" in their dealings with whites. Fowler writes, "Cheyennes and Arapahos were aware of the prevailing Indian imagery and not averse to making use of it, particularly the romantic images, in political contexts. They were also prepared to reject this imagery, in the context of both federal and local settler discourses."[46] Not just Cheyennes and Arapahos but Native peoples across Oklahoma and throughout the United States manipulated simulations for political and personal gain.

To be sure, Blue Eagle's public persona embodied the ambivalent position of Native Americans in the twentieth century—caught between white expectations and an emerging political agency—but he also expressed a broader transformation in American culture, which historian Warren Susman described as the shift from a culture of "character" to a culture of "personality"—focused on consumption, leisure, and individualistic self-realization that defined the self as fundamentally performative. As Susman writes of the emerging culture of personality in the 1920s and 1930s:

> Every American was to become a performing self. . . . Everyone was expected to impress and influence with trained and effective speech. Special books and courses were developed to meet demands in this area alone. In these books and articles exercise, proper breathing, sound eating habits, a good complexion, and grooming and beauty aids were all stressed. At the same time, clothing, personal appearance, and "good manners" were important, but there was little interest in morals. Poise and charm top the list of necessary traits, and there was insistence that they could be learned and developed through careful practice. The new stress on the enjoyment of life implied that true pleasure could be attained by making oneself pleasing to others.[47]

We might also consider the notion of the performative "persona" itself. The notion of a "persona" (in Latin, *per* is "through" and *sonare* is "sound") dates to ancient traditions of masked performance. In its classical use it referred to both the actor and the masks employed by the actor to perform different roles. By speaking through a mask the actor assumed a specific theatrical role. An individual might play many roles and inhabit many selves, each of them relationally and situationally authentic.[48]

Blue Eagle's response to a legacy of Indian Removal, cross-cultural traffic, hybridity, and his own family's experience of diaspora was to

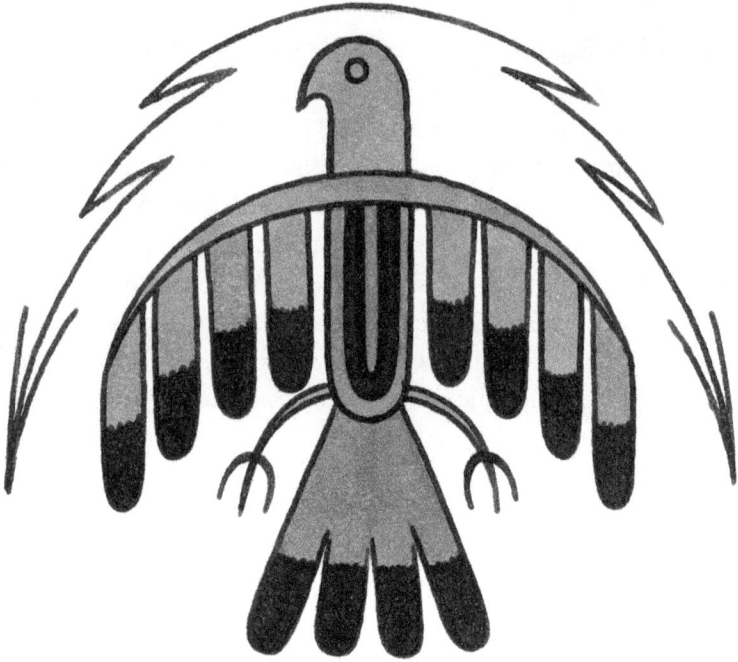

Fig. 13.7. "Blue Eagle Trademark," n.d., painting. Manuscript Acee Blue Eagle Papers: Painting and Drawings by Blue Eagle, National Anthropological Archives, Smithsonian Institution, NAA INV 08765100.

create a persona—a performative self—a project that may have had its origins in his stage career but then became the basis for his public identity as an artist, performer, and public figure. Indeed, many of the details of Blue Eagle's early life may be apocryphal. Stories relate that a boyhood nickname Ah-Say or Ah-See—reportedly "look there!" in Creek language—was "Anglicized" to Acee at his first English-language boarding school. However, Blue Eagle was born Alex C. McIntosh, and Acee more likely derives from the initials A.C. Further evidence of a later date for the invention of the name is the reported story that as an art student at the University of Oklahoma, Alex McIntosh fell under the spell of Spanish painting and signed his early artworks "Antonio Cortez Macintosh." Later, when crafting another persona, the initials A.C. became Ah-Say or Ah-See (cf. Blue Eagle's later speeches and poems in dialect), which resolved

Fig. 13.8. Pin with National Recovery Administration's blue eagle logo, n.d., Author's Collection.

at some point to Acee. The new name, according to one biographical sketch, fit the aspiring artist "like a kid glove."[49]

Likewise, published accounts of the name "Blue Eagle" differ, suggesting another, later invention. Biographical sketches indicate that Alex McIntosh's parents died when the artist was a young boy, and that the youngster was subsequently raised by grandparents, from whom he claimed to have adopted the name "Blue Eagle." Accounts vary here, too.[50] According to some, "Blue Eagle" was the name of a paternal grandfather; others link the name to the artist's maternal line. Moreover, the *Sooner* feature published in 1933 pointed to the similarity of Blue Eagle's name and trademark-like graphic logo he began using in the early 1930s and that of the National Recovery Act, launched in 1933 as one of the first major components of Roosevelt's New Deal. The author noted that the artist was "shoved into the limelight recently by the similarity of his name to the national emblem of recovery."[51] (The Blue Eagle name and logo may have served as a personal symbol of "recovery" for the artist at a key moment of cultural and political revival for Native peoples and communities across North America.) At any rate, by the time of the artist's death, the name Alex C. McIntosh had all but disappeared; the name does not appear at all in Blue Eagle's 1959 anthology *Oklahoma Indian Painting-Poetry*.

Conclusion: Blue Eagle's Legacy?

The reason we no longer think about Blue Eagle might be found in the changing climate of the late 1950s and 1960s—a period that saw dramatic transformations in the Native American art world, as well as in Native American cultural politics generally. Oscar Howe's argument against the notion that Native artists—and Native people—should calibrate their selves to white expectations became a manifesto for the new Native American art that was already emerging. In the aftermath of Howe's letter to the Philbrook Museum—and after Blue Eagle's death—Blue Eagle's work and his showman's persona were seen as being out of step with the changing times. The transformations at the Indian Annual presaged the emergence of a "New Indian Painting," which was seen as more in step with the contemporary circumstances of Indian people, new ideas about what an Indian was, as well as burgeoning political struggles for self-determination, land and treaty claims, and cultural and political militancy. The 1960s saw the bold and thoroughly contemporary paintings of artists such as T. C. Cannon and Fritz Scholder. Blue Eagle and a generation of midcentury Native artists were forgotten or dismissed as "kitsch."

But what does Blue Eagle teach us today? Is he relevant for today's Native artists? Blue Eagle was written out of the history of Native American art, but his performative seems to find a contemporary analogue in the work of Toronto-based painter and performance artist Kent Monkman (Cree, b. 1965), whose alter ego Miss Chief Eagle Testickle is an ironic riff on the history of primitivizing performances by figures such as Molly Spotted Elk (Molly Nelson Dellis, Penobscot, 1903–1977). A significant number of Native American postmodernists

Fig. 13.9. Kent Monkman, "The Emergence of a Legend," 2006. Detail from a series of five photographs (chromogenic prints on metallic paper) 4.5 × 6.5 inches / 16 × 13.25 inches (framed). Signed edition of 25 with 5 proofs in collaboration with photographer Chris Chapman. Courtesy of the artist.

Fig. 13.10. Kent Monkman, "The Emergence of a Legend," 2006. Detail from a series of five photographs (chromogenic prints on metallic paper) 4.5 × 6.5 inches / 16 × 13.25 inches (framed). Signed edition of 25 with 5 proofs in collaboration with photographer Chris Chapman. Courtesy of the artist.

have emerged in recent years, producing work that engages issues of identity and persona, drawing from an archive of mass-media images and stereotypes of the Indian. Monkman's work might teach us to see Blue Eagle's carefully cultivated persona not as kitsch but as a deliberate engagement with pervasive images and received knowledge—a relational and situational Indianness that is not a simulation but rather a canny assertion of what Vizenor terms Native "survivance" amid a settler-colonial culture of personality. At the very least, Blue Eagle's complicated performance deserves our renewed attention.

Notes

1. Gerald Vizenor, *Manifest Manners: Narratives on Postindian Survivance* (Lincoln: University of Nebraska Press, 1999).

2. "Why Injun Artist Me," published posthumously in Acee Blue Eagle, *Oklahoma Indian Painting-Poetry* (Tulsa: Acorn Publishing Company, 1959), n.p. For a discussion of Blue Eagle's poem in the tradition of Native dialect writers, see Timothy Petete and Craig S. Womack, "Thomas E. Moore's *Sour Sofkee* in the Tradition of Muskogee Dialect Writers," *Studies in American Indian Literature* 18, no. 4 (2006): 1–37.

3. Joseph Roach, *It* (Ann Arbor: University of Michigan Press, 2007).

4. "Emperor Takes Back Blue Eagle Art Work," *Muskogee Sunday Phoenix and Times Democrat*, July 11, 1954, Manuscript Acee Blue Eagle Papers, Box 16, National Anthropological Archives, Smithsonian Institution.

5. Bruce Bernstein and W. Jackson Rushing, *Modern by Tradition: Native American Painting in the Studio Style* (Santa Fe: Museum of New Mexico Press, 1995).

6. Howe quoted in Bill Anthes, *Native Moderns: American Indian Painting, 1940–1960* (Durham NC: Duke University Press, 2006), xi–xii.

7. Bill Anthes, "Contemporary Native Artists and International Biennial Culture," *Visual Anthropology Review* 25, no. 2 (2009): 109–27.

8. For a discussion of expressions of diasporic identity in Native American culture, see Bill Anthes, "Learning from Foxwoods: Visualizing the Mashantucket Pequot Tribal Nation," *American Indian Quarterly* 32, no. 2 (2008): 204–18. On the "culture of personality," see Warren Susman, "Personality and the Making of Twentieth Century Culture," in *Culture as History: The Transformation of American Society in the Twentieth Century* (New York: Pantheon Books, 1984), 271–85.

9. Anthes, *Native Moderns*, xi–xii. See also Philip J. Deloria, *Indians in Unexpected Places* (Lawrence: University Press of Kansas, 2004). For alternative histories of modernist art, see the series organized by the Institute of International

Visual Arts, Annotating Art's Histories: Cross-Cultural Perspectives in the Visual Arts, ed. Kobena Mercer (Cambridge MA: MIT Press): *Cosmopolitan Modernisms* (2005); *Discrepant Abstraction* (2006); *Pop Art and Vernacular Cultures* (2007); and *Exiles, Diasporas, and Strangers* (2008).

10. Alongside this fluorescence of material and visual expressions, the Reservation Era also saw the emergence of traditionalist religious movements such as the Ghost Dance, syncretic institutions such as the Native American Church, and the development of other new social forms such as the intertribal powwow and Fourth of July celebrations and other nonceremonial dance and performance events that could take place safely under the watchful eyes of Indian agents and missionary keepers.

11. Moreover, Berlo and Phillips note that drawing distinctions based on Euro-American notions of "art" and "non-art" is itself inherently problematical for pre-nineteenth-century objects produced for community use prior to the large-scale production of objects produced for circulation or trade. As they explain, "the distinction imposes a Western dichotomy on things made by people who do not make the same categorical distinction and whose own criteria for evaluating objects have often differed considerably." Janet C. Berlo and Ruth B. Phillips, *Native North American Art* (Oxford: Oxford University Press, 1998), 7–8.

12. Walter Benjamin, "The Work of Art in the Age of Mechanical Reproduction" (1936), in *Art in Theory, 1900–2000: An Anthology of Changing Ideas*, ed. Charles Harrison and Paul Wood (Malden MA: Blackwell Publishing, 2003), 520–27.

13. See, for example, W. Jackson Rushing, *Native American Art and the New York Avant-Garde: A History of Cultural Primitivism* (Austin: University of Texas Press, 1995); Molly Mullin, *Culture in the Marketplace: Gender, Art, and Value in the American Southwest* (Durham NC: Duke University Press, 2001); and Elizabeth Hutchinson, *The Indian Craze: Primitivism, Modernism, and Transculturation in American Art, 1890–1915* (Durham NC: Duke University Press, 2009).

14. Mourning Dove, *Mourning Dove: A Salishan Autobiography*, ed. Jay Miller (Lincoln: University of Nebraska Press, 1990), 3. Quoted in Frederick Hoxie, "Exploring a Cultural Borderland: Native American Journeys of Discovery in the Early Twentieth Century," *Journal of American History* 79, no. 3 (1992): 969.

15. Hoxie, "Exploring a Cultural Borderland," 969–70. See also Joy Porter, "Progressivism and Native American Self-Expression in the Early Twentieth Century," in this volume.

16. Renato Rosaldo, "Imperialist Nostalgia," *Representations*, no. 26 (1989): 107–22; Alfred Haworth Jones, "The Search for a Usable American Past in the New Deal Era," *American Quarterly* 23, no. 5 (1971): 710–24.

17. "Acee Blue Eagle," *Sooner Magazine* (Norman OK), December 1933, 65.

18. See chapter on Blue Eagle in David Randolph Milsten, *Thomas Gilcrease* (San Antonio: Naylor Company, 1969), 267.

19. "Acee Blue Eagle Indian Artist," University Extension Division, University of Kansas, Lawrence, n.d., Manuscript Acee Blue Eagle Papers, Box 21.

20. Milsten, *Thomas Gilcrease*, 266.

21. For the history of Chilocco and other boarding schools, see K. Tsianina Lomawaima, *They Called It Prairie Light: The Story of Chilocco Indian School* (Lincoln: University of Nebraska Press, 1994).

22. Painter Lois (Bougetah) Smoky (1907–1981) is also often cited as a member of the group, although she did not participate in their dance performances.

23. Oscar Jacobson, *Kiowa Indian Art* (Nice, France: C. Szwedzicki, 1929).

24. Janet Catherine Berlo, "The Szwedzicki Portfolios of American Indian Art, 1929–1952: Kiowa Indian Art, Pueblo Indian Painting, and Pueblo Indian Pottery," *American Indian Art Magazine* 34 (2009): 36–45.

25. *Sooner Magazine*, December 1933, 65.

26. Blue Eagle quoted in the *Oxford Mail*, August 15, 1935, Manuscript Acee Blue Eagle Papers, Box 16. Blue Eagle also claimed membership in the Kiowa Five in his 1959 book, *Oklahoma Indian Painting-Poetry*. In his introduction, "Oklahoma's Finest Indian Artists," Blue Eagle wrote, "The original Kiowa artists were Monroe Tsa-to-ke, Spencer Asah, Steven Mopope, Jack Hokeah, and Bou-ge-tah Smoky. Later this group was joined by James Auchiah and Acee Blue Eagle" (n.p.).

27. "Creek Indian Sails to Teach at Oxford," *New York Times*, August 1, 1935, clipping from Manuscript Acee Blue Eagle Papers, Box 16.

28. Clipping dated December 14, 1936, from Manuscript Acee Blue Eagle Papers, Box 16.

29. Anthes, *Native Moderns*, xi–xii.

30. Blue Eagle quoted in the *Oxford Mail*, August 15, 1935, clipping from Manuscript Acee Blue Eagle Papers, Box 16.

31. Blue Eagle, *Oklahoma Indian Painting-Poetry*, n.p.

32. Acee Blue Eagle, "American Indian Art," undated manuscript, Manuscript Acee Blue Eagle Papers, Box 23.

33. Blue Eagle, "American Indian Art," undated manuscript.

34. Blue Eagle, "American Indian Art," undated manuscript.

35. Acee Blue Eagle, "Plans for Work," October 13, 1938, Manuscript Acee Blue Eagle Papers, Box 24.

36. Acee Blue Eagle, "American Indian Art."

37. *Northeast Oklahoma TV and Radio News*, Muskogee OK, vol. 1, no. 3 (October 10–16, 1954): 3. Clipping from Manuscript Acee Blue Eagle Papers, Box 9.

38. Letter, Blue Eagle to Jack Schurch, n.d., Acee Blue Eagle Papers, Folder 30, Gilcrease Museum, Tulsa.

39. Curiously, no published sources list the artist's middle name, only the initial "C." It is possible that Alex McIntosh's middle name was "Chillicothe," for Chillicothe "Chilli" McIntosh, the artist's paternal ancestor, the former chief of the Creek Nation. See Tamara Liegerot Elder, *Lumhee Holot-Tee: The Art and Life of Acee Blue Eagle* (Edmond OK: Medicine Wheel Press, 2006), 4.

40. "Acee Blue Eagle's Birthplace," *Chronicles of Oklahoma* 39, no. 1 (1961): 80–81.

41. Rob Martindale, "Muskogee Paying Tribute to Blue Eagle," n.d., clipping in Arthur and Shifra Silberman Native American Art Collection, Box 127, Folder 5, Dickinson Research Center, National Cowboy and Western Heritage Museum, Oklahoma City.

42. "Acee Blue Eagle Biographical Data," typescript notes, Silberman Native American Art Collection, Box 127, Folder 4.

43. "Info from [Woody] Crumbo 5/18/75," typescript notes, Silberman Native American Art Collection, Box 127, Folder 4. On Silberman, see Joyce Szabo, *Art from Fort Marion: The Silberman Collection* (Norman: University of Oklahoma Press, 2007), 3.

44. Blue Eagle, *Oklahoma Indian Painting-Poetry*, n.p.

45. Moreover, it should be noted that the name McIntosh has a long history among the Creek (also as noted above), which suggests that Blue Eagle's Creek identity likely came through his paternal line. Elder traces the McIntosh lineage to Captain John McIntosh, who emigrated from Scotland to Georgia in 1736. Elder, *Lumhee Holot-Tee*, 4.

46. Loretta Fowler, *Tribal Sovereignty and the Historical Imagination: Cheyenne-Arapaho Politics* (Lincoln: University of Nebraska Press, 2002), 76.

47. Susman, "Personality and the Making of Twentieth Century Culture," 280–81.

48. My discussion here draws from feminist art criticism. See Lynn Gumpert, introduction to *Inverted Odysseys: Claude Cahun, Maya Deren, Cindy Sherman*, ed. Shelley Rice (Cambridge MA: MIT Press, 1999), x. In a similar vein, Judith Butler has argued that gender is fundamentally performative: "First, what is meant by understanding gender as an impersonation? Does this mean that one puts on a mask or persona, that there is a 'one' who precedes that 'putting on,' who is something other than its gender from the start? Or does this miming, this impersonating precede and form the 'one,' operating as its formative precondition rather than its dispensable artifice?" Judith Butler, *Bodies that Matter: On the Discursive Limits of Sex* (New York: Routledge, 1993), 231.

49. Marcel Lefebvre, "Acee Blue Eagle," *Chronicles of Oklahoma* 39, no. 1 (1961): 81–84.

50. Some sources indicate that Blue Eagle may not have been orphaned.

51. *Sooner Magazine*, December 1933, 65, 68.

Chapter 14

Asserting a Global Indigenous Identity
Native Activism Before and After the Cold War

Daniel M. Cobb

> The United States operates on incredibly stupid premises.
> VINE DELORIA JR., *Custer Died for Your Sins*

The assertion of a global indigenous identity stands among the most potentially transformative aspects of the struggle for tribal sovereignty during the Cold War era (1945–1991). Advocates achieved this, in part, by adopting a language of nationalism, anticolonialism, and decolonization. This critically important rhetorical stance connected the past experiences, present concerns, and future aspirations of American Indians to those of other indigenous peoples in the Western Hemisphere and beyond. It also served as an impetus for locating Native issues in the context of international laws governing human rights, a "postcolonial vision" that Lumbee legal scholar Robert A. Williams Jr. calls "the neglected Fifth Element of the Marshall Model of Indian Rights."[1]

Twenty-first-century perspectives on Native politics attest to the decisiveness of the shift. Mainstream newspapers, radio broadcasts, and websites—from *Indian Country Today* and *News from Indian Country* to *Native America Calling* and *indianz.com*—regularly address global indigenous issues. The National Congress of American Indians (NCAI) and the Assembly of First Nations, national advocacy organizations in the United States and Canada, respectively, have coordinated their efforts since 2001 in keeping with the "Declaration of Kinship and Cooperation among the Indigenous Peoples and Nations of North America." The idea of tribal governments having a presence in United Nations forums strikes us as commonplace rather than controversial. After decades of effort, the UN General Assembly's endorsement of the Declaration on the Rights of Indigenous Peoples no longer represents an insurmountable obstacle but a battle won.[2]

But how much do we really know about the antecedents to these accomplishments? How well do we understand the history that makes the assertion of an international identity a *reassertion*, the connection to other indigenous peoples a *reconnection*, and the locating of issues in a global context a *relocating*? Political scientist Benedict Anderson's work on nation-states as "imagined communities" allows us to see the articulation of Native and global indigenous rights movements as a *reimagining* as well. Native nations, no less than those of Europe, Africa, Asia, or the Western Hemisphere, represent imagined political communities. The contemporary individuals, governments, and organizations involved in the tribal sovereignty movement represent not "a new" but "the next" generation. They continue a centuries-long tradition of constructing and reconstructing the boundaries of nationhood, of defining and redefining its meaning. Some have done so consciously and others have not.[3]

This chapter acknowledges the deep history of thinking globally about the rights of indigenous peoples and offers a detailed look at how that process evolved over the course of the twentieth century. A concluding section asks why the legacy of this important political tradition remains unfixed and uncertain, even as it continues into the twenty-first century. The central characters include individuals associated with the Society of American Indians (SAI), Inter-American Indian Institute, National Congress of American Indians (NCAI), Association on American Indian Affairs (AAIA), National Indian Youth Council, International Indian Treaty Council (IITC), and Working Group on Indigenous Populations. Does it make sense to place these historical figures and the larger political tradition to which they contributed

in a diasporic context? Dakota intellectual Charles Eastman (Ohiyesa) answered that question when, at the beginning of the twentieth
century, he described himself as a "stranger in a strange country."[4]
In a physical sense, many of the Native individuals featured in this
chapter lived *in* diaspora—that is, they resided in communities far removed from the ancestral homelands of their people. Others stayed
but found the world around them made strange *by* diaspora—exiled
without ever leaving. Both circumstances emerged from the fact that
in the present-day United States, colonists arrived intent on becoming the new Natives.[5]

Antecedents

American Indians did not need the presence of Europeans to engage
in international politics. Much has been written about whether concepts such as "nation" and "sovereignty," given their European deri-
vation, adequately describe indigenous self-conceptions at the time
of contact. Whatever one concludes, it does not change the fact that
Native communities had clear senses of community, belonging, governance, law, authority, exchange, and place for themselves and in
contradistinction to neighbors both near and far. From this essential definition of self and others grew diplomatic relationships, trade
agreements, and political and military alliances that certainly can
be thought of as the hallmarks of international affairs. The arrival
of newcomers—be they English, Dutch, French, Spanish, American,
Russian, Canadian, or indigenous—altered the dynamics of these relations, but they did not create them sui generis.[6]

    Consider the proliferation of alliances among indigenous commu-
nities during the two centuries around contact with Europe. The term
"tribe," for instance, is not autochthonous but instead a designation ascribed to Native people, and many of the groups defined as such lived
in autonomous villages bound together by linguistic and kinship ties.
The Creek Confederacy in the Southeast, the Iroquois Confederacy,
or Haudenosaunees, in the Northeast, the Council of Three Fires organized by the Ojibwes, Odawas, and Potawatomis in the Great Lakes
region, the United Indian Nations in the Ohio Country, and the All

Indian Pueblo Council in the Southwest represented intentional confederations consisting of autonomous political communities. More re-
vealing still, these confederations did not hesitate to turn outward to
engage in the politics of European empire when it became necessary
to do so. Indeed, some were born of it. Through diplomatic encounters in Native North America and across the Atlantic, they leveraged
their allied strength in an attempt to manipulate European nations
whose far-flung geopolitical contests for global supremacy threatened
their lands, resources, and livelihoods. Indigenous communities continued to forge similar alliances for mutual defense in regions from
the Northern and Southern Plains to the Pacific Northwest throughout the nineteenth and early twentieth centuries.[7]

During this entire period, nation-to-nation agreements, embodied
in the treaty-making process, reinforced the fact that the same tradition governing international relations elsewhere in the world governed
them in Native North America. The thrust of United States Indian law
from the early nineteenth century forward, however, focused on do-
mesticating Native communities. The application of the term "tribe"
and the use of the modified "tribal nations" revealed the ethnocentric underpinnings of European and later American attitudes toward
indigenous communities. Supreme Court chief justice John Marshall
gave voice to them when he answered his own question of whether the
Cherokee Nation constituted a "foreign state in the sense of the constitution" in *Cherokee Nation v. Georgia* (1831). "In general, nations not
owing a common allegiance are foreign to each other," he reasoned.
"But the relation of the Indians to the United States is marked by peculiar and cardinal distinctions which exist nowhere else." "Though
the Indians are acknowledged to have an unquestionable, and here-
tofore, unquestioned right to the lands they occupy . . . it may well be
doubted whether those tribes which reside within the acknowledged
boundaries of the United States can, with strict accuracy, be denominated foreign nations," Marshall continued. "They may, more correctly, perhaps, be denominated domestic dependent nations."[8]

Native people controlled more than half the North American continent in 1832, making Marshall's definition of the limited nature of

tribal sovereignty aspirational at best. Nonetheless, as the U.S. government increased its political, economic, and military power over Native America, it also gained the ability to reinforce this definition of indigenous communities as less than fully sovereign. By the late nineteenth century, Supreme Court justices wrote opinions that referred to Indians in the infantilizing language of wards and children, as savage and backwards, as helpless and hapless, as incompetent and incapable of being independent. It should come as no surprise that the United States proclaimed an end to treaty making in 1871. In time, Marshall's notion of "domestic dependent nations" paved the way for pernicious ideas such as the doctrine of plenary power, which held that the U.S. Congress had the "right" to take whatever action it chose—regardless of tribal consent—so long as it deemed that action to be in a community's "best interest."[9]

By the early twentieth century, federal lawmakers had performed a work of magic that would have stunned even the great Harry Houdini, a contemporary of theirs. For through legislative, executive, and judicial mechanisms, they created an illusion in which the only "real" nation in the United States was the United States. With regard to the consequences, anthropologist Thomas Biolsi observed, "The term 'nation' disappeared from discourse in Indian affairs, and it would be many decades before anyone would speak again—at least in English—of native sovereignty." Citizens of indigenous nations did not fail to see these deceptions for what they were. Quite to the contrary, tribes went on asserting their treaty rights and refused to abandon the legitimate exercise of self-governance and self-determination.[10]

The advent of the First World War (1914–18) and the rise of Wilsonian internationalism reignited—or at least gave more visibility to—appeals to a global indigenous identity. Consider the efforts of Robert Yellowtail, a Crow tribal leader who appeared before Congress in 1919 to defend his reservation from being reduced through hostile legislative action. "Mr. Chairman, I hold that the Crow Indian Reservation is a separate semisovereign nation in itself, not belonging to any State, nor confined within the boundary lines of any State of the Union," he argued. "The history of all nations tell us that they have grown only better just in proportion as they have grown free, and I am here, gentlemen, to advocate that proposition for the American Indian, who still is held in bondage as a political slave."[11]

The Society of American Indians, formed in 1911, also drew upon the language of internationalism, national self-determination, and anticolonialism. Perhaps ironically, some of its leading members, including Yavapai physician Carlos Montezuma, used the First World War to demand U.S. citizenship for Native people. When Indians fought, they fought as Indians, he argued, but they also fought as Americans. In light of this, he saw the denial of U.S. citizenship abhorrent. Other tribes, such as the Standing Rock Sioux, Ojibwes, Pamunkeys, Mattaponis, Goshutes, and Creeks, had members resist the draft, while the Iroquois independently declared war upon the Triple Alliance and agreed to serve as allies. The Iroquois, in particular, had no interest in gaining U.S. citizenship as a result.[12]

Another critical dimension of Native activism during and after the war grew out of President Woodrow Wilson's Fourteen Points. Americans adopted everything from strict isolationist and neutral stances to limited nonmilitary interventionism during the first three years of the war. Enunciated in a special address to Congress in January 1918, the Fourteen Points gave meaning to American participation in the Great War. Wilson believed that the sacrifice in American lives and national wealth would prevent another war of its magnitude. Among the principles of the Fourteen Points were the right of national self-determination, the adjustment of colonial claims, and the formation of an international body "for the purpose of affording mutual guarantees of political independence and territorial integrity to great and small states alike." This internationalist position ran counter to the swelling isolationist impulse in the United States, and Congress refused membership in the League of Nations.[13]

That did not stop Indian rights advocates such as Dakota writers and Society of American Indian members Zitkala Ša and Charles Eastman from seizing upon Wilsonian ideals to defend Indian rights. In the pages of SAI's *American Indian Magazine*, Ša called upon the spirit of the negotiations following the armistice to advocate for Indian rights. "The eyes of the world are upon the Peace Conference sitting in Paris. Under the sun a new epoch is being staged," she proclaimed. "Little peoples are to be granted the right of self determination!" Charles Eastman, who along with W. E. B. DuBois also attended the First Universal Races Congress in London in 1911, called upon the U.S. government to fulfill its role as "the champion of the 'little peoples'" by extending full citizenship rights to American Indians. "The Indian Bureau, instead of being the servant of the people and of the Indians in accordance with treaty stipulations, has grown into a petty autocracy," Eastman contended. "We do not ask for territorial grant or separate government. We ask only to enjoy with Europe's sons the full privileges of American citizenship."[14]

A less conciliatory attempt at gaining international recognition came from the Iroquois living in the Six Nations Reserve on the Grand River in Canada. During the First World War, the Canadian government conscripted Iroquois citizens to serve in the military and then set aside portions of the reserve for veterans to own upon their return. The arbitrary enfranchisement and removal of Indian status, authorized by amendments to the Indian Act, further incensed the Confederacy Council of the Six Nations. Their inability to work through these violations of Iroquois sovereignty via the Canadian Department of Indian Affairs prompted Cayuga hereditary chief Deskaheh (Levi General), speaker of the Confederacy Council, to take their case before the League of Nations in Geneva in 1923. At the heart of the conflict rested the question of whether the Iroquois were allies or subjects of the Crown. Despite winning the support of key member states, Deskaheh could not convince the League of Nations to accept the argument that the Six Nations represented an independent state. After more than a year of lobbying, Deskaheh returned home in defeat and died shortly thereafter.[15]

The 1930s brought renewed political interest in hemispheric thinking about indigenous peoples. In 1934 President Franklin Delano Roosevelt inaugurated the New Deal and appointed an eccentric reformer named John Collier as commissioner of Indian affairs to oversee its implementation in Indian Country. Collier did this and more. In addition

to driving the Indian Reorganization Act through Congress, he spear-
headed the formation of the Inter-American Indian Institute (IAII)
in 1940. The IAII provided a means through which the governments
belonging to the Pan American Union (predecessor to the Organization of American States) coordinated their policies toward indigenous
communities and collaborated on research projects. While this reflected Collier's strong belief in the connection between the indigenous
peoples of North and South America, it did not fulfill its promise. In
the final analysis, the IAII existed first to promote social scientific research in areas of health, medicine, and social psychology. Moreover,
the IAII typically avoided taking public stances on matters of indigenous political rights.[16]

The IAII did, however, shape the thinking of a generation of Native activists, one of the most important being D'Arcy McNickle, a
Flathead tribal member who began his tenure in the Bureau of Indian Affairs (BIA) in 1935. Six years later, President Roosevelt established
the National Indian Institute to represent the United States to the
IAII, and Collier appointed McNickle to serve on several occasions
as the BIA's liaison and acting director. Clearly affected by this exposure to hemispheric conceptualizations of indigenous peoples, Mc-
Nickle contributed essays in the IAII's journal, *América Indígena*, into
the 1950s. He also worked with other BIA employees to found the National Congress of American Indians. Established in 1944, the NCAI
stands as the oldest and most influential pan-tribal Indian rights organization in the United States. McNickle's contributions tended to
be behind the scenes rather than center stage, but this did not lessen
their impact. Instead, he emerged as one of the Cold War era's pre-
eminent voices in favor of extending the model of international aid
to Native America.[17]

Patriotic Parallels

Between 1954 and 1962, tensions between the United States and the
Soviet Union ran extraordinarily high. It saw the Eisenhower administration articulate the idea of "brinkmanship," the advent of "mutually assured destruction," the expansion of covert counterinsurgency

campaigns in Latin America, the Middle East, and Southeast Asia, the construction of the Berlin Wall, the Bay of Pigs fiasco, the Cuban missile crisis, and the long descent into Vietnam. The ideological and economic struggle between capitalism and communism simultaneously played out in the realm of humanitarian aid. Here the contest revolved around winning the "hearts and minds" of what policy makers called the "developing nations" of the "Third World."[18]

Domestic contests over what freedom and democracy meant at home carried profound implications for the ability of the United States to make and defend claims to moral superiority. Over the past several years, scholars have demonstrated how many interested parties aggressively pointed this out—and how central the domestic became to the international as a result. From the Truman administration forward, federal policy makers understood the stakes. Soviet propaganda suggested that the Russians did, as well. And if that were not enough, civil rights activists did not fail to point out the importance of racial justice for black Americans either.[19] Within this charged political environment, proponents of tribal sovereignty related the concerns of reservation-based tribal communities to international affairs. As with the black freedom struggle, they hoped to move federal-Indian relations from the margins to the center of politics in Cold War America.[20]

From 1945 to 1961, the National Congress of American Indians and Association on American Indian Affairs emerged at the forefront of the effort. Neither organization immediately seized upon decolonization as an obvious metaphor for improving upon the status quo. The parallel with international politics evolved in uneven, inconsistent, and sometimes contradictory ways. Moreover, the meanings assigned to the various metaphors shifted along with the social, cultural, political, and economic milieu of the 1950s, 1960s, and 1970s. A closer look at the rhetoric of the NCAI and AAIA in the wake of the Second World War suggests the complexity of the shift.

In the immediate aftermath of the war, Native rights advocates overwhelmingly drew patriotic parallels with U.S. foreign policy— and for good reason. The Allies had finally emerged victorious after several years of bloodshed in the European and Pacific theaters, and the nation seemed for the moment to be beyond reproach as a beacon of freedom. That sense of moral superiority revealed its darker side, as it fueled sentiments of national self-righteousness and mobilized interest groups that drew upon intolerance as their raison d'être. Anticommunism embodied both of these impulses at their worst and contributed to an all-out attack on dissent in the United States. Some advocates of Native rights fully internalized this worldview, while those less persuaded understood what implications it carried for them. They would have to critique the present state of affairs and call for reform delicately—in ways that would not be perceived as anything less than 100 percent American, to use the parlance of the day.[21]

Be that as it may, Indian Country faced a host of crises that needed to be confronted immediately. The legacies of colonialism manifested themselves across Native America: an educational system controlled by outsiders and predicated on the doctrine of assimilation; inadequate health care; dire poverty and virtually no federal efforts to promote economic development; a tribal land base that in many areas had been allotted and fractionated so thoroughly that it could not support a family, much less a nation; rampant corruption and mismanagement on the part of BIA agency superintendents and employees; disempowered tribal governments and internal political divisions at the local level. To make matters worse, some members of Congress, many of whom represented western states, pressed for a policy called "termination," in which the federal government would no longer recognize its legal relationship with and responsibilities toward tribal communities. This malicious effort sought to refute tribal sovereignty in order to open reservation lands and resources to individual and corporate exploitation.[22]

To combat the threat of termination and advocate for reform, the Association on American Indian Affairs appealed to the public's sense of humanitarianism. But they went further by suggesting that promoting the welfare and defending the rights of Native people was not merely an ethical thing to do, it was the *patriotic* thing to do. Consider an AAIA poster featuring a photograph of several Native American soldiers marching somewhere in the Pacific theater. Words across the top of the picture read: "American Indians Protect You! Do You Protect Them?" By connecting the narrative of Native rights to the struggle to defeat threats to American security posed by totalitarianism, the AAIA tapped into the rhetoric of the "double victory." In the spirit of reciprocity, they beseeched Americans to do their part to protect freedom in a dangerous world, just as Native soldiers had done for them.[23]

The National Congress of American Indians adopted the language of patriotism to appeal for reform, as well. Indeed, NCAI members could make an even more legitimate claim upon the need for reciprocity, given that so many of them had served in the military. Among its leaders were veterans of the twentieth century's two global wars. A critical problem the NCAI grappled with revolved around how to present Native communities as sovereign nations without alienating a general public that rarely thought about Indians, much less their unique legal place within the federal system. The idea of nations within a nation simply did not occur to the general population, and if it did, it would have been deemed unfathomable, abhorrent, or both. This sentiment drove proponents of termination like Nevada senator George Malone, who likened tribalism to communism and Utah senator Arthur V. Watkins, who argued that the only way to secure "equal rights" for Native people would be to destroy every vestige of tribal sovereignty.[24]

This inflammatory rhetoric and irrational logic put the NCAI in a precarious position. The organization needed to advocate for tribal sovereignty in ways that avoided charges of un-Americanism. Historian Paul Rosier has shown how NCAI leaders did this via "A Declaration of Indian Rights." Issued in response to a round of new termination legislation in 1954, the NCAI statement contended that "some of *our fellow Americans* think that our reservations are places of confinement." "Nothing could be farther from the truth," it continued. "Reservations do not imprison us. They are ancestral homelands, retained by us for our perpetual use and enjoyment. We feel we must assert our right to maintain ownership in our own way, and terminate it only by our consent."[25]

The NCAI also took advantage of broad support for the European Recovery Act, popularly known as the Marshall Plan. In mainstream newspapers, the NCAI solicited support with a cartoon featuring two Indians sitting on a dock, empty-handed and bewildered. Meanwhile, in the distance a ship steamed toward the horizon, surrounded by dollar signs with the words "3½ Billion Foreign Aid" above it. In the top center, the heading read "Leave Some for Us!!" The NCAI also reminded readers of where to focus their priorities: "Help! Remind Our Government That Many Solemn Obligations Still Remain Unfilled at Home." If the United States could expend capital on rebuilding European nations and provide training and technical assistance abroad, the NCAI reasoned, then surely it could contribute to the economic revitalization of Indian Country. The allusion to nation building may not have been obvious, but it was there nonetheless.[26]

As the push for termination accelerated during the 1950s, the NCAI seized upon aid to Puerto Rico as still another alternative. Considered an "unincorporated territory" of the United States, this small island's economy relied primarily on agriculture. "Operation Bootstrap," initiated in 1947, provided a host of incentives to American industries as a mechanism to promote rapid industrialization. By the mid-1950s, it appeared to be a tremendous success. Operation Bootstrap raised the standard of living for the island's inhabitants, fostered a strong tourist industry, and led to the construction of new hospitals, schools, and infrastructure. Hopeful that a similar kind of economic development project could be started in Indian Country, the NCAI sent delegates on a tour of Puerto Rico in 1958. The organization also worked with Congressman E. Y. Berry of South Dakota on legislation patterned after Operation Bootstrap. After many years of fruitless effort, as well as evidence that the modernization of Puerto Rico came at considerable cost to Puerto Rican laborers, the NCAI abandoned the campaign.[27]

Though the AAIA only modestly joined the NCAI on advancing Puerto Rico as a model for economic development, its members did refer to other pressing matters of foreign policy in their newsletter. "We petition the Administration and the new 85th Congress to face the American Indian problem and its meaning," read an editorial appearing in *Indian Affairs*. "Looked at through a haze of wish-fulfillment, it is only the little question of 450,000 stiff-necked people who would have no trouble if they would simply stop being Indians. Seen in this way, the Indian question is hardly an item for a Governmental agenda that will include the authorization to send armed forces to block Soviet imperialism." "Looked at squarely," the editorial countered, "the Indian problem is a problem of conquest and colonialism, deeply involving us and our ideal of ourselves as a nation." Taking a stance in opposition to termination, the AAIA asserted, "The cruel situation should be met with humane measures by the Administration and Congress." "The warmhearted electorate will not be more niggardly with the dispossessed American Indians than with the dispossessed Hungarians," they reasoned. "The United States is well able to take care of both and to support an economic aid program in the Middle East to boot."[28]

The connection to nations emerging from colonialism crystallized in the 1950s, in large measure as a response to President Harry S. Truman's Point 4 Program. In his inaugural address in 1949, Truman pledged to provide U.S. support in the form of training and technical assistance to Latin America, Africa, and the Middle East. This initiative, carried out under the auspices of the Agency for International Development, was guided by what historian Michael Latham calls "modernization ideology." Though clothed in the rhetoric of altruistic humanitarianism, it grew out of a profoundly ethnocentric conception of American cultural, economic, and political superiority. It also had geopolitical value vis-à-vis the Soviet Union's own attempts to build alliances in these regions. If America could show so-called underdeveloped nations how to compete in and benefit from the global market economy, it could also demonstrate to the rest of the world the advantages of capitalism over communism.[29]

Over the course of the next few years, a movement for an American Indian Point 4 Program gained momentum. In 1951 Flathead author and NCAI founding member D'Arcy McNickle called for a plan modeled after the Agency for International Development. The idea gained new life in 1954 and again in 1956 and 1957 when the AAIA and NCAI joined forces to press for the adoption of Senate Concurrent

Resolution 3, the "American Indian Point Four Program." AAIA executive director LaVerne Madigan's personal epiphany in relation to the concept captured the general mood of those who supported it. After reading a newspaper story regarding President Dwight D. Eisenhower's intention of extending Point 4 to economically depressed areas within the United States, Madigan wrote to a colleague, "It seemed to me that the Point IV angle gives us a much more positive, challenging issue on which to hang our resounding appeal for Indian rights. . . . After all, Point IV is modern America at its best and most sympathetic." For Madigan, the AAIA, and the NCAI, Point 4 epitomized the patriotic parallel with American foreign policy.[30]

The joint AAIA-NCAI drive for Senate Concurrent Resolution 3 ultimately foundered, but the Point 4 analogy did not disappear. D'Arcy McNickle later infused the text of the "Declaration of Indian Purpose," the document drafted for the American Indian Chicago Conference in June 1961, with its spirit. The final version of the declaration made an overt connection to other nationalist movements. It proclaimed that tribal communities meant "as earnestly as any small nation or ethnic group . . . to hold on to identity and survival" and emphasized the central importance of self-government, treaties, the preservation and reconsolidation of the tribal land base, and the fulfillment of trust obligations. In an effort to reinforce the notion that theirs was no small concern, the Declaration of Indian Purpose asserted, "The problem we raise affects the standing which our nation sustains before world opinion." In August 1962, delegates from the Chicago conference presented their collective call for self-determination to President John F. Kennedy at a formal ceremony on the South Lawn of the White House.[31]

The Declaration of Indian Purpose did not immediately impact policy as the organizers of the Chicago conference hoped. Indeed, the Kennedy and Lyndon B. Johnson administrations' emphasis on Native issues, in general, fell short of their high expectations. Advocates of tribal self-determination sustained the connection with the international scene nonetheless. Vine Deloria Jr., a Standing Rock Sioux who served as the NCAI's executive director from 1964 to 1967, consistently urged the organization's members to "talk the language of the larger world" and to "say we're nations." Cognizant of the Point 4 analogy, his successor, John Belindo (Kiowa-Navajo), followed suit. In a newspaper editorial published in the *Oklahoma Journal*, Belindo reinvoked its spirit. "The 'American Indian Point IV Program' is a dream that is still far from becoming a reality," he wrote. "But it promises to be the answer to the Indians' world—an impoverished underdeveloped country in the midst of the richest nation in history. . . . In a country that somehow left them behind, the American Indian Point IV program seems to be a plan of rehabilitation that would allow them to catch up."[32]

Confronting Colonialism, 1961–1968

By the mid-1960s, the NCAI's and AAIA's patriotic parallels lost their edge. The latter lost two of its most influential leaders to tragic deaths and found its ability to influence federal Indian policy slipping. Meanwhile, under Vine Deloria's direction, the NCAI adopted a more critical stance toward the Johnson administration. Platitudes about Marshall Plans and Operation Bootstraps disappeared from the NCAI *Sentinel* during the mid-1960s. In its place, Deloria inserted straight talk about self-government, self-determination, treaty rights, nationalism, and sovereignty. In response to the controversial Indian Resources and Development Act of 1967, a piece of legislation that targeted trust lands as collateral on loans to entice outside industries onto reservations, the NCAI called once again for an approach modeled after international aid to emerging nations. "Let us develop a model for the former colonial world and avoid their mistakes," an NCAI resolution stated.[33]

During this transitional period, another group of American Indian activists emerged. They were even less persuaded by arguments in favor of the inherent goodness of development and more circumspect about the promise of modernization. They called for decolonization. Here again caution is necessary. These assertions mislead insofar as they do not acknowledge the messy process through which ideas gain articulation. Rather than linear, simple, and methodical, it proved to be sprawling, complicated, multifaceted, and exploratory. Some thoughts were nonstarters, others false starts. More than a few were half-baked. A sense of this messy reality can be found in the experiences of Native students involved in the Workshop on American Indian Affairs and National Indian Youth Council (NIYC).

The workshop originated in the concerns of social scientists at the University of Chicago. As termination continued to cast its long shadow over Indian Country during the 1950s, they proposed a summer program for Native college students which, they hoped, would cultivate a generation of leaders to see their communities through these perilous times, resist termination, and, if necessary, accommodate to the radically changed circumstances of having the federal government turn its back on its trust obligations to tribes. Between its inaugural year in 1956 and the early 1960s, the Workshop on American Indian Affairs metamorphosed into something far more ambitious. The six-week summer program, held most years at the University of Colorado, became a meeting place and ideological training ground for many of the people involved in the founding of the National Indian Youth Council, the leading edge of the Red Power movement.[34]

A number of different scholars led the workshops during the 1950s. But Cherokee anthropologist Robert K. Thomas focused the curriculum on comparative colonialisms. From his perspective, American Indians represented a folk people who had been forced to adjust to being overwhelmed by an urban industrial society, a position he later developed in an essay entitled "Colonialism: Classic and Internal." The workshops afforded an opportunity for Thomas and others to assign readings and present lectures that encouraged students to confront the devastating impact this system—and the culture that produced it—had on tribal values and identities the world over.[35]

During the 1962 workshop, Thomas wrote essay questions that asked students to "Describe the consequences for the world and social relations of a folk people under a colonial administration." Others asked, "Is it possible for a government, given a colonial situation to determine the destiny of the governed people and also to terminate their colonial status with success?"; "Using examples, relate colonialism to your community"; and "How did nationalism come about and what are some of the advantages of Nationalism?" Thomas made the connection again in 1963 with this prompt: "Compare the structure and consequences of colonialism or minority group status in one of the following: India, Kenya, Ghana, Maori in New Zealand, aboriginal people in the Philippines, with the structure and consequences of the relationship between either American Indians or a specific group and the wider American society." While some students resisted the analogies, others wrote essays that demonstrated how deeply they felt the connections.[36]

The youths at the workshop who most aggressively pursued the parallel with colonialism also belonged to the National Indian Youth Council. The NIYC originated from the optimism and disillusionment they felt after attending the American Indian Chicago Conference in June 1961. By the mid-1960s, the organization took a more outspoken stance in protesting the state of federal Indian affairs and adopted direct action techniques similar to those found in the black freedom struggle. This included an alliance with the fishing rights movement in the Pacific Northwest that culminated in fish-ins and large demonstrations in Washington State. The NIYC also committed itself to raising awareness of Native rights on college campuses, congressional hearings, and other public forums.[37]

The language deployed by Clyde Warrior, a Ponca from Oklahoma who attended the workshop twice and served as NIYC president, epitomized the abandonment of the patriotic parallels of the past. Speaking before non-Indian college students, he referred disparagingly to the "act of America" and referred to many of the participants of the Chicago conference as "finks" and "little brown Americans" whose blind patriotism caused them to "go around pledging the allegiance." In September 1966, upon assuming the presidency, he told reporters at a press conference that NIYC intended to "seek radical and drastic changes in Indian affairs in order that the nature of our situation be recognized and made the basis of policy and action." From his point of view, the federal agencies in control of Indian affairs were not only structurally flawed but "full of white colonialists, racists, fascists, uncle tomahawks, and bureaucrats . . . who could not care less about the average Indian." "Negroes, Mexican-Americans, and Puerto Ricans could only take colonialism, exploitation, and abuse for so long; then they did something about it," he added. "Will American Indians wait until their reservations and lands are eroded away and they are forced into urban ghettos before they start raising hell with their oppressors???"[38]

The Poor People's Campaign from April to late June 1968 served as the pinnacle of this generation's brand of anticolonialism. Health complications prevented Clyde Warrior from attending. In his absence, NIYC executive director Mel Thom, a Walker River Paiute, and Hank Adams, an Assiniboine central to the fishing rights campaigns, conveyed the sentiments of the Native participants in the campaign. The moment of crystallization came when Thom presented a position paper before interior secretary Stewart Udall and commissioner of Indian affairs Robert L. Bennett (Oneida). "Our chief spokesman in the federal government, the Department of Interior, has failed us. In fact it began failing us from its very beginning," Thom stated. "The Interior Department began failing us because it was built upon and operates under a racist, immoral, paternalistic, and colonialistic system." "There is no way to improve upon racism, immorality and colonialism; it can only be done away with," he continued. "Indian people have the right to separate and equal communities within the American system—our own communities, that are institutionally and politically separate, socially equal and secure within the American system."[39]

Continuing the Tradition, 1968–2007

Throughout the remainder of the decade, Native rights organizations persistently advocated for a global indigenous identity predicated on the shared experience of being subjected to colonialism. The National Indian Youth Council pursued connections with Indian communities in Latin America. The organization's newsletter, *Americans Before Columbus*, revealed an avid interest in finding common ground during the 1970s and after. Meanwhile, peripatetic author Stan Steiner's *The New Indians*, published in 1968, brought the voices of American Indian nationalists—the first generation of NIYC leaders in particular—to the reading public. The period between 1961 and 1968, in his mind, represented a collective journey in which the idea of nationalism, which had been thoroughly "submerged" but never "destroyed," resurfaced through their identification with anticolonial movements the world over. While Steiner overstated the case when he claimed that the NCAI's statement in January 1967 stood as "the first time in the history of Indian affairs" that "tribes had publicly likened their status to that of colonial nations," he captured a larger truth about what had transpired after the Second World War.[40]

Former NCAI executive director Vine Deloria Jr., one of Steiner's inspirations, gave the Indian rights movement greater visibility when he published *Custer Died for Your Sins* in 1969. This groundbreaking "manifesto" took no prisoners and advanced "modern tribalism" as one of its guiding analytical themes. Deloria pursued a similar line of argumentation in *Behind the Trail of Broken Treaties: An Indian Declaration of Independence.* "The proposal to restore the Indian tribes to a status of quasi-international independence with the United States acting as their protector strikes most Americans as either radical or ridiculous," he observed in a chapter entitled "The Size and Status of Nations." "In fact, it is neither." The chapter, and the book taken as a whole, set out to demonstrate how the nations of Native North America compared favorably to small nation-states across the globe, from Belgium and Luxembourg to Barbados and Zambia. In characteristically perspicacious fashion, Deloria explained why "a return to the sovereign relationship" between tribes and the United States had "every justification from an international point of view."[41]

With that said, it was one thing to make an intellectual case for nationalism and quite another to work out a program for action. The creation of such a mechanism through the United Nations stands as the hallmark achievement of the post-1960s era. Established in 1945, the UN brought to fruition the ideals and aspirations of the defunct League of Nations. But like its forebear, it failed to provide formal representation for indigenous peoples among the family of nations, despite the acceleration of the decolonization movement during the 1950s and 1960s. Two organizations founded in the 1970s, the World

Council of Indigenous Peoples and the International Indian Treaty Council, took it upon themselves to remedy the UN's oversight. They continued the longstanding tradition of sending Native diplomats to the center of global geopolitics in hopes of securing the rights of indigenous peoples. And this in turn gave rise to the Working Group on Indigenous Populations and the crafting of the Declaration on the Rights of Indigenous Peoples.[42]

By the early 1970s, the American Indian Movement (AIM) exploded onto the political scene. Its militant action and radical rhetoric struck contemporary observers as unique, unprecedented, and unrivaled. For contemporary observers and later scholars, AIM seemed to sweep away all that had come before it. It represented a rupture with the past—the beginning of Indian protest and activism. This could not have been further from the truth. Yes, AIM used a language that bespoke the radicalization of racial politics in America. And yes, its members also managed to grasp the attention of the public in a way that earlier activists had not. But they were also inheritors of a tradition of dissent, direct action, and ideational parallel making. Many people are aware of AIM's most visible acts of resistance—the occupation of the Bureau of Indian Affairs building and issuing of the Twenty Points in 1972, the Wounded Knee confrontation in 1973, the Mount Rushmore and military base occupations, and the Longest Walk in 1978. Less well known but no less important was the creation of the International Indian Treaty Council.[43]

In June 1974 an estimated five thousand representatives from more than ninety indigenous nations gathered on the Standing Rock Sioux Reservation to forge an alliance that would allow indigenous peoples of the Western Hemisphere to speak in one voice. The document they produced to convey their shared vision carried an instructive title, "The Declaration of Continuing Independence." Echoing the words of Mel Thom and AIM's Twenty Points, the declaration stated, "World concern must focus on all colonial governments to the end that sovereign people everywhere shall live as they choose; in peace with dignity and freedom." In 1977 the IITC gained consultative status with the United Nations Economic and Social Council as a nongovernmental organization (NGO). It has steadfastly promoted the human rights of indigenous peoples in a number of international forums ever since.[44]

Movement within the United Nations itself intersected with the activism of the IITC and the World Council of Indigenous Peoples during the 1970s and 1980s. In 1982 the UN formed the Working Group on Indigenous Populations within the Subcommission on the Promotion and Protection of Human Rights to advance the human rights for indigenous peoples agenda. The Working Group was charged with "facilitating and encouraging dialogue between governments and fundamental freedoms of indigenous peoples," reporting to the subcommission on events relating to indigenous rights, and giving "particular attention to changes in international standards relating to the human rights of indigenous peoples."[45] The efforts of the Working Group, the product of robust consultation with numerous indigenous representatives, resulted in the Draft Declaration on the Rights of Indigenous Peoples in 1993.

Though bolstered by the inauguration of the International Decade of the World's Indigenous Peoples in 1995, it took more than twelve years for the document to secure final approval. The breakthrough occurred in June 2006, the first year of the second International Decade of the World's Indigenous Peoples, when the United Nations Human Rights Council adopted the document. On September 13, 2007, the Declaration on the Rights of Indigenous Peoples went before the General Assembly. One hundred forty-three nations endorsed the document, while only four voted against it. Despite the resounding victory, the negative votes may have spoken the loudest, for they came from Australia, New Zealand, Canada, and the United States, settler states with large indigenous populations. Australia and New Zealand eventually reversed their stances, and in the wake of the 2010 Olympic Winter Games in Vancouver, the Canadian government stated its intention of following suit. In April 2010 the United States, responding in part to President Barack Obama's campaign pledges in 2008 and in part to the embarrassment of being the only nation on record unequivocally against the declaration, announced that it, too, would reevaluate its stance. Finally, in December 2010,

the Obama administration announced its endorsement of the UN
declaration.[46]

Visions Clarified and Obstructed

Even with unanimous support, the realization of the declaration's
promise has not come easily. As the initial round of voting showed,
some opponents point to pedantic matters, such as the definitions of
"indigenous" and "peoples." Other critics raise questions about how
to reconcile international standards with existing legal mechanisms.
And in an act of self-congratulation, Canada and the United States actually suggested that the declaration proved redundant because it reiterated principles already governing their relations with indigenous
nations.[47] But there remains an even deeper conceptual obstruction.
For the document did not simply enumerate a list of rights. It advanced a narrative of persistent, independent, self-governing indigenous communities that fundamentally contradicted narratives of
disappearances and vanishing acts, total defeats and subordinations,
domestications and dependences first manufactured, then edited and
revised, and finally internalized and taken for granted by a majority
of the population in the settler states.[48]

These two narratives, along with the imagined political communities they intend to substantiate, have yet to be reconciled. It remains
to be seen whether they can. The stakes, however, could not be higher. For if the United States continues to operate on what Vine Deloria
termed "incredibly stupid premises," then indigenous sovereignty and
nationhood will continue to be seen as second class—as something
not to be taken seriously. Whatever outcome results from the ongoing
struggle will assuredly flow from a multifaceted, complex, uneven, and
at times contradictory process of negotiation. At the forefront will be
Native people who either live in diaspora or who reside in ancestral
homelands, returning to Charles Eastman's words, made strange by
diaspora. Powerful external forces will shape the contexts in which
future political action takes place, just as they did in the wake of the
Second World War. The next generation of activists, like their predecessors in the National Congress of American Indians, Association

on American Indian Affairs, National Indian Youth Council, International Indian Treaty Council, and Working Group on Indigenous Populations will seek to deflect, harness, manipulate, or turn them to their advantage. In so doing, they will engage in an autochthonous political tradition of asserting a global indigenous identity that began long before and will continue long after the Cold War.

Notes

1. Robert A. Williams Jr., *Like a Loaded Weapon: The Rehnquist Court, Indian Rights, and the Legal History of Racism in America* (Minneapolis: University of Minnesota Press, 2005), 161–95, quote at 165.

2. For a text of the joint NCAI-AFN declaration, see the AFN's website, http://www.afn.ca/article.asp?id=55 (accessed March 10, 2010).

3. Benedict Anderson, *Imagined Communities: Reflections on the Origins and Spread of Nationalism*, rev. ed. (New York: Verso, 1991), 1–7. On the continuity of activism in Native America, see Daniel M. Cobb, "Continuing Encounters: Historical Perspectives," in *Beyond Red Power: American Indian Politics and Activism since 1900*, ed. Daniel M. Cobb and Loretta Fowler (Santa Fe: School for Advanced Research Press, 2007), 57–69. For another important perspective on defining the boundaries of sovereignty as a co-constitutive process, see Kevin Bruyneel's *The Third Space of Sovereignty: The Postcolonial Politics of U.S.-Indigenous Relations* (Minneapolis: University of Minnesota Press, 2007).

4. Charles Eastman, *From the Deep Woods to Civilization: Chapters in the Autobiography of an Indian* (Boston: Little, Brown, 1916), 54.

5. On this process, consider Jean M. O'Brien, *Firsting and Lasting: Writing Indians Out of Existence in New England* (Minneapolis: University of Minnesota Press, 2010).

6. Nancy Shoemaker, *A Strange Likeness: Becoming Red and White in Eighteenth-Century North America* (Oxford: Oxford University Press, 2004), 6–8; Vine Deloria Jr., "Self-Determination and the Concept of Sovereignty," in *Native American Sovereignty*, ed. John Wunder (New York: Garland, 1999), 118–24; David E. Wilkins, *American Indian Politics and the American Political System* (New York: Rowman and Littlefield, 2002), 339; Taiaiake Alfred, *Peace, Power, Righteousness: An Indigenous Manifesto* (New York: Oxford University Press, 1999); Tom Holm, Diane Pearson, and Ben Chavez, "Peoplehood: A Model for the Extension of Sovereignty in American Indian Studies," *Wicazo Sa Review* 18, no. 1 (2003): 7–24.

7. Shoemaker, *A Strange Likeness*, 6–8, 64–68, 83–103; Raymond D. Fogelson, "The Context of American Indian Political History: An Overview and Critique,"

in *D'Arcy McNickle Center for the History of the American Indian Occasional Papers in Curriculum Series*, no. 11: *The Struggle for Political Autonomy* (Chicago: Newberry Library, 1989), 15–17; Willard B. Walker, "Creek Confederacy Before Removal," in *Handbook of North American Indians*, vol. 14: *Southeast*, ed. Raymond D. Fogelson (Washington DC: Smithsonian Institution, 2004), 373–92; Robert A. Williams Jr., *Linking Arms Together: American Indian Treaty Visions of Law and Peace, 1600–1800* (New York: Oxford University Press, 1997); Daniel K. Richter, *Ordeal of the Longhouse: The Peoples of the Iroquois League in the Era of European Colonization* (Chapel Hill: University of North Carolina Press, 1992); Gregory Evans Dowd, *A Spirited Resistance: The North American Indian Struggle for Unity, 1745–1815* (Baltimore: Johns Hopkins University Press, 1991); Joe S. Sando, *The Pueblo Indians* (San Francisco: Indian Historian Press, 1976), 12; Alexandra Harmon, *Indians in the Making: Ethnic Relations and Indian Identities around Puget Sound* (Berkeley: University of California Press, 1998); and Jeffrey Ostler, *The Plains Sioux and U.S. Colonialism from Lewis and Clark to Wounded Knee* (New York: Cambridge University Press, 2004).

8. For a text of Marshall's decision, see Jill Norgren, *The Cherokee Cases: Two Landmark Federal Decisions in the Fight for Sovereignty* (Norman: University of Oklahoma Press, 2004), 165–69.

9. See David E. Wilkins and K. Tsianina Lomawaima, *Uneven Ground: American Indian Sovereignty and Federal Law* (Norman: University of Oklahoma Press, 2001), 64–97 and 98–116; Taiawagi Helton and Lindsay G. Robertson, "The Foundations of Federal Indian Law and Its Application in the Twentieth Century," in Cobb and Fowler, *Beyond Red Power*, 36–38; David E. Wilkins, *American Indian Sovereignty and the U.S. Supreme Court: The Masking of Justice* (Austin: University of Texas Press, 1997).

10. Thomas Biolsi, "Political and Legal Status ('Lower 48' States)," in *A Companion to the Anthropology of American Indians*, ed. Thomas Biolsi (Malden MA: Blackwell Publishing, 2004), 235.

11. Frederick E. Hoxie, ed., *Talking Back to Civilization: Indian Voices from the Progressive Era* (Boston: Bedford/St. Martin's, 2001), 133–38.

12. Hoxie, *Talking Back to Civilization*, 123–33; Thomas A. Britten, *American Indians in World War I: At Home and at War* (Albuquerque: University of New Mexico Press, 1997), 51–72.

13. David M. Kennedy, *Over Here: The First World War and American Society* (New York: Oxford University Press, 1980), 332, 354, 358–63. For the full text, see President Wilson's Message to Congress, January 8, 1918, Records of the United States Senate, Record Group 46, National Archives, http://www.ourdocuments .gov/doc.php?flash=old&doc=62 (accessed May 11, 2010).

14. Quoted in Hoxie, *Talking Back to Civilization*, 129–33.

15. Harvard Project on American Indian Economic Development, *The State of the Native Nations: Conditions Under U.S. Policies of Self-Determination* (New York: Oxford University Press, 2008), 84; Joëlle Rostkowski, "The Redman's Appeal for Justice: Deskaheh and the League of Nations," in *Indians and Europe: An Interdisciplinary Collection of Essays*, ed. Christian Feest (1989; repr., Lincoln: University of Nebraska Press, 1999), 435–53; Annemarie Shimony, "Alexander General, 'Deskahe,' Cayuga-Oneida, 1889–1925," in *American Indian Intellectuals of the Nineteenth and Early Twentieth Centuries*, ed. Margot Liberty (1978; repr., Norman: University of Oklahoma Press, 2002), 187–89; Donald B. Smith, "Deskaheh (Levi General)," *Dictionary of Canadian Biography Online*, www.biographi.ca?009004-119.01-e.php?BioId=42238&query= (accessed May 11, 2010). Also see Bruyneel, *Third Space*, 97–121.

16. On the Indian New Deal, see Vine Deloria Jr. and Clifford M. Lytle, *The Nations Within: The Past and Future of American Indian Sovereignty* (1984; repr., Austin: University of Texas Press, 1997). On John Collier's hemispheric vision, see John Collier, *The Indians of the Americas* (New York: W. W. Norton, 1947), esp. 291–314; Kenneth R. Philp, *John Collier's Crusade for Indian Reform, 1920–1954* (Tucson: University of Arizona Press, 1977), 206–8; and William Willard, "The Plumed Serpent and the Red Atlantis," *Wicazo Sa Review* 4, no. 2 (1988): 17–30. On the IAII, see Dorothy R. Parker, *Singing an Indian Song: A Biography of D'Arcy McNickle* (Lincoln: University of Nebraska Press, 1992), 82–85; Russel Lawrence Barsh, "The Ninth Inter-American Indian Congress," *Journal of International Law* 80, no. 3 (1986): 682–85; Carlos Salomon, "Indigenismo across Borders," *Journal of the West* 48, no. 3 (2009): 48–52; and http://www.state.gov/www/background_notes/oas_0398_bgn.html (accessed May 11, 2010). Christian McMillen has found that the Collier administration proved fundamental to getting the Hualapai's land claim case before the Supreme Court. The *United States v. Santa Fe Pacific Railroad* decision in 1941, in turn, has carried global implications for indigenous claims litigation. Christian McMillen, *Making Indian Law: The Hualapai Land Case and the Birth of Ethnohistory* (New Haven CT: Yale University Press, 2007), esp. 166–83.

17. For the executive order establishing the IAII, see Charles J. Kappler's *Indian Affairs: Laws and Treaties*, which is available full-text online at http://digital.library.okstate.edu/kappler/vol7/html_files/v7p1439b.html (accessed May 11, 2010). On McNickle and the NCAI, see Daniel M. Cobb, *Native Activism in Cold War America: The Struggle for Sovereignty* (Lawrence: University Press of Kansas, 2008), 10–11; Thomas W. Cowger, *The National Congress of American Indians: The Founding Years* (Lincoln: University of Nebraska Press, 1999), 24–48; and Parker, *Singing an Indian Song*, 106–9.

18. James T. Patterson, *Grand Expectations: The United States, 1945–1974* (New York: Oxford University Press, 1996), 276–310, 486–523; David Kaiser, *American Tragedy: Kennedy, Johnson, and the Origins of the Vietnam War* (Cambridge MA: Belknap Press), 2000.

19. Mary L. Dudziak, *Cold War Civil Rights: Race and the Image of American Democracy* (Princeton NJ: Princeton University Press, 2000); Thomas Borstelmann, *The Cold War and the Color Line: American Race Relations in the Global Arena* (Cambridge MA: Harvard University Press, 2001); Brenda Gayle Plummer, ed., *Window on Freedom: Race, Civil Rights, and Foreign Affairs, 1945–1988* (Chapel Hill: University of North Carolina Press, 2003); Brenda Gayle Plummer, *Black Americans and United States Foreign Affairs, 1935–1960* (Chapel Hill: University of North Carolina Press, 1996); Gerald Horne, *Black and Red: W. E. B. DuBois and the Afro-American Response to the Cold War, 1944–1963* (Albany: State University of New York Press, 1986); Penny Von Eschen, *Race Against Empire: Black America and Anticolonialism, 1937–1957* (Ithaca NY: Cornell University Press, 1997); Carol Anderson, *Eyes Off the Prize: African Americans, the United Nations, and the Struggle for Human Rights, 1944–1952* (Columbus: Ohio State University Press, 1995); Melani McAlister, "On Black Allah: The Middle East in the Cultural Politics of African American Liberation, 1955–1960," *American Quarterly* 51, no. 3 (1999): 622–56; and Robin D. G. Kelley, "'But a Local Phase of a World Problem': Black History's Global Vision, 1883–1950," *Journal of American History* 86, no. 3 (1999): 1045–77; Thomas F. Jackson, *From Civil Rights to Human Rights: Martin Luther King Jr. and the Struggle for Economic Justice* (Philadelphia: University of Pennsylvania Press, 2007).

20. Daniel M. Cobb, "Indian Politics in Cold War America: Parallel and Contradiction," *Princeton University Library Chronicle* 67 (2006): 392–419; Cobb, "Talking the Language of the Larger World: Politics in Cold War (Native) America" in Cobb and Fowler, *Beyond Red Power*, 161–77; Paul C. Rosier, "'They Are Ancestral Homelands': Race, Place, and Politics in Cold War Native America," *JAH* 92 (2006): 1300–26; Paul C. Rosier, *Serving Their Country: American Indian Politics and Patriotism in the Twentieth Century* (Cambridge MA: Harvard University Press, 2009), 109–220.

21. See Peter Kuznick and James Gilbert, eds., *Rethinking Cold War Culture* (Washington DC: Smithsonian Institution Press, 2001); and Stephen J. Whitfield, *The Culture of the Cold War*, 2nd ed. (Baltimore: Johns Hopkins University Press, 1996).

22. Donald L. Fixico, *Termination and Relocation: Federal Indian Policy, 1945–1960* (Albuquerque: University of New Mexico Press, 1986); Kenneth R. Philp, *Termination Revisited: American Indians on the Trail to Self-Determination, 1933–1953*

(Lincoln: University of Nebraska Press, 1999); R. Warren Metcalf, *Termination's Legacy: The Discarded Indians of Utah* (Lincoln: University of Nebraska Press, 2002).

23. Pamphlet, ca. 1944–1945, folder 3, box 123, Association on American Indian Affairs Records, Seeley G. Mudd Manuscript Library, Princeton University, Princeton NJ. This photograph is reproduced in Cobb, "Indian Politics in Cold War America," 395.

24. Cowger, *National Congress of American Indians*, 88; Rosier, "'They Are Ancestral Homelands,'" 1308–9.

25. Quoted in Rosier, "'They Are Ancestral Homelands,'" 1316.

26. "Leave Some For Us" cartoon, "Cartoons and Caricatures" folder, box 34, Helen L. Peterson Papers, National Anthropological Archives, Smithsonian Institution, Suitland MD. A reprint of this ad can be found in Rosier, *Serving Their Country*, 194.

27. Cowger, *National Congress of American Indians*, 122–23. A critique of Puerto Rico as a model for Indian Country is Guy B. Senese, *Self-Determination and the Social Education of Native Americans* (New York: Praeger, 1991), 22–24, 27–30. Operation Bootstrap was born of the "modernization ideology" guiding other foreign aid programs in that it was predicated on a model that intended to profit outside (American) investors and industrialists more than the indigenous populations, who were often seen as little more than cheap labor. Also see Ismael García-Colón, "Buscando Ambiente: Hegemony and Subaltern Tactics of Survival in Puerto Rico's Land Distribution Program, *Latin American Perspectives* 23, no. 1 (2006): 42–65.

28. Editorial, *Indian Affairs*, no. 19 (1957): 1.

29. Cobb, *Native Activism in Cold War America*, 8–9, 27–29; Michael E. Latham, *Modernization as Ideology: American Social Science and "Nation Building" in the Kennedy Era* (Chapel Hill: University of North Carolina Press, 2000).

30. LaVerne Madigan to Oliver La Farge, March 9, 1956, folder 6, box 151, AAIA Records. For more on the American Indian Point Four Program see, Cobb, *Native Activism*, 8–22; Cobb, "Indian Politics in Cold War America," 392–416; Cowger, *National Congress of American Indians*, 122–23; and Rosier, *Serving Their Country*, 191–201.

31. For a full account of the Chicago conference, see Cobb, *Native Activism*, 30–57, 69, quotes at 52.

32. On Deloria's role as NCAI executive director, see Cobb, *Native Activism*, 102–46. The Deloria quotes are from Vine Deloria Jr., interview by author, tape recording, Golden CO, October 18, 2001; John Belindo, "Changing Profile," *Oklahoma Journal*, November 1, 1965, folder 11, box 4, American Indian Institute Collection, Western History Collections, University of Oklahoma, Norman.

33. For a text of the NCAI resolution, see Stan Steiner, *The New Indians* (New York: Dell, 1968), 297–99. On this period, also see Bruyneel, *Third Space*, 123–69.

34. For a more comprehensive account of the Workshop on American Indian Affairs, see Cobb, *Native Activism*, 24–27, 62–79.

35. Robert K. Thomas, "Colonialism: Classic and Internal," *New University Thought* 4, no. 4 (1966/1967): 37–44.

36. Cobb, *Native Activism in Cold War America*, 63, 73. For student responses, see Cobb, *Native Activism*, 64–66 and 73–75.

37. On NIYC and the fishing rights campaign, see Bradley G. Shreve, "'From Time Immemorial': The Fish-In Movement and the Rise of Intertribal Activism," *Pacific Historical Review* 78, no. 3 (2009): 403–34. For an organizational history of the NIYC, see Bradley G. Shreve, *Red Power Rising: The National Indian Youth Council and the Origins of Native Activism* (Norman: University of Oklahoma Press, 2010).

38. Clyde Warrior Lecture on Social Movements, Monteith College, February 4, 1966, audio recording, Albert L. Wahrhaftig Papers, author's possession; Clyde Warrior, interview by Stan Steiner, ca. summer 1966, tape 15, Stan Steiner Papers, Department of Special Collections, Stanford University Libraries, Stanford CA; NIYC Press Release, n.d., folder 30, box 3, National Indian Youth Council Records, Center for Southwest Research, University of New Mexico, Albuquerque. Another perspective on Warrior is Paul McKenzie-Jones, "'We Are among the Poor, the Powerless, the Inexperienced and the Inarticulate': Clyde Warrior's Campaign for a 'Greater Indian America,'" *American Indian Quarterly* 34, no. 2 (2010): 224–57.

39. "Statements of Demands for Rights of the Poor Presented to Agencies of the U.S. Government by the Southern Christian Leadership Conference and Its Committee of 100," April 29–30 and May 1, 1968, folder 30 [1 of 3], box 48, Carl Albert General Collection, Carl Albert Center for Congressional Research and Studies, University of Oklahoma, Norman. For an extended analysis of the Poor People's Campaign, see Cobb, *Native Activism*, 147–92.

40. See *Americans Before Columbus*, generally; Steiner, *New Indians*, 268–89, quote at 285. On NIYC activism during the 1970s, see Bradley G. Shreve, "Up Against Giants: The National Indian Youth Council, the Navajo Nation, and Coal Gasification, 1974–1977," *American Indian Culture and Research Journal* 30, no. 2 (2006): 17–34. For a general description of NIYC activism, see "NIYC History," http://www.niyc-alb.org/history.htm and "The NIYC at the United Nations," http://www.niyc-alb.org/activities.htm (accessed May 13, 2010).

41. Vine Deloria Jr., *Custer Died for Your Sins: An Indian Manifesto* (New York: Avon Books, 1969); Vine Deloria Jr., *Behind the Trail of Broken Treaties: An Indian*

Declaration of Independence (1974; repr., Austin: University of Texas Press, 1985), 161–86, quotes at 161 and 186.

42. Harvard Project, *State of the Native Nations*, 84–85; S. James Anaya, *Indigenous Peoples in International Law*, 2d ed. (New York: Oxford University Press, 2004), 51–54. According to the United Nations, since 1945 more than eighty colonized territories with a population of more than 750 million gained their independence from foreign rule. United Nations Department of Public Information, "United Nations and Decolonization," February 2005, http://www.un.org/Depts /dpi/decolonizations/Decolonization_brochure.pdf (accessed May 13, 2010). For a list of trust and non-self-governing territories, from 1945 to 1999, see http://www .un.org/Depts/dpi/decolonization/trust2/htm (accessed May 13, 2010).

43. On the American Indian Movement, see Paul Chaat Smith and Robert Allen Warrior, *Like a Hurricane: The Indian Movement from Alcatraz to Wounded Knee* (New York: New Press, 1996).

44. Wilkins, *American Indian Politics*, 211–12; Randel D. Hanson, "Contemporary Globalization and Tribal Sovereignty," in *A Companion to the Anthropology of American Indians*, ed. Thomas Biolsi (Malden MA: Blackwell Publishing, 2004), 284–303; http://www.treatycouncil.org/about.htm (accessed May 12, 2010). For a text of the Declaration of Continuing Independence, see http://www.treatycouncil .org/pdfs/declaration_of_continuing_independence.pdf (accessed May 12, 2010).

45. Harvard Project, *State of the Native Nations*, 85; International Working Group for Indigenous Affairs website, http://www.iwgia.org (accessed May 12, 2010).

46. International Working Group for Indigenous Affairs website; Harvard Project, *State of the Native Nations*, 85–86; Daniel M. Cobb, "Memory and the Winter Olympics," *Chronicle of Higher Education* 56, no. 28 (March 26, 2010): B9–B11; and Valerie Taliman, "United States Re-Examines Opposition to UN Declaration," April 23, 2010, *Indian Country Today*, http://www.indiancountrytoday .com/global/91903174.html (accessed May 12, 2010).

47. For more on the issue of "indigenous," see Jeff J. Corntassel, "Who is Indigenous? 'Peoplehood' and Ethnonationalist Approaches to Rearticulating Indigenous Identity," *Nationalism and Ethnic Politics* 9, no. 1 (2003): 75–100. For Canadian and U.S. statements explaining their initial negative votes, see "Statement by Ambassador McNee to the General Assembly on the Declaration on the Rights of Indigenous Peoples," September 13, 2007," http://www.canada international.gc.ca (accessed May 13, 2010) and "Explanation of Vote by Robert Hagen, U.S. Advisor, on the Declaration on the Rights of Indigenous Peoples, to the UN General Assembly," September 13, 2007, http://www.archive.usun.state .gov/press_releases/20070913_204.html (accessed May 13, 2010).

48. Which goes a long way in explaining why UN Special Rapporteur on the Rights of Indigenous Peoples James Anaya could not secure an audience with members of Congress during his U.S. tour in April and May 2012 and why his effort is not known outside of a limited circle of scholars interested and activists engaged in the global indigenous rights movement. See Jenni Monet, "James Anaya: A Sit-Down with the UN's Man in Indian Country," *Indian Country Today*, May 9, 2012, http://indiancountrytodaymedianetwork.com (accessed September 3, 2012) and Chris McGreal, "U.S. Should Return Stolen Land to Indian Tribes, Says United Nations," *The Guardian*, May 4, 2012, http://www.guardian.co.uk (accessed September 3, 2012).

| Chapter 15

From Tribal to Indian
American Indian Identity in the Twentieth Century

Donald L. Fixico

When I lived in Los Angeles and was shopping in a supermarket one afternoon, an elderly white woman approached me and said, "I just returned from a vacation from Asia and it was wonderful! I bet you are Chinese? Japanese? Korean?" I shook my head no each time; then I thought, she thinks I am a foreigner and she is actually the one that is the foreigner and my people have been here long before hers. This has happened more than once. Being Indian is hard. It is a personal struggle that is also waged in the face of being told what you are supposed to be by mainstream America. The core of Native identity had always been grounded within the communities, but this infrastructure changed during the course of the nineteenth and twentieth centuries. Explaining this transformation from community identity to tribal identity to Indian identity is the central focus of this discussion, which uses an internal-external model to illustrate how Native identity functions and how it has changed due to external influences.

Being Indian in modern America is a personal experience often involving internal and external pressures. Since the late nineteenth century, outside pressures on Indians to assimilate into the American mainstream have played an important role in altering the identity of Native people from tribalness to a generic Indianness. Bureaucrats designed federal policies to colonize Native people, thereby undermining their identity.

Being Indian is always finding one's self outnumbered by the majority of society and frequently feeling lonely and surrounded. The Native person feels more like the Lone Ranger than Tonto. Learning how to cope is important for finding balance within one's self and accepting one's own Indian identity. Learning how to get along, often playing the white man's game, can become critical, but learning the rules is of the utmost importance. A Native person struggles with the internal pressures inside himself or herself and faces rhetoric, historical stereotypes, and other outside influences that must be balanced. To understand one's own inner self is essential before coping with such external pressures. The work of Edward Said in his *Orientalism* is helpful here for understanding how outsiders view a people and control the perception of the people's identity.[1]

Being Indian is finding humor even during the most strenuous circumstances. The long history of American Indians and their suppressive relationship with the United States is not a pretty one; it is one that is filled with tremendous loss of lands, massacres, brainwashing in boarding schools, soul stealing by churches. Being Indian in modern American is often finding one's self alone, the only Native person in a meeting, the only one on a team, the only one on an elevator surrounded by non-Indians. What it is like to feel surrounded is one case of "what to do in a difficult situation," like when the Lone Ranger turns to Tonto and says "Tonto, we're surrounded by Indians." Tonto replies, "What do you mean 'we,' white man?" This is an Indian joke and Indians find it funny, but to others it may not be so humorous. To be Indian is to learn to laugh at one's self, to not take one's self so seriously. It is the circumstance that is humorous, so even non-Indians can laugh at the Lone Ranger joke. Furthermore, Tonto and the Lone Ranger had been partners for nearly twenty years and they shared many experiences. In such a relationship of an Indian and non-Indian, the latter sees himself or herself as being a part of the Indian experience or even being Indian.

Originally Native people lived in communities, either sedentary or nomadic. These communities were also called towns, villages, bands, or camps. This community identity changed in the nineteenth century when bureaucrats began to hold treaty councils and grouped communities together because they spoke the same language and the communities had kinship ties to each other. For example, all the Muscogee Creek communities in the Southeast, which operated as separate towns, became recognized as the Muscogee Creek tribe. The exception occurred when the same linguistic communities spread over a very large area, such as the Ojibwas or Lakotas; hence, bureaucrats approached them as more than one tribe of Ojibwas and Lakotas. This reorganization of Native communities in this fashion created tribes that Native people themselves adopted in the reordering of their communities as the government placed them on newly created reservations throughout the nineteenth century.

Tribal Native identity is based on the infrastructure of communities that can be illustrated by using a model like a circle. Within the circle can be any Native community, but within the community are six internal elements that are bonded together. These six elements are (1) self or people, (2) family or extended family, (3) clan or society, (4) community or town or village, (5) tribe, and (6) spirituality. To help demonstrate this infrastructure, I use the Seminoles as an example. The Seminoles had a host of towns or communities in the Southeast that once included lower Alabama, although most towns were in Florida.

The key to Native identity is defined by the collective six elements mentioned above. The first internal element is the self or individual Seminole who finds security from being a part of the community or town. The Seminole person also receives his or her identity from the community or town. At the same time, each Seminole seeks to maintain a balance within himself or herself. I also propose in this chapter that a natural dichotomy exists between left and right, male and female, light and dark, right and wrong, which are universal in the Seminole worldview. Furthermore, the individual Seminole seeks balance with the rest of the internal elements of the community or town.

The second element is the Seminole extended family, which was a crucial component of identity among early Native peoples up until the early twentieth century, although the familial composition has changed since then. Extended families became more nuclear, without the extra relatives living in a single household in the post—World War II era, although the extended family has remained quite common in many tribal communities throughout Indian Country. The nuclear family has also changed in the late twentieth century as the single-parent family became increasingly common alongside the two-parent family.

The clan or society is the third internal element of the tribal community. Most Eastern Woodland tribes, including the Florida Seminoles, have clans named after animal and plant totems that their peoples have studied for generations.[2] Such clan totems include the wolf, deer, bear, and so forth. Among western Indians, military societies or age-group societies existed and functioned much the same as clans. Among the Lakotas, the young bull society, old shields society, elk society, and old bulls society are examples.[3] In the Southwest, the Navajo and Pueblo communities have clan systems as well as the Crows of the northern Great Plains.

The fourth element is the community or town itself. It consists of the other three previous elements and it can act as a tribe, if one community constitutes a tribe. Due to this possibility, the fourth and fifth elements may be the same element, but only if one community is the tribe. In the case of the Seminole, twenty to twenty-five towns or communities constituted the Seminole tribe.

The next element is the tribe or tribal community. A tribe is a sociopolitical construction that was produced by political negotiations and other contact with the American mainstream, which found it convenient to refer to Native groups as tribes. A tribe also might be called nation, perhaps nation-state in political jargon, but it is interesting that Native people have embraced the term "tribe" of late and made it their own. Native people have adopted the term "tribe" to the extent that an impressive amount of pride is associated with being Seminole, Cherokee, Navajo, and so forth.

The final element is spirituality. This element is an energy that bonds the rest of the internal elements together. The Seminole tribal or community members' spirituality compels them to have faith in their belief system, which is based within a physical and metaphysical reality.[4] In this indigenous context, visions and dreams are accepted as a part of daily reality.

It is proposed here that forces outside the Seminole tribal community cause the internal elements within the circle to come together and solidify to thwart the external pressures. Throughout American Indian history, external forces as agents of change have acted upon the tribal community. These forces include military attacks by other tribes and Euro-American powers, cultural materialism from European trade, foreign diseases, boarding schools, missionary conversion efforts, and various federal Indian policies and programs. The tribal community within the circle remains intact, unless one or more of the internal elements begins to fracture or yields to the outside pressures described. Indian tribal identity is based on belonging to a community, and maintaining connection to that community is imperative to a person's identity.

The U.S. government forcefully removed sixty-seven tribes, including the Seminoles, to Indian Territory (present-day Oklahoma) during the nineteenth century. More tribes were removed to other areas. This action produced the Reservation Era. From an external position, the federal government and the U.S. military carried out federal Indian policies and government programs that promoted "tribal" identity and simultaneously undermined the importance of "community" or "town" in the case of the Seminoles. In the supervision of Indian affairs, the Bureau of Indian Affairs and the military treated various similar communities as "nation-states" or tribes. To simplify situations, the government wanted to negotiate treaties with as few leaders as possible for each tribe. For example, each of the removed Seminole towns functioned under its own autonomy, although the U.S. government treated them as one tribe because they spoke the same language and lived in the same area. At the same time, the various Seminole towns fought as allies against the United States, giving the appearance that they were one tribe or nation.[5]

After removal and placement on reservations, the boundaries of the tribes' new homelands encompassed all the Seminole towns. This definition of new homelands occurred with other tribal communities. Two exceptions were the Cheyennes[6] and Arapahos, who had communities or bands removed to Indian Territory while the others remained in their original homeland. The separations resulted in the Northern and Southern Cheyennes and the Northern and Southern Arapahos. Other exceptions include the Ojibwas, whose communities were placed on reservations in Minnesota, Wisconsin, Michigan, and South Dakota. The Potawatomis had a similar experience as government officials assigned them to reservations in Michigan, Wisconsin, Kansas, and Oklahoma.

These years proved difficult for Native people due to war with the United States and a forceful anti-Indian attitude confirmed by General Phil Sheridan's infamous misquoted statement, "The only good Indian is a dead Indian."[7] Theodore Roosevelt reinforced this negative view in 1886 when he stated, "I don't go so far as to say that the only good Indians are dead Indians, but I believe nine out of ten are, and I shouldn't like to inquire too closely in the case of the tenth."[8]

The United States' efforts to remove Indians and place them on reservations produced an "othering" process that historian Robert Berkhofer Jr. described in his classic *The White Man's Indian: Images of the American Indian from Columbus to the Present.*[9] Beginning with the first impression observed by Christopher Columbus about Native people, Indians were defined and identified by those who wrote history and others who made observations about them. By 1900, Americans had redefined the identity of indigenous people, as the U.S. population approached 76.5 million whereas Indians spiraled toward a zero population.[10] The imagery is powerfully painted via art like George Catlin's works and words in newspapers and books that depicted Native people being inferior to white civilization.[11] The "othering" process produced deep attitudes of hatred toward Indians and the U.S. government's authorization of 1,679 wars, skirmishes, and battles against Native people in the United States.[12] By the end of the nineteenth century, the United States had waged two major periods of war against Native peoples east of the Mississippi River and in the West, resulting in nearly two hundred reservations set aside to segregate indigenous people from white Americans.

At the turn of the twentieth century, the imagery, identity, and destruction witnessed a pivotal moment for indigenous people. Reformers,

Christians, and humanitarians felt sorry for Native people as they seemed to begin to vanish from the face of the earth. The end of the wild savage as observed via the Wounded Knee Massacre in 1890 and the volunteer surrender of Ishi, the last of his Yahi people, gave credence to James Earl Fraser's sculpture *The End of the Trail*. The total indigenous population reached its lowest ever—less than 238,000 people from an original estimated 15 million. Postcolonial America had developed thirty-four negative stereotypes about American Indians in its attempt to assimilate the surviving Native people. Since the arrival of Columbus over five hundred years ago, the European perception and accompanying American view berated Native people, thus resulting in a Euro-American superiority complex.

At this stage of Indian-white relations, Native people held tightly to their own identities, which, as mentioned, encompassed a variety of factors such as family, tribe, and community, yet the American mainstream had developed its own view of indigenous people as "Indians." These competing understandings of Native identity continued into the following decades, with Native people clinging to their tribal identities.

In the early twentieth century, the First World War produced many changes, including changes throughout Indian Country. An estimated twelve thousand Indian men fought for the United States, the majority of them not U.S. citizens.[13] The Act of 1919 took care of this issue and offered U.S. citizenship to all honorably discharged Indians from the armed services.[14] At the same time, the First World War pulled the men away from their communities. The General Citizenship Act of 1924 was aimed as an external influence to break down tribal communities through assimilation and individualizing Native people to become like mainstream Americans. For the remaining one-third of the Native people who were not citizens, this act of Congress gave blanket U.S. citizenship to all Indians.[15]

Within tribal communities, Native people continued to operate on a daily basis on their reservations or in their rural home areas. During these years, community and culture continued to render "identity" to a Native person. Although the location of one's home remained important, the interrelatedness of one's family, friends, and kinspeople placed a person within the context of kinship and membership in the community. This combination perpetuated the nature of tribal identity and balance in a traditional sense.

In the early modernization era of Indian Country, following American Progressivism and during the Great Depression years, the duality of tribal identity and Indian identity became more evident as many Native people sought to become a part of the mainstream, at least as needed. More specifically, the majority of Native people lived in tribal communities, thereby perpetuating tribal identity, while many opted to become a part of the mainstream as Indians. Because the majority of Americans possessed little knowledge about Native people, white society "Indianized" them, according to Berkhofer's "othering" process. Specifically, mainstream Americans called all Native people "Indians" because they did not know their tribal identities. This homogenization of Americans occurred repeatedly, for example, as all people from Italy in the United States became Italian Americans without regard to what part of Italy they came from, ignoring the fact that some came from northern Italy or from Sicily or other places. American homogenization was applied to all people coming from various countries to the United States, as they would ultimately be known just as "Americans."

Yet the Americanization process caused concern for Native people. Within each Native person, with the progression of a modern Indian Country, identity became more of a struggle. Modern indigenous identity is the struggle of a Native person to realize his or her balance within the self and to maintain this balance outside the tribal community and in the mainstream. To maintain a healthy identity as a minority in a non-Indian mainstream is the supreme test for Native people in two ways. First, the Native person must maintain a healthy psychological balance. Second, the Native person has to find balance among non-Natives, who will either accept or reject him or her. In each case, sustaining the Native voice or perspective is a struggle in the non-Indian world whose mainstreamers deem Indians not relevant to their lives. So, non-Indians neglect or dismiss what Native people may think or believe. In other words, the tribal worldviews are foreign to mainstream Americans.

Throughout the 1930s, tribal identities generally remained intact. Native people remained in their tribal communities and remained connected to their families and kinship clans or societies. At the same time, the Great Depression impacted the entire United States and the rest of the world, including tribal communities everywhere in Indian Country. More to the point, the Indian New Deal implemented by commissioner of Indian affairs John Collier and the Franklin Roosevelt presidential administration posed a serious threat to tribal identities and tribal communities. During these years, mainstream Americans, bureaucrats, and others called Native people "Indians." The success of Collier's Indian New Deal reform measures and restructuring of tribal communities modeled after the U.S. government, in fact, nationalized Native groups. Thus, Collier's success undermined communal infrastructure, according to Native traditions. While Collier admired and respected Native peoples, he wanted to preserve their communities as he deemed most suitable.

American involvement in the Second World War began in 1941 and acted as a catalytic force that threatened the tribal communities. More than twenty-five thousand Native men served in the armed services, and several hundred Native women joined them. An estimated forty thousand Native people joined the labor force in the war industries that exposed them to the American mainstream.[16]

This great exodus from Indian Country introduced many Native people to the "off reservation" experience for the first time in their lives. The Second World War represented the first critical agent of change in permanently replacing tribal identity with Indian identity. Separated from their families and communities, Native men and women were at a distance from the elements that had previously served to inform their identity.

Following the war, the early 1950s witnessed a backlash against American freedom with the rise of McCarthyism and the Red Scare during the Cold War. Anyone or any organization that did not fully personify American values was viewed as un-American and discriminated against, sometimes beaten up, and blacklisted as being a communist.

From 1950 to 1954 Senator Joseph McCarthy's movement charged more than nine thousand people with being communists. The paranoia of McCarthyism strove to homogenize all Americans based on a conservative attitude that idealized society and excluded anyone of color.

The anti-Indian and antiminority years did not deter Native people from entering the service to fight for the United States during the Korean War. When this conflict ended on July 27, 1953, an estimated ten thousand Native men had served. Charles George, Raymond Harvey, and Mitchell Red Cloud earned the Medal of Honor.

The perception of color made a difference. Indians who looked Indian, with black hair and brown skin, suffered from public discrimination as conservative Americans stigmatized minorities of color. Conservativism entered Congress with the election of Republicans like Arthur V. Watkins from the state of Utah to the Senate and the presidential appointment of Dillon S. Myer as the commissioner of Indian affairs in 1950. Both individuals led a political bloc in Congress called terminationists that established the most dreadful federal Indian policy called termination. The policy deliberately intended to abrogate the "trust" protection guaranteed by 374 U.S.-Indian ratified treaties in exchange for Indians ceding 98 percent of the land in the country to the U.S. government.

In Congress, Senator Henry Jackson of Washington introduced House Concurrent Resolution 108 and Representative William Harrison of Wyoming sponsored the measure in the House of Representatives. The termination policy was established in House Concurrent Resolution 108, which stated:

> Whereas it is the policy of Congress, as rapidly as possible, to make the Indians within the territorial limits of the United States subject to the same laws and entitled to the same privileges and responsibilities as are applicable to other citizens of the United States, to end their status as wards of the United States and to grant them all of the rights and prerogatives, pertaining to American citizenship; and Whereas the Indians within the territorial limits of the United States should assume their full responsibilities as American citizens.[17]

Bureaucrats tried to present termination to Indians as a liberation of trust restrictions that kept them from having full control of their business affairs. Yet when the Menominees of Wisconsin became the first terminated tribe in 1961, tribal members lost huge amounts of timber properties to white opportunists. The same occurred to the timber rich Klamath tribe in Oregon and other vulnerable tribes possessed of oil, gas, uranium, and coal on their tribal lands.

This difficult time for Indians became worse when the same Eighty-third Congress and the Bureau of Indian Affairs introduced the federal relocation program on a voluntary basis to all Native people between the ages of eighteen to forty-five. Many Native people who volunteered felt forced to leave their homes and participate in the program because their reservations had nothing to offer—no jobs, only poverty. There was no choice but to move to the cities where the government offered temporary housing, mostly apartment living, and to take whatever jobs were available, which often turned out to be manual labor or seasonal work, with no real future.

From 1953 to 1972, Congress terminated 109 cases of trust status for tribes, communities, villages, bands, and individuals. These years of conservativism and a backlash of activism made life difficult for minorities, including women, and Indians especially in border towns, on reservations, and in rural areas. "Indian" became a bad word due to the mainstream's response to Native activism and the rise of the American Indian Movement (AIM). From 1953 to 1972, two-thirds of the total Indian population became urbanized mostly through relocation.

These were tough years for Indians. Much of this difficulty continued with the next generation of Native people. Given the circumstances, it was good to have lots of relatives and to have family. In spite of discrimination, Native families found security through stories, many of them funny, told on the front porch, at the kitchen table, or other gathering place, making everyone laugh and sometimes feel sad when accounts of tragedy were recalled. Many times the stories were about discrimination. Because Native people were so outnumbered, outsiders had a strong intervening influence on Indian families.

Interestingly, brothers and sisters did not always have the same skin color. Sometimes one was lighter than a brother or sister. But it was the one with the darker skin that encountered the brunt of discrimination and ill treatment. Many Indians lived with a daily awareness that whites might violate them.[18] Unfortunately one sibling sometimes witnessed a brother or sister being unfairly treated while he or she was not, simply because one sibling might not have looked Indian and the racist did not know that the two siblings were of the same family. In one case, one mother who had three children told how her two full-blood sons would "get called 'Black Indian' ever so often," and that their feelings were hurt.[19] If mainstream racism is not bad enough, internal racism occurred among Native people. For example, conservative Native people called full bloods "apples"—Indians who tried to be "white" in the way they dressed and acted.

This is always sad, but the one with the lighter skin did not always get off so easy, especially those who were mixed-blood. To be part Indian and part white or another race created a lot of confusion for the mixed-blood. Most of the time, the mixed-blood chooses his or her Indian part and tries to deny the white part of himself or herself. This kind of denial sometimes leads to self-hatred, making the person wish that he or she were all Indian, which might be called the underdog syndrome.

The worst that can happen is suicide. Occasionally, the pressure of not being white finally gets to individuals. They become alcoholic, have low self-esteem, and feel like they are worthless. They become addicted to drugs, abuse others, abuse themselves, and many give up hope and do not want to go on anymore. Death becomes a welcomed relief.[20]

As more Indians moved to cities, a new Native identity arose—the urban Indian. At the same time, urban Indians mostly tried to remain connected to their relatives on the reservations and make new Native friends.[21] As Indians continued to live in cities and as more arrived, more Indians lived in urban areas than on reservations by the 1980s. In the cities, tribal barriers dissolved as an Indian person was glad to see another Indian. At first it mattered, but in the end it did not matter that the other Native person might be of a different tribe, even a historical rival tribe.

In the cities, urban Indians became invisible. People confused them with others of the same or similar skin color. Many full-blood Indians, who physically look Indian, were mistaken for people of other groups. Often, other people mistook full bloods for Hawaiians, Koreans, Chinese, or Japanese. For example, to be asked if one is a foreigner, when one is obviously Indian, provokes an emotional sense of irony. Since this country was originally all Indian, the non-Indian who questions a full-blood Indian's identity is the real foreigner. To be called a minority in one's own country is indicative of cultural imperialism.

Clyde Bellecourt, a leader and cofounder of the American Indian Movement, encountered an identity crisis as a young man. Clyde is Ojibwa from White Earth reservation in northern Minnesota. He is one of eleven children whose father was totally disabled during the First World War, and his family was poor when he grew up. As a reckless youth, Clyde went from boarding school to reformatory when he was arrested for the first time at age eleven. His next stop was at Minnesota Training School for Boys at Red Wing and then to St. Cloud Reformatory. Clyde's small crimes led to stealing cars. He was convicted and sent to Stillwater State Penitentiary in Minnesota, where he lost all hope. Feeling all was lost, Clyde entered a deep mental depression. "I was convinced," Bellecourt said, "that I was an ignorant, dirty savage—so I just gave up." Clyde hated his Indianness, hated himself, and vowed that he would never eat again. He wanted to die.

Fortunately Clyde Bellecourt met Eddie Benton Benai, an Ojibwa medicine man. Eddie was a trustee in the prison. He visited Clyde frequently and they talked at length about many things. Clyde's outlook on life changed and Eddie told Clyde about the proud history of their Ojibwa people. Eddie had seen what had happened to Clyde more than once with other Indian people. He said, "The [American] system beats Indian people down. It robs them of their self-respect. It demoralizes and discards them, and too often leads to resignation and defeat."

With a new perspective and newfound pride, Clyde's life changed. "I realized that I wasn't a savage," he said. "I wasn't filthy and I wasn't

ignorant. I was smart and capable." Upon his release, he returned to
Minneapolis where he helped to found the American Indian Movement during the summer of 1968.

Activist John Trudell, Santee Sioux, observed:

> I have seen people from the tribes, "Indians," that don't have the con-
> nection. Somehow it got taken from them. They may have certain blood
> degrees, but they don't have the connection. So it has to do with be-
> ing separated from our relationship to the earth entirely. . . . Besides,
> none of us are "Indians" so it's a meaningless quarrel about who's the
> "most Indian" or who's the "Best Indian." We're the People—we come
> from the tribes, and that's who the ancient ones were and who the an-
> cestors were—the People.[22]

In the same year of the founding of the American Indian Movement, President Lyndon B. Johnson delivered his "Forgotten American" speech to Congress on March 31, 1968. From a poor background
himself, and in spite of his unpopularity due to the controversial Vietnam War and civil rights unrest, Johnson's "Great Society" program
included programmatic efforts to alleviate the poverty on reservations largely in the West and in Appalachian communities existing
in thirteen states.

The late 1960s and early 1970s were the presidential years of Richard Nixon. He befriended Native people, perhaps due to his poor
background growing up on the wrong side of the tracks in Yorba
Linda, a small town in southern California. In spite of the Water-
gate scandal, Nixon did much for Indians, and his administration introduced a new policy of self-determination. While most presidents
only gave lip service to Indians at best, Nixon listened to Native people's many concerns and different articulations of Indianness. During
this tumultuous time, Foster Hood, a Shawnee activist in the Indian community in Los Angeles, explained that there are four kinds of
Indians: legal Indians, biological Indians, psychological Indians, and
Hollywood Indians.[23] Many young people challenged societal values
at this time. Because of the struggle of being Indian, many wanted

to be a part of the uphill battle against the mainstream and the so-called establishment.

On July 8, 1970, Nixon delivered a special message to Congress calling for federal Indian policy that embraced Indian self-determination. President Nixon began his speech stating,

> The first Americans—the Indians—are the most deprived and most isolated minority group in our nation. On virtually every scale of measurement—employment, income, education, health—the condition of the Indian people ranks at the bottom. This condition is the heritage of centuries of injustice. From the time of their first contact with European settlers, the American Indians have been oppressed and brutalized, deprived of the ancestral lands and denied the opportunity to control their own destiny. Even the Federal programs which are intended to meet their needs have frequently proven to be ineffective and demeaning. . . . It is long past time that the Indian policies of the Federal government began to recognize and build upon the capacities and insights of the Indian people. Both as a matter of justice and as a matter of enlightened social policy, we must begin to act on the basis of what the Indians themselves have long been telling us. The time has come to break decisively with the past and to create the conditions for a new era in which the Indian future is determined by the Indian acts and Indian decisions.[24]

With all good intentions, President Nixon addressed a better future for American Indians, but it was uncertain who were the Indians. The misidentification of Indian people, and the stereotypes, racism, and prejudice against Native American men and women, caused greater confusion over Indian identity. For example, Native people often found themselves being confused with other people of color when they were among Mexican Americans or Chinese Americans. The irony is that the questioner rarely guesses American Indian, especially when other ethnic groups are common in the area.

Being Indian is actually a process involving three thematic concepts—image, identity, and self. The way Native people see themselves, the image they project, and the way other people—particularly non-Indians—see them, especially those of a different race, influences the shaping of Indian identity. In this sociocultural context of life, the human process of perception also involves self-image. In addition, understanding the various kinds of Native identity are important. Finally, it is about results of human perception of racial differences and analyzing the negative impact called racism. Incongruence is a human flaw in which anything of the "other" must be a threat of some sort to the majority, which in 2010 is mainstream America with 306 million people and 4.5 million Indians.

Philosophical differences between American Indian intellectualism and American mainstream intellectualism help to explain the binary of Indian-white relations. Yet the difference is not accurately between Indian intellectualism and mainstream intellectualism, but between mainstream intellectualism and the different tribal intellectualisms. This may seem obvious, but often stereotypes negate the multiple differences between the various tribal nations and their cultures, promoting a generic "Indianness."

Stares and questioning looks from non-Indians can be troubling for Indians, but this is a part of human nature in any part of the world. Most people have preconceived attitudes, especially about mixed-race marriages and mixed-race couples. Older conservative people are less willing to accept mixed couples, although increasingly, mixed-race marriages are occurring in various parts of the United States and the world.

Perhaps the above observation will help non-Indians gain some insight into "being Indian." It may help non-Indians learn about the complexity of Native identity, especially in relationships with non-Indians. At the same time, it will help some Indians to feel better about themselves, mixed bloods, full bloods, and those not certain about their tribal ways and unsure about their identities.

In the early 1970s, the Vietnam War finally approached an end. Integration of schools nationwide invited harsh feelings between African Americans and whites, but it put other people of color on the defensive as well. These were the pivotal years when Indians, knowing full well their tribal identities, increasingly identified with all Indians. But this was not easy.

Trying to not be Indian is harder than being Indian, especially when one looks like an Indian. As George Mitchell, a full-blood Ojibwa and AIM cofounder explained, "I was constantly frustrated when I was trying to be a white man." Mitchell stated, "I am proud of my Indian dress. I'd rather see this country become a rainbow culture. I'd like for us to be able to see different peoples and their different ways."[25]

As a young man, former assistant interior secretary of Indian affairs Louis Bruce noted he struggled with being an Indian among whites, but he could not be like them. He had to be himself among them. He said,

> Americans unquestioningly are the greatest salesmen on earth. So I set out, grimly, to become a salesman. I signed up for merchandising courses and got myself a spare-time job selling on commission at Peck & Vinney, a man's clothing store in Syracuse. Each night I practiced putting myself across in front of my mirror. What a ridiculous Indian, I thought! Sometimes I felt like slinking back to the reservation. At the store, each customer looked like an unassailable monster. I would clinch my fists and wade into him with my most practiced smile. . . . When, in the third week, I managed to sell to a traveling salesman, who wanted "something around $35," a $60 suit, I decided that maybe even an Indian could learn to sell. I wrote my final college thesis on "the Manufacture of Men's Clothing."[26]

Richard West, the late famous Cheyenne artist who served as the director of the art department at Bacone College outside Muskogee, Oklahoma, for many years, and in 1980 served as director of art at Haskell Junior College in Lawrence, Kansas, rendered similar advice. West shared his wisdom with Roger Axford, dean of faculty at Bacone Junior College. "He told me at one time that an Indian starts out in life with already one strike against him, and that an Indian has to strive harder than the non-Indian. He said that if an Indian could prove himself, he is just as capable of being accepted as any member of his community."[27]

The establishment of the American Indian Movement in 1968, the Native fish-ins a few years earlier, and the takeover of Alcatraz rocked the American status quo and the U.S. government. At this time, Vine Deloria's book *Custer Died for Your Sins: An Indian Manifesto* sharply criticized the government and society for its ill treatment of Indians at the time and in the past. At the same time, N. Scott Momaday's novel *House Made of Dawn* also helped to create an Indian renaissance. The literary awakening received its greatest boost with another significant book. Dee Brown's *Bury My Heart at Wounded Knee*, which became the most popular book on Indians, was released in 1970. Since then, *Bury My Heart at Wounded Knee* has sold over five million copies in seventeen languages worldwide and continues to sell.[28]

During the high point of Indian activism and at the initiation of American Indian studies programs and departments, such as the one at San Francisco State University in 1968, literature about Indian identity increased in volume. Non-Native scholars have laid the groundwork through such books as Roy Harvey Pearce's *Savages of America: A Study of the Indian and the Idea of Civilization* (1953) and *Savagism and Civilization: A Study of the Indian and the American Mind* (1967); Hazel Hertzberg's *The Search for Indian Identity: Modern Pan-Indian Movements* (1971); Joseph H. Cash and Herbert Hoover's *To Be an Indian: An Oral History* (1971); Robert F. Berkhofer Jr.'s *The White Man's Indian: The History of an Idea from Columbus to the Present* (1978); James Clifton's *Being and Becoming Indian: Biographical Studies of North American Frontiers* (1989) and *Invented Indian: Cultural Fictions and Government Policies* (1990); and Joane Nagel's *American Indian Ethnic Renewal: Red Power and the Resurgence of Identity and Culture* (1996). A particularly enlightening work is Sherry Smith's *Reimagining Indians: Native Americans through Anglo Eyes, 1880–1940* (2000). These major works have brought important attention to the evolving Indian identity of many types, and they suggest more about image than Native identity. For example, they offer valuable insight into the American mind and specifically how white Americans have viewed Native peoples.

A much smaller number of Indian scholars have written about Native identity. These scholars include Philip Deloria whose book *Playing*

Indian (1998) is a major study to help balance the scale. Additional works have come to print that urge attention to be given to this important subject, including Patricia Penn Hilden's *When Nickels Were Indians: An Urban, Mixed-Blood Story* (1995) about one person's experiences; Jay Leibold's *Surviving in Two Worlds: Contemporary Native American Voices* (1997), a collection of Native views; Alexandra Harmon's *Indians in the Making: Ethnic Relations and Indian Identities around Puget Sound* (1998), a regional study with sound analysis; and Jacquelyn Kilpatrick's *Celluloid Indians: Native Americans and Film* (1999) with its focus on Native image, not identity.

The dual reality of Indians and the mainstream continues for many Native people. The American dream is not the same for American Indians. Rather, Native people learned this the hard way and defined an American Indian dream for themselves in a postmodern world. The urbanization of Native people only added strife to new Indian communities forming in cities. One Native woman felt frustrated trying to learn to live like mainstream whites. She explained,

> I wasn't happy unless, I was suppose to live like the whites. And you look around and see what they have. I wouldn't even let anyone come in my house unless I have that electric percolator, if I didn't have that new dress. And how can you compete with them and all this. One day I thought to hell with it, I'm an Indian, I'm going to be an Indian. And I'm happy. I don't give a darn. I don't care if I have [materialistic things]. I just want happiness, and go out sit on the lawn and enjoy the air, and you feel so good then you go away from the bustle of the city, and go down along the creek and remember the times when you were just a kid.[29]

Although this chapter includes the othering process of mainstream pressures on Native identity, producing related terms such as "Native," "Native American," "First American," "savage," "noble savage," "red man," "Indigenous," "tribe," and "First Nations," the emphasis is on the personal experience of being Native or being *Indian*. Other terms related to the "Indian experience" such as "assimilation," "acculturation," "ethnicity," "diversity," "multiculturalism," and "colonization" are included in this introspection of being Indian in the context of Indian-white relations, but the objective here is not to address the impact of Anglo-America on Native America. It is more important to understand what being Indian is like and how Native people have become "Indian" on their own terms. This discourse is about being Indian from an internal viewpoint, encompassing the personal experiences of those who look Indian and are Indian.

Delbert Broker, an Ojibwa businessman, viewed economics and education as the means for Indians asserting and establishing their identity. He said that "the educational institution was the only mechanism we had to gain skills, [and] knowledge, to develop self-worth or identity." He continued, "I feel the Indian people have to recognize themselves as Indians, and not let someone else tell them they are. This is my philosophy. I feel Indianness is an individual thing."[30]

In 1976 Pat Locke, Ojibwa-Lakota and former director of planning resources in minority education for the Western Interstate Commission for Higher Education, stated that "today's Indians must learn to walk both the white path and the red path. Both are important for survival."[31]

There are people who are not even Indian, but they are Indian in their hearts. They have worked with and for Indians all their lives. These individuals are so devoted that they are more Indian than some people who are Indian by blood.

For those who are not and those who want to be, this is an insider's version of Indian identity, including an introspective analysis. A part of this effort strives to analyze the "whys" and "hows" for the several types of Native identity and how they have developed. Simultaneously, the personal experience of being Indian needs to be placed in the larger context of Native identity by examining types of Native identity, including Native women's identity, government depiction of Indian identity, as well as the media versions of Native Americans. Again, the outside pressures have a continuing influence on Native identity while the Indian person has his or her struggle with accepting an "Indian" identity. This acceptance of Indianness must be on one's own terms, or the internal identity crisis continues. Many Native

Americans, however, will concur and confirm these same feelings regarding being Indian in modern America.

The politics of defining Indian identity is complicated by the presence of other groups such as those from India. Many East Indians who have been born in the United States claim that they are Indian Americans, so American Indians cannot call themselves by this term. This is an example of "losing the box" on government forms asking for identification, where the choice that often appears is American Indian/Alaska Native.

In this chapter I have attempted to share insights into personal experiences of "being Indian," focusing on the individuality of being Indian rather than being a member of an Indian tribe or Indian community. This ethnohistorical examination is a cultural analysis of the problem of American Indian identity within the mainstream society. Although the "Indian" individual is discussed here in the context of tribalism or communalism, the emphasis is on a person being Indian or Native American, rather than on the use of "Indian" to refer to a tribe or community. Furthermore, the term "Indian" has evolved in history due to the European colonization of the Western Hemisphere, and during the 1960s and 1970s the focus has been on how Native people defined "Indian" on their own terms with considerable pride by turning a negative into a positive.

Notes

1. Edward W. Said, *Orientalism* (New York: Vintage Books, 1978), 3.

2. The Seminoles had ten original clans and lived in twenty to twenty-five towns in Florida.

3. Royal B. Hassrick, *The Sioux: Life and Customs of a Warrior Society* (Norman: University of Oklahoma Press, 1955), 3–31.

4. Donald L. Fixico, *The Invasion of Indian Country in the Twentieth Century: American Capitalism and Tribal Natural Resources* (Niwot: University Press of Colorado, 1998), 3–142.

5. The Seminoles in Florida engaged the United States in three wars: First Seminole War, 1817–18; Second Seminole War, 1835–41; and Third Seminole War, 1855–58.

6. For Cheyenne social structure, see E. Adamson Hoebel, *The Cheyennes Indians of the Great Plains* (New York: Holt, Rinehart and Winston, 1960), 20–36.

7. General Phil Sheridan, nicknamed "Little Phil," at five foot five inches tall, made the bold statement, "The only good Indians I ever saw were dead ones," to Comanche leader Tosawi (Silver Knife) in 1869.

8. Originally quoted in Herman Hagerdorn, *Roosevelt in the Bad Lands* (Boston: Houghton Mifflin, 1921), 355.

9. Robert Berkhofer explains the book's purpose is "to present the implications of the ideas and imagery used by Whites to understand the peoples they call Indians." See Robert F. Berkhofer Jr., *The White Man's Indian: Images of the American Indian from Columbus to the Present* (New York: Alfred A. Knopf, 1978), xiv.

10. The 1893 World's Columbian Exposition in Chicago and Frederick Jackson Turner's frontier thesis advanced an American imperialism that promoted the idea of the vanishing American Indian. Shari M. Huhndorf, *Going Native: Indians in the American Cultural Imagination* (Ithaca NY: Cornell University Press, 2001), 52–64.

11. Huhndorf, *Going Native*, xv.

12. For literature on Indian destruction, one can turn to Roy Harvey Pearce, *Savagism and Civilization: A Study of the Indian and the American Mind* (Baltimore: Johns Hopkins University Press, 1953), paperback printings, 1971, 1977; Richard Drinnon, ed., *Facing West: The Metaphysics of Indian-Hating and Empire-Building* (New York: New American Library, 1980); Gary Anderson, *The Conquest of Texas: Ethnic Cleansing in the Promised Land, 1820–1875* (Norman: University of Oklahoma Press, 2005); and Ned Blackhawk, *Violence Over the Land: Indians and Empires in the Early American West* (Cambridge MA: Harvard University Press, 2006).

13. See Thomas A. Britten, *American Indians in World War I: At Home and At War* (Albuquerque: University of New Mexico Press, 1997).

14. "Citizenship for World War I Indian Veterans Act," November 6, 1919, 41 U.S. Statutes at Large 350.

15. "Indian Citizenship Act," June 2, 1924, 43 U.S. Statutes at Large 253.

16. See Alison R. Bernstein, *American Indians and World War II: Toward a New Era in Indian Affairs* (Norman: University of Oklahoma Press, 1991); and Jere Bishop Franco, *Crossing the Pond: The Native American Effort in World War II* (Denton: University of North Texas Press, 1999).

17. House Concurrent Resolution 108, August 1, 1953, 67 *U.S. Statutes at Large* B132.

18. The Indian group identity involved white hate crimes against Indians on a daily basis due to cultural imperialism. Barbara Perry, *Silent Victims: Hate Crimes Against Native Americans* (Tucson: University of Arizona Press, 2008), 75.

19. Arlene Poemoceah, interview by Christine Valenciana, April 10, 1971, La Mirada CA, Interview 1087, Box 56, Acc. No. 24, Doris Duke Indian Oral History Collection, Marriott Library, University of Utah, Salt Lake City.

20. David Lester observed that the Indian suicide rate was higher in communities where there were more rather than fewer Indians. David Lester, *Suicide in American Indians* (New York: Nova Science Publishers, 1997), 94.

21. Donald L. Fixico, *The Urban Indian Experience in America* (Albuquerque: University of New Mexico Press, 2000), 172–90.

22. John Trudell, "One of the People," in *Dreaming the Dawn: Conversations with Native Artists and Activists*, ed. E. K. Caldwell (Lincoln: University of Nebraska Press, 1999), 6–7.

23. Quote in Fred William Gabourie, "Justice and the Urban Indian," *Black Politician* 3, no. 1 (1971): 70.

24. Richard Nixon, "Special Message to Congress," July 8, 1970, *Public Papers of the Presidents: Richard M. Nixon, 1970*, 565–76.

25. Elizabeth Wheeler, "Indians Have Found a Mecca in Minneapolis," *Rocky Mountain News*, Denver, September 13, 1976.

26. Louis Bruce Jr., "A Mohawk Indian Tells What America Means to Me," *American Magazine* 148 (1949): 19, 123.

27. Roger W. Axford, ed., *Native Americans: 23 Indian Biographies* (Indiana PA: A.G. Halldin Publishing Company, 1980), 101.

28. Dee Brown, *Bury My Heart at Wounded Knee: An Indian History of the American West* (New York: Holt, Rinehart and Winston, 1970).

29. Muriel Waukazoo, interview by Stephen Ward, July 13, 1972, Rapid City, SD, Interview No. 68, Part 2, Tape No. 853, American Indian Research Project, Doris Duke Indian Oral History Collection, University of South Dakota, Vermillion.

30. Axford, *Native Americans*, 27.

31. Josephine Robertson, "Pat Locke—Liaison Between Two Cultures," *Christian Science Monitor*, February 2, 1976.

| Contributors

BILL ANTHES is associate professor of art history at Pitzer College in Claremont, California. His first book, *Native Moderns: American Indian Painting, 1940–1960*, was published by Duke University Press in 2006. He is currently writing the first monograph on the career of the Cheyenne-Arapaho contemporary artist Hock E Aye Vi Edgar Heap of Birds.

JAMES TAYLOR CARSON is professor of history at Queen's University in Kingston, Ontario. He has published two books on the ethnohistory of the American South: *Searching for the Bright Path: The Mississippi Choctaws from Prehistory to Removal* (1999) and *Making an Atlantic World: Circles, Paths, and Stories from the Colonial South* (2007).

DANIEL M. COBB is associate professor of American studies at the University of North Carolina at Chapel Hill. Previously he was assistant professor of history at Miami University in Oxford, Ohio (2004–10), and assistant director of the Newberry Library's D'Arcy McNickle Center for American Indian and Indigenous Studies (2003–4). His first book, *Native Activism in Cold War America* (2008), won the inaugural Labriola Center American Indian National Book Award. He is currently at work on a biography of Ponca activist Clyde Warrior.

DUANE CHAMPAGNE (Turtle Mountain Band of Chippewa, North Dakota) is professor of sociology and American Indian studies at the University of California–Los Angeles. He is the author of many books, some of which include *Social Order and Political Change:*

Constitutional Governments among the Cherokee, the Choctaw, the Chickasaw, and the Creek (1992); *The Native North American Almanac* (2001); *Social Change and Cultural Continuity among Native Nations* (2007); *and Notes from the Center of Turtle Island* (2010).

FELICITY DONOHOE undertook her PhD at the University of Glasgow and gained her MLitt and MA from the University of Dundee. Her thesis focused on ritual violence and Native American women. She has published in the *Journal of Early American Studies* and in the edited collection *Debating the Difference: Gender, Representation, and Self Representation* (2009). She has held several grants and fellowships in the United Kingdom and United States, including the McNeil Center for Early American Studies, the American Philosophical Society, and the International Center for Jefferson Studies. She also edited *US Studies Online* postgraduate journal from 2008 to 2010.

KATHERINE ELLINGHAUS is a Monash Fellow in the School of Philosophical, Historical, and International Studies at Monash University. She is the author of *Taking Assimilation to Heart: Marriages of White Women and Indigenous Men in the United States and Australia* (2006) and a forthcoming book that explores the discourse of "blood" in Native American assimilation policy. Her current research compares the indigenous assimilation policies of Australia and the United States.

LINFORD D. FISHER is assistant professor of history at Brown University. He received his doctorate from Harvard University in 2008 and is the author of *The Indian Great Awakening: Religion and the Shaping of Native Cultures in Early America* (Oxford, 2012). His essays have appeared in *Ethnohistory* and the *New England Quarterly*, and his research has been supported by the National Endowment for the Humanities, the Massachusetts Historical Society, and the American Antiquarian Society.

DONALD L. FIXICO (Shawnee, Sac and Fox, Muscogee Creek, and Seminole) is Distinguished Foundation Professor of History and affiliate faculty in American Indian studies at Arizona State University. He has worked on nearly twenty documentaries. He is also the author of numerous books, some of which are *Termination and Relocation: Federal Indian Policy, 1945–1960* (1986); *The Invasion of Indian Country in the Twentieth Century: American Capitalism and Tribal Natural Resources* (1998); *The Urban Indian Experience in America* (2000); and *The American Indian Mind in a Linear World: Traditional Knowledge and American Indian Studies* (2003).

CLAUDIA B. HAAKE is senior lecturer in history at La Trobe University in Melbourne, Australia. She is the author of *The State, Removal and Indigenous Peoples in the United States and Mexico*, coeditor (with Richard Bessel) of *Removing Peoples: Forced Migration in the Modern World*, and has written numerous articles on indigenous issues in the United States and Mexico. Her current research centers on questions of forced migration, land, and identity among several Native American tribes of the United States in the removal era.

REBECCA HORN teaches in the department of history at the University of Utah. She is a specialist on colonial Spanish America, especially the Nahuatl-speaking peoples of central Mexico. She is the author of *Postconquest Coyoacan: Nahua-Spanish Relations in Central Mexico, 1519–1650* (Stanford University Press, 1997); "Mundane Documents in Nahuatl," and "Nahuatl and Spanish Sources on Coyoacan" in *Sources and Methods for the Study of Postconquest Mesoamerican Ethnohistory* (2007). She is also coauthor of an essay on comparative approaches to the early modern Americas, "Territorial Crossings: Histories and Historiographies of the Early Americas," *William and Mary Quarterly* (2010), and coauthor (with John Kicza) of the second edition of *Resilient Cultures: America's Native Peoples Confront European Colonialism, 1500–1800* (2013).

KERRI A. INGLIS is associate professor of history at the University of Hawai'i at Hilo, where she teaches courses in Hawaiian and Pacific history. Her research interests are in the fields of disease and medicine. She is author of *Ma'i Lepera: Disease and Displacement in Nineteenth-Century Hawaii* (2013).

MICHAEL A. MCDONNELL is associate professor of history at the University of Sydney. He is the author of *The Politics of War: Race, Class, and Conflict in Revolutionary Virginia* (published by the Omohundro Institute of Early American History and Culture, 2007), which won the New South Wales Premier's History Award in 2008, and numerous articles on the American Revolution in the *Journal of American History*, the *William and Mary Quarterly*, and the *Journal of American Studies*. He won the Lester Cappon Prize for the best article published in the *William and Mary Quarterly* in 2006, and his work is featured in the Organization of American Historians Best American History Essays (2008). His most recent works include *Negotiating Empires: French, Anishinaabe, and Métis Communities in the Making and Unmaking of the Atlantic World* (2014) and, as coeditor with Clare Corbould, Frances Clarke, and W. Fitzhugh Brundage, *Remembering the Revolution: Memory, History, and Nation-Making from Independence to the Civil War* (2013).

BROOKE N. NEWMAN is assistant professor of history at Virginia Commonwealth University and a 2010–11 National Endowment for the Humanities Long-Term Fellow at the John Carter Brown Library, Brown University. She has published articles in *Gender and History*, *Slavery and Abolition*, and *Sargasso* and is currently at work on a book-length project exploring issues of gender, race, and identity in metropolitan Britain and the British West Indies during the long eighteenth century.

VERA PARHAM is an assistant professor of history at the University of Hawai'i at Hilo. She gained her PhD in Native American history from the University of California, Riverside. Her research focuses on the use of protest by various Native American groups and individuals of the Pacific Northwest in the quest to preserve and protect culture and heritage. Her recent articles delve into the fishing rights struggles and "fish-ins" of the 1960s as well as the Fort Lawton protest occupation in Seattle. She continues to work on revisions to her PhD dissertation.

JOY PORTER writes on Native American Indian history, literature, and culture and is professor of indigenous history at teh University of Hull, United Kingdom. She is the author of *Native American Freemasonry: Associationalism and Performance in America* (2011) and *Land and Spirit in Native America* (2012). She was an AHRC Fellow during 2010–11, working on a new monograph, *The American Indian Poet of the First World War: Modernism and the Indian Identity of Frank "Toronto" Prewett*. During 2011–12 she was a BA Mid-Career Fellow working on the research project "The American Presidency and Tribal Diplomacy in the Twentieth Century."

GREGORY D. SMITHERS teaches history at Virginia Commonwealth University. He specializes in comparative race relations and indigenous studies. He is the author of *Science, Sexuality, and Race in the United States and Australia, 1780s–1890s* (2009); *Slave Breeding: Sex, Slavery, and Memory in African American History* (2012); and coauthor (with Clarence E. Walker) of *The Preacher and the Politician: Jeremiah Wright, Barak Obama, and Race in America* (2009). His most recent book is *The Cherokee Diaspora* (2014).

Index

adoption, 153, 159, 188, 213

African Americans, 11, 13, 210, 215, , 285, 290, 299, 303–5, 319

Africans, 3, 11–13; in the Caribbean, 110, 112, 121–38; and intermarriage, 172, 174, 290; and migrations, 34. *See also* African Americans; Indian slavery; "Maroon Negroes"; Middle Passage; slavery

agriculture, 33, 48–49, 239, 253–56, 327, 454; and Christian missionaries, 170; and Dawes Act, 280; and plantations, 17; and reservations, 360; and subsistence, 193

Alabama, 187, 210, 215–17, 219–23, 226–27, 475

altepetl, 35–40, 44, 47, 60, 62, 65

Algonquian–Iroquois Wars, 82, 90, 92

Algonquians, 80, 82, 88–89, 92–93

All Indian Pueblo Council, 445–46

allotment, 173, 254, 275, 298–99, 301, 303, 308, 358, 361–62

American Indian Defense Association, 287

American Indian Movement (AIM), 8–9, 462, 483, 485, 490

Americanization, 480. *See also* assimilation

American Revolution, 98, 114, 134, 166, 175, 176, 191, 212

American settlements, 152–53, 187, 275, 278

Americas, mainland, ix, 3, 4, 6, 7, 11, 15, 17, 31, 32, 34, 81, 137, 154. *See also* United States

Andes, 31

Anishinaabeg, 81–93, 95, 97, 98, 300, 303

Arapahos, 285, 430–31, 440, 478

Argentina, 31

Articles of Agreement (1874), 251

assimilation, 318, 391, 430, 479, 491; and British policy, 118; cultural, 273, 377, 452; and Progressivism, 277–83, 285, 287, 292;

and racial mixing, 297–311; and United States policy, 318, 350–54, 373–74, 418–19; and wage labor, 320, 326, 328, 334

Association on American Indian Affairs (AAIA), 444, 451–57, 464

Aztecs, 34–35

Banderas, Juan, 255–56

Baptists, 211, 423

Black Caribs, 14, 109–41. *See also* Garifuna

"blood," 11–12, 488–89; and "blood law," 2; and "blood quantum," 354, 358, 386, 418; and identity, 14, 123, 290–91, 304–9, 486, 491–92; and kinship, 97, 123; race mixture, 11, 174, 177, 281, 289, 290–91, 297–301, 484–85, 486, 488–89, 491–92

blood quantum, 14, 300, 303, 354, 358, 386, 418, 486

Blue Eagle, Acee, 4, 411–37

boarding school movement, 276, 420

boarding schools, 10, 285, 298, 358, 413, 420, 477; and Christianity, 283, 285, 298, 364; as a form of cultural genocide, 474; erasing Native languages, 377; Western worldview of, 354

Board of Indian Commissioners, 278

Boas, Franz, 280, 319, 335

borderlands, 12, 235–65

Bosque Redondo, 239–66

Boudinot, Elias, 1–2, 13, 18, 223

Brothertown, 151–78. *See also* Eeyawquittoowauconnuck, New Stockbridge

Brothertown movement, 151–78

British colonialism, 109–41, 151–78

Brunias, Agostino, 127–29, 130, 136–37

Bureau of Indian Affairs (BIA), 368–70, 378; and labor, 326–27; and mixed-race people, 308–10; Native opposition to, 9–10, 482, 483; and New Deal policies, 449–50, 452, 481;

Bureau of Indian Affairs (BIA) (*cont.*)
relocation program of, 483; suppressing
Native culture, 283. *See also* Office of
Indian Affairs

Burke Act, 275

cabecera, 37–39, 53–54, 63
cabildo, 37, 39, 40–41, 46, 50, 55–56, 59–
60, 64

Cabot, John, 152

Cajeme, 255–56

Calhoun, John C., 216

Caribbean, ix, 3, 6, 7, 15, 17, 39, 109–41

Caribs, 109–41. *See also* Black Caribs

Carlisle Indian Industrial School, 290

cartography, 36, 61

Cass, Lewis, 222

Catawbas, 13, 154, 156

Cayugas, 156–57, 449

Ceded Islands, 109, 116–18. *See also* Dominica; Grenada; St. Vincent; Tobago

Chamorros, 396–99, 405–6

Champlain, Samuel de, 90–91

Chatoyer, Joseph, 118, 127–29, 133, 139–40

Cherokee Constitution, 212–13, 215

Cherokee Nation v. Georgia (1831), 446

Cherokee Phoenix, 218, 223

Cherokees, 4, 18, 290–91, 428–30, 446, 458;
and colonial warfare, 156; and diplomacy,
209–10, 215–27; and identity, ix, 1–2, 15,
476; and land, 14; and literacy, 215–19;
Nativist movements of, 190; population of,
277; and race, 213; and social change, 13.
See also Cherokee Constitution

Cheyennes, 425, 430–31, 477–78, 489

Chickahominy, 305

Chickasaws, 201, 210, 212–13, 215–16, 219–
21, 223, 225, 303–5

Chinooks, 322

Chippewas, 102–3, 300–302, 309

Choctaws, 210–15, 283, 430; diplomacy of,
14; and freedmen, 304; and race, 190, 304;
and Redstick War, 193; and U.S. expansion,
221–26. *See also* Mississippi Choctaws

Christianity, 16, 54–59, 152, 157–60, 163,
168, 283

churches: Baptists, 211, 413, 423; Catholics,
116–17; Methodism, 115, 125, 211; Protestantism, 157–59, 353, 387

citizenship, 225, 308, 355–59, 482; and allotment, 275; and assimilationist policies,

351–52; and Cherokees, 218–19; dual, 355,
367–71, 374; and identity, 279; and Native
military service, 287, 448–49. *See also*
Indian Citizenship Act (1924)

clan, 81–86, 209, 352, 355, 359, 363, 481; as
"body politic," 377; and California Indians,
372–73; and Cherokees, 13; and Choctaws,
221; and Creeks, 188–89, 194, 196, 199–
202, 422, 430; as source of community,
475–76. *See also* doodem

Clendinnen, Inga, 7

Clifford, James, 4

cofradías, 57

Cold War, 443–65

Collier, John, 283, 288, 292, 362, 449–50, 481

colonial encounters, 5, 7, 12, 111, 113–14,
132, 153

colonialism, ix, 3–7, 15–18, 79, 81, 386–89,
398, 455; and anticolonialism, 443; 448,
460; and the British, 12, 14, 97–99, 108–
39, 151, 155, 161, 169–70, 178, 192, 195,
220, 223, 324, 390–92; and Christianity,
154, 157, 160; and cultural imperialism,
214, 385–86, 389–92, 406, 455, 485; and
disease, 8, 9–10, 12, 18, 119, 138, 151,
154–55, 211, 225, 239, 244, 274–75, 279,
325, 385–406, 477; and the Dutch, 17, 109,
121, 152–53, 445; and the French, 12, 13,
16, 17, 79–100, 108, 113–20, 123, 126,
132, 135, 138–40, 152–53, 161, 172, 192,
425, 430, 445; and imperialism, 79–81,
88, 119, 214, 385–405, 455; legacies of,
452, 455, 457–60; and settler colonialism,
4–7, 9–11, 14, 16, 109, 114–18, 123–26,
131–41, 159–60, 190, 236, 281, 305, 309,
320, 386–88, 418–20, 430–31, 437, 487;
and the Spanish, 12, 16, 17, 31–65, 121,
152, 153, 211, 235–67, 394–97, 432, 445;
and the United States, 1, 9, 15–17, 98, 191,
211–28, 235–38, 241–42, 250–51, 254,
256, 279–82, 300, 311, 350–58, 392–96,
430–31, 443–64, 463–64, 476–93; and
venereal disease, 262, 320–26, 340, 405

Columbian Exposition (1893), 289

Columbus, x, 3, 121–22, 152, 478–79, 491

Comanches, 4, 13, 242–44, 262,

Coolidge, Sherman, 285

corn, 87, 97–98, 175, 195, 221, 351

Council of Three Fires, 445

Coweta, 209

Creeks, 14, 412, 418–22, 428–30, 432, 445, 475; and ethnogenesis, 13; and gendered identities, 187–201; and the Tuscarora War, 156; and the United States, 209–10, 212–17, 219–20, 221–22, 225
Crows, 293, 447, 476
Curtis Act (1898), 303

Dakotas, 89, 290, 417, 445, 448
Dawes Act (1887), 17, 275, 280, 298, 303–4
Declaration of Indian Purpose, 456
Declaration on the Rights of Indigenous People, 375, 444, 462–63
Delawares, 157, 181, 190
Deloria, Vine, Jr., 443, 456–57, 461, 464, 490
diaspora, x, 16, 431–32, 445, 464; definition of, 3–5; and Mesoamerica, 34; and removal, 235, 266–67, 412; and wage laborers, 318–19
Dillingham Commission, 279
disease. See colonialism: and disease; epidemics
dispossession, 7, 8, 18, 100, 111–12, 119, 154, 214, 227–28
Dominica, 109, 128, 132
doodem, 81, 84–90, 92–97, 99
Dove, Morning, 290, 421
Durant, Benjamin, 189, 192, 193
Durant, Sophia, 187–201
Duwamish, 325, 330–31

Eastman, Charles A. (Ohiyesa), 275, 283–84, 290, 303–5, 445, 449, 464
Eeyawquittoowauconnuck, 151, 176. See also Brothertown
Eisenhower, Dwight D., 366, 370, 450, 456
El Salvador, 33
encomienda, 37, 54
Enlightenment, 12, 114
epidemics, 154, 391–95, 400, 405
ethnicity, 174, 394, 492; and African ethnicity, 121; in Mesoamerica, 36, 39, 62–65; Native, 310
ethnogenesis, 12–13, 112, 135, 152–57, 178
European traders, 16, 152, 190, 192, 324; and the French, 13, 81, 88, 90, 94, 96, 98; and intermarriage with Native peoples, 13. See also trade
exile, 445; and disease, 398, 400, 402–3, 405; and Navajos, 230–67
"expansion with honor," 17, 189–90

First Carib War, 119, 137–38
First Great Awakening, 158, 161

First World War, 282–83, 287, 396, 421, 447–49, 479, 485
Five Nations of the Iroquois Confederacy, 156
Folsom, David, 221
Fort Defiance, 238, 253
Fox, 89, 92, 93
freedmen, 303–4. See also African Americans

Garifuna, 14, 112, 141
Garroutte, Eva Marie, 10, 11, 298
genealogy, 31–32, 61, 430
George III (King), 113, 117
Georgia, 191, 209, 210, 215–19, 221–24, 226–27
Gilmer, George, 224
Great Lakes region, 79–100, 446. See also pays d'en haut
Greenblatt, Stephen, 12
Grenada, 109, 162
Guadeloupe, 109, 124, 140
Guam, 386, 393–99, 405
Guatemala, 33
Guzman, Don Juan de, 44–45, 51–52

Haidas, 331
Hämäläinen, Pekka, 7
Harmon, Alexandra, x, 4
Hawaii, ix, 385–406, 485
Hawaiians, Native, 325, 385–406
Hawkins, Benjamin, 191–92, 197, 199
Hicks, Elijah, 218
Hicks, George, 217
homeland, 10, 14, 274, 340, 389; and diaspora, 318–19, 445, 464; of Cherokees, 2; of Choctaws, 226; of Navajos, 248; of Oneidas, 151, 176; removal from, 5, 222; reservation, 276, 453, 477–78; of Yaquis, 254–55, 261. See also land
Honduras, 33, 113, 141
Honolulu, 391, 400
Hopi, 279, 363
hop pickers, 317–42
Hurons, 82, 91, 94, 104

identity, 350–55, 357; and art, 411–37; in British Caribbean, 112, 121, 126, 131; and Brothertown movement, 151–53, 156–57, 173, 177; and Cherokees, 2; and Cold War, 443–65; and colonialism, 12–14; complexity of, 2–4, 15, 93–95, 100, 237; and Creek women, 190, 193, 199; cultural, 353; and diaspora, 4–5; and disease, 404;

identity (*cont.*)
  indigenous, ix, 6–8, 10–11, 15–17, 95,
    273–93, 358, 361, 367, 386, 412, 475–76;
    in Mesoamerica, 34, 36, 38, 48–49, 58,
    59–65; mixed-race, 297–311; and Navajos,
    235, 240, 247, 254, 266; in *pays d'en haut*,
    79, 81, 84, 86–87; and wage labor, 318–42;
    and Yaquis, 236–37, 257, 260, 263–67
Indian Citizenship Act (1924), 283, 361–63, 479
Indianness, 2–4, 281, 338, 418, 430, 437,
    473, 485–88, 492
Indian Reorganization Act (1934), 297–98,
    361–62, 367, 449, 479
Indian Rights Association, 287
Indian slavery, 93, 211. *See also* slavery;
    Middle Passage
Indian Territory, 227, 239, 247–48, 303–4,
    308, 422, 477
Inter-American Indian Institute, 444
intermarriage: and assimilation policy, 301,
    304, 306, 324; and British Caribbean, 132;
    and Brothertown movement, 152–53, 160,
    172, 177; and the French, 84, 87–88, 97
International Indian Treaty Council (IITC),
    444, 461–62, 463–64
Iroquois, 80–87, 90–92, 156, 176, 284, 287,
    325, 445–49

Jackson, Andrew, 218–19, 221, 223–24, 226,
    422
Jamestown, 152–53
Jennings, Francis, 8
Jesuit missionaries. *See* missionaries: Jesuit
Johnson, Emily Pauline, 289
Johnson, Lyndon B., 368, 456, 486
Justice, Daniel Heath, 10

Kalaupapa settlement, 400–409
Kennedy, John F., 368, 456
Kiowa, 415, 421, 424, 457
King Philip's War, 155
kinship, 5, 12, 353–54, 359–63, 370, 377–78;
    and Anishinaabeg, 81–85, 87, 96–100; and
    Brothertown movement, 153–54, 178; and
    community, 444–45, 475, 480; and Dako-
    tas, 290; and marriage, 324; and Nahuatl
    terminology, 50–52; among Navajos, 238;
    among Southeastern Indians, 213; and trade,
    337. *See also* clan; doodem
Klamath, 366, 483
Kupperman, Karen Ordahl, 7

labor, 6, 237, 352, 358, 454, 481; and Broth-
    ertown movement, 155, 159, 172; in Carib-
    bean, 116, 129, 133, 138; gendered division
    of, 48–50, 133, 352; in Mesoamerica, 37–
    38, 40–49, 54–55, 63–64; among Navajos
    and Yaquis, 255–58, 264, 278; wage, 199,
    317–42, 371
Lake Ontario, 91
land, 1–10, 16–18, 280–81, 289, 318–20,
    352–62, 482–83, 487; and allotment, 275,
    301, 305; and Black Caribs, 110–41; and
    "blood," 303, 305, 309, 311; and Brother-
    town movement, 151–52, 154–56, 158–62,
    164–70, 175–77; loss of, 292, 298–99;
    and Mesoamerica, 31–36, 40–49, 57, 60;
    Native protection of, 366–69, 421, 446,
    452, 456–57; and Oceania, 387, 402; and
    "otherness," 12; and Pacific Northwest, 327;
    and *pays d'en haut*, 86, 92; reservation,
    239, 242–66, 275–76, 279, 281–87, 298,
    301, 325–28, 333–34, 339, 349, 354–77,
    418–22, 429, 447, 451–53, 457, 460, 462,
    475, 477–79, 483–89; and Southeast, 195–
    96, 199, 209–10, 211–12, 214–27; and
    Southwest borderlands, 239, 241, 243–67.
    See also homeland
Langlade, Charles, 97–98
language, 41, 47–49, 52–65, 162, 264, 418,
    432, 490; and cultural diversity, 323; and
    cultural mixture, 13–15, 122, 134; identity
    expressed through, 10, 84, 94, 329, 334, 354,
    360, 377, 421–22, 475; and nationalist ideals,
    448, 453, 459; political uses of, 201, 209–28,
    290, 360, 375, 477; and visual signals, 125,
    428. *See also* Spanish-language sources
LeFlore, Greenwood, 221, 224, 227
leprosy (Hansen's disease), 394–406. *See also*
    colonialism: and disease
Lesser Antilles, 109, 124
literacy, 60–65, 158, 210, 214, 215, 304, 389;
    and illiteracy, 285. *See also* language
Lockhart, James, 7, 55–56
Long Lance, Sylvester Clark, 290–91
Lummi, 331

Mahicans, 157, 176
Makahs, 328
Manuelito, 238, 248–54
"Maroon Negroes," 14, 115, 131, 136–38
Martinique, 109, 117, 133, 134, 139, 140
massacres, 98, 122, 276, 474, 479

matrilineal society, 188–89, 191, 193, 196–97, 199–200

Mattaponi, 305

Mayas, 31–65, 264

McDonald, James, 223–24

McGillivray, Alexander, 187–88, 215

McNickle, D'Arcy, 450, 455–56

memory, 55, 61, 210, 214, 248, 267, 404, 427

Merchand, Sehoy, 188

Mesoamerica, 31–65

Mexican Revolution, 260, 265

Mexico, 31, 33, 35, 37, 47, 54, 57–58, 235–39, 259, 265

Michilimackinac, 81–88, 92, 94–95, 97–99

Mico, Tukabatchee, 220

"middle ground," 5, 79–81, 88

Middle Passage, 122

migration, 2, 17, 81, 274, 278–79, 324, 326–27, 341; and Brothertown movement, 151–52, 155–56, 159–171, 175–78; and identity, 10, 327; and Mesoamerica, 34–35, 42, 61; and *pays d'en haut*, 86, 89; and Southwest borderlands, 240; uncertainty experienced in, 5, 12–13, 360

Miles, Tiya, 11

missionaries, 16–17, 276, 358, 418, 477; and assimilation, 334, 387, 388; and Brothertown, 158, 161–62, 164, 169; in the Caribbean, 115–16, 125, 134; Jesuit, 81–82, 91, 93–94, 395; and missionary schools, 290

Mississippi, 210, 215, 217, 219–23, 225–27, 310, 371, 376

Mississippi Choctaws, 371. *See also* Choctaws

mixed race, 13, 14, 15, 289–91, 327, 395, 430, 484, 488; and Black Caribs, 111–12, 123, 126–27, 131; and Brothertown, 172–75, 177; and identity, 17, 281, 297–311, 484; and Mesoamerica, 34, 62; and *pays d'en haut*, 87, 91, 95, 97; and tribal membership, 10–11

Mixtecs, 31–65

Mohawks, 157

Mohegans, 152–55, 157, 160–65, 168–69, 172–73, 176–77

Momaday, N. Scott, 289, 490

Montauketts, 154, 160, 163–66, 168, 176–77

Montezuma, Carlos, 280, 285, 448

Morgan, Lewis Henry, 280

Mucho, Ganado, 242, 244–45, 251, 253

Musgrove, Mary, 200–201

Nahuatl, 31–65

Nanticokes, 157

Narragansetts, 154–56, 160–61, 163–64, 167–69, 172, 174, 176–77

National Congress of American Indians (NCAI), 367–68, 370, 443–44, 450, 451–57, 461

National Indian Youth Council (NIYC), 444, 458–60, 464

Native Americans. *See individual Native groups*

Native women, 225, 287, 290, 400, 419, 481, 483, 487, 492; and Black Caribs, 110, 111, 122, 129; and Brothertown, 163, 168; and Creek women, 188–91, 201; and Mesoamerica, 45–46, 48–50, 52–53, 57; and *pays d'en haut*, 88; and work, 274, 319, 328, 335, 339

Navajos (Diné), 13, 235–67, 365, 419, 476

Neolin, 158–59

New Deal, 283, 288, 292, 357, 362–66, 433, 449. *See also* Indian Reorganization Act (1934)

New England, 151, 152, 155, 157–61, 163–77

New Stockbridge, 177

Niantics, 154–55, 157, 160, 163, 164, 168, 177

Nixon, Richard M., 369–70, 486–87

Oaxaca City, 33

O'Brien, Jean, 7

Occom, Samson, 152, 154, 163–72, 176

Oceania, 385–406

Odawas, 83–99

Office of Indian Affairs, 221, 287, 299, 301, 309, 354, 357–60, 375

Oglethorpe, James, 209

Ohio Valley, 98

Ojibwes, 83, 84, 86, 90, 92, 94, 98, 99, 445, 448

Oklahoma, 15, 285–86, 304, 412–13, 417, 421–25, 428–31, 477–78, 489

Oneidas, 91, 151, 156–57, 161–62, 164–67, 173, 175–77, 460

oral tradition, 214, 290

Pacific Islands, ix, 3, 6, 7, 18, 384–96, 405

Pacific Northwest, 83, 317–42, 446, 459, 501

Pagden, Anthony, 7

Pamunkey, 305, 448

Parker, Arthur Caswell, 284–88, 290

pays d'en haut, 79–100
Pequots, 153–60, 163–64, 168, 378
Pequot War, 154
Perdue, Theda, 11
Pickawillany, 97–99
Plecker, Walter A., 306–9
Pocahontas, 153, 310
"Pocahontas rule," 305–6
Pokagon, Simon, 288–89
Pontiac, 99, 158
population, 275, 322, 324–26, 331, 367,
    371, 418, 478–79; of Black Caribs, 110–11,
    114–16, 122–24, 129, 131, 138, 140; of
    Brothertown, 152, 172–73; and depopula-
    tion, 5–6, 9, 18, 37, 46–47, 151, 154–56,
    225, 277, 386, 388, 390, 392–96, 402;
    increase, 310; of Mesoamerica, 34, 37, 62;
    of *pays d'en haut,* 83; and racial bias, 299–
    300, 305–6; of Southeast, 210, 213, 216,
    235–36; urbanized, 483
Potawatomis, 84, 95, 99, 376, 425, 445, 478
potlatch, 276, 320–29, 335, 337
Powhatan, 153, 155, 310. *See also* Wahunse-
    nacawh (Chief)
Progressive Era, 274–93, 420
Puyallup, 317, 328, 330–32, 337

Quileutes, 322

Racial Integrity Act (1924), 305
racial stereotypes, 13, 15–16, 124–26, 412,
    447, 479, 487–88
Rappahannock, 305
Redstick War, 193
removal, 1, 100, 177, 305, 430–31, 477;
    and Black Caribs, 110, 118–19, 131; from
    Southeast, 211, 221–23, 225, 229; and
    Southwest borderlands, 235–67
Removal Act (1830), 17, 221–23
Richter, Daniel, 7, 10, 81
Ridge, John, 2, 224
Rio Grande, 242
Roanoke, 152–53
Roe Cloud, Henry, 285
Roosevelt, Eleanor, 297
Roosevelt, Franklin, 288, 326, 366, 433,
    450, 481
Roosevelt, Theodore, 275, 279, 478
Ross, John, 217–18, 224, 227

Ša, Zitkala, 283–84, 290, 448
Salish, 324–25, 421

Sammamish, 331, 333
Sault Sainte Marie, 83, 91, 94
Second Carib War, 140
Second World War, 364, 390, 396, 413, 415,
    451, 461, 464, 481
self-determination, 282, 283, 285, 418, 434,
    447–49; and American Indian Movement
    (AIM), 9; as U.S. Indian policy, 350, 357,
    369–78, 456–57, 486–87
Seminoles, 4, 14, 16, 425, 475–77
Seven Years' War, 98, 109, 113, 116, 134
"shatter zones," 12, 80
Shawnees, 4, 13, 98, 157, 190, 486
Six Nations of the Iroquois Confederacy, 156,
    449
slavery, 93, 110–11, 122, 124, 126, 211, 213,
    220, 221, 224, 226–28. *See also* Indian
    slavery; Middle Passage
Smith, John, 153
Snoqualmies, 322, 333
Society of American Indians (SAI), 283–88,
    290, 444, 448
Sonora, 237, 254–59, 261–63, 265
Southwest borderlands, 235–67, 419, 421,
    446, 476
sovereignty, 9, 18, 290, 320, 367, 418,
    445; in British Caribbean, 111, 130; and
    Brothertown Indians, 154, 173, 178; in Me-
    soamerica, 35, 55, 59; in Pacific Northwest,
    325, 341; in Southeast, 212, 219–20, 225;
    and tribal governments, 372, 374–75, 378,
    444, 447, 449, 451, 453, 457, 464
Spanish-language sources, 31–38. *See also*
    language
Spokane, 331
Squaxins, 322
Standing Bear, 18
Steiner, Stan, 460–61
St. Vincent, 109–41
Sujetos, 38

Taylor, Alan, 7
Tenochtitlan, 34, 60
termination, 357, 366–71, 374, 452–55, 458,
    482–83
Tlingits, 331
Tobago, 109, 128
Treaty of Dancing Rabbit Creek (1830), 225
Treaty of Indian Springs (1825), 216–17, 219
Treaty of New Echota, 1–2
Treaty of Washington (1826), 216–17

Treaty of Versailles (1783), 139
tribal institutions, 348–78
"tribal nations," 156, 300, 308, 488, 491;
    and Creeks, 196; and institution building,
    349–78; in New England, 151, 157, 160;
    and sovereignty, 443–47, 453, 456, 461
Truman, Harry, 366, 451, 455
Turner, Frederick Jackson, 278
Tuscaroras, 156–59, 285
Tuscarora War, 156–57

United Indian Nations, 445
United States, 1, 9, 15–17, 98, 474, 493;
    and Cold War era, 443–56, 461, 463–64;
    Indian agents of, 191; and Native art, 418,
    425, 431; and Oceania, 391, 394, 396; and
    Progressive Era, 276–77, 279, 282; and race
    mixing, 300, 311, 325, 488; and removal,
    211–12, 215–19, 221–23, 228–29, 477–82;
    and Southwest borderlands, 235–38, 241–
    42, 250–51, 254, 256, 265–66; and tribal
    institutions, 350, 352, 355–58, 361, 375
Usner, Daniel, 7, 10, 319, 340

Vietnam War, 228, 451, 488

violence, 3, 5, 8–10, 17, 18, 98, 112, 122,
    138, 261–62, 272. See also massacres
Virgin of Guadalupe, 57–58, 65

wage laborers, 317–42, 371
Wahunsenacawh (Chief), 153
Warrior, Clyde, 459–60
White, Richard, 7, 10, 79–80, 82, 85, 99
Whitney, Eli, 210
Wild West show, 286
Wilson, Woodrow, 282, 448
Wimpey, Elijah, 165, 167, 170
Winnebagos, 89, 285
Winnemucca, Sarah (Thocmentony), 275
Wichita, 422, 429
Wolfe, Patrick, 6
Wounded Knee (1890), 276, 462, 479, 490

Yakama, 331, 338
Yaqui (Yoemes), 235–67
Yarbrough, Fay, 11
Yoholo, Opothle, 220
Yucatan, 33, 36, 39–40, 42, 48, 54, 62, 237

Zuni, 370

www.ingramcontent.com/pod-product-compliance
Lightning Source LLC
Chambersburg PA
CBHW021841290326
41932CB00064B/337